The
EDUCATIONAL
GRANTS
DIRECTORY

2006/07

Alan French
Tom Traynor
Sarah Johnston

DIRECTORY OF SOCIAL CHANGE

Published by

Directory of Social Change

24 Stephenson Way

London NW1 2DP

Tel. 08450 77 77 07; Fax 020 7391 4804

E-mail publications@dsc.org.uk

www.dsc.org.uk

from whom further copies and a full books catalogue are available.

Directory of Social Change is a Registered Charity no. 800517

First published 1988

Second edition 1992

Third edition 1994

Fourth edition 1996

Fifth edition 1998

Sixth edition 2000

Seventh edition 2002

Eighth edition 2004

Ninth edition 2006

ISBN-10 1 903991 75 7
ISBN-13 978 1 903991 75 6

British Library Cataloguing in Publication Data

A catalogue record for this book is available from the British Library

Cover design by Keith Shaw

Text designed by Gabriel Kerne

Typeset by CPI Tradespools, Chippenham

Printed and bound by Page Bros., Norwich

Other Directory of Social Change departments in London:
    08450 77 77 07

Directory of Social Change Northern Office:
    Federation House, Hope Street, Liverpool L1 9BW
    Courses and conferences 08450 77 77 07
    Policy & Research 0151 708 0136

CONTENTS

INTRODUCTION

The *Educational Grants Directory* is now in its ninth edition. The main focus of the guide is to provide a comprehensive list of sources of non-statutory help for people in education who are in financial need. This edition contains information on over 1,500 grant-making trusts, which accumulatively distribute over £60 million in grants. A total of 50 new trusts are included in this guide.

The funds outlined in the guide are becoming increasingly important to higher education students who may find themselves getting deeper into debt as state support for them drops still further. Students leaving university in 2006 graduated with an average debt of around £13,000.

Many students undertake work to assist with their living costs and fees, although many have to turn to other sources of funding to ease the financial burden that a university career now presents. It is often students with children of their own or those from low-income backgrounds who leave their university education because they can not afford to continue. Until a more balanced funding system is introduced, the limited help available from grant-making trusts will continue to be crucial. Some trusts offer small grants to help with tuition fees, others offer scholarships based on their own, often strict criteria, however, there is always stiff competition for the limited funds available.

People at other stages of their education will also find trust money useful for providing grants for needs not covered by the state. This often includes school uniforms, which for many parents the costs run into hundreds of pounds a year.

Trusts can meet needs ranging from school clothing and books for schoolchildren to equipment and materials for people starting work. Individuals are more likely to be helped with extras like these, rather than with fees or living expenses. Funding to enable people with few qualifications to re-enter education are also popular. Very few trusts can meet the full costs of tuition fees and loans (see *How can trusts help?*).

Which trusts are included?

Those which give:

- at least £500 a year in education grants to students (most give considerably more)
- grants for up to and including first degree level
- grants based on need rather than merely academic performance
- grants to students of more than one school or college.

Not those which give:

- grants solely for postgraduate study
- awards or scholarships for academic excellence, except where these appear to be particularly relevant to people in need.

Many of the trusts support individuals for non-educational causes as well. These are all included in the sister guide to this book, *A Guide to Grants for Individuals in Need*. Some trusts support organisations such as schools or educational charities. Entries in this guide concentrate only on trusts' educational grants to individuals.

How trusts are ordered in the guide

National section

National trusts are classified according to:

- *need*, for example, independent & boarding schools, illness/disabilities and overseas students p17
- *occupation*, of parent or applicant p51
- *subject*, being studied p67

To find relevant trusts, individuals should initially use the flow chart p10, or go to the indexes on p291.

Local sections

Local sections start on p93; see pp89–91 for how to use these sections.

Before approaching trusts for grants

Before approaching trusts for grants, always enquire after any other possible sources of funds. Several trusts make this a prerequisite for considering applications.

Parents or students should first ask the school/college/university concerned whether they offer any financial help. Many have at least some funds for cases of need, even though they may not be publicised.

Other possible sources of funding are included in more detail at the back of the guide.

Supporting information

The guide also contains:

- a basic guide to the statutory entitlements and support for people in education p271
- information on company sponsorships and career development loans p277
- a description of some of the options available for boarding and independent school education (particularly state maintained boarding schools) p279
- a list of education authorities p283
- sources of further information and advice p289

How can trusts help?

Most trusts in this guide can only give supplementary help.

Trusts typically help with the cost of books, small-scale fees such as RSA, GCSE and A-level exam fees, and supplementary awards. It is very rare for a trust to fund fees and maintenance throughout an individual's academic career.

Creative use of the resources available in this guide can, however, have far-reaching effects on an individual's education.

Grants are usually for one of the following purposes:

- to enable individuals to study at any educational establishment (including for study or training of a professional, technical or vocational nature) – these grants are usually for fees or to buy books or equipment

- to help with the cost of travel for educational purposes (for example field studies, visits to museums)
- to help with extracurricular activities which are aimed at the physical and social development of the individual (such as outdoor centres, voluntary work overseas).

Loans of money, for buying musical instruments for example, can also be made.

Schoolchildren

Children who come from families which have severe financial needs can miss out on educational benefits such as books or school outings. This often puts the child at a social as well as an educational disadvantage to his or her peers. Grants from trusts do not address the causes of such situations, but they do help to redress some of the balance.

Grants can be made, for instance, for:

- children who struggle academically but have potential in extracurricular activities (for example, grants for musical instruments or sports equipment could help them to develop their potential in those areas)
- children with learning difficulties, who may be helped with grants towards extra lessons
- children with disabilities, who may be able to get grants for equipment related to their disabilities not otherwise available from statutory sources.

Many such grants will be for less than £100, but make a great difference to those concerned.

Students in further and higher education

Student loans now constitute the main source of funding for students and the demand for trust grants and other non-statutory sources of funding is higher than ever. Trust funds can help to relieve some of the debt students face, by making grants for:

- childcare costs
- books, equipment and materials
- travel, such as fieldwork or during gap years
- fees.

People starting work/apprentices

Many of the older educational trusts were originally set up to give grants to apprentices or to those 'entering a trade or profession'. These days, this means that grants are made to school-leavers and people leaving further or higher education, who are starting work.

Grants can be awarded to buy tools and equipment to help people in their trade, for example, arts materials, clothing or books/manuals. This can be extremely valuable to people who have student loans to repay.

Welfare to work is in many ways a modern apprenticing system. It may be that some educational charities can help individuals through this scheme.

Which trusts should I apply to?

Applications should not be made to trusts which clearly state the applicant is not eligible to receive a grant.

Trusts usually have very tight restrictions on who they can make grants to. These are usually set through legally defined criteria which cannot be altered. Eligibility can depend on various factors such as birthplace or parental occupation, as well as more obscure criteria such as surname! More commonly it is a matter of family background and where you were born or now live.

Trusts in this guide are listed thematically (parental occupation, geographical area of benefit, and so on). This is also done to emphasis that individuals should not apply to those trusts which clearly state that they would NOT be eligible to receive a grant. Individuals who do contact such trusts waste their own money and annoy trustees, who either feel obliged to reply (using their trust's money) or, as we would recommend, put the letter straight in the bin.

Approaching trusts

When you have found relevant trusts which may be worth looking into further (see *How to use this guide*, p9), read the entries through carefully. Many trusts have several criteria which potential applicants must meet. Some trusts publish guidelines to assist applicants. If so, get hold of them before making an application, along with an application form if there is one.

Some trusts welcome an initial telephone call from the individual or a third party, to enquire whether the application is suitable. Many of the correspondents for local trusts, however, administer the trust in their free time from home and may not be available during the day.

How to make an application on p11 goes into these issues in more detail.

How trusts work

Applications should not be made to trusts which clearly state the applicant is not eligible to receive a grant.

A trust can only make grants for the purposes outlined in its objects, defined when the trust is formed. One or two trusts in this guide are restricted to making grants to inhabitants of relatively wealthy parishes and appear to have great difficulty finding individuals in need of financial support.

Most trusts, however, receive a constant flow of applications for worthy causes. Where the objects of the trust permit it, we would like to see trusts increasingly forming clear policies on who they do support, targeting those most in need, across a range of academic ability, stages of education and types of need – from paying for school trips for schoolchildren to supporting the childcare costs of mature students on vocational courses.

The effectiveness of charities

While some charities, particularly national charities, produce clear guidelines, others (especially local charities) do not. We would like to make several suggestions as to ways in which educational charities, particularly local charities, could seek to encourage greater fairness in funding:

- Local charities could seek to expand their resources to meet new or more widespread needs.
- If trustees can only meet twice a year, they should aim to cover the peak periods. Although educational needs arise throughout the year, there are obvious peak times, notably around November (when people have started their course and have a much clearer idea of how much money they need) and May (when people are running out of money at the end of the academic year).
- Charities should also aim to ensure that needs can be met as rapidly as possible, for example by empowering the clerk or a small number of trustees to make payments up to a certain limit (say £100).
- Charities should ensure they are very well known in their area of benefit.

We recommend that each charity (depending on its eligibility restrictions) writes to at least the following: all welfare agencies (especially Citizens Advice); all community centres and other public meeting points; and the offices of the relevant education authority.

There are also a few trusts where the need in the area of benefit is not sufficient for all the income to be spent and/or the needs have changed from those that the trust was originally set up to meet. In this case the trust can consider extending its area of benefit or altering (expanding) the type of help it can give.

Acknowledgements

We are extremely grateful to the many trust officers and others who have helped compile this guide. However, although drafts of all the entries were sent to the charities concerned, and any corrections noted and incorporated, the text and any mistakes within it remain ours rather than theirs.

A request for further information

The research for this book was done as fully and carefully as we were able, but there will be relevant charities that we have missed and some of the information will be incomplete or will become out-of-date.

If any reader comes across omissions or mistakes in this guide, please let us know so that they can be rectified in future editions.

A telephone call to the research department of the Directory of Social Change (0151 708 0136) is all that is needed.

How to use this GUIDE

Below is a typical trust entry, showing the format we have used to present the information obtained from each of the trusts.

On the following page is a flowchart. We recommend that you follow the order indicated on the flow chart to look at each section of the guide and find trusts which are relevant to you.

Individuals should therefore initially look at the charities which give nationally, firstly in the section classified by occupation of parent. Once you have found any charities in that section we advise you to look in the section classified by subject, followed by the section classified by need. Individuals should then look in the local section of the guide, which relates to where they live, or at any other areas with which they have a connection.

Eligibility

This states who is eligible to apply for a grant. It can include restrictions on age, family circumstances, occupation of parent, subject to be studied, stage of education, ethnic origin, or place of residence.

Exclusions

This field gives information on what the trust will not fund.

Annual grant total

The total amount of money given in grants to individuals in the last financial year for which figures were available. Other financial information may be given where relevant.

Correspondent

The main person to contact, nominated by the trustees. Often the correspondent is the trust's solicitors or accountants, who may just pass applications on to the trustees and therefore will not be able to help with telephone enquiries.

The Fictitious Trust

Eligibility: Children/young people up to 25 years of age who are in need. Preference is given to children of single parent families and/or those who come from a disadvantaged or unstable family background.

Types of grants: Small one-off grants, to assist in cases of short-term need. The trust gives grants for a wide range of needs, including school uniform, books, equipment and educational trips in the UK and abroad. The maximum grant is £250.

Exclusions: No grants for school/college or university fees.

Annual grant total: 140 grants totalled £25,000 in 2005/06.

Applications: On a form available from the correspondent, submitted either directly by the individual or by the parent or guardian for those under 18. Applications are considered in January, April, July and October.

Correspondent: Mrs I M Helpful, Charities Administrator, 7 Pleasant Road, London SN0 0ZZ (020 7123 4567; Fax: 020 7123 4568).

Other information: The trust also gives relief-in-need grants to individuals.

Types of grants

Specifies whether the trust gives one-off or recurrent grants, the size of grants given and what grants are actually given for, e.g. school uniform, travel to school/ other educational establishment, living expenses, college fees, tools/ instruments, books and so on.

Applications

Including how to apply, who should make the application (i.e. the individual or a third party) and when to submit an application.

Other information

This contains miscellaneous further information about the trust.

How to identify sources of help
Quick reference flowchart

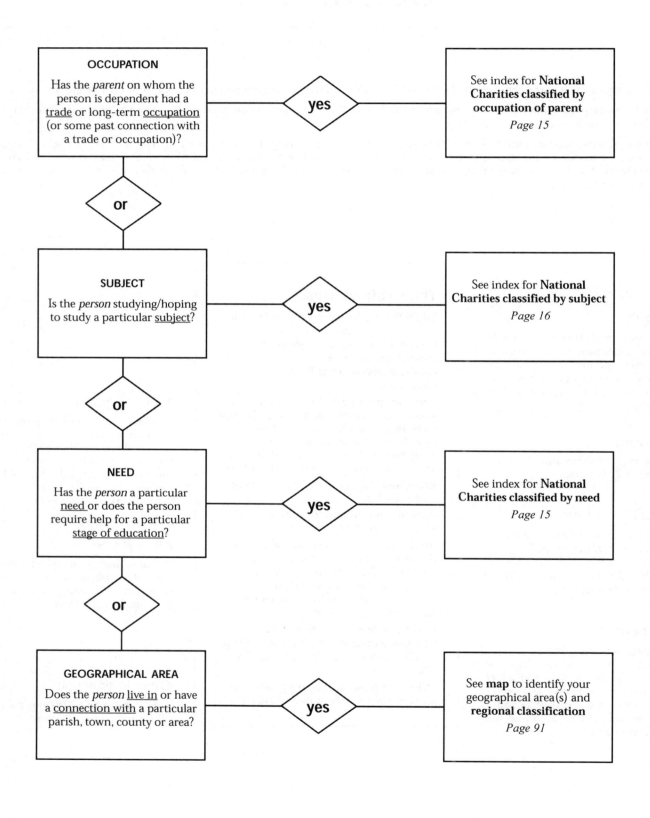

OCCUPATION

Has the *parent* on whom the person is dependent had a <u>trade</u> or long-term <u>occupation</u> (or some past connection with a trade or occupation)?

yes → See index for **National Charities classified by occupation of parent** *Page 15*

or

SUBJECT

Is the *person* studying/hoping to study a particular <u>subject</u>?

yes → See index for **National Charities classified by subject** *Page 16*

or

NEED

Has the *person* a particular <u>need</u> or does the person require help for a particular <u>stage of education</u>?

yes → See index for **National Charities classified by need** *Page 15*

or

GEOGRAPHICAL AREA

Does the *person* <u>live in</u> or have a <u>connection with</u> a particular parish, town, county or area?

yes → See **map** to identify your geographical area(s) and **regional classification** *Page 91*

HOW TO MAKE AN APPLICATION

In general, applicants should:

1. Exhaust other sources of funds

All sources of statutory funding should have been applied for and/or received before applying to a charity. Applications, therefore, should include details of these sources and any refusals. Where statutory funding has been received, but is inadequate, an explanation that this is the case should be made. A supporting reference from a relevant agency may also be helpful.

Educational establishments should also have been approached to see if they have any funds or can give a reduction in fees.

2. Give details of any unforeseen circumstances

Where relevant, try and show how the circumstances you are now in could not have been foreseen (for example, illness, family difficulties, loss of job and so on). In general, charities are reluctant to help people who start a course knowing that they have not got the money to complete it.

3. Ask for a suitable amount

Ask for an amount which the trust is able to give. Most trust grants are under £300, and local charities often give much less. If a trust only makes small grants, try asking for help with books, travel, childcare expenses and such like, and apply for fees elsewhere.

4. Give clear, honest details about any savings, capital or compensation

Most trustees will consider the applicant's savings when they are awarding a grant, although sometimes this does not need to affect trustees' calculations. In circumstances where you are certain that your savings are not relevant to grant calculations, you should explain this in the application.

5. Tailor the application to suit the particular charity

For example, if someone is applying to a trade charity on behalf of a child whose father had lengthy service in that particular trade, then a detailed description (and, where possible, supporting documentation) of the father's service would be highly relevant. If an application for the same child was being made to a local charity on another occasion, it would not.

6. Remember each charity has different deadlines for applications

Some charities can consider applications throughout the year, others may meet monthly, quarterly or just once a year. Very urgent applications can sometimes be considered between the main meetings. Where the trust has provided us with information about their deadlines, we have included it in the entry.

7. Mention applications to other charities

Explain that other charities are being approached, when this is the case, and state that any surplus money raised will be returned.

8. Make sure the appropriate person submits the application

Some trusts specify that they wish the application to be made directly by the individual and others request that the application is submitted via a third party, for example, a professional such as a teacher or educational welfare officer, or a parent/guardian.

9. Offer to supply references

For example, from a teacher, college tutor and/or another independent person. If the individual is disabled or has medical needs then a report from a doctor would be necessary.

10. Complete the trust's application form if there is one

The entry in this Guide should state if there is an application form available and how to obtain it.

Over the page is a general purpose application form. It can be photocopied and used whenever convenient and should enable applicants to state clearly the basic information required by most trusts. Alternatively, it can be used as a check-list of points to include in a letter. For notes on using the form see page 14.

11. Be honest and realistic, not moralising and emotional

Too many applications try to morally bribe trustees into supporting the application, or launch tirades against the current political regime. It is best to confine your application to clear and simple statements of fact.

12. Be as concise as possible and provide sufficient detail

Give as much relevant information as possible, in the most precise way. For example, 'place of birth' is sometimes answered with Great Britain, but if the trust only gives grants in Liverpool, to answer 'Great Britain' is not detailed enough and the application will be delayed pending further information. Applications are dealt with in the strictest confidence.

13. Write neatly and clearly; do not use jargon

Do not make it difficult for trustees to understand your application, they often have a lot of applications to read.

Please see page 14 for notes on the model application form.

Model application form

PURPOSE FOR WHICH GRANT IS SOUGHT	AMOUNT SOUGHT FROM £ THIS APPLICATION
APPLICANT (Name)	Occupation/School
Address Telephone no.	
Date of birth	Age Place of birth
Nationality	Religion (if any)

☐ Single   ☐ Married   ☐ Divorced   ☐ Partnered   ☐ Separated   ☐ Widow/er

FAMILY DETAILS: Name	Age	Occupation/School
Parents/ Partner	....	....
Brothers/Sisters/ Children..	....	....
....	....	....
....	....	....
Others (specify)..	....	....

INCOME (weekly)	£	p	EXPENDITURE (weekly – *excluding course fees*)	£	p
Father's/husband's wage	....		Rent/mortgage	....	
Mother's/wife's wage	....		Council tax	....	
Partner's wage	....		Water rate	....	
Income Support	....		Electricity	....	
Job seekers allowance	....		Gas	....	
Child benefit	....		Other fuel	....	
Family Credit	....		Insurance	....	
Attendance allowance	....		Fares/travel	....	
Disability living allowance	....		Household expenses (food, laundry etc).	....	
Housing benefit	....		Clothing	....	
Maintenance payments	....		School dinners	....	
Pensions	....		Childcare fees	....	
Other income (specify)............................	....		HP commitments	....	
....	....		Telephone	....	
....	....		TV rental	....	
....	....		TV licence	....	
			Other expenditure (specify)..................	....	
			....	....	
			....	....	
			....	....	

TOTAL WEEKLY INCOME   £ [   ]   TOTAL WEEKLY EXPENDITURE   £ [   ]

NAME OF SCHOOL/COLLEGE/UNIVERSITY:

Address

COURSE:

Is the course ☐ full-time? ☐ part-time?

Date of starting course: Date of finishing course:

NAME OF LOCAL EDUCATION AUTHORITY:

Have you applied for a grant?   ☐ YES ☐ NO

What was the outcome of the application?

Give details of any other grants or scholarships awarded:

Have you applied to your school/college/ university for help?   ☐ YES ☐ NO

What was the outcome of the application?

Have you applied to any other trusts? ☐ YES ☐ NO

What was the outcome of the application?

Have you applied for any loans? ☐ YES ☐ NO

What was the outcome of the application?

HOW MUCH ARE YOUR SCHOOL/COLLEGE FEES?

£

Have they been paid in full?   ☐ YES ☐ NO

If NO, please give details:

Other costs (e.g. books, clothing, equipment, travel etc.):

How much money do you need to complete the course? £

EXAMINATIONS PASSED & OTHER QUALIFICATIONS

PREVIOUS EMPLOYMENT (with dates)

ANY OTHER RELEVANT INFORMATION (*please continue on separate sheet if necessary*)

Signature: **Date:**

Notes: model application form

1. Because this form is designed to be useful to the wide range of people who apply for education grants, not all the information asked for will be relevant to every application. If, for example, an applicant is not in receipt of state benefits, or does not have credit debts, he/she should write 'N/A' (not applicable) in the box or line in question.

2. If, similarly, you do not have answers for all the questions at the time of applying, for example, if you have applied to other trusts and are still waiting for a reply, you should write 'Pending' under the question "Have you written to any other trusts? What was the outcome of the application?".

3. The first page is relevant to all applications; the second page is only relevant to people applying for school or college fees. If you are applying for clothing or books for a schoolchild then it may be worth filling out only the first page of the form and submit a covering letter outlining the reasons for the application.

4. Filling out the weekly income and expenditure parts of the form can be worrying or even distressing. Expenditure when itemised in this way is usually far higher than people expect. It is probably worth filling out this form with the help of a trained welfare rights worker.

5. You should always keep a copy of the completed form in case the trust has a specific query.

6. This form should not be used where the trust has its own form which must be completed.

NATIONAL & GENERAL SOURCES OF HELP

The entries in this section are arranged in three groups classified by need, occupation of parent (or applicant) and subject. Generally, trusts which occur in the second and third classification are not listed in the first, which is reserved for more general trusts. However, they may have been cross referenced where appropriate.

The breakdown aims to make it easy to identify trusts which might be of relevance and as such as have attempted to make the terms as specific as possible. In doing so, there will be some cross-over between categories as, for instance, mature university students could identify trusts in the 'Adult & continuing education' and 'further & higher education' sections, with various other categories possibly being relevant dependent on personal circumstances. There were, however, a number of trusts which did not fall into any specific category and these have been listed at the front of the guide.

The trusts are arranged alphabetically within each category. Readers are warned not to use these lists by themselves as a guide to sources of money. Each main entry must also be read carefully because in most cases there will be further specific requirements to be met. The trusts in each category tend to be in contact with each other, and any applicant who just writes to them all, regardless of their particular policies, will meet with limited sympathy.

Classification by subject

NATIONAL CHARITIES CLASSIFIED BY NEED

The Gustav Adolph & Ernest Koettgen Memorial Fund

Eligibility: British-born subjects who wish to educate themselves or to obtain tuition for a higher commercial career but whose means are insufficient for them to obtain such education or tuition at their own expense.

Types of grants: Students and mature students of British nationality who are studying in this country and are in higher education can apply for financial help towards the costs of books, fees, living expenses and childcare. Applicants are only considered if they are in the final year of a course and if they have managed to raise almost the whole amount needed, or if they encounter unexpected difficulty, as these grants are only intended to be supplementary.

Exclusions: Grants cannot be given for postgraduate study.

Annual grant total: In 2004/05 the fund had an income of almost £8,000 and a total expenditure of £6,900.

Applications: On a form available from the correspondent, submitted directly by the individual and supported by an academic reference. Trustees meet monthly.

Correspondent: Ms Fiona Macgillivray, Family Welfare Association, 501–505 Kingsland Road, Dalston, London E8 4AU (020 7254 6251; Fax: 020 7249 5443; e-mail: grants.enquiry@fwa.org.uk; website: www.fwa.org.uk)

Lawrence Atwell's Charity

Eligibility: Young people who have reached the age of 16 but who are under 27 at the date of application. Assistance will not be given to applicants whose parents' joint income exceeds £25,000 a year, plus £2,750 for each other dependent child under 18 years, nor to individuals with full LEA (or other) awards for fees and additional maintenance funding available to them, in the form of grants or loans. Applicants must be British citizens or refugees with indefinite leave to remain. Only students undertaking vocational training will be considered for funding.

Types of grants: The charity was founded over 400 years ago (1588) to 'set poor people upon work'. Grants are made for books, fees, travel, living costs and childcare. Grants can include those towards the cost of an apprentice's tools as well. In general, need as much as merit is taken into account when deciding to make grants.

Grants are usually one-off or recurrent and range from £200 to £3,000. Grants can be made for courses lasting more than one year. If the applicant is on a 2 or 3-year course, he/she may be asked to re-apply before the start of each year. If the applicant's costs are very high, they will be expected to show how they intend to raise the funds needed. The trustees will not make an award if they feel that finances are not feasible. Loans are rarely made.

Exclusions: Grants are not made for: study abroad; expeditions in the UK or abroad for any reason; intercalated degrees; clinical years of study (where LEA/NHS funding is in place) or electives; research, PhD degrees or non-vocational masters; business ventures; those already qualified for work; computer equipment (unless studying IT); students on dance or drama courses which are not accredited by the National Council for Drama Training or the Council for Dance Education and Training; students of music who have already had a year of postgraduate study (excluding voice students); students studying for A levels, GCSE's and GNVQ's; and students seeking to help cover debts or loans that have already been taken out.

Annual grant total: In 2004/05 it had assets of £15 million and an income of £567,000. Grants for educational purposes were made to 201 individuals totalling £262,000. Grants for other purposes totalled £126,000.

Applications: On a form available from the correspondent to be submitted directly by the individual. Guidelines for applicants, the application form, explanatory notes and a family finance form are also available to download from the charity's website www.skinnershall.co.uk/lawrenceatwell.htm.

Applications require proof of age and nationality, evidence of parental income and the support of two referees, which will be taken up in writing. Applications are considered in every month. The charity recommends that applications should be made as early as possible and to bear in mind that August, September and October are their busiest months. For courses finishing in June/July, the deadline for applications is Easter.

Correspondent: Gemma Garret, Atwell Administrator, The Skinners' Company, Skinners' Hall, 8 Dowgate Hill, London EC4R 2SP (020 7213 0561; Fax: 0207 236 5629; e-mail: atwell@skinners.org.uk; website: www.skinnershall.co.uk/lawrence_atwell.htm)

The Alfred Bourne Trust

Eligibility: Students aged under 30, who have lived in the UK for at least two years, are not in receipt of a mandatory grants and are in need for one course year only.

Types of grants: Help is to students in school, college or university.

Annual grant total: About £1,000 is available each year for individuals.

Applications: In writing to the correspondent, enclosing an sae.

Correspondent: J Kidd, Director, Maybrook House, Godstone Road, Caterham, Surrey CR3 6RE (01883 331177)

The Coffey Charitable Trust

Eligibility: People in need in the UK.

Types of grants: One-off and recurrent grants according to need.

Annual grant total: In 2004/05 the trust had an income of £6,000 and a total expenditure of £4,300.

Applications: The trust has previously stated that funds are fully committed.

Correspondent: C H Green, 24 Portman Gardens, Uxbridge, Middlesex, UB10 9NT

Other information: This trust also makes grants to organisations.

Conservative and Unionist Agents' Benevolent Association

Eligibility: Children of deceased Conservative or Unionist Agents or Women Organisers.

Types of grants: One-off and annual grants towards books, equipment, instruments and fees for schoolchildren.

Annual grant total: In 2004/05 the association had assets of £2.1 million, an income of £110,000 and a total expenditure of £83,000. Grants to individuals for welfare and educational purposes totalled £67,000.

Applications: Initial telephone calls are welcomed and application forms are available on request. Applications can be made either directly by the individual or their parent/guardian, or through a member of a management committee or local serving agent. All beneficiaries are allocated a 'visiting agent' for their award reassessment. More frequent visits may be made as necessary. Applications should be submitted in January and June for consideration in February and July.

Correspondent: The Secretary, Conservative Central Offices, 32 Smith Square, London SW1P 3HH (020 7984 8172; e-mail: jofarrell@ conservatives.com)

The Gillian Diamond Charitable Fund

Eligibility: People in need in the UK and developing countries.

Types of grants: One-off cash grants in the range of £100 and £300. Grants are given to schoolchildren, mature students, people with special educational needs and overseas students, including those for books and equipment/instruments.

Exclusions: Grants are not paid for fees or debts. No loans are made.

Annual grant total: In 2004/05 the fund had assets of £160,000 and an income of £5,000. The sum of £5,500 was distributed in welfare and education grants.

Applications: In writing to the correspondent to be submitted either directly by the individual or a family member, through an organisation such as Citizens Advice or school or through a third party such as a social worker or teacher. Applications are considered on an ongoing basis.

Correspondent: Gillian Diamond, PO Box 49849, London, NW5 9AJ (020 7485 6522; Fax: 020 7482 1384)

Other information: Grants are also made to organisations.

Essex Awards Trust

Eligibility: Applicants must have lived in Essex for at least two years prior to application, and must be undergoing a course of study in further or higher education beyond school-leaving age or are in attendance at a secondary school in Essex.

Types of grants: Grants are given to those in financial need in secondary school, further or higher education for fees, books and equipment, study abroad, living expenses and educational outings.

Annual grant total: Grants are made totalling about £1,000 each year.

Applications: On a form available from the correspondent. Applications should be made by the 15th of June, October and February.

Correspondent: The Student & Pupil Financial Support Manager, Student & Pupil Financial Service, PO Box 5287, County Hall, Chelmsford CM1 1LT

Other information: Two small trusts, the Florence Knapton Scholarship and the Cicely Courtauld & Ashdown Scholarships, have been incorporated into this trust.

The Fenton Trust

Eligibility: British-born subjects who are dependants of a member of the professional classes and are undergoing a course of education or training approved by the trustees; or poor members of the professional or middle class.

Types of grants: Grants are one-off and range between £100 and £500. They are only intended to be supplementary, therefore applicants are only considered if they are in the final year of a course and if they have managed to raise almost the whole amount needed, or if they encounter unexpected difficulty. Grants can go to students and mature students for help with costs of books, fees, living expenses, travel and childcare.

Exclusions: Grants are not given towards postgraduate study.

Annual grant total: In 2004/05, the trust had an income of £19,000 and a total expenditure of £8,300.

Applications: On a form available from the correspondent, to be submitted directly by the individual and supported by an academic reference. Trustees meet monthly.

Correspondent: Ms Fiona Macgillivray, Educational Grants Advisory Service, Family Welfare Association, 501–505 Kingsland Road, Dalston, London E8 4AU (020 7254 6251; Fax: 020 7249 5443; e-mail: grants.enquiry@fwa.org.uk; website: www.fwa.org.uk)

The Gane Charitable Trust

Eligibility: Students of arts and crafts, or design and social welfare. There is a preference for applicants from Bristol and south Wales.

Types of grants: College students, vocational students and mature students can receive help towards fees, books and equipment/instruments. Grants range from £200 to £500 and are normally one-off.

Annual grant total: In 2004 the trust had assets of £702,000, an income of £23,000 and a total expenditure of £19,000. The sum of £17,000 was distributed in 24 grants to individuals.

Applications: On a form available from the correspondent. Applications are considered in January, May and September.

Correspondent: Mrs R Fellows, The Secretary, c/o Bristol Guild, 68–70 Park Street, Bristol, BS1 5JY (0117 926 5548)

The General Federation of Trade Unions Educational Trust

Eligibility: Members of a trade union. Grants will only be considered for the subjects of economic history and theory; industrial law; and the history and principles of industrial relations.

Types of grants: Full-time and part-time students undertaking a course nominated by the recipient's trade union receive a grant of up to £150 (full-time), £50 (part-time) or £100 (Open University). Open University students will be supported after completing the first year. Grants may be paid annually.

Annual grant total: Grants are given to around 15 individuals totalling about £1,500 annually.

Applications: A nomination form is available from the correspondent and must be signed by the general secretary from the applicant's trade union. Applications are considered quarterly. Proof of trade union membership may be required. Forms signed by lay representatives and local officials are not valid.

Correspondent: Michael Bradley, Secretary, GFTU Educational Trust, Central House, Upper Woburn Place, London WC1H 0HY (020 7387 2578; Fax: 020 7383 0820; e-mail: gftuhq@gftu. org.uk; website: www.gftu.org.uk)

The N & P Hartley Memorial Trust

Eligibility: People who are disabled, older or terminally ill. Priority is firstly given to those living in West Yorkshire, secondly to individuals living in the north of England and thirdly to those elsewhere in the UK and overseas.

Types of grants: One-off grants for vocational training for vocational employment.

Exclusions: No support is given to animal rights or welfare.

Annual grant total: In 2003/04 the trust had assets of £844,000 generating an income of £39,000. Grants to six individuals totalled £4,100.

Applications: In writing to the correspondent, preferably through a social worker, Citizens Advice or other welfare agency, for consideration twice yearly. Reapplications from previous beneficiaries are welcomed.

Correspondent: J E Kirman, Trustee, Arabesque House, Monks Cross Drive, Huntington, York YO32 9GW

Other information: Grants are mainly made to organisations (£53,000 in 2003/04).

The Nora Henry Trust

Eligibility: Students from any country with a preference for students from developing countries who are studying subjects which will be of use when the student returns to that country.

Types of grants: One-off grants usually ranging from £100 to £200 can be given towards books, fees, living expenses, travel and childcare.

Exclusions: No grants for study or travel overseas for British students, or for student exchanges.

Annual grant total: In 2004/05, the trust had an income of £48,000 and total expenditure of £44,000.

Applications: On a form available from the correspondent. Applications should be submitted directly by the individual and supported by an academic referee. They are considered all year round.

Correspondent: Ms Fiona Macgillivray, Educational Grants Advisory Service, Family Welfare Association, 501–505 Kingsland Road, Dalston, London E8 4AU (020 7254 6251; e-mail: grants.enquiry@ fwa.org.uk; website: www.fwa.org.uk)

Kentish's Educational Foundation

Eligibility: Young people aged 11 to 35 who have the name of Kentish or who are related to the founder Thomas Kentish (died 1712) and require financial help. There are also limited opportunities to award grants to children/young people not named Kentish from Hertfordshire and Bedfordshire only (Thomas Kentish was associated with these counties).

Types of grants: One-off and recurrent grants ranging from £200 to £1,000. Grants for young people at secondary school for uniforms/clothing, books, educational outings, equipment and special help with disabilities which affect education. Further/ higher education awards are towards books, fees, equipment, study or travel abroad or student exchange. Grants to people starting work can be for travel, books, equipment/instruments or expenses arising from apprenticing. Because of the limited number of grants available, grants for postgraduate study are awarded only in special cases. Grants are not normally awarded to young people in the age group eligible for the Educational Maintenance Allowance.

Annual grant total: In 2004/05 the trust had assets of £544,000, an income of

£22,000 and a total expenditure of £24,000. Grants were made totalling £20,000 to 26 individuals.

Applications: A form is supplied on request and can be submitted by the individual or their parents/guardians. A copy of a school or tutor's report is required, together with copies of birth or marriage certificates if the applicant claims kinship with the founder but does not have the surname Kentish. Applications are to be submitted by the end of August for consideration in October.

Correspondent: Mrs M D Roberts, Clerk to the Trustees, 7 Nunnery Stables, St Albans, Hertfordshire AL1 2AS

The Leverhulme Trade Charities Trust

Eligibility: Undergraduates who are in need and are the dependants of people who have been employed for at least five years as commercial travellers, chemists (members of the Royal Pharmaceutical Society) or grocers. This includes the offspring, spouses, widows and widowers of such people.

Types of grants: Grants of up to £3,000 a year to full-time first degree students for needs such as tuition fees, books, travel costs and accommodation. Grants can be one-off or last for the duration of the course.

Annual grant total: In 2004 grants were made to 61 undergraduates (from 67 applications) and totalled £330,000. A further £564,000 was given in grants to organisations.

Applications: Undergraduate applications must be made through their university rather than directly by the individual, with the grants paid to the institutions to pass through to the successful applicants. The deadlines for the trust receiving the completed applications are 1 March and 1 November, with decisions made and funds available by the end of the month. Potential applicants should contact their student support services department for details of how to apply.

Correspondent: The Secretary, 1 Pemberton Row, London EC4A 3BG

P & M Lovell Charitable Settlement

Eligibility: People in need in education.

Types of grants: One-off grants of £50 to £500.

Annual grant total: In 2004/05 it had assets of £1.3 million and an income of £43,000. Grants to 8 individuals totalled £900 and a further £13,000 was given to 71 organisations.

Applications: In writing to the correspondent.

Correspondent: c/o Mike Haynes, KPMG, 100 Temple Street, Bristol BS1 6AG (0117 905 4000; Fax: 0117 905 4065)

Moody Charitable Trust

Eligibility: Students in need in the UK.

Types of grants: One-off and recurrent grants according to need.

Annual grant total: In 2004 the trust had an income of £4,000 and a total expenditure of £22,000. Grants totalled about £20,000.

Applications: In writing to the correspondent.

Correspondent: T J Mines, Thomas David, Orchard House, 5 The Orchard, Hertford SG14 3HQ

Other information: Grants are also made to organisations.

Richard Newitt Fund

Eligibility: Students aged between 24 and 45 with an intention to live and work in Britain.

Types of grants: One-off and recurrent grants according to need.

Exclusions: Grants are not normally awarded for the first year on an undergraduate course.

Annual grant total: In 2003/04 the fund had an income of £56,000 and a total expenditure of £87,000. Grants totalled about £80,000.

Applications: In writing to the correspondent.

Correspondent: Chris Gilbert, Kleinwort Benson, PO Box 57005, 30 Gresham Street, London EC2P 2US (020 3207 7356; Fax: 020 3207 7001)

The Noon Foundation

Eligibility: People in education.

Types of grants: One-off and recurrent grants according to need.

Annual grant total: In 2004, the foundation had net assets of £3.5 million, an income of £123,000 and a total expenditure of £73,000. During the year the foundation made grants to institutions totalling £54,000.

Applications: Application forms are available from the foundation.

Correspondent: The Trustees, 25 Queen Anne's Gate, St James' Park, London SW1H 9BU (020 7654 1600; Fax: 020 7654 1601; e-mail: secretary@ noongroup.co.uk)

The Osborne Charitable Trust

Eligibility: People in education in the UK and overseas.

Types of grants: One-off and recurrent grants according to need and one-off grants in kind. Grants are given to schoolchildren for equipment/instruments and special needs education for fees and equipment/instruments.

Exclusions: No grants for religious or political purposes.

Annual grant total: In 2004/05 the trust had an income of £8,300 and a total expenditure of £73,000.

Applications: This trust does not respond to unsolicited applications.

Correspondent: Jet Eaton, 57 Osborne Villas, Hove, East Sussex BN3 2RA

The Tim Rice Charitable Trust

Eligibility: People in need in the UK on academic or cultural courses.

Types of grants: One-off and recurrent grants of up to £1,000, but typically around £500 each. Grants can be for the costs of music and sport, school fees and for other educational purposes.

Annual grant total: In 2004/05, the trust had an income of about £40,000. A direct charitable expenditure of £34,000 was distibuted in grants made to individuals of £9,250, and to organisations totalling £24,800.

Applications: In writing to the correspondent.

Correspondent: Mrs E Heinink, Trustee, Ivy House, 31 The Terrace, Barnes, London SW13 0NR (020 7580 7313; Fax: 020 7580 2179)

The Rivendell Trust

Eligibility: British students studying in the UK who have started a course and are unable to complete it. Preference is given to prisoners, musicians and people who are disabled.

Types of grants: Grants of up to £1,000 towards books, equipment and travel, but not usually for course fees.

Exclusions: No grants for people starting work, overseas students, refugees, or people studying abroad.

Annual grant total: In 2004/05, the trust had a total income of £24,000 and an expenditure of £362,000. There was no further information concerning grants total.

Applications: On a form available from the correspondent, who will also give applicants further information about how to apply. Applications are considered four times a year.

Correspondent: The Trustees, Bircham, Dyson, Bell, 50 Broadway, London, SW1H OBL (020 7227 7000; Fax: 020 7227 3480)

Scarr-Hall Memorial Trust

Eligibility: People in education in the UK.

Types of grants: One-off grants according to need, usually in the range of £100 and £500.

Annual grant total: About £10,000.

Applications: In writing to the correspondent.

Correspondent: c/o C Kane, DPC, Vernon Road, Stoke-on-Trent, Staffordshire, ST4 2QY (01782 744144)

Shell Personal Development Awards

Eligibility: Students not yet in the final year of a university course, studying in the UK, the Republic of Ireland or the Netherlands.

Types of grants: One-off grants of £500 (€750) to help towards developing a talent in sport, music or performance art. Grants are also available towards expedition costs and learning a language or another skill.

Annual grant total: About £30,000 is available each year for grants to 60 individuals.

Applications: On a form available from the Shell website.

Correspondent: Shell Recruitment, Shell International, HRDR, Rowlandsway House, Manchester M22 5SB (0845 6001819; e-mail: graduates@shell.com; website: www.shell.com/careers)

Southdown Trust

Eligibility: Individual ventures of general educational benefit.

Types of grants: One-off and recurrent grants and loans ranging from £20 to £1,000. Grants are to 'support individual ventures of general educational benefit'. Previously grants have been made, for example, to fund a teaching assistant at a primary school, and to provide a scholarship for a university student.

Exclusions: No grants are made for art, dance, sociology, theatre, law, journalism, counselling, media studies, PhDs or materials.

Annual grant total: In 2005/06 the trust had assets of £800,000 and both an income and a total expenditure of £34,000, all of which was given in 110 grants.

Applications: In writing to the correspondent enclosing full information and an sae. Applications should be made directly by the individual.

Correspondent: J G Wyatt, 'Holmbush', 64 High Street, Findon, West Sussex BN14 0SY

The Mary Trevelyan Fund

Eligibility: Hardship grants are available for living costs for students from developing countries studying in London. Students must be in their final year of study and intend to return home on completion of their course. Students with outstanding tuition fees will not generally be considered. Preference is given where the institution is a member of International Students House.

Types of grants: Grants of up to £1,000 are available to those who experience difficulties due to unexpected financial hardship.

Annual grant total: In 2005/06 grants were made totalling £15,000. Between 15 and 20 individuals are supported each year.

Applications: On an application form available from the correspondent. Applications can be submitted directly by the individual or through a social worker, Citizens Advice or other welfare agency at any time. The trust states that an application will have a greater chance of success if it is supported by the student's own college/university advice or welfare service.

Correspondent: Peter Anwyl, Welfare Service, International Students House, 229 Great Portland Street, London W1W 5PN (020 7631 8369; Fax: 020 7631 8307; e-mail: welfare@ish.org.uk; website: www.ish.org.uk)

UNIAID Foundation

Eligibility: Higher education students and prospective students experiencing extreme financial hardship.

Types of grants: Support towards the financial challenges of higher education by provision of accommodation bursaries. One-off in kind grants are made.

Exclusions: No grants for postgraduate study.

Annual grant total: In 2005 the foundation had a total expenditure of £328,000. Grants usually total about £60,000.

Applications: Applications forms can be found on the foundation's website to be submitted directly by the individual. Also see the website for full guidelines.

Correspondent: Suite 210, Waterloo Business Centre, 117 Waterloo Road, London SE1 8UL (0870 600 0858; e-mail: info@uniaid.org.uk; website: www.uniaid.org.uk)

The Vardy Foundation

Eligibility: People in need in who live in the UK.

Types of grants: One-off and recurrent grants according to need.

Annual grant total: In 2004/05 the trust had assets of £14 million and an income of £2.3 million. Grants to 30 individuals for education and welfare purposes totalled £42,000.

Applications: In writing to the correspondent.

Correspondent: Sir Peter Vardy, Chair of the Trustees, Houghton House, Emperor Way, Doxford International Business Park, Sunderland SR3 3XR (0191 516 3636; e-mail: foundation@regvardy.com)

Other information: Grants are also made to organisations (£580,000 in 2005).

The Thomas Wall Trust

Eligibility: UK nationals in financial need, who wish to undertake educational studies which are vocational, short courses of professional training, or in a broad sense are concerned with social service and which will lead to paid employment.

Types of grants: One-off grants, up to £1,000, to supplement assistance from other sources. The trustees also need to be satisfied that the cost of the course is reasonable and that the intended result cannot be equally well obtained at less cost. Although the courses will normally be full-time, some vocational part-time courses will also be considered.

Exclusions: Grants are not given:

- to those who qualify for support from the Student Loan Company for undergraduate study
- for travel, study or work experience abroad
- for elective periods or intercalated courses
- for attendance at conferences
- for research or study for higher degrees by research
- to schoolchildren.

Annual grant total: In 2004/05 the trust had assets of £2.6 million and an income of £94,000. Grants were made to 45 individuals totalling £41,000. Organisations received £26,300.

Applications: On a form available for downloading from the website or by sending an sae to the correspondent. Applications are considered from January until September, or until funds run out. Only successful applicants will be notified by the trust. All information on the trust is available on its website.

Correspondent: The Director, PO Box 52781, London EC2P 2UT (website: www.thomaswalltrust.org.uk)

Other information: Grants are also given to charitable organisations in the field of education and social welfare, especially small ones or those of a pioneering nature.

The Wall Trust

Eligibility: Students, including students from overseas who are studying in the UK, who are aged 16 and over and are nominated by an organisation with which the trust has a scholarship scheme (see Applications section). Individuals may be undertaking further, higher or postgraduate education or vocational training in the performing arts and be studying music, drama or dance.

Types of grants: Normally grants are paid for each year of a scholar's course – on average for three years. Grants normally range between £1,000 and £3,000 a year and are limited to training or tuition fees.

Annual grant total: In 2004/05 the trust had an income of £40,000. Expenditure on scholarships and grants totalled £37,000.

Applications: Applications should only be made via an organisation with which the trust has a scholarship scheme. These are the Royal Ballet School, London Studio Centre, RADA, Royal College of Music, Royal Northern College of Music and the Purcell School. The trust stated in 2006 that all its funds were allocated.

Correspondent: Charles Wall, 19 Waterside Point, 2 Anhalt Road, London SW11 4PD (020 7978 5838; e-mail: charles@thewalltrust.org)

The Wingate Scholarships

Eligibility: People aged 24 or over on 1 September in the current year who are citizens of the UK, or another Commonwealth country, Ireland or Israel; or citizens of the EU who have been resident in UK for at least three years. Applicants must be living in the UK at the time of application. Applicants must satisfy the scholarship committee that they need financial support to undertake the work projected and, where relevant, show good reason why Research Council, British Academy or major agency support cannot be expected.

Types of grants: Wingate Scholarships are awarded to individuals of great potential or proven excellence who need financial support to undertake pioneering or original work of intellectual, scientific, artistic, social or environmental value, and to outstandingly talented musicians for advanced training. The work to be undertaken may or may not be in the context of a higher degree.

They are designed to help with costs of a specified project which may last up to three years, including grants for living expenses/fees, study or travel abroad and overseas students studying in the UK. Grants average about £6,500 each and the maximum available in any one year is £10,000.

Exclusions: Awards are not made for medical research, taught courses, including those at art, drama or business schools or those leading to professional qualifications or for electives.

Fine artists are not eligible for Wingate Scholarships, but those engaged in art history, craft or other related research can apply.

Annual grant total: About £400,000. In 2005 between 40 and 50 awards were made averaging £6,500 each.

Applications: More detailed information and application forms will be sent on written request to the correspondent. An A4 sae (45p) should be enclosed. Alternatively, application forms and information are available on the website. Applications should be submitted between 1 October and 1 February for consideration in March/April. Interviews of shortlisted candidates are carried out in London in May.

Correspondent: Faith Clark, Administrator, 2nd Floor, 20–22 Stukeley Street, London WC2B 5LR (website: www.wingate.org.uk)

Mrs Wingfield's Charitable Trust

Eligibility: People who are in need. Individuals in Shropshire have priority over the rest of the country.

Types of grants: Grants are given to schoolchildren, further and higher education students, vocational students, mature students and people with special educational needs, including those towards the cost of uniforms/clothing, fees, books and equipment/instruments.

Annual grant total: In 2003/04 the trust had assets of £498,000 and an income of £28,000. The sum of £14,000 was distributed in four educational grants. A further £690 was distributed in three relief-in-need grants.

Applications: In writing to the correspondent, directly by the individual. Cases are considered at regular meetings of the trustees. Refusals are not always acknowledged due to the cost involved. If a reply is required, please enclose an sae.

Correspondent: John Dodds, Dyke Yaxley, 1 Brassey Road, Old Potts Way, Shrewsbury SY3 7FA (01743 241281; Fax: 01743 235794; e-mail: info@dykeyaxley.co.uk; website: www.dykeyaxley.co.uk)

The Zobel Charitable Trust

Eligibility: People in education in the UK, particularly in the Christian field.

Types of grants: One-off and recurrent grants according to need.

Annual grant total: About £1,500 a year.

Applications: This trust does its own research and does not always respond to unsolicited applications.

Correspondent: S D Scott, Tenison House, Tweedy Road, Bromley, Kent BR1 3NF

Other information: Grants are also made to organisations.

Adult & continuing education

The Adult Education Bursary Scheme

Eligibility: People over 20, attending full-time courses of at least one year of liberal adult education at one of the following residential colleges: Coleg Harlech, Harlech, Wales; Fircroft College, Birmingham; Hillcroft College, Surbiton, London; Newbattle Abbey, Dalkeith; Northern College, Barnsley; and Ruskin College, Oxford. Applicants must have been offered a place on certificate and diploma courses at one of the colleges, and have been recommended for a bursary.

Types of grants: These colleges offer to relatively small numbers each year the opportunity of full-time university-type education in the broad field of social sciences and liberal studies. Students accepted by the colleges for one year courses are normally eligible for the bursaries covered by this scheme. These cover tuition fees and a maintenance grant and dependants' allowances. Grants for travel of over £80 a year are considered for the journey between the home and the residential college, or daily travel fees for students living at home during term-time.

Grants are also available to students who are disabled, including:

- a special equipment allowance of up to £4,795 towards buying, leasing or repairing special equipment
- a non-medical personal helper's allowance of up to £12,135 for non-medical helpers such as lip-readers or note-takers
- a general disabled student's allowance of up to £1,605 towards items such as printer inks, disks, braille paper and so on to supplement other grants.

Annual grant total: Grants total about £250,000 each year.

Applications: Most of the colleges have an annual intake of students each September or October, with some offering intakes in January or April. Intending applicants should write initially to the college of their choice for a guideline to applying. Their addresses are listed above. English and Welsh students' application forms will be allocated by the college once they have been accepted on the course.

English and Welsh students wishing to study in Coleg Harlech should contact: The Student Grant Officer, Coleg Harlech, Harlech, Gwynedd LL46 2PU.

Correspondent: Christine Francis, Awards Officer, Adult Education Bursaries, c/o Ruskin College, Walton Street, Oxford OX1 2HE (01865 554331; Fax: 01865 556362; e-mail: awards@ruskin.ac.uk)

Other information: The addresses of the colleges are as follows:

Coleg Harlech, Harlech, Gwynedd LL46 2PU (01766 780363).

Fircroft College, 1018 Bristol Road, Selly Oak, Birmingham B29 6LH (0121 472 0116).

Hillcroft College, South Bank, Surbiton, Surrey KT6 6DF (020 8399 2688).

Newbattle Abbey College, Dalkeith,

Midlothian EH22 3LL (0131 663 1921).

Northern College, Wentworth Castle, Stainborough, Barnsley, South Yorkshire S75 3ET (01226 776000).

Ruskin College, Walton Street, Oxford OX1 2HE (01865 554331).

The Gilchrist Educational Trust

Eligibility: Two categories of tertiary level students are eligible for consideration:

(i) those who have made proper provision to fund a degree or higher education course but find themselves facing unexpected financial difficulties which may prevent the completion of it. Applicants will normally be in the last year of the course;

(ii) those who, as part of their degree course, are required to spend a short period studying in another country. Examples are the fieldwork necessary for a thesis or dissertation, or medical students' elective periods study.

Types of grants: Grants are modest and are given once only. Adult study grants (see (i) above) are up to £1,000. Travel study grants (see (ii) above) are up to £500.

Exclusions: Assistance cannot be offered to the following: part-time students; those seeking funds to enable them to take up a place on a course; students seeking help in meeting the cost of maintaining dependents; students who have, as part of a course, to spend all or most of a academic year studying in another country; those wishing to go abroad under the auspices of independent travel, exploratory or educational projects.

Annual grant total: In 2005/06 the trust had assets of £1.9 million, an income of £86,000 and a total expenditure of £82,000. Grants were given to 43 individuals totalling £30,000. A further £24,000 went to organisations.

Applications: There is no application form. In response to an initial enquiry, the trust sends a sheet listing the information required to enable an application to be considered. They can be submitted at any time of the year.

Correspondent: The Secretary, 28 Great James Street, London WC1N 3EY (020 7404 1672; e-mail: gilchrist.charity@btinternet.com; website: www.gilchristgrants.org.uk)

Other information: This is a small trust with limited funds; grants have to be very modest and applicants are expected to be seeking help from other sources as well. A large number of applications are received each year, but only a few students can be helped.

The Sure Foundation

Eligibility: Christians seeking to share their faith in the UK or overseas and people needing a new start in employment, such as ex-offenders. Preference is given to

those training to promote Christian work and faith.

Types of grants: Grants in the range of £50 to £200 are given towards training for various aspects of Christian ministry and to people restarting work for equipment, tools and so on.

Exclusions: Grants are not made to individuals with previous vocational or professional qualifications or for higher education.

Annual grant total: In 2004/05 the trust had assets of £12,000 and an income of £1,100 and a total expenditure of £4,600.

Applications: In writing to the correspondent directly from the individual. References are considered helpful when assessing applications. Applications are considered in February, May, August and November.

Correspondent: The Trustees, Hobbs Green Farm, Odell, Bedfordshire MK43 7AB

Business start-up & apprentices/ vocational training

The Oli Bennett Charitable Trust

Eligibility: Young people between 18 and 30, who are self-employed and are UK residents.

Types of grants: Grants in the range of £1,000 and £1,500 for people starting up their own businesses.

Annual grant total: In 2004 the trust had an income of £2,500 and a total expenditure of £9,300.

Applications: Application forms are available on the trust's website. Applications are considered every three months. A business plan is required to assess the viability of the idea.

Correspondent: Mrs B J Bennett, 'Camelot', Penn Street, Amersham, Buckinghamshire HP7 0PY (01494 717702; e-mail: info@olibennett.org.uk; website: www.olibennett.org.uk)

Other information: The trust was set up in memory of Oli Bennett, who died in the September 11 2001 attacks in New York.

The Prince's Trust

Eligibility: See below.

Types of grants: The Prince's Trust helps young people overcome barriers and get their lives working.
Through practical support including

training, mentoring and financial assistance, The Prince's Trust helps 14-30 year olds to realise their potential. The trust focuses its efforts exclusively on those who have struggled at school, been in care, been in trouble with the law, or are long-term unemployed. The trust runs a variety of opportunities to help these young people to succeed.

In terms of cash support, these grants are available:

● Development awards – cash awards of £50–£500 combined with advice and support, so young people can access education, training or work.

● Group awards – cash awards of between £250 and £1,000 (for groups of young people aged 14–16) and £500 and £5,000 (for groups aged 16–25) for projects of a useful nature in the local community.

● Business start-up assistance – low interest loans, grants and other business start-up support for 18–30 year olds.

Annual grant total: In 2004/05, the trust had net assets of £15.9 million. It had an income of £42.6 million and a total expenditure of £39.6 million. Grants were given to 41,680 individuals totalling £1.8 million.

Applications: An online contact form is available on each of the trust's programmes on its website, or Freephone 0800 842 842.

Correspondent: Ms Nicola Brentnall, Secretary, 18 Park Square East, London NW1 4LH (020 7543 7480; Freephone: 0800 842 842 – for details of how to apply; Fax: 020 7543 1200; website: www.princes-trust.org.uk)

The Women's Careers Foundation (Girls of The Realm Guild)

Eligibility: Women only, who are UK citizens. Applicants should be seeking assistance to begin or continue studies for a career and should be 21 or over, except for music or dancing when the minimum age is 16.

Types of grants: One-off grants ranging from £250 to £400 are made to eligible beneficiaries, as are loans of up to £1,000 repayable over four years at 2.5% interest. Smaller grants averaging around £50 are also made. All these grants can help with any costs relating to further education relevant to a career.

Exclusions: Grants are not given for PhD study or postgraduate studies if the subject indicates a complete change of direction.

Annual grant total: In 2005 grants were made to 18 individuals totalling £6,100. The trust also made 3 loans totalling £2,300.

Applications: In writing to the correspondent. Applications should be submitted between the 1 September and 31 January for the following academic year. An sae is essential. The correspondent has stated that timing is crucial: 'so many people write for immediate help which we cannot give'. Applications must be submitted well in advance.

Correspondent: Mrs B Hayward, Secretary, 2 Watchoak, Blackham, Tunbridge Wells, Kent TN3 9TP (01892 740602)

Children & young people

The French Huguenot Church of London Charitable Trust

Eligibility: Young people, usually in secondary or higher education, but applications for younger children can be considered. For all categories, where there are two or more claimants of equal merit, the trustees have the following order of priority:

(a) people who, or whose parents are, members of the Church

(b) people of French Protestant descent

(c) other people as trustees think fit.

Grants can be given for the education of:

(i) children of members of the church

(ii) French Protestant children attending French schools in London

(iii) those under 25 of proven French Protestant descent

(iv) girls at schools of the Girls' Public Day School Trust and the Church Schools Company Ltd

(v) boys at selected independent day schools

(vi) choristers at schools of the Choir Schools Association

(vii) people under 25 for individual projects, at home or abroad.

Types of grants: (i) Bursaries at the schools mentioned above; these do not usually exceed the value of one term's fees. (ii) Project grants [as in (vii) above]; these do not usually exceed £250 and may be less.

Annual grant total: In 2004, the trust had net assets of £7,6 million, a total income of around £400,000, and a total expenditure of £383,000. The trust gave educational grants to 89 individuals totalling £134,000

Applications: Applications for categories (i) and (ii) above should be made to the Secretary of the Consistory, 8–9 Soho Square, London W1V 5DD. Correspondence regarding categories (iii) and (vii) should be sent to the correspondent. Applications for categories (iv), (v) and (vi) should be sent to the head of the school concerned, mentioning the applicant's connection (if any) with the French Protestant Church.

Correspondent: Penny Chapman, 50 Broadway, Westminster, London SW1H 0BL (020 7227 7123; Fax: 020 7222 3480; e-mail: pennychapman@bdb-law.co.uk)

Other information: The trust also awards an annual scholarship for Huguenot Research at the Institution of Historical Research at the University of London, and has endowed an annual scholarship to support students under 25 wishing to undertake projects relevant to modern Europe (Peter Kirk Memorial Fund).

The William Gibbs Trust

Eligibility: Young people in education who are of British nationality.

Types of grants: One-off and recurrent grants according to need.

Annual grant total: In 2004 the trust had an income of £9,700 and a total expenditure of £44,000. Grants totalled about £40,000.

Applications: This trust states that it does not respond to unsolicited applications as the funds are already allocated. Please do not telephone the trust.

Correspondent: Antonia Johnson, Administrator and Trustee, Manor Farm, Middle Chinnock, Crewkerne, Somerset TA18 7PN

The Glebe Charitable Trust

Eligibility: Children and young people up to the age of 18 who are disabled or disadvantaged in some way in addition to being in financial need. Please note, financial need alone is not sufficient.

Types of grants: One-off grants in the range of £250 and £1,000.

Exclusions: Grants are not made towards fees for higher education, for gap year activities or for dyslexia.

Annual grant total: In 2004 the trust had assets of £357,000 and an income of £25,000. Grants to eight individuals totalled £4,000.

Applications: The trust states that it: 'receives applications beyond its capacities, both administrative and financial. The trustees have therefore taken the reluctant decision that they can no longer consider unsolicited applications from either charities or individuals.' Its current policy is to make grants to organisations known to the trustees, which give practical help to disabled/disadvantaged children.

Correspondent: The Trustees, PO Box 38078, London SW19 5WS (020 7405 1234; Fax: 020 7831 1525)

Other information: Grants to organisations in 2004 totalled £11,000.

The Eleanor Hamilton Educational Trust

Eligibility: Priority is given to children who are either in their second year of GCSEs or their second year at A-level. Consideration is also given to students (under 30) who are dyslexic or have other special needs and are estranged from their parents.

Types of grants: One-off grants in the range of £100 and £500 towards fees for schoolchildren and people with special educational needs and towards living expenses for college student, undergraduates, vocational students and people with special educational needs.

Annual grant total: In 2005 the trust's assets totalled £4.6 million and its income was £149,000. During the year 208 educational grants were made to students, totalling £104,000. In addition, organisations received grants totalling £1,500.

Applications: On a form available form the correspondent at any time.

Correspondent: The Trustees, 62 Park Lane, Norwich NR2 3EF (01603 614945)

The Jeremi Kroliczewski Educational Trust

Eligibility: People under 25 who are in education and live in England or Wales. There is a preference for people who are of Polish origin, although the trust states that all funds are fully committed years in advance.

Annual grant total: In 2005/06 the trust had both an income and a total expenditure of around £7,000.

Applications: The trust states that all funds are fully committed.

Correspondent: Simeon Emmanuel Arnold, Solicitor, 37–38 Haven Green, Ealing, London W5 2NX

The Mercers' Company Educational Trust Fund

Eligibility: (i) Children:

Children in their final years of a GCSE course or the final year of an A–level course can receive support for fees at an independent school approved by the trust. The child's family must have met unexpected financial misfortune.

(ii) Students:

People resident in the UK who are under 25 years at the date of application and are pursuing a full-time course leading to a vocational degree, diploma or other qualification at an educational institution approved by the trust in the UK.

The company makes bursary awards directly to a number of institutions of further and higher education, and consequently applications from individual students cannot be accepted for courses in performing arts, law, business and management studies, journalism, BTec, City and Guilds, intercalated degrees or elective study. Grants are restricted to students under the age of 25 who are not in receipt of a local authority or state grant and taking a vocationally-orientated degree or diploma.

There are a further four small funds for students at Oxford and Cambridge universities.

Annual grant total: In 2005, the trust had net assets of £1.3 million. It had an income of £1 million, and a total expenditure of £737,000; grants and bursaries to individuals in further education totalled £600,000.

Applications: On forms obtainable from the correspondent. Forms should be submitted by the individual or through the educational establishment or a welfare agency, for consideration in March, June, September and December.

Correspondent: Clare Fuchs, Education Manager, Mercers' Company, Mercers' Hall, Ironmonger Lane, London EC2V 8HE (020 7726 4991; Fax: 020 7600 1158; e-mail: mail@mercers.co.uk; website: www.mercers.co.uk)

Other information: The trust receives about 1,000 applications per month. Eligibility does not ensure a grant.

Professional Classes' Aid Council

Eligibility: The dependants of people of professional background who are in financial distress.

Types of grants: Weekly allowances of £5 to £20, and one-off gifts according to need.

Annual grant total: In 2004 the trust had assets of £2.3 million and an income of £314,000. Grants to 456 individuals, 317 of which were existing beneficiaries, totalled £138,000 and were made for education and welfare purposes.

Applications: On a form available from the correspondent, submitted either by the individual, or via a third party such as a social worker, Citizens Advice or other welfare agency.

Correspondent: Miss Nerina Inkson, 10 St Chrisopher's Place, London W1U 1HZ (020 7935 0641)

Red House Youth Projects Trust

Eligibility: Young people between the ages of 10 and 21 who are resident in Norfolk.

Types of grants: Grants do not normally exceed £500.

Annual grant total: In 2004/05 the charity had an income of £30,000 and made grants to individuals totalling £725. A further £21,000 went to organisations.

Applications: In writing to the correspondent. Grants are considered four times a year in March, July, October and December.

Correspondent: Robert N Marsh-Allen, Grants Administrator, c/o Marguerite Smith, 12 Spruce Avenue, Ormesby, Great Yarmouth, Norfolk, NR29 3RY (01493 731976; Fax: 01493 731976)

Reynolds Memorial Scheme

Eligibility: Young people aged between 16 and 21 who: (i) are estranged or orphaned; (ii) have continuing responsibility for the care of sick or disabled parents or relatives; (iii) are looked after by adoptive parents; (iv) are living with single parents; (v) are cared for by family members or friends; or (vi) have been granted full refugee status or indefinite leave to remain.

Types of grants: Assistance provided for the acquisition of academic, professional, trade or vocational qualifications. Grants towards living costs such as rent, food, clothing, transport, books and materials or equipment where these cannot be provided from statutory sources or family. Help with fees is only considered where no statutory funding is available or it is insufficient. No grants towards debts, childcare, overseas study, intercalated degrees or computer purchase.

Exclusions: Young people who are looked after by a local authority, live outside the UK, are overseas or postgraduate students, or whose single fundamental problem is financial hardship, are not eligible.

Annual grant total: In previous years grants to around 200 individuals have been made totalling about £200,000. No recent financial information was available.

Applications: In writing to the correspondent, including age and date of birth of the applicant, home and student addresses, course and place of study or training, dates of start and completion of course, and grounds of eligibility, together with a full account of the problems faced and family circumstances.

Correspondent: The Clerk, Reynolds Memorial Committee, The Buttle Trust, Audley House, 13 Palace Street, London SW1E 5HX (020 7828 7311; Fax: 020 7828 4724; e-mail: karenm@ buttletrust.org)

The T A K Turton Charitable Trust

Eligibility: Students in the final year of GCSE or A-level courses, where a sudden loss of parental income would mean they are unable to complete the course.

Types of grants: Grants are from between £500 and £2,500.

Annual grant total: In 2005 the trust had assets of £327,000 and an income of £14,000, all of which was given in grants to around 16 individuals.

Applications: Applications should be submitted through a school, college or educational welfare agency at any time. They must be sent to the following address:

Joint Educational Trust, 6 Lovat Lande, London, EC32 8DT (Tel: 020 7626 4583).

Correspondent: C T O Turton, Trustee, Egypt Farm Bungalow, Rushlake Green, Heathfield, Sussex TN21 9QT (01435 830478)

Further & higher education

The Follett Trust

Eligibility: Students in higher education.

Types of grants: One-off and recurrent grants according to need.

Annual grant total: In 2005, the trust had net assets of £71,000, an income of £246,000, a total expenditure of £188,000. The trust gave grants to individuals totalling £11,000.

Applications: The trust states, 'A high proportion of donees come to the attention of the trustees through personal knowledge and contact rather than by written application. Where the trustees find it impossible to make a donation they rarely respond to the applicant unless a stamped addressed envelope is provided'.

Correspondent: M D Follett, 17 Chescombe Road, Yatton, Bristol BS49 4EE (01934 838337)

The Gen Foundation

Eligibility: Postgraduates and students in further education studying modern languages, music, art and natural sciences. Usually only people who live in the UK or Japan are considered. Applications that promote cultural exchange between Japan and the UK are given priority.

Types of grants: One-off grants and scholarships.

Annual grant total: In 2004/05, the foundation had net assets of £1 million, a total income of around £53,000 and a total expenditure of £26,000. The foundation split a total budget of £17,500 between ten sucessful individuals.

Applications: On a form available from the correspondent. Applications should include an essay proposal.

Correspondent: Masanori Wada, The Gen Foundation, 45 Old Bond Street, London W1S 4DN (020 7495 5564; Fax: 020 7495 4450; e-mail: info@ genfoundation.org.uk; website: www. genfoundation.org.uk)

George Heim Memorial Trust

Eligibility: People aged under 30 who are in further education.

Types of grants: Grants range from £100 to £1,000.

Annual grant total: In 2004/05 the trust had an income of £960 and a total expenditure of £1,400. Grants totalled about £1,000.

Applications: In writing to the correspondent.

Correspondent: Paul Heim, Wearne Wyche, Picts Hill, Langport, Somerset TA10 9AA

The Hockerill Educational Foundation

Eligibility: People aged 18 to 50 who are, or intend to become, teachers of religious education (or work related to religious education), and young people at college or university who are in financial need.

Types of grants: Grants of £500 to £2,000 are available for students in further/higher education for help with fees, books, living expenses and travel.

Exclusions: No grants to schoolchildren, those studying for Christian ministry or mission unless continuing in teaching, and for visits, study or conferences abroad, gap year activities, courses in counselling, therapy or social work, or for courses leading specifically to non-teaching careers such as medicine, law or accountancy. Grants are no longer made to overseas students.

Annual grant total: In 2004/05 the trust had assets of £5.7 million and an income of £235,000. Grants to 26 individuals totalled £21,000.

Applications: On a form available from the correspondent, to be returned by 1 March.

Correspondent: Colin Broomfield, 16 Hagsdell Road, Hertford SG13 8AG (01992 303053; Fax: 01992 425950; e-mail: hockerill.trust@ntlworld.com)

Other information: The charity states that the majority of annual funding is committed to long-term projects or activities in education, but limited funding is also available to organisations for projects relating to churches' educational work (£116,000 in 2004/05).

The Humanitarian Trust

Eligibility: British citizens and overseas students under 30 years old on a recognised course of study in the UK and who hold a basic grant for the course.

Types of grants: Grants of £200 are available to graduates and postgraduates and are awarded for 'academic subjects only', and top up fees.

Exclusions: No grants for domestic expenses such as childcare, overseas courses, fieldwork or travel, theatre, music, journalism or art, drama, sociology, youth work or sports.

Annual grant total: In 2004/05 the trust had assets of £3.2 million and an income of £87,500. Grants were made to 45

individuals totalling £1,600. A further £56,300 was given to organisations.

Applications: In writing to the correspondent including a cv, income and expenses and total shortfall and two references (from course tutor and head of department).

Correspondent: Mrs M Myers, 27 St James's Place, London SW1A 1NR

Helena Kennedy Foundation

Eligibility: Students attending a further education college in the UK who are progressing to university education and who may be disadvantaged in some way. Applicants must be intending to undertake a higher diploma or undergraduate degree for the first time

Types of grants: One-off bursaries of £1,000.

Annual grant total: There were 48 bursaries made totalling £48,000 in 2005.

Applications: Applicants are encouraged to visit the website www.hkf.org.uk, or send a short email to enquire about eligibility criteria. The application deadline is the end of April.

Correspondent: Rachel Watters, Development and Fundraising Offic, 101 Windsor Street, Wolverton, Milton Keynes MK12 5AN (01908 321155; e-mail: enquiries@hkf.org.uk; website: www.hkf.org.uk)

The Sidney Perry Foundation

Eligibility: The trust aims primarily to help first degree students. Students must be younger than 35 when the course starts. Eligible foreign students studying in Britain can also apply. Postgraduates may also receive support (see under Types of grants).

Types of grants: One-off and recurrent grants with the maximum award of £700 reserved for exceptional cases. Grants are usually towards books and equipment/ instruments. Applicants can reapply in further years.

Distance learning, correspondence, part-time and short-term courses may be considered according to circumstances.

Exclusions: The foundation is unable to assist: students in the first year of a (three or four year) first degrees; medical students during their first year if medicine is their second degree; medical students during elective periods and intercalated courses; any second degree courses where the grade in the first degree finals was lower than a 2:1; second degree courses, unrelated to first degrees, unless they are a necessary part of professional training such as medicine or dentistry; expeditions overseas; cases where a full LEA funding has been awarded; GCSE and A-level courses; students on Access, ESOL, HNC, HND, BTEC, GNVQ and NVQ Levels 1-4 and foundation courses.

Annual grant total: In 2004 the foundation had an income of £171,000 and a total expenditure of £124,000.

Applications: Applications can be made at any time on official forms available from the correspondent and directly by the individual. Incomplete forms will be disregarded. Enclosure of an sae would be appreciated. 'Students are expected to have a confirmed placement at college and have the bulk of their funding before approaching the foundation. We will not contact referees on an applicant's behalf: candidates should ensure an academic reference (not a photocopy) is included'. Previous beneficiaries of grants should include details of the previous grant i.e. amount of grant, year received and grant number.

Correspondent: Mrs L A Owens, PO Box 2924, Faringdon SN7 7YJ (e-mail: sidneyperryfound@cs.com)

Other information: The foundation is unable to deal with student debt or financial problems needing a speedy resolution.

The Wilfred Maurice Plevins Charity

Eligibility: Sixth form students, who are children of professional men or women, whose education or career training has been prejudiced by financial misfortunes not of their own making. The father is required to be or have been a member of a professional institute or association having disciplinary control over members in the event of professional misconduct. This includes commissioned members of the armed forces.

Types of grants: Preference is currently given to A-level students. Grants are made on an annual or short-term basis with a discretionary maximum of half-fees. (The average grant paid in 2004/05 was £1,417.)

Exclusions: Grants are not given for first degree courses or in circumstances where parents were not in a position to fund the fees when entering the child for the school.

Annual grant total: In 2004/05, the charity had assets of £3.2 million and an income of £96,000. The sum of £61,000 was paid in 43 grants to individuals.

Applications: In writing to the correspondent including full financial details of parents (capital and income), full details of other awards, grants, scholarships, and so on, and school reports. Applications should be submitted by the applicant's parents, normally by 31 March for the following September.

Correspondent: The Trustees, c/o Chantrey Vellacott, Prospect House, 58 Queens Road, Reading, Berkshire RG1 4RP

Other information: The correspondent also administers the Thornton-Smith Young People's Trust (see separate entry).

Fred and Pat Tuckman Foundation

Eligibility: Support is given to a range of further and higher education students studying in the UK who are academically talented and in financial need, including mature students and postgraduates. There may be a preference for foreign students who are studying in the UK and are either on a course they are unable to take in their own country, or able to benefit from experiencing a democratic way of life in the UK. There is some preference for Jewish students.

Types of grants: Average annual grants are of £500 each and are made to about six individuals a year. Further smaller grants are made to well-established charities.

Annual grant total: In 2004/05 the foundation had an income of £2,400 and a total expenditure of £5,400. Education grants to individuals average £2,500 to £3,000 in total each year.

Applications: On a form available from the correspondent – requests must be accompanied by an sae. The trust requires information giving an outline of the applicant's achievements, details of goals and the extent of the financial shortfall. Applications should be submitted directly by the individual, preferably by the end of May, for consideration between July and August.

Correspondent: F A Tuckman, 6 Cumberland Road, Barnes, London SW13 9LY (020 8748 2392)

Williamson Memorial Trust

Eligibility: Students on first degree courses.

Types of grants: Grants of not more than £200 a year are made to people not known to the trustees for help with books, fees, living expenses and study or travel abroad. Grants limited to £200 a year to overseas students; the trust is not able to make a more significant contribution towards the higher fees and living expenses that overseas student incur. Grants are rarely made for student exchange or postgraduate study.

Annual grant total: In 2005/06 the trust predicts an income of £5,800 from donations, educational grants to 25 individuals totalling £4,800 and welfare grants to 18 individuals totalling £1,500.

Applications: Due to a reduction of its funds and the instability of its income, the trust regrets that very few new applications will be considered to ensure it can meet its existing commitments. In 2005, for example, over 500 letters were acknowledged regretting inability to help. Support will generally only be given to cases known personally to the trustees and to those individuals the trust has existing commitments with.

Correspondent: C P Williamson, Little Cluny, The Street, Ightham, Sevenoaks, Kent TN15 9HE

S C Witting Trust

Eligibility: Schoolchildren under 15, undergraduates and mature students who live England.

Types of grants: One-off grants are made for uniforms/clothing, books and equipment/instruments.

Exclusions: No grants towards debts or loans.

Annual grant total: About £300,000 in 2004.

Applications: In writing to the correspondent, through a third party such as a social worker or teacher including a short case history, reason for need and the amount required. University students must have a letter of support indicating financial need. Unsuccessful applications are not acknowledged unless an sae is included.

Correspondent: The Administrator, Friends House, 173 Euston Road, London NW1 2BJ

Illness & disability

The British Association of Health Services in Higher Education Student Disability Assistance Fund

Eligibility: Students in an institution of higher education who are wholly or mainly engaged in a course of study. The study must have been affected by illness, accident or disability and grants are only given to help students who need extra assistance due to this problem. No grants to people under the age of 18.

Types of grants: Grants are generally given to first degree students, although postgraduates can be funded. 'We stress that we are not able to award grants for tuition, maintenance or fees. We prefer a grant to buy a specific item, aid or piece of equipment. Funding for more expensive items must be pledged from other sources before our contribution is released.' The trust gives one-off grants of up to £500. Grants can also be used towards extra travel, books or instrument expenses.

Exclusions: Grants are not given towards living expenses, taxes or examination fees.

Annual grant total: Between £9,000 and £10,000.

Applications: Further details and application forms are available from the correspondent. Applications can be submitted directly by the individual or by a relevant third party, for example, RNIB, RNID and social workers. The trust also requires a reference from the applicant's tutor and a doctor's letter, stating the area of disability or problem due to illness or accident. Applications should be made in triplicate; an sae is preferred. No telephone contact is possible. Deadlines for applications to be considered are 1 March, 1 June and 1 November.

Correspondent: Dr K. Cockerill, 35 Hazlewood Road, Bush Hill Park, Enfield EN1 1JG (website: www.bahshe.demon.co.uk)

David Hyman Charitable Trust

Eligibility: University students, under 25 years of age, who are severely disabled (wheelchair bound) or blind.

Types of grants: One-off grants of up to £200, depending on circumstances. Grants can be towards university fees, books and equipment.

Annual grant total: In 2003/04 the trust had an income of £2,400 and a total expenditure of £56,000.

Applications: In writing to the correspondent with full proof of disability and educational opportunity.

Correspondent: David Hyman, 101 Flood Street, London SW3 5TD

The MFPA Trust Fund for the Training Of Handicapped Children in the Arts

Eligibility: Children with physical or mental disabilities living in the UK between the ages of 5 and 18.

Types of grants: One-off and recurrent grants towards participation in painting, music, or drama, for example, books, educational outings and school fees. The maximum grant available is £5,000.

Annual grant total: About £28,000.

Applications: In writing to the correspondent for consideration throughout the year. Applications can be made directly by the individual or through a third party such as their school, college or educational welfare agency. Applications should enclose a letter explaining their needs and a doctor's letter confirming disability.

Correspondent: Florence Bunn, Trustee, 180 Bispham Road, Blackpool, FY2 0LA

The Silverwood Trust

Eligibility: Children and young people of school age with physical or learning disabilities.

Types of grants: One-off or small recurrent grants according to need. (Normally restricted to people known to the trustees.)

Exclusions: No grants for computers or school fees.

Annual grant total: Around £1,000 is given each year in educational grants.

Applications: In writing to the correspondent.

Correspondent: J N Shergold, Trustee, 35 Orchard Grove, New Milton, Hampshire BH25 6NZ

The Snowdon Award Scheme

Eligibility: Physically disabled students (including sensory disabilities) between 17 and 25 years of age who are in or about to enter further or higher education or training in the UK, and because of their disability have financial needs which are not met elsewhere. Students above the age of 25 can also apply for grants, subject to available funds.

Types of grants: Bursaries are awarded annually for a period of one or two years. Grants are normally between £250 and £2,000 and are given towards costs such as equipment, travelling, interpreters and books. Foreign students studying in Britain may be eligible. Help with fees/living expenses may be given in exceptional circumstances.

Exclusions: Grants are not made to students studying overseas.

Annual grant total: In 2004/05 the trust had assets of £657,000, an income of £125,000 and a total expenditure of £156,000. Grants were made to 70 individuals totalling £118,000.

Applications: All applications must be made by the individual on a form available from the website or from the administrators in printed, CD, tape or Braille format. The closing date for completed applications is 31 May for consideration in July; late applications will be accepted until 31 August for consideration in September, funds permitting. Completed forms should be addressed to Nicky Allison together with: medical confirmation of disability; an academic reference; confirmation of a place at college or university; and a personal reference.

Correspondent: Nicky Allison, Administrator, 22 City Business Centre, 6 Brighton Road, Horsham, West Sussex RH13 5BB (01403 211252; Fax: 01403 271553; e-mail: info@snowdonawardscheme.org.uk; website: www.snowdonawardscheme.org.uk)

Student Disability Assistance Fund (formerly British Students Educational Assistance Fund)

Eligibility: Students engaged in a course of study, in any subject, at a higher or postgraduate level, who are affected by illness, disease, injury or physical infirmity. Priority will be given to those who are not eligible for funding from LEAs. Mature students can also be supported.

Types of grants: One-off grants of up to £500 towards educational aids made necessary by the student's disability, for example special computer equipment, extra travel costs for those with mobility problems, cost of note-takers or signers and other special equipment.

Exclusions: Grants will not be made for the payment of fees or general living expenses.

Annual grant total: Previously £6,000.

Applications: On a form available from the correspondent, preferably submitted directly by the individual with a letter of support from a tutor/member of disability staff/ disability adviser and a doctor's letter confirming illness or disability. Guidelines for applicants are available from the correspondent on request, enclosing an sae. Deadlines for applications are 1 March, 1 June and 1 November.

Correspondent: Dr Kathy Cockerill, c/o Mrs Sandra Furmston,, Administrative Secretary, BAHSHE Office, 35 Hazelwood Road, Bush Hill Park, Enfield EN1 1JG (e-mail: s.furmston@mdx.ac.uk; website: www.bahshe.demon.co.uk)

Paul Vander-Molen Foundation

Eligibility: People who are disabled and need financial assistance in order to 'realise their adventurous aspirations. Explorers are also assisted in their search for new expedition techniques.'

Types of grants: Grants of between £200 and £1,000 to enable people to enjoy and participate in adventurous activities. Grants have been towards, for example, sub-aqua training, an Arctic canoe race for people with disabilities, and expeditions in Canada, Chile and India.

Annual grant total: About £1,000 is available each year.

Applications: In writing to the correspondent at any time.

Correspondent: Michael Coyne, 92 Belgrave Road, Wanstead, London E11 3QP

Illness & disability – Blindness

Gardner's Trust for the Blind

Eligibility: Registered blind or partially-sighted people who live in England and Wales.

Types of grants: Grants are mainly for computer equipment, music equipment or course fees.

Exclusions: No grants for loan repayments.

Annual grant total: In 2003/04 the trust had assets of almost £2 million and an income of £68,000. Out of a total expenditure of £53,000, the sum of £38,000 was distributed to individuals.

Applications: In writing to the correspondent. Applications can be submitted either directly by the individual or by a third party, but they must also be supported by a third party who can confirm the disability and that the grant is needed. They are considered in March, June, September and December and should be submitted at least three weeks before the meeting.

Correspondent: Angela Stewart, Boundary House, 117 Charterhouse Street, London EC1M 6PN (020 7253 3757)

The Webster and Davidson Educational Trust

Eligibility: People who are blind or partially sighted undertaking higher or further education at universities or other educational institutions. Applicants must be resident in Scotland. Help can only be given to students currently in the education system until they complete or leave their course.

Types of grants: Although the trust has powers to make cash grants, its funds are limited, so priority is given to students who may be helped by the loan of equipment, for example, computers, scanners, printers, magnification software, desktop synthesisers and so on.

Annual grant total: In 2005 the trust had a total income of £7,400. Details concerning grants for individuals were unavailable; previously £1,000 has been awarded in grants to individuals.

Applications: Application forms are available from: Mrs L A Gray, 43 Kilnburn, Newport-on-Tay, Fife DD6 8DE (01382 543287; e-mail: lesley.gray@talk21.com). Applications can be made at any time. The grants committee meets four times a year.

Correspondent: Louise Fraser, Thorntons WS, 50 Castle Street, Dundee DD1 3RU (01382 229 111)

Illness & disability – Cancer

Sargent Cancer Care for Children

Eligibility: Children and young people under the age of 21 living in the UK who

have cancer or have been under treatment in the past six months.

Types of grants: Grants of up to £170 to alleviate crises or help with the quality of life of the child and/or family during treatment. Exceptional grants of up to £400 may be issued where no other support is available.

Annual grant total: In 2003/04 grants totalled £320,000.

Applications: On a form, to be completed by the Sargent Care Professional working with the family.

Correspondent: Grants Department, 161 Hammersmith Road, London W6 8SG (020 8752 2800; e-mail: grants@sargent. org; website: www.sargent.org)

Other information: The charity also provides respite holidays. Details of grants holidays and other services are available from the Sargent Care Professional.

Illness & disability – Deafness

The Peter Greenwood Memorial Trust for Deaf People

Eligibility: Post-school applicants (over 16) for courses in higher and further education and training, who are deaf or whose hearing is impaired, and who live in England and Wales.

Types of grants: Grants of under £200 towards books, videos, software and equipment. Students can be enrolled on any university course. Mature students and post-graduates can also be supported.

Annual grant total: In 2004, the fund had an income of £3000 and an expenditure of £2,600.

Applications: On a form available from the correspondent, to be received before 1 October, together with a letter from a sponsor who can verify the applicant's deafness and need. Late applications will not be considered.

Correspondent: Peter Robinson, MR Peter Robinson, Manesty, Bradford Road, Burley in Wharfedale, Ilkley, West Yorkshire LS29 7PZ (01943 864819; website: www. pgmtrust.org.uk)

Other information: Applicants are requested to ask their LEA for assistance before contacting the trust as they often offer special help to deaf students.

The National Deaf Children's Society

Eligibility: Deaf children between the ages of 4 and 18 who are in full-time education.

Types of grants: The society has a limited fund that is able to provide equipment to deaf children that will support their educational or social development. This excludes equipment that would normally be provided by the education, health or social services. Only one grant per family is allowed.

Annual grant total: Previously around £250,000 was given in grants to individuals for educational and welfare purposes.

Applications: On a form available from the fund coordinator. The application form includes an income declaration section. Support from relevant professionals, such as social workers, teachers of the deaf, IT teacher and so on is necessary. Evidence of the child's type and level of deafness is required.

Correspondent: Yvonne Tysoe, Fund Coordinator, 15 Dufferin Street, London EC1Y 8UR (Freephone family information and helpline: 0808 800 8880 voice & text; Fax: 020 7251 5020; e-mail: yvonne@ndcs. org.uk; website: www.ndcs.org.uk)

Other information: The society also runs the Blue Peter Loan Scheme, which loans out radio aids, environmental aids and other equipment for children to access in the comfort of their own homes. Please contact Jeremy Hine at the above address.

Illness & disability – Meningitis

Meningitis Trust

Eligibility: UK residents in need with meningitis or meningococcal diseases, or who are disabled as a result of meningitis.

Types of grants: One-off and recurrent grants towards equipment, re-education and special training.

Exclusions: No grants towards domestic bill arrears or clothing.

Annual grant total: In 2004/05 the trust had net assets totalling £1.7 million, an income of £2.2 million and a total expenditure of £3 million. Grants totalled £124,000 including those for re-education and training.

Applications: Each applicant needs a third party professional representative (such as a GP, nurse, health visitor or social worker) who knows their background and history well. The representative needs to contact the trust for an application form.

Clients can also contact the helpline (0845 6000 800) in the first instance, requesting information regarding the application process.

Correspondent: Mr P Kirby, Fern House, Bath Road, Stroud GL5 3TJ (01453 768000; Fax: 01453 768001; e-mail: grants@ meningitis-trust.org; website: www. meningitis-trust.org)

Illness & disability – Renal

The British Kidney Patient Association

Eligibility: Renal patients of UK nationality. The association covers all renal patients, whether on dialysis or not. The association will not pay loans, court fines or bills already paid.

Types of grants: Grants to help with the cost of books and materials, computers, board and lodgings, university and college fees and educational trips in the UK and overseas.

Annual grant total: In 2004 the trust had assets totalling £26 million and an income of £2.3 million. Grants were made totalling £937,000, including £310,000 to individuals.

Applications: Via a social worker or medical staff on a form available from the correspondent, or which can be downloaded from the BKPA website. Applications are considered on an ongoing basis.

Correspondent: Mrs Elizabeth Ward, Bordon, Hampshire GU35 9JZ (01420 472021/2; Fax: 01420 475831; website: www.britishkidney-pa.co.uk)

Illness & disability – Special educational needs

The Royal Eastern Counties Schools Limited

Eligibility: People under 25 with special educational needs, particularly those with emotional and behavioural difficulties. Preference is given to people living in Essex, Suffolk, Norfolk, Cambridgeshire and Hertfordshire.

Types of grants: One-off grants are given to people with special educational needs for uniforms/clothing, fees, study/travel

overseas, equipment/instruments, maintenance/living costs and educational outings in the UK.

Exclusions: Normally no grants are made for recurring costs.

Annual grant total: In 2004/05 the charity had an income of about £79,000 and a total expenditure of about £84,000.

Applications: Application forms can be obtained from the correspondent. Applications should normally be submitted during October for consideration between November and March, although urgent applications can be considered at other times. Applications should be made through an organisation. Unsuccessful applicants will not be informed unless an sae is provided.

Correspondent: A H Corin, Company Secretary, Brook Farm, Wet Lane, Boxted, Colchester, Essex CO4 5TN (01206 273295)

Independent & boarding schools

The Athlone Trust

Eligibility: Adopted children under the age of 18 who are in need.

Types of grants: The trust gives grants for school fees, but not for people at college or university. Occasionally one-off grants are given to help with the cost of education essentials for schoolchildren.

Annual grant total: In 2005 the trust had an income of £6,200 and a total expenditure of £6,700. Grants totalled about £5,000.

Applications: In writing to the correspondent. Applications should be submitted by the applicant's parents and are usually considered in May and November.

Correspondent: Peter Canney, Stoakes Cottage, Hastingleigh, Ashford, Kend, TN25 5HG

The Combined Trusts Scholarships Trust

Eligibility: Sixth form pupils between the ages of 16 and 18 who demonstrate academic ability.

Types of grants: The trust awards two-year scholarships to help pupils; who can demonstrate that they will benefit from pursuing an A-level course; who have been accepted by a fee-paying school to take such a course; and whose families are unable to meet the entire cost. Grants range between £1,000 and £3,000. The trust makes no other kinds of awards and candidates already started on the course are not considered.

Annual grant total: In 2004/05 the trust had assets of £204,000, an income of £279,000 and a total expenditure of £97,000. Scholarships were awarded to 57 individuals totalling £90,000.

Applications: Must be made through the school at which the A-level course is to be followed. The trustees place great weight on the recommendation of the head of the school. Each school may make one application only. Application forms may be obtained only by heads of schools from the correspondent. 'It is regretted that for administrative reasons, application forms cannot be sent to parents direct.' The closing date for applications is 31 January each year.

Correspondent: Dr Richard Gliddon, Scholarship Administrator, 36 Grange Court Road, Westbury-on-Trym, Bristol BS9 4DR (0117 962 0412; e-mail: rgliddon@blueyonder.co.uk; website: www.plans-ltd.co.uk/ctst)

The Emmott Foundation Limited

Eligibility: Young people aged 16 to 18 starting or completing sixth form education, whose parents have experienced unforeseen hardship from death, illness, divorce, redundancy and so on.

Types of grants: Grants are given to enable children to start or complete A-level courses at independent day or boarding schools and at maintained sector boarding schools. Applicants should usually expect to go to university or other higher educational establishment. Grants are usually of between £400 and £1,000 per term.

Grants are subject to regular review of academic progress and confirmation that the family's financial resources have not materially changed.

Annual grant total: In 2005/06 the foundation had an income of £365,000 and awarded 87 grants totalling £327,000.

Applications: Application forms are sent to individuals if there is the possibility of a grant being made. Except in cases of extreme emergency, all requests should be received by the end of November for grants to be made for the following September. The trustees meet in March and June to consider applications.

Correspondent: Guy Dodd, Education Officer, Brill, Tregew Road, Flushing, Falmouth, Cornwall TR11 5TF (01326 375383; e-mail: emmottfoundation@btopenworld. com)

Other information: This trust also makes contributions to other educational organisations and charities (£38,000 in 2005/06).

The Fishmongers' Company's Charitable Trust

Eligibility: Children/young people up to 19 years of age in need of a sum of money to complete schooling. Preference is given to children of single-parent families and/or those with a learning difficulty or disability, or those who come from a disadvantaged or unstable family background.

Types of grants: Small, one-off grants to assist in cases of short-term need. The company gives assistance with school fees. The maximum grant is £1,800.

Exclusions: No grants for further/higher education.

Annual grant total: In 2004 the trust had assets of £8.8 million and an income of £860,000. There were 36 educational grants made to individuals totalling £60,000. A further 47 welfare grants to individuals totalled £16,000. Grants to organisations totalled £945,000.

Applications: On a form available from the correspondent, to be submitted directly by the individual or by the parent or guardian for those under 18.

Correspondent: The Clerk, Fishmongers' Hall, London Bridge, London EC4R 9EL (Fax: 020 7929 1389; e-mail: clerk@fishhall.co.uk; website: www.fishhall.co.uk)

Other information: The company also administers Gresham's School in Norfolk, a fee-paying public school.

The Haberdashers' St Catherine Foundation

Eligibility: Children between the ages of 15 and 19 years old attending fee-paying schools, whose parents are unable to maintain the necessary payments due to unexpected changes in financial circumstances. Help is only given to people in the final year of GCSEs or A-levels.

Types of grants: Grants towards tuition fees to enable children to complete the final year of their secondary education at a fee-paying school in cases where the family's financial circumstances have recently changed adversely. This can include a state boarding school where fees are charged. Grants range from £250 to £500 a year. Such bursaries are paid direct to the schools concerned.

Annual grant total: In 2004/05 the foundation had assets of £1.4 million, an income of £132,000 and a total expenditure of £101,000. Grants were made to 78 individuals totalling £98,000.

Applications: Applicants should write briefly with reasons for application or telephone for guidance. A comprehensive application form will then be sent if the necessary criteria are met. Applications should be submitted at least one calendar month before meetings, which normally take place in May, September and December.

Correspondent: Mrs J Burns, Director, Joint Educational Trust, 6 Lovat Lane, London EC3R 8DT (020 7283 3445; Fax: 020 7283 3446; e-mail: admin@ jetcharity.org)

Joint Educational Trust

Eligibility: Children aged between 7 and 13 who are likely to benefit from a place in an independent school and whose families cannot meet the financial demands of this.

Types of grants: Grants of free and reduced fee places at an independent school are awarded. They may also provide grants if there is a shortfall in funding. Grants are for £500 a term.

Grants in the past have been awarded to allow two young boys in a custody battle to be educated in a boarding school while their father worked away from home, and for a young girl whose sister was disabled and prone to violent acts, and whose mother had cancer, to get the support she needed.

'The Joint Education Trust helps children who have suffered tragedy or trauma at home or are at risk in some way. JET enables these children to attend independent schools where they have a real chance of making a new start.'

Exclusions: The trust states it will not help in cases of financial difficulty or learning need alone – there must also be a social need.

Annual grant total: In 2005 the trust had an income of £195,000 and a total expenditure was £277,000, with 158 grants made totalling £154,000.

Applications: On a form available from the correspondent. Applications are considered in March, June and October, and can be submitted by the individual, through a social worker, the individual's school or educational welfare agency, or a third party such as a doctor or minister of religion, at any time.

Correspondent: Mrs Julie Burns, 6 Lovat Lane, London EC3R 8DT (020 7283 3445; Fax: 020 7283 3446; e-mail: admin@ jetcharity.org; website: www.jetcharity.org)

Other information: The trust also administers grants to individuals through four other charitable institutions.

The Lloyd Foundation

Eligibility: The children (between 5 and 25 years old) of British citizens where the family are necessarily living/working overseas.

Types of grants: Grants ranging between £300 and £3,000 a year to enable such children to attend the nearest English-medium school. Where no such school exists the foundation may give some help with fees for a school in the UK. Grants for schoolchildren, further/higher education and special educational needs are for educational expenses, such as fees, books, equipment and living expenses.

Exclusions: No help can be given for children under the age of five or for those taking postgraduate courses.

Annual grant total: In 2004/05 the trust had assets of £2.7 million and an income of £125,000. Total expenditure was £124,000, with 81 grants being awarded totalling £124,000.

Applications: On a form available from the correspondent, to be submitted directly by the individual or through a third party. Applications are considered quarterly.

Correspondent: The Secretary, Fairway, Round Oak View, Tillington, Herefordshire HR4 8EQ (01432 760409; Fax: 01432 760409)

The McAlpine Educational Endowments Ltd

Eligibility: Schoolchildren aged 13 to 18 who are in need.

Types of grants: Grants of up to £1,800 a year, mainly towards the cost of independent school fees for children of academic ability, sound character and leadership potential who, for reasons of financial hardship, would otherwise have to leave the school. Grants are paid each term while the child is at school (subject to an annual review) and are limited to children attending 10 schools selected by the trustees.

Exclusions: There are no grants for students at college or university, nor for people at specialist schools (such as ballet or music schools, or schools for children with learning difficulties).

Annual grant total: In 2004/05, the charity had an income of £11,000 and a total expenditure of £3,900. Grants total about £3,500, given to individuals and organisations.

Applications: In writing to the correspondent. Applications must be submitted through one of the 10 schools where applicants are supported by the trust but, because of the long-term nature of the trust's commitments, very few new grants can be considered each year. Applications are considered during the summer before the new academic year. A list of the schools involved is available from the correspondent.

Correspondent: G L Prain, Eaton Court, Maylands Avenue, Hemel Hempstead, Hertfordshire, HP2 7TR (01442 233444 ext 2919; Fax: 01442 234316)

The Ogden Trust

Eligibility: Academically gifted young people in the areas of science and maths who wish to attend a selection of independent secondary schools at sixth form level. Grants are also made to undergraduates. Applicants must be British.

Types of grants: (i) Educational scholarships covering at least 50% of school fees, paid half by the trust and matched by the school, which is a condition of their participation. The bursaries fund the pupils through the two years of their A-levels. (ii) Undergraduate scholarships of £1,500 per annum for up to four years of undergraduate study and are payable in two annual instalments (October and February).

Annual grant total: In 2004/05, the trust had assets of £26 million and an income of £246,000. Bursaries and scholarships totalled £58,000. A further £604,000 was distributed in 'general grants'.

Applications: The sixth form scholarships operate through schools associated with the trust, a list of which can be found on its website. The list is not closed and new schools may submit candidates.

In 2006, undergraduate scholarships were only open to specific categories of candidate. See the trust's website for further details.

Correspondent: Tim Simmons, Hughes Hall, Wollaston Road, Cambridge CB1 2EW (01223 518164; Fax: 01223 518173; e-mail: ogdentrust@ hughes.cam.ac.uk; website: www. ogdentrust.com)

The Reedham Trust

Eligibility: Children aged up to 16 who, due to the death, disability or absence of one or both of their parents (whether natural or through adoption) or of their own disablement or other domestic or personal circumstances, are in need of boarding care. Help will continue after the age of 16 only in exceptional circumstances.

The trust does not support day pupils or children of two-parent families, unless one or both parents are totally incapacitated in some way.

Grants are only given where there is a social need for boarding, not an educational need. Assistance is only available where the Local Educational Authority has no statutory duty to help.

Types of grants: Grants towards boarding fees, of up to £2,000 per year.

Annual grant total: In 2004/05 the trust had assets of £6 million and an income of £342,000. Total expenditure was £372,000, with 138 grants being awarded to individuals totalling £294,000.

Applications: On a form available from the Caseworker. Guidelines are available from the correspondent. Applications may be submitted directly by the individual, a parent/guardian, through the applicant's school or an educational welfare agency. They are considered throughout the year. Applications need confirmation from a professional that boarding school education is in the best interests of the applicant.

Correspondent: Mrs J Watkins, Secretary, The Lodge, 23 Old Lodge Lane, Purley, Surrey CR8 4DJ (020 8660 1461; Fax: 020 8763 1293; e-mail: info@ reedham-trust.org.uk; website: www. reedham-trust.org.uk)

Royal Wanstead Children's Foundation

Eligibility: Children aged 11 to 18 years who have lost one or both parents and whose home circumstances make boarding essential. Grants are restricted to children living within the UK and in respect of schools also situated in the UK.

Types of grants: Recurrent grants towards school fees of up to £1,000 per term.

Emphasis is on boarding need rather than on educational need. The foundation does not discriminate between state and independent education and where a place is secured at a state boarding school, the foundation is prepared to consider help with the boarding element of the fees if necessary.

Only orphans or children from one-parent homes are eligible and if the parent subsequently marries, re-marries or in some other way creates a two-parent home, the grant may cease. A one-parent situation is not by itself sufficient grounds for this foundation's support. The case for boarding must be made out by reference to the specific needs of the child (rather than of the parent) which cannot be provided at home for him or her as a day pupil.

Annual grant total: In 2004/05 the foundation had assets of £19 million, an income of £913,000 and a total expenditure of £617,000. There were 240 grants made in the year totalling £423,000.

Applications: Applications should be made in writing by the person having legal responsibility for the child. Initial enquiries can be made to the correspondent.

Correspondent: Mrs Susan Mary Rigby, Director, Sandy Lane, Cobham, Surrey KT11 2ES (01932 868622; Fax: 01932 866420; e-mail: clerk@ royalwanstead.org.uk)

School Fee Support Scheme

Eligibility: Secondary school children who are facing severe social, emotional or health problems 'within a limited set of family circumstances', or who are experiencing acute distress by the serious illness or death of a parent and are: (i) looked after by adoptive parents; (ii) cared for by family members or friends; (iii) living with single parents.

The trust cannot help children who: (i) live with two parents (except where adopted); (ii) can have their needs met within the state system, perhaps through a change of school; (iii) have learning difficulties with needs which can be met within the state system; (iv) are at a fee-paying school on parental preference for a particular type of education; or (v) are normally resident outside the UK. In addition assistance is not offered on intellectual, sporting or artistic grounds.

Where the need is evident, help may be given at an earlier age (although help with boarding fees of primary-aged children is rare) and help is rarely given to young people in sixth form. Children who attend school where the religious instruction and ethos are not Christian cannot be considered.

Types of grants: Help with fees at a boarding school where the child has serious family difficulties or special needs so the child has to be educated away from home. Help with day fees in case where serious loss of self-esteem, suicidal tendencies or chronic school phobia has resulted from the failure of a state school to cater for the needs of the child, or protect from bullying (the trust will only help in cases where a change of state school would not solve the problem and there is a possibility of serious long-term damage to the child).

Annual grant total: In 2004/05 the scheme made 221 school fee grants totalling £426,000.

Applications: In writing to the correspondent, giving the date of birth of the child, a description of the family circumstances, the problems faced by the child and the reasons why the proposed school has been chosen (if at that stage). Reports from professionals such as doctors, educational psychologists and teachers should also be included. Applicants considered eligible will be asked to complete a form giving full details of the family finances, and will be visited to discuss the case.

Applications should be directed to the trust's offices as follows:

For applicants in England: The Director, The Buttle Trust, Audley House, 13 Palace Street, London SW1E 5HX (020 7828 7311; e-mail: aland@buttletrust.org).

For applicants in Wales: The Regional Secretary, PO Box 7, Rhayader, Powys, LD6 5WB (01597 870060; e-mail: wales@buttletrust.org).

For applicants in Scotland: The Regional Secretary, PO Box 5075, Uplawmoor, Renfrewshire G78 4WA (01597 870060; e-mail: scotland@buttletrust.org).

For applicants in Northern Ireland: The Regional Secretary, PO Box 484, Belfast BT6 0YA (02890 641164; e-mail nireland@buttletrust.org).

If you are resident in Wales, Scotland or Northern Ireland, please contact the offices above for their criteria on school fee support.

Correspondent: Geraldine McAndrew, Audley House, 13 Palace Street, London, SW1E 5HX (020 7828 7311; Fax: 020 7828 4724)

Other information: The trust was founded by Revd W F Buttle in 1953. It publishes useful 'Notes for the guidance of social agencies or others applying for a Buttle Trust grant'.

The Thornton-Smith Young People's Trust

Eligibility: Children of above average ability already attending fee-paying public schools and whose parents have experienced an adverse change in financial circumstances. Currently the trustees only support sixth formers studying A-levels.

Types of grants: Grants follow a means test of the parental resources and are paid per term, subject to reasonable progress. The average award is up to half the total fees. Preference is given to short-term applications primarily in relation to A-levels.

Grants are not given for first degree courses or in circumstances where parents were not in a position to fund the fees when entering the child for the school.

Annual grant total: In 2004/05, the trust had assets of £4.8 million and an income of £141,000. The sum of £136,000 was given in grants to individuals.

Applications: In writing to the correspondent, including details of education and parents' financial situation. If an applicant is considered eligible further inquiries are made. Applications are normally considered by 31 March to commence in September.

Correspondent: The Trustees, c/o Chantrey Vellacott, Prospect House, 58 Queens Road, Reading, Berkshire RG1 4RP

Other information: The correspondent also administers The Wilfred Maurice Plevins Charity (see separate entry).

Orders

The Journal Children's Fund (in conjunction with the Royal Antediluvian Order of Buffaloes)

Eligibility: 'The education and preferment of orphan or necessitous children of deceased members of the Royal Antediluvian Order of Buffaloes Grand Lodge of England.' The fund's activities extend worldwide.

Types of grants: Help with the cost of books, clothing and other essentials for schoolchildren. Grants may also be available for those at college or university who are eligible.

Annual grant total: In 2004/05 the fund had net assets of around £300,000. Total income was £64,300, with an expenditure

of £70,000. The fund gave grants totalling £40,700.

Applications: Initial enquiries regarding assistance can only be made through the individual's branch of attendance.

Correspondent: Stuart Steele, Grant Secretary, RAOB GLE Trust Corporation, Grove House, Skipton Road, Harrogate, North Yorkshire HG1 4LA (01423 502438; e-mail: hq@raobgle.org.uk; website: www.raobgle.org.uk)

Royal Masonic Trust for Girls and Boys

Eligibility: Generally the children of Freemasons. The objects of the trust are to relieve poverty and to advance education. Those eligible for assistance are the children of any age (including adopted children, step-children and children of the family) of Freemasons under the United Grand Lodge of England who are considered to be in need of such help.

The trust also has power, provided sufficient funds are available, to help children who are not the offspring of a Freemason. Such assistance is usually only given by way of grants to other children's charities.

Types of grants: Any necessary kind of assistance. The children concerned are usually, but not always, in state education. Help with the costs of a boarding education can only be given if there is a specific and demonstrable boarding need. Grants can go towards school uniforms, school clothing, books, educational outings, maintenance costs, living expenses, childcare and study or travel overseas.

Exclusions: No grants are available for student exchanges.

Annual grant total: In 2004 the trust had an income of £7 million and a total expenditure of £10.2 million. During the year the trust supported 2,801 children and young people in schools, colleges and universities through its various schemes, bursaries and subsidiary funds. Grants to individuals totalled at least £1.2 million.

Applications: Applications should be made in the first instance to the nearest Masonic authority or, where that is not known, a preliminary enquiry may be addressed to the correspondent.

Correspondent: Mr Leslie Hutchinson, 31 Great Queen Street, London WC2B 5AG (020 7405 2644; Fax: 020 7831 4094; e-mail: info@rmtgb.org; website: www.rmtgb.org)

Overseas students (by place of origin)

The British & Foreign School Society – International Award Scheme – see entry on page 46

Correspondent: Charles Crawford, Director, Maybrook House, Godstone Road, Caterham, Surrey CR3 6RE (01883 331177; Fax: 01883 344429; e-mail: britforeign@aol.com; website: www.bfss.org.uk)

British Government & British Council Award Schemes – Scholarships for Overseas Students & Trainees

Eligibility: Specified foreign nationals resident outside of the UK.

Types of grants: There are various awards/schemes. The following two scholarships may be awarded to undergraduates:

(i) DFID Shared Scholarship Scheme

Eligibility: Students from developing Commonwealth countries who are of high academic calibre and intend studying subjects of developmental relevance but who are unable to support their studies in Britain. Normally under 35 years of age; they must be able to speak English fluently.

No grants to people who are employed by their government or by an international organisation.

Types of grants: Awards are for taught courses at postgraduate level. Very exceptionally, awards for undergraduate study may be made available where the course of training satisfies the conditions of the scheme but is not available in the student's own country or at a nearby regional institution.

Applications for awards should be made directly to the participating British institutions. These usually vary from year to year, as can each institution's individual closing date for receipt of applications. A revised list of institutions is normally available from December onwards from the Association of Commonwealth Universities, the Department for International Development, and British High Commissions and British Council representatives in the Commonwealth countries concerned.

Applicants must be resident in a developing Commonwealth country at the time of application and, if successful, are required to return there on completion of their awards.

Further details are available from the correspondent.

(ii) Commonwealth Scholarships and Fellowship Plan (CSFP)

Eligibility: People who live in either a Commonwealth country or a British dependent territory.

Types of Grants: The scholarships are normally for postgraduate study or research, so applicants must have a university degree or equivalent qualification. If there are no undergraduate courses in a particular subject in a country or regional university, it may sometimes be possible to apply to do a first degree course under this scheme.

Grants are for one to three years and usually cover the cost of travel, tuition fees and living expenses. In some cases additional allowances may be available for help with books or clothes. An allowance may be paid to help with the cost of maintaining a spouse.

Applications for awards should be made through the Commonwealth Scholarship Agency in the individual's home country. Agency addresses are listed in the 'Commonwealth Universities Yearbook', available from the address below. If you are already in the UK the ACU can help you with general information concerning the scheme, but it cannot issue application forms to international students.

Further details from the correspondent.

Other postgraduate awards include:

British Chevening Scholarships, British Council Fellowship Programmes, Overseas Research Students Awards Scheme and Royal Society Fellowships.

Correspondent: The Association of Commonwealth Universities, Woburn House, 20-24 Tavistock Square, London WC1H 9HF (website: www.acu.ac.uk)

Churches Commission on Overseas Students: Hardship Fund

Eligibility: Full-time students from developing countries attending British or Irish institutions for first-degree or postgraduate studies lasting a minimum of one academic year, who are within six months of completing their course but face unexpected financial problems. They are required to confirm their intention to return to their home country immediately after their course.

Types of grants: Grants are typically £500 but do not exceed £800; the same person is not funded twice.

Exclusions: The fund will not consider students from industrialised countries, asylum seekers or refugees, or those whose studies relate to arms manufacture or experimentation on live animals.

Annual grant total: Grants are made to individuals each year totalling about £150,000.

Applications: Initial enquiries should be made to the grants secretary and should contain basic information about the student, particularly related to eligibility. Applicants should be able to show that with the help of a small grant, they will be able to complete their course. Application documents are sent to those who appear likely to meet the criteria. The hardship fund committee decides on grants three times a year, in February (for studies finishing April-July), June (for August-November) and October (for December-March).

Correspondent: David Philpot, Grants Secretary, 121 George Street, Edinburgh EH2 4YH (0131 225 5722 ext 300; Fax: 0131 226 6121; e-mail: dphilpot@cofscotland.org.uk)

Zibby Garnett Travelling Fellowship

Eligibility: People living in the UK studying the conservation off: historic buildings; historic landscapes, gardens and open spaces; historic and decorative crafts and artefacts.

Types of grants: Grants for foreign study scholarships.

Exclusions: Generally grants are given for practical work in preference to pure study or research.

Annual grant total: In 2004/05 the fellowship had an income of £4,900 and made 10 grants totalling £7,200.

Applications: On a form available from the trustees to be submitted directly by the individual. The deadline for applications is 1 March for consideration that month.

Correspondent: The Trustees, The Grange, Norwell, Newark, Nottinghamshire NG23 6JN (01636 636288; Fax: 01636 636760)

Ruth Hayman Trust

Eligibility: Adults (aged over 16) who live in the UK and who speak a language other than English as their first language. In practice, most beneficiaries are refugees and asylum seekers.

Types of grants: One-off and recurrent grants ranging from £20 to £300. First priority is given to tuition and examination fees, but small grants can also be made towards books and materials. Grants towards travel costs are also made to people who have disabilities.

Exclusions: No grants to overseas students for fees, higher degrees, or for childcare or living costs.

Annual grant total: In 2004/05 the trust had an income of £14,000 and a total expenditure of £20,000, all of which was given in grants.

Applications: On a form available from the correspondent on request either by letter or e-mail. Applications are considered in June, September, December

and March. Deadlines for applications are posted on the trust's website. Applicants must provide a reference.

Correspondent: The Trustees, PO Box 17685, London N6 6WD (website: www.ruthhaymantrust.com)

The Florence and Don McGregor Trust

Eligibility: Young people under the age of 35 years who have not studied at higher education level and are not planning to do so.

Types of grants: One-off grants ranging from £150 to £300 to enable the individual to travel overseas on a project which might promote greater international understanding. Grants are towards projects which benefit the overseas host community and which last for at least six months. The trust does not normally fund study trips.

Annual grant total: The trust has an income of about £4,000 and gives around 10 grants each year.

Applications: Applicants should send a letter of application with details and costing of the proposed project, including a cv and supporting information, plus names and addresses of two referees. There are no application forms or deadlines.

Correspondent: Maurice Plaskow, 57 Telephone Road, Southsea, Hampshire PO4 0AU (023 9273 6848)

The Professor D G Montefiore Trust

Eligibility: Grants to students from developing countries, principally those undertaking postgraduate medical work in the UK before returning to their own countries. Normally grants are in the form of single payments in time for the start of the academic year and can be for up to £500.

Types of grants: Grants are given to asylum seekers who need retraining in this country at any level, from language courses to medical exams.

Annual grant total: In 2004/05, the trust had both an income and total expenditure of £11,800. About £9,000 given in grants.

Applications: Applications must be made through the university or college and provide details of how all other costs, including living expenses, are going to be met. Applications from individuals will not be considered without confirmation from the university including references and cvs. Applications are considered monthly.

Correspondent: Miss Jean M Bogaardt, 17 Market Street, Crewkerne, Somerset, TA18 7JU (01460 74401; Fax: 01460 73988)

Other information: The trust prefers all correspondence to be received in writing.

The Nurses Association of Jamaica (NAJ) (UK)

Eligibility: Primarily people from black and ethnic minority groups, especially African-Caribbean groups, who are aged 18 or over. The trust will consider any studies to promote the practice of nursing, midwifery and health visiting. This may range from students undertaking studies in health education, nursing courses at degree, diploma, certificate and attendence levels, sociology, psychology, nursing and other health and health science related programmes, in particular where the course of study will impact positively on the health and health care of ethnic minority groups. The trust also considers the following funding priorities: business schools and pre-school education; IT training; special needs education; and training for community development. Preference is given to people living in Birmingham, London, Nottingham and internationally.

Types of grants: One-off grants ranging between £50 and £300 towards books, fees, educational outings in the UK, study or travel abroad, student exchanges and people who are black or part of an ethnic minority group studying in the UK.

Priority is given to part-funding for one year or less, although a period of up to two years may be considered.

Annual grant total: In 2004 the association had an income of £23,600 and a total expenditure of £18,000. Grants totalled about £15,000.

Applications: Initial contact by telephone to head office (below) or branch to request an application form. Application forms can be submitted directly by the individual, through a school/college or educational welfare agency, or through another third party. All applications should be supported with a reference. The completed form can be returned in February or August, with supporting statements to justify the purpose of the application, costings and how the money will be used, and specific details about the study/projects supported. They are considered in September and March.

Correspondent: NAJ (UK), PO Box 652, Sherington, Newport Pagnell, Buckinghamshire MK16 9ZY (Fax: 01908 613776; e-mail: cim@btinternet.com)

Prisoners of Conscience Appeal Fund

Eligibility: Prisoners of conscience and their families in the UK and worldwide. The fund makes grants to individuals and/or their families, who have suffered persecution for their conscientiously held beliefs. The fact that the person is seeking asylum or has been a victim of civil war is not sufficient grounds in itself.

Types of grants: Mainly one off grants to a usual maximum of £500 each for travel, resources and equipment and so on. Grants are also made for vocational conversion courses.

Exclusions: No support to people who have used or advocated violence or supported a violent organisation. No grants for university fees.

Annual grant total: In 2005 the sum of £48,000 was distributed in educational grants in the UK.

Applications: Application forms are available from the correspondent and should be submitted through an approved agency on behalf of the individual. Applications should include evidence of identification of the applicant and of costs.

Correspondent: The Grants Officer, PO Box 36789, London SW9 9XF (020 7738 7511; e-mail: info@prisonersofconscience.org; website: www.prisonersofconscience.org)

Other information: The fund was initially established in 1962 as the relief arm of Amnesty International, but is now a charity in its own right.

Overseas students (by place of origin) – Africa

The Africa Educational Trust

Eligibility: Students of African descent. Most of the trust's work is carried out in Africa.

Types of grants: (i) Full-time and part-time scholarships

The trust currently has extremely limited funds therefore enquiries regarding both full- time and part- time scholarships must be made before application.

(ii) Emergency small grants for students from Africa

Candidates for the small emergency grants programme should be in the final few months of their course and need a small amount of money to enable them to complete the course. The average grant under this programme is £350. Applicants should be studying in the UK and hold a student's visa.

The trust is also usually able to provide a number of small grants each year with funds received from donors and individuals. The availability, criteria and restrictions for these vary from fund to fund.

Annual grant total: In 2004/05 the trust had assets of £834,000, an income of £1.4 million and a total expenditure of £1.3 million. Grants were made to 50 individuals through the UK Grants Programme totalling £21,000.

Applications: Candidates can contact the trust for information concerning its programmes at any time during the year.

Correspondent: Ms J Landymore, 38 King Street, London WC2E 8JR (020 7836 5075/7940; Fax: 020 7379 0090; e-mail: info@africaeducationaltrust.org; website: www.africaeducationaltrust.org)

Other information: The trust also offers a free educational advice service to migrants and refugees with an African background.

Overseas students (by place of origin) – Armenia

The Armenian General Benevolent Union London Trust

Eligibility: Children of an Armenian parent(s) studying recognised undergraduate or postgraduate courses in British universities or educational institutions, including specific vocational courses. Preference is given for courses in Armenian studies or subjects which may benefit the Armenian community.

Types of grants: Student loans are normally for educational fees, otherwise, a contribution can be made towards the cost of books or some maintenance costs. All loans are interest free and subject to a maximum set by the trustees reflecting the current income available. Student grants are occasionally given to Armenians with significant financial hardship or for refugees in the UK.

Special grants are available for people to attain Armenian university education or to pursue Armenian studies at university.

Annual grant total: £30,000 in 2004 in grants and loans.

Applications: On a form available from the correspondent, to be submitted by 15 June each year.

Correspondent: The Chair, c/o Student Loans Committee, 25 Cheniston Gardens, London W8 6TG

Other information: Support is also given to Armenian schools, nurseries and cultural groups in the UK and overseas, usually towards running costs for Armenian language, history and culture classes. Occasionally welfare grants can be given to people in need.

The Armenian Relief Society of Great Britain Trust

Eligibility: Poor, sick or bereaved Armenians, worldwide.

Types of grants: One-off and recurrent grants of £150.

Annual grant total: In 2003/04 the trust had an income of £62,000 and a total expenditure of £55,000. Grants, all to relief centres and organisations which provide relief for disasters for Armenians, totalled £20,000.

Applications: In writing to the correspondent.

Correspondent: Mrs O Saroukhanoff, 8 Southbourne Close, Pinner, Middlesex HA5 5BA

The Benlian Trust

Eligibility: Children of Armenian fathers; applicants must be members of the Armenian Church studying at universities in Great Britain.

Types of grants: Grants for people studying on undergraduate degree courses and apprenticeships. Grants may also be given to help with the cost of articles, but otherwise priority is given to undergraduates.

Annual grant total: In 2005, the trust had net assets of 1.5 million, an income of £150,000, with a total expenditure of £170,000. The Trustees have granted a total of £66,650 in scholarships towards the 'fees and/or living expenses of 30 students studying at various colleges and universities in England.

Applications: On a form available from the correspondent, completed applications must be returned before 30 April.

Correspondent: S Ovanessoff, Administrator, 15 Elm Crescent, Ealing, London W5 3JW (020 8567 1210; Fax: 020 8567 1210)

The Mihran Essefian Charitable Trust

Eligibility: University students of Armenian origin studying in Armenia. In previous years help has also been given to Armenian university students in the UK.

Types of grants: Scholarship grants are made ranging from £100 to £4,500.

Annual grant total: In 2005, the trust had net assets of £1.5 million. It had an income of around £90,000 and a total expenditure of £76,000. The fund gave grants to 453 individuals totalling £45,000 and a further £21,500 to educational institutions.

Applications: In writing to the correspondent by 30 April each year.

Correspondent: Stephen Ovanessoff, Administrator, 15 Elm Crescent, Ealing, London W5 3JW (020 8567 1210)

Overseas students (by place of origin) – Asia

The Bestway Foundation

Eligibility: Higher education students who are of Indian, Pakistani, Bangladeshi or Sri Lankan origin.

Types of grants: One-off and recurrent grants according to need.

Annual grant total: In 2004/05, the foundation had assets of £3.5 million, an income of around £500,000, and a total expenditure of £200,000. The trustees gave grants to individuals totalling £85,000.

Applications: In writing to the correspondent enclosing an sae. Applications are considered in March/April. Telephone calls are not welcome.

Correspondent: A K Bhatti, Bestway Cash & Carry Ltd, 2 Abbey Road, Park Royal, London NW10 7BW

The Hammond Trust

Eligibility: Students from Asia between the ages of 18 and 45 who are studying in the UK. Grants are intended to provide financial assistance so that students may complete their studies in the UK when those studies are threatened with interruption owing to unexpected financial difficulties beyond the control of the student. Applicants must be in their final six months of study for a degree, diploma or other professional qualification at a recognised institution. Preference will be given to those following a course of study that will be of benefit to the applicant's own country. Applicants are expected to make every effort to meet their commitments from their own resources

Types of grants: One-off and recurrent grants, generally of £500.

Exclusions: Grants will not be awarded for help with tuition fees.

Annual grant total: Grants of about £500 are awarded to around 10 individuals.

Applications: On an application form available from the correspondent. The course tutor or supervisor must give a report on the applicant in part B of the application form which must be sent through the academic institution's authority and be endorsed with the official stamp.

Correspondent: International Student Services Unit, British Council, Bridgewater House, 58 Whitworth Street, Manchester M1 6BB (0161 957 7279)

Overseas students (by place of origin) – Australia

The Britain-Australia Society Education Trust

Eligibility: Individuals 18 or under (usually of secondary school age) living in the UK who have a connection with Australia.

Types of grants: Grants contributing towards the expenses (but not fares) of educational projects leading to better British-Australian understanding. Grants are also given to schoolchildren for uniforms/clothing, fees, study/travel overseas and books. Grants range from between £250 to £500.

Annual grant total: About £2,000 to £3,000 a year in grants, given to schools and individuals.

Applications: In writing to the correspondent, including details of the funding required. The deadline for applications is 31 March for consideration through May.

Correspondent: The Trustees of the Education Trust, The Britain-Australia Society, Swire House, 59 Buckingham Gate, London SW1E 6AJ (020 7630 1075; Fax: 020 7828 2260; e-mail: britaus@ britain-australia.org.uk; website: www. britain-australia.org.uk)

Overseas students (by place of origin) – Belgium

The Royal Belgian Benevolent Society

Eligibility: Belgian students who are living/ studying in Britain and are in need.

Types of grants: One-off grants of £500 to £2,000 towards the costs of further/higher education and postgraduate study.

Annual grant total: In 2004 the society had an income of £14,000 and a total expenditure of almost £10,000.

Applications: On a form available from the correspondent, submitted directly by the individual.

Correspondent: Mrs S Ault, Chair, Anglo-Belgian Club, c/o 60 Knightsbridge, London SW1X 7LF (Fax: 020 7245 9470)

Overseas students (by place of origin) – British Commonwealth

The Sir Ernest Cassel Educational Trust: Mountbatten Memorial Grants

Eligibility: Overseas students from Commonwealth countries studying in the UK who are in the final year of their studies and are experiencing unforeseen financial difficulties. Grants are only given to students in higher education (at college or university) in the UK.

Types of grants: Grants of £200 to £500 for living or general expenses.

Exclusions: Overseas students who are UK-registered for fees purposes are not eligible; applicants must have paid course fees as an overseas student. Grants are not given for the actual course fees themselves.

Annual grant total: In 2005 the trust had assets of £1.3 million, an income of £56,000 and a total expenditure of £53,000. Grants were made to 75 individuals totalling £27,000.

Applications: The grants are administered by 10 universities and institutions on behalf of the trust. Potential applicants should consult their student welfare officer for further details. Students at universities and institutions not included in the scheme may also apply through their student welfare officers to the address below

Correspondent: David Constable, 199 West Malvern Road, Malvern, Worcestershire WR14 4BB (01684 572437)

Other information: Grants are also made to organisations.

Overseas students (by place of origin) – Canada

The Canadian Centennial Scholarship Fund

Eligibility: Canadian post-secondary school students studying in the UK, who are both in need and of high academic ability. Preference is given to students taking courses which are 'of relevance to Canada'.

Students must already be enrolled in a UK educational institution before applying for a grant.

Types of grants: One-off grants of £500 to £2,500 for fees, study or travel abroad, books, maintenance and living expenses.

Annual grant total: In 2005 the trust had assets totalling £160,000, an income of £24,000 and a total expenditure of £23,000. Grants were made to 13 individuals totalling £22,000.

Applications: Further information and application forms are also available from the fund's website. Applications must be received, with references, by 15 March. Interviews for those shortlisted are the first week of June and scholarships are paid out in late September.

Correspondent: Mrs Julia Montgomery, Chair, Canadian Women's Club, 1 Grosvenor Square, London W1K 4AB (020 7258 6344; e-mail: info@canadianwomenlondon.org; website: www.canadianscholarshipfund.co.uk)

Overseas students (by place of origin) – Costa Rica

Ronaldo Falconer Charitable Trust

Eligibility: Further and higher education Costa Rican students, including mature students, who are studying in the UK, with a preference for technical courses.

Types of grants: Scholarships and bursaries.

Annual grant total: In 2004/05 the trust had an income of £7,300 and a total

expenditure of £53,000. Grants totalled about £50,000.

Applications: In writing to the correspondent. Applications are considered in September or October.

Correspondent: The Manager, NatWest Trust and Estate Services, 153 Preston Road, Brighton BN1 6BD (01273 545064; Fax: 01273 545075)

Overseas students (by place of origin) – Egypt

Egyptian Community Association in the United Kingdom

Eligibility: People in need who are Egyptian or of Egyptian origin and are living in or visiting the UK.

Types of grants: One-off and recurrent grants towards course fees, clothing, books, and so on.

Annual grant total: In 2003 the trust had an income of £39,000 and a total expenditure of £44,000. Grants to individuals for educational purposes totalled £2,400. A further £370 was given to individuals for Eid and Ramadan.

Applications: In writing to the correspondent.

Correspondent: Dr Wafik Moustafa, 38 Birbeck Road, London, W3 6BQ

Other information: The association arranges seminars and national and religious celebrations, as well as offering other services. It also gives grants to individuals for general welfare purposes.

Overseas students (by place of origin) – Greece

The Schilizzi Foundation

Eligibility: Greek nationals pursuing an undergraduate degree course or vocational training in Great Britain where there is a real need for financial assistance. Priority is given to students in their final year of study and second year students will only be considered in exceptional circumstances.

Types of grants: One-off grants ranging from £250 to £2,000, awarded in cases of hardship or special need during the final year of study for books, fees and living expenses. Other cases will be considered only in exceptional circumstances of serious or unforeseen hardship. (Major scholarships for further education in the UK are also awarded to selected students; no direct applications will be considered.)

Exclusions: Postgraduates are not eligible for funding.

Annual grant total: In 2004/05 the trust had assets of £1.4 million, an income of £56,000 and a total expenditure of £39,000. A total of £29,000 was given to 19 individuals during the year.

Applications: On a form available from the secretary. Applications can be submitted directly by the individual or a parent/guardian, or through an organisation such as a school or an educational welfare agency. They are considered up to 1 April in the final year, although earlier applications are preferred.

Correspondent: Bryan P Smith, Secretary, Rowan, Turweston, Brackley, Northamptonshire NN13 5JX (website: www.schilizzifoundation.org.uk)

Overseas students (by place of origin) – India

The Northbrook Society

Eligibility: Nationals of India who are studying in the UK and returning to India to related employment.

Types of grants: One-off grants ranging between £250 and £750 to students in further and higher education, including mature students, towards books, fees and living expenses.

Annual grant total: In 2005, the society had an income of £5,000 and a total expenditure of £9,000.

Applications: In writing to the correspondent directly by the individual. The applicant must provide evidence of a return to India on completion of the course, and a reference from a supervisor or tutor.

Correspondent: Ms B Weller, Secretary, Northbrook Society, 37 Neatherd Road, Dereham, Norfolk, NR20 4AU (01362 692150; Fax: 01362 699714)

The Charles Wallace India Trust

Eligibility: People of Indian nationality and citizenship, aged between 25 to 38,

normally resident in India and intending to return to India at the end of their study. Certain short-term awards are available for people aged between 25 to 45.

Types of grants: Only in the arts and humanities, with particular emphasis on fine arts, music, theatre, crafts and design, conservation of historical buildings and materials, anthropology, the preservation of archives, letters, history and the history of ideas.

Most awards are at postgraduate level to supplement other sources of funding or constitute completion of study awards for those whose scholarships have run out. A limited number of post-doctoral or post-professional research grants are awarded.

Exclusions: Studies relating to economic development or leading to professional legal, business or administrative qualifications are not considered.

Annual grant total: In 2005 the trust has net assets of £5.1 million. The trust had an income of £176,000 and a total expenditure of £208,000, from which scholarships were made to individuals totalling £160,000.

Applications: In writing to the correspondent. Detailed information and application forms can be downloaded from the website

Correspondent: R H Alford, 36 Lancaster Avenue, London, SE27 9DZ, Alternatively: c/o The British Council, 10 Spring Gardens, London SW1A 2BN (020 8670 2825; e-mail: cwit@btinternet.com; website: www.britishcouncil.org/india)

Other information: The separate and smaller Charles Wallace Trusts for Bangladesh, Burma and Pakistan are administered by William Crawley, who can be contacted for further information at 22 Holyoake Walk, London, N2 0JX.

Overseas students (by place of origin) – Turkey

Hazel Heughan Educational Trust

Eligibility: Students and academics in further, higher or postgraduate education who usually live in Turkey and are from poor backgrounds.

Types of grants: One-off and recurrent grants towards education at university, and for trips to the UK (usually Edinburgh) to further studies in the English language and, if possible, gain work experience. This can

include grants for travel expenses, books, equipment and instruments, fees and maintenance and living expenses.

Annual grant total: About £14,000 a year.

Applications: In writing to the correspondent at any time, for consideration usually in May and November. Applications should be submitted by a third party.

Correspondent: The Trustees, 14 Camus Avenue, Edinburgh EH10 6QT

Overseas students (by place of origin) – Uganda

The Uganda Welfare Action Group

Eligibility: Ugandans living in the UK undertaking further or higher education to enable them to become qualified.

Types of grants: Help for students to acquire skills and to train for possible employment and future progress when they return to Uganda. Grants are given towards the cost of books and fees/living expenses. Preference is given to mature students. Grants range from £250 to £300 and are one-off.

Annual grant total: No financial information is currently available.

Applications: In writing to the correspondent, including proof of the offer of a place at college or university and the intended course of study. Applications are considered in July and August.

Correspondent: Stephen Lwerango, Flat 4 Cricket Court, 13 Elderbury Way, London, E6 6JJ (0795 0644 5510)

Personal development & adventure training

Jim Bishop Memorial Fund

Eligibility: People under 19 who wish to participate in any adventure activity.

Types of grants: Grants of between £50 and £150.

Exclusions: University expeditions will not be supported.

Annual grant total: Previously £2,000.

Applications: On a form available from the correspondent, or as a download from the Young Explorers' Trust website. Applications are considered in late February.

Correspondent: Maggie Brown, c/o Young Explorers Trust, 10 Larch Close, Bingham, Nottinghamshire NG13 8GW (website: www.theyet.org)

The Duveen Trust

Eligibility: Individuals aged up to 25 who wish to get involved with projects which require initiative and which give something back to the community, and who are in need of support because self-help has proved to be insufficient.

Types of grants: One-off grants of £100 to £500.

Annual grant total: The trust gives about £15,000 each year in grants to individuals.

Applications: Application forms and guidelines are available from the correspondent. The deadlines for applications are just before the trustees' meetings, three times a year.

Correspondent: The Trustees, 26 Beechwood Avenue, London N3 3AX (Fax: 020 8349 9649; website: www. theduveentrust.org.uk)

The David Finnie & Alan Emery Charitable Trust

Eligibility: People between the ages of 18 and 25 who are in need and are permanently resident in the UK and are of British nationality.

Types of grants: Grants of £500 to £3,000 are given towards education, personal achievement and development.

Exclusions: No grants where alternative funding was or should be made available by other agencies, government or otherwise. No support for: loans and non-specific cash sums; expeditions, conference attendance and seminars; general cases of hardship falling outside the stated criteria; requests for holiday trips, family reunions and the like; debts of any kind; house removal or funeral expenses; TV, car and animal licences; nursing and/or residential care fees (including for people who are homeless); furniture and fixtures, treatment that should be provided by the NHS; overseas funding; religious purposes; building work of any kind; wheelchairs; or pushchairs.

Annual grant total: In 2004/05 the trust had assets of £1.9 million and an income of £76,000. Educational grants to 23 individuals totalled £26,000, whilst a further £4,000 went in 10 welfare grants. Grants to organisations totalled £35,000.

Applications: Initially, in writing to the correspondent. Applications can be submitted directly by the individual or through a social worker, Citizens Advice,

other welfare agency or other third party. They are considered in April and October each year, and, if successful, an application form is forwarded for completion.

Correspondent: John A Buck, 4 De Grosmont Close, Abergavenny, Monmouthshire NP7 9JN (01873 851048)

The Leadership Trust Foundation

Eligibility: Young people, primarily those aged 16 to 25, living within 25 miles of the trust's office who are undertaking activities designed to enhance their personal and leadership skills with a recognised charity.

Types of grants: Grants are given to individuals embarking on activities with Raleigh International, Duke of Edinburgh's Award, GAP, British Schools Expedition Society, Jubilee Sailing Trust and so on.

Annual grant total: In 2004, the foundation had net assets of £7.4 million and both an income and a total expenditure of £3.4 million; this was given in grants totalling £129,000.

Applications: Initially in writing to the correspondent, who will then send an application form to relevant applicants. Completed forms are considered quarterly.

Correspondent: The Grants Department, The Leadership Trust, Weston Under Penyard, Ross-on-Wye, Herefordshire HR9 7YH (01989 767667; Fax: 01989 768133; e-mail: grantmaking@ leadership.co.uk; website: www.leadership. org.uk)

The Quest Trust

Eligibility: People embarking upon exchange schemes in rural areas.

Types of grants: Grants of up to £500 are available for travel and subsistence costs.

Annual grant total: In 2005 the trust had an income of £289,500 and an expenditure of £285,300. Grants totalled about £280,000.

Applications: In writing to the correspondent.

Correspondent: Simon Buxton, 1 Belmont, Lansdown Road, Bath BA1 5DZ (01225 466 222; Fax: 01225 315904; website: www.quest-net.org/)

The Vandervell Foundation

Eligibility: Medical students and other gap year students.

Types of grants: One-off grants averaging £300 to £500 towards students taking medical electives and gap year projects.

Exclusions: Grants are not made where the foundation already makes a major grant directly to the organisation, such as Raleigh International.

Annual grant total: In 2004 the trust had an income of £279,000 and made 649 grants to individuals totalling £218,000.

Applications: In writing to the correspondent, enclosing a CV and a budget. Trustees meet about every fortnight to consider applications from individuals.

Correspondent: Ms Sheila Lawler, Bridge House, 181 Queen Victoria Street, London EC4V 4DZ

Other information: Grants are also made to organisations (£152,000 in 2004)

Prisoners/ex-offenders

The Aldo Trust

Eligibility: People in need who are being held in detention pending their trial or after their conviction. The applicant must still be serving the sentence. Applicants must have less than £25 in private cash.

Types of grants: Education grants of £10 to help with items such as books, course fees, equipment, audio/visual and other training equipment and tools for employment. Those eligible can only receive one grant a year.

Annual grant total: Around £18,000 a year for educational and welfare purposes.

Applications: On a form available from the correspondent. Applications must be made through prison service personnel (for example, probation, chaplaincy, education), and should include the name and number of the prisoner, age, length of sentence and expected date of release. No applications direct from prisoners will be considered. Applicants may apply once only in each twelve-month period, and applications are considered monthly.

Correspondent: c/o NACRO, 169 Clapham Road, London SW9 0PU

Other information: NACRO also offers a fund for people on probation; see separate entry in this guide.

The Longford Trust

Eligibility: Ex-prisoners undertaking higher education courses to degree level. (Eligibility remains open for up to five years after release.) Applicants must be at a UK university or equivalent UK institute.

Types of grants: Scholarships are worth a maximum of £5,000 per annum, extendable for up to three years on receipt of suitable reports of academic progress. Grants are intended to cover both the cost of tuition fees on higher education courses and offer a contribution to living expenses for books, course material and basic sustenance.

Exclusions: No grants for postgraduate study.

Annual grant total: In 2004, the trust had an income of £57,000. Scholarship costs totalled £2,100. A further £7,000 was distributed to organisations.

Applications: Application forms can be downloaded from the trust's website, or are available by contacting the trust in writing. Applications for courses beginning in the September of any year must be made by the start of June in that year.

Correspondent: Peter Stanford, 42 Callcott Road, London, NW6 7EA (website: www.longfordtrust.org)

Other information: The trust also administers the Patrick Pakenham Educational Awards, for ex-prisoners wishing to study law to degree level.

The National Association for the Care & Resettlement of Offenders (NACRO)

Eligibility: Ex-offenders and their partners and families.

Types of grants: One-off grants of up to £100 for study and employment training fees, course materials, work wear and tools required for training.

Young offenders, aged under 30 years, can also be supported towards expenses associated with education and training. Most of these grants are one-off and for up to £100, but support can also be given for successive years for a two or three-year course.

Annual grant total: £50,000

Applications: Either directly by the individual or through a probation service, social service department, citizen's advice bureau or registered charity. Applications are considered every two months.

Correspondent: Finance Director, 169 Clapham Road, London SW9 0PU (020 7840 6431; Fax: 020 7840 6720; website: www.nacro.org.uk)

The Prisoners' Education Trust

Eligibility: Prisoners aged 18 and above who are in custody in England and Wales and still have at least six months of their sentence to serve. Only prisoners serving in one of 60 specific prisons are eligible (this number is increased as funds allow). For a list, contact the correspondent.

Types of grants: One-off and recurrent grants of between £25 and £750 to pay course fees for a range of Open University, A-level, GCSE, City and Guilds or other approved courses.

The trust also gives the Allt Award which purchases educational books and other vital equipment for a small number of applicants.

Annual grant total: In 2005, the trust had net assets of £227,000, an income of around £503,000 and a total expenditure of £493,000. In total it gave educational grants of £575,200 to individuals.

Applications: Applications should be submitted on a form available from the trust or through a prison education department, for consideration monthly. Initial telephone enquiries are welcome. Applicants should check with their prisoner education department that the prison is in the scheme and will contribute 10% towards course fees.

Correspondent: Ms Ann Creighton, Director, Ground Floor, Wandle House, Riverside Drive, Mitcham, Surrey CR4 4BU (020 8648 7760; Fax: 020 8648 7762; e-mail: ann@ prisonerseducation.org.uk; website: www. prisonerseducation.org.uk)

The Royal London Society

Eligibility: Offenders, both before and after discharge from prison, their families and young people 'at risk' (that is young people under a supervision order or who have come to the attention of the police). Grants are only made to people living or serving a sentence in the London area.

Types of grants: One-off grants that will help lead to employment in the immediate future or within the next six months. Donations may be made for training, work clothing, tools and equipment and travel expenses.

Exclusions: Grants are not given for books, university courses, clothing, maintenance/ living expenses or debts.

Annual grant total: In 2005, the society had net assets of £1 million, an income of £68,000 and a total expenditure of £121,000. 42 individuals received grants totalling £59,000.

Applications: On a form available from the correspondent. An authority, such as a welfare agency or probation officer, must support all applications; grants are made through that authority (not directly to the beneficiary). Applications are considered in March, June, September and December.

Correspondent: Veronica Eades, 16 Manor Road, Bexhill-on-Sea, East Sussex, TN40 1SP (01424 218097)

SACRO Trust

Eligibility: Ex-offenders in Scotland who are in need.

Types of grants: Grants are usually to a maximum of £150, including those for fees, driving lessons, books and equipment.

Exclusions: No grants are made where financial help from other sources is available.

Annual grant total: In 2004/05 grants to 49 individuals totalled £6,000.

Applications: On a form available from the correspondent. Applications can only be accepted if they are made through a local authority, voluntary sector worker, health visitor or so on. They are considered every two months. No payment can be made directly to an individual by the trust;

payment will be made to the organisation making the application. Other sources of funding should be sought before applying to the trust.

Applications for grants up to £200 can be made at any time, although assessments are made quarterly; applications for larger sums will be considered at two trustees' meetings held in June and December.

Correspondent: Trust Fund Administrator, 1 Broughton Market, Edinburgh EH3 6NU (0131 624 7258; Fax: 0131 624 7269; website: www.sacro. org.uk)

The Paul Stephenson Memorial Trust

Eligibility: People who have served at least two years of imprisonment and are near the end of their sentence or have been released recently.

Types of grants: One-off grants of up to £100 for tools for work or assistance with college fees.

Exclusions: Grants are not given for recreational activities, setting up small businesses or becoming self employed, or for existing debts.

Annual grant total: In 2004 the trust had an income of £970 and a total expenditure of £300. Grants totalled about £200.

Applications: On a form available from the correspondent, which must be submitted via a probation officer, prison education officer or voluntary associate. Applicants should mention other trusts or organisations that have been applied to and other grants promised or received, including any statutory grants. Trustees usually meet twice a year.

Correspondent: Pauline Austin, The New Bridge, 27A Medway Street, London SW3 2BD

Refugees

Aid for Jewish Refugees

Eligibility: Refugees, and in particular Jewish refugees, living in the UK.

Types of grants: Grants may be spent on vocational training courses, fees, books and equipment for any future career.

Annual grant total: In 2003/04 the trust had an income of £750 and a total expenditure of £4,700.

Applications: In writing to the correspondent.

Correspondent: Henry Jonas, Flat 17 Greenleaf Court, 17 Oakleigh Park North, Whetstone, London N20 9AQ (020 8445 1694)

The Airey Neave Trust

Eligibility: Refugees or those with exceptional leave to remain in this country.

Types of grants: Grants of £1,000 to £1,500 towards English language classes, and help towards the cost of postgraduate courses or research.

Exclusions: Grants are not given to asylum seekers, overseas students or British citizens.

Annual grant total: In 2004/05 the trust had assets of £800,000, an income of £50,000 and a total expenditure of £72,000. Education grants were given to 16 individuals and totalled £17,000, with a further £22,000 given in grants for other purposes.

Applications: In writing to the correspondent. Applications should be submitted before the end of April for consideration in July. They can be submitted either directly by the individual, or through the British Refugee Council or other related bodies.

Correspondent: Hannah Scott, PO Box 36800, 40 Bernard Street, London WC1N 1WJ (020 7833 4440; e-mail: hanthoc@aol. com; website: www.aireyneavetrust.org.uk)

Ruth Hayman Trust – see entry on page 33

Correspondent: The Trustees, PO Box 17685, London N6 6WD (website: www. ruthhaymantrust.com)

The Elizabeth Nuffield Educational Fund

Eligibility: Women between the ages of 21 and 50 years who have children and are studying for a qualification which will improve their employment prospects. Applicants must have lived in the UK for three years for purposes other than studying, or be a recognised refugee, and be undertaking a course at a LEA recognised college or university. Applicants previously turned down by the fund, or with an household income over £22,010, are not eligible.

Students must be studying business/ administration, catering, childcare, humanities, languages, law, medicine and health, science and technology, social care, social work, social science or teacher-training (excluding PGCE).

Types of grants: Grants are given for childcare only, and are for a maximum of £3,000 a year for students who are in receipt of NHS bursaries and a maximum of £2,000 for people on other educational courses.

Exclusions: No grants are available to graduates or for intercalated degrees, distance learning, complementary medicine, counselling, hairdressing/beauty therapy courses, dance, drama or music courses, visual arts, crafts, fashion or interior design, ESOL/TEFL or adult returner courses. The foundation website has further information on eligibility criteria.

Annual grant total: Grants totalling £429,000 were awarded to 134 individuals in 2005.

Applications: Applicants are advised to check the website for current eligibility criteria. Application forms are also available from the site. The selection committee meets in March and November each year, with closing dates for application forms approximately 10 weeks in advance.

Correspondent: Suzanne Berry, The Administrator, 28 Bedford Square, London WC1B 3JS (020 7631 0566; Fax: 020 7323 4877; website: www. nuffieldfoundation.org)

The Russian Refugees Aid Society

Eligibility: Refugees and asylum seekers from the area that was formerly the Russian Empire and their families who are in need, and now live in Great Britain.

Types of grants: One-off grants, usually around £50. Grants are awarded for books and equipment/instruments. Schoolchildren can also receive grants towards the cost of uniform. Grants are particularly given for English language courses.

Annual grant total: In 2005, the trust had net assets of £1.4 million and an income of around £64,000. With a total expenditure £122,400, £97,000 of this was paid out in charitable grants.

Applications: In writing to the correspondent. Applications can be submitted directly by the individual or through the individual's school, college or an educational welfare agency. Applicants must show proof that they have applied to the Home Office for asylum. They are considered at any time.

Correspondent: Barbara Margaret Irvine, Room G03, Britannia House, 11 Glenthorne Road, Hammersmith, London, W6 0LH (020 8735 6511)

Religion – Christian

The Alexis Trust

Eligibility: Members of the Christian faith.

Types of grants: Grants of between £50 and £100 are available, mostly for Christian-based activities.

Annual grant total: In 2004/05 the trust gave grants totalling £45,000 from an income of £46,000. Around 10% of the grant total is usually given to individuals each year.

Applications: In writing to the correspondent.

Correspondent: Prof. D W Vere, 14 Broadfield Way, Buckhurst Hill, Essex IG9 5AG

Other information: The grants given to individuals are usually from the surplus funds from the grants to organisations. Applicants should contact the correspondent for further information before making an application.

The Britland Trust

Eligibility: People involved in the advancement of Christianity, mission work and Christian education and training.

Types of grants: One-off and recurrent grants according to need.

Annual grant total: In 2004, the trust had an income of £32,000. No charitable donations were made during the year. Previously grants have been made to organisations and individuals.

Applications: In writing to the correspondent.

Correspondent: J M P Colman, Trustee, 20 Henderson Road, Wandsworth, London SW18 3RR (e-mail: jcolman@lineone.net)

The Groves Charitable Trust

Eligibility: Individuals undertaking Christian education or training, at any level, who are in need.

Types of grants: One-off grants ranging from £200 to £1,000 towards Christian education and training.

Annual grant total: About £16,000 for welfare and educational purposes.

Applications: Applications should be made in writing, explaining the purpose for which the grant is being sought.

Correspondent: R Humphrey, c/o Messrs Grant Thornton, 125 High Street, Crawley, West Sussex RH10 1DQ

Other information: Support is also given to Christian missionaries and their work.

The Podde Trust

Eligibility: Individuals involved in Christian work in the UK and overseas.

Types of grants: One-off and recurrent grants.

Annual grant total: In 2004/05 the trust has an income of £28,000. There were 27 grants to individuals totalling £7,200.

Applications: In writing to the correspondent: please note, the trust states that it has very limited resources, and those it does have are mostly already committed. Requests from new applicants therefore have very little chance of success.

Correspondent: P B Godfrey, 68 Green Lane, Hucclecote, Gloucester GL3 3QX (01452 613563)

Other information: Organisations involved in Christian work are also supported (£21,000 in 2004/05).

The Stewardship Trust Ripon

Eligibility: People connected with Christian causes living in the UK, with a preference for Yorkshire.

Types of grants: One-off and recurrent grants, for example, for training in Christian ministry.

Annual grant total: In 2004/05, the trust had an annual income of £27,000 and an expenditure of £22,000.

Applications: In writing to the correspondent. The trust's funds are usually fully committed and new applications are only considered if there is 'extreme need'.

Correspondent: W B Metcalf, Chair, Hutton Hill, Hutton Bank, Ripon, North Yorkshire, HG4 5DT (01765 602887)

Religion – Church of England

The St George's Trust

Eligibility: People involved in work 'for the furtherance of the Church of England and churches in communion with her'.

Types of grants: Grants are small, one-off and made towards a specific project or theological course, e.g. young people undertaking voluntary Christian work abroad and clergymen planning special work during a sabbatical.

Exclusions: Restoration projects or any long-term financial support.

Annual grant total: About £15,000 to £18,000 is given in grants each year.

Applications: In writing to the correspondent, giving details of the project, its likely cost and with a note of any funds available towards it. An sae is required for a reply.

Correspondent: St Edward's House, 22 Great College Street, London SW1P 3QA

Religion – Huguenot

Charities in connection with the Society of St Onge & Angoumois

Eligibility: Young people aged 16 to 25 who live in the UK, with preference for those who are descended from French Protestants (Huguenot) and in particular those who have at any time lived in the province of St Onge and Angoumois in France, who are in need, and who are preparing for, entering upon or engaged in any profession, trade or service.

Types of grants: One-off grants to enable beneficiaries to train for a trade or occupation in order to help them to advance in life or earn their living. Grants are only given on proof of purchase, for example, for books, equipment, daily travel and clothing for people on a training course, and for books, equipment and daily travel for students in further or higher education. Grants range from £100 to £400.

Exclusions: No grants to foreign students studying in the UK.

Annual grant total: In 2004/05 the trust had an income of £2,200 and a total expenditure of £1,900. Grants totalled about £1,500.

Applications: On a form available from Mr A Squire, 26 Blaisdon, Weston-super-Mare, Somerset, BS22 8BN. Applications should be submitted directly by the individual or by a parent or guardian. They are considered in April and May.

Correspondent: Mrs P J Lane-Gilbert, Flat 19, Amberley Court, Angell Road, London SW9 7HL

Religion – Jewish

The Anglo Jewish Association

Eligibility: Jewish students studying at a UK university, regardless of nation of origin, who are in need.

Types of grants: Grants ranging between £500 and £3,000 a year for students at either undergraduate or postgraduate level.

Annual grant total: About £100,000 each year.

Applications: On a form available from the correspondent in January, or from the website, to be submitted by 30 April. Applications must include academic references, a cv and details of the applicant's personal history.

Correspondent: Ms J Samuel, Suite 4, 107 Gloucester Place, London W1U 6BY (020 7486 5155; e-mail: info@anglojewish. co.uk; website: www.anglojewish.co.uk)

Finnart House School Trust

Eligibility: Jewish children and young people aged over 14 years who are in need. Bursaries and scholarships are for those with ability, who, because of family circumstances, may otherwise be unable to achieve their potential.

Types of grants: Bursaries are awarded through schools. Awards may be made regularly each term, or may be one-off.

Grants range between £100 and £1,500. Scholarships are awarded for higher education until the completion of the course and range up to £5,000 a year.

Exclusions: Only members of the Jewish faith can be supported.

Annual grant total: In 2004/05 it had assets of £3.9 million, which generated an income of £148,000. Grants to 16 individuals totalled £109,000, all for educational rather than welfare needs. A further £31,000 went to organisations.

Applications: Bursaries are awarded via schools. Scholarship applications are made by the individual on a form available from the correspondent, to be submitted by April.

Correspondent: Peter Shaw, 707 High Road, London N12 0BT (020 8445 1670; Fax: 020 8446 7370; e-mail: info@finnart. org)

Other information: This trust also makes grants for relief-in-need purposes and to organisations which work with children and young people of the Jewish faith who are in need.

Gur Trust

Eligibility: People connected to the Jewish faith in the UK.

Types of grants: One-off and recurrent grants according to need.

Annual grant total: In 2003/04 the trust had an income of £22,000 and a total expenditure of £56,000. Grants are made to organisations and individuals.

Applications: 'Funds are raised by the trustees. All calls for help are carefully considered and help is given according to circumstances and funds then available.'

Correspondent: The Trustees, c/o 479 Holloway Road, London N7 6LD

The Jewish Widows & Students Aid Trust

Eligibility: Jewish students from the UK, France, the Commonwealth and Israel who are aged 10 to 30 years old. Grants may occasionally be given to poor widows if they have young children.

Types of grants: Mainly interest-free loans ranging from £250 to £1,000. Awards are made on the basis of academic excellence and need. Students can be given grants towards fees, living expenses, books or travel. On rare occasions grants can also be given to schoolchildren.

Annual grant total: In 2004/05 the trust had assets of £521,000 and an income of £38,000. Grants were made to 28 individuals totalling £27,000.

Applications: In writing to the correspondent requesting an application form, including a cv and confirmation of acceptance at an educational establishment. Applications should be submitted directly by the individual to be considered at any time.

Correspondent: Alan Philipp, Marlborough House, 298 Regents Park Road, London N3 2UU (020 8349 9988)

The Charities of Moses Lara

Eligibility: Spanish and Portuguese Jews, born in wedlock and living in the UK. There may be a preference for people whose principal place of worship is a Sephardi Synagogue.

Types of grants: Help with the cost of books, clothing and other essentials for college and university students. Preference may be given to those promoting the study of texts and so on of Judaism involving the Rabbinic Law. The trust also assists residents in Beth Holim (Wembley).

Annual grant total: In 2004/05 the trust had assets of £250,000, and both an income and a total expenditure of about £12,000. Grants were made to 12 individuals totalling £10,000.

Applications: In writing to the correspondent.

Correspondent: B C Musikant, Vestry Office, 2 Ashworth Road, London W9 1JY (020 7289 8780)

The Spanish & Portuguese Jews Children's Fund

Eligibility: People under 26 who are in need and are Sephardi Jews or are accustomed to congregate with them.

Types of grants: One-off and recurrent grants for schoolchildren and people in further and higher education.

Annual grant total: In 2005 grants totalled £12,000.

Applications: In writing to the correspondent. Applications are considered twice a year, and are to be submitted by 31 March or 30 September.

Correspondent: H Miller, Secretary, Spanish & Portuguese Jews Congregation, 2 Ashworth Road, London W9 1JY (Fax: 020 7289 2573: 020 7289 2709)

The Benjamin Winegarten Charitable Trust

Eligibility: People involved in the advancement of the Jewish religion and religious education.

Types of grants: One-off and recurrent grants according to need.

Annual grant total: In 2005, the trust had net assets of £501,000, an income of around £160,000, and a total expenditure of £114,000. Grants to individuals totalled £5,500.

Applications: In writing to the correspondent.

Correspondent: B A Winegarten, 25 ST. Andrew's Grove, London, N16 5NF (020 8800 6669)

Religion – Protestant

William and Mary Hart Foundation

Eligibility: Baptist Christians under the age of 25. Preference shall be given to persons who live in the parish of Collingham or who have a parent or parents living there.

Types of grants: One-off and recurrent grants and loans to school children, undergraduates and vocational students.

Annual grant total: In 2004 the foundation had a gross income of £1,300 and a total expenditure of £350. Grants totalled about £250.

Applications: In writing to the correspondent.

Correspondent: David Marshall, 2 Keats Drive, Hucknall, Nottingham, NG15 6TE (0115 963 5428)

The Mylne Trust

Eligibility: Members of the Protestant faith, individuals engaged in evangelistic work or Christian workers whose finances are inadequate. Married ordinands with children are also supported when all other sources of funding have failed to cover their needs.

Types of grants: Grants are given towards educational training at theological colleges, for the cost of books and living expenses to undergraduates and overseas students.

Annual grant total: In 2004/05 the trust had assets of £1.5 million and an income of £48,000. Grants totalled £41,000.

Applications: On a form available from the correspondent, or which can be downloaded from the trust's website. The trustees meet quarterly to consider applications.

Correspondent: The Trustees, Hadfields Butt & Bowyer, 104 West street, Farnham, Surrey GU9 7ET (e-mail: admin@ mylnetrust.org.uk; website: www. mylnetrust.org.uk)

Religion – Quaker

The Friends Educational Foundation

Eligibility: Members of Britain Yearly Meeting of the Religious Society of Friends (Quakers) or those closely associated with the society (for example, regular attenders).

Types of grants: Two types of award exist: (i) bursaries for children attending Quaker schools; and (ii) grants for Quakers pursuing courses of further or higher education.

Exclusions: Retrospective applications or applications for more than a year ahead cannot normally be considered.

Annual grant total: Previously £98,000.

Applications: For bursaries for children attending Quaker schools – via the Quaker schools upon entry; and for grants for Quakers pursuing courses of further or higher education – to the correspondent in the year before the course begins.

The closing dates for applications each year is 30 April. Initial enquiries by telephone, e-mail or letter.

Correspondent: Debbie Taylor, Friends House, 173 Euston Road, London NW1 2BJ (020 7663 1000; e-mail: debbiet@ quaker.org.uk)

Religion – Roman Catholic

The Duchess of Leeds Foundation for Boys and Girls

Eligibility: Orphaned or fatherless Catholic children aged between 11 and 18 who attend fee-paying Catholic schools and are in need. Children must live in England, Wales or the Channel Islands. Help is concentrated on secondary education; children in primary and secondary school are helped only in exceptional circumstances.

Types of grants: Grants to help with the cost of school fees only. Grants may continue until the end of an A-level course. Current maximum annual grants are £1,158 for boarders and £999 for day pupils.

Annual grant total: In 2005 the foundation had assets of £437,000 and an income of £19,000. There were 45 grants made totalling £36,000.

Applications: On a form available form the correspondent to be submitted directly by the individual or a parent/guardian. The deadline for applications in 31 January.

Correspondent: B L Cawley, Clerk, 15 High Oaks, Enfield, EN2 8JJ (020 8367 1077; Fax: 020 8367 1077)

Religion – United Reformed Church

Milton Mount Foundation

Eligibility: The children of ministers of the United Reformed Church, the Congregational Federation, the Evangelical Fellowship of Congregational Churches and the Unaffiliated Congregational Churches; also daughters of members of these churches.

Types of grants: The foundation gives bursaries towards school fees for children aged 11 to 18, both at United Reformed Church and Congregational schools, and at other independent boarding or day schools approved by the trustees. Grants may also be given towards the cost of school uniform for eligible boys or girls on entry to secondary school at both independent and maintained schools. Women taking up further/higher education at a later stage can also receive grants towards books and fees. Up to one third only of the income may be spent on boys as the funds arise from the sale of a girls' school, thereby limiting the number of bursaries available to the sons of ministers.

Annual grant total: In 2004/05 the trust had assets of £2.7 million, generating an income of just £93,000. Grants were made to 22 individuals totalling £110,000

Applications: On a form available from the correspondent, with information about total family income. Applications are considered in May and June.

Correspondent: Rev. Erna Stevenson, 11 Copse Close, Cippenham, Slough, Berkshire SL1 5DT (01753 748713)

Sport

The Francis Drake Fellowship

Eligibility: Dependants of members of the fellowship who have died.

Types of grants: Allowances of £52 per month per child is given to children in full-time education, up to the end of their A-levels.

Annual grant total: In 2005 the fellowship had assets of £187,000, an income of £37,000 and gave grants to 37 individuals, all for welfare purposes, totalling £16,000.

Applications: In writing to the correspondent, requesting an application form. Applications should be submitted through the bowling club's Francis Drake Fellowship delegate. Applications are

accepted two years after the date of the members death.

Correspondent: Joan Jupp, 24 Haldane Close, London N10 2PB (020 8883 8725)

The Rugby Football Union Charitable Fund

Eligibility: Individuals injured while participating in any sport and any dependant of any person who was killed while participating in any sport.

Types of grants: One-off grants of up to £500 towards, for instance, hospital visits, personal and domestic expenses and educational expenses.

Annual grant total: In 2004 the trust had an income of £19,000 and a total expenditure of £35,000.

Applications: On a form available from the correspondent.

Correspondent: Carol Collins, 41 Station Road, North Harrow, Middlesex HA2 7SX

Other information: Grants are made to organisations and individuals.

Vegetarian

The Vegetarian Charity

Eligibility: People under the age of 26 who are vegetarian or vegan and are sick or in need.

Types of grants: One-off and recurrent grants of £250 to £1,000 for general educational purposes.

Annual grant total: In 2004/05 the charity had assets of £945,000 and an income of £36,000. There were 29 educational grants made totalling £13,000. A further 18 welfare grants were made totalling £1,200

Applications: On a form available from the correspondent, including details of any other grants received, a CV, a letter of recommendation from a tutor, school reports, covering letter and three references. Applications are considered throughout the year.

Correspondent: Margaret Chatfield, Cobblers Cottage, Chapel Lane, Cox Bank, Audlem, Cheshire CW3 0EU (e-mail: maggiechat@hotmail.com)

Other information: Grants are also made to organisations which promote vegetarianism among young people and to vegetarian children's homes.

Volunteers

The Alec Dickson Trust

Eligibility: Young people under 30 years of age and living in the UK, involved in volunteering or community service.

Types of grants: 'The trust's mission is to support young people who are able to demonstrate that through volunteering or community service projects they can enhance the lives of others, particularly those most marginalised by society. The trust particularly welcomes applications from innovative projects in the spirit of Alec Dickson – projects which young people themselves have devised and which are unlikely to be funded by other charitable trusts. As a result, it is unlikely that applications from young people embarking on organised gap year" projects overseas or requesting a grant for college/university course fees will match with the trust's funding criteria.' Grants are generally between £100 and £250."

Annual grant total: Around £3,000 each year.

Applications: Directly by the individual on a form available from the correspondent. Applications are considered in April and October.

Correspondent: Miss Angela Lazenbury, Flat 11, Barbrook House, Chatham Place, London E9 6PE (020 7643 1338)

The Emmaus Charitable Trust

Eligibility: Christians involved in voluntary projects. Grants are given internationally but in practice there is a preference for Greater London.

Types of grants: One-off and recurrent grants according to need.

Annual grant total: In 2004/05 the trust made £6,800 available for grants, of which £6,100 was given to nine organisations, and £500 was awarded to individuals. In any given year the trust can only provide support for one or two individuals.

Applications: In writing to the correspondent.

Correspondent: R J Silman, Trustee, 4 Church Avenue, Lancaster LA1 4SP (01524 368824)

The New Durlston Trust

Eligibility: Students undertaking gap year projects or youth work in conjuction with Chrisitan charities.

Types of grants: One-off gants of around £100 each.

Annual grant total: In 2004/05 it had assets of £50,000 and an income of £27,500. Grants were made totalling £31,000, mostly to organisations but around 50 grants were given to individuals.

Applications: In writing to the correspondent, including confirmation from the charity that the applicant will be working with. They are considered every three to four months.

Correspondent: N A H Pool, Trustee, 95 Fleet Road, Fleet, Hampshire GU51 3PJ (01252 620444; Fax: 01252 622292)

The Princess Royal Trust for Carers

Eligibility: Unpaid carers in the UK, especially those who live near a Princess Royal Trust for Carers Centre.

Types of grants: One-off grants towards educational bursaries.

Annual grant total: About 650 grants are made each year.

Applications: Applications are made via your local Princess Royal Trust for Carers Centre.

Correspondent: The Clerk, 142 Minories, London EC3N 1LB (020 7480 7788; website: www.carers.org)

Women

The Altrusa Careers Trust

Eligibility: Women in the UK and Eire who wish to further their career prospects or to retrain after bringing up a family, and who are in extreme need or facing an emergency.

Types of grants: A loan or grant of up to £500.

Exclusions: Grants are not available to those still at school and there is probably a restriction on those going on to do a second degree.

Annual grant total: Between £2,000 and £5,000 is available each year for grants.

Applications: On a form available from the correspondent. Applications are reviewed after 31 March each year. A shortlist is drawn up and references taken up. Applicants are requested to keep in touch with the trustees once a year so that their progress can be noted.

Correspondent: Ms Grace Franklin, YAM Publications, Suite 9, 2nd Floor, 73 Robertson Street, Glasgow G2 8QD

The Golden Jubilee Fellowship

Eligibility: Women who live 'permanently' within the boundaries of Soroptimist International of Great Britain and Ireland, who need not be Soroptimists. The countries are: Anguilla, Antigua and Barbuda, Bangladesh, Barbados, Cameroon, Gambia, Grenada, Guernsey, India, Isle of Man, Jamaica, Jersey, Republic of Ireland, Malawi, Malta, Mauritius, Mozambique, Nigeria, Pakistan, Seychelles, Sierra Leone, South Africa, Sri Lanka, St Vincent and the Grenadines, Trinidad & Tobago, Turks & Caicos Islands, Uganda, UK and Zimbabwe.

Types of grants: Preference is given to women seeking to improve their skills or gain new ones to seek employment after years in the home, or to enter a field where prospects of employment and advancement are greater. One-off grants of £100 to £500 are awarded each year. About 30 awards, usually in the range of £100 to £500 are made each year.

Annual grant total: The annual income of the trust amounts to around £4,500. Grants total around £4,000.

Applications: On an application form, to be requested by writing to the correspondent, enclosing an sae. Completed forms should be returned by 15 April each year for the academic year beginning the following autumn. The committee meets to consider applications in May/June and successful applicants are informed by the end of July. Please enclose an sae/international reply coupon.

Correspondent: The Chair, Soroptimist International Great Britain and Ireland, 127 Wellington Road South, Stockport SK1 3TS (0161 480 7686; Fax: 0161 477 6152; e-mail: hq@ soroptimistgbi.prestel.co.uk; website: www.soroptimist-gbi.org)

The Mary MacArthur Educational Trust

Eligibility: Non-graduate women over the age of 20 who have shown desire and aptitude for further education by attendance since age 16 at educational courses or establishments including trade union, cooperative society or political courses. Priority is given to women whose early education was limited and who left school at an early age but have since, through their own efforts, tried to further their education.

Types of grants: (i) One-year scholarship awards of approximately £900 for women who gain a place at one of the following adult residential colleges:

Coleg Harlech, Gwynedd

Fircroft College, Birmingham

Hillcroft College, Surbiton

Newbattle Abbey College, Dalkeith

Northern College, Barnsley

Ruskin College, Oxford.

(ii) Exceptionally, if the grant total is not exhausted by awards of type (i) a few awards may be made of smaller bursaries or grants for women to attend summer schools, lectures or other activities to promote further education up to degree level. These are to help cover costs of books, transport, childminding and so on.

Exclusions: No grants for study or travel abroad or foreign students studying in the UK, nor for the study of second degrees.

Annual grant total: In 2005, the trust had an income of £3,000 and a total expenditure of £2,200. About £1,800 was given in grants.

Applications: (i) Through the adult residential college at which you have been given a place, on a form supplied and signed by the college, for consideration normally in July/August.(ii) To the correspondent in January, May or August for consideration in March, July or October. An sae must be enclosed if there is to be any response to the applications. Two testimonials from referees should be included.

Correspondent: Meg Tritton, Hon. Secretary, Central House, Upper Woburn Place, London WC1H 0HY (020 7388 0852)

Other information: All correspondence must include an sae for a reply.

The Hilda Martindale Educational Trust

Eligibility: 'Women of the British Isles whose intention it is to fit themselves for some profession or career likely to be of use or value to the community, and for which vocational training is required.' Applicants under 21 are not considered. Grants are not available to women doing wholly academic courses, academic research, short courses, access courses, courses outside the UK, elective studies, intercalated BSc years during a medical, dental, veterinary or nursing course, special projects in the UK or abroad, or Masters' courses immediately after a first degree. Candidates eligible for career development loans are expected to have tried this option before applying. Students eligible for grants from research councils, British Academy or other public sources are also ineligible.

Types of grants: One-off grants are of between £200 and £1,000. Grants can be used for books, equipment, fees, living expenses or childcare.

Annual grant total: Previously grants were awarded to 36 individuals totalling £30,000.

Applications: On a form available from the correspondent. Applications must be returned by 1 March for the following academic year, with the results of application announced in mid-June. Applications should be submitted directly by the individual including a reference.

Correspondent: Miss J L Hurn, Secretary to the Trustees, c/o Registry, Royal Holloway University of London, Egham, Surrey TW20 0EX (01784 434455; Fax: 01784 473662)

Other information: Due to a large number of applicants, in general only 10% of applications are funded. People who do not exactly suit the eligibility criteria are asked not to apply.

The Elizabeth Nuffield Educational Fund – see entry on page 40

Correspondent: Suzanne Berry, The Administrator, 28 Bedford Square, London WC1B 3JS (020 7631 0566; Fax: 020 7323 4877; website: www. nuffieldfoundation.org)

President's Fund

Eligibility: Women in their final year of study for a degree (postgraduate or undergraduate) at a British university who face unexpected financial hardship.

Types of grants: One-off grants between £150 and £500. Applicants receive only one award which is for current study. Grants are intended to help with costs of books, equipment and maintenance/living expenses.

Exclusions: Grants are not given towards access courses, diplomas, certificates, study or work outside the UK, childcare, any year of study other than final year, one year undergraduate and one year postgraduate degrees.

Annual grant total: The trust has an annual income of about £10,000, the greater part of which is given in grants.

Applications: On a form only available by writing to the correspondent. Requests for application forms must be submitted directly by the applicant (not third parties). The trustees meet to consider applications in February, April/May, October and November.

Correspondent: Mrs Alison MacLachlan, Hon. Secretary, Flat 5, 6 Craigleith Avenue South, Edinburgh EH4 3LQ

Other information: The trust stated that 'applications which disregard the exclusions listed above will not be acknowledged'.

The Women's Careers Foundation (Girls of The Realm Guild) – see entry on page 23

Correspondent: Mrs B Hayward, Secretary, 2 Watchoak, Blackham, Tunbridge Wells, Kent TN3 9TP (01892 740602)

Yorkshire Ladies' Council of Education (Incorporated)

Eligibility: British women who are aged 21 or over 'who can present a case of special need in funding their further or higher education at a British institution'.

Types of grants: Grants in the range of £200 and £300 a year are made towards fees.

Exclusions: YLCE members and their dependants are not eligible for support.

Annual grant total: In 2004/05 the trust had assets of £452,000, an income of £22,000 and a total expenditure of £26,000. Grants were offered to 69 totalling £15,000.

Applications: Applications forms can be requested from the correspondent, or are available to download from the charity's website. Completed forms should be submitted directly by the individual by the first of January, March, June or September for consideration later in the month.

Correspondent: The Chairman, YLCE Awards Committee, Forest Hill, 11 Park Crescent, Leeds LS8 1DH (0113 269 1471; website: www.ylce.org.uk)

Work/study overseas

The Melanie Akroyd Trust

Eligibility: Young people aged 22 to 27 years who are living in the UK.

Types of grants: Travel scholarships for educational or personal development purposes, up to a maximum of £1,500. The applicant must begin their journey alone and will have to demonstrate that (i) they have been earning their own living for some years, (ii) that there are no financial resources available to them from their family which could go towards the trip, and (iii) that they have earned and saved funds for the trip which are equal to the funds which the trust will provide. Candidates' trips must cover a period of at least six months and must be in developing countries.

Annual grant total: In 2004/05 the trust had an income of £3,000 and a total expenditure of £2,000.

Applications: This trust does not accept unsolicited applications.

Correspondent: R M Tasher, Trustee, 9 Cambrian Place, Llandidloes, Powys, SY18 6BX (07711 178 162; Fax: 44 845 280 6007; e-mail: robert. tasher@btinternet.com)

Lady Allen of Hurtwood Memorial Trust

Eligibility: Individuals wishing to carry out a specific travel project that will help them gain specific additional knowledge and experience which will enhance the quality and the nature of their work with young children (particularly those who are deprived or disabled) and their families.

Types of grants: Travel awards, ranging from £500 to £1,000.

Annual grant total: About £2,000 is available each year for grants to individuals.

Applications: On a form available, with guidelines for applicants, from the correspondent. Applicants must have a specific project in mind and offer positive evidence of how the award will help them, and how the knowledge gained will be shared with others. Shortlisting is in February and the awards are made in March.

Correspondent: Mrs Caroline Richards, Hon. Secretary, 89 Thurleigh Road, London SW12 8TY

The Barnabas Trust

Eligibility: People embarking on Christian mission activities, and people on religious education courses.

Types of grants: One-off grants according to need.

Annual grant total: In 2004/05 the trust had assets of £3.3 million, which generated an income of £164,000. Grants to 10 individuals totalled £10,000. A further £300,000 went to bible colleges.

Applications: In writing to the correspondent. Applications should be submitted by the end of February. Trustees meet quarterly.

Correspondent: Mrs Doris Edwards, 63 Wolsey Drive, Walton-on-Thames, Surrey KT12 3BB (01932 220622)

Captain F G Boot Scholarships

Eligibility: School leavers aged 17 to 20, or university students.

Types of grants: These scholarships enable school leavers to spend at least six months abroad to learn or to improve a foreign language prior to further education. Each scholarship may be for an amount up to £1,000. Grants are not given to Project Trust applicants.

Annual grant total: Previously £5,000.

Applications: Application forms can be downloaded from the Worshipful Company of Cutlers website.

Correspondent: The Clerk, The Worshipful Company of Cutlers, Cutlers' Hall, Warwick Lane, London EC4M 7BR (website: www.cutlerslondon.co.uk)

The British & Foreign School Society – International Award Scheme

Eligibility: Individuals from the UK who wish to engage in educational activities in developing countries, and vice versa. Most UK awards are made to young people who volunteer to teach abroad for an academic year. Most awards in developing countries are made to individuals of any age who want to visit the UK for an academic year to acquire specific skills and knowledge. All awards are channelled through existing links and organisations to ensure volunteers are fully briefed and supported.

Types of grants: Grants of up to £2,000 per individual. Other grants have been given to support or sponsor individuals engaging in educational activities overseas. About £25,000 is available each year for grants to individuals.

Annual grant total: In 2004 the society had assets of £9.5 million, an income of around £500,000, and a total expenditure £400,000. Thirty- two individuals received grants totalling £2,900 overall.

Applications: Guidelines for applications are available from the correspondent.

Correspondent: Charles Crawford, Director, Maybrook House, Godstone Road, Caterham, Surrey CR3 6RE (01883 331177; Fax: 01883 344429; e-mail: britforeign@aol.com; website: www.bfss.org.uk)

Harold Buxton Trust

Eligibility: People undertaking projects, particularly study/exchange visits, which will promote mutual understanding and interchange between the Anglican, Roman Catholic and Orthodox Churches.

Types of grants: One-off grants of £100 to £1,000 for travel expenses for study/ exchange visits to and from Eastern Europe, countries of the former Soviet Union and the Middle East.

Annual grant total: In 2004/05 the trust had assets of £158,000, an income of £7,000 and a total expenditure of £3,300. Grants totalled £2,900.

Applications: Contact the secretary by letter or telephone, giving brief details of the project. If it falls within the remit of the trust, an application form and guidelines will be sent. Applications should be submitted by February, May or September for consideration in the following month; they cannot be considered between meetings.

Correspondent: Mrs Pat Phillips, c/o SPCK, 36 Causton Street, London SW1P 4ST (020 7592 3900; Fax: 020 7592 3939; e-mail: pphillips@spck.org.uk)

The Winston Churchill Memorial Trust

Eligibility: Men and women from all walks of life who wish to travel overseas and learn about the life, work and people of other countries. Each year the trust selects a group of different categories from which candidates for that year will be chosen.

Types of grants: 'Travelling Fellowships are awarded for originality, quality of character, enterprise and a sense of responsibility. The primary consideration is whether the contribution which candidates can make to their trade, industry, profession, business, community or calling will be increased by personal travel overseas. The awards are open to any man or woman who is a UK citizen and resident in the UK, regardless of age. Everyone has an equal chance. Those who are selected travel to all corners of the world as representatives of this country, in

the name of Sir Winston Churchill.' Details of the current categories can be obtained from the trust's website, or from the address below. In the past they have covered the widest possible range of activities. The categories supported change each year.

Exclusions: The trust cannot award grants for attending courses or academic studies, nor for student grants; this includes electives, degree placements and post-graduate studies unless it is clear that the proposed fellowship would meet the principles set out under 'types of grants' above. Applications under the guise of a 'gap' year will not normally be considered.

Annual grant total: In 2005/06 the trust had assets of £26 million and an income of £974,000. There were 107 grants made totalling £847,000.

Applications: The categories for the following year are published in June of the preceding year and applications should be received by the end of October. Information about the categories and an application form is available on sending a 9 inch x 4 inch sae to the correspondent, or via e-mail through the trust's website.

Correspondent: The Director General, 15 Queen's Gate Terrace, London SW7 5PR (020 7584 9315; Fax: 020 7581 0410; e-mail: office@wcmt.org.uk; website: www. wcmt.org.uk)

The Norman Evershed Trust

Eligibility: Young people undertaking educational expeditions overseas.

Types of grants: One-off grants averaging £500 each.

Annual grant total: In 2004/05 the trust had an income of £6,000 and a total expenditure of £122,000.

Applications: In writing to the correspondent, although the trust has stated that no funds are currently available.

Correspondent: Mrs C A Evershed, Trustee, 35 Lemsford Road, St Albans, Hertfordshire AL1 3PP (01727 852019)

Other information: The trustees are intending to give away all the funds and close the trust before April 2008.

Reg Gilbert International Youth Friendship Trust (GIFT)

Eligibility: UK residents who are aged 14 to 25 and are visiting a developing country on a trip lasting at least four weeks. Applicants must be unable to afford the cost, be planning to live with an indigenous family in the host country as an ordinary member of the family, and be aiming to develop friendship. The trust stresses that there must be an indigenous homestay element within the programme to be eligible for any funding.

Types of grants: The aim of the trust is to help with the personal development of

young people by assisting them in gaining firsthand experience of a different culture, thereby developing friendships with, and an understanding of, people of that culture. The more applicants can show they will have a clear association with indigenous people, the more likely they are to get a bursary.

Bursaries range between £100 and £300.

Exclusions: No grants for proposals leading to academic or vocational qualifications.

Annual grant total: In 2004/05 the trust had an income of £15,000 and a total expenditure of £2,000, all of which was given in grants to individuals.

Applications: Potential applicants who will be living with an indigenous family in a developing country should send an outline proposal. An application form and guidelines will then be sent out. Please enclose an sae.

Applications are considered in November and June.

Correspondent: Reg Gilbert, 67 Nunney Road, Frome, Somerset BA11 4LE (e-mail: rgilb@beeb.net)

The Gilchrist Educational Trust – see entry on page 22

Correspondent: The Secretary, 28 Great James Street, London WC1N 3EY (020 7404 1672; e-mail: gilchrist.charity@ btinternet.com; website: www. gilchristgrants.org.uk)

Roger and Miriam Pilkington Charitable Trust

Eligibility: Grants are given to 'enterprising' people aged 18 to 25, particularly those who are undertaking imaginative projects abroad which could be said to broaden horizons, giving them experiences which they may not otherwise have; increase awareness of other cultures and ways of living; or help them understand something of social problems outside their immediate environment. Suitable projects include British Schools Exploring Society, Raleigh International, Project T and Trek Aid.

Types of grants: Donations are usually in the range of £300 to £500.

Exclusions: The trustees favour making awards for medical electives and VSO projects. The trustees do not take on responsibilities which are properly those of the education authorities. Long-term funding is not given.

Annual grant total: In 2004/05 the trust had an income of £24,000. Grants were made to individuals and schools totalling about £20,000.

Applications: In writing, directly by the individual to the correspondent at any time, for consideration in March and August. All grants are contingent on the applicant raising a significant proportion of the funds through their own efforts.

Correspondent: Alison Houghton, c/o Brabners Chaffe Street, 1 Dale Street, Liverpool L2 2ET (0151 600 3443; Fax: 0151 600 3300; e-mail: alison. houghton@brabnerscs.com)

The Rotary Foundation Scholarships

Eligibility: Scholarships overseas to further international understanding, for vocational study, graduates, undergraduates who have completed two years of university study, teachers of people with disabilities or professional journalists.

Types of grants: The purpose of the scholarships is to further international understanding and friendly relations among peoples of different countries, rather than to enable beneficiaries to achieve any particular qualification. About 30 scholarships, each for about nine months' study overseas, are awarded each year. Candidates are selected at the level of rotary districts only. Each of the 29 rotary districts in the UK can award one such scholarship as of right each year. Normally one applicant is chosen with another on 'standby'. It is possible that applicants may be offered a place for courses, institutions or even in countries other than those for which they have originally applied. It is important to realise that these are not academic awards and to read carefully the first paragraph of the full description below.

Applicants will be selected by local rotary districts on the basis of their personal qualities as ambassadors of international goodwill. They must be prepared to present themselves in this capacity.

The Rotary Foundation publishes the following information about these scholarships, which is quoted extensively though not in its entirety:

'The purpose of Rotary Foundation scholarships is to further international understanding and friendly relations among peoples of different countries. Both men and women may apply for one of the three types of foundation scholarships to complete one academic year of study or training in another country where Rotary clubs are located. During the time of study abroad, Rotary scholars are expected to be outstanding ambassadors of good will to the people of the host country through both formal and informal appearance before rotary clubs and districts, school and civic organisations, and other forums. After the period of study has been completed, the scholar is expected to share the experiences of understanding acquired during the scholarship with the people of his/her home country and the Rotarians who sponsored the scholarship.

'The three types of Rotary Foundation scholarships are:

(1) The Academic-Year Ambassadorial Scholarships

Awarded for one academic year of study abroad at an institution assigned by the foundation. The foundation will provide round-trip airfare, plus a scholarship of up to £14,000 to be used for tuition fees, living expenses and one month of intensive language training if assigned by the Rotary Foundation.

(2) Multi-Year Ambassadorial Scholarships

Awarded for two or three years of specific degree-orientated study abroad and coursework which relates directly to the completion of the degree. The foundation will provide a flat grant of £6,400 to be used for costs related to the pursuit of an academic degree.

(3) Cultural Ambassadorial Scholarships

This is awarded for three to six months of intensive language study and cultural immersion in another country. Study must be in a country where Rotary Clubs are located. Funding is subject to successful academic progress and submission of satisfactory reports. The foundation will provide funding for round-trip airfare, tuition and fees and reasonable living expenses. University applicants must have completed at least two years of university coursework when the scholarship begins. Those pursuing practical training or vocational study must have a secondary education and have been employed in a recognised vocation for at least two years when the scholarship begins. No grants for Rotarians, Honorary Rotarians, employees of Rotary Clubs, districts or other Rotary entity or members of their families.

'The Rotarian counsellors

A benefit not found in other scholarships is the scholar's association with Rotary clubs and Rotarians. Each scholar is assigned both a sponsor and a host Rotarian counsellor who provides orientation, advice, and assistance in preparing for and completing a successful study period in another country.

'Terms of scholarship

The basic period of the scholarship is the regular academic year (usually nine months) at the assigned study institution. The award cannot be held over, extended, or postponed beyond the period for which it is originally granted, because the primary purpose of the scholarship is to contribute to international understanding and since the foundation's sponsorship ends after one academic year, an award does not necessarily enable the recipient to earn a degree, certificate, or diploma.

'Rotary Foundation scholarships include round-trip transportation between the scholar's home and study city, all required academic fees, some necessary educational supplies, on-campus double-occupancy room (or approved off-campus accommodations if on-campus housing is not offered), on-campus board (or off-campus, if the study institution does not offer meals), limited educational travel during the award year, and limited contingency expenses. Personal preferences which lead to higher expenses will not be paid for by the foundation.

'A candidate whose native language is other than that of the proposed study institution and country must submit evidence of ability to read, write, and speak the host language(s). The candidate may also be required to successfully pass a language ability examination determined by the foundation.

'A scholarship may be undertaken for almost any field of study. This includes short-term training for scholars from developing countries going to developed countries. However, it may not be used by a person intending to do unsupervised research, or during the period of medical internship or residency. Scholars are not permitted to be employed on a full-time basis in the host country.

'Study or training must be undertaken in a country or territory in which there are Rotary clubs, but not in the country of the sponsoring Rotary club. An applicant must be a citizen of a country in which there is a Rotary club.

'Applicants are strongly encouraged to study in a country where they have not previously lived, thereby broadening international experience. If assignment to a country of previous residence is requested, the applicant must supply an explanation why such an assignment better fulfils the foundation's objective of improved international understanding than one to a country in which the applicant has not lived or studied. Although applicants are asked to list their school preferences, the trustees of the Rotary Foundation reserve the right to make assignment to any suitable study institution in order to ensure the widest possible geographical distribution of scholarships.

'A Rotary Foundation scholarship does not include personal living expenses. Scholars must apply sufficient personal funds for all expenses not covered by the award.

'Spouses and children may accompany scholars (other than undergraduate scholars), but only at their own expense.'

Annual grant total: In 2004/05 the foundation had both an income and a total expenditure of around £2.2 million.

Applications: Applications can only be made through a rotary club in the district where the applicant lives, studies or works. All selection of candidates is done at the level of one of the 29 rotary districts in Great Britain and Ireland. Where possible, applicants are recommended to apply in the district where they have lived for a substantial time and of which they could present themselves as a potentially convincing representative and ambassador. Candidates going forward from their place of study are likely to have a substantially harder task in convincing the local district of their value in this respect. If potential applicants are unaware of how to contact a local rotary club, they should write to the correspondent.

Correspondent: R Freeman, The Secretary, Rotary International in Great Britain & Ireland, PO Box 2747, Alcester, Warwickshire B49 5BR (01789 765411; Fax: 01789 756570; e-mail: secretary@ribi. org; website: www.rotary.org)

The Tropical Agricultural Association Award Fund

Eligibility: UK graduates, people with a diploma or senior students up to the age of 30 wishing to spend at least six months working on a rural development project in a developing country. Usually grant recipients have had a training in agriculture, forestry, agroforestry, environmental science or geography.

Types of grants: Grants of up to a maximum of £2,000 to help with airfares or living costs arising from their proposed projects (paid or unpaid).

Annual grant total: In 2004/05 the association had an income of about £43,000 and a total expenditure of £36,200. Grants totalled about £35,000.

Applications: Application forms are available from the association's website. Applications are considered every two months.

Correspondent: The Secretary, 144 Mostyn Road, London, SW19 3LR (020 8543 7563; Fax: 020 8543 7563; e-mail: general_secretary@taa.org.uk; website: www.taa.org.uk)

The WR Foundation

Eligibility: Undergraduates and people undertaking educational trips overseas.

Types of grants: One-off grants averaging £1,000 each.

Annual grant total: In 2004/05 the foundation had an income of about £16,000 and a total expenditure of £20,000. Grants totalled about £10,000.

Applications: In writing to the correspondent.

Correspondent: J Malthouse, Trustee, Malthouse & Co, America House, Rumford Court, Rumford Place, Liverpool L3 9DD (0151 284 2000)

Other information: The trust makes grants to organisations and individuals.

Work/study overseas – Antarctic

The Trans-Antarctic Association

Eligibility: Citizens of the UK, Australia, South Africa and New Zealand.

Types of grants: Cash grants of up to £1,500 may be made to people seeking to further knowledge or exploration of the Antarctic.

Exclusions: No grants for Arctic work or for people who are not nationals of the countries named above.

Annual grant total: In 2005 the association had an income of about £11,000 and a total expenditure of £7,300. Grants totalled about £6,000.

Applications: Applications should be made by 31 January each year on a form available from the correspondent.

Correspondent: Dr Mike Curtis, C/O Verity Barnes, St Johns Innovation Centre, Cowley Road, Cambridge, BB4 0WS (01223 422 144; Fax: 01223 422 146; e-mail: kelly.verity@veritybarnes.co.uk; website: www.transantarctic.org.uk)

Work/study overseas – Europe

The Peter Kirk Memorial Fund

Eligibility: Citizens of any European country aged between 18 and 26 years.

Types of grants: One-off grants of between £750 and £1,500 to help young people increase their understanding of Europe by undertaking a project on any aspect of modern European life. This must involve active research in at least one other European country for two to three months.

Annual grant total: In 2004/05 the fund had an income of £21,000 and a total expenditure of £16,000, that was distributed in scholarships.

Applications: On a form available from the correspondent, by e-mail or on receipt of an sae. Appliaction forms can also be downloaded from the website. Projects must be submitted by 16 Feb, with selection/interviews normally being completed by the end of April. Interviews take place in London at the applicant's expense. The fund would prefer

applications to be submitted by e-mail if possible.

Correspondent: Mrs Angela Pearson, Secretary, 17 St Paul's Rise, Addingham, Ilkley LS29 0QD (01943 839210; Fax: 01943 839210; e-mail: mail@kirkfund. org.uk; website: www.kirkfund.org.uk)

SOCRATES-ERASMUS: Mobility Grants to Students

Eligibility: Students who are members of an EU, EEA or associated nation (see list below), or possess a valid UK residence permit, and are registered at a UK institution of higher education and have completed their first year of study and have not received a previous Erasmus grant. Applications are encouraged from students who have disabilities or special needs.

Types of grants: Grants are available for students wishing to spend 3 to 12 months studying at an institution in another participating country to contribute towards the extra costs arising from studying abroad. No tuition fees are paid to the host institution. Additionally, for students who study in a partner institution for a whole academic year, home tuition fees may be waived.

Students gain academic recognition from their home university of the work they do overseas and remain entitled to any loans or grants they would have received from the national authorities for study at their home university.

Individual grant totals depend on the length of exchange and the country concerned. The maximum each individual can receive is €500 per month.

Annual grant total: Educational grants to individuals totalled £7,000.

Applications: Students should enquire about the Socrates-Erasmus programme at their home university department, International/European office, or the UK Socrates-Erasmus Council.

Correspondent: Information Officer, UK Socrates-Erasmus Council, Rothford, Giles Lane, Canterbury, Kent CT2 7LR (01227 762712; Fax: 01227 762711; e-mail: info@erasmus.ac.uk; website: www. erasmus.ac.uk)

Other information: Students registered at institutions in other participating countries who wish to spend a Socrates-Erasmus study period at a UK institution should approach the National Agency in the country of their home institution. Socrates-Erasmus grants are provided by the European Community as part of their education policy.

Countries eligible for the scheme are Austria, Belgium, Bulgaria, Cyprus, Czech Republic, Denmark, Estonia, Finland, France, Germany, Greece, Hungary, Iceland, Ireland, Italy, Latvia, Liechtenstein, Lithuania, Luxembourg, Malta, Netherlands, Norway, Poland,

Portugal, Romania, Slovenia, Slovakia, Spain, Sweden, Turkey and the UK.

W W Spooner Charitable Trust

Eligibility: Young people who are taking part in voluntary overseas projects and expeditions, with a preference for those living in Yorkshire – especially West Yorkshire.

Types of grants: One-off and recurrent grants towards voluntary work overseas.

Annual grant total: In 2005 the 'Wordsworth charitiable trust projects' totalled £7,800. In the same year 'Hardcore grants and donations' totalled £49,000 and 'single appeals' totalled £15,500. Total expenditure was £73,000.

Applications: In writing to the correspondent by the end of March, July or October.

Correspondent: M H Broughton, Co Addleshaw Goddard, Sovereign House, Sovereign Street, Leeds LS1 1HQ (0131 209 2000)

The Trades Union Congress Educational Trust

Eligibility: Members of TUC affiliated trade unions who are attending a course and are not in receipt of other grants.

Types of grants: The European study bursary offers two bursaries of £800 each to allow members to visit an EU country to study an aspect of trade unionism, industrial relations, training or employment or to write a report for for the TUC educational service.

Annual grant total: In 2004, the trust had a total income of about £80,000 and a total expenditure of £170,000. No information concerning grants was available.

Applications: Applications should be made through the participating colleges. The closing date for applications is 1 September.

Correspondent: Miss L Reece, Congress House, 23-28 Great Russell Street, London WC1B 3LQ (020 7467 1344; Fax: 020 7467 1353; e-mail: jscott@tuc.org.uk)

Other information: This trust also gives one-year TUC Educational Awards in association with Mary MacArthur Educational Trust. For more information, see entry in the National section.

The trust spends approximately £800,000 annually on developing and providing courses for union representatives through colleges and the WEA.

Work/study overseas – New Zealand

The Link Foundation

Eligibility: People wishing to participate in a vocational exchange between the UK and New Zealand, through specific joint schemes such as Equine Fertility, Hospitality Awards and Social Sciences Awards. The schemes are advertised through the governing bodies and specialist press belonging to these areas.

Types of grants: Grants of between £200 and £10,000 towards educational and cultural exchange linked to a vocation, including for research.

Exclusions: Grants are not made to individuals seeking funds for one-off trips such as medical residencies or to applicants wishing to visit countries other than Britain or New Zealand. Grants are not usually made for study.

Annual grant total: In 2004/05, the foundation had an income of £73,000 and a total expenditure of around £93,000.

Applications: In writing to the correspondent or to the organisation with which the foundation is jointly offering the award. Applications can be submitted directly by the individual or through the school/college or educational welfare agency.

Correspondent: Francis King, Executive Officer, New Zealand Link Foundation, New Zealand House, Haymarket, London SW1Y 4TQ (020 7839 3423; e-mail: linkuknz@dircon.co.uk)

Work/study overseas – Scandinavia

CoScan Trust Fund

Eligibility: British people aged between 15 and 25 who are undertaking a project of an educational nature involving travel between the UK and Scandinavia and within Scandinavia. Only short visits will be considered.

Types of grants: One-off grants of between £75 and £150.

Annual grant total: In 2005 grants were made to 14 individuals totalling £1,400.

Applications: On a form available from the correspondent, accompanied by a personal letter. Applications are considered

once a year and should be submitted by 31 March for consideration in April/May.

Correspondent: Dr Brita Green, 103 Long Ridge Lane, Nether Poppleton, York YO26 6LW (01904 794438)

Work/study overseas – Sweden

Anglo-Swedish Literary Foundation

Eligibility: Individuals wishing to participate in study visits connected to research on Swedish literature. The foundation aims to encourage cultural exchange between Sweden and the British Isles by promoting and diffusing knowledge and the appreciation of Swedish art and literature in the UK.

Types of grants: Grants may be spent on study visits connected with research on Swedish literature. Grants may also be used for translations and publishing subsidies and so on.

Annual grant total: In 2004/05 the trust had assets of £133,000, an income of £8,900 and a total expenditure of £4,700. No educational grants were made during the year.

Applications: In writing, outlining your project or activity and stating required funding and any other sources of funding.

Correspondent: c/o Embassy of Sweden, 11 Montagu Place, London W1H 2AL (020 7917 6400)

NATIONAL CHARITIES CLASSIFIED BY OCCUPATION OF PARENT

Airline Pilots

The British Airline Pilots' Association Benevolent Fund (BALPA)

Eligibility: Dependants of retired or deceased commercial pilots and flight engineers, who are or have been members of BALPA.

Types of grants: Limited grants are made towards the cost of books, uniforms and associated educational expenses.

Exclusions: Grants are not given for school fees.

Annual grant total: In 2004/05 the trust had assets of £765,000 and an income of £27,000. Grants totalled £4,000. A further £8,900 was given in interest-free loans.

Applications: In writing to the correspondent requesting an application form. Applications are considered quarterly.

Correspondent: Gillian Pole, 81 New Road, Harlington, Hayes, Middlesex UB3 5BQ (020 8476 4000; Fax: 020 8476 4077)

The Guild of Air Pilots Benevolent Fund

Eligibility: Members of the guild and those who have been engaged professionally as air pilots or air navigators in commercial aviation, and their dependants.

Types of grants: Grants or loans can be given towards, for example, school fees. Grants range between £250 and £2,000. Loans above about £2,000 may need some security.

Exclusions: Training and higher education is not usually supported.

Annual grant total: In 2004/05 the trust had assets of £808,000 and an income of £28,000. Over £13,000 was distributed in 'regular' and 'occasional' grants to beneficiaries.

Applications: On a form available from the correspondent. Applications are considered in January, April, July and October. The fund has helpers and visitors who can help applicants fill in the form (details required include the individual's financial situation and proof of an aviation career). The trust attaches great importance to the comments and recommendations of helpers.

Correspondent: Peter Davis, Secretary, Cobham House, 9 Warwick Court, Gray's Inn, London WC1R 5DJ (020 7404 4032; Fax: 020 7404 4035; e-mail: gapan@gapan. org; website: www.gapan.org)

Other information: The fund works closely with the other aviation trusts for individuals (both military and civilian). If an applicant has approached another such trust, they should say so in their application to this fund.

Artists

The Artists' Orphan Fund

Eligibility: Children of a professional artist (for example, painter, sculptor, illustrator or designer) who has died. Applicants should be under 25 and in full-time education.

Types of grants: Recurrent grants according to need. Individuals can be supported throughout their education but they must reapply each year.

Annual grant total: In 2004/05 the fund had assets of £1.3 million, an income of £44,000 and a total expenditure of £67,000. It gave £54,000 in grants to 14 individuals.

Applications: In writing to the correspondent, including career details of qualifying parent and the present financial position of the family. Appropriate applicants will receive a form which they will need to complete, and are considered upon receipt.

Correspondent: Miss April Connett-Dance, Secretary, Burlington House, Piccadilly, London W1J 0BB (020 7734 1193; Fax: 020 7734 9966)

Equity Trust Fund

Eligibility: Professional performers (under Equity or ITC contracts) with a minimum of 10 years experience as an adult (work performed below the age of 16 is not counted).

Types of grants: Grants to enable people to pursue a new career. They can be used towards books, equipment, instruments, fees, living expenses or childcare.

Exclusions: No grants to amatuer performers, musicians or drama students.

Annual grant total: In 2004/05 it had assets of £8.1 million and an income of £335,000. Educational grants totalled £121,000, with a further £56,000 distributed in welfare grants.

Applications: On a form available from the correspondent. There are normally three meetings each year, with the first one taking place normally around about the middle of May.

Correspondent: Keith Carter, Secretary, 222 Africa House, 64 Kingsway, London WC2B 6BD (020 7404 6041; Fax: 020 7831 4953; e-mail: keith@ equitytrustfund.freeserve.co.uk)

Other information: Grants are also made to organisations.

Kraszna-Krausz Foundation

Eligibility: Writers, film-makers and researchers involved in the fields of photography or the moving image.

Types of grants: One-off grants in the range of £1,000 and £3,000 to encourage a higher standard of research, publishing and other projects. Grants are not made for courses but for living expenses and study or travel overseas for research purposes.

Annual grant total: In 2004/05 the trust had an income of £37,000 and a total expenditure of £36,000. Grants totalled £2,000.

Applications: Application forms are available from the correspondent. They are considered twice a year – applications for consideration in July should reach the foundation by 1 May and those for consideration in December by 1 October.

Correspondent: Andrea Livingstone, Administrator, 122 Fawnbrake Avenue, London SE24 0BZ (020 7738 6701; e-mail: awards@k-k.org.uk; website: www. k-k.org.uk)

The Geoffrey Parsons Memorial Trust

Eligibility: Concert pianists and people with the ability to become concert pianists, who have a particular interest in the accompaniment of song or in chamber music. There is a preference for people under 35.

Types of grants: One-off and recurrent grants, usually of sums up to £2,000, towards piano lessons with pre-eminent teachers and the purchase of music (i.e. sheet music and scores).

Annual grant total: In 2004/05 the trust had an income of £2,400. Grants were made to two individuals totalling £4,000.

Applications: Unsolicited applications will not be considered.

Correspondent: B P Griffin, 50 Broadway, Westminster, London SW1H 0BL (020 7227 7000; Fax: 020 7222 3480)

Peggy Ramsay Foundation

Eligibility: Writers for the stage who have been produced publicly, are 'of promise' and are in need of time to write which they cannot afford, or are in need of other assistance. Applicants must live in the British Isles (including Republic of Ireland and the Channel Islands).

Types of grants: One-off grants. Individual awards rarely exceed £5,000 for writing time or £1,000 for word processors.

Exclusions: No grants towards production costs or to writers who have not been produced. Drama students or other artists learning their trade are not supported, just experienced writers who could not otherwise follow their career. No grants are made for writing not intended for the theatre.

Annual grant total: In 2004 the trust had assets of £4.5 million and an income of £220,000. Grants to 56 individuals totalled £112,000.

Applications: Apply by writing a short letter to the correspondent, submitted with a CV directly by the individual. Scripts and publicity material must not be included. Applications, which are always acknowledged, are considered four or five times a year.

Correspondent: G Laurence Harbottle, Trustee, Hanover House, 14 Hanover Square, London W1S 1HP (020 7667 5000; Fax: 020 7667 5100; e-mail: laurence. harbottle@harbottle.com; website: www. peggyramsayfoundation.org)

Other information: Grants to organisations totalled £93,000.

TACT Education Fund

Eligibility: Dependants of members of the theatrical profession who are over the age of 18 and who wish to pursue higher education in the arts.

Types of grants: Grants of up to £1,200 to students in further and higher education, including mature students and postgraduates.

Exclusions: Grants are not available for drama school fees or study abroad.

Annual grant total: In 2005/06 grants to individuals totalled £19,000.

Applications: On a form available from the correspondent. Applications are to be submitted directly by the individual for consideration at any time, and should include details of the theatrical parent's cv.

Correspondent: Robert Ashby, Africa House, 64 Kingsway, London WC2B 6BD (020 7242 0111; Fax: 020 7242 0234; e-mail: robert@tactactors.org; website: www.tactactors.org)

Bankers

The Bankers Benevolent Fund

Eligibility: Children of bank employees who have died or are not able to work because of ill health.

Types of grants: Help towards the education and maintenance of children who are at school or are studying for a first degree or similar qualification. Most children helped are being educated within the state system, with help towards all normal schooling expenses including fares, lunches, sports equipment, school trips and extra-curricular activities together with regular clothing allowances and, to those on low incomes, additional maintenance allowances. Grants are given towards school fees only in certain limited circumstances. Help is also given to students in higher/further education to supplement loans. Grants are usually reviewed annually.

Exclusions: The fund does not provide assistance for debt repayment, business ventures, private medical treatment or situations where statutory or other sources of funding are available.

Annual grant total: In 2004/05 the trust had an income of £1.6 million. It made grants totalling £605,000 towards towards child-related causes, such as for clothing, maintenance, school fees and expenses and to students for studying. Grants to older people totalled £267,000.

Applications: Application forms are available from the fund; they can also be downloaded from its website. Once the form has been received it will be reviewed by staff. Additional contact may be required to obtain further information or clarification. The trustees meet quarterly to consider new cases.

Correspondent: Pinners Hall, 105–108 Old Broad Street, London EC2N 1EX

The Alfred Foster Settlement

Eligibility: Employees and former employees of banks and their dependants who are in need. Applicants must be students aged under 28 years.

Types of grants: One-off grants, for example, to help with university fees, books, travel costs and living expenses while in further education.

Annual grant total: In 2004/05 the trust had an income of £25,000 and a total expenditure of £16,000. Grants totalled about £15,000.

Applications: In writing to the correspondent. Applications can be submitted directly by the individual or through the school/college or educational welfare agency.

Correspondent: Russell Jones, Barclays Bank Trust Co Ltd, Executorship & Trustee Service, Osborne Court, Gadbrook Park, Rudheath, Northwich CW9 7UE

Barristers

The Barristers' Benevolent Association

Eligibility: The dependants of past or present practising members of the Bar in England and Wales, who are in need.

Types of grants: Educational grants for dependants are only given in the most exceptional circumstances, for example where the death or disability of a barrister leaves his or her children stranded in mid-education. Grants or loans are given to schoolchildren towards fees, books, educational outings, maintenance or school uniforms or clothing; students in further/higher education for help with books, fees and living expenses; mature students for books, travel, fees or childcare; and people starting work for books, equipment, clothing and travel.

Annual grant total: In 2004 the trust had assets of £7.1 million, an income of £702,000 and its total expenditure was £481.000. A total of £278,000 was given in welfare and educational grants.

Applications: In writing to the correspondent. Applications are considered throughout the year and should include the name and address of the chambers where they last practised as a barrister.

Correspondent: Janet South, Director, 14 Gray's Inn Square, London WC1R 5JP (020 7242 4764; e-mail: enquiries@the-baa. com; website: www.the-bba.com)

Book retail

The Book Trade Benevolent Society

Eligibility: People in need who have worked in the book trade in the UK for at least one year (normally publishing/distribution/book-selling), and their dependants.

Types of grants: One-off and recurrent grants of up to £1,500 are given to help retrain people from the book trade who have been made redundant. These grants are given to mature students where a welfare need is evident. The society is a relief-in-need charity, with retraining of such people as part of their work. Therefore, general educational grants are not made.

Annual grant total: In 2005 the society has assets of £2.1 million and an income of £406,000. From a total expenditure of £377,000, grants to nearly 100 individuals totalled £100,000.

Applications: On a form available from the correspondent. Applications can be submitted by the individual or through a recognised referral agency (social worker, Citizens Advice, doctor and so on) and are considered quarterly.

Correspondent: David Hicks, Chief Executive, The Foyle Centre, The Retreat, Abbots Road, Kings Langley, Hertfordshire WD4 8LT (01923 263128; Fax: 01923 270732; e-mail: btbs@booktradecharity.demon.co.uk; website: www.booktradecharity.demon.co.uk)

Building trade

Norton Folgate Trust

Eligibility: People who engaged in or studying the craft of carpentry or any branch of the building industry.

Types of grants: Grants, to a usual maximum of about £100, (a) for school pupils to help with the cost of books, equipment, clothing or travel and (b) to help with school, college or university fees or to supplement existing grants.

Annual grant total: In 2004/05 the trust had assets of £3.5 million, an income of £164,000 and a total expenditure of £100,000. Educational grants were made to eight individuals totalling £16,000.

Applications: On a form available from the correspondent.

Correspondent: The Clerk, Carpenter's Company, Carpenter's Hall, 1

Throgmorton Avenue, London EC2N 2JJ (020 7588 7001)

Other information: Grants are also made to organisations and individuals for welfare purposes.

Civic & public services

The Water Conservation Trust

Eligibility: People who are working or intending to work in the water and environment industry.

Types of grants: One-off grants for approved projects and courses of study.

Exclusions: Unsolicited applications are not accepted.

Annual grant total: In 2004/05, the trust had an income of £23,000 and a total expenditure of £7,000. Grants totalled about £5,000.

Applications: When funds are available the trustees invite applications for scholarships through the water and environmental press.

Correspondent: The Secretary, Watermans Hall, 16 St Mary at Hill, London, EC3R 8EF (0208 421 0305; Fax: 0208 421 0305; e-mail: waterclo@aol.com)

Other information: Grants are also made towards research and to organisations.

Coalminers

The Miners' Welfare National Educational Fund

Eligibility: People who are at least 17 years old and (i) employed in the coalmining industry of Great Britain (including any activity conducted by British Coal) or who have ceased to be so employed by reason of age or disability or who, having ceased to be so employed for any other reason, have not subsequently changed their occupation; or (ii) the dependant sons and daughters (and other dependants) of those described above.

Types of grants: Grants of not more than £500 a year to help with the costs of taking educational courses at degree or equivalent level. For applicants in category (i) above, all full-time courses and Open University courses are eligible. Otherwise the course must be one for which local education authority grants are mandatory. Grants are only considered for those taking postgraduate courses directly after and related to a first degree where it is essential for entry into a profession.

Annual grant total: In 2004/05, the trust had net assets of £1.1 million, and it had an income of £47,000 and a total expenditure of £79,000. The fund gave grants to individuals in two categories totalling £427,300; 'A' candidates received £1,000, with the remainder going to 'B' candidates.

Applications: Application forms are available from the correspondent to be submitted by the individual's school/college for considered at any time from August through to March. Confirmation of A-level results and confirmation of award of student support must be included.

Correspondent: V O S Jones, Secretary, The Old Rectory, Rectory Drive, Whiston, Rotherham, South Yorkshire S60 4JG (01709 728115; e-mail: mwnef@ciswo.org.uk)

Other information: Grants awarded are not recurrent. Applicants must reapply in each academic year of an eligible course.

Commerce

The George Drexler Foundation

Eligibility: People who have a direct link with commerce, i.e. who have owned and run their own commercial business. Applicants whose parents or grandparents have this link can also be supported. This does not include professional people such as doctors, lawyers, dentists, architects or accountants. No exceptions can be made. Preference is given to schoolchildren with serious family difficulties so that the child has to be educated away from home, and to people with special educational needs.

Types of grants: One-off and recurrent grants of £500 to £6,000. Schoolchildren, further and higher education students, including mature students, and postgraduates can receive support for books, fees and study or travel abroad. Grants can also be made to; schoolchildren for uniforms or other school clothing and educational outings in the UK; further and higher education students for maintenance/living expenses and equipment/instruments; and mature students and postgraduates for maintenance/living expenses.

Annual grant total: In 2004/05 the trust had an income of £226,000 and an expenditure of £187,000. Educational grants totalled £93,000 and welfare grants totalled £66,000.

Applications: On a form available from the correspondent, submitted directly by the individual, enclosing an sae. Applications should be submitted in May for consideration in June/July.

Correspondent: The Trustee, 35–43 Lincolns Inn Fields, London, WC2A 3PE

The Ruby & Will George Trust

Eligibility: The dependants of people in need who have been or who are employed in commerce. Preference is given to people who live in the north of England.

Types of grants: One-off and recurrent grants of up to £5,000 towards maintenance and fees.

Exclusions: Expeditions, study visits and student exchanges are not funded.

Annual grant total: In 2004/05 the trust had assets of £2.9 million and an income of £83,000. Grants to 105 individuals totalled £156,000, given for welfare and educational purposes.

Applications: In writing to the correspondent in the first instance, requesting an application form. Applications are considered at quarterly intervals in February, May, August and November. Applications should be submitted three weeks prior to the beginning of these months.

Correspondent: David John Simpson, Administrator, 18 Ghyll Edge, Lancaster Park, Morpeth, Northumberland NE61 3QZ (01670 516657)

Farming

The Dairy Crest and NFU Fund

Eligibility: Children of farmers, ex-farmers, smallholders and ex-smallholders, 16 years old or over, living in Cornwall, Devon, Dorset and Somerset. The applicant must be studying a dairy-related topic in further education, which will contribute to the future industry.

Types of grants: This fund aims to promote and encourage 'practical and scientific education in dairying and dairy farming'. Grants usually range from £200 up to £2,000 a year and can be for books, fees, equipment and maintenance/living expenses.

Annual grant total: In 2002/03 the trust had an income of £34,000. Educational grants to individuals totalled £23,000.

Applications: On a form available from the correspondent; two references will be required. Applications should be submitted by the individual by August each year; for consideration in September.

Correspondent: Mrs C Booth, Higher Moorlake Cottage, Crediton, Devon, EX17 5EL

Fire service

The Fire Services National Benevolent Fund

Eligibility: Orphans who have lost a parent who was a member, or in certain circumstances was a retired member, of the Fire Service, or widows/widowers whose spouse was a member, or in certain circumstances was a retired member, of the Fire Service.

Types of grants: Grants of £550 to £850 to help with items such as books for students in higher or further education. Grants may be paid directly to the student, but do take into account parental/guardian's financial status.

Exclusions: Grants are not made to clear debts.

Annual grant total: Grants to individuals for educational purposes total around £80,000 a year.

Applications: In writing to the benevolent fund officer at the local county fire brigade headquarters, or to the address below. Applicants should contact the fund before they apply.

Correspondent: Grants and Services, Marine Court, Fitzalan Road, Littlehampton, West Sussex BN17 5NF (01903 736062; Fax: 01903 731095; e-mail: administration@fsnbf.org.uk; website: www.fsnbf.org.uk)

Other information: This fund was founded in 1943 to help all types of fire-fighters and their widows or widowers and young dependants. It also provides short-term convalescence, rehabilitation, therapy and sheltered housing, but does not have residential or nursing homes.

Institution of Fire Engineers

Eligibility: People living and working within the UK who are studying fire-fighting, fire engineering, fire protection or fire research.

Types of grants: One-off grants according to need.

Annual grant total: The income for the trust is donated by another charity, and varies greatly. In 2004 grants were made totalling around £40,000.

Applications: In writing to the correspondent. Applications are considered four times a year.

Correspondent: Professional Development Officer, London Road, Moreton-in-Marsh, Gloucestershire GL56 0RH

Furnishing trade

Furnishing Trades Benevolent Association

Eligibility: People whose parents are or were employed in any capacity in the furnishing and allied trades (including carpets and floorcovering) for at least two years.

Types of grants: One-off grants in the range of £200 and £500 are given to schoolchildren for uniforms, books, instruments/equipment and maintenance/living expenses, and to college students for these later two categories. Preference is given to children with special needs.

Annual grant total: In 2004 no educational grants were made, however a total of £150,000 was distributed in 380 welfare grants.

Applications: On a form available from the benefits coordinator at the address above. Applications should be submitted through a third party such as a social worker or teacher, or through an organisation such as Citizens Advice or a school. Applications are considered in March, May, August and November. However, emergency applications can be dealt with quickly, if necessary.

Correspondent: Jonathan Seddon-Brown, Chief Executive, Furniture Maker' Hall, 4th Floor, 12 Austin Friars, London, EC2N 2HE (020 7256 5954; Fax: 020 7256 6035; e-mail: welfare@ftba.co.uk; website: www.ftba.co.uk)

Other information: The trust states that grants are mainly for the relief of need; education grants are of secondary importance.

Furniture trade

The Worshipful Company of Furniture Makers Company

Eligibility: Young people working or studying to work in the furniture industry.

Types of grants: There are awards for each branch of the industry, for example, design, manufacturing and retail. Students intending to enter the industry are eligible and there are awards for postgraduate studies. Grants can be made towards fees, study/travel abroad, equipment and instruments and range between £500 and £1,000 each. It also gives awards for excellence.

Exclusions: No grants are given for childcare.

Annual grant total: In 2005/06 the trust had assets of £1 million and an income of

£94,000. No grants were made to individuals during the year.

Applications: On a form available from the correspondent to be submitted directly by an individual or a parent/guardian. Applications are considered throughout the year.

Correspondent: The Clerk, Furniture Maker' Hall, 12 Austin Friars, London, EC2N 2HE (020 7256 5558; Fax: 020 7256 5155; e-mail: clerk@ furnituremkrs.co.uk; website: www. furnituremakers.co.uk)

Other information: Grants are also made for group college projects.

Gardeners

Royal Gardeners' Orphan Fund

Eligibility: Children in need, particularly orphans, whose parents are or have been employed full-time in horticulture. The associated Constance Spry Fund can assist such children who go on to full-time further/higher education. Applicants should be under 25. Assistance is also given to children of horticulturalists who are mentally or physically disabled.

Types of grants: Quarterly allowances to orphans still in full-time education. Grants can be given towards school uniforms, books, educational outings, maintenance fees, school fees and study and travel overseas. Each case is assessed individually by the executive committee.

Annual grant total: In 2004 the trust had assets of £725,000 and an income of £100,000. Grants to individuals for educational and welfare needs totalled £96,000.

Applications: Ideally, applicants should obtain an application form to be submitted at least two weeks before one of the committee meetings, which take place in March, September and November each year. Applications can be submitted directly by the individual or through the individual's school/college or educational welfare agency, with details of parents' and/or applicant's income and expenditure.

Correspondent: Mrs Kate Wallis, Secretary, 10 Deards Wood, Knebworth, Hertfordshire, SG3 6PG (01438 813939; Fax: 01438 813939; e-mail: rgof@ btopenworld.com)

The Constance Spry Fund

Eligibility: See the entry for the Royal Gardeners' Orphan Fund above.

Horse-racing and breeding

National Trainers Federation Charitable Trust

Eligibility: People in need who work or have worked in the thoroughbred horse-racing and breeding industry, and their dependants.

Types of grants: Mainly ongoing grants towards course fees for retraining.

Annual grant total: In 2004/05 the trust had assets of £431,000, an income of £10,000 and a total expenditure of £5,500. Grants were made to two individuals totalling £2,800.

Applications: In writing to the correspondent, with details of the course you wish to pursue, proof you have approached your local authority for a grant and been unsuccessful, and two referees who are authorities connected with the industry.

Correspondent: The Trustees, 20b Park Lane, Newmarket, Suffolk CB8 8QD (01638 560763; Fax: 01638 565240; e-mail: info@racingwelfare.co.uk; website: www.racingwelfare.co.uk)

Insurance

The Insurance Charities – The Orphans' Fund

Eligibility: University students whose parents have been in the insurance industry for at least five years.

Types of grants: Help may be given to first degree students towards day-to-day expenses.

Annual grant total: In 2004/05 the trust had assets of £22 million, an income of £1.2 million and a total expenditure of £953,000. Grants to individuals totalled £629,000.

Applications: An initial form can be completed online, or can be downloaded from the trust's website.

Correspondent: Mrs A J Thornicroft, 20 Aldermanbury, London EC2V 7HY (020 7606 3763; Fax: 020 7600 1170; e-mail: info@theinsurancecharities.org.uk; website: www.theinsurancecharities.org. uk)

Meat Trade

The Worshipful Company of Butchers' Educational Charity

Eligibility: People involved in the meat trade who are studying courses related to the trade.

Types of grants: One-off grants towards further and higher education fees.

Annual grant total: In 2004/05 the trust had assets of £246,000, an income of £10,400 and a total expenditure of £9,700. Grants to individuals totalled £550. Grants to organisations totalled £8,000.

Applications: In writing to the correspondent. Applications should be submitted directly by the individual for consideration monthly.

Correspondent: The Clerk, Butchers' Hall, 87 Bartholomew Close, London EC1A 7EB (020 7600 4106; Fax: 020 7606 4108; e-mail: clerk@butchershall.com; website: www.butchershall.com)

Media

The Chartered Institute of Journalists Orphan Fund

Eligibility: Orphaned children of institute members who are in need, aged between 5 and 22 and in full-time education.

Types of grants: Grants are given for schoolchildren towards the cost of school clothing, books, educational outings and school fees. Grants are also given to students in further or higher education towards the cost of books, help with fees/ living expenses and study or travel abroad. Grants are also given for birthdays, Christmas and summer holidays.

Annual grant total: In 2004 grants to individuals totalled £32,000.

Applications: Applications should be submitted by the child's surviving parent or other third party. Applications are considered quarterly.

Correspondent: Norman Barlett, The Honorary Treasurer, 2 Dock Offices, Surrey Quays Road, London SE16 2XU (020 7252 1187; e-mail: memberservices@ cioj.co.uk; website: www.cioj.co.uk)

Other information: This fund also gives grants for relief-in-need purposes.

The Journalists' Charity

Eligibility: The dependants of journalists in need.

Types of grants: This fund mainly supports welfare, not educational causes, although there is often some crossover.

Exclusions: Vocational support will only be made if the parent of the child is/was a journalist and there is evidence of need.

Annual grant total: In 2004 the fund had assets of £13 million and an income of £1.1 million. Total expenditure was £1.6 million, with £227,000 being given in welfare grants to individuals. No grants were made for educational purposes.

Applications: On a form available from the correspondent, to be submitted directly by the individual or a family member. Applications should include details of the career in journalism and are considered monthly.

Correspondent: David Ilott, Director, Dickens House, 35 Wathen Road, Dorking, Surrey RH4 1JY (01306 887511; Fax: 01306 888212)

Other information: The fund also runs residential homes in Dorking.

Medicine

The Chartered Society of Physiotherapy Members' Benevolent Fund

Eligibility: Members and past members of the society, including full and assistant members and students.

Types of grants: Grants towards retraining costs.

Exclusions: No grants towards payment of debts or when statutory help is available.

Annual grant total: In 2004 grants totalled £60,000.

Applications: On a form available from the correspondent. Applications should be submitted directly by the individual or by a third party such as a carer or partner. Applications are considered in January, April, July and October.

Correspondent: Christine Cox, 14 Bedford Row, London WC1R 4ED (020 7306 6642; Fax: 020 7306 6643; e-mail: coxc@csp.org. uk; website: www.csp.org.uk)

The Dain Fund

Eligibility: Children of doctors or deceased doctors (not nurses or physiotherapists and so on) who are at a critical stage of their education and are in need.

Types of grants: One-off and recurrent grants to: (i) children who are in private education already and approaching public examinations; (ii) children in state schools towards the cost of uniform, field trips and such like; (iii) students, though rarely, to supplement local education authority grants. If students have been supported by the fund throughout their degree course, they may receive an interest-free loan for the final year instead of a grant.

Normally support will be given to only one child in a family.

Annual grant total: In 2005 the fund had assets of £1.2 million, an income of £62,000 and a total expenditure of £59,000. Grants were made totalling £33,000.

Applications: On a form available from the correspondent, to be submitted directly by the individual or a parent/guardian or through a social worker, Citizens Advice or other welfare agency

Correspondent: Mrs Linda Dluska-Miziura, BMA Charities, BMA House, Tavistock Square, London WC1H 9JP (020 7383 6142; Fax: 020 7554 6334; e-mail: info.bmacharities@bma.org.uk; website: www.bma.org.uk)

Other information: This fund is designed to help families in an emergency and is not a scholarship trust.

The Hume Kendall Educational Trust

Eligibility: The sons or daughters (natural or adopted) of any doctor or dentist, whose fathers are deceased or permanently incapacitated, where there is great hardship through family tragedy.

Types of grants: Contributions towards the cost of the education of beneficiaries up to and including first degree level.

Annual grant total: In 2004/05, the trust had an income of £4,000 and a total expenditure of £1,000. Grants totalled about £700.

Applications: In writing to the correspondent. Applications can be made at any time.

Correspondent: H M Green, Hon. Secretary, c/o Finance Department, King's College London, Room G37, James Clerk Maxwell Building, 57 Waterloo Road, London SE1 8WA

The Nightingale Fund

Eligibility: Nurses and hospital attendants seeking further training.

Types of grants: One-off and recurrent grants in the range of £300 to £3,000.

Annual grant total: In 2004/05 the fund had assets of £484,000, an income of £23,000 and made 17 grants totalling £27,000.

Applications: On a form available form the Honorary Secretary to be submitted directly by the individual in January, May or September. Two references are required.

Correspondent: Mrs J Chambers, Honorary Secretary, 55 Recreation Road, Shortlands, Bromley, Kent, BR2 0DY

The Royal Medical Benevolent Fund

Eligibility: Registered medical practitioners, their wives, husbands, widows, widowers and dependant children

who are in need and are resident in Great Britain. The registered medical practitioner's name must appear in a General Medical Council (GMC) register. Preference is given to schoolchildren with serious family difficulties resulting in them being educated away from home and children with special educational needs.

There is also a medical student bursary scheme which helps medical students in their second or third year of study.

Types of grants: Schoolchildren may receive help towards school uniform and clothing, books and travel to school. People starting work can be awarded grants for books, equipment/instruments and clothing. In exceptional cases, the fund may assist with fees and expenses.

Bursaries of £2,000 each are awarded for three academic terms. Beneficiaries are expected to attend an initial induction event, an end-of-year review, promote the fund to other medical students and undertake research into medical student debt.

Exclusions: Children of working parents cannot be considered for help, nor can children who are not (or whose parents are not) already beneficiaries of the fund. No assistance is given with any of the following: second degree/postgraduate courses; fees/living expenses; travel abroad; and PLAB (Professional & Linguistic Assessment Board) and associated fees/ living expenses for doctors not on the GMC register.

Annual grant total: In 2005, the fund had net assets of £951,000. Grants were made to individuals totalling £571,000; total expenditure was £1,322,000.

Applications: For general educational grants: On a form available from the correspondent, which can be submitted either directly by the individual or through a medical colleague or other medical and general charities. Applications are considered almost every month. Two references are taken up (at least one of which should be from a medical practitioner). All applicants are visited before a report is submitted to the case committee. Income/capital and expenditure are fully investigated, with similar rules applying as for those receiving Income Support.

For bursaries: on a form available from the correspondent, to be returned by early February each year. Applicants are interviewed before a bursary is awarded (reasonable travel expenses paid).

Correspondent: The Senior Case Manager, 24 King's Road, Wimbledon, London SW19 8QN (020 8540 9194; Fax: 020 8542 0494; e-mail: seniorcaseworker@rmbf.org; website: www.rmbf.org)

Other information: Voluntary visitors liaise between beneficiaries and the office.

The Royal Medical Foundation

Eligibility: Dependants, aged up to 18, of medical practitioners who are in need.

Types of grants: Grants of between £500 and £15,000 are given to schoolchildren and college students towards fees. Preference is given to pupils with family difficulties so that they have to be educated away from home, pupils with special educational needs and medical students.

Annual grant total: In 2004/05 the foundation had assets of £4.3 million and an income of £310,000. Educational grants to 40 individuals totalled £185,000 and 19 welfare grants totalled £37,000.

Applications: On a form available from the correspondent, for consideration throughout the year. Applications can be submitted either by the individual or a family member, through a third party such as a social worker or teacher, or through an organisation such as Citizens Advice or a school. The trust advises applicants to be honest about their needs. All applicants are means tested.

Correspondent: John Higgs and Nickie Colville, College Road, Epsom, Surrey KT17 4JQ (01372 821010; Fax: 01372 821013; e-mail: caseworker@ royalmedicalfoundation.org; website: www.royalmedicalfoundation.org)

The Society of Apothecaries' General Charity

Eligibility: Members or potential members of the medical and pharmaceutical professions who are in the penultimate or final year of their studies and are in need.

Types of grants: Grants of between £500 and £1,000 are given to medical students in need. Only very limited funds are available for small-scale help.

Exclusions: Grants are not considered for electives or those taking a second degree.

Annual grant total: In 2005 the society had net assets of £1 million. It had an income of around £95,000, and a total expemditure of £39,000. Grants were made to 27 individuals totalling £27,000.

Applications: In writing to the correspondent via the dean of the school. Supporting evidence of need is required from the college being attended. Applications should be submitted by 30 June and are considered in July for the following academic year.

Correspondent: R J Stringer, The Clerk, Apothecaries' Hall, Black Friars Lane, London EC4V 6EJ (020 7236 1189; Fax: 020 7329 3177; e-mail: clerk@ apothecaries.org; website: www. apothecaries.org)

Metal trades

The Institution of Materials, Minerals & Mining

Eligibility: Members of the institution and former members and their dependants.

Types of grants: One-off and recurrent grants and one-off grants in kind towards educational needs. Grants are made to schoolchildren for fees and to college students for fees, books and equipment/ instruments.

Annual grant total: In 2005 the charity had assets of £1.6 million, an income of £65,000 and a total expenditure of £70,000. There were 46 welfare grants made totalling £52,000, with £3,200 distributed in four educational grants.

Applications: On a form available from the correspondent for consideration at any time.

Correspondent: David Oxley, c/o The Institution of Materials, Minerals & Mining, 1 Carlton House Terrace, London, SW1Y 5DB (website: www.iom3.org)

Mining

Mining Institute of Scotland Trust

Eligibility: Members or former members of the Mining Institute of Scotland who are taking a university course with a mining element in it. The trust has a preference for supporting people from Fife in the first instance, and, secondly, those who are of Scottish origin, although other people can be considered. Applicants who are not already members of the institute will be invited to join. Members of the Mining Institute of Scotland, and their dependants, can also receive 'hardship grants'.

Types of grants: Educational grants are one-off or recurrent, normally of £1,500 a year. A recent grant was made, for example, towards an engineering course that had a mining element to it. Grants can be for the student's general upkeep, or for course fees, and so on.

Hardship grants are one-off or recurrent of up to £1,000 a year. A recent grant was made, for example, to the son of a member for travel to university.

Annual grant total: The trust has about £25,000 available to give in grants each year for both education and hardship.

Applications: In writing to the correspondent in the first instance, to request an application form.

Correspondent: 2 Ashfield Gardens, Kelty, Fife KY4 0JY

Other information: Schools are also supported.

The Warwickshire Miners' Welfare Fund

Eligibility: Mineworkers and former mineworkers who have worked within the coal industry in Warwickshire and their dependants.

Types of grants: One-off grants from £50 to £300 towards convalescent holidays, hospital visits to spouse (or applicant), electrical appliances such as cookers and vacuum cleaners, carpets, beds and other furniture, wheelchairs, inhalers, electric hoists and so on, and medical reports for industrial diseases.

Exclusions: No death grants or grants to people who have received redundancy pay in the last 10 years. Grants will not be given for any purpose for which the DWP will pay.

Annual grant total: In 2004 the trust had an income of £23,000 and a total expenditure of £17,000.

Applications: In writing to the correspondent. Applications can be submitted directly by the individual or through a social worker, Citizens Advice or other welfare agency or other third party. Applications should include weekly income and medical proof from doctor (if applicable). They are considered at any time.

Correspondent: The Secretary, CISWO, 142 Queens Road, Stoke-on-Trent ST4 7LH (01782 744996)

Police

The Gurney Fund for Police Orphans

Eligibility: Children under 18 of deceased or incapacitated police officers from 22 subscribing forces in southern and south midland areas of England and South and Mid-Wales, excluding the Metropolitan and City of London Police Forces.

Types of grants: Grants are available for students up to 18 years old; applications from older students will be considered in certain circumstances at the discretion of the trustees. Grants can be for books, uniforms, equipment, educational travel, school trips, music lessons, sport and other extra-curricular activities. No grants for school fees, but consideration may be given to children with special needs. Grants can be both one-off cash grants for amounts of up to £1,800 each, or recurrent, ranging from between £10 and £60 per week.

Exclusions: No grants for school fees or skiing holidays.

Annual grant total: In 2004/05 the fund had assets of £5.2 million, an income of £533,000 and a total expenditure of

£402,000. There were 21 donations made for educational purposes totalling £31,000.

Applications: Applications can be made at any time and are considered in February, May, August and November. They must include a copy of the child's birth certificate and successful applicants will be asked to complete an income and expenditure form and provide receipts when assistance with specific expenditure is requested. A force welfare officer or local representative then assesses the application for a later decision by the trustees.

Correspondent: Miss C McNicol, The Director, 9 Bath Road, Worthing, West Sussex, BN11 3NU (01903 237256)

The National Police Fund

Eligibility: Children of serving, retired or deceased members of police forces in England, Wales and Scotland who are aged over 18 years.

Types of grants: One-off and recurrent grants for general assistance to students in further or higher education, up to a maximum of £800. Grants are sometimes, though rarely, given to mature students and younger children.

Annual grant total: In 2004/05, the trust had net assets of £2.3 million. It had an income of around £270,000 and a total expenditure £91,000. Grants were given to individuals totalling £63,800.

Applications: Application forms can be obtained from the welfare officer of the police force where the officer is serving or has served. Applications must be returned by the individual in November for consideration in December. A reference from the student's college or university must be included.

Correspondent: Mrs Hannah Muella, National Police Fund, 3 Mount Mews, High Street, Hampton TW12 2SH (020 8941 7661; Fax: 020 8979 4323; e-mail: office@nationalpolicefund.org.uk; website: www.nationalpolicefund.org.uk/)

Police Dependants' Trust

Eligibility: (i) Dependants of current police officers or former police officers who died from injuries received in the execution of duty.

(ii) Police officers or former police officers incapacitated as a result of injury received in the execution of duty, and/or their dependants.

Types of grants: Grants are available for retraining and to the children of police officers who are at college or university. This is a relief-in-need charity, so most of the grants are given for welfare rather than educational purposes.

Annual grant total: In 2004/05 the trust had assets of £25 million and an income of £1.6 million. Grants mainly for welfare purposes totalled £1.8 million.

Applications: On a form available from the chief executive, to be submitted through one of the force's welfare officers. Applications are generally considered every two months although urgent decisions can be made between meetings.

Correspondent: David French, Chief Executive, 3 Mount Mews, High Street, Hampstead, Middlesex TW12 2SH (020 8941 6907; Fax: 020 8979 4323; e-mail: office@policedependantstrust.org.uk; website: www.policedependantstrust.org.uk)

Precious metals

The Johnson Matthey Educational Trust

Eligibility: People over the age of 16 with a parent or grandparent currently connected with the precious metals industry.

Types of grants: Grants to college students and undergraduates for fees, books, equipment and maintenance/living expenses. Grants are usually for between £400 and £500.

Exclusions: Grants are not made to students studying second degrees or mature students.

Annual grant total: In 2004/05 the trust had assets of £475,000, and an income and expenditure of £24,000, all of which was given in 86 grants.

Applications: On a form available from the correspondent. Applications should be submitted by the relevant parent or grandparent, if possible, on behalf of the individual in October for consideration in December. Advertisements appear in the relevant trade journals.

Correspondent: R Hewitt, Johnson Matthey PLC, 40–42 Hatton Garden, London EC1N 8EE (020 7269 8124; Fax: 020 7269 8129; e-mail: hewittr@matthey.com)

Railway workers

Railway Benevolent Institution

Eligibility: The dependants of railway employees (active or retired) in the UK and Republic of Ireland. Unless there are very special circumstances, grants are not made to anyone with capital in excess of £16,000.

Types of grants: One-off grants ranging from £100 to £1,650 to schoolchildren, college students, people starting work and those with special educational needs towards uniforms, clothing, books and equipment and maintenance/living expenses.

Annual grant total: In 2005 the institution had assets of over £4 million, an income of £402,000 and a total expenditure of £541,000. A total of 777 grants were made totalling £403,000.

Applications: On a form available from the correspondent. Applications can be submitted either directly by the individual or a family member, through a third party such as a social worker or teacher, or through an organisation such as Citizens Advice. They are considered on a monthly basis. Applicants must be able to provide verification of railway service.

Correspondent: B R Whitnall, Director, Electra Way, Crewe Business Park, Crewe, Cheshire CW1 6HS (01270 251316; Fax: 01270 503966)

Other information: This is mostly a welfare charity, and these educational grants are part of its wider welfare work.

Religious workers

Children of the Clergy Trust

Eligibility: Children of deceased ministers of the Church of Scotland, based anywhere.

Types of grants: One-off or recurrent grants in the range of £500 and £1,000 for any educational need.

Annual grant total: In 2005 the trust had assets of £38,000 and an income of £2,100. There were two grants of £1,000 each. One for relief-in-need purposes and one for education.

Applications: In writing to the correspondent. Applications should be submitted directly by the individual to be considered at any time, and should include information about the applicant's ministerial parent, general family circumstances and other relevant information.

Correspondent: Revd Iain U Thomson, The Manse, Manse Road, Kirkton of Skene, Westhill, Aberdeenshire AB32 6LX (01224 743277; Fax: 01224 743277)

The Corporation of the Sons of the Clergy

Eligibility: Dependant children (under 25 years of age) of Anglican clergy of the dioceses of the UK and Ireland and of the diocese in Europe or of the widows/widowers and separated or divorced spouses of such clergy. Grants are made only to the parent, not the child.

Types of grants: Grants are available to help with tuition and boarding fees when there is a demonstrable need for independent education for the child in question. The maximum amount of such a grant is £4,200 a year, paid in three instalments at the start of each term. The usual minimum age at which help can be given is 11 and the grants are renewable from year to year, subject to the applicant's circumstances, up to the GCSE (or equivalent) examination.

The corporation is also able to consider help in the following areas associated with the education of children over the age of 11 in both the independent and maintained sectors:

(a) towards the cost of school uniforms

(b) towards the cost of school trips where the school concerned provides a letter of support confirming that the trip is an essential part of the curriculum

(c) towards the cost of travel to and from day schools

(d) towards the cost of music lessons and the provision of a musical instrument.

The corporation is able to help with special outfits or equipment (but not books) required by a child who has left school and is undertaking vocational training.

Annual grant total: At the end of 2005 the corporation had assets of £33 million with an income and total expenditure of £1.5 million. About £1 million is given in grants to individuals annually, divided roughly between relief-in-need and educational purposes.

Applications: An information leaflet and application form are available from the correspondent. Applications for grants towards tuition and boarding fees should be submitted at least two clear terms before the grant is required. All applications are means-tested.

Correspondent: Robert Welsford, Registrar, 1 Dean Trench Street, Westminster, London SW1P 3HB (020 7799 3696; Fax: 020 7222 3468; e-mail: registrar@sonsoftheclergy.org.uk)

Other information: This charity incorporates The Clergy Orphan Corporation.

The CPAS Ministers in Training Fund

Eligibility: Evangelical Anglican ordinands who are in financial need during their training.

Types of grants: Recurrent grants, one per academic year, to help with maintenance and personal expenses. They range between £50 and £500.

Annual grant total: In 2004/05 the fund had both an income and a total expenditure of £17,000.

Applications: Application forms are available from the correspondent. Applications should be submitted in October or January. Applicants are asked for two referees and a completed budget form to detail income and expenditure.

Time should be allowed for references to be taken up.

Correspondent: Mrs Pauline Walden, CPAS, Athena Drive, Tachbrook Park, Warwick CV34 6NG (01926 458480; Fax: 01926 458459; e-mail: pwalden@cpas.org.uk; website: www.cpas.org.uk)

The EAC Educational Trust

Eligibility: Children of Church of England clergymen and of single parent families, aged 8 to 16. Preference is often given to the sons of clergymen.

Types of grants: Grants are almost exclusively for school fees including boarding. The trust has a close link with one particular school which specialises in educating the families of clergy. However, it accepts applications from other sources especially for the education of children in choir schools or other establishments with musical or dramatic emphasis. Individual grants almost never exceed one-third of the pupil's annual fees.

Annual grant total: About 20 grants each year totalling £32,000.

Applications: In writing to the correspondent. Applications are considered in the spring.

Correspondent: Julian Bewick, 1 Church Cottages, Monkton Combe, Bath, BA2 7HB (01225 723583; e-mail: julian@bewick.org)

The Friends of the Clergy Corporation

Eligibility: The children of Anglican clergy who are under 23 years old.

Types of grants: One-off grants towards primary school clothing and pre-school nursery fees. University maintenance costs can also be supported. However, most of the funds are given towards relief-in-need.

Annual grant total: In 2004/05 the trust had assets of £24 million and an income of £1.1 million. Grants totalling £605,000 were made to 734 individuals, including £116,000 for university maintenance and £32,000 for school clothing.

Applications: On a form available from the correspondent to be submitted directly by the individual or by a social worker, dependant or so on, if the individual is unable to do so. Applications are considered each month.

Correspondent: Robert Welsford, Registrar, 1 Dean Trench Street, Westminster, London SW1P 3HB (020 7799 3696; Fax: 020 7222 3468; e-mail: registrar@sonsoftheclergy.org.uk)

The Silcock Trust

Eligibility: Children of clergy with learning and/or other difficulties.

Types of grants: Help with maintenance and fees for schoolchildren. Preference will be given to children with serious family

difficulties and special educational needs. Grants range from £250 to £2,000.

Annual grant total: In 2004, the trust had an income of £8,000 and a total expenditure of £5,600.

Applications: In writing to the correspondent.

Correspondent: A R T Hancock, Trustee, 4 Church Street, Old Isleworth, Middlesex TW7 6BH

Wells Clerical Charity

Eligibility: People in need who are under 25 years old who are children of members of clergy of the Church of England who are serving (or who have retired or died and last served) in the former archdeaconry of Wells as constituted in 1738.

Types of grants: Grants are made to support eligible individuals in preparing for entering any profession or employment by paying travel fees, the costs of clothing/uniform or maintenance costs.

Annual grant total: Previously about £6,000.

Applications: In writing to the correspondent.

Correspondent: Revd Martin Lee, The Rectory, 3 Ash Trees, East Brent, Highbridge, Somerset TA9 4DQ

Women's Continuing Ministerial Education Trust (formerly The Deaconess Trust Funds)

Eligibility: Ordained women, accredited female lay workers in the Church of England (including Church Army Sisters) and religious sisters (both lay and ordained).

Types of grants: Grants usually help with continuing education expenses including part-time degree course fees, conferences, sabbaticals and workshops, and also some welfare needs. Grants are intended to supplement funds available from the applicant's diocese. Grants range from £500 to £1,000.

Annual grant total: In 2004 the trust had assets of £1.4 million, an income of £48,000 and made 73 grants totalling £46,000. Grants were broken down as follows: £37,000 towards individual's courses; £4,300 on sabbaticals and study visits; £2,300 towards conferences and consultations; £1,000 towards retreats and £1,800 on pilgrimages.

Applications: Applications must be made on the form available from the correspondent, and endorsed by the Diocesan CME Officer or Dean of the Women's Ministry. Application deadlines are two weeks before the quarterly meetings during which they will be considered. Meetings take place at the end of March, June, September and December.

Correspondent: Ven. Dr Gordon Kuhrt, Director of Ministry, Ministry Division, Church House, Great Smith Street, London SW1P 3NZ (020 7898 1391; e-mail: ros.miskin@mindiv.c-of-e.org.uk)

Sales representatives

The Royal Pinner School Foundation

Eligibility: Grants to help with the educational expenses, mainly in state schools, of the children, preferably under 25, of travelling sales representatives and manufacturer's agents, where the family has experienced adversity or hardship.

Types of grants: Help is given in the following ways:

(i) Education: maintenance allowances or grants tenable at any school, college, university or other place of learning approved by the trustees. Most beneficiaries attend local state schools, or special schools in the case of disabled children, with parents awarded grants per term to cover books, equipment, travel and so on.

(ii) Careers: financial assistance, outfits, clothing, tools, instruments or books to help beneficiaries on leaving school, university or other educational establishment to prepare for or to assist their entry into a profession, trade or calling.

(iii) Travel: awards to assist beneficiaries to travel, whether in this country or abroad, in order to further their education and to participate in school-sponsored visits and field courses.

(iv) The arts: financial assistance to enable beneficiaries to study music or other arts.

(v) Continued education: in otherwise promoting the education (including social and physical training) of beneficiaries.

Grants range from £300 to £3,500.

Exclusions: No loans are given and no help for part-time education.

Annual grant total: In 2005, the foundation had net assets of £5.2 million and an income of £281,000. Total expenditure was £511,600, of which 211 individuals received about £380,000 in grants from the trustees.

Applications: Application forms may be obtained from the correspondent, and should be submitted directly by the individual throughout the year. Note that no applications can be considered except those applying for the sons and daughters of travelling sales representatives or manufacturer's agents.

Correspondent: David Crawford, Secretary, 110 Old Brompton Road, South Kensington, London SW7 3RB (020 7373 6168)

Other information: The Royal Pinner School, which was formerly the Royal Commercial Travellers' Schools, was closed in 1967. The foundation was endowed with the proceeds of the closure.

Science

Royal Society of Chemistry Benevolent Fund

Eligibility: People who have been members of the society for the last three years, or ex-members who were in the society for at least 10 years, and their dependants, who are in need.

Types of grants: This fund is essentially a relief-in-need charity which also makes grants for education. It offers regular allowances, one-off grants and loans towards needs such as school uniforms and educational trips.

Exclusions: Anything which should be provided by the government or local authority is ineligible for funding.

Annual grant total: In 2004 the fund's income was £369,000. Direct charitable expenditure totalled £99,000.

Applications: In writing or by telephone in the first instance, to the correspondent. Applicants will be requested to provide a financial statement (forms supplied by the secretary) and include a covering letter describing their application as fully as possible. Applications can be made either directly by the individual, or through a third party such as a social worker or citizen's advice bureau. They are considered every other month, although urgent appeals can be considered at any time.

Correspondent: Jane Banning, Benevolent Fund Manager, Thomas Graham House, Science Park, Milton Road, Cambridge CB4 0WF (01223 432144; Fax: 01223 432269; e-mail: banningj@rsc.org; website: www.rsc.org)

Other information: The fund is acts as an advisory service, as well as a grant provider.

Seafarers

Royal Liverpool Seamen's Orphan Institution

Eligibility: Children of deceased British merchant seafarers, who are of pre-school age or in full-time education (including further education).

Types of grants: Monthly maintenance and annual clothing grants. Help may also be given for school fees.

Annual grant total: In 2004 the trust had assets of £3.4 million and an income of £185,000. Grants totalled £282,000 made up of maintenance grants (£270,000), clothing grants (£9,000) and education fee grants (£3,000).

Applications: On a form available from the correspondent, to be considered at any time. Applications can be submitted either directly by the individual, or by the parent or guardian. They need to include confirmation of the seafarer's death, the child's birth certificate and proof of their educational status.

Correspondent: Mrs Linda Gidman, Secretary, 2nd Floor, Tower Building, 22 Water Street, Liverpool L3 1AB (0151 227 3417; e-mail: enquiries@rlsoi-uk.org; website: www.rlsoi-uk.org)

The Royal Merchant Navy School Foundation

Eligibility: Children in need who have a parent who has served or is serving as a seaman of any grade in the British merchant service for not less than six years. The child's parents are expected to contribute towards the educational costs of their children according to their means. All beneficiaries must have British nationality. Full eligibility requirements are available from the correspondent.

Types of grants: One–off and recurrent grants are made. Grants are tailored to meet the needs of each individual and are usually paid directly to schools and colleges. Schoolchildren are awarded grants for general educational needs. College and vocational students may receive support for uniform and other school clothing, fees, books and equipment/instruments. Vocational students can also be awarded grants for maintenance/living expenses. Higher education students can receive help for fees, study or travel abroad, books, equipment and maintenance/living expenses.

Annual grant total: In 2005, the foundation had assets of £737,000 and an income of £644,000. Total expenditure was £647,000; supporting 27 young people to a total cost of £8,200.

Applications: On a form available from the correspondent. Applications can be submitted at any time, either by the individual or their parent/guardian. Information about the parents' employment and financial situation is required. The application procedure normally includes a visit by the correspondent to the applicant's home.

Correspondent: T J Manzi, Clerk to the Trustees., Bearwood, Wokingham,

Berkshire RG41 5BG (0118 974 8380; Fax: 0118 974 8384; e-mail: admin@ merchantnavy.org.uk; website: www. merchantnavy.org.uk)

The Sailors' Families' Society

Eligibility: People under 22 who are the dependants of UK seafarers who are in one-parent families with children aged below 16 years. Grants can also be given if the seafarer is in a two-parent family, but is permanently disabled. Usually, the only source of income for the family is Income Support or Incapacity Benefit.

Types of grants: (i) Discretionary clothing grants payable per child twice a year – £75 in August and £40 in January – to help children to start off the new school year and to buy a new winter coat. (ii) Educational holiday grants of up to £250 per child for holidays 'with a difference' (Outward Bound Courses, Sail Training Association trips) where the experience can be character building. (iii) Special equipment grants of up to £250 to help with non-academic abilities such as musical instruments and sports equipment, or for training in special skills which may benefit them in securing employment.

Annual grant total: In 2004/05 the society had assets of £2.5 million and an income of £1.5 million. Out of a total expenditure of £1.7 million, the sum of £269,000 went to seafarers' families.

Applications: On a form available from the correspondent, with details about children, income and expenditure, home environment and with copies of relevant certificates, for example, birth certificates and proof of seafaring service. Applications can be submitted directly by the individual or through a social worker, Citizens Advice, other welfare agency, or through seafaring organisations. Applications are considered every other month, beginning in February.

Correspondent: Ian Scott, Welfare Manager, Newland, Cottingham Road, Hull HU6 7RJ (01482 342331; Fax: 01482 447868; e-mail: info@sailors-families.org.uk; website: www.sailors-families.org.uk)

Other information: This trust is essentially set up to give relief-in-need to seafarers, but some of their grants are of an educational nature.

Service/ex-service

The Army Benevolent Fund

Eligibility: Members and ex-members of the British Army and their dependants who are in need.

Types of grants: Mature student education/training grants for ex-soldiers who are unemployed and receiving training or education to enhance their prospect of gaining long-term employment. Such assistance is also available to soldiers who became disabled whilst with the army or after service and need to change their vocation.

Bursaries are also available in exceptional circumstances for the private education of dependants. Preference is given to orphans or children with only one parent, especially if the parent was killed in service. Other priorities include those where a parent is severely disabled or where the child has special needs, which may include where the home environment is such that the child has to be educated away from home.

Annual grant total: Bursaries totalling £80,000 were available for 2004/05. In that year the fund's income was £4 million and its total expenditure was £3.7 million.

Applications: Applications are considered as need arises, but all are reviewed annually in July. The fund does not deal directly with individual cases which should be referred initially to the appropriate corps or regimental association. Enquiries may be made directly to the fund to determine the appropriate corps or regimental association.

Correspondent: The Director of Grants and Welfare, 41 Queen's Gate, South Kensington, London SW7 5HR (020 7591 2060 (Grants Department); Fax: 020 7584 0889; website: www. armybenfund.org)

Other information: The trust also gives grants to individuals for relief-in-need purposes and to organisations.

The Association of Royal Navy Officers (ARNO)

Eligibility: Officers and retired officers of the Royal Navy, Royal Marines, WRNS, QARNNS and their Reserves, who have joined and are members of the association, and their dependants.

Types of grants: One-off grants for educational purposes.

Annual grant total: In 2004 grants for educational purposes totalled £6,700.

Applications: In writing to the correspondent.

Correspondent: Cmdr Ridley, 70 Porchester Terrace, Bayswater, London

W2 3TP (020 7402 5231; e-mail: arno@ eurosurf.com)

Greenwich Hospital

Eligibility: Dependants, aged between 7 and 18 years old, of members and former members of the Royal Navy and Royal Marines.

Types of grants: Grants are given in the following categories:

(i) Grants to children of officers. Grants are available to help with the education and maintenance of the sons and daughters of deceased or distressed commissioned officers of the Royal Navy or Royal Marines.

(ii) Grants for children of ratings. Grants are available in aid of the education and maintenance of children of non-commissioned officers, petty-officers and men, the children of such people if they are deceased or distressed, and children of members of the Naval or Marine reserve forces killed in service.

Grants are up to a maximum of £1,500 a year for help with school or college fees. Preference is given to schoolchildren with serious family difficulties so the child has to be educated away from home.

Annual grant total: About £15,000.

Applications: On a form available from the correspondent.

Correspondent: John Gamp, Charity Director, Greenwich Hospital, 40 Queen Anne's Gate, London SW1H 9AP

Other information: Greenwich Hospital is a charity responsible to the Admiralty Board. Its main functions are supporting the Royal Hospital School near Ipswich (an independent boarding school for the children and grandchildren of seafarers) through meeting the cost of fees, building sheltered housing for elderly naval families, and granting pensions and bursaries to those in need.

Lloyd's Patriotic Fund

Eligibility: Dependants of ex-servicemen and women (Royal Navy, Army, Royal Marines and Fleet Air Arm, but excluding Royal Air Force personnel) who served for at least five years, or less if they served during wartime. Preference is given to schoolchildren with serious family difficulties so that the child has to be educated away from home, and people with special educational needs.

Types of grants: Bursaries ranging from £800 to £1,500 per year for school fees at nominated schools.

Annual grant total: In 2005 the fund, which stands at £1.8 million, donated £47,000 in 193 welfare grants to individuals. A further £15,000 was distributed in 14 educational grants to individuals.

Applications: Applications should be made to the relevant school, not to the fund.

Correspondent: The Secretary, Lloyd's, One Lime Street, London EC3M 7HA (020 7327 5921; Fax: 020 7327 6368; e-mail: communityaffairs@lloyds.com; website: www.lloyds.com)

The Officers' Association

Eligibility: Dependants of anyone who has held a commission in HM Forces.

Types of grants: Assistance towards school fees will not normally be given unless the father has died, or become unemployed, at a stage in the children's education when it would seriously prejudice their future for them to be moved to non-fee-paying schools. In such cases, the applicant will be expected to apply first to the county education officer for a grant and to the school for reduced fees. Advice can be given about other charities specialising in educational assistance.

Exclusions: The association does not assist with the cost of further education.

Annual grant total: In 2003/04 the trust had assets of £8 million, an income of £2 million and a total expenditure of £2.7 million. Grants to individuals totalled £945,000, mostly for relief-in-need purposes.

Applications: On a form available from the Benevolence Secretary at the address below. Applications can be submitted either directly by the individual or via a third party. The association has a network of honorary representatives throughout the UK who will normally visit the applicant.

Correspondent: General Secretary, 48 Pall Mall, London SW1Y 5JY (020 7930 0125; e-mail: postmaster@oaed.org.uk; website: www.officersassociation.org.uk)

Other information: For applicants in Scotland: See entry for the Officers' Association Scotland.

The RN & RM Children's Fund

Eligibility: People under 25 who are the dependants of somebody who has served in the Royal Navy or Royal Marines.

Types of grants: One-off and recurrent grants are made to schoolchildren, college students, undergraduates, vocational students and people with special educational needs. Grants given include those towards uniforms/clothing, fees, books, equipment/instruments, maintenance/living expenses and childcare.

Annual grant total: In 2004/05 the fund had assets of £8.7 million, an income of £1 million and a total expenditure of £852,000. The sum of £825,000 was distributed in 1,114 relief-in-need grants with a further £547,000 distributed in 120 educational grants.

Applications: On a form available from the correspondent. Applications can be submitted directly by the individual or through the individual's school/college, an educational welfare agency or any other third party. They are considered on a monthly basis.

Correspondent: Ms Monique Bateman, 311 Twyford Avenue, Portsmouth PO2 8RN (023 9263 9534; Fax: 023 9267 7574; e-mail: mab52@btconnect.com; website: www.rnrmchildsfund.org.uk)

Royal Air Force Benevolent Fund

Eligibility: The children (aged 8 to 18) of officers and airmen who have died or were severely disabled while serving in the Royal Air Force. Additionally, help may be considered in those circumstances where the parent dies or becomes severely disabled after leaving the Royal Air Force.

Types of grants: Grants to enable the education plans commenced or envisaged by the child's parents to be fulfilled. Help with the costs of boarding school fees may be given from the age of 8 years up to the end of secondary phase only (i.e. up to A-level examinations). Educational assistance from the fund is subject to a parental contribution which is reviewed annually. Grants range from £250 to over £20,000. Where, at the time of the parent's death or disablement, the child has already commenced a 'critical stage' of education at a fee-paying school, education assistance may be provided to the end of the GCSE or A-level course; where the child is not at a 'critical stage', appropriate assistance may be provided only to the end of the current academic year. A 'critical stage' is the two-year course leading to GCSE examinations or A-level examinations. Those children eligible for help with education costs will also be eligible for a modest scholarship to assist with their studies towards a first degree or equivalent.

Exclusions: No grants for private medical costs or for legal fees.

Annual grant total: In 2005 the trust had assets of £160 million and an income and total expenditure of £20 million. Grants to 5,700 individuals for welfare purposes totalled £6 million and a total of £390,000 was distributed to 75 individuals in educational grants.

Applications: By telephoning the fund or through RAFA, SSAFA or other ex-service welfare agencies. Applications are considered weekly.

Correspondent: The Director Welfare, 67 Portland Place, London W1B 1AR (020 7580 8343; Fax: 020 7636 7005; e-mail: mail@rafbt.org.uk; website: www.raf-benfund.org.uk)

Other information: The fund maintains a short-term care home in Sussex and a further three homes in Northumberland, Avon and Lancashire which are operated jointly with the RAFA.

Royal Artillery Charitable Fund

Eligibility: Dependants of members of the Royal Regiment of Artillery who are unable to work due to illness or death.

Types of grants: This is a relief-in-need charity, which as part of its welfare work supports the children of its members who have started private education before the family's 'breadwinner' became unable to earn – and therefore unable to help them continue their education. It also supports specialist clothing and fees for mature students and people starting work.

Exclusions: No grants towards loans, credit card debts or telephone bills.

Annual grant total: In 2005 it had assets of £14 million and an income of £1.2 million. Educational grants to two individuals totalled £10,000. Welfare grants to 2,001 individuals totalled £6420,000. A further £51,000 went to organisations.

Applications: In writing to SSAFA Forces Help (details of local branches can be found in telephone directories or from Citizens Advice). Applications can also be made to the Royal British Legion in England and Wales or to Earl Haig Fund in Scotland (see Scotland section of this guide). Applications can be considered at any time.

Correspondent: The Welfare Secretary, Artillery House, Artillery Centre, Larkhill, Salisbury, SP4 8QT (01980 634309; Fax: 01980 634020)

Royal British Legion Women's Section Children's Fund

Eligibility: Dependant children of serving or ex-service personnel who are aged 21 or under and are living in England, Wales, Northern Ireland or the Republic of Ireland (for Scotland see the entry for the Earl Haig Fund Scotland in the Scotland general section of the book).

Applications are also considered from ex-servicewomen wishing to complete educational courses or retraining schemes.

Types of grants: Help is provided to assist the children of serving and ex-Service personnel with grants for school clothing (including shoes and uniforms for youth organisations), extra curricular activities, school educational trips & outbound courses (UK only), and other needs as required. A weekly allowance may also be considered in certain cases.

Annual grant total: In 2002/03 the fund had an income of £1.1 million and gave £15,000 in grants to individuals.

Applications: Initial enquiries by telephone or in writing to request an application form are welcomed.

Correspondent: Christine McLeod, Welfare Advisor, The Royal British Legion Women's Section, 48 Pall Mall, London SW1Y 5JY (020 7973 7225; Fax: 020 7839 7917; e-mail: women@

britishlegion.org.uk; website: www. britishlegion.org.uk)

Other information: Grants are made through the Women's Section which is an autonomous organisation within the Royal British Legion, concentrating on the needs of widows and ex-servicewomen and dependent children of ex-service personnel. It works in close association with the Legion but has its own funds and its own local welfare visitors.

Royal British Legion Women's Section President's Award Scheme

Eligibility: Dependant children of serving or ex-service personnel who are living in England, Wales, Northern Ireland or the Republic of Ireland (for Scotland see the entry for the Earl Haig Fund Scotland in the Scotland general section of this book).

Types of grants: Scholarships of £1,500 per year are made to young people aged 9 to 25. These are recurrent but require a new application at various times in the person's education (broadly speaking at the ages of 13 and 18). It also provides educational grants of up to £1,000 each to people over 21, such as mature students seeking full or part-time education, people on a retraining programme or those seeking support for other educational opportunities.

Annual grant total: Previously £25,000, although his figure varies from year to year.

Applications: Initial enquiries by telephone or in writing requesting a visit by a welfare visitor who will submit an application form, which includes a financial statement. Applications must be submitted by the end of May, August or December, for consideration within a month.

Correspondent: Jessica Cooper, Welfare Advisor, The Royal British Legion Women's Section, 48 Pall Mall, London SW1Y 5JY (020 7973 7333; e-mail: woman@britishlegion.org.uk; website: www.britishlegion.org.uk)

Other information: Grants are made through the Women's Section which is an autonomous organisation within the Royal British Legion, concentrating on the needs of widows and ex-servicewomen and dependant children of ex-service personnel. It works in close association with the Legion but has its own funds and its own local welfare visitors.

Royal Naval Benevolent Trust

Eligibility: Serving and ex-serving men and women of the Royal Navy and Royal Marines (not officers) and their dependants.

Types of grants: Educational grants are available to schoolchildren and people wishing to change their careers. This is a welfare charity which makes these educational grants as part of its wider work.

Annual grant total: In 2004 a total of £2 million was given in welfare grants to 4,065 individuals. The sum of £21,000 was given in 28 educational grants.

Applications: On a form available from the correspondent, to be submitted through a social worker, welfare agency, SSAFA Forces Help, Royal British Legion or any Royal Naval Association branch. Applications are considered twice a week.

Correspondent: The Grants Administrator, Castaway House, 311 Twyford Avenue, Portsmouth PO2 8NR (023 9266 0296; Fax: 023 9266 0852; e-mail: rnbt@rnbt.org.uk; website: www. rnbt.org.uk)

Other information: The trust advises that: 'The very wide discretionary powers of the Grants Committee are such that there are but few cases of genuine distress to which the committee is unable to bring prompt relief. Once a need is known to exist and the applicant is deemed to be eligible to benefit and deserving of help, the trust's aim is to provide assistance at a sufficiently high level to enable the beneficiary to make a fresh start with a reasonable prospect of avoiding a further set-back often, however, no such satisfactory solution is possible. [Many] face the prospect of long-term unemployment or low living standards and there is little that can be done to improve their lot. Occasional grants can be made to meet exceptional circumstances but frequently recurring applications have to be discouraged because the trust's resources cannot be stretched to permit a regular supplementation of income.'

The Royal Naval Reserve (V) Benevolent Fund

Eligibility: The children of members or former members of the Royal Naval Volunteer Reserve, Women's Royal Naval Volunteer Reserve, Royal Naval Reserve and the Women's Royal Naval Reserve who are serving or who have served as non-commissioned rates.

Types of grants: One-off grants mainly for schoolchildren who, because of the poverty of their families, need help with clothes, books, equipment or necessary educational visits, and, secondly, for eligible children with aptitudes or disabilities which need special provision. Grants are normally limited to a maximum of £200 for any applicant.

Annual grant total: About £2,000.

Applications: In writing to the correspondent.

Correspondent: Commander J M D Curteis, Hon. Secretary and Treasurer, The Cottage, St Hilary, Cowbridge, Vale of Glamorgan CF71 7DP (01446 771108)

The Royal Patriotic Fund Corporation

Eligibility: Orphans and dependants (aged 5 to 18) of officers and men of the armed forces.

Types of grants: Assistance with the payment of day or boarding school fees. Preference is given to schoolchildren with serious family difficulties so the child has to be educated away from home and to people with special educational needs.

Annual grant total: In 2005 the corporation has assets of £3.1 million and an income of £180,000. The sum of £202,000 was made available to 364 individuals for welfare purposes with a further £13,000 distributed among 12 individuals for educational purposes.

Applications: Normally through service sources such as SSAFA Forces Help and or Royal British Legion. Information required includes annual income and expenditure of applicant, details of the serviceman/ woman's military service and the reason why the child needs help. Applications are considered fortnightly.

Correspondent: Col. R J Sandy, 4 North Street, Wilton, Salisbury, Wiltshire, SP2 0HE (01722 744030; Fax: 01722 744150; e-mail: rpat@fish.co. uk)

The WRNS Benevolent Trust

Eligibility: Ex-Wrens and female serving members of the Royal Navy (officers and ratings) who joined the service between 3 September 1939 and 1 November 1993 who are in need. People who deserted from the service are not eligible.

Types of grants: This charity is essentially a relief-in-need charity which offers grants for educational purposes. These are usually given to schoolchildren for uniforms and other clothing and to students in further or higher education, including mature students, towards books, equipment, instruments, fees and maintenance.

Annual grant total: In 2004 the trust had assets of £2.6 million and an income of £257,000. Grants, mainly for welfare purposes, totalled £224,000. Grants for educational purposes total about £10,000 each year.

Applications: Applications can be made direct to the correspondent, or through SSAFA.

Correspondent: Mrs Sheila Tarabella, General Secretary, Castaway House, 311 Twyford Avenue, Portsmouth, Hampshire PO2 8RN (023 9265 5301; Fax: 023 9267 9040; e-mail: admin@ wrnsbt.org.uk; website: www.wrnsbt. ukonline.co.uk)

Shipping

The Bonno Krull Fund

Eligibility: Individuals connected to the shipping industry.

Types of grants: One-off according to need.

Annual grant total: In 2004/05, the fund had an income of £20,000 and a total expenditure of £27,000.

Applications: In writing to the correspondent.

Correspondent: Mark Soutter, The Baltic Exchange, St Mary Axe, London EC3A 8BH

Social work

The Social Workers' Educational Trust

Eligibility: Registered social workers, with at least two years' post-qualifying experience, involved with improving social work practice.

Types of grants: One-off and recurrent grants from £100 to £300 for fees, travel costs, childcare and books. Up to £1,500 is available for scholarships.

Exclusions: The trust cannot assist those undertaking initial social work training or qualifications.

Annual grant total: In 2003/04 the trust has assets of £70,000, an income of £10,900 and a total expenditure of £6,700. Grants and scholarships were given to 24 social workers totalling £6,000.

Applications: On a form available from the correspondent. Applications are considered in February, June and October.

Correspondent: Mrs Gill Aslett, Hon. Secretary, 16 Kent Street, Birmingham B5 6RD (0121 622 3911; website: www. basw.co.uk/swet)

Other information: The trust also makes awards from specific bequests (one or two a year) following a competition; details are available in the Professional Social Worker journal and from the Hon. Secretary.

Solicitors

The Solicitors' Benevolent Association

Eligibility: Solicitors on the Roll for England and Wales, and their dependants, who are in need.

Types of grants: One-off and recurrent grants, and interest-free loans where applicable, towards welfare needs, which may be used towards educational needs if appropriate.

Exclusions: Solicitors who have been considered to have brought the profession into disrepute are not eligible.

Annual grant total: In 2004 over £1 million was distributed to 354 beneficiaries, this included 80 students, 66 dependent children and 7 people in residential or nursing care.

Applications: By application form available on request from the correspondent.

Correspondent: Adrian Rees, 1 Jaggard Way, Wandsworth Common, London SW12 8SG (020 8675 6440; Fax: 020 8675 6441; e-mail: bensec@sba. org.uk; website: www.sba.org.uk)

Stationers

The Stationers & Newspaper Makers Educational Charity

Eligibility: UK residents under the age of 25 who are in need of financial assistance with their education. Preference is given to: children of the Stationers and Newspaper Makers Company's liverymen; and students intending to enter the stationery, printing, newspaper or any allied industries.

Types of grants: All applications from eligible individuals are considered, provided that they are not otherwise eligible for state grants. The company can also make two annual travel scholarships for young men and women in the printing, publishing or paper industries.

Annual grant total: In 2004/05, the charity had net assets of £2.8 million, and an income of £127,000. Grants totalled £79,000, of which around £25,000 went to individuals.

Applications: On a form available from the correspondent, they are considered quarterly.

Correspondent: P Thornton, Secretary, The Old Dairy, Adstockfields, Adstock, Buckingham MK18 2JE (01296 714886; Fax: 01296 714711)

Tailoring

The Merchant Taylors' Company

Eligibility: 'Owing to the enormous demands for grants, the company limits its support to members of the company; the tailoring trade; and the schools with which the company has an association or interest.'

Types of grants: There are two charitable trusts: (i) The Marler Trust (cc no. 1094923); and (ii) Merchant Taylors' Consolidated Loans Charities. Only one application is required for consideration by both charities.

Annual grant total: In 2004 the combined assets of both charities was £201,000, generating a combined income of £28,000. Grants from the Consolidated Loan Charities totalled £24,000; grants from the Marler Trust totalled £550.

Applications: Applications may be made to the correspondent at any time.

Correspondent: The Clerk, Merchant Taylors' Hall, 30 Threadneedle Street, London EC2R 8AY

Other information: The company is also associated with the Merchant Taylors' School, Northwood, Middlesex; St Helen's Girls School in Northwood, Middlesex; Merchant Taylors' School for Boys and Girls in Crosby, near Liverpool; Wolverhampton Grammar School; and Foyle & Londonderry College; and Wallingford School, Oxford.

Tallow chandlers

Tallow Chandlers Benevolent Fund

Eligibility: People in need who have a connection with the company in the City of London and adjoining boroughs.

Types of grants: Recurrent grants of between £500 and £5,000.

Annual grant total: In 2004/05 the fund had assets of £3.2 million, an income of £265,000 and a total expenditure of £187,000. Grants were made to six individuals totalling £4,000, with grants to organisations totalling £134,000.

Applications: In writing to the correspondent. Applications are considered every three months.

Correspondent: The Clerk, Tallow Chandlers Hall, 4 Dowgate Hill, London EC4R 2SH (020 7248 4726; Fax: 020 7236 0844; e-mail: clerk@ tallowchandlers.fsnet.co.uk)

Other information: The trust mostly makes grants to schools and charities for educational purposes and rarely supports individuals. Individuals are eligible for support via school/college selected and supervised bursaries and scholarships.

Textile workers

Textile Industry Children's Trust

Eligibility: Children and young people under 20 whose parents work or have worked for at least five years in the retail or manufacturing sectors, principally selling clothing or household textiles (not footwear). Wholesalers, distributors and service providers are excluded.

Types of grants: The trust concentrates its grant giving on 'the essential costs of education'; in practice this means particularly, but not exclusively, the payment of school fees. It also includes grants for clothing, books, travel costs to attend school and educational trips. There are preferences for those with serious family difficulties so the child has to be educated away from home, people with learning difficulties and pupils at a 'critical stage' of their education such as GCSEs or A-levels. Grants usually range from £250 to £1,500 a term.

Exclusions: No grants towards study/travel abroad; overseas students studying in Britain; student exchange; or people starting work.

Annual grant total: In 2004/05 the trust had assets of almost £7 million and an income of £386,000. Educational grants to 130 individuals totalled £239,000 and 169 welfare grants totalled £39,000.

Applications: On a form available from the correspondent. Applications can be submitted at any time either directly by the individual or a family member, through a third party such as a social worker or teacher, or through an organisation such as Citizens Advice or a school.

Correspondent: G Sullivan, Director, Lynnhaven House, Columbine Way, Gislingham, Eye, Suffolk IP23 8HL (01379 788644; Fax: 01379 788644; e-mail: textilect@aol.com)

Actuary

Company of Actuaries Charitable Trust Fund

Eligibility: Further and higher education students progressing towards actuarial qualifications.

Types of grants: One-off grants of around £600 each to help students with course/ exam fees so that they can complete their training for the profession.

Annual grant total: In 2004/05 the charity had assets of £247,000 and an income of £66,000. Grants for educational purposes totalled £17,000.

Applications: In writing to the correspondent supported by a tutor's report. Applications are mainly considered in October, but also in January, April and July.

Correspondent: G H Lockwood, 34 Howe Drive, Beaconsfield, Buckinghamshire HP9 2BD (01494 673451; Fax: 01494 673451)

The Institute of Actuaries Research and Education Fund

Eligibility: Overseas students who are studying or researching in actuarial science or related fields in the UK.

Types of grants: Small travel grants.

Annual grant total: In 2004/05 the trust had an income of £6,900 and its total expenditure was £2,500.

Applications: Applicants should normally be nominated by an actuarial authority abroad.

Correspondent: Miss P A Hargreaves, Institute of Actuaries, Staple Inn Hall, 1–3 Staple Inn, London WC1V 7QJ (website: www.actuaries.org.uk)

Other information: An annual research grants programme also supports actuarial research in universities at postdoctoral and PhD level. Applications for this programme should be made via the relevant university department.

Agriculture & related rural issues

Association of Professional Foresters Education and Provident Fund

Eligibility: Members of the Forestry and Timber Association (or Association of Professional Foresters or Timber Growers Association) and their dependants who are in need. Members must have been involved with the association for at least one year.

Types of grants: One-off grants of up to £500 towards courses, excursions and professional development.

Annual grant total: In 2004 the fund had assets of £94,000 and an income of £7,400. Just one grant totalling £440 was made during the year, for educational purposes.

Applications: In writing to the correspondent.

Correspondent: Ms J Karthaus, Woodland Place, West Street, Belford, Northumberland NE70 7QA (01668 213937; e-mail: jane@apfs.demon. co.uk; website: www.forestryandtimber. org)

The Dick Harrison Trust

Eligibility: Further and higher education, mature and postgraduate students who are in need and are training in livestock auctioneering and/or rural estate management and who were born in Cumbria, Northumberland or Scotland, or who are (or whose parents or guardians are) at the time of the award living in any of these places.

Types of grants: One-off grants towards fees, books, equipment/instruments, maintenance/living expenses and study or travel abroad.

Annual grant total: In 2003/04, the trust had an income of £970 and a total expenditure of £600. Grants totalled about £500.

Applications: On a form available from the correspondent, or from the trust's website. Applications should be submitted directly by the individual and are considered at any time.

Correspondent: R Addison, Secretary, Harrison and Hetherington Ltd, Borderway Mart, Rosehill, Carlisle CA1 2RS (01228 590490; Fax: 01228 640901; website: www. dickharrisontrust.org.uk)

The Institute of Chartered Foresters Educational & Scientific Trust

Eligibility: Students of forestry and related disciplines.

Types of grants: Grants of £50 to £400 to enable recipients to study forestry at home or abroad, assisting them to qualify or improve their qualifications for a career in forestry. The trust aims to promote public lectures, demonstrations and exhibitions on forestry subjects.

Annual grant total: The amount given in grants varies from year to year. Recent grants have totalled about £1,500.

Applications: On a form available from the correspondent.

Correspondent: The Secretary, 7a St Colme Street, Edinburgh EH3 6AA (0131 225 2705; Fax: 0131 220 6128; e-mail: icf@charteredforesters.org; website: www.charteredforesters.org)

Nuffield Farming Scholarships Trust

Eligibility: UK residents aged 25 to 40 who are working in farming, growing, forestry, fish farming, and countryside management businesses and ancillary to these, and people in positions to influence them.

Types of grants: Grants are given to study topics of interest to rural industry, which can be worldwide. The grants cover a period of eight weeks, and are for travel and subsistence costs.

Exclusions: Full-time education and research projects will not be funded.

Annual grant total: In 2004/05 the trust had an income of £268,000 and a total expenditure of £251,000. Scholarships awarded to individuals totalled £109,000.

Applications: Awards are advertised in October each year. Write or telephone for an application form.

Correspondent: John G Stones, Blaston Lodge, Blaston, Market Harborough, Leicestershire LE16 8DB (e-mail: nuffielddirector@aol.com; website: www.nuffieldscholar.org)

The John Oldacre Foundation

Eligibility: Undergraduates and postgraduates who are carrying out research in the agricultural sciences which is meaningful to the UK agricultural industry. The research must be published.

Types of grants: One-off and recurrent grants according to need towards structured research in the UK and overseas. Grants are not made towards other types of overseas travel.

Annual grant total: In 2004/05, the trust's assets totalled £3.4 million and it had an income of £100,000. Grants totalled £88,000 including two grants to individuals totalling £3,000.

Applications: In writing to the correspondent through the individual's college/university. Applications are usually considered twice a year, in the autumn and spring.

Correspondent: Henry Bonner Shouler, Hazleton House, Hazleton, Cheltenham, Gloucester GL5 4EB

The Royal Bath & West of England Society

Eligibility: People studying any aspect of agriculture, horticulture, forestry, conservation or any form of food production or marketing.

Types of grants: Grants are usually linked to research scholarships which have different criteria each year. For information on what is available contact the correspondent.

Up to £10,000 is available for each scholarship.

Annual grant total: In 2003/04, the fund had net assets of £2 million with an income of £2.4 million and a total expenditure of £2.5 million. No further information was available concerning grants total.

Applications: On a form available from the correspondent. Applications can be submitted either directly by the individual or through a research organisation, with scholarships considered in December and grants in August. Applications tend to be oversubscribed each year.

Correspondent: Jane Guise, The Showground, Shepton Mallet, Somerset BA4 6QN (01749 822201; Fax: 01749 823169; e-mail: jane.guise@bathandwest.co.uk)

The Studley College Trust

Eligibility: 'Those who are training for a career in agriculture, horticulture, forestry and allied land-based industries whose progress is barred by insufficient financial resources. Applicants should be British nationals aged 17 to 30, with priority being given to those seeking their initial technical qualification (postgraduate and veterinary studies are only awarded grants in special cases). Pre-course practical experience is regarded as essential and students on industrial placements are not assisted as they are expected to be worth a wage and therefore self-supporting. The trust annually sponsors a number of scholarships. It also has an emergency fund to help eligible students for whom changed circumstances and a financial crisis threatens their continued studies.

Types of grants: One-off and recurrent grants towards fees, books, travel and maintenance for students in the above subjects. Grants can be for up to £2,000 according to circumstances. Applicants must be studying in public sector institutions within the UK and must be providing a contribution to the cost of their proposal.

Annual grant total: In 2005 the trust had gave £49,000 in 30 educational grants.

Applications: Applications should be made directly by the individual on a form available from the correspondent, for consideration in May, July or October. Deadlines are the first days of April, June and September respectively. Applications should include eligibility details and names of two referees. Applicants will be interviewed by the administrator.

Correspondent: D J Brazier, Hill View, Chapel Lane, Ratley, Banbury OX15 6DS (01295 670397; e-mail: david.brazier@homecall.co.uk; website: www.studleytrust.co.uk)

Jack Wright Memorial Trust

Eligibility: Young people wishing to travel overseas to study aspects of water management in agriculture, including irrigation.

Types of grants: One or more scholarships awarded annually, with a maximum value of £1,750.

Annual grant total: About £2,000.

Applications: Further details can be obtained by writing to the correspondent.

The successful applicants will have prepared a 'well thought out and costed proposal, which highlights how they, and the wider community, will benefit from the award.' Short-listed candidates will be asked to defend their proposal at interview.

Correspondent: John Gowing, Secretary, c/o Centre for Water Resources, Food and Rural Development, University of Newcastle NE1 7RU

Archaeology/ antiquarian studies

Society of Antiquaries of London

Eligibility: People in higher education, including postgraduates, with an interest in archaeological and antiquarian subjects.

Types of grants: A limited range of awards are available for a variety of study levels in archaeological and antiquarian subjects. Grants are of up to £2,000.

Annual grant total: In 2004/05 the society had assets of £12.9 million, an income of £1 million and a total expenditure of £1.4 million. Grants were made to individuals totalling £52,000.

Applications: On a form available from the correspondent or via website. Applications should be submitted directly by the individual in December for consideration in March.

Correspondent: The General Secretary, Burlington House, Piccadilly, London W1J 0BE (020 7734 0193; Fax: 020 7287 6967; e-mail: admin@sal.org.uk; website: www.sal.org.uk)

Arts

The Aquarius Trust Ltd

Eligibility: Artists worldwide.

Types of grants: One-off and recurrent grants according to need.

Annual grant total: In 2004 income totalled £270 and the total expenditure was £700. Grants totalled about £500.

Applications: In writing to the correspondent.

Correspondent: The Secretary, Sanson Seal, Dualla Road, Cashel, County Tipperary, Eire (00353 6263 765)

The William Barry Trust

Eligibility: People engaged, or about to engage in technical, craft and artistic occupations.

Types of grants: One-off cash grants in the range of £600 and £1,000, including those for fees and maintenance/living expenses.

Annual grant total: In 2004/05, the trust had assets of £1.2 million, an income of £37,000 and made grants totalling £17,000.

Applications: In writing to the correspondent. Applications should be submitted directly by the individual or a family member.

Correspondent: W S Barry, 56 Avenue Close, London NW8 6DA (020 7722 3974)

Henry Dixon's Foundation for Apprenticing

Eligibility: Apprentices or students under 25 studying in the fields of music, technical textiles and art.

Types of grants: One-off grants ranging from £100 to £2,000. Grants are made to four London music colleges and one London art college.

Annual grant total: In 2004/05 it had an income of £44,000 and made grants totalling £73,000.

Applications: The trust makes block grants to educational institutions, who then administer the grants. Therefore grant recipients must apply to their educational institutions rather than the trust.

Correspondent: Charities Administrator, Drapers' Company, Drapers' Hall, London EC2N 2DQ (020 7588 5001; Fax: 020 7628 1988; website: www.thedrapers.co.uk)

Other information: This trust was formerly called Drapers' Educational Foundation.

The Ann Driver Trust

Eligibility: Young people from the EU wishing to pursue an education in the arts, particularly music.

Types of grants: The trust makes awards to institutions on a rota basis which changes annually.

Annual grant total: £20,000 to £25,000 per year.

Applications: Application forms should be requested by the principle or head of department at place of study

Correspondent: Kay Tyler, Administrator, PO Box 2761, London, W1A 5HD

Other information: The trust selects different institutes for support in May of each year. A copy of the list of institutes can be obtained from the administrator by sending an sae.

The Fenton Arts Trust

Eligibility: People who are making, or who aspire to make, a worthwhile contribution to the artistic and cultural life of the UK. Grants are made towards the creative arts, principally painting and drama. Students should have British nationality and be aged under 35.

Types of grants: Scholarships/bursaries are awarded for a one-year period to final year or postgraduate students undertaking arts courses. Grants are also made for individual works, activities, performances, exhibitions or prizes.

Annual grant total: The trust makes grants, mainly to organisations, totalling around £50,000 a year.

Applications: Applications for The Fenton Arts Trust Scholarships/Bursaries may come from any institution which provides appropriate study opportunities and wishes to offer its students the scholarships/bursaries. (Individuals should only apply via their institution.)

Applications for other grants can be made in writing directly by the individual to the administrator at the address below. Requests should include a fully budgeted proposal with the amount requested and information regarding other sponsors to the project.

Applications should preferably be sent nine months to a year in advance.

The trustees meet to discuss applications four times a year.

Correspondent: Shelley Baxter, PO Box 135, Leatherhead, Surrey KT24 9AB (website: www.moxie.u-net.com/fentonarts/)

The Gordon Foundation

Eligibility: Young people up to the age of 30. 'To support their education in the fine or performing arts, particularly music, drama or design, or to allow them to engage in educational travel which involves physical challenge and endeavour.'

Types of grants: One-off and recurrent grants according to need.

Annual grant total: In 2004/05 the foundation had assets of £1.1 million and an income of £46,000. Grants to organisations and individuals totalled £101,000.

Applications: In writing to the correspondent.

Correspondent: Gillian Hoyle, Administrator, PO Box 214, Cobham, Surrey, KT11 2WG (01483 579108; e-mail: gordon.foundation@btinternet.com; website: www.gordon.foundation.btinternet.co.uk)

Other information: The foundation also owns and maintains two long wheelbase Land Rovers which it loans without charge to groups of young people for expeditions or field trips.

The Haworth Charitable Trust

Eligibility: Young musicians and painters in their final year of full-time study or the first year of their professional career. Preference is given to applicants from the north west of England, Herefordshire, Shropshire, The Wrekin and London. Mature musicians and painters, even if they are students, will not be funded.

Types of grants: Grants of £1,000 to £2,000 for one year only, paid in instalments over the year. Grants are for any purposes to further the establishment of a career in music, painting and the fine

arts. Grants are not made for general welfare purposes.

Exclusions: Loans are not made.

Annual grant total: About £3,000.

Applications: Applications should be made by letter, with a cv, to the correspondent, and must be supported by a recommendation of a tutor of a full-time course.

Correspondent: Rooks Rider Solicitors, Rooks Rider Solicitors, Challoner House, London EC1R 0AA

The Martin Smith Foundation

Eligibility: People undertaking further, higher or postgraduate training in ecology, environment and natural resources, music or performing arts.

Types of grants: One-off grants, of up to £2,500, towards books, equipment, fees, bursaries or fellowships.

Exclusions: Travel expenses are not funded.

Annual grant total: Previously around £4,000 a year.

Applications: The trustees state that they do their own research and do not consider unsolicited applications.

Correspondent: Miss G Conneely, PO Box 22507, London W8 7ZF

The Society for Theatre Research

Eligibility: Applicants should be aged 18 or over. There are no restrictions on status, nationality, or the location of the research, but it must be concerned with the history, historiography, art and practice of the British theatre, including music-hall, opera, dance, and other associated performing arts.

Exclusively literary topics are not eligible, nor are applications for course fees unless for specific professional training in research techniques.

Applications are not restricted to those engaged in formal academic work and academic staff, postgraduate students, theatre professionals and private researchers are all equally eligible.

Types of grants: Annual theatre research awards ranging between £200 and £1,000. Grants can go towards research costs, study or travel overseas and foreign students studying in the UK.

Exclusions: No grants for course fees or purely for subsistence

Annual grant total: In 2004/05 grants totalled £4,500 and were made to 10 individuals.

Applications: Further information and an application form are available from the correspondent from 1 October. Completed forms should be returned by 1 February, with a detailed breakdown of costing and the names of two referees. Applications received later than this date, for whatever reason, will not be admitted. However, the form may also be submitted online.

Correspondent: Eileen Cottis, Hon. Secretary, c/o The Theatre Museum, 1e Tavistock Street, London WC2E 7PR (website: www.str.org.uk)

The South Square Trust

Eligibility: Students aged 18 years and over studying full-time practical degree courses in the fine and applied arts, especially those related to gold, silver and metalwork, but also music, drama and dance. The trustees prefer to help people commencing their academic studies at undergraduate level. Assistance is given to postgraduates but they do not support individuals undertaking research degrees at PhD level. Courses have to be within the UK. Preference is given to UK nationals.

Types of grants: One-off and recurrent grants for assistance with fees or living expenses. Grants to individuals range from £500 to £2,000. No assistance will be given to individuals where a bursary has been set up with a school. No grants are made for expeditions, travel bursaries, courses outside the UK or short courses.

Exclusions: No grants for: people under 18; part-time or short courses; expeditions, travel or shoes; courses outside the UK; or courses not concerned with fine or applied arts.

Annual grant total: In 2004/05 the trust had assets of £3.7 million and an income of £157,000. Grants were made to 23 individuals totalling £22,000, with a further £56,400 given to schools and colleges for their bursary/scholarship funds. Grants to other organisations totalled £43,000.

Applications: On a form available from the correspondent, for submission from January to April for consideration in May for courses starting in September. Initial enquiries by telephone are welcomed. Two references and a photograph are required for submission with the application form (along with photographs of work if on an arts-related course).

Correspondent: Mrs Nicola Chrimes, Clerk to the Trustees, PO Box 67, Heathfield, East Sussex TN21 9ZR (01435 830778; Fax: 01435 830778)

Other information: Various bursaries have been set up with schools connected with the fine and applied arts. These are as follows: Byam Shaw School of Art; West Dean College (Metalwork); The Slade School of Fine Art; The Royal Academy Schools; London Metropolitan University (Silversmithing and Metalwork); Royal College of Music; Bristol Old Vic Theatre School; GSA Conservatoire; Royal Academy of Dramatic Art (RADA); School of Jewellery, Birmingham Institute of Art & Design; Guildhall School of Music & Drama; Royal Academy of Music; Royal College of Art; Textile Conservation Centre; and Royal Northern College of Music.

The Talbot House Trust

Eligibility: Individuals undertaking courses in the performing arts, such as drama, dance and music. Only UK residents will be awarded grants, for study in the UK.

Types of grants: One-off grants to students in further/higher education to help with the cost of fees. In exceptional circumstances a contribution towards equipment and instruments or maintenance and living costs will be considered.

Exclusions: No grants to postgraduates.

Annual grant total: In 2004/05, the trust had assets totalling £185,000, an income of £6,700 and a total expenditure of £6,800.

Applications: On a form available from the correspondent. All completed application forms must be received by March for consideration in May. The applicant should provide any detail of financial or other hardship, and any reason why special consideration should be given to their application.

Correspondent: Mrs Jayne Day, Pothecary & Barratt, 25c North Street, Bishop's Stortford, Hertfordshire, CM23 2LD (01279 506421; Fax: 01279 657626; e-mail: charities@pothecary.co.uk)

S D Whitehead's Charitable Trust

Eligibility: Children under 16 with special artistic talents, especially in music, dance or ballet.

Types of grants: Grants are available to help pay school fees or to help fund one-off purchases (for example musical instruments) for talented children, and range from £500 to £2,500.

Annual grant total: In 2004/05 the trust had assets of £862,000 and an income of £34,000. Grants were made to 14 individuals totalling £22,000.

Applications: On a form available from the correspondent, to be submitted directly by the individual for consideration in June.

Correspondent: Andy Mullett, Moore Stephens, Chartered Accountants, 30 Gay Street, Bath, BA1 2PA (01225 486100; e-mail: andy.mullett@moorestephens.com)

Arts – Crafts

The Queen Elizabeth Scholarship Trust

Eligibility: People involved in modern or traditional crafts who are reasonably well-established in the field, rather than those who are starting off. Applicants must be permanently resident in the UK.

Types of grants: One-off and staged grants, over a maximum of four years, of up to £10,000 each for further education, such as work experience and training and can include related travel and research costs. About £85,000 is available to be given in grants to individuals a year, made in two distributions a year in the spring and autumn.

Exclusions: Grants are not made for tools, leasing studios/workshops, materials, staging exhibitions or for general educational courses.

Annual grant total: In 2005 the trust had assets of £3 million, an income of £123,000 and a total expenditure of £130,000. Grants totalling £83,000 were made to 14 individuals.

Applications: On an application form available on written request with an A4 sae from the correspondent, and from the website. Applications are considered in March/April and June/July and should be submitted by mid-January and mid-June respectively.

Correspondent: Col. C J Pickup, 1 Buckingham Place, London SW1E 6HR (020 7828 2268; website: www.qest.org.uk)

Arts – Dance

The Lionel Bart Foundation

Eligibility: Drama students (undergraduate and postgraduate).

Types of grants: One-off grants towards fees are given in the range of £1,000 to £3,000. About 12 grants are made each year.

Annual grant total: In 2004/05, the foundation had an income of £42,000, and a total expenditure of £30,000; £29,400 was given in grants to individuals.

Applications: In writing to the correspondent to be received by May 15 each year. Applications are considered in late May.

Correspondent: John Michael Roth Cohen, 55 Drury Lane, London WC2B 5SQ (e-mail: jc@clintons.co.uk)

The Adaline Calder Memorial Trust

Eligibility: People aged 16 to 19 who are resident in Scotland and are taking or about to undertake a three year, full time training course in dance.

Types of grants: The trust awards a single scholarship of £700 each year to a nominated 'winner' after holding auditions in June. The purpose of the scholarship is to enable the successful candidate to receive assistance for one year. It can be used towards the purchase of dancewear, books, training, return home travel fares and any other item necessary to pursue a career in dance. Any remaining income, which is generated by the audition fees, is given to the runner–up candidate.

Annual grant total: £700 each year to the winner of the scholarship. A second grant is dependent on income.

Applications: In writing to the correspondent, requesting an audition in June.

Correspondent: The Trustees, c/o 5 Rutland Square, Edinburgh, EH1 2AX

The Lisa Ullmann Travelling Scholarship Fund

Eligibility: Individuals working in all areas of movement and dance. Scholarships are awarded to dancers, choreographers, administrators, teachers, therapists, journalists, photographers and others. Travel must originate in, and return to, the UK.

Types of grants: Scholarships are awarded to fund the travel of individuals abroad or in the UK to attend conferences, to pursue a research project, or undertake a short course of study in the field of movement or dance. The average scholarship is £500.

Exclusions: The following are not supported:

- fees for courses or conferences are not paid;
- fees or travel for 'long' courses, e.g. courses extending over one, two or three years; these include, for example, most diploma, certificate, degree and postgraduate courses;
- individuals under the age of 18;
- projects which directly support the work of companies, institutions or organisations;
- set up costs of projects or festivals;
- those not resident in the UK for a minimum of two years continuously prior to the application;
- previous recipients of LUTSF scholarships are considered for a second award only after at least five years have passed and/or in exceptional circumstances.

Annual grant total: In 2004/05 the fund had an income of £11,000, most of which was given in grants to 16 individuals.

Applications: On a form available from the correspondent upon receipt of an A5 sae, or from the fund's website. Four copies of the form must be sent by post to arrive no later than 25 January. Forms not received by this date cannot be considered. Forms sent by email or fax are not acceptable.

Correspondent: The Secretary, 24 Cuppin Street, Chester CH1 2BN (website: www. ullmann-trav.fsnet.co.uk)

The Jeremy & Kim White Foundation

Eligibility: Young people in the performing arts with a special emphasis on jazz and classical ballet.

Types of grants: One-off scholarships according to need.

Annual grant total: In 2005, the foundation had an income of £6,600 and a total expenditure of £2,200. Grants totalled about £2,000.

Applications: In writing to the correspondent.

Correspondent: c/o C L White, 102 Alwoodley Lane, Leeds LS17 7PP (website: www.whitefoundation.com)

Arts – Fine arts

Rootstein Hopkins Foundation

Eligibility: British people studying or working in the fine arts, particularly painting and drawing. Applications must have been resident in Britain for at least three years.

Types of grants: Grants are given towards artist's travel, special projects, sabbaticals, exchange students and mature students.

Exclusions: Grants are no longer given for fine arts conversion courses from HND to BA.

Annual grant total: In 2004 the foundation had assets of £6 million, an income of £134,000 and a total expenditure of £109,000. Grants were made to five individuals totalling £27,000.

Applications: On a form, available with guidelines, from the correspondent in November. The application then has to be submitted by mid-January.

Correspondent: The Secretary, PO Box 194, Wallington SM6 0WT (e-mail: info@ rhfoundation.org.uk; website: www. rhfoundation.org.uk)

Other information: Three institutions also received grants totalling £44,000.

Arts – Music

The Tom Acton Memorial Trust

Eligibility: People up to the age of thirty involved in music.

Types of grants: Grants and loans according to need.

Annual grant total: In 2004/05 the trust had an income of £3,800 and a total expenditure of £2,500. Grants totalled about £2,000.

Applications: In writing to the correspondent.

Correspondent: A T Gage, Hamilton House, Cobblers Green, Felsted, Dunmow, Esssex, CM6 3LX

The Alper Charitable Trust

Eligibility: Young musicians in full-time education.

Types of grants: The trust usually gives an interest-free loan (generally £200 to £500) to help buy a musical instrument.

Exclusions: People on postgraduate courses are ineligible for help.

Annual grant total: Around £6,200 is available each year.

Applications: Write to the correspondent for an application form (enclosing an sae). Applications can be submitted directly by the individual at any time. Two references are essential.

Correspondent: Simon Alper, Chilford Hall, Linton, Cambridge CB1 6LE (01223 895600; Fax: 01223 895605; e-mail: simonalper@chilfordhall.co.uk)

Australian Music Foundation in London

Eligibility: Australian singers and instrumentalists under 30 years of age for study in Europe. Students should either be resident in Australia or the UK.

Types of grants: Grants of up to £12,000 are available in two instalments of £6,000, for study in Europe.

Annual grant total: In 2004 the foundation had an income of £20,000. Grants were made totalling £16,700.

Applications: In writing to the correspondent. Applications should be submitted by the end of January each year.

Correspondent: Guy Parsons, Blackfriars, 17 Lewes Road, Haywards Heath, West Sussex, RH17 7SP (01444 454773; Fax: 01444 456192)

The Busenhart Morgan-Evans Foundation

Eligibility: Young musicians at the start of their professional career.

Types of grants: One-off and recurrent grants towards equipment, instrument and fees.

Annual grant total: In 2004/05, the foundation had an income of £18,000 and a total expenditure of £27,000. Grants are made to organisations and individuals.

Applications: Through the individual's college, to be submitted to the Worshipful Company of Musicians, 6th Floor, 2 London Wall Buildings, London EC2M 5PP (020 7496 8980).

Correspondent: John F Bedford, Trustee, Brambletye, 455 Woodham Lane, Woodham, Surrey KT15 3QG (01932 344806; Fax: 01932 343908; e-mail: johnbedford@compuserve.com)

The Choir Schools' Association Bursary Trust Fund

Eligibility: Pupils or proposed pupils, aged 8 to 13, at a member school.

Types of grants: Grants are available to pay the fees to choristers attending CSA schools. Applications are means tested. Grants range from £300 to £2,400.

Annual grant total: In 2005 the trust had net assets of £140,000, an income of around £200,000 and a total expenditure of £185,000.

Applications: On an application form to the headmaster of the choir school concerned. Applications should be submitted by 15 March, 31 August and 15 December for consideration in May, October and February.

Correspondent: Mrs W A Jackson, Administrator, The Minster School, Deangate, York YO1 7JA (01904 624900; Fax: 01904 557232; e-mail: info@ choirschools.org.uk; website: www. choirschools.org.uk)

The Else & Leonard Cross Charitable Trust

Eligibility: Students of music who have considerable potential as pianists and are in financial need.

Types of grants: The trust makes scholarships to musical institutes which are in turn passed on to individuals.

Annual grant total: In 2004/05, the trust had an income of £14,000 and a total expenditure of £41,000. Grants are made to organisations and individuals.

Applications: Applications must be made through the college the student is with, not directly to the trust.

Correspondent: Mrs H Gillingwater, Trustee, The Wall House, 2 Lichfield Road, Richmond, Surrey TW9 3JR (020 8948 4950)

The EMI Music Sound Foundation

Eligibility: Young people in the UK who are undertaking music education.

Types of grants: Grants to a maximum of £2,500 to schoolchildren towards uniforms/clothing and equipment/ instruments. The trust also operates a bursary scheme paying fees for college students.

Exclusions: No grants are given to applications from outside the UK, or that relate to community projects or music therapy.

Annual grant total: In 2004/05 it had assets of £6 million, an income of £255,000 and a total expenditure of £427,000. Grants are made to individuals and organisations and total around £200,000 each year.

Applications: On a form available from the correspondent, or which can be downloaded from the website. Completed forms can be submitted either directly by the individual or through the individual's school. The trustees meet every six months, in March and September, and applications need to be received three weeks before the relevant meeting, with references and supplier's quotes. Applications for bursaries are considered by the colleges themselves.

Correspondent: Ms Janie Orr, Administrator, 27 Wrights Lane, London W8 5SW (020 7795 7000; Fax: 020 7795 7296; e-mail: orrj@ emigroup.com; website: www. emimusicsoundfoundation.com)

Fame Academy Bursary Trust

Eligibility: Young people involved in music.

Types of grants: The bursary funds students while they pursue careers in music (£37,500 for three years). The scheme is open to players of all styles of music. Applicants must be aged between 16 and 30 on the opening day of applications.

Instrument and equipment awards are also available, worth up to £1,200 each, for applicants aged 11-15.

Annual grant total: In 2004/05 the trust had assets of £2.3 million, an income of £237,000 and made grants totalling £382,000.

Applications: Full guidelines can found on the BBC website.

Correspondent: Gilly Hall, Room 6080, BBC Television Centre, Wood Lane, London, W12 7RJ (e-mail: gilly.hall@bbc. co.uk; website: www.bbc.co.uk/newtalent/ music/fameacademybursary/)

The Gerald Finzi Charitable Trust

Eligibility: Students of music of any age who are in need.

Types of grants: Scholarships and prizes for music students to further their musical education, including the purchase of musical instruments. Grants usually range between £200 and £400.

Grants are not given for degree courses or postgraduate study, but short courses and overseas study are considered.

Exclusions: No grants are made for fees or living expenses. Applications from students of other art forms will not be supported.

Annual grant total: In 2003/04 the trust had assets of £177,000, an income of £75,000 and a total expenditure of £44,000.

Grants were made to 12 individuals totalling £3,100.

Applications: In writing to the correspondent with full supporting information (proof of income, a cv and the names and addresses of three referees). Applications are considered throughout the year.

Correspondent: Elizabeth Pooley, PO Box 21, Hereford HR1 3YQ (0845 241 0369; website: www.geraldfinzi.org)

The Simon Fletcher Charitable Trust

Eligibility: People studying music, usually singers under 30, studying at a recognised music academy. Grants are made in the UK and Australia.

Types of grants: One-off grants of up to £1,000. Grants are made to schoolchildren for books and equipment/instruments and to college students, undergraduates, vocational students, mature students and overseas students for fees, study/travel abroad and maintenance/living expenses.

Annual grant total: In 2005 the trust made educational grants to individuals totalling £2,000.

Applications: On a form available from the correspondent. Applications can be submitted directly by the individual.

The trust also administers the Simon Fletcher Award, an annual award given to one individual, usually of £1,000. This is awarded after a process of application, audition and interview, usually in June.

Correspondent: Miss V Fletcher, 74 Hamstead Road, London NW1 2NT (e-mail: info@simonfletcher.org.uk; website: www.simonfletcher.org.uk)

Other information: Grants are also made to schools for the purchase of instruments, music and so on.

The Michael James Music Trust

Eligibility: This trust supports the advancement of education in music, particularly in a Christian context.

Types of grants: One-off and recurrent grants are given towards tuition fees and expenses.

Annual grant total: In 2004/05 the trust had an income of £14,000 and a total expenditure of £13,000. Grants totalled about £10,000.

Applications: On an application form available from the correspondent. Applications should be received by 30 April each year.

Correspondent: Edward Monds, 4 Onslow Gardens, Wimborne, Dorset, BH21 2QG (01202 842103)

The Kathleen Trust

Eligibility: Young musicians of outstanding ability who are in need.

Types of grants: Loans in the form of musical instruments and sometimes bursaries to attend music courses.

Annual grant total: In 2004/05, the trust had net assets of £1 million. Total income was £31,000, with an expenditure of £59,000.

Applications: In writing to the correspondent.

Correspondent: Edward Perks, Secretary, Currey & Co, 21 Buckingham Gate, London SW1 6LS (020 7828 4091; Fax: 020 7828 5049)

The Macfarlane Walker Trust

Eligibility: Music students who are in need with a preference for those who live in Gloucestershire.

Types of grants: One-off grants ranging from £500 to £2,000, for the purchase of musical instruments for music students.

Annual grant total: In 2004/05 the trust had assets of £530,000, an income of £20,000 and a total expenditure of £25,000. One grant was made to an individual totalling £1,300. Grants to organisations totalled £23,000.

Applications: In writing to the correspondent, directly by the individual, giving the reason for the application and an outline of the project with a financial forecast. An sae and references from an academic referee must accompany the initial application.

Correspondent: Mrs Sara Walker, Secretary, 50 Courthope Road, London NW3 2LD

The Music Libraries Trust

Eligibility: Music librarians involved in education or training, or people carrying out research into music librarianship and music bibliography.

Types of grants: One-off and recurrent grants according to need. No grants are made for music courses or instruments.

Annual grant total: In 2004, the trust had an income of £3,000 and a total expenditure of £2,000. During the year the trust gave grants to three individuals totalling £1,650.

Applications: In writing to the correspondent. Applications can be submitted directly by the individual or through the school/college or educational welfare agency.

Correspondent: Claire Kidwell, Secretary, Trinty College of Music, King Charles Court, Old Royal Naval College, King William Walk, London SE10 9JF (020 8305 4425; Fax: 020 8305 9425; e-mail: ckidwell@tcm.ac.uk; website: www.musiclibrariestrust.org)

The Ouseley Trust

Eligibility: Children aged 9 to 16 who are choristers in recognised choral foundations in the Church of England, Church of Ireland or Church in Wales.

Types of grants: Grants towards choir school fees for up to three years. Grants usually range from £1,000 to £5,000.

Exclusions: No grants for music lessons. Help is unlikely to be available for chorists at Rochester, Ely or St Albans where the trust has donated funds to be used for scholarships. It does not usually award further grants to successful applicants within a two-year period.

Annual grant total: In 2005 the trust had assets of £3.3 million, an income of £120,000 and a total expenditure of £115,000. Grants were given to nine individuals totalling £23,000. Grants to nine organisations totalled £76,000.

Applications: On a form available from the correspondent by the school or choral foundation concerned, not by the chorister or his/her parents. A statement of financial resources by the child's parents or guardian will be required. Applications should be submitted by the end of January or June for consideration in April or October. The trust states that applicants are strongly advised to obtain and study the guidelines for applications.

Correspondent: Martin Williams, 127 Coleherne Court, London SW5 0EB (020 7373 1950; Fax: 020 7341 0043; website: www.ouseleytrust.org.uk)

Other information: Grants are also made towards projects that promote the use of the choral liturgy, for example, for organ repairs and purchase of music.

The Geoffrey Parsons Memorial Trust – see entry on page 52

Correspondent: B P Griffin, 50 Broadway, Westminster, London SW1H 0BL (020 7227 7000; Fax: 020 7222 3480)

The Pratt Green Trust

Eligibility: Hymn writers, church musicians and people studying religious music.

Types of grants: Scholarships, bursaries, prizes, research expenses and other grants.

Annual grant total: In 2004/05, the trust had an income of £36,000. Out of a total expenditure of £41,000 the trust made three grants to individuals totalling £400. Only three applications were received during the year.

Applications: In writing to correspondent.

Correspondent: Revd Brian Hoare, 5 Flaxdale Close, Knaresborough, North Yorkshire, HG5 0NZ (01423 860750; e-mail: brianhoare@ntlworld.com)

Other information: Grants are also made to organisations (£5,100 in 2004/05).

The Royal College of Organists

Eligibility: Students of organ playing who are members of the Royal College of Organists.

Types of grants: There are various scholarships and awards as follows: (i) Various Open Award Bequests.

Group A

Eligibility: Students training to become organists. There is usually a preference for those under 19 years of age.

Types of grants: Grants may be used towards the cost of lessons with teachers approved by the college, organ music and attendance at approved short courses, fees to attend summer school for organists, and other similar events. Grants are usually awarded in respect of one academic year but consideration may be given to applications from students for a second or further award. Grants range from £50 to £200.

Group B

Eligibility: Normally full-time music students at undergraduate or postgraduate level.

Types of grants: Grants may be used towards the cost of additional courses or lessons for which the holder receives no local authority or government grant, and may be used in this country or abroad. Grants are usually awarded in respect of one academic year but consideration may be given to applications from students for a second or further award. Grants are of at least £400 each.

(ii) William Robertshaw Exhibition

A grant of at least £120 a year for up to three years tenable by an organ student for use towards tuition fees and/or the cost of purchasing music.

(iii) R J Pitcher Scholarship

A scholarship of at least £350 a year tenable alternately at the Royal College of Music and the Royal Academy of Music. The scholarship may be held by any one student for up to three years.

(iv) Sir John Goss Exhibition

A grant of at least £150 tenable at the Royal Academy of Music by a male ex-chorister. May be held by any one student for up to three years.

(v) Mary Layton Organ Exhibition

Grants up to a maximum of £2,000 a year to female organists only. Tenable for one year at either the Royal College of Music, the Royal Academy of Music or the Royal Northern College of Music.

(vi) Dr D E Braggins Prize

A grant of at least £500 to be competed for annually by female organists under the age of 21.

(vii) Forsyth-Grant/Hurford Travelling Scholarship

Eligibility: Members of the Royal College of Organists aged between 18 and 26 years of age who may be of any nationality but ordinarily resident in the UK or Republic of Ireland.

(viii) The Eddie Palmer Memorial Award

Awards of £400 a year are available to any organist under the age of 25 living in the UK for the furtherance of the study of the organ, particularly with the intention of taking any college examination. Preference will be given to those living, studying or working in Oxfordshire, Buckinghamshire or Northamptonshire.

Types of grants: Successful applicants will receive around £750 to enable them to spend at least 18 days examining and playing organs in one or more European countries and to take at least one consultation lesson with a recognised teacher of high repute. On return, the holder of the award is required to write a dissertation on what they have discovered and learnt from their experience.

Annual grant total: In 2005, the trust had net assets of £1.2 million and grants totalled £121,800. Gross income for the year was £727,400 with an expenditure of £1.2 million.

Applications: On a form available from the correspondent, to be submitted by the individual or the individual's school, college, educational welfare agency, or another third party, with a reference from the applicant's organ teacher. Applications close by the end of April each year, and they are considered in May or June.

Correspondent: The Registrar, Millennium Point, Curzon Street, Birmingham, B4 7XG (0121 331 7222; Fax: 0121 331 7220; e-mail: admin@rco. org.uk; website: www.rco.org.uk)

The Rushworth Trust

Eligibility: People who live in a 60-mile radius of Liverpool.

Types of grants: One-off grants of up to £300 to help with the cost of the study of music and to stimulate and encourage beneficiaries in their musical pursuits. Grants are awarded to composers, young conductors, young performers, student singers and instrumentalists, and choirs and choir singers, for assistance with publication, copying, training, promotion, equipment, instruments, music tours, apprenticeships, concerts and maintenance. Only single payments are made and can only be given if the individual is not eligible for grants from any other sources. Awards are not usually repeated.

Exclusions: No grants for course fees or maintenance costs of higher education.

Annual grant total: In 2003/04 the trust had assets of £100,000, an income of £4,200 and a total expenditure of £3,100, all of which was given in grants, mostly to individuals.

Applications: By the individual on a form available from the correspondent, including all relevant information and documentary evidence. Applications are considered in March, June, September and December, and applications should be received before the start of the month. Applicants are advised of the outcome by the last day of the same month.

Correspondent: The Grants Team, Liverpool CVS, 14 Castle Street, Liverpool L2 0NJ (Helpline: 0151 653 0550; Fax: 0151 258 1153; e-mail: grants@lcvs. org.uk)

Other information: The trust has been formed by the merging of The William Rushworth Trust, The Thew Bequest and The A K Holland Memorial Award.

The Schools Music Association of Great Britain

Eligibility: Musicians in full-time education up to the age of 18 who are in financial need.

Types of grants: Help towards buying musical instruments, summer schools, short courses and so on. Grants are one-off and usually range from £50 to £150.

Exclusions: Ongoing courses cannot be funded.

Annual grant total: In 2004/05, the trust had an income of around £31,000, and a total expenditure of £33,000. Grants totalled about £30,000.

Applications: On a form available from the correspondent. Applications must be supported in writing by a headteacher, principal, music teacher or music adviser/ inspector, and by a member of the Schools Music Association.

Grants can be made upon receipt of written evidence of the expenditure having been made during the 12 months following the date of application, for example, a receipt for an instrument bought, or a summer school certificate of attendance. Grants are not normally made for expenditure before the date of application.

Correspondent: Maxwell Pryce, Educamus, 71 Margaret Road, New Barnet, Hertfordshire EN4 9NT (0208 440 6919; e-mail: maxwellpryce@educamus.free-online.co.uk; website: www.schoolsmusic. org.uk)

John Wates Charitable Trust

Eligibility: Further and higher education students, including mature students and postgraduates, who are studying music and singing and live in London or the south east of England.

Types of grants: One-off grants ranging from £500 to £1,000 for fees and maintenance/living expenses.

Exclusions: No grants are made for expeditions or travel.

Annual grant total: In 2004/05 the trust had assets of £195,000 and its income from investments was £4,300 (a further £128,000 came from donations). A total of nine grants were made to students totalling £20,000.

Applications: In writing to the correspondent. Applications should be submitted directly by the individual for consideration on a rolling basis.

Correspondent: The Trustees, c/o Slater Maidment, 7 St James's Square, London, SW1Y 4JU

Other information: Grants are also made to organisations.

Arts – Performing arts

The Elizabeth Evans Trust

Eligibility: Young people between 16 and 26 who wish to pursue a professional career in the performing arts – as an actor, singer, instrumentalist or within stage management. Priority will be given to applicants who can demonstrate a close association, or connection with Carmarthenshire.

Types of grants: Funding may be applied for either a college or university course at both undergraduate and postgraduate level, or alternately for a short-term project such as a summer course or private study.

Annual grant total: Around £5,000

Applications: Application forms can be downloaded from the trust's website. Nearly all the trust's correspondence is done via e-mail.

Applicants will not be means tested, but an applicant's personal circumstances may be a factor determining the amount and extent of any award.

Applications received by e-mail or exceptionally by post will be considered between the 1 January and 30 April in any year. Consideration of applications received at other times will be deferred until the 1 January following receipt of the application, unless sufficient reason can be established for expediting the application.

Correspondent: The Trust Secretary, c/o Ungoed Thomas and King, Gwynne House, 6 Quay Street, Carmarthen, SA31 3AD (e-mail: hazelthorogood@ theelizabethevanstrust.co.uk; website: www.theelizabethevanstrust.co. uk)

Arts – Theatre

The Actors' Charitable Trust (TACT)

Eligibility: Children (aged under 21) of people in the theatrical profession who are in financial need.

Types of grants: One-off and recurrent grants of up to £2,000 towards educational 'extras', for example music lessons, uniforms and so on. Grants are also made in the form of gift vouchers and payments to service providers.

Exclusions: No grants are made towards private school fees.

Annual grant total: In 2004/05 the sum of £160,000 was given to individuals for welfare purposes. A further £880 went to individuals for education. Over 1,000 grants are made each year.

Applications: On a form available from the correspondent. Applications can be considered at any time, and can be submitted either by the individual or a parent. Forms are also available on the trust's website.

Correspondent: Robert Ashby, Africa House, Kingsway, London WC2B 6BD (Fax: 020 7242 0111, 020 7242 0234; e-mail: advice@tactactors.org; website: www.tactactors.org)

The Costume Society

Eligibility: Students and researchers in history and theory of design (fashion and textiles) and in theatre wardrobe and costume design. Support is given to students engaged in full or part-time study on further, higher and postgraduate courses and individuals engaged in relevant research.

Types of grants: Two grants support research, offering travel, modest living costs, inter-library loans etc. One grant supports attendance at *The Symposium*, the society's annual conference, offering full attendance and accommodation. A grant, about to be offered in 2006 for the first time, offers support for a student on a museum placement.

Each of the three grants is for a maximum of £500, to be spent in one academic year.

Annual grant total: The society offers a maximum of £500 per each of the three grants. Each grant may be made to one individual or shared between several applicants.

Applications: Application information is available on the society's website and is published in *Costume*, the annual journal of the society. Information can also be obtained by writing to the correspondent.

Correspondent: Chairman of the Education Sub-committee, St Paul's House, 8 Warwick Lane, London EC4P

4BN (website: www.costumesociety.org.uk)

TACT Education Fund – see entry on page 52

Correspondent: Robert Ashby, Africa House, 64 Kingsway, London WC2B 6BD (020 7242 0111; Fax: 020 7242 0234; e-mail: robert@tactactors.org; website: www.tactactors.org)

The John Thaw Foundation

Eligibility: People wishing to pursue a career in the theatre.

Types of grants: Funding for arts-based training courses.

Annual grant total: In 2004/05 the foundation had an income of £167,000 and a total expenditure of £215,000. The charity works with a number of partner organisations to help achieve its objectives. Grants are also made to organisations and individuals with eight students receiving help during the year.

Applications: In writing to the correspondent.

Correspondent: The Trustees, PO Box 38848, London, W12 9XH

Carpentry & construction

The Carpenters Company Charitable Trust

Eligibility: The trust is set up to 'support the craft' i.e. people wishing to set up in or to study carpentry.

Types of grants: One-off grants up to amounts of £3,000 each, to help with fees, maintenance, equipment and other necessities.

Annual grant total: In 2004/05 the trust had assets of £16 million, an income of £660,000 and a total expenditure of £550,000. About 250 grants are made each year, 'totalling around £50,000'.

Applications: On a form available from the correspondent. Applications are considered in November, February and June.

Correspondent: Miss Mead, Charities Administrator, Carpenters Hall, 1 Throgmorton Avenue, London EC2N 2JJ (020 7588 7001)

Other information: Grants are also made to organisations.

Norton Folgate Trust – see entry on page 53

Correspondent: The Clerk, Carpenter's Company, Carpenter's Hall, 1 Throgmorton Avenue, London EC2N 2JJ (020 7588 7001)

Clockmaking

Clockmakers Museum and Educational Trust

Eligibility: Intending clockmakers from 18 to 22 years of age. Applicants must be British, be intending to work in the horological industry in the UK, and expect to have a reasonable working life at the end of three years' training.

Types of grants: One-off grants of between £400 and £1,200 are available to horology students in further/higher education for help with fees and living expenses.

Annual grant total: Grants are made each year totalling about £2,000.

Applications: In writing to the correspondent. Applications can be submitted at any time by the individual and will be considered within three months; meetings are organised when there are sufficient applications to justify one.

Correspondent: J W H Buxton, Salter's Hall, Fore Street, London EC2Y 5DE (020 7638 5500; e-mail: clockmakersco@aol.com; website: www.clockmakers.org)

Commerce

The Worshipful Company of Chartered Secretaries and Administrators General Charitable Trust Fund

Eligibility: Chartered secretaries and administrators who are undertaking studies connected with commerce.

Types of grants: Scholarships of £1,000 and prizes of between £50 and £500 for commercial education at various universities. No grants for people studying medicine, or any other profession.

Annual grant total: The trust had an income of £45,000 and a total expenditure of £17,000. Grants totalled about £16,000.

Applications: In writing to the correspondent. Grants are considered every three months, usually January, April, July and October.

Correspondent: The Chairman, Weaves End, Church Lane, Haslemere, Surrey,

GU27 2BJ (01428 651421;
Fax: 01428 641307)

The London Chamber of Commerce & Industry Commercial Education Trust

Eligibility: Scholarships are open to all candidates worldwide who have obtained at least one LCCIEB qualification. There is no age restriction.

Types of grants: The LCCIEB Scholarship is for applicants who hold at least one LCCIEB certificate and wish to take further LCCIEB qualifications. Grants are to cover tuition and examination fees.

The Charles R E Bell Scholarship is for holders of LCCIEB Third or Fourth Level qualifications who are resident in the UK and wish to enter into an undergraduate business degree at a recognised UK university.

Annual grant total: In 2003/04, the trust had net assets of £5.9 million, an income of £330,000 and a total expenditure of £326,000. Sixteen individuals received grants from the foundation totalling £18,600.

Applications: Application forms for both scholarships are available from the correspondent. Applications for the Charles R E Bell Scholarship must be received by 30 June each year.

Correspondent: Secretary to the Director of Commercial Development, London Chamber of Commerce and Industry Examinations Board, Commercial Education Trust, 22 Queen Street, London EC 4R 1AP (0207 203 1909; Fax: 020 8302 4169; e-mail: rbooth@ londonchamber.co.uk; website: www. lccieb.org.uk)

Engineering

The Douglas Bomford Trust

Eligibility: EU citizens who are or will be professional engineers or scientists applying their skills to mainly rural engineering problems.

Types of grants: Mainly grants for travel, language training and conference attendance. Some discretionary awards in cases of hardship or for special projects, and some research projects.

Annual grant total: In 2005, the trust had net assets of £1.1 million, an income of £38,000, and a total expenditure of £35,700. The trust gave grants to fourteen individuals totalling £6,000.

Applications: There is no application form or particular format, and no deadline for applications. Initial telephone or e-mail queries are welcome.

Correspondent: Peter L Redman, Secretary, 44 Drove Road, Biggleswade, Bedfordshire, SG18 8HD (01767 315429; e-mail: redmanpl@aol.com; website: www. iagre.org)

The Bernard Butler Trust Fund

Eligibility: Students studying in the field of engineering.

Types of grants: One-off and recurrent grants in the range of £700 and £2,000. About 12 grants are made each year. Grants are given to college students, undergraduates, vocational students and mature students for fees, study/travel abroad, books, equipment/instruments and maintenance/living expenses.

Annual grant total: In 2004/05, the trust had an income of £16,000 and a total expenditure of £18,000.

Applications: Application forms are available from the correspondent, alternatively they can be downloaded from the fund's website, or completed online. They should be submitted directly by the individual or a family member and are considered in May and November.

Correspondent: The Secretary, 37 Oasthouse Drive, Fleet, Hampshire GU51 2UL (e-mail: info@ bernardbutlertrust.org; website: www. bernardbutlertrust.org)

Other information: Grants are also made to organisations.

The Coachmakers and Coach Harness Makers Charitable Trust 1977

Eligibility: People studying/working in the aerospace, automotive, carriage building and associated trades.

Types of grants: Bursaries of £2,500 each for college students and undergraduates for study/travel overseas and maintenance/ living expenses and to mature students for awards for excellence.

Annual grant total: In 2004/05 the trust had an income of £44,000. Grants to one individual totalled £3,000, with a further £8,000 to organisations.

Applications: In writing to the correspondent. Application deadlines are in December for consideration in January and October for consideration in November.

Correspondent: Grp Capt. Gerry Bunn, Clerk, Woodlands House, The Clump, Chorley Wood, Hertfordshire WD3 4BB (website: www.coachmakers.co.uk)

The Worshipful Company of Engineers Charitable Trust Fund

Eligibility: Final year undergraduates and postgraduate students who are in need and taking courses related to the science and

technology of engineering; principally those who are in the UK.

Types of grants: One-off grants of between £500 and £1,000. Grants are given for one year only or as a top-up to people nearing the end of their course, towards fees, maintenance/living costs or awards for excellence.

Annual grant total: In 2004 the trust's assets totalled £284,000, its income was £37,000 and its total expenditure was £28,000. The sum of £3,500 was distributed in one educational grant with a further £500 was distributed in one relief-in-need grant.

Applications: In writing to the correspondent at any time providing as much detail about your circumstances as possible. For hardship on completing a course, support from the Dean of Engineering is required. Applications are considered throughout the year.

Correspondent: Air Vice-Marshal G Skinner, The Worshipful Company of Engineers, Wax Chandlers Hall, 6 Gresham Street, London EC2V 7AD (020 7726 4830 (no); Fax: 020 7726 4820; e-mail: clerk@ engineerscompany.org.uk; website: www. engineerscompany.org.uk)

Other information: Grants are also made to charities with educational roles and to individuals in need.

The Caroline Haslett Memorial Trust

Eligibility: Women undertaking a full-time course in electronic, electrical and mechanical or allied engineering subjects leading to a HND or Incorporated Engineer-level degree. People on sandwich courses, involving periods in industry, are also eligible, but the award is available only for the academic parts of the course.

Types of grants: Scholarships of £1,000 a year.

Annual grant total: In 2004/05, the trust had an income of £24,000 and a total expenditure of £27,000.

Applications: On a form available from the correspondent, to be returned by 16 October. Applicants may be required to attend an interview in London (reasonable travel costs will be met) and applicants are required to submit a report on their progress at the end of each academic year.

Correspondent: A F Wilson, The Institution of Engineering and Technology, Savoy Place, London WC2R 0BL (0207 344 5415; e-mail: afwilson@theiet. org; website: www.theiet.org)

The Institution of Electrical Engineers (IEE)

Eligibility: The following regulations apply to the scholarships and prizes listed below (but candidates should see the guidelines for the particular scholarship they are interested in, which are available from the website

(i) Students must be studying or about to study (in the next academic session) on an IEE-accredited degree course at a UK university.

(ii) Each candidate must be nominated by the head of the educational or training establishment, the course tutor, the university head of department or by a chartered member of the IEE.

(iii) A candidate who is shortlisted for an award may be required to attend an interview at the IEE.

(iv) During the tenure of an award, the professor or other person under whom the grant holder is studying will be asked to certify that the holder is making satisfactory progress.

(vi) The scholarship will be paid in instalments, as determined by the IEE. It will be withdrawn and any unpaid instalments withheld if the holder leaves the course.

(vii) Successful candidates must not hold any other IEE scholarships or grants at the same time.

(viii) Candidates must start their studies within one month of the planned start date unless they have approval otherwise from the IEE.

(ix) The application must be made on a form and must be returned by the closing date (see below).

Types of grants: (a) IEE Undergraduate Scholarships and Grants

Eight scholarships of £1,000 a year are available annually to outstanding students, tenable for the final year of the degree course. One scholarship is available to an eligible candidate who is studying in the Republic of Ireland.

A limited number of grants are also available to assist students requiring financial assistance to complete their studies. When applying for a grant the parent or guardian of a candidate selected for interview will be asked to submit a confidential statement of income for the three years immediately preceding the date of the interview.

Closing date: 30 June.

(b) IEE Grants

Three grants of £1,000 each are available to eligible students who are in need of financial support. They are tenable for one year of the degree course. Final year students must apply for an IEE Undergraduate Scholarship or Grant.

Closing date: 30 June.

(c) The Lord Lloyd of Kilgerran Memorial Prize

Two prizes, each worth £1,000, are available to final year undergraduate students who can demonstrate an interest and commitment to mobile radio and RF engineering. Candidates must agree to undertake final year courses and a project

which are relevant to mobile radio. The tenure of the prize shall be one year. At the discretion of the trustees, and in the event that mobile radio may change direction, the funds may be used to fund further study in the area of mobile communications including by satellite.

Closing date: 30 June

Annual grant total: During 2006 the institution plans to make payments to 180 individuals totalling £356,000.

Applications: Further details and application forms are available from the website. Applications are usually made by IEE members or people applying for membership.

Correspondent: Scholarships & Prizes, The IEE, Michael Faraday House, Six Hills Way, Stevenage, Hertfordshire, SG1 2AY (website: www.iee.org/scholarships)

Other information: The IEE also administers the following:

(a) The Princess Royal Scholarship

One grant of £1,000, to help an IEE member to use his or her professional knowledge and experience to provide a benefit to an underprivileged community, or similar, in a developing country. The closing date for this award is 30 April.

(b) J R Beard Travelling Fund

Six grants of £500 are available, preferably to younger members, to assist them to travel overseas to further the objects of the IEE and to broaden their horizons, especially in manufacturing techniques. This could be achieved, for example, by a study tour, by working in industry or by participation in an international conference or seminar.

(c) Hudswell Bequest Travelling Fellowship

Four fellowships of £500 to fund travel overseas in furtherance of research being undertaken. Applicants should have financial security in respect of maintenance and research fees and demonstrate a genuine need for the award. Applications can only be considered if submitted through the applicant's head of department.

(d) Postgraduate scholarships

Several scholarships; further details available from the IEE. Value of awards varies from £1,250 to £10,000.

Full details can be found on the IEE website.

Institution of Mechanical Engineers (IMechE)

Eligibility: Members of IMechE who are studying or who are about to study mechanical engineering at degree level (see below).

Types of grants: Awards for undergraduates:

Student Hardship Awards

Grants of up to £1,000 to affiliated

members of an IMechE accredited degree programme who are experiencing financial hardship. Students must be making good progress. Applicants must be recommended by a professor or head of department, and must show that their difficulty lies outside the scope of other sources of financial aid. Applicants are required to submit detailed information about their budget. Applicants should normally be resident in the UK. There are normally 10 awards made each year.

IMechE Undergraduate Scholarship

IMechE offers 50 scholarships valued at £2,000 each, usually paid at £500 per year for four years, for exceptional students who have achieved excellent A-level (or equivalent) results, and wish to pursue an IMechE accredited degree. Students must be living in the UK.

Overseas/Third World Engineering Projects Award

Grants of up to £1,000 towards overseas voluntary or project work to assist the developing world. Applicants must be student members of the institution and hold or be studying for a degree accredited by the institution.

Annual grant total: About £42,000 is given each year by the above funds.

Applications: Applicants should request the appropriate form from the correspondent. Three months are needed to process applications; this should be three months prior to when a decision is required, not necessarily the date of the activity. Closing dates are determined by the approximate dates of the committee meetings, which are held in March, June and September. Applicants requiring an interview will be notified.

Correspondent: Prizes and Awards Department, Northgate Avenue, Bury St Edmunds, Suffolk IP32 6BN (01284 763277 ext 617 or 619; Fax: 01284 765172; e-mail: prizesandawards@imeche.org.uk; website: www.imeche.org.uk)

Other information: The institution makes a number of other awards to postgraduates and for research purposes and for travel and attending conferences, including the Overseas Study Awards and Flatman Grants towards travel overseas for undergraduate mechanical engineers.

The Worshipful Company of Scientific Instrument Makers

Eligibility: Undergraduates and postgraduates with outstanding ability in science and mathematics and a creative and practical interest in branches of engineering connected with instrumentation and measurement. Students must attend one of the following universities: Brunel, Cambridge, City, Glasgow Caledonian, Imperial, Oxford, Teesside, UCL, UMIST, Warwick.

Types of grants: The company awards prizes to encourage third year undergraduates taking courses which will equip them to work in the instrumentation and measurement industry. These are worth £500.

Additionally the company awards bursaries for postgraduate students taking MSc courses in metrology. These bursaries are worth £1,000 for one year. Students reading for a PhD are eligible for these scholarships.

Annual grant total: In 2004/05 the trust had an income of £63,000 and a total expenditure of £57,000. Grants to individuals totalled about £30,000.

Applications: All applications must be made through the applicants' university and not directly to the company.

Correspondent: N J Watson, 9 Montague Close, London SE1 9DD (020 7407 4832; Fax: 020 7407 1561; e-mail: theclerk@ wcsim.co.uk; website: www.wcsim.co.uk)

Other information: The company stated: 'no individual applications are accepted without following the procedure outlined above'. Furthermore 'there is no additional funding for any applicants outside the above universities.'

The Water Conservation Trust – see entry on page 53

Correspondent: The Secretary, Watermans Hall, 16 St Mary at Hill, London, EC3R 8EF (0208 421 0305; Fax: 0208 421 0305; e-mail: waterclo@aol.com)

Environmental studies

The Karen Hanssen Trust

Eligibility: UK citizens between 16 and 25 who are taking part in a project which is not part of their formal education to do with nature, the environment, art or the natural world.

Types of grants: One-off grants are given, but individuals can reapply each year.

Exclusions: Non-UK citizens are ineligible.

Annual grant total: In 2004/05, the trust had an income of £13,000 and a total expenditure of £11,000.

Applications: In writing to the correspondent.

Correspondent: The Trustees, Butt Miller & Co, 12 Park Street, Camberley, Surrey, GU15 3NY (01276 25542; Fax: 01276 686441; e-mail: maurice@ hanssen.co.uk)

The Martin Smith Foundation – see entry on page 69

Correspondent: Miss G Conneely, PO Box 22507, London W8 7ZF

Esperanto

Norwich Jubilee Esperanto Foundation

Eligibility: Students under 26 who are in need of financial help, who have a high level of Esperanto and are prepared to use it for travel abroad. Preference among non-Britons is normally given to those whose native language is not English, since contact with such is more useful to British students of Esperanto.

Types of grants: One-off grants of between £40 and £500 are given to British students for travel to approved venues including insurance, conference fees and accommodation; and to overseas students for travel in the UK and simple accommodation where this is not provided by host groups. Grants to overseas students are only given towards the costs of travel to and from the UK in exceptional circumstances.

Research grants are given to teachers of Esperanto of any age on similar conditions.

Annual grant total: About £4,000.

Applications: Letters of applications should be in Esperanto, including if possible some details of travel plans, and preferably letters of support from one or two referees. Applications showing no knowledge of or interest in Esperanto are not normally acknowledged.

Correspondent: Dr K M Hall, Secretary, 37 Granville Court, Cheney Lane, Oxford OX3 0HS (website: www.esperanto.org/uk/ nojef/)

Other information: All grants are conditional on the recipient sending a written report in Esperanto on the visit. A proportion of the grant may be withheld until the report is received.

Furniture

The Worshipful Company of Furniture Makers Company – see entry on page 54

Correspondent: The Clerk, Furniture Maker' Hall, 12 Austin Friars, London, EC2N 2HE (020 7256 5558; Fax: 020 7256 5155; e-mail: clerk@ furnituremkrs.co.uk; website: www. furnituremakers.co.uk)

Gas engineering

The Institution of Gas Engineers Benevolent Fund

Eligibility: UK and overseas students wishing to study gas engineering.

Types of grants: A range of awards are on offer.

Annual grant total: In 2005 the trust had assets of £237,000 and an income of £9,500. Grants totalled £5,000.

Applications: In writing to the correspondent.

Correspondent: Lesley Ecob, Charnwood Wing, Holywell Park, Ashby Road, Loughborough, Leicestershire LE11 3GR (01509 282728; e-mail: lesley@igem.org.uk; website: www.igem.org.uk)

Geography

Royal Geographical Society (with the Institute of British Geographers)

Eligibility: Scientists, including non-academics, who are over 19 and are carrying out geographical research in the UK and overseas. Travel awards are also available.

Types of grants: Grants are normally one-off, but can be recurrent. Some grants are restricted to teams or to fellows of the society. Grants range from £750 to £15,000.

Annual grant total: In 2004 the society had an income of £5.9 million and a total expenditure of £3.4 million. Grants to individuals total about £100,000 a year.

Applications: In writing, or via e-mail, to the correspondent. All grant details, guidelines and forms can be obtained from the website.

Correspondent: D J Riviere, 1 Kensington Gore, London SW7 2AR (020 7591 3088; Fax: 020 7591 3031; e-mail: d.riviere@rgs. org; website: www.rgs.org)

Other information: The society is a primary source of funding for geographical research projects in the UK and overseas. Grants include Ralph Brown Expedition Award, Neville Shulman Challenge Award, Gilchrist Fieldwork Award, The Expedition Research Grant Scheme, Journey of a Lifetime Award, Small Research Grants Programme, Innovative Geography Teaching Grants and a number of small travel awards and bursaries.

Greece

The Hellenic Foundation

Eligibility: Students studying the culture, tradition and heritage of Greece.

Types of grants: One-off and recurrent grants for projects involving education, research, music and dance, books and library facilities and university symposia. Grants for individuals rarely exceed £5,000 each.

Annual grant total: In 2003 the foundation had an income of £36,000. Grants totalled £59,000, including £2,000 to individuals.

Applications: In writing to the correspondent.

Correspondent: G D Lemos, Hon. Secretary, St Paul's House, Warwick Lane, London EC4P 4BN

Other information: Grants are also made to organisations.

Home economics

The British & Foreign School Society – Berridge Bursary Fund

Eligibility: Students of home economics, food and nutrition or dietetics.

Types of grants: One-off grants according to need.

Annual grant total: About £1,500 is available each year for grants to individuals.

Applications: In writing to the correspondent directly by the individual. The application should be submitted with an sae and the names and addresses of two referees.

Correspondent: Charles Crawford, Director, Maybrook House, Godstone Road, Caterham, Surrey CR3 6RE (01883 331177; website: www.bfss.org.uk)

Horticulture/ botany

The Merlin Trust

Eligibility: UK and Irish nationals, aged between 20 and 35, who are horticulturists or botanists and wish to extend their knowledge of plants, gardens and gardening by travelling. Other nationalities are only eligible if they are studying full time at a UK horticultural establishment.

Types of grants: Grants of up to £750 towards visiting gardens in different parts of the country or abroad, or travelling to see wild plants in their native habitats. Previous support has been awarded for an expedition to southern Chile to observe the range of beautiful plants, a trip to New York's community gardens and a visit to Peru in search of orchids.

Exclusions: Grants are not given towards postgraduate study or to fund highly technical laboratory-based research.

Annual grant total: In 2004/05 the trust had assets of £430,000 and an income of £18,000. Grants to 17 individuals totalled £12,000.

Applications: On a form available from the correspondent. Applications can be considered at any time and must include a cv, itinerary, budget, correspondence with host and two references.

Correspondent: Fiona Crumley, 55 Deodar Road, London, SW15 2NU (020 8874 7636; Fax: 020 8874 7636)

Other information: Successful applicants are required to submit a report on their trip, which will be housed in the RHS Lindley Library, 80 Vincent Square, London SW1P 2PE. For enquiries ring 020 7821 3050. Reports are also available for reference at the Royal Geographical Society, 1 Kensington Gore, London SW7 2AR (Tel: 020 7591 3030). Annual awards of £500 are awarded to the author of the best report and the report with the best photographs.

The Royal Horticultural Society

Eligibility: People who have an interest in horticulture. Preference is given to applicants between 20 and 35 years of age.

Types of grants: Grants are given to UK residents for study abroad and to people living abroad for study in the UK. Grants are not for university courses, but are towards horticultural projects and can also occasionally be towards the costs of attending horticultural conferences and research. Applicants are expected to obtain additional funding from other sources for high cost projects.

Exclusions: Grants are not made for salary costs, tuition fees, exam fees or living costs for educational courses.

Annual grant total: In 2005/06 grants totalling £68,000 were awarded to 75 individuals. Grants range from £200 to £2,000.

Applications: On a form available from the correspondent. Applications should be submitted directly by the individual in December, March, June and September for consideration in February, May, August and November. Applicants are expected to demonstrate clear objectives, provide a cv, full costings and evidence of other funding sources.

Correspondent: The Secretary, Bursaries Committee, The Royal Horticultural Society's Garden, Wisley, Woking, Surrey GU23 6QB (01483 212380; Fax: 01483 212382; e-mail: bursaries@rhs.org.uk; website: www.rhs.org.uk)

Hospitality trades

The Savoy Educational Trust

Eligibility: People entering or working in the hospitality industry throughout the UK. People starting work, further and higher education students, mature students and postgraduates can be supported.

Types of grants: Individuals can receive up to £500 for uniforms or other school clothing, books, equipment, instruments, fees, educational outings in the UK and study or travel abroad. In addition, two or three Reeves-Smith scholarships of £5,500 each are given to young men and women to help with their training for the industry. In 2004/05 a total of 33 grants were made to individuals.

Annual grant total: In 2004/05 the trust had assets of £36 million, an income of £980,000 and a total expenditure of £963,000 million. About £12,000 is given to individuals each year.

Applications: On a form available from the correspondent. A college application must always accompany the application. Meetings of the trustees are held in March, July, October and December, and applications can be submitted directly by the individual or through a third party such as the individual's school, college or educational welfare agency throughout the year.

Correspondent: Margaret Georgiou, 1 Savoy Hill, London WC2R 0BJ (020 7420 2310; Fax: 020 7420 2338; e-mail: info@savoyeducationaltrust.org.uk; website: www.savoyeducationaltrust.org.uk)

Other information: Regular grants are made to educational institutions and associations connected with the hospitality industry.

Information technology

Misys Charitable Foundation

Eligibility: People in need who are studying or wish to study IT, both in the UK and internationally. Mainly undergraduates are supported. Beneficiaries have high academic ability and financial need. Grants are only made to people attending certain universities, colleges and schools that are partners of this foundation. This includes certain colleges of Oxford and Cambridge universities.

Types of grants: Grants are given to fund IT scholarships and to fund university courses for people who would otherwise be unable to afford them.

Annual grant total: About £200,000

Applications: Applications should not be made directly to the foundation in any circumstance. Grants are only made via the institutions that work in partnership with the foundation, who recommend beneficiaries to the foundation.

Other information: The foundation only makes awards on the recommendation of partner institutions.

International affairs

Gilbert Murray Trust: International Studies Committee

Eligibility: People who are studying, or have studied, international relations (or international law) at an institution of higher education in the UK. Applicants should be 25 years or younger on 1 April of the year they are applying, although other people can receive grants if they are able to put forward special reasons for their delayed education.

Types of grants: Awards are 'given to support a specific project (such as a research visit to the headquarters of an international organisation, to a particular country or a short course at an institution abroad) which will assist the applicant in his or her study of international affairs in relation to the purposes and work of the United Nations'. Up to 10 junior awards can be given, each of £300. The trust stresses that the junior awards are not intended as general financial support for the study of international affairs.

Exclusions: No grants to assist with fees or maintenance costs for people studying international affairs.

Annual grant total: In 2004/05 the trust had an income of £4,100 and a total expenditure of £6,800. Grants from the International Studies Committee totalled £3,000.

Applications: In writing to the correspondent by 1 April. The letter should be supported by a short cv, a statement of career intentions and a description of the project for which the award is sought, with an estimate of its total cost and the sources of additional funding if required. (Preference will be given to applications where the award will cover all or the greater part of the project.) An assessment by a person in a position to judge the applicant in his or her suitability for the award is also necessary. All of this information should be submitted with four other copies, in typed form, only using one side of the paper.

Correspondent: Mrs Mary Bull, Hon. Secretary, International Studies Committee of the Gilbert Murray Trust, 5 Warnborough Road, Oxford OX2 6HZ (01865 556633)

Languages

The John Speak Trust Foreign Languages Scholarships

Eligibility: People who are over 18 and who have a sound basic knowledge (at least GCSE) of the foreign language they wish to study. Applicants must be British born.

Types of grants: Grants to help with the cost of studying a foreign language abroad, normally for a continuous period of six months. They are aimed at people who are intending to follow a career connected with the export trade of the UK, so applicants should usually be (or should stand a reasonable chance of becoming) a representative who will travel abroad to secure business for the UK. The applicant is expected to obtain a post as an unpaid volunteer with a respectable firm or to attend a school, college, university or be on another suitable training course. The value of the ten-month scholarship is approximately £1,800 (to cover living and travel expenses).

Annual grant total: In 2004/05 the trust had an income of £13,500, and a total expenditure of £16,000.

Applications: The scholarships are advertised in February, May and October each year. Applicants will be expected to read, translate and converse in their chosen language (at least to GCSE level) in their interview.

Correspondent: Mrs S Needham, Bradford Chamber of Commerce, Devere House, Vicar Lane, Bradford, West Yorkshire, BD1 5AH (01274 230090; Fax: 01274 224549)

Leather industry

Dr Dorothy Jordan Lloyd Memorial Trust

Eligibility: People employed in the production of leather or research directly relevant to this sector. Non-UK students must be fluent in English and intend to return to their home country to work in the leather industry. The fellowship may not be offered to an applicant resident in, or a citizen of, a country which restricts free trade in hides, skins or leather. Applicants must be aged 20 to 40.

Types of grants: Grants ranging from £100 to £1,500 each are made towards travel and international exchange among young people involved in the leather industry. It does not aim to support students in following standard courses of education.

Annual grant total: Grants are made totalling about £4,000 each year to around 10 individuals.

Applications: In writing to the correspondent, to be submitted by the individual for consideration at any time.

Correspondent: Paul Pearson, Leather Trade House, Kings Park Road, Moulton Park, Northampton NN3 6JD (01604 679999; Fax: 01604 679998; e-mail: paul_p@blcleathertech.com)

Levant

Council for British Research in the Levant

Eligibility: British citizens or those ordinarily resident in the UK, Isle of Man or the Channel Islands carrying out arts, humanities and social sciences research in connection with the countries of the Levant (Cyprus, Israel, Jordan, Lebanon, Palestine and Syria). Students registered on a full-time undergraduate or postgraduate degree in a UK university are eligible to apply for travel grants.

Types of grants: Research awards are open to individuals seeking support for advanced research at postdoctoral or equivalent level. Travel grants are open to individuals undertaking study or research at undergraduate, postgraduate or postdoctoral level.

Exclusions: No grants towards maintenance, fees, conferences, language courses, field schools/group tours, books or equipment.

Annual grant total: In 2004/05 the trust had assets of £195,000, an income of £488,000 and a total expenditure of

£466,000. It gave £85,000 in research grants and £8,000 in travel grants.

Applications: On a form available from the correspondent or available to download from the website. Research award forms to be submitted by 1 December; travel grant forms to be submitted by 31 January.

Correspondent: The UK Secretary, The British Academy, 10 Carlton House Terrace, London SW1Y 5AH (020 7969 5296; Fax: 020 7969 5401; e-mail: cbrl@britac.ac.uk; website: www.cbrl.org.uk)

Other information: For further details or advice, please contact the UK secretary (cbrl@britac.ac.uk) or the Director (b.finlayson@cbrl.org.uk).

Littoral

The British Institute of Archaeology at Ankara

Eligibility: British undergraduates and postgraduates studying the Turkish and Black Sea littoral in all academic disciplines within the arts, humanities and social sciences. Scholars from Turkey and the countries surrounding the Black Sea who are studying in the UK can also be supported.

Types of grants: The trust gives for the following purposes: (i) support visits to the UK or the Institute's library in Ankara for scholars from Turkey or the countries surrounding the Black Sea; (ii) travel grants of up to £500 to British undergraduates and postgraduates studying archaeology and related subjects to enable them to travel to and in Turkey (although grants for participation in archaeological projects are not given); and (iii) grants of up to £400 to enable British undergraduates and postgraduates to participate in an excavation or survey that relates to Hellenic studies (in its widest sense).

Annual grant total: In 2004/05 the institute had assets of £324,000 and income of £35,000. There were 59 grants to individuals made totalling £91,000.

Applications: For scheme (i) above, on a form available from the correspondent, to be completed with references by the first week of November for a decision by the start of the following April when the grant will be paid. For schemes (ii) and (iii), on a form available from the correspondent, which must be returned with two academic references by the start of February.

Correspondent: Gina Coulthard, 10 Carlton House Terrace, London SW1Y 5AH (020 7969 5204; Fax: 020 7969 5401; e-mail: biaa@britac.ac.uk; website: www.biaa.ac.uk)

Other information: It also runs a number of schemes solely for postgraduates as well as overseeing a number of other funds. Please see the fund's website for further details.

Marxism, socialism & working class history

The Barry Amiel & Norman Melburn Trust

Eligibility: Groups and individuals working to advance public education in the philosophy of Marxism, the history of socialism, and the working class movement.

Types of grants: Grants to individuals and organisations range from £200 to £7,000, and are paid for a range of archiving, research, printing, publishing and conference costs.

Exclusions: The trust does not award funds to subsidise the continuation or running of university/college courses, or subsidise fees/maintenance for undergraduate/postgraduate students.

Annual grant total: In 2004 the trust had net assets of £1.5 million, an income of £63,000, and a total expenditure of £39,000. Previously grants totalled £30,000.

Applications: On a form available from the correspondent. The trustees meet twice a year to consider applications, usually in January and June.

Correspondent: Willow Grylls, 8 Wilton Way, London, E8 3EE (020 7254 1561; Fax: 020 7254 1561; e-mail: williow.grylls@companypictures.co.uk)

Media

The Grace Wyndham Goldie (BBC) Trust Fund

Eligibility: Employees and ex-employees engaged in radio or television broadcasting or an associated activity, and their dependants.

Types of grants: One-off grants to help with educational costs such as school or college fees, travelling expenses, school uniforms, books and equipment, living expenses or to supplement existing educational awards.

Exclusions: Recurrent grants are not made.

Annual grant total: About £25,000 is given in grants for educational and welfare purposes per annum.

Applications: On a form available from the correspondent. The deadline for applications is 31 July; they are considered in September. As the income of the fund is limited, and to ensure help can be given where it is most needed, applicants must be prepared to give full information about their circumstances.

Correspondent: Christine Geen, BBC Pension and Benefits Centre, Broadcasting House, Cardiff CF5 2YQ (029 2032 3772; Fax: 029 2032 2408)

George Viner Memorial Fund

Eligibility: British black and asian students wishing to gain employment in radio, print and photo journalism.

Types of grants: Grants for course fees, books or travel payments.

Annual grant total: In 2004/05 the fund had an income of £20,000 and a total expenditure of £15,000.

Applications: On a form available form the fund.

Correspondent: The General Secretary, Headland House, 308–312 Grays Inn Road, London WC1X 8DP (020 7278 7916; e-mail: georgeviner@nuj.org.uk; website: www.georgeviner.org.uk)

Other information: The trust also provides mentoring, course and careers guidance.

The Welsh Broadcasting Trust

Eligibility: People who wish to expand their knowledge of the media. Applicants must have been fully resident in Wales for at least two years prior to making the application, have been born in Wales, or be Welsh speakers.

Types of grants: Participation in appropriate training or career development courses, full or part-time, for example writing workshops/specialist technical skills/business development; attendance of educational courses at higher degree level; travel grants to accredited festivals/markets; projects which enrich the cultural experience through the medium of television, film, radio and new media.

Exclusions: The trust does not fund undergraduate entry to courses.

Annual grant total: In 2004, the trust had an income of £16,000 and a total expenditure of £15,000. Grants totalled about £14,000.

Applications: Application forms are available from trust's website, or contact the trust for a printed application form.

The trustees meet twice a year, usually at the end of March and beginning of September to assess applications.

Correspondent: The Secretary, Islwyn, Lôn Terfyn, Morfa Nefyn, Pwllheli, Gwynedd, LL53 6AP (01758 720 132 (after 6pm); e-mail: info@wbt.org.uk; website: www. ydg.org.uk)

Other information: Grants are also made to training bodies or companies which offer specific training/educational programmes.

Medicine, including medical research, nursing & veterinary studies

The Worshipful Society of Apothecaries General Charity Limited

Eligibility: Penultimate and final year medical and pharmaceutical students who are in need.

Types of grants: One-off and recurrent grants of about £1,000 a year.

Annual grant total: In 2004/05 the trust had an income of £94,500 and an expenditure of about £38,800. Grants totalled about £37,000.

Applications: Every year the trustees write to the dean of every medical school in the country requesting nominations of eligible students, to be submitted by 30 June. The committee considers the recommendations in July, and the grants are disbursed in August.

Correspondent: Andrew Wallington Smith, Apothecaries Hall, Black Friars Lane, London EC4V 6EJ (020 7236 1189)

Other information: Organisations are also supported.

British Society for Antimicrobial Chemotherapy

Eligibility: Postgraduate and undergraduate students involved in research and training in antimicrobial chemotherapy.

Types of grants: One-off and recurrent grants according to need. Grants include:

- Vacation grants to enable undergraduates in the middle year of a full-time degree course to undertake a research project over the summer vacation. The student would receive a grant of £150 a week for up to 10 weeks

and the department would receive £500 towards the cost of consumables

- Travel grants, towards travel to national or international conferences to give presentations or poster presentations. They are available to UK and overseas residents and can be for up to £1,500.

Annual grant total: In 2005 the society had assets of £4.3 million, an income of £2.1 million and a total expenditure of £1.5 million. Only a small proportion of this is given to undergraduates, with the bulk of the money spent on research projects. During the year research grants (including for travel) were made totalling £126,000, while grants directly to 11 individuals totalled £21,000.

Applications: On a form available from the correspondent, or on-line. Apart from travel grants, all grants have to be made via the institution attended by the student. The closing dates for submission of applications for travel grants are 31 August and 31 January each year; applicants will be informed of the result of their application in January and May of each year respectively.

Correspondent: Tracey Guest, 11 The Wharf, 16 Bridge Street, Birmingham B1 2JS (0121 633 0410; Fax: 0121 643 9497; e-mail: tguest@bsac.org.uk; website: www. bsac.org.uk)

The Roger & Sarah Bancroft Clark Charitable Trust

Eligibility: People studying in the UK, including overseas students.

Types of grants: Grants are mainly for medical and dental electives, and for overseas voluntary aid work.

Exclusions: Grants are not made for overseas outward bound activities and expeditions.

Annual grant total: In 2005, the trust had net assets of £5 million, an income of around £230,000 and a total expenditure of £225,000. Grants were given to 274 individuals totalling £70,900.

Applications: In writing to the correspondent, enclosing an sae. Applications are considered about three or four times a year. Applicants cannot receive more than one grant a year.

Correspondent: Mike Haynes, K P M G, 100 Temple Street, Bristol, BS1 6AG (0117 9054694; Fax: 0117 9054065; e-mail: lynette.cooper@clarks.com)

Dr Gardner's Charity for Sick Nurses *see entry on page 179*

Correspondent: Dr P L Boardman, Hon. Secretary, 3 Mayfield Park, Shrewsbury SY2 6PD (01743 232768)

Hospital Saturday Fund Charitable Trust

Eligibility: Medical students who live in the UK and the Republic Ireland.

Types of grants: Medical elective grants of £25 to £100 each.

Annual grant total: In 2004/05 it had an income of £380,000. Educational grants to 27 individuals totalled £2,400. Welfare grants were made to 174 individuals and totalled £11,000.

Applications: In writing to the correspondent. If the application is made directly by the individual, a supporting letter from a welfare agency, social worker or other third party is required. Applications are considered at meetings held every six weeks.

Correspondent: K R Bradley, Administrator, 24 Upper Ground, London SE1 9PD (020 7928 6662; Fax: 020 7928 0446; e-mail: trust@hsf.eu. com)

Other information: Grants are also made to medical educational projects and medical charities (£152,000 in 2004/05) and individuals who are ill or disabled.

The Dr Robert Malcolm Trust

Eligibility: Students studying for a medicine degree. Grants are only given for first degrees. Applicants do not have to be in Scotland.

Types of grants: Grants towards the cost of medical education.

Annual grant total: The trustees state that this is a 'small family trust with limited assets'.

Applications: In writing to the correspondent. Recently the trustees have found it more successful to directly target potential applicants through referral from school headteachers. The headteachers must give details of the students' potential ability and their funding needs.

Correspondent: Ian Brash, Trustee, Fa'side Castle, Tranent, East Lothian EH33 2LE (0131 665 7654)

Sandra Charitable Trust

Eligibility: People pursuing a career in nursing.

Types of grants: One-off and recurrent grants according to need.

Annual grant total: In 2003/04 the trust had assets of £11.3 million, an income of £376,000 and a total expenditure £389,000, most of which was given in grants to organisations. Grants were given to 80 nurses totalling £42,000.

Applications: In writing to the correspondent, although the trust's funds are largely committed. The trustees meet on a frequent basis to consider applications.

Correspondent: Keith Lawrence, Moore Stephens, St Paul's House, Warwick Lane, London EC4P 4BN (020 7334 9191; Fax: 020 7651 1953)

The Society for Relief of Widows & Orphans of Medical Men

Eligibility: Medical students who have at least one parent who is a doctor, and whose family is in financial need.

Types of grants: One-off and recurrent grants of £500 to £3,000 to college students, undergraduates, vocational and mature students for fees, books, maintenance/living expenses, instruments/equipment and clothing (not to mature students), and to schoolchildren and people starting work for maintenance/living expenses.

Exclusions: Grants are not normally given for second degrees.

Annual grant total: In 2004 the trust had assets of £3.3 million and an income of £115,000. Grants totalled £35,000.

Applications: On a form available from the correspondent. Applications should be submitted directly by the individual and are considered in February, May, August and November.

Correspondent: Mrs C Darby, Secretary, Medical Society of London, Lettsom House, 11 Chandos Street, Cavendish Square, London W1G 9DE

Sir John Sumner's Trust

Eligibility: People studying nursing or medicine, including veterinary studies, who are in need and living in the UK, although there is a strong preference for the Midlands.

Types of grants: Grants of up to £400 towards equipment, instruments, fees or living expenses.

Exclusions: No grants towards religious or political causes.

Annual grant total: In 2004/05 the trust had assets of £784,000 and an income of £36,000. Grants totalled £29,000, about two-thirds of which went to individuals for education and welfare purposes.

Applications: In writing to the correspondent, through the individual's college or a welfare agency. Two referees should be provided, one of whom must be from the relevant educational establishment. Applications can be considered at any time.

Correspondent: A C Robson, The Secretary to the Trustees, No. 1 Colmore Square, Birmingham, B4 6AA

Other information: The trust was planning to move offices in January 2007.

Metal work & metal jewellery

The Goldsmiths Arts Trust Fund

Eligibility: Apprentices and students studying silversmithing and precious metal jewellery at art colleges.

Types of grants: Bursaries for specific projects of £100 to £500. Previous donations have been made for financing exhibitions, assistance with educating apprentices, bursaries, masterclasses and courses.

Exclusions: Grants are not normally made for fees or subsistence on standard courses at further or higher education institutions. Grants are not made to overseas students studying in the UK.

Annual grant total: In 2004/05 the trust had assets of £68,000 and an income of £930,000. Grants to individuals totalled £28,000 with a further £664,000 given to organisations.

Applications: In writing to the correspondent, through an organisation such as a college or university. Applications are considered quarterly.

Correspondent: The Clerk, The Goldsmiths' Company, Goldsmiths' Hall, Foster Lane, London EC2V 6BN (020 7606 7010; Fax: 020 7606 1511; e-mail: the.clerk@thegoldsmiths.co.uk; website: www.thegoldsmiths.co.uk)

The South Square Trust – see entry on page 70

Correspondent: Mrs Nicola Chrimes, Clerk to the Trustees, PO Box 67, Heathfield, East Sussex TN21 9ZR (01435 830778; Fax: 01435 830778)

Postal history

The Stuart Rossiter Trust Fund

Eligibility: Anyone of any nationality undertaking original research into postal history with a view to publication. English language is preferred in published or electronic form to promote accessibility.

Types of grants: Grants range from £500 to £5,000 and may be spent on: translations; cost of hire of researchers; publication costs; and costs of research. Part or the entire grant may be recovered from sales of the publication.

Exclusions: The trust only gives grants for research into postal history with a view to publication.

Annual grant total: In 2005 the trust had assets of £343,000 and an income of £15,000. Three grants to individuals totalled almost £5,000.

Applications: Application forms are available from the correspondent, or from the trust's website.

Correspondent: R Pizer, 6 Drews Court, Churchdown, Gloucestershire, GL3 2LD (website: www.rossitertrust.com)

Religion/ministry

The Andrew Anderson Trust

Eligibility: People studying theology.

Types of grants: One-off and recurrent grants according to need.

Annual grant total: In 2004/05 the trust had assets of £8 million, which generated an income of £217,000. Grants to five theology students totalled £11,000, with a further £30,000 given in 66 welfare grants. Organisations received £173,000 in total.

Applications: The trust states that it rarely gives to people who are not known to the trustees or who have been personally recommended by people known to the trustees. Unsolicited applications are therefore unlikely to be successful.

Correspondent: The Trustees, 84 Uphill Road, Mill Hill, London NW7 4QE (020 8959 2145)

Other information: Grants are also made to organisations (£173,000 in 2004/05).

The Aria (Portsmouth) Trust

Eligibility: Men under 35 in Great Britain who intend to enter the Anglo-Jewish ministry and attend a recognised educational establishment.

Types of grants: One-off grants according to need.

Annual grant total: In 2004/05 the trust had an income of £5,100 and a total expenditure of £400.

Applications: In writing to the correspondent, directly by the individual.

Correspondent: Mrs Joanna Benarroch, Adler House, 735 High Road, London N12 0US (020 8343 6301; Fax: 020 8343 6310; e-mail: info@ chiefrabbi.org; website: www.chiefrabbi. org)

The Elland Society

Eligibility: Men and women in training for the ordained ministry of the Church of England who are evangelical in conviction and outlook. Priority for grants is given to ordinands from dioceses in the province of York or who will serve their title in that province.

Types of grants: Grants are given to those who have already started training at theological college, be it residential or non-residential, and who have financial needs outside their anticipated agreed budget relating to actual items of expenditure. Recent grants given were towards, for example, family educational expenses, postgraduate study, car expenses where it was needed for training or a spouse's job, replacement of fridge and dental treatment. Grants to individuals seldom exceed £500 per person.

Annual grant total: In 2004/05 the trust had an income of £4,700 and a total expenditure of £1,500, all of which was distributed in grants.

Applications: In writing to the correspondent.

Correspondent: Revd C I Judd, Secretary, 57 Grosvenor Road, Shipley, West Yorkshire BD18 4RB (01274 584775; e-mail: www.thejudds@saltsvillage. wanadoo.co.uk; website: www. ellandsociety.co.uk)

The Lady Hewley Trust

Eligibility: Young men or women preparing for Baptist or United Reformed Church ministries. Preference will be given to students who were born in the north of England.

Types of grants: Exhibitions are given to students who are approved by the relevant church authorities and attend one of the following colleges: Northern Baptist College, Manchester; Northern College, Manchester; Mansfield College, Oxford; Westminster College, Cambridge; or The Queen's Foundation, Birmingham. The size of grants given is related to other income, although the usual maximum is £300 to £400.

Exclusions: No grants will be given when local authority funds are available.

Annual grant total: About £30,000 given to a maximum of 75 people.

Applications: Should be made on a form available from the college concerned. Applications should be submitted via the college by 15 July for the meeting of the trustees in November.

Correspondent: D R Wharrie, Clerk, Woodside House, Ashton, Chester CH3 8AE (01829 751544)

Lady Peel Legacy Trust

Eligibility: Individuals training to be priests in the Anglo-Catholic tradition.

Types of grants: One-off or recurrent grants according to need.

Annual grant total: In 2005 about £4,000 was given towards both educational and welfare purposes.

Applications: In writing to the correspondent. The closing dates for applications are 1 April and 1 November each year. Telephone contact is not invited.

Correspondent: Revd Preb James Trevelyan, Bridge End, Barbon, Carnforth LA6 2LT

Powis Exhibition Fund

Eligibility: People who are training as ordinands in the Church in Wales. Applicants must: have an adequate knowledge of the Welsh language; and have been born, or be resident, in Wales.

Types of grants: Grants of up to £700 annually, for no longer than the period of study.

Annual grant total: In 2003/04 the fund had an income of £7,900 and a total expenditure of £2,100. Grants totalled about £1,500.

Applications: Application forms are available form the correspondent or from individual dioceses.

Correspondent: John Richfield, 37–39 Cathedral Road, Cardiff CF11 9XF (029 2034 8200; Fax: 029 2038 7835; e-mail: johnrichfield@churchinwales.org. uk)

St Christopher's College Educational Trust

Eligibility: People studying religious education connected with promoting the objects of the Church of England/Wales.

Types of grants: One-off and recurrent grants in the range of £250 and £2,000.

Exclusions: No grants to students studying overseas.

Annual grant total: In 2004, grants, all to organisations, totalled £21,000.

Applications: In writing to the correspondent.

Correspondent: The Trustees, c/o The National Society, Church House, Great Smith Street, Westminster, London SW1P 3NZ

The Foundation of St Matthias

Eligibility: Further and higher education students, including mature students and occasionally postgraduates, who are studying in accordance with the doctrine of the Church of England. Preference is given to people studying teaching or religious education who are living in the dioceses of Bristol, Bath & Wells and Gloucester. In practice funding is absorbed by people who meet these preferences.

Types of grants: One-off grants usually ranging from £100 to £750. Grants can be for books, fees, maintenance/living expenses, childcare and for some study or travel abroad. Foreign students studying in the UK may also be supported (but not at postgraduate level).

Annual grant total: In 2004/05, the foundation had net assets of £5.6 million, an income of184,000, and a total expenditure of around £180,000. The

foundation gave grants to 42 individuals totalling £17,300.

Applications: Applicants should telephone in the first instance to discuss the nature of study and so on. Applications must be made on a form available from the correspondent. They should be submitted directly by the individual by 1 January, 1 June and 1 September for consideration in February, July and October, respectively.

Correspondent: Lynette Cox, Church House, 23 Great George Street, Bristol BS1 5QZ (0117 906 0100; e-mail: lynette. cox@bristoldiocese.org)

Other information: Grants can also be given to educational organisations and schools with a Christian focus.

The Thornton Fund

Eligibility: Students at Unitarian colleges or training for Unitarian ministry.

Types of grants: Grants between £250 and £1,500 to help with books, equipment, instruments, living expenses, study exchange and study or travel abroad.

Annual grant total: In 2004 the charity had assets of £383,000 and an income of £18,000. There were 12 educational grants made totalling £11,000.

Applications: In writing to the correspondent through a third party such as a minister, including the total and annual estimated costs of study. They are considered on an ongoing basis.

Correspondent: Dr Jane Williams, 93 Fitzjohn Avenue, Barnet, Hertfordshire EN5 2HR (020 8440 2211)

Other information: Grants are also made to organisations (£6,200 in 2004).

Torchbearer Trust Fund

Eligibility: People engaged in full-time Christian instruction or training. Preference is given to students and former students of Torchbearer Bible schools.

Types of grants: One-off grants and bursaries according to need.

Annual grant total: In 2004/05 the trust had assets of £143,000 and an income of £40,000. Grants totalled £44,000.

Applications: In writing to the correspondent.

Correspondent: The Secretary, Capernwray Hall, Carnforth, Lancashire LA6 1AG (01524 733908; Fax: 01524 736681; e-mail: info@ capernwray.org.uk; website: www. capernwray.org.uk)

Other information: Grants are also available for missionary work.

Seafaring

The Corporation of Trinity House, London

Eligibility: Candidates with five GCSE or equivalent passes at grade C or better, including mathematics, physics or dual award science, English language and two other academic subjects. Applicants must be applying to become an officer in the Merchant Navy.

Types of grants: Full scholarships of £7,000 under the Trinity House Cadet Training Scheme.

Annual grant total: In 2005, the corporation had net assets of £96 million, an income of £4.6 million, and a total expenditure of £4.3 million. Scholarships were awarded to 14 individuals totalling £98,000.

Applications: Details of the scholarship scheme are available upon application in writing to the correspondent.

Correspondent: Roger Haworth, Chiltern Maritime Ltd, The Red House, 84 High Street, Buntingford, Hertfordshire SG9 9AJ (01763 272202; e-mail: chilternmaritime@ compuserve.com)

The Honourable Company of Master Mariners

Eligibility: People who are serving or intending to serve in the Merchant Navy.

Types of grants: Grants to encourage the education, instruction and training of applicants.

Annual grant total: Around £14,000 a year.

Applications: On a form available from the correspondent. Applications can be submitted directly by the individual, through a social worker, Citizens Advice, or other welfare agency, or by a friend or relative. They are considered throughout the year.

Correspondent: The Clerk to the Honourable Company, HQS Wellington, Temple Stairs, Victoria Embankment, London WC2R 2PN (020 7836 8179; Fax: 020 7240 3082; e-mail: info@hcmm. org.uk; website: www.hcmm.org.uk)

The Marine Society and Sea Cadets

Eligibility: Professional seafarers, active or retired. Those who, while not professional seafarers, would prepare themselves to join sea services in time of emergency.

Types of grants: 'It is the society's policy to help where financial hardship is evident. If the applicant is likely to be employed or re-employed then interest-free loans may be given rather than grants. The award of a loan or grant is usually made to an applicant who is attempting to improve his career prospects, or who has to change his career due to unforeseen circumstances.' In addition, the society offers a scholarship scheme for seafarers or prospective seafarers.

Exclusions: Recurrent grants are not made.

Annual grant total: In 2004/05 the trust had assets of £12 million, an income of £7.9 million and a total expenditure of £8.2 million. Grants to individuals totalled £476,000.

Applications: On a form obtainable from the correspondent. Applications are considered as they arrive.

Correspondent: Capt. Ian Smith, Director, 202 Lambeth Road, London SE1 7JW (020 7654 7000; e-mail: enq@ms-sc.org; website: www.ms-sc.org)

Shipbuilding

The Worshipful Company of Shipwrights' Educational Trust

Eligibility: UK citizens, preferably under 25, who are involved in any craft or discipline connected with ship and boatbuilding, design or research.

Types of grants: Grants range from assistance given to apprentices in the boatbuilding trade to postgraduate research costs. Many grants are to individuals to develop their skills rather than for help with professional education for which local education authority grants are usually available. Grants range from £500 to £2,000.

Exclusions: No grants to non-UK citizens.

Annual grant total: In 2004/05 the trust had assets of £827,000, an income of £459,000 and a total expenditure of £37,000 all of which was given in grants to around 50 individuals.

Applications: Application forms are available from the correspondent and are considered quarterly. They can be submitted directly by the individual. Applications should include career details, plans for the study or work concerned, and the names of appropriate referees.

Correspondent: The Clerk, Ironmongers' Hall, Barbican, London EC2Y 8AA (020 7606 2376)

Sport

The Dickie Bird Foundation

Eligibility: Disadvantaged young people under the age of 18 who are participating in sport.

Types of grants: One-off grants of £500 to £5,000 according to need.

Annual grant total: The foundation was established in March 2004. At the time of writing (February 2006) no accounts had yet been submitted to the Charity Commission and it is still unclear what the total level of grantmaking will be.

Applications: Application forms can be downloaded from the foundation's website. Applicants need to show that they are unable to raise the finance necessary through any other means. Applications also need to be supported by two independent referees.

Correspondent: The Grants Officer, 47 Ripon Road, Earlsheaton, Dewsbury, West Yorkshire, WF12 7LG (e-mail: info@ thedickiebirdfoundation.org; website: www.thedickiebirdfoundation. org)

The Monica Elwes Shipway Sporting Foundation

Eligibility: Schoolchildren engaged in sporting activities who live in England and Wales and have limited resources.

Types of grants: One-off grants ranging from £100 to £250 to schoolchildren towards school clothing, equipment and fees.

Annual grant total: In 2004/05 the trust had assets of £110,000, an income of £4,400 and a total expenditure of £2,700. Grants to four individuals totalled £1,700. Organisations received a further £1,000.

Applications: In writing to the correspondent, for consideration throughout the year.

Correspondent: S Goldring, 23 Tufton Road, Gillingham, Kent ME8 7SH (01634 260012; Fax: 01634 263575)

Stationery

The Stationers & Newspaper Makers Educational Charity – see entry on page 64

Correspondent: P Thornton, Secretary, The Old Dairy, Adstockfields, Adstock, Buckingham MK18 2JE (01296 714886; Fax: 01296 714711)

Surveying

Company of Chartered Surveyors 1991 Trust

Eligibility: Further and higher education students of the surveying profession who live in the UK.

Types of grants: One-off grants ranging from £100 to £500 for books, fees and maintenance/living expenses.

Annual grant total: In 2004/05 the trust had assets of £850,000. It had both an income and total expenditure of £60,000. The sum of £10,000 was given in four educational grants.

Applications: In writing to the correspondent. Applications can be submitted at any time in the year directly by the individual or through the individual's college, university or educational establishment. Letters of support from the individual's tutor or head of department must be provided. Applications are considered quarterly, in January, March, June and September.

Correspondent: Mrs A Jackson, 75 Meadway Drive, Horsell, Woking, Surrey GU21 4TF (01483 727113; Fax: 01483 720098; e-mail: wccsurveyors@ btopenworld.com)

Other information: This trust also gives grants to universities to be given to students as prizes.

Teaching

All Saints Educational Trust

Eligibility: People aged 18 or over who are training to be teachers, or are connected with education, in home economics or related subjects, and in religious subjects including multi-cultural and inter-faith matters. Applicants must be UK or EU citizens at UK institutions. Serving teachers who are seeking further relevant qualifications are also supported.

Types of grants: One-off and recurrent grants are given to help with fees, maintenance, books and travel costs. The trust only gives partial funding. Students on part-time or one-year courses take preference over people on longer courses. Grants usually range from £300 to £10,000.

Exclusions: No grants are made people who are: classified as an overseas student (grants to overseas students who are Commonwealth citizens, engaged in one-year courses at postgraduate level, enrolled in a UK higher education institution, will be received with effect from September 2007); under 18 years of age; hoping to have a career in business/management,

engineering, law, medicine, nursery nursing, social or welfare care; intending to train for ordination; requesting a Sabbatical period; or eligible for government assistance, such as an NHS bursary.

Annual grant total: Grants committed to individuals in 2005/06 totalled £107,000.

Applications: On an initial form available from the website, or by sending an A4 sae to the correspondent. Once it has been verified that the candidate is eligible, a full application form will be sent. The closing date for this completed form is 31 March. Applicants are advised to complete the initial form as early as possible as extensions to the final deadline are only made at the clerk's discretion.

Correspondent: The Clerk, St Katharine Cree Church, 86 Leadenhall Street, London EC3A 3DH (020 7283 4485; Fax: 020 7261 9758; e-mail: enquiries@aset. org.uk; website: www.aset.org.uk)

Other information: The trust was formed following the closure and sale of the College of All Saints in 1978. The college itself had been formed in 1964 from St Katharine's College, Tottenham (founded by the Society for Promoting Christian Knowledge) and Berridge House (founded by the National Society For Promoting Religious Education).

The Bell Educational Trust Ltd

Eligibility: Funds are used for providing opportunities for the English language learning and teacher training to students and teachers from overseas who would not otherwise have the chance to benefit from this educational oportunity. Providing scholarships is only a small part of the trust's activities.

Types of grants: Attendance at a relevant Bell course.

Annual grant total: In 2004 the trust had an income of £15.3 million and a total expenditure of £15.1 million. Scholarships to 11 individuals totalled £3,000.

Applications: In writing to the correspondent or via the ESU or British Council.

Correspondent: Chief Executive, Hillscross, Red Cross Lane, Cambridge CB2 3QX (01223 212333; website: www. bell-centres.com)

The British Cotton Growing Association: Work People's Collection Fund

Eligibility: Anyone, including postgraduates, undertaking approved study and/or research of a medical, nursing or social nature beneficial to workers in the UK textile industry.

Types of grants: Research grants, of up to £30,000 per year, for approved study or research of a medical, nursing or social

nature which will benefit the industry, including PhD studentships. The association also considers fees, maintenance costs and foreign students living and studying in the UK.

Annual grant total: Previously the association made grants totalling £88,000.

Applications: In writing to the correspondent. Applications (1- 2 pages) should include full details of the proposed research, background, relevant publications, costings and the names of two referees. Applications should be submitted by mid-April for consideration in May.

Correspondent: Steven Delderfield, Research & Graduate Support Unit, Christie Building, University of Manchester, Oxford Road, Manchester M13 9PL (e-mail: steven.delderfield@ manchester.ac.uk; website: www.campus. manchester.ac.uk/researchoffice/finding/ cotton/)

Textiles

Coats Foundation Trust

Eligibility: University students living in the UK who are studying textile and thread-related subjects.

Types of grants: One-off grants according to need. Grants are made to college students, undergraduates and mature students for fees, books and equipment/ instruments. Schoolchildren may also receive grants for books and equipment/ instruments.

Annual grant total: In 2004/05 the trust had an income of £62,000 and its total expenditure was £60,000. Grants to 35 individuals totalled £48,000.

Applications: In writing to the correspondent enclosing a cv, an sae, details of circumstances (e.g. student status, name of college), the nature and amount of funding required and referee names and addresses. There is no formal application form. Only applicants enclosing an sae will receive a reply. Applications are considered four times a year.

Correspondent: Jenny Mcfarlane, Coats plc, Pension Office, Pacific House, 70 Wellington Street, Glasgow G2 6UB (0141 207 6821; Fax: 0141 207 6856; e-mail: jenny.mcfarlane@coats.com)

Other information: Grants are also made to organisations (£11,000 in 2004/05)

The Costume Society – see entry on page 75

Correspondent: Chairman of the Education Sub-committee, St Paul's House, 8 Warwick Lane, London EC4P

4BN (website: www.costumesociety.org.uk)

Henry Dixon's Foundation for Apprenticing – see entry on page 69

Correspondent: Charities Administrator, Drapers' Company, Drapers' Hall, London EC2N 2DQ (020 7588 5001; Fax: 020 7628 1988; website: www.thedrapers.co.uk)

The Weavers' Company Textile Education Fund

Eligibility: Students of weaving technology or design. Applications are invited from undergraduates who have completed at least one year of study and from postgraduate students. Applicants must be British subjects.

Types of grants: Scholarships of between £200 and £1,500.

Annual grant total: About £5,000 a year.

Applications: On a form which can be downloaded from the company's website. Applications must be supported by two references, one of which must be an academic reference, provided by a course tutor or head of department. The written references must be submitted with the application form.

A scholarship holder's report must be submitted at the end of the academic year for which the grant is awarded.

Correspondent: The Clerk, The Worshipful Company of Weavers, Saddlers' House, Gutter Lane, London EC2V 6BR

Other information: Grants are also made to educational establishments in the UK to encourage the quality of textile teaching. In addition, it offers a range of awards to those working within the industry.

Town and country planning

Royal Town Planning Institute

Eligibility: People under the age of 30 wishing to study town and country planning or some aspect of planning theory or practice.

Types of grants: The Royal Town Planning Institute Trust administers the George Pepler International Award. It is open to overseas candidates who wish to visit the UK, or anyone in the UK who wishes to visit an overseas country, in order to spend time (three to four weeks) studying some particular aspect of town and country planning. This award is made every two years. The award is not for basic support

for students or for postgraduate studies or those working for a doctorate. Such applications are unlikely to be successful.

Annual grant total: Each year one successful candidate is awarded £1,500 which is paid in two instalments.

Applications: Contact the correspondent for guidelines, an application form and a list of past award winners.

Correspondent: Judy Woollett, 41 Botolph Lane, London EC3R 8DL (020 7929 9473; Fax: 020 7929 8197; e-mail: judy.woollett@rtpi.org.uk)

LOCAL CHARITIES

This section lists local charities giving grants to individuals for educational purposes. The information in the entry applies only to educational grants and concentrates on what the charity actually does rather than on what its trust deed allows it to do. It does not give a complete picture of the charity's work.

All the charities listed have a grant-making potential of £500 a year for individuals; most are spending considerably more than this.

Regional classification

We have divided the UK into nine geographical areas, as numbered on the map overleaf. Scotland, Wales and England have been separated into areas or counties in a similar way to previous editions of this guide. Overleaf, we have included a list under each such area/county of the unitary and local authorities they include.

The Northern Ireland section has not been subdivided into smaller areas. Within the other sections, the trusts are ordered as follows.

Scotland:

- Firstly, the charities which apply to the whole of Scotland, or at least two areas in Scotland.

- Secondly, Scotland is sub-divided into five areas. The entries which apply to the whole area, or to at least two unitary authorities within, appear first.

- The rest of the charities in the area are listed in alphabetical order of unitary authority.

Wales:

- Firstly, the charities which apply to the whole of Wales, or at least two areas in Wales.

- Secondly, Wales is sub-divided into three areas. The entries which apply to the whole area, or to at least two unitary authorities within, appear first.

- The rest of the charities in the area are listed in alphabetical order of unitary authority.

England:

- Firstly, the charities which apply to the whole area, or at least two counties in the area.

- Secondly, each area is sub-divided into counties. The entries which apply to the whole county, or to at least two towns within it, appear first.

- The rest of the charities in the county are listed in alphabetical order of parish, town or city.

Please note, in the North East section, we have included a section called Teesside for this edition, incorporating Hartlepool and Stockton-on-Tees (which we previously listed under County Durham) and Middlesbrough and Redcar & Cleveland (which we listed as North Yorkshire).

London:

- Firstly, the charities which apply to the whole of Greater London, or to at least two boroughs.

- Secondly, London is sub-divided into the boroughs. The entries are listed in alphabetical order within each borough.

Please note, within each county/area section, the trusts are arranged alphabetically by the unitary or local authority which they benefit in Scotland and Wales, while in England they are listed by the city/town/parish.

To be sure of identifying every relevant local charity, look first at the entries under the heading for your:

- unitary authority for people in Scotland and Wales

- city/town/parish under the relevant regional chapter heading for people living in England

- borough for people living in London.

People in London should then go straight to the start of the London chapter, where trusts which give to individuals in more than one borough in London are listed.

Other individuals should look at the sections for trusts which give to more than one unitary authority/town before finally considering those trusts at the start of the chapter which make grants across different areas/counties in your country/region.

For example, if you live in Liverpool, firstly establish which region Merseyside is in by looking at the map on page 91. Then having established that Merseyside is in region 5, look at the list overleaf and see which page entries for Merseyside are on. Then look under the heading for Liverpool to see if there are any relevant charities. Next check the charities which apply to Merseyside generally. Finally, check under the heading for the North West generally.

Having found the trusts covering your area, please read carefully any other eligibility requirements. While some trusts can and do give for any need for people in their area of benefit, most have other criteria which potential applicants must meet.

1. NORTHERN IRELAND

Aisling Bursaries

Eligibility: Students over 18 in West Belfast going into full-time or part-time further or higher education or vocational training courses. Bursaries are not available for people repeating all or part of a course unless it is due to medical or personal reasons.

Types of grants: One-off and recurrent grants of up to £1,000 each. The trust also administers bursaries sponsored by local businesses.

Annual grant total: In 2005 grants were made totalling £42,000. The amount given each year depends on the number of sponsors.

Applications: In writing to the correspondent. Deadlines are advertised in the Andersonstown News, usually in March for consideration in June/July. Grants are only awarded once per individual, although previous applicants not supported may reapply.

Correspondent: West Belfast Partnership Board, 218–226 Falls Road, Belfast BT12 6FB

Bank of Ireland Millennium Scholars Trust

Eligibility: People aged 16 or over who have been resident in Ireland or Northern Ireland for at least one year prior to the date of their application, or who can demonstrate a real and substantial connection with the region, and who, because of economic circumstances or other barriers such as disability, are prevented or held back from reaching their full potential.

Applicants should be: students in their final year of secondary education, mature students or other candidates preparing to enter higher education; students in higher education who would be unlikely to continue their courses without financial support; or people with exceptional ability in the creative/performing arts who face obstacles to fulfilling their potential through advanced study or training.

Types of grants: Scholarships of up to €6,300 a year towards living expenses. Total scholarships to one individual over a number of years can not exceed €38,000.

Annual grant total: 50-60 scholarships are given each year.

Applications: Applications must be made through one of the trust's nominating bodies, which are Irish organisations and groups approved by the trust to support potential applicants. A full list of these nominating bodies are available on the trust's website. Applications should then be made on a form available with guidelines from the correspondent, to be returned with an appropriate reference. Suitable applicants will be interviewed.

Correspondent: Bank of Ireland Millennium Scholars Trust Office, National College of Ireland, Mayor Street, Dublin 1 (00 3531 449 8500; Fax: 00 3531 497 2200; e-mail: boischolars@ncirl.ie; website: www. boi.ie)

Other information: This trust was established to award 60 scholarships annually for the first 10 years of the 21st century.

The Belfast Association for the Blind

Eligibility: People in Northern Ireland who are registered blind.

Types of grants: Grants for educational needs such as computers, course fees and so on. Grants are also given for welfare purposes, for holidays, house repairs and visual aids

Annual grant total: In 2005 the trust had assets of over £1 million and an income of £66,000. There were 95 grants to individuals made totalling £20,000.

Applications: In writing to the correspondent, through a social worker or from the secretary of an organisation. Applications are considered throughout the year.

Correspondent: R Gillespie, Hon. Secretary, 30 Glenwell Crescent, Newtownabbey, County Antrim BT36 7TF (028 9083 6407)

Other information: Grants are also made to organisations (£43,000 in 2005).

Educational Trust

Eligibility: Ex-prisoners, ex-offenders and their immediate relatives from Ireland who are seeking access to education and/or

training and for whom no other sources of funding are available.

Types of grants: One-off and recurrent grants towards degrees, postgraduate qualifications, NVQs and HGV driving licences.

Exclusions: No grants are made towards computer hardware, capital equipment or setting-up costs of small business initiatives.

Annual grant total: About £1,000 is given in grants each year.

Applications: On a form available from the correspondent. They are considered every four to six weeks.

Correspondent: The Administrator, c/o NIACRO, 4 Amelia Street, Belfast BT2 7GS (028 9032 0157; e-mail: edtrust@niacro.co. uk)

EMMS International

Eligibility: Medical, nursing, dental and paramedical students at universities in Scotland, Northern Ireland or the third world who are undertaking a placement abroad for their elective period, usually in mission hospitals in developing countries. Applicants should normally be in the later stages of the course of study so that the benefits are maximised.

Types of grants: Bursaries of £100 to £250.

Exclusions: Students studying at universities in England and Wales are not eligible.

Annual grant total: In 2005 the trust had assets of £2.8 million and an income of £1.2 million. Total expenditure was £1.1 million, including £5,100 given in about 26 grants to students.

Applications: On a form available from the correspondent, including an active Christian testimony. Applications are considered every month.

Correspondent: Robin G K Arnott, Chief Executive, 7 Washington Lane, Edinburgh EH11 2HA (0131 313 3828; Fax: 0131 313 4662; e-mail: info@emms. org; website: www.emms.org)

The Presbyterian Orphan and Children's Society

Eligibility: Children aged 23 or under who are in full or part-time education, living in Northern Ireland and Republic of Ireland, usually in single parent families. One parent must be a Presbyterian.

Types of grants: One-off and recurrent grants according to need. For recurrent grants a scale is used for the total given to a family each year, in quarterly payments with Christmas and summer bonuses. In 2004 these levels were £650 for a one-parent family with one child and £840 for a one-parent family with two children, for example.

Annual grant total: About £400,000.

Applications: Applications are made by Presbyterian clergy; forms are available from the correspondent. They are considered in March/April and September/October. As recurrent grants are means tested, applications should be submitted with details of the applicant's income and expenditure.

Correspondent: Dr Paul Gray, Glengall Exchange, 3 Glengall Street, Belfast, BT12 5AB (028 9032 3737)

The Royal Ulster Constabulary Benevolent Fund

Eligibility: Members and ex-members of the Royal Ulster Constabulary and their dependants who are in need.

Types of grants: Support is given to schoolchildren, college students, undergraduates, mature students, people with special educational needs and overseas students towards uniforms, fees, study/travel overseas, books and equipment.

Annual grant total: About £800,000.

Applications: In writing to the correspondent at any time. Applications must be submitted via a regional representative. Grants below £500 are considered throughout the year, while larger donations up to £10,000 are assessed monthly.

Correspondent: The Secretary, Police Federation for Northern Ireland, 77–79 Garnerville Road, Belfast BT4 2NX (028 9076 4200; Fax: 028 9076 1549; e-mail: benfund.pfni@btconnect.com; website: www.rucbenevolentfund.org)

The Society for the Orphans and Children of Ministers & Missionaries of the Presbyterian Church in Ireland

Eligibility: Children and young people aged under 26 who are orphaned and whose parents were ministers, missionaries or deaconesses of the Presbyterian Church in Ireland.

Types of grants: One-off grants of £300 to £2,000 for general educational purposes.

Annual grant total: Grants to individuals for educational and welfare purposes total about £30,000.

Applications: On a form available from the correspondent. Applications should be submitted directly by the individual in March for consideration in April.

Correspondent: Paul Gray, Glengall Exchange, 3 Glengall Street, Belfast, BT12 5AB (028 9032 3737)

Other information: The trust also gives welfare grants to the children of deceased ministers, missionaries and deaconesses.

The Sydney Stewart Memorial Trust

Eligibility: People in Northern Ireland who are involved in voluntary work.

Types of grants: One-off grants of between £100 and £250 to individuals interested in volunteering in projects in developing countries for at least one month. Preference is given to people going to the Indian sub-continent.

Annual grant total: In 2004/05 the trust had assets of £110,000 and an income of £8,000. Total expenditure was £6,900, with 16 individuals receiving £1,400.

Applications: On a form available from the correspondent.

Correspondent: The Correspondent, Sydney Stewart Memorial Trust, VSB, 34 Shaftesbury Square, Belfast BT2 7DB

Other information: This trust also gives grants to organisations.

The Victoria Homes Trust

Eligibility: Young people under 21 who live in Northern Ireland. The trust prefers to fund groups or organisations for a specific project involving young people under 21 years old, rather than funding individual young people.

Types of grants: One-off and recurrent grants of £200 to £2,500 to help with problems associated with homelessness, alcohol and drug abuse and towards the cost of counselling for young people. Grants are occasionally made for educational purposes.

Annual grant total: In 2004/05 the trust had assets of £1 million and an income of £50,000. Grants totalled £40,000.

Applications: On a form available from the correspondent. Applications should be submitted through a social worker, Citizens Advice or other welfare agency. They are considered twice a year.

Correspondent: Derek H Catney, Secretary, 2 Tudor Court, Rochester Road, Belfast BT6 9LB (028 9079 4306; e-mail: derek.catney1@btinternet.com)

2. SCOTLAND

The Arrol Trust

Eligibility: Young people aged 16 to 25.

Types of grants: Grants are given to people wishing to broaden their horizons through travel in the UK or overseas, for gap year projects and so on.

Exclusions: No grants are made for course fees or other educational expenses.

Annual grant total: The trust has an annual income of about £3,000, all of which is available in grants.

Applications: Application forms may be obtained from the correspondent and must be supported by a reference from the applicant's teacher or employer. Applicants must be willing to attend an interview with the trustees and be willing to report back on the completion of their trip.

Correspondent: C S Kennedy, Lindsays, Caledonian Exchange, 19a Canning Street, Edinburgh, EH3 8HE (0131 229 1212)

The June Baker Trust

Eligibility: Individuals working in the conservation of historic and artistic artefacts in Scotland, or those training to do so.

Types of grants: Awards of £200 to £500 each will be available for travel, training, fees, purchase of equipment, short courses and other suitable projects to students, mature and vocational students and people starting work.

Exclusions: Fees for long, full-time courses are not given.

Annual grant total: The trust has an annual income of £1,000, all of which is usually given in four educational grants.

Applications: On a form available from the correspondent. Applicants may have to attend an interview. A cv and two referees should also be provided. Applications are considered in June, and should be submitted directly by the individual.

Correspondent: Mrs Priscilla Ramsey, Goose Croft House, Kintore, Aberdeenshire AB51 0US (01467 632337; e-mail: ramseyph@tiscali.co.uk)

The Black Watch Association

Eligibility: Serving and retired Black Watch soldiers, their wives, widows and children.

Types of grants: One-off grants in the range of £250 and £500. Grants can be made to schoolchildren, people starting work and students in further/higher education for equipment/instruments, fees, books and maintenance/living expenses.

Exclusions: No grants towards council tax arrears, loans or large debts.

Annual grant total: Varies, up to £10,000.

Applications: On an application form to be completed by a caseworker from SSAFA Forces Help (19 Queen Elizabeth Street, London SE1 2LP. Tel: 020 7403 8783; Fax: 020 7403 8815; website: www.ssafa.org.uk). Applications are considered on a monthly basis.

Correspondent: Maj. A R McKinnell, Balhousie Castle, Hay Street, Perth PH1 5HR (01738 623214; Fax: 01738 643245)

The Buchanan Society

Eligibility: People with any of the following surnames: Buchanan, McAuslan (any spelling), McWattie or Risk.

Types of grants: Bursaries for students in severe financial difficulties of about £1,000. One-off grants can also be given for general educational purposes.

Annual grant total: About 70 people are supported each year. In 2004 the society had an income of £41,000.

Applications: On a form available from the correspondent, to be submitted either directly by the individual or a family member, or through a third party such as a social worker or teacher. Applications are considered throughout the year.

Correspondent: Mrs Fiona Risk, Secretary, 18 Iddesleigh Avenue, Milngavie, Glasgow G62 8NT (0141 956 1939; Fax: 0141 956 1939)

Other information: The Buchanan Society is the oldest Clan Society in Scotland having been founded in 1725. Grantmaking is its sole function.

The Carnegie Trust for the Universities of Scotland

Eligibility: For fee assistance: undergraduates taking a first degree at, a Scottish university who were born in Scotland, or had a parent born in Scotland, or have had at least two years of secondary education in Scotland.

For grants: graduates and members of staff of any age at a Scottish university.

For scholarships: graduates of any age of a Scottish university with a first-class honours degree.

Types of grants: Fee assistance: help with tuition fees for a first degree course at a Scottish university.

Grants: given mainly for personal research in most fields covered by the university curriculum, and towards the travel and accommodation costs that this incurs.

Scholarships: maintenance grants, tuition fees and some other costs while undertaking three years postgraduate research at a university within the UK (normally Scotland).

Annual grant total: In 2004/05 the trust had assets of £58 million generating an income of £2 million. Overall, £1.8 million was given in grants.

Applications: Directly by the individual, on a form available from the correspondent or the website. A preliminary telephone call may be helpful.

Applications are considered as follows:

Fee assistance: from 1 April to 30 September for the following session; applications received after 1 October will not be considered.

Grants: closing dates for applications are 15 January, 15 May and 15 October.

Scholarships: 15 March for the following session.

Correspondent: The Secretary, Cameron House, Abbey Park Place, Dunfermline, Fife KY12 7PZ (01383 622148; Fax: 01383 622149; e-mail: jgray@carnegie-trust.org; website: www.carnegie-trust.org)

Other information: This trust is one of the major grant-giving foundations in the UK.

Churchill University Scholarships Trust for Scotland

Eligibility: Students in Scotland.

Types of grants: Grants are given for one-off educational projects of benefit to the community, for example, medical electives or voluntary work overseas in a student's gap year or holiday.

Exclusions: Grants are not made for any other educational needs, such as course fees, books or living expenses.

Annual grant total: £10,000

Applications: In writing to the correspondent.

Correspondent: Kenneth MacRae, McLeish Carswell, 29 St Vincent Place, Glasgow G1 2DT (0141 248 4134)

The James Clark Bequest Fund

Eligibility: Members (including student members) of the Educational Institute of Scotland.

Types of grants: One-off cash grants up to a maximum of £500 each. Between one and four grants are made a year.

Annual grant total: In 2004/05 the charity had assets of £58,000 and an income of £2,000. One grant of £500 was distributed.

Applications: On a form available from the correspondent to be submitted directly by the individual or a family member. Applications are considered five times a year.

Correspondent: The General Secretary, Educational Institute of Scotland, 46 Moray Place, Edinburgh EH3 6BH (0131 225 6244; Fax: 0131 220 3151; e-mail: sharris@eis.org.uk; website: www.eis.org.uk)

The Cross Trust

Eligibility: Young people aged 16 to 35 who are of Scottish birth or parentage.

Types of grants: Grants of £150 to £1,500 for university or college costs (some courses are subject to restrictions), grants for travel and study abroad in respect of approved projects, and support for vacation projects and study visits. The trustees will consider proposals from university students for study at an overseas institution. Attendance at conferences, symposia and extra-curricular courses can be considered. Voluntary work performed through a recognised charity, such as gap year activities, can also be funded.

Annual grant total: In 2005, the trust had an income of £164,000. Previously the trust gave grants totalling £166,000, of which 80% went to individuals and 20% to organisations.

Applications: On a form available from the correspondent with guidelines.

Correspondent: Mrs Dorothy Shaw, Assistant Secretary, 25 South Methven Street, Perth PH1 5ES (01738 620451; Fax: 01738 631155)

Allan Currie Memorial Trust

Eligibility: Young business people with a preference for those living in Glasgow, although people living in other parts of Scotland will be considered.

Types of grants: One-off and recurrent grants for business training.

Annual grant total: The trust has an income of around £1,500. Grants totalled about £1,000.

Applications: In writing to the correspondent.

Correspondent: W Cairns, Messrs Cairns Brown Solicitors, 112 Main Street, Alexandria, Glasgow G83 0NZ (01389 756979; Fax: 01389 754281; e-mail: b.cairns@cairnsbrown.co.uk)

ECAS – Challenger Children's Fund

Eligibility: Children under 18 who live in Scotland and are physically disabled. The fund aims to help by meeting expenses caused by the child's disability or which has a direct bearing on the child's welfare.

Types of grants: One-off grants for maintenance, education, clothing and general welfare, typically about £200, however larger amounts may be considered.

Exclusions: The following disabilities alone are not eligible: learning difficulties, developmental delay, Down's Syndrome, cystic fibrosis, autism and visual or hearing impairment.

No grants to pay for items which have already been bought, or to repay loans.

Annual grant total: In 2004 grants totalled £32,000 and were given towards both educational and welfare purposes.

Applications: On a form available from the correspondent with parental income and expenditure and a GP's report. Applications are normally received from the parent/guardian of the child through a social worker, health visitor or other professional who is currently aware of the child's needs. Applications are limited to one per person per year and the trust cannot give regular help to any family. They are considered monthly.

Correspondent: Wendy Dunn, Barstow Miller, Midlothian Innovation Centre, Pentlandfield, Roslin, Midlothian, EH25 9RE (0131 440 9030)

Other information: In 2004 the fund made a grant of £10,000 to the Jubilee Sailing Trust to meet the cost of a crew of six disabled children and three buddies travelling aboard The Lord Nelson taking part in the European leg of the Tall Ships Race.

EMMS International *see entry on page 93*

Correspondent: Robin G K Arnott, Chief Executive, 7 Washington Lane, Edinburgh EH11 2HA (0131 313 3828; Fax: 0131 313 4662; e-mail: info@emms.org; website: www.emms.org)

The Esdaile Trust

Eligibility: Ministers of the Church of Scotland or Deaconesses of the Church of Scotland who are widows and missionaries appointed or nominated by the Overseas Council of the Church of Scotland with daughters at secondary school and university.

Types of grants: Annual grants towards the cost of education.

Annual grant total: Grants are made totalling around £20,000 each year.

Applications: In writing to the correspondent.

Correspondent: R Graeme Thom, 17 Melville Street, Edinburgh EH3 7PH (e-mail: graeme.thom@scott-moncrieff.com)

The Ferguson Bequest

Eligibility: Ministers, or people intending to become ministers, who live in south west Scotland.

Types of grants: Scholarships are given.

Annual grant total: In 2004 the trust had assets of £3.5 million and an income of £166,000. Grants made during the year totalled £144,000. Previously only a small proportion of this has been given to individuals.

Applications: On a form available by writing to the correspondent, to be considered at any time.

Correspondent: Ronald D Oakes, Secretary, 182 Bath Street, Glasgow G2 4HG

The Caroline Fitzmaurice Trust

Eligibility: Young women under the age of 23 who live in the diocese of St Andrews, Dunkeld and Dunblane. Broadly speaking, the diocese covers the whole of Perthshire and Fife, part of Stirlingshire and a small part of Angus, including Forfar and the towns to the west of Forfar, but excluding Dundee.

The trust states that applicants must show both financial need and evidence of, or the promise of, excellence.

Types of grants: Grants of between £200 and £5,000 are given if there is a specific need. The trust aims 'to assist applicants who show promise of future excellence in their educational, cultural or social fields; applicants are expected to show the intention, in their turn, to contribute to the community wherever they may settle;

and are endeavouring to raise funds through their own personal efforts'.

Annual grant total: In 2004/05 payments to three individuals totalled £2,300.

Applications: On a form available from the correspondent. Written references and details of parents' financial situation are required. The trustees meet once a year. The closing date for full, complete applications (including referees' reports and reports on parents' means) is 30 April.

Correspondent: The Secretaries, Pagan Osborne Solicitors, 12 St Catherine Street, Cupar, Fife KY15 4HN (01334 653777; Fax: 01334 655063; e-mail: enquiries@pagan.co.uk)

James Gillan's Trust

Eligibility: People training for the ordained ministry in the Church of Scotland who have lived in, or whose parents have lived in, Moray or Nairn for at least three years. There is a preference for those native to the parishes of Forres and Dyke, Kinloss, Rafford, Edinkillie and Dallas.

Types of grants: Grants of up to £1,000.

Annual grant total: About £2,000.

Applications: In writing to the correspondent.

Correspondent: Stewart Michael Murray, Solicitor, c/o R & R Urquhart, 121 High Street, Forres IV36 0AB (01309 672216)

The Glasgow Highland Society

Eligibility: Students who have a connection with the Highlands (for example, lived or went to school there) and who are now studying in Glasgow. Grants are normally given for first degrees only, unless postgraduate studies are a natural progression of the degree.

Types of grants: Grants of around £100 help with fees for people at college or university or who are in vocational training (including mature students). Grants may also be given for Gaelic research projects and apprenticeships.

Annual grant total: In 2005 the trust had assets of £128,000, generating an income of £6,600. Grants were given to 63 individuals and totalled £6,300.

Applications: On a form available from the correspondent or downloadable from the website. Applications should be submitted directly by the individual by 30 November and are considered in December.

Correspondent: The Secretaries, Alexander Sloan & Co, 144 West George Street, Glasgow G2 2HG (0141 354 0354; Fax: 0141 354 0355; e-mail: kt@alexandersloan.co.uk; website: www.alexandersloan.co.uk/ghs)

The Glasgow Society of the Sons of Ministers of the Church of Scotland

Eligibility: Children of ministers of the Church of Scotland who are in need, particularly students and the children of deceased ministers.

Types of grants: One-off and recurrent grants according to need.

Annual grant total: About £40,000 a year is given in educational and welfare grants to individuals.

Applications: On a form available from the correspondent. Applications from students are considered in August.

Correspondent: R Graeme Thom, Secretary and Treasurer, Scott-Moncrieff, 17 Melville Street, Edinburgh EH3 7PH (0131 473 3500; Fax: 0131 473 3535; e-mail: graeme.thom@scott-moncrieff.com)

The Grand Lodge of Antient, Free & Accepted Masons of Scotland

Eligibility: Children of members and deceased members.

Types of grants: Grants for people entering further education.

Annual grant total: About £155,000 is given in welfare grants each year and £25,000 in educational grants.

Applications: On a form available from the correspondent, or by direct approach to the local lodge. They are considered three times a year, although urgent requests can be dealt with between meetings.

Correspondent: D M Begg, Grand Secretary, Freemasons Hall, 96 George Street, Edinburgh EH2 3DH (0131 225 5304)

Other information: The trust also runs care homes for older people.

The Highlands & Islands Educational Trust

Eligibility: Applicants should be living in the counties of Argyll, Bute, Caithness, Inverness, Orkney, Ross and Cromarty, Sutherland or Shetland and be of the protestant faith. Applicants should be in the fifth or sixth form at school and about to leave on to university or other institution of further education. Preference is given to Gaelic speakers.

Types of grants: Grants of £120 to £160 a year are given to students about to study for a first degree at college/university, towards their university/college books and maintenance. Bursaries are awarded at the discretion of the governors on merit, based on the results of the 'Higher' grade examinations. In determining the award, parental means are taken into account.

Annual grant total: About £7,000.

Applications: In writing to the correspondent. Applications should be submitted through the individual's school between March and June inclusive and include: confirmation that the applicant is of the protestant faith; details of the occupation and gross income of parent/guardian; ability at Gaelic, if any; university/college course to be undertaken; and intended career of the applicant. Decisions are made in September.

Correspondent: The Trustees, c/o Tods Murray LLP, Edinburgh Quay, 133 Fountainbridge, Edinburgh, EH3 9AG

Jewish Care Scotland

Eligibility: Schoolchildren, people starting work and students in further or higher education, including mature students, who are Jewish and live in Scotland.

Types of grants: One-off grants are given towards uniforms, other school clothing, equipment, instruments, fees, maintenance and living expenses. There is a preference for schoolchildren with serious family difficulties so that the child has to be educated away from home.

Exclusions: No grants are given to postgraduates.

Annual grant total: This charity has an annual income of around £500,000. Educational grants to individuals usually total around £18,000.

Applications: In May 2006 the charity stated that it was not accepting applications for the foreseeable future.

Correspondent: Ethne Woldman, May Terrace, Giffnock, Glasgow G46 6LD (website: www.jcarescot.org.uk)

Other information: The board also helps with friendship clubs, housing requirements, clothing, meals-on-wheels, counselling and so on.

The Lethendy Trust

Eligibility: Young people in need who live in Scotland, with a preference for Tayside.

Types of grants: One-off and recurrent grants of £50 to £350 towards educational and development activities.

Annual grant total: In 2005, the trust had assets of £1.4 million and an income of £40,000. Grants were made to five organisations and 36 individuals totalling £37,500.

Applications: In writing to the correspondent. The trustees usually meet to consider grants in July.

Correspondent: George Hay, Henderson Loggie, Chartered Accountants, Royal Exchange, Panmure Street, Dundee DD1 1DZ (01382 200055; Fax: 01382 2212410; e-mail: ghay@hendersonloggie.co.uk)

The Dr Thomas Lyon Bequest

Eligibility: Scottish orphans, aged 5 to 18, of members of Her Majesty's Forces and those of the Mercantile Marine, who are in need.

Types of grants: Grants are given towards primary and secondary education for school uniforms, other school clothing, books, educational outings and school fees. They range from £500 to £1,000.

Annual grant total: In 2004/05, the charity had an income of £7,900. Grants totalled £2,000.

Applications: In writing to the correspondent. Applicants must state their total income, the regiment/service of their parent and the cause and date of their death.

Correspondent: The Secretary, The Merchant Company, The Merchants' Hall, 22 Hanover Street, Edinburgh EH2 2EP (0131 225 7202)

The Catherine Mackichan Trust

Eligibility: People who are researching various aspects of Scottish history, including archaeology, genealogy and language studies.

Types of grants: Grants of up to £500 are given to: schoolchildren for books and educational outings; and students in further or higher education, including mature and overseas students, towards books, living expenses and study or travel overseas.

Exclusions: No grants are given to people whose education or research should be funded by statutory sources.

Annual grant total: In 2005/06 the trust made grants totalling £1,500 to five individuals.

Applications: On a form available from: The Landsdowne Clinic, 25 Landsdowne Terrace, Gosforth, Newcastle upon Tyne, NE3 1HP. Applications should arrive by 15 April for consideration in April/May.

Correspondent: The Administrator, 21 Cowan Road, Edinburgh EH11 1RL

Other information: Grants are also given to schools and local history societies for local history and archaeological purposes

The Mathew Trust

Eligibility: Adults in need who live in the local government areas of the City of Dundee, Angus, Perth and Kinross and Fife.

Types of grants: One-off grants for study/travel abroad are given to college students, undergraduates, vocational students, mature students, people starting work, overseas students and people with special educational needs.

Annual grant total: In 2004/05 the trust had assets of £5.8 million and an income of £181,000. Grants to 22 individuals totalled £8,800. Grants to organisations totalled £63,000.

Applications: In writing to the correspondent. Applications can be submitted directly by the individual for consideration every two months.

Correspondent: Mrs Fiona Bullions, Henderson Loggie, Chartered Accountants, Royal Exchange, Panmure Street, Dundee DD1 1DZ

Other information: Grants are also made to organisations (£63,000 in 2004/05).

The McGlashan Charitable Trust

Eligibility: Students of music, other arts studies, medicine, veterinary science, architecture, law, together with science and technology, aged 16 to 30 who were born in, or are studying or working in, Scotland.

Types of grants: One-off and recurrent grants in the range of £250 and £1,000 are given to people in further or higher education, including mature, vocational and overseas students and undergraduates, towards fees, books, equipment, instruments and living expenses.

Exclusions: No grants are given towards sports.

Annual grant total: Previously, the trust had a total expenditure of £44,000, of which £36,000 was given in 58 grants to individuals and £7,500 to organisations.

Applications: Initially, in writing to the correspondent directly by the individual. Initial applications must be comprehensive enough for trustees to decide on issuing a formal application form or not. Applications are considered at irregular times during the year.

Correspondent: The Administrator, PO Box 16057, Glasgow G12 9XX

James McMorran Bursary

Eligibility: Students of music who live in the Inverness, Nairn and Moray area.

Types of grants: The trust provides grants for schoolchildren and school leavers seeking a future in music for fees, instruments and maintenance. Grants range between £50 and £150.

Annual grant total: Grants are made to individuals totalling about £1,000.

Applications: In writing to the trust at the following address: The Minister, Nairn Parish Church, The Manse, Manse Road, Nairn, Highland. Adverts are placed in the local papers when applications are being considered, although they should usually arrive by March, for consideration in April.

Correspondent: J B Rodger, Secretary & Treasurer, Westerwood, Marine Road, Nairn, Highland IV12 4EA (01667 451998)

The Muirhead Trust

Eligibility: Female students in Scotland.

Types of grants: Grants for those studying to become doctors or dentists. Grants are primarily given to students who are studying medicine after obtaining a first degree in another subject. These grants are for two years, after which the student is eligible for a statutory grant for the further three years.

Annual grant total: In 2005, the trust had an income of £7,000. No further information was available.

Applications: On a form available from the correspondent. Applications should arrive in September for consideration in October.

Correspondent: Clerk to the Trust, 24 St Enoch Square, Glasgow G1 4DB (0141 226 3000)

North of Scotland Quaker Trust

Eligibility: Children of people who are associated with the Religious Society of Friends in the North of Scotland Monthly Meeting area.

Types of grants: Grants are given to schoolchildren and to people studying in further or higher education for books, equipment, instruments and educational outings.

Exclusions: No grants are given to people studying above first degree level.

Annual grant total: About £10,000 for educational and welfare purposes.

Applications: In January 2004 the trust stated that due to maintenance and building costs the trust will be unable to make any substantial grants over the next four years. The level of grant-making is therefore likely to be significantly reduced.

Correspondent: Michael Baker, Clerk, 2 Thornton Place, Watson Street, Banchory, Aberdeenshire, AB31 5UU

Other information: This trust was previously known as The Aberdeen Two Months' Meeting Trust.

The Royal Air Force Benevolent Fund (Scottish Branch)

Eligibility: Ex-RAF people (and their direct dependants) in Scotland who are in need or financial distress.

Types of grants: The type of grant is determined by the need of the eligible applicant and may consist of a one-off grant, small regular allowance, or loan.

Annual grant total: About £320,000 in educational grants.

Applications: In writing to the correspondent. Applications can be made at any time, submitted either directly by the individual or through RAFA, SSAFA, war pensions or a social worker. Confirmation of RAF service, or sufficient details to allow a search of RAF service records, should be included.

Correspondent: The Director, 20 Queen Street, Edinburgh EH2 1JX (0131 225 6421)

Other information: Applications from serving RAF people and those involving sums over £7,500 (rare) are handled by the London HQ of the RAF Benevolent Fund, 67 Portland Place W1N 4AR (see separate entry).

The fund also gives to organisations (2003: £5.2 million) and operates a residential nursing home on Deeside.

The Royal Incorporation of Architects in Scotland

Eligibility: Architects and students of architecture.

Types of grants: Student prizes and other awards open to architects. Some funds are open to members of the RIAS generally.

Annual grant total: In 2005 the charity had a gross income of £1.4 million. The RIAS Millennium Awards closed in June 2004 with final grants totalling about £200,000 paid during the year; no grants are being made until the charity's reserves are built up.

Applications: In writing to the correspondent. Applications for awards and prizes are considered in November to February.

Correspondent: Mary Wren, Chief Executive, 15 Rutland Square, Edinburgh EH1 2BE (0131 229 7205; website: www. rias.org.uk)

Other information: Awards are given for particular achievements in some aspect of study, not for general academic or subsistence support.

The Royal Scottish Corporation (also known as The Scottish Hospital of the Foundation of King Charles II)

Eligibility: Scottish people, their children and widows, who are in need and live within a 35-mile radius of Charing Cross.

Types of grants: This welfare charity gives training grants to enable people to secure qualifications with a view to gaining employment. Support is also given to students on low incomes or from deprived backgrounds.

Annual grant total: In 2004/05 the trust had assets of £33 million and an income of £1.7 million. Student and training grants of up to £1,500 each were made to 42 individuals.

Applications: On a form available from the trust; upon receiving the completed form, which should include copies of the birth/wedding certificates, the corporation decides whether to submit the application for consideration at the trustees' monthly meeting. They may also decide to visit or ask the applicant to visit the corporation's office to discuss their case.

Correspondent: Willie Docherty, Chief Executive, 37 King Street, Covent Garden, London WC2E 8JS (020 7240 3718 (UK helpline 0800 652 2989); Fax: 020 7497 0184; e-mail: enquiry@ royalscottishcorporation.org.uk; website: www.royalscottishcorporation. org.uk)

SACRO Trust *see entry on page 39*

Correspondent: Trust Fund Administrator, 1 Broughton Market, Edinburgh EH3 6NU (0131 624 7258; Fax: 0131 624 7269; website: www.sacro. org.uk)

Scottish Arts Council – Professional Development Fund

Eligibility: People working at professional level in the arts in Scotland. Volunteers aged over 16 may also apply.

Types of grants: Grants of £75 to £2,000 are given of up to 75% of the total amount needed (people working in the industry are expected to receive a contribution from their employer). Grants can be towards short-term or one-off training courses, conference fees, masterclasses, mentoring and other experiences which will improve the individual's creative, technical or professional skills, such as travel to see work, undertaking research or establishing contacts. Eligible costs include travel in the UK or overseas, accommodation, subsistence, childcare and course or entrance fees.

Exclusions: No grants can be given towards activities which have already started, or which will not begin before the end of the following March. No grants are issued to those in higher education.

Annual grant total: About £300,000 is available each year.

Applications: On a form available from the correspondent, or downloadable from the website. Applications can be submitted either directly by the individual or by the organisation they work for. Applicants are usually made aware of the decision 15 working days after the receipt of the form. A percentage of applicants are asked to report back on how their grant was used.

Correspondent: Carol Ashworth, Grants Administration Department, Scottish Arts Council, 12 Manor Place, Edinburgh EH3 7DD (0845 603 6000/ 0131 226 6051; e-mail: help.desk@scottisharts.org.uk; website: www.scottisharts.org.uk)

The Scottish Chartered Accountants' Benevolent Association

Eligibility: The dependents of members of the Institute of Chartered Accountants of Scotland who are at school, college, university and are in financial need.

Types of grants: One-off grants towards fees, maintenance and living expenses.

Annual grant total: About £120,000 a year for educational and welfare purposes.

Applications: On a form available from the correspondent.

Correspondent: R Linton, Hon. Secretary, 53 Bothwell Street, Glasgow, G2 6TS

The Society for the Benefit of Sons & Daughters of the Clergy of the Church of Scotland

Eligibility: Ministers of the Church of Scotland with children at secondary school and university.

Types of grants: Annual grant towards the cost of education.

Annual grant total: £20,000.00

Applications: In writing to the correspondent.

Correspondent: R Graeme Thom, Secretary, 17 Melville Street, Edinburgh EH3 7PH (e-mail: graeme.thom@scott-moncrieff.com)

John Suttie Memorial Fund

Eligibility: People who live in Moray and Nairn, with preference for people under 30 who are starting on an agricultural or veterinary career.

Types of grants: Grants towards further or higher education.

Annual grant total: The fund has a total income of about £12,000 a year with grants totalling £500.

Applications: Information regarding awards is circulated annually to schools and through agricultural and veterinary organisations. Applications should be made in writing to the correspondent.

Correspondent: S M Murray, Solicitor, 117–121 High Street, Forres, Moray IV36 1AB (01309 672216; Fax: 01309 673161; e-mail: stewartmurray@r-r-urquhart.com)

John Watson Foundation Trust

Eligibility: One parent families in Scotland with children in secondary education.

Types of grants: One-off and recurrent grants, mainly towards school fees for three to four schoolchildren a year.

Annual grant total: About £6,000 a year.

Applications: In writing to the secretary: Mrs M M Gordon, Secretary, 28 Craigmount View, Edinburgh EH12 8BT. Please note the trust states that funds are fully committed. The trustees meet on a number of occasions throughout the year.

Correspondent: Dr I S M Smart, 13a Viewbank View, Bonnyrigg EH19 2HU

John Watson's Trust

Eligibility: Children or young people under the age of 21 who have a physical or learning disability or are socially disadvantaged and who live in Scotland. There is a preference for people who live in or are connected with the Lothian region.

Types of grants: Help in connection with special tuition, educational trips, computers for people with special educational needs, books, tools or expenses for further training and education, and equipment, travel and other activities contributing to education and advancement in life.

The trust also gives grants towards the cost of a boarding education for children normally resident in Scotland who are experiencing serious family difficulties and who would benefit from an education away from home.

Grants are one-off and range from £50 to £2,000, apart from boarding school grants which range from £300 to £1,000 a year and may be recurrent.

Exclusions: No grants for day school fees.

Annual grant total: In 2005 the trust had assets of £3.7 million, generating an income of £186,000. Grants to 115 individuals and 66 organisations totalled £131,000.

Applications: On a form available from the correspondent or from the trust's website. Applications can be submitted directly by the individual, or through a social worker, Citizens Advice, other welfare agency or through another third party on behalf of an individual. Applications must include full details and dates and locations of any trips being undertaken. They are considered in February, late March, June, August and October.

Correspondent: Ms I Wilson, Signet Library, Parliament Square, Edinburgh EH1 1RF (0131 220 1640; Fax: 0131 220 4016; e-mail: johnwatson@ onetel.com; website: www.johnwatsons. com)

Aberdeen & Perthshire

The Aberdeen Endowments Trust

Eligibility: Secondary schoolchildren who live in the former Grampian region, and adult students in Aberdeen.

Types of grants: Grants of up to £200 are available to children in secondary school in the former Grampian region according to need and academic performance, with most of the support given to pupils at Robert Gordon's College. Grants are also given towards adult education.

Annual grant total: In 2005 the trust had a gross income of £810,000. There was no grant total available.

Applications: On a form available from the correspondent. Applications are considered nine or ten times a year.

Correspondent: William Russell, Clerk, 19 Albert Street, Aberdeen AB25 1QF (01224 640194; Fax: 01224 643918)

Dr John Calder's Fund

Eligibility: People in need who live in the parish of Machar, or within the city of Aberdeen, including people only resident for their education and people from the area studying elsewhere.

Types of grants: Grants for educational needs.

Annual grant total: Around £2,000 is available for individuals. A further £8,000 is given in grants towards educational projects or organisations.

Applications: The trust stated in January 2006 that funds were fully committed and that this situation was likely to remain so for the medium to long term.

Correspondent: Clive Phillips, Paull & Williamsons, New Investment House, 214 Union Row, Aberdeen AB10 1QY

The Brian & Margaret Cooper Trust

Eligibility: Journalists under 30, born or working in Aberdeen, the north east and north of Scotland (the area north of Stonehaven), who may need assistance for the furthering of his/her education by way of travel or instruction. Support is also given to their dependants.

Types of grants: Usually one-off payments according to need. Maximum grant is normally in the region of £1,000.

Annual grant total: £1,000, mostly given in welfare grants.

Applications: In writing to the correspondent.

Correspondent: Alan J Innes, 100 Union Street, Aberdeen AB10 1QR (01224 428000)

The Anne Herd Educational Trust

Eligibility: Pupils at Merchiston Castle School, Harrogate College, High School of Dundee or other independent schools.

Types of grants: Payment of school fees when parents would not have otherwise been able to afford the full tuition fees.

Annual grant total: About £10,000.

Applications: Applicants should contact the schools named in 'eligibility', but more information can be obtained from the correspondent.

Correspondent: The Trustees, Messrs Bowman, 27 Bank Street, Dundee DD1 1RP

The Anne Herd Memorial Trust

Eligibility: People who are blind or partially sighted who live in Broughty Ferry (applicants from the city of Dundee, region of Tayside or those who have connections with these areas and reside in Scotland will also be considered).

Types of grants: Grants are usually given for educational equipment such as computers and books. Grants are usually at least £50.

Annual grant total: The trust gives approximately £25,000 a year in grants.

Applications: In writing to the correspondent, to be submitted directly by the individual in March/April for consideration in June.

Correspondent: The Trustees, Bowman Solicitors, 27 Bank Street, Dundee DD1 1RP (01382 322267; Fax: 01382 225000)

The Morgan Trust

Eligibility: Children of people who: (i) were born or educated in the former royal burghs of Dundee, Forfar, Arbroath and Montrose; or (ii) have been resident in one or more these burghs for five years immediately before applying for an award or immediately before his/her death.

Types of grants: One-off and recurrent grants of up to £200, usually for maintenance/living expenses. Grants are reviewed each year. In May 2002 the trustees decided to increase the minimum grant to £100 and to give larger grants to fewer people.

Exclusions: Grants are not given to people with an income of more than £10,000, unless there are exceptional circumstances.

Annual grant total: In 2005, the trust has an income of £12,000.

Applications: On a form available from the correspondent, for completion on behalf of the applicant with full details of their financial situation. Applications are usually considered at May and November meetings.

Correspondent: Michael R F Clark, Clerk & Factor, Miller Hendry, 13 Ward Road, Dundee DD1 1LU (01382 200000; Fax: 01382 200098; e-mail: mikeclark@ miller-hendry.co.uk)

The Gertrude Muriel Pattullo Advancement Award Scheme

Eligibility: Young people aged 16 to 25 who are physically disabled and live in the city of Dundee or the county of Angus.

Types of grants: One-off and recurrent grants of £100 to £500 to schoolchildren and students in further or higher education towards books, equipment, instruments, fees and educational outings in the UK.

Exclusions: No grants are given towards the repayment of debts.

Annual grant total: In 2004/05 the trust had assets of £122,000, an income of £4,300 and a total expenditure of £5,100. No grants were made to individuals during the year. Grants totalling £3,300 were made to organisations working with young people who are disabled.

Applications: On a form available from the correspondent at any time. Applications can be submitted directly by the individual or through any third party.

Correspondent: Mrs Beth Anderson, Help Unit, Blackadders Solicitors, 30–34 Reform Street, Dundee DD1 1RJ (01382 229222; Fax: 01382 342220; e-mail: beth.anderson@ blackadders.co.uk)

Aberdeen & Aberdeenshire

Aberdeenshire Educational Trust

Eligibility: Residents of, or schoolchildren or students whose parents reside in, the former county of Aberdeen.

Types of grants: Grants of between £10 and £200 are given as: postgraduate scholarships for research work or advanced study; supplementary bursaries to students at university, central institution or a college of education in cases of need; grants towards travel, fees, books or equipment for apprentices; grants to student apprentices at university or central institution; travel grants for educational purposes (including educational outings for primary school pupils); further education grants for courses not usually recognised by LEAs or further educational bursaries; special grants to people over 21 applying for university places; grants promoting education in arts, music and drama; and grants to help individuals to undertake educational experiments and research which will be for the educational benefit of people in the county.

Annual grant total: In 2004/05 the trust had an income of £76,000, of which £39,000 was given in grants to organisations and individuals.

Applications: On a form available from the correspondent, to be considered throughout the year.

Correspondent: St Leonards, Sandyhill Road, Banff AB45 1BH

Other information: Grants are also made to clubs, schools and other educational establishments.

Huntly Educational Trust 1997

Eligibility: People in the district of Huntly.

Types of grants: Grants are given for the education and training of individuals and average £200.

Annual grant total: Grants totalled £4,000.

Applications: In writing to the correspondent for consideration at a monthly meeting.

Correspondent: A B Mitchell, Stuart Wilson Dickson & Co, Huntly Business Centre, Huntly AB54 8ES (01466 792101)

Kincardineshire Educational Trust

Eligibility: People who live in Kincardine County, and schoolchildren and young people who either attend schools or further educational centres there or whose parents live there.

Types of grants: Grants of up to £200 are given to: schoolchildren towards books, equipment, instruments and educational outings; and people in further or higher education, including mature students and postgraduates, towards books, equipment, instruments, fees, living expenses, student exchanges and educational outings and trips in the UK and overseas.

Annual grant total: In 2004/05 the trust had an income of £4,000. Grants to individuals have previously totalled about £1,400.

Applications: On a form available from the correspondent, to be received by 30 November for consideration in March.

Correspondent: Amanda Watson, Aberdeenshire Finance, Trust Section, St Leonard's, Sandyhill Road, Banff, AB45 1BH

Other information: Grants are also made to clubs, schools and other educational establishments.

Angus

Angus Educational Trust

Eligibility: Students and mature students attending a university who live in Angus.

Types of grants: Grants are given to supplement existing grants. Household income is taken into account in determining whether or not a grant is awarded.

Annual grant total: In 2004/05 the trust had an income of £22,000. No further information was available.

Applications: On a form available from the correspondent. The governors meet twice a year in April and September to consider applications.

Correspondent: The Clerk, Education Offices, County Buildings, Forfar, Angus DD8 3WE (01307 473212)

The David Barnet Christie Trust

Eligibility: Men or women aged up to 40, preferably living in or originating from the Arbroath area (or failing this Angus), who are about to enter into an engineering apprenticeship, have already taken up such or similar training, or wish to progress by taking further engineering qualifications.

Types of grants: One-off grants to people starting work or students in further or higher education, including mature students and postgraduates, towards books, study or travel abroad, equipment, instruments, maintenance and living expenses.

Annual grant total: In 2004/05 the trust had assets of £43,000 and an income of £2,500. Grants were made to three individuals totalling £800.

Applications: On a form available from the correspondent. Applications should be submitted directly by the individual by the end of September each year.

Correspondent: Graham McNicol, Thorntons WS, Brothockbank House, Arbroath DD11 1NF (01241 872683; Fax: 01241 871541)

The Duncan Trust

Eligibility: Candidates for the Ministry of the Church of Scotland, especially those who have a connection with the former Presbytery of Arbroath.

Types of grants: Cash grants to student applicants studying for their first degree.

Exclusions: Postgraduate studies.

Annual grant total: About £5,000.

Applications: In writing to the correspondent to request an application form, to be returned by 31 October each year.

Correspondent: G J M Dunlop, Solicitor, Thorntons Solicitors, Brothockbank House, Arbroath, Angus DD11 1NE (01241 872683)

Dundee Masonic Temple Trust

Eligibility: Children of Freemasons who are, or who were immediately prior to death, members of Lodges in Angus.

Types of grants: Recurrent grants of £200 to £500 to students in further or higher education, including mature students, for living expenses.

Annual grant total: Previously about £1,600.

Applications: On a form available from the correspondent. Forms should be returned directly by the individual in October for consideration in November/December.

Correspondent: The Trustees, 2 India Buildings, 86 Bell Street, Dundee DD1 1JQ

Dundee

City of Dundee Educational Trust

Eligibility: Students in further or higher education who have a strong connection with Dundee. Priority is given to students who do not receive a mandatory award.

Types of grants: Grants of around £300 each.

Annual grant total: About £12,000.

Applications: On a form available from the correspondent, to be accompanied by a full cv. Applications should be submitted at least two weeks before the quarterly meetings in March, June, September and December.

Correspondent: J Hope, Miller Hendry, 13 Ward Road, Dundee DD1 1LU (01382 200000)

The Polack Travelling Scholarship Fund

Eligibility: People over 17 attending an educational institution within Dundee or the surrounding area.

Types of grants: To enable attendance on courses or conferences abroad to study foreign languages, international law, management studies or aspects of company and commercial education. Grants are one off and range from £250 to £400.

Annual grant total: In 2005, the fund had an income of £1,500. Previously, the fund had assets of £28,000 and grants were made to four individuals totalling £1,200.

Applications: In writing to the correspondent directly by the individual. Applications are to be submitted by 30 April for consideration in May.

Correspondent: Ian R Johnston, Henderson Loggie, Royal Exchange, Dundee DD1 1DZ (01382 200055; Fax: 01382 200764; e-mail: irj@hendersonloggie.co.uk)

Moray

The Banffshire Educational Trust

Eligibility: Residents of the former county of Banffshire, people who attend schools or further education centres in the former county, and school pupils whose parents live in the former county of Banffshire. Grants are means tested to those earning £25,000 a year or less.

Types of grants: One-off grants of between £15 and £200 are given towards postgraduate scholarships, higher education bursaries, mature students, apprentices and trainees, travel scholarships for people studying outside

Scotland, and travel and educational excursions for schoolchildren and people in adult education.

Annual grant total: In 2005/06 the trust had assets of £385,000 and an income of £15,900. Grants were made totalling £8,700 to 50 individuals.

Applications: On a form available from the correspondent which should be submitted by 30 September for consideration in November/December.

Correspondent: Jean-Anne Goodbrand, Administrative Officer, Educational Services, Moray Council Headquarters, High Street, Elgin, Moray IV30 1LL (01343 563151; Fax: 01343 563478; e-mail: jeananne.goodbrand@moray.gov.uk; website: www.moray.gov.uk)

The Dick Bequest

Eligibility: Teachers within local authority schools in the former county of Morayshire.

Types of grants: Grants are given for training purposes.

Annual grant total: No information was available.

Applications: On a form available from: Mrs Susan Masterton, Clerk to the Governors, 15 Young Street, Edinburgh EH2 4HU. Applications should be made by 30 April for consideration in May.

Correspondent: Jean-Anne Goodbrand, Administrative Officer, Educational Services, Moray Council Headquarters, High Street, Elgin, Moray IV30 1LL (01343 563151; Fax: 01343 563478; e-mail: jeananne.goodbrand@moray.gov.uk; website: www.moray.gov.uk)

Moray and Nairn Educational Trust

Eligibility: People who have lived in the former counties of Moray and Nairn for at least five years. No grants are given to people whose household earnings are over £20,000 a year, less £800 for each dependent child.

Types of grants: One-off grants, ranging from £50 to £200, are available to schoolchildren for educational outings in the UK and study or travel abroad and to students in further or higher education, including mature students and postgraduates, for any purpose.

Annual grant total: In 2005/06 the trust had assets of £333,000 and an income of £14,000. Grants were made to individuals totalling £5,900. Grants were also made to organisations totalling £2,200.

Applications: On a form available from the correspondent and should be submitted by 30 September each year for consideration in November/December.

Correspondent: Jean-Anne Goodbrand, Administrative Officer, Educational Services, Moray Council Headquarters,

High Street, Elgin, Moray IV30 1LL (01343 563151; Fax: 01343 563478; e-mail: jeananne.goodbrand@moray.gov.uk; website: www.moray.gov.uk)

Ian Wilson Ski Fund

Eligibility: Young people aged under 21 who are in full time education in a school run by Moray council. Preference is given to families with a restricted income.

Types of grants: One-off grants are given to advance education by promoting outdoor activities, including sport and related studies.

Annual grant total: In 2004/05 the trust had assets of £10,000, an income of £1,400 and a total expenditure of £1,600, all of which was given in grants to seven individuals.

Applications: On a form available from the correspondent. Applicants are encouraged to apply in plenty of time, in October through to December for consideration by the trustees in January, as there are a limited number of grants available. Applications can be submitted either directly by the individual or through his or her school, college, educational welfare agency, or another third party.

Correspondent: Ian Hamilton, Hon. Secretary & Treasurer, Slack Villa, King Edwards Terrace, Portknockie, Moray AB56 4NX (01542 840551; e-mail: ianptk@tiscali.co.uk)

Perth & Kinross

The Guildry Incorporation of Perth

Eligibility: People in need who live in Perth.

Types of grants: Grants ranging between £100 and £500.

Annual grant total: In 2004/05 the trust had an income of £172,000 and distributed about £80,000 in donations, pensions and bursaries. These were broken down as follows: weekly pensions (£18,000); quarterly pensions (£8,500); coal allowances (£4,800); school prizes (£4,500); charitable donations (£29,000); and bursaries (£15,000).

Applications: Application forms can be requested from the correspondent. They are considered at the trustees' meetings on the last Tuesday of every month.

Correspondent: Lorna Peacock, Secretary, 42 George Street, Perth PH1 5JL (01738 623195)

Miss Isabella MacDougall's Trust

Eligibility: Students who were born within the former county of Perth and are studying first degree courses in the faculty of arts at the following universities:

Edinburgh, Glasgow, St Andrews, Aberdeen, Dundee, Sterling and Strathclyde.

Types of grants: A maximum bursary of £200 per year for a period not exceeding three years.

Exclusions: No grants are made to postgraduates.

Annual grant total: Previously about £800 in bursaries.

Applications: In writing to the correspondent.

Correspondent: A G Dorward, Messrs Miller Hendry, 10 Blackfriars Street, Perth PH1 5NS (01738 637311)

Other information: Bursaries will be awarded on the basis of academic achievement within the state education system plus a further examination or interview by the trustees.

Perth & Kinross Educational Trust

Eligibility: Students in further or higher education, including mature students and postgraduates, who were born or attended school in Perth and Kinross.

Types of grants: Grants of up to £150 towards books, fees, living expenses and study or travel abroad.

Annual grant total: About £8,000.

Applications: On a form available from the correspondent. Applications should be received by mid-May for consideration in June. The exact closing date can be found on the application form. Late applications cannot be considered.

Correspondent: Tracy Dowie, Finance Section, Education & Children's Services, Perth & Kinross Council, Pullar House, 35 Kinnoull Street, Perth PH1 5GD (01738 476767; Fax: 01738 476210)

Central Scotland

Clackmannanshire

Clackmannanshire Educational Trust

Eligibility: People who live in the county of Clackmannanshire.

Types of grants: Grants of up to £100 towards education travel (in the UK or overseas) and adult education.

Annual grant total: Grants total about £500 each year.

Applications: Directly by the individual on a form available from the facilities, schools & welfare team at the address above. Applications are considered on the first

Thursday of January, April, July and October.

Correspondent: Facilities, Schools and Welfare Team, Services to People, Clackmannanshire Council, Lime Tree House, Alloa FK10 1EX (01259 452363; Fax: 01259 452440)

Paton Educational Trust

Eligibility: People (usually aged 16 to 26) who live in the burgh of Alloa or Clackmannanshire or whose parent was employed by Patons & Baldwins Ltd – Alloa or who are members or adherents of West Church of Scotland – Alloa or Moncrieff U F Church – Alloa.

Types of grants: Supplementary grants of £50 to £100 per year for students in further and higher education. Grants can go towards books and fees/living expenses. Grants can also sometimes be given for study or travel abroad or for student exchanges.

Annual grant total: About £400.

Applications: On a form available from the correspondent. Applications are usually considered in September/October.

Correspondent: William Jarvis, Solicitor, 27 Mar Street, Alloa FK10 1HX (01259 723408)

Fife

Fife Educational Trust

Eligibility: People who have a permanent address within the Fife council area and who attended a secondary or primary school there.

Types of grants: Support for individuals below postgraduate level is usually restricted to travel grants where this is an integral part of the course of study, but can also be given for music, drama and visual arts. Grants range from £50 to about £75.

Annual grant total: About £1,200.

Applications: In writing to the correspondent. Applicants must give their permanent address, details of schools they attended within Fife with dates of attendance, and details of other money available. Applications are considered in March.

Correspondent: Education Services, Fife Council, Rothesay House, Rothesay Place, Glenrothes KY7 5PQ

New St Andrews Japan Golf Trust

Eligibility: Children and young people in need living in the county of Fife who are undertaking sports and recreational activities.

Types of grants: One-off and recurrent grants ranging from £200 to £1,500, for sports equipment, travel, accommodation

and coaching assistance to individuals, and university fees for sports scholarships.

Annual grant total: In 2003/04 the trust had assets of £80,000 and an income of £8,000. Grants were made to organisations totalling £2,500, with a further £5,500 being given to individuals.

Applications: In writing to the correspondent, providing the contact details of two referees.

Correspondent: David S D Robertson, Secretary, Chestney House, 149 Market Street, St Andrews, Fife KY16 9PF (01334 472255)

Stirling

The Stirlingshire Educational Trust

Eligibility: People who were born in, or have lived for five years in, Stirlingshire and are in need.

Types of grants: Grants are made to schoolchildren for study/travel abroad and excursions and to college students, undergraduates, vocational students and mature students, including those for clothing/uniforms, fees, study/travel abroad, books, equipment/instruments and excursions.

Grants range from £150 to £500.

Annual grant total: About £85,000.

Applications: On a form available from the correspondent. Applications must be received by February, May, August and November for consideration on the first Wednesday of the following month.

Correspondent: The Clerk/Treasurer, 68 Port Street, Stirling FK8 2LJ (01786 474956 The office is only staffed on Tuesdays and Thursdays)

Edinburgh, the Lothians & Scottish Borders

The Avenel Trust

Eligibility: Children in need under 18 and students of nursery nursing living in the Lothians.

Types of grants: Grants for childcare costs.

Exclusions: Grants are not given for holidays, toys or household furnishings.

Annual grant total: In 2004/05 the trust had an income of £13,000. The sum of £9,000 was distributed to around 100 individuals for welfare purposes, with a further £1,000 distributed in two educational grants.

Applications: Applications should be submitted through a tutor or third party such as a social worker or teacher.

Correspondent: Alison Kennedy, 75 Comiston Drive, Edinburgh EH10 5QT (0131 447 2250)

Other information: Grants are also made to organisations (£3,000 in 2004/05).

City of Edinburgh

City of Edinburgh Charitable Trusts

Eligibility: People in need who live in Edinburgh, mostly people of pensionable age.

Types of grants: One-off and recurrent grants, generally of £10 to £100. The charity is made up of approximately 135 trusts, all of which give different types of grants with different eligibility criteria.

Annual grant total: In 2004/05 the combined assets of the individual trusts totalled £16 million. Income stood at £524,000, while grants were made to organisations and individuals totalling £453,000.

Applications: Initially in writing to the correspondent. The application criteria for each trust varies.

Correspondent: Marlyn McConaghie, Investment and Treasury Division, City of Edinburgh Council, 12 St Giles Street, Edinburgh EH1 1PT (0131 469 3518; Fax: 0131 225 6356; e-mail: marlyn. mcconaghie@edinburgh.gov.uk)

The James Scott Law Charitable Fund

Eligibility: Young people, aged between 5 and 18 years who attend primary or secondary Edinburgh Merchant Company Schools.

Types of grants: Grants are given for school fees, clothing, books and allowances. The maximum award is about £2,000.

Annual grant total: Grants totalled about £6,000.

Applications: On a form available from the correspondent for consideration in August, a bursar at their school usually interviews applicants.

Correspondent: Alistair Beattie, Merchants' Hall, 22 Hanover Street, Edinburgh EH2 2EP (0131 225 7202)

East Lothian

East Lothian Educational Trust

Eligibility: People in education who live in the former county of East Lothian and are in need.

Types of grants: One-off grants in the range of £100 and £700 are given to: schoolchildren, college students, undergraduates, vocational students, mature students and people with special educational needs, including those towards uniforms/clothing, fees, study/travel abroad, books, equipment/instruments, maintenance/living expenses and excursions.

Annual grant total: In 2004/05 the trust had assets of £1.2 million, an income of £53,000 and a total expenditure of £40,000. Grants to 55 individuals totalled £24,000 and £11,000 was given to organisations.

Applications: On a form available from the correspondent. Applications can be submitted directly by the individual or a parent/guardian, through a third party such as a teacher, or through an organisation such as a school or an educational welfare agency. Applications should be submitted between August and October for consideration between September and November.

Correspondent: K Brand, Clerk, John Muir House, Council Buildings, Haddington, East Lothian EH41 3HA

The Red House Home Trust

Eligibility: Young people who are aged under 22 and live in East Lothian.

Types of grants: The trust promotes the education and training of disadvantaged young people under the age of 22, to help them into independent living.

Annual grant total: The trust has an income of around £15,000 each year. Grants are made to individuals totalling about £3,000.

Applications: On a form available from the correspondent.

Correspondent: Graeme Thom, Secretary, Scott-Moncrieff, 17 Melville Street, Edinburgh EH3 7PH (0131 473 3500; Fax: 0131 473 3500; e-mail: graeme.thom@ scott-moncrieff.com)

Other information: Grants are also made to organisations.

Scottish Borders

The Elizabeth Hume Trust

Eligibility: People in need who live in the parish of Chirnside.

Types of grants: Grants are made to schoolchildren for uniforms/clothing and equipment/instruments and to undergraduates for fees and books.

Annual grant total: In 2005 the trust had assets of £250,000 and an income of £10,000. No grants were made during the year.

Applications: Applications can be made either directly by an individual or family member, through a third party such as a social worker or teacher, through an organisation such as a Citizens Advice or school or through a church elder.

Correspondent: The Minister, The Manse, Chirnside, Duns, Berwickshire TD11 3XL

Charities Administered by Scottish Borders Council

Eligibility: Within the Scottish Borders there are four educational trusts corresponding to the four former counties of Berwickshire, Peeblesshire, Roxburghshire and Selkirkshire. Grants may be awarded for a variety of educational purposes to people who are ordinarily living in the above areas.

Types of grants: One-off and recurrent grants are made under the following headings: (i) educational excursions; (ii) special grants; (iii) travel grants; (iv) adult education; and (v) drama, visual arts and music. Grants range between £20 and £250.

Annual grant total: Previously over £5,000.

Applications: On a form available from the correspondent. Applications are considered all year round.

Correspondent: The Trustees, Education and Lifelong Learning, Newtown St Boswells, Melrose, Roxburghshire TD6 0SA (01835 824000; Fax: 01835 825091)

Other information: Grants are also given to schools.

West Lothian

The West Lothian Educational Trust

Eligibility: People who live in the former county of West Lothian.

Types of grants: Grants are given towards books and equipment, fees, maintenance, travel abroad and travel to/from college for students in further and higher education. Grants are also given to mature students, part-time students and for short course attendance.

Annual grant total: In 2003/04 it had assets of £183,000 and an income of £15,000. The trust made grants to both organisations and individuals totalling £9,800 which was distributed as follows: Prize money – £1,700; John Newland bursaries – £1,000; Anderson bursary – £1,200; Educational awards – £5,900.

Applications: Application forms are available from the correspondent. Applications must be received by 1 February, 1 May and 1 September each year.

Correspondent: Janice Cooper, Secretary, Scott-Moncrieff, Chartered Accountants, 17 Melville Street, Edinburgh EH3 7PH (0131 473 3500; Fax: 0131 473 3535)

Glasgow & West of Scotland

The Ayrshire Educational Trust

Eligibility: People who live in the former county of Ayrshire.

Types of grants: Grants are given to students in further/higher education for travel in either the UK or abroad for educational purposes. Grants can also be made to buy special equipment for mentally or physically disabled students. Equipment for pilot projects or of an experimental nature will be considered. Grants are also given to schoolchildren for educational outings or for Scottish Youth Theatre or Scottish Youth Choir.

Exclusions: Assistance cannot be given towards personal equipment or to help with student's course fees when following full-time or part-time courses of education.

Annual grant total: In 2004/05 the trust awarded about 25 grants to individuals totalling £11,000.

Applications: On a form available from the correspondent. Applications are usually considered four times a year. They should be submitted directly by the individual.

Correspondent: Mrs Catherine Martin, Principal Administration Officer, Community Learning and Development, East Ayrshire Council, Rennie Street Office, Rennie Street, Kilmarnock KA1 3AR (01563 578106; Fax: 01563 576269)

Dunbartonshire Educational Trust

Eligibility: People who live in the old county area of Dumbarton district aged 16 and over. There is a preference for people from deprived areas and a policy of positive discrimination (for instance, people who are disabled or children of single parents).

Types of grants: Grants towards fees, maintenance, travel and equipment for students in further or higher education and to obtain practical experience of trades, for example the cost of books during an apprenticeship. Generally grants range from £25 to £50; the maximum given is £100 in exceptional circumstances.

Annual grant total: About £2,000 is available each year.

Applications: On a form available from the correspondent. Applications can be considered at any time, but students usually apply before the start of the course.

Correspondent: The Trustees, West Dunbartonshire Council, Council Offices, Garshake Road, Dumbarton G82 3PU

The Glasgow Society for the Education of the Deaf & Dumb

Eligibility: Children over school age who are deaf and/or speech impaired and live in the west of Scotland.

Types of grants: Grants to help with the cost of providing tutors to support deaf people, courses (for example, sign language, lip reading), holidays, radio aids, computers and so on.

Annual grant total: In 2004/05 the society had assets of £905,000, an income of £38,000 and distributed £33,000 in 68 educational grants.

Applications: On a form available form the correspondent, or from the society's website. Applications can be submitted at any time directly by the individual or through a social worker.

Correspondent: I Mowat, Treasurer and Secretary, Alexander Sloan Chartered Accountants, 144 West George Street, Glasgow G2 2HG (0141 354 0354; Fax: 0141 354 0355; website: www.gsedd.org.uk)

Other information: The society also gives grants to organisations and schools (£14,000 in 2004/05).

The Logan & Johnstone School Scheme

Eligibility: Students in further/higher education, including mature students, people starting work and postgraduates, who live in the former Strathclyde region.

Types of grants: One-off grants for books, equipment, instruments and fees.

Exclusions: Grants are not made towards living or travel expenses.

Annual grant total: About £5,000.

Applications: On a form available from the correspondent. Applications should be submitted directly by the individual between April and June for consideration in August.

Correspondent: Dorothy Mullen, Education Services, Wheatley House, 25 Cochrane Street, Merchant City, Glasgow G1 1HL (0141 287 3602)

Colonel MacLean Trust Scheme

Eligibility: Students in further/higher education, including mature students and postgraduates, who live in the former Strathclyde region.

Types of grants: One-off grants for books, equipment, instruments and fees.

Annual grant total: In 2005/06 the trust had an income of £5,100, all of which was given in grants to 11 individuals.

Applications: On a form available from Marianne Hosie, Principal Officer (Finance), at the address below. Applications should be submitted directly by the individual between April and June for consideration in August.

Correspondent: Dorothy Mullen, Education Services, Wheatley House, 25 Cochrane Street, Merchant City, Glasgow G1 1HL (0141 287 3602)

Renfrewshire Educational Trust

Eligibility: People who have lived within either the Renfrewshire, East Renfrewshire or Inverclyde areas for the last three years or have come from one of the aforementioned areas but currently live elsewhere in order to undertake their course of studies. Student's family income must not exceed £30,000 per annum. For children's excursions the minimum criteria is receiving free school meals.

Types of grants: Scholarships and grants towards fees and maintenance for students in further and higher education, including mature students and travel grants for study in the UK or overseas, such as medical electives. Schoolchildren can receive help with the costs of educational outings. Grants usually range from £400 to £750, but larger grants can be considered.

Exclusions: No grants for individuals whose household income is £30,000 or over.

Annual grant total: In 2005/06 the trust had a total expenditure of £24,000, £10,000 of which was given in educational grants to individuals, with the remainder being given in grants for music, drama and sport.

Applications: On a form available from the correspondent. (Separate application forms are available for general grants and travel grants.) Details of household income are requested. Applications can be submitted either directly by the individual or via their school. Applications are considered every six weeks.

Correspondent: Alex Hewitson/Sarah White, Renfrewshire Council, Council Headquarters, North Building, Cotton Street, Paisley PA1 1RT (0141 840 3147/ 0141 847 3630; Fax: 0141 840 3335)

The Spiers Trust

Eligibility: People in need who live in the parishes of Beith, Dalry, Dunlop, Kilbirnie, Lochwinnoch and Neilston. Preference is given to students from families with restricted income.

Types of grants: Awards known as Spier Grants to help secondary school pupils and students in further/higher education to meet the cost of attending a course or obtaining special tuition in any academic, artistic, scientific or technological subject or subjects, in or outside of Scotland. Grants may also be given to help with travelling costs. Grants range from £50 to £200.

Annual grant total: Previously £2,200.

Applications: Applications can be submitted directly by the individual on an application form available by phoning the correspondent. Evidence of need will have to be shown. Each year applications are considered regularly until all the funds have been spent.

Correspondent: The Head of Service, North Ayrshire Council, Educational Services, Resources Section (Finance), Cunninghame House, Irvine KA12 8EE (01294 324428)

Argyll & Bute

The Argyll Educational Trust

Eligibility: People who live in the former county of Argyll.

Types of grants: Grants ranging from £100 to £250 to people receiving no other types of student support. Most grants given are at postgraduate level, but grants may be given to undergraduates for travel, uniform (nurses and so on), equipment, books and so on.

Annual grant total: In 2005/06 the trust had assets of £240,000, an income of £12,000 and a total expenditure of £10,000, all of which was given in grants to 100 individuals.

Applications: On a form available from the correspondent. The trustees meet every couple of months to consider applications.

Correspondent: The Trustees, Education Offices, Argyll House, Alexandra Parade, Dunoon, Argyll PA23 8AJ (01369 704000; Fax: 01369 708584)

Charles & Barbara Tyre Trust

Eligibility: People aged 18 to 25 who live in the former county of Argyll and are of the protestant faith.

Types of grants: Grants of up to £1,500 are made for a wide variety of purposes to college students, undergraduates, vocational students and people with special educational needs.

Annual grant total: In 2004/05 the trust had assets of £651,000 and an income of £28,000. The sum of £23,000 was distributed in 23 educational grants.

Applications: In writing to the correspondent including references, by 31 May for consideration in August/September. Proof of continued attendance of the course must be produced at the start of each term.

Correspondent: The Clerk, c/o Wylie & Bisset Chartered Accountants, 160 Argyll Street, Dunoon, PA23 7NA (01369 703888)

City of Glasgow

Glasgow Educational & Marshall Trust

Eligibility: People over 18 years old who are in need and who have lived in the city

of Glasgow (as at the re-organisation in 1975) for a minimum of five years (excluding time spent studying in the city with a home address elsewhere).

Types of grants: Grants range from £100 to £1,000, although in exceptional cases higher awards have been made. They are given towards: educational outings for schoolchildren; books, course fees/living expenses, study/travel abroad for people in further/higher education; and course fees, travel, books, equipment/instruments for people wishing to undertake vocational training. Mature students can also qualify for assistance with childcare costs, books, travel and fees.

Grants can be one-off or recurrent and are normally given for courses where a Scottish Education Department grant is not available, or where such grants do not cover the total costs.

Exclusions: No grants are given retrospectively or for courses run by privately owned institutions.

Annual grant total: In 2005/06 the trust made around 60 awards to individuals totalling about £36,000.

Applications: Directly by the individual on a form available from the trust, together with two written references.

The main meetings of governors are held on the first Wednesday of March, June, September and December. Interim meetings may be held if required as a result of the number of applications received.

Correspondent: Mrs Avril Sloane, Secretary & Treasurer, 21 Beaton Road, Glasgow G41 4NW (0141 423 2169; Fax: 0141 424 1731)

The JTH Charitable Trust

Eligibility: People in need who live in Glasgow and are undertaking education which enhances the cultural and social fabric of society with a view to meeting unmet local needs which are not municipal, governmental or religious.

Types of grants: One-off grants ranging from £100 to £1,000 to schoolchildren for study/travel overseas, books, equipment/instruments and maintenance/living expenses, to college students, undergraduates, vocational students and mature students for fees, study/travel overseas, books, equipment/instruments, maintenance/living expenses and childcare, to overseas students for fees, books, equipment/instruments and maintenance/living expenses and to individuals with special educational needs for excursions.

Exclusions: Grants are unlikely to be made to people at Glasgow or Strathclyde Universities or Royal Scottish Academy of Music and Dance as the trust makes block payments to the hardship funds of these institutions. Grants are also not normally awarded towards medical electives, second or further qualifications, payments of

school fees or costs incurred at tertiary educational establishments.

Annual grant total: In 2004/05, the trust had assets of £4.3 million and an income of £174,000. Grants to 39 individuals totalled £11,000 ranging between £100 and £500 each. Grants to organisations totalled £173,000.

Applications: An application form to be submitted together with a summary in the applicant's own words, extending to no more than a single A4 sheet, of the purpose and need of the grant. The possible costs and financial need should also be broken down.

The trustees meet four times a year normally in March, June, September and December, but this can vary. All applications should be submitted one month prior to the meeting.

It is a condition that with any grant given, a report should be made as to how the funds have been used. Grants not used for the purposes stated must be returned. Applicants receiving help one year may expect to be refused in the next.

Correspondent: Lynne Faulkner, Biggart Baillie, Dalmore House, 310 St Vincent Street, Glasgow G2 5QR (0141 228 8000)

The Trades House of Glasgow

Eligibility: People in need who live in Glasgow.

Types of grants: Grants to encourage promising young people in university or colleges.

Annual grant total: In 2004/05 the charity had assets of £14 million and an income of £422,000, including £90,000 from fundraising activities. The sum of £97,000 was distributed in 283 relief-in-need grants to individuals. A further £15,000 went in 82 educational grants to individuals.

Applications: In writing to the correspondent.

Correspondent: The Clerk, Administration Centre, North Gallery – Trades Hall, 85 Glassford Street, Glasgow, G1 1UH (0141 553 1605; Fax: 0141 553 1233)

Other information: Grants are also made to organisations (£183,000 in 2004/05).

Dumfries & Galloway

The Dumfriesshire Educational Trust

Eligibility: People normally living in Dumfriesshire who have had at least five years of education in Dumfriesshire.

Types of grants: Grants of up to £60, usually recurrent, are given to: schoolchildren towards educational outings; students in further/higher education for books, fees/living expenses, study/travel abroad and student exchanges;

and mature students towards books and travel.

Exclusions: Grants are not available for childcare for mature students or foreign students studying in the UK.

Annual grant total: About £18,000 a year is given to individuals and organisations.

Applications: On a form available from the correspondent, for consideration in March, June, September or December. Applications should be submitted in the preceding month directly by the individual or through the relevant school/college/educational welfare agency or through another third party and signed by the applicant.

For recurrent grants, applicants must reapply each academic year.

Correspondent: Alex Heswell, Dumfries and Galloway Council, Municipal Chambers, Buccleuch Street, Dumfries DG1 2AD (01387 260000; Fax: 01387 245961)

The Holywood Trust

Eligibility: Young people aged 15 to 25 living in the Dumfries and Galloway region, with a preference for people who are mentally, physically or socially disadvantaged.

Types of grants: One-off and recurrent grants of £50 to £500 to schoolchildren, people in further or higher education, vocational students, people with special educational needs and people starting work for books, equipment, instruments, fees, living expenses, childcare, educational outings and study or travel overseas. Applications which contribute to their personal development are more likely to receive support. This could include financial or material assistance to participate in education or training, access employment, establish a home or involve themselves in a project or activity which will help them or their community.

Exclusions: No grants are given towards carpets or accommodation deposits.

Annual grant total: In 2003/04 the trust had assets of £15 million and an income of £945,000. Grants to individuals and organisations totalled £348,000.

Applications: On a form available from the correspondent, or which can be downloaded from the trust's website. Applications are considered at least four times a year. The trust encourages applicants to provide additional information about any disadvantage which affects them where their application form has not given them an opportunity to do so. It also welcomes any supporting information from third party workers.

Correspondent: Peter Robertson, Director, Mount St Michael, Craigs Road, Dumfries DG1 4UT (01387 269176; Fax: 01387 269175; e-mail: funds@ holywood-trust.org.uk; website: www. holywood-trust.org.uk)

Other information: The trust also supports groups and project applications which benefit young people.

The John Primrose Trust

Eligibility: Young people in need with a connection to Dumfries and Maxwelltown by parentage or by living there.

Types of grants: Grants to students to help with educational needs or help for people starting work.

Annual grant total: About £10,000, half of which is given to individuals for relief-in-need and educational purposes.

Applications: On an application form available from the correspondent, to be considered in June and December.

Correspondent: The Trustees, Primrose & Garden, 92 Irish Street, Dumfries DG1 2PF

The Stewartry Educational Trust

Eligibility: Persons belonging to the Stewartry of Kirkcudbright (i.e. the area of the Stewartry of Kirkcudbright prior to local government re-organisation in 1975).

Types of grants: One-off grants are given to schoolchildren for educational outings in Scotland and for general study costs to people starting work and students in further or higher education, including mature students and postgraduates.

Annual grant total: In 2005, the trust had a total income of £3,500.

Applications: On a form available from the correspondent with details of any grants available from other sources. Applications can be submitted directly by the individual or through a parent/ guardian, social worker, Citizens Advice, other welfare agency or other third party. They should be submitted in February, May or August for consideration in the following month.

Correspondent: Alex Haswell, Clerk, Corselet College, Buittle, Castle Douglas, DG7 1NJ (01557 330291; Fax: 01557 332536; e-mail: christim@ dumgal.gov.uk; website: www.dumgal.gov. uk)

The John Wallace Trust Scheme

Eligibility: Young people who live in the following areas: the electoral wards of Kirkland, Kello, Crichton, Douglas, Cairn, Morton and that part of Dalswinton Ward lying outside the parish of Dumfries and all in the local government area of Nithsdale District.

Types of grants: Bursaries for educational costs and travel grants for visits of an educational nature.

Annual grant total: In 2004/05 educational grants were made to 31 individuals totalling £4,000.

Applications: Application forms are available from the correspondent. The closing date is 31 December each year.

Correspondent: Director of Education, Education and Community Services, Woodbank, 30 Edinburgh Road, Dumfries DG1 1NW (01387 260485)

Wigtownshire Educational Trust

Eligibility: People who live in the former county of Wigtownshire and are unemployed, receiving benefits or disabled. Grants are only given to those who can demonstrate personal hardship and that no other source of funding is available.

Types of grants: Grants, ranging from £50 to £300, to school children, college students, undergraduates, vocational students, mature students and people with special educational needs. Grants given include those towards, clothing/uniforms, fees, study/travel abroad, books, equipment/instruments and excursions. Assistance is also given towards gaining practical experience of trades and promoting education in the visual arts, music and drama.

Annual grant total: In 2005 the sum of £1,600 was distributed in 10 grants.

Applications: On a form available from the above address. Applications are considered throughout the year. If the applicant is a child/young person, details of parental income are required.

Correspondent: Council Secretariat, Area Management Wigtown, Dumfries and Galloway Council, Council Offices, Sun Street, Stranraer DG9 7JJ (01776 702151 ext 61207)

East, North & South Ayrshire

The Robert Cummings Bequest

Eligibility: Young people aged under 21 who are orphans and originate from Ayrshire.

Types of grants: Grants in the range of £10 and £50, including those towards clothing, educational fees and books and equipment.

Annual grant total: In 2004/05 the charity had assets of £2,300 and an income of £130. Grants to 18 individuals totalled £930.

Applications: Applications should be submitted directly by the individual or guardian. They should be accompanied by the exact certificate of birth of the applicant and the exact certificate(s) of death of father and/or mother. Any guardian must submit satisfactory evidence as to their right to act in this capacity.

In February 2006 the trust stated that 'It is anticipated that the fund will be fully expended in the near future however applications will continue to be considered up until that time.'

Correspondent: Administration Manager, East Ayrshire Council, Council Headquarters, London Road, Kilmarnock KA3 7BU (01563 576093; Fax: 01563 576245; e-mail: gillian.hamilton@east-ayrshire.gov.uk)

The John Longwill Education Trust

Eligibility: Scholars or students who are attending Higher grade school or university in Scotland and who are native to Dalry and of Scottish descent.

Types of grants: Payments of about £100 each.

Annual grant total: In 2005, the trust had an income of £750; grants totalled about £400.

Applications: In writing to the correspondent at any time.

Correspondent: James McCosh, J & J McCosh Solicitors, Clydesdale Bank Chambers, Dalry, Ayrshire KA24 5AB

The C K Marr Educational Trust

Eligibility: People who currently live in Troon or the Troon electoral wards.

Types of grants: Mainly bursaries, scholarships and educational travel grants for those at college or university.

Annual grant total: In 2004/05 the trust had assets of £7.2 million and an income of £451,000. Out of a total expenditure of £369,000, the sum of £228,000 was distributed in over 800 grants.

Applications: On a form available from the correspondent to be submitted either directly by the individual, or through an organisation such as a school or an educational welfare agency.

Correspondent: Alan A Stewart, Clerk, 1 Howard Street, Kilmarnock KA1 2BW (01563 572727; Fax: 01563 527901)

North & South Lanarkshire

Loaningdale School Company

Eligibility: Children and young people aged 12 to 20 who are in need and live within the Clydesdale local area of South Lanarkshire.

Types of grants: One-off grants ranging from £100 to £1,000 towards furthering the individual's education or employment prospects. Priority is given to creative or outdoor pursuits for young people, young unemployed people and post-school education and training of young people.

Annual grant total: The trust has an annual income of around £10,000. Grants total around £6,000, about £1,500 of which is given to individuals

Applications: On a form available from the correspondent, with guidelines for applicants. Applications are considered in March, June, September and December, and should be submitted in the previous month.

Correspondent: R Graeme Thom, Scott-Moncrieff, 17 Melville Street, Edinburgh EH3 7PH (0131 473 3500; e-mail: graeme.thom@scott-moncrieff.com)

Other information: Grants are also made to organisations.

Highlands & Islands

The Fresson Trust

Eligibility: People wishing to further their career in aviation who are living in, or visiting, the Highlands and Islands.

Types of grants: Grants in the past have been given to assist in the payment of flying lessons and in the form of a scholarship bursary. One-off grants can be given to help people starting work to buy books, equipment and clothing and help with their travel expenses. Students in further or higher education may be provided with money for books, fees or living expenses. Mature students can receive grants for books, travel, fees and childcare.

Annual grant total: About £500.

Applications: In writing to the correspondent at any time. Applicants should state how they can assist in the development of aviation in the Highlands and Islands.

Correspondent: The Secretary, 24 Drumsmittar Road, North Kessock, Inverness IV1 3JU (website: www.fressontrust.org.uk)

Highland

The Highland Children's Trust

Eligibility: Children and young people in need who are under 25 and live in the Highlands.

Types of grants: One-off grants of £50 to £500, although a loan may be considered. Assistance may be provided towards: the costs of school children participating in educational outings; the education and training costs for students in further or higher education and people on vocational courses; obtaining employment; setting up in business; the provision of holidays; the purchase of computers, preference being given to people with special educational needs.

Exclusions: Grants are not given for postgraduate study, to pay off debts, nor to purchase clothing, footwear, food, furniture or cars and so on.

Annual grant total: In 2003/04 the trust had assets of £897,000, an income of £41,000 and a total expenditure of £42,000. Educational grants to 82 individuals totalled £15,000 and 24 welfare grants totalled £4,000.

Applications: On a form available from the correspondent. They can be submitted at any time either directly by the individual or through a social worker, Citizens Advice or other welfare agency. Applications must include details of income and savings and are considered at board meetings held on a regular basis.

Correspondent: Mrs Alison Harbinson, 105 Castle Street, Inverness IV2 3EA (01463 243872; Fax: 01463 243872; e-mail: info@hctrust.co.uk; website: www.hctrust.co.uk)

The Morar Trust

Eligibility: People who live in the community of Morar.

Types of grants: Funds are used to support educational, social and charitable occasions in the local community. The trust has in the past assisted with payments for educational equipment, trips and festivities, along with supporting the hospital, ambulance and welfare purposes. Grants are given as one-off payments.

Annual grant total: £1,000 for educational and welfare purposes.

Applications: In writing to the council via the correspondent or through a social or medical worker.

Correspondent: Mrs Deidre Roberts, 3 Bracare, Morar PH40 4PE

Isle of Lewis

Ross & Cromarty Educational Trust

Eligibility: People who live on the Isle of Lewis.

Types of grants: Grants range from £50 to £200 for: (a) books, fees and living expenses and study or travel abroad for students in further and higher education; (b) books, equipment, instruments and clothing for people starting work; (c) books, travel and fees for mature students; and (d) books and educational outings for schoolchildren. Grants are sometimes considered for various social, cultural and recreational purposes for individuals.

Annual grant total: The trust has an income of about £10,000 each year, all of which is available in grants to individuals and organisations.

Applications: In writing to the correspondent at any time.

Correspondent: The Director of Education, Comhairle nan Eilean, Sandwick Road, Stornoway, Isle of Lewis HS1 2BW (01851 709498)

Orkney Islands

Orkney Educational Trust Scheme 1961

Eligibility: People on postgraduate courses, in further education or on apprenticeships who live in the former county of Orkney.

Types of grants: Subsidiary grants of £8 to £50 to help with travel, material costs and fees/living expenses for further education students. Grants are also made to people starting work to help with books, equipment/instruments, clothing and travel costs, and to schoolchildren to help with books and educational outings. Grants may also be given for the promotion of education in the community.

Annual grant total: Grants totalling about £2,500 are made to around 50 individuals each year.

Applications: In writing to the correspondent. Applications are considered in October.

Correspondent: The Director of Education, Orkney Islands Council, Education Department, Council Offices, School Place, Kirkwall, Orkney KW15 1NY (01856 873535; Fax: 01856 876327)

3. WALES

The Cambrian Educational Foundation for Deaf Children

Eligibility: Deaf and partially hearing children aged between 3 and 25 who live or whose parents live in Wales. Beneficiaries can be in special classes (units) in ordinary and special schools in Wales; students in further education; and people entering employment.

Types of grants: One-off and occasionally annual grants of £100 to £500. Grants have been provided to schoolchildren for school uniforms, occasionally for educational outings in the UK and for study or travel abroad, to people starting work and to further and higher education students for books.

Exclusions: Grants are not given for leisure trips.

Annual grant total: In 2005 the trust had both an income and a total expenditure of around £21,000, all of which was given in grants to around 50 individuals.

Applications: Applications, on a form available from the correspondent, can be submitted directly by the individual, or through their school/college/educational welfare agency or other third party. They are considered throughout the year.

Correspondent: Mrs Pamela Brown, Montreux, 30 Lon Cedwyn, Sketty, Swansea SA2 0TH (01792 207628; e-mail: pamela@brown.fsworld.co.uk)

The Cambrian Educational Trust Fund

Eligibility: People under the age of 21 who are blind or partially-sighted and were born in, or live in, Wales.

Types of grants: One-off grants to promote education, such as towards care and maintenance costs.

Annual grant total: Grants totalled £2,000 in 2003.

Applications: On a form available from the correspondent. Applications are considered quarterly. The trust welcomes telephone enquiries from potential applications to discuss suitability and how to apply.

Correspondent: Owen Williams, Wales Council for the Blind, 3rd Floor, Shand House, 20 Newport Road, Cardiff CF24 0DB (029 2047 3954; Fax: 029 2043 3920; e-mail: technology@wcb-ccd.org.uk; website: www.wcb-ccd.org.uk/)

The James Pantyfedwen Foundation

Eligibility: Candidates for Christian ministry from Wales and Welsh postgraduate students.

Types of grants: One-off and recurrent grants according to need.

Annual grant total: In 2004/05 the foundation had assets of £9.5 million, which generated an income of £439,000. Grants were made to 29 individuals totalling £72,000. A further £269,000 was given to various organisations, including religious organisations.

Applications: On a form available from the correspondent. The closing date is 30 June preceding the academic year for which the application is being made. Applications are considered in July.

Correspondent: Richard H Morgan, Executive Secretary, Pantyfedwen, 9 Market Street, Aberystwyth SY23 1DL (01970 612806; Fax: 01970 612806; e-mail: pantyfedwen@btinternet.com)

Other information: This trust mostly supports organisations.

The Michael Sobell Welsh People's Charitable Trust

Eligibility: People in need who live in Wales.

Types of grants: One-off and recurrent grants ranging from £40 to £500.

Annual grant total: In 2004/05, the association had an income of £11,000 and a total expenditure of £16,900. No information concerning grants total was available from the Charity Commission.

Applications: In writing to the correspondent.

Correspondent: Mrs S E Davies, Dolenog, Old Hall, Llanidloeas, Powys SY18 6PP

Other information: The trust makes grants to both individuals and organisations.

The Welsh Broadcasting Trust
see entry on page 81

Ymddiriedolaeth Bryntaf (the Bryn-Taf Trust)

Eligibility: Children of school age (2 to 16) who have some special educational need and are either Welsh speaking or are receiving Welsh medium education or the parents desire such provision for their child.

Types of grants: Educational expenses for children in special schools or hospitals. This includes the cost of equipment and travel costs for parents to visit children, the cost of school clothing, books, educational outings and school fees. Grants range from £100 to £500.

Annual grant total: In 2004/05 the trust had assets of £18,000. No grants have been made during the past few years, although this may change in the near future.

Applications: On a form available from the correspondent. Applications can be submitted either through the individual's school/college/educational welfare agency on behalf of the child or parent, directly by the individual or by another third party on their behalf.

Correspondent: D Roberts-Young, Hon. Secretary, Pen Roc, Rhodfa'r Mor, Aberystwyth SY23 2AZ

Other information: Grants are also given towards conferences and research on Welsh language issues in special education.

Mid-Wales

Ceredigion

The Brecknock Association for the Welfare of the Blind

Eligibility: Blind and partially-sighted people living in Brecknock.

Types of grants: One-off grants at Christmas and for special equipment/special needs, for example, cookers, talking books and college fees.

Annual grant total: In 2004/05 the association had an income of £3,500 and a total expenditure of £3,400. Grants totalled about £3,000.

Applications: In writing to the correspondent, to be considered when received.

Correspondent: E J Vince, Ken Dy Gwair, Aber, Talybont-on-Usk, Brecon, LD3 7YS

The Cardiganshire Intermediate & Technical Educational Fund

Eligibility: Applicants must have, at any time, been in attendance for at least two years at a maintained secondary school in the Ceredigion area (the former county of Cardiganshire). They must also be over the age of 25.

Types of grants: Grants of £100 to £150 a year, to help with college or university fees or to supplement existing grants.

Annual grant total: About £4,000.

Applications: Application forms are available from the correspondent from August, to be submitted by 30 November.

Correspondent: Gerwyn Richards, The Students Awards Section, Education Department, County Offices, Ceredigion County Council, Marine Terrace, Aberystwyth SY23 2DE (e-mail: e-mail gerwynr@ceredigion.gov.uk)

Powys

The Thomas John Jones Memorial Fund for Scholarships and Exhibitions

Eligibility: People under the age of 26 whom, for a period of at least two years, have both lived and attended a secondary school in the former county of Brecknockshire.

Types of grants: Preference is given to applicants undertaking courses of study or training in civil engineering at universities or colleges.

Annual grant total: Previously £44,000.

Applications: In writing to the correspondent.

Correspondent: D Meredith, Clerk to the Trustees, Cilmery, The Avenue, Brecon, Powys LD3 9BG

Edmund Jones' Charity

Eligibility: People under the age of 25 who live or work within the town of Brecon.

Types of grants: Help towards the cost of education, training, apprenticeship or equipment for those starting work and grants tenable at any Brecon town

secondary school, training college for teachers, university or other institution of further education approved by the trustees. Grants range from £50 to £300.

Annual grant total: About 120 grants totalling £18,000.

Applications: On a form available from the correspondent giving details of the college/course/apprenticeship and the anticipated cost, together with details of any other grants received or applied for. Applications may be submitted by the individual, parent or college. They are considered at any time, but mainly in October.

Correspondent: Mrs Gail Elizabeth Rofe, Secretary, The Guildhall, Lion Street, Brecon, Powys LD3 7AL (01874 622884; e-mail: brecon.guildhall@btinternet.com)

The Llanidloes Relief-in-Need Charity

Eligibility: Students who live in the communities of Llanidloes and Llanidloes Without. No support to students not living within three miles of the town, or to foreign students studying in the area.

Types of grants: Grants to help with the cost of books, living expenses and other essential items for those at college or university.

Annual grant total: In 2004/05 the charity had an income of £1,700 and a total expenditure of £1,200. Grants totalled about £1,000.

Applications: In writing to the correspondent.

Correspondent: Mrs S J Jarman, Clerk, Llwynderw, Old Hall, Llanidloes, Powys SY18 6PW (01686 412636)

The Owen Lloyd Educational Foundation

Eligibility: People between 16 and 25 who live in the parishes of Penrhoslligwy, Moelfre or the neighbouring civil or ecclesiastical parishes. Preference is given (larger grants) to residents of Penrhoslligwy, as this was the original area covered by the trust's deed.

Types of grants: Grants are given to help with: books, fees/living expenses, travel costs (but not for study/travel abroad) and tools and equipment for students in further/higher education; apprenticeship costs such as books, equipment, clothing and travel.

Annual grant total: In 2004, the foundation had a gross income of £5,700, and a total expenditure of £5,800.

Applications: On a form available from the correspondent, including details of income and expenditure. Applications are considered in October. Grants are given in June.

Correspondent: Emlyn Evans, Nant Bychan Farm, Moelfre, Gwynedd LL72 8HF

The Powys Welsh Church Acts Fund

Eligibility: People less than 25 years living in Powys.

Types of grants: Grants, ranging from £50 to £250 for those wishing to follow a course of study at college or university for; uniforms/clothing, fees, study/travel aboard, equipment/instruments and books. Help may also be available for those preparing for, or entering a trade, profession or calling.

Annual grant total: In 2005 the fund had fixed assets of £1.7 million an income of £51,000 and an expenditure of £52,000. Grants totalled about £30,000.

Applications: On a form available from the correspondent to be submitted directly by the individual.

Correspondent: Neil McNeil, Powys County Council, County Hall, Llandrindod Wells, Powys LD1 5LG (01597 726000)

North Wales

Doctor William Lewis' Charity

Eligibility: Students under the age of 25 who live in the former counties of Anglesey, Caernarvon, Merioneth, Montgomery, Flint and Denbigh.

Types of grants: A portion of the income of the foundation is used to make awards for students at Oxford, Cambridge or the University of Wales and St David's University College, Lampeter. Grants are also given to applicants who are in training for a profession or trade.

Annual grant total: In 2003/04 the charity had an income of £1,900 and a total expenditure of £1,600. Grants totalled about £1,500.

Applications: On a form available from the correspondent, to be submitted directly by the individual by the beginning of October.

Correspondent: The Secretary, The Diocesan Centre, Cathedral Close, Bangor, Gwynedd LL57 IRL

The Wrexham (Parochial) Educational Foundation

Eligibility: People under 25 who live in the county borough of Wrexham and who attended for at least two years one of the following: Minera and Brymbo Aided Primary School or St Giles Voluntary Controlled Infant and/or Junior Schools, Wrexham.

Types of grants: Grants to help students in secondary and further education, and those starting an apprenticeship or training. Grants have included supporting a student with disabilities who was living at home and unable to receive a statutory grant.

Annual grant total: In 2005 the foundation had £12,500 available for grants to individuals.

Applications: In writing to the correspondent. Applications must be submitted directly by the individual.

Correspondent: P J Blore, 49 Norfolk Road, Wrexham LL12 7RT (01978 356901)

Anglesey

The Ynys Mon Trust Fund

Eligibility: People under the age of 25 who are in need, have lived in Anglesey for not less than two years and have received at least two years of their secondary education in Anglesey.

Types of grants: Grants to help with school, college or university fees or to supplement existing grants.

Annual grant total: In 2004/05 it had net assets of £1.8 million and an income of £35,000. A total of £33,000 was awarded to 185 former pupils.

Applications: In writing to the correspondent. Applications are considered at meetings of the committee, and meetings are arranged in accordance with the number of applications. It is advisable to submit applications through the college/tutor/head of department.

Correspondent: David Elis-Williams, Corporate Director, Anglesey Further Education Trust Fund, Isle of Anglesey County Council, County Offices, Llangefni, Ynys Mon, LL77 7TW (01248 752 600; Fax: 01248 752 696)

Conwy

The Sir John Henry Morris-Jones Trust Fund

Eligibility: People living in the former municipal borough of Colwyn Bay, as existing on 31 March 1974 (that is, prior to the reorganisation of local government in 1974). Applicants must be under the age of 19 on the 31 March.

Types of grants: Applicants have to satisfy the trustees, at a personal interview, of their degree of excellence in one of the following activities: arts and crafts; sport; academic and research; science and technology; industry and commerce; and any other field of activity that applicants may feel would meet the requirements of the trustees. Grants are one-off.

Annual grant total: In 2004/05 the trust had an income of £1,100 and a total expenditure of around £1,800.

Applications: On a form available from the correspondent. Applications are considered in April/May.

Correspondent: J M Roberts, Clerk to the Trustees, Town Hall, 7 Rhiw Road, Colwyn Bay LL29 7TG (01492 532248)

Richard Owen Scholarships

Eligibility: People aged under 25 who live in Llandudno. Preference is given to undergraduates at University of Bangor, but not exclusively so.

Types of grants: Grants, ranging from £70 to £100 are given towards clothing, tools, instruments or books for people leaving education and preparing for work. Student bursaries are also available as are grants towards educational travel abroad.

Annual grant total: In 2005 the trust had an income of £680 and a total expenditure of £630, all of which was given in seven grants to individuals.

Applications: On a form available from the correspondent, to be submitted in September for consideration in August.

Correspondent: Toby G Prosser, Llandudno Town Council, Town Hall, Lloyd Street, Llandudno, Gwynedd LL30 2UP (01492 879130; Fax: 01492 879130)

Denbighshire

The J E Buckley Jones Trust (Denbighshire)

Eligibility: People in need at college or university, including mature students, who have lived, or whose parents have lived, in the former county of Denbighshire (as constituted pre-1974) for at least 10 years.

Types of grants: Grants towards tuition fees, books and/or living costs. Grants ranged from £50 to £400.

Annual grant total: In 2004/05, the trust had an income of £1,900. There has been no expenditure in recent years.

Applications: Application forms are available from the website. They should be submitted directly by the individual by 1 August each year, for consideration in August/September.

Correspondent: Andrew Black, Directorate of Lifelong Learning, Denbighshire County Council, Council Offices, Wynnstay Roath, Ruthin LL15 1YN (website: www.denbighshire.gov.uk)

Other information: There is another trust with the same name and objectives for people who live in the former county of Flintshire (as constituted pre-1974); see separate entry. If you have any confusion over which one to apply to, please contact one of the correspondents.

The Robert David Hughes Scholarship Foundation

Eligibility: University students who were either born in the community of Denbigh, or had a parent or parents resident in the area at the time of his or her birth, or at the date of the award have a parent or parents resident in the area who have lived there for at least ten years. Full documentary evidence is required.

Types of grants: Grants are made according to need to university students.

Exclusions: Individuals attending colleges of further education do not qualify for a grant.

Annual grant total: In 2005/06 the trust made 59 grants to individuals totalling £18,600.

Applications: On a form available from the correspondent, to be submitted not later than 30 September. Applications are considered in November each year. Grants are made each term on receipt of completed certificates of attendance, signed by the principal or registrar of the university. After the first year, applicants are automatically sent forms for subsequent years.

Correspondent: E. Emrys Williams, Clerk, Highfield, 2 Llewellyn's Estate, Denbigh LL16 3NR (01745 812724)

The Llanynys Educational Foundation

Eligibility: People under 25 who live in the community of Llanynys Rural, and that part of the community of Ruthin which was formerly the parish of Llanynys Urban.

Types of grants: One-off and recurrent grants up to £100 for students in further and higher education to assist with books, fees/living expenses, and study/travel abroad.

Annual grant total: About £600 is available each year.

Applications: The charity places advertisements in the local press shortly after A-level results are published. Applications are considered in September. If a large number of requests are received in relation to the funds available, preference is given to first time applicants.

Applicants should include in their application their age; place of residence; course to be followed; qualification pursued; institution attended; and the purpose to which the grant will be put.

Correspondent: Robert Ian Kinnier, Rhewl Post Office, Ruthin, Denbighshire LL15 1TH (01824 702730)

John Matthews Educational Charity

Eligibility: People under 25 who live in the district of Glyndwr and the borough of Wrexham Maelor, both in the county of Denbighshire and the borough of Oswestry in the county of Shropshire.

Types of grants: Usually to enable a desirable or necessary course of education to be followed which would otherwise be financially impossible, with the emphasis on development of exceptional talents. Grants range from £150 to £2,000.

The charity favours postgraduate or second degree students who are not getting other financial support, although undergraduates can be supported.

Annual grant total: In 2005 the trust had assets of £324,000, an income of £10,000 and a total expenditure of £4,800. Grants were made to four individuals totalling £3,500.

Applications: In writing to the correspondent. Applicants must provide information about their parents' financial circumstances once their eligibility has been established.

Correspondent: Paul B Smith, Bursar, Ruthin School, Mold Road, Ruthin, Denbighshire LL15 1EE (01824 702543; Fax: 01824 707141; e-mail: secretary@ ruthinschool.co.uk)

Flintshire

The J E Buckley Jones Trust (Flintshire)

Eligibility: People in need at college or university who have lived, or whose parents have lived, in the former county of Flintshire (as constituted pre-1974) for at least 10 years.

Types of grants: Grants are given towards tuition fees and/or the cost of living.

Annual grant total: About £500.

Applications: In writing to the correspondent.

Correspondent: Philip Latham, Flintshire County Council, Flintshire County Hall, Shire Hall, Mold, Flintshire CH7 6ND

Other information: There is another trust with the same name and objectives that is for people who live in the former county of Denbighshire (as constituted pre-1974); see separate entry. If you have any confusion over which one to apply to, please contact one of the correspondents.

Gwynedd

The Caernarfonshire Further Education Trust Fund

Eligibility: People living in the former administrative county of Caernarfonshire

who have received their education at a secondary school within the former county.

Types of grants: Grants of around £20 to help with college or university fees or to supplement existing grants.

Annual grant total: About £500 in grants to individuals.

Applications: In writing to the correspondent. Applications are considered at committee meetings which are arranged in accordance with the number of applications. It is advisable to submit applications through the college/ tutor/head of department.

Correspondent: Peter Williams, Youth & Community/ Student Support Section, Education, Culture and Leisure Department, Council Offices, Caernarfon, Gwynedd LL55 ISH (01286 679190; Fax: 01286 679183; e-mail: plw@gwynedd. gov.uk)

The Griffith Charles Jones Trust Fund

Eligibility: Pupils or former pupils of the Sir Hugh Owen School, Caernarfon; the Segontoum School, Caernarfon; Brynrefail School, Llanrug; Dyffryn Nantlle School, Penn-y-Groes. Applicants must be following or entering an advanced course at a recognised establishment of further education and be under the age of 21 at the start of the course.

Types of grants: Grants of £30 to £60 for the first year only. The size of the grant is dependent on the applicant's A-level results.

Annual grant total: About £1,500.

Applications: The head teachers of the local schools submit names of potential beneficiaries before 31 May each year. Awards are decided at the trustees' meeting in November. Late applications will only be considered if funds are available after the first distribution of income.

Correspondent: Peter Williams, Youth & Community/ Student Support Section, Education, Culture and Leisure Department, Council Offices, Caernarfon, Gwynedd LL55 ISH (01286 679190; Fax: 01286 679183; e-mail: plw@gwynedd. gov.uk)

The Morgan Scholarship Fund

Eligibility: People born or living in the civil parish of Llanengan who are under the age of 25. When funds permit, the area of benefit may be extended to include other parishes in the rural district of Lleyn.

Types of grants: Preference is given to undergraduates of the University College of North Wales. However, grants are also given for the following purposes: for those at college or university (to a usual maximum of about £60); for those going abroad to pursue their education; financial assistance, clothing, tools, instruments or

books to help those leaving school, college or university to prepare for, or enter, a profession, trade or calling.

Annual grant total: About £1,000.

Applications: On a form available from the correspondent. Applications are considered in September.

Correspondent: Peter Williams, Youth & Community/ Student Support Section, Education, Culture and Leisure Department, Council Offices, Caernarfon, Gwynedd LL55 ISH (01286 679190; Fax: 01286 679183; e-mail: plw@gwynedd. gov.uk)

The R H Owen Memorial Fund (Gronfa Goffa R H Owen)

Eligibility: People aged between 12 and 25 who were born in, or whose parents have lived for at least five years in, the parish of Llanberis and Brynrefail Comprehensive School catchment area.

Types of grants: Recurrent grants are given to schoolchildren, undergraduates, vocational students and people starting work for any academic or vocational need.

Annual grant total: In 2004/05 the fund had an income of £850 and a total expenditure of £550. Grants total around £500 a each year.

Applications: On a form available from the correspondent which should be submitted directly by the individual. The closing date for applications is 31 August.

Correspondent: J H Hughes, Tan-y-Clogwyn, Llanberis, Caernarfon, Gwynedd LL55 4LF (01286 871562)

Dr Daniel William's Educational Fund

Eligibility: People under 25 attending college or university, particularly schoolchildren with serious family difficulties and people with special educational needs. Preference for (i) former pupils or close relatives of former pupils of Dr William's School, Dolgellau and (ii) people who live, or who have a parent who lives, in the district of Meirionnydd. This preference is strictly applied in view of the demands on the trust's income.

Types of grants: Recurrent grants towards the cost of books, equipment, fees/living expenses and study or travel abroad for students who are part of or linked to an educational course. Awards are usually of a maximum of £500.

Annual grant total: Over 150 grants awarded each year totalling around £30,000.

Applications: In writing, directly by the individual to the correspondent, requesting an application form.

Correspondent: T Meirion Wynne, Clogwyn Hal, Betws-y-coed, Gwynedd LL24 0BL (01690 710264)

Wrexham

Dame Dorothy Jeffreys Educational Foundation

Eligibility: People in need aged between 16 and 25 who live in the former borough of Wrexham or the communities of Abenbury, Bersham, Broughton, Bieston, Brymbo, Esclusham Above, Esculsham Below, Gresford, Gwersyllt and Minera.

Types of grants: Grants of £50 minimum. Grants for general education purposes are given to schoolchildren, further/higher education students, people starting work and vocational students. Mature students, up to the age of 25, can also receive grants.

Annual grant total: In 2005 the foundation had assets of £4,800, an income of £3,500 and a total expenditure of £3,600. Grants were made totalling £3,500 to nine individuals.

Applications: On a form available from the correspondent to be submitted directly by the individual. Applications are considered in November/December and should be submitted by 1 October.

Correspondent: P J Blore, 49 Norfolk Road, Wrexham LL12 7RT (01978 356901)

The Ruabon & District Relief-in-Need Charity

Eligibility: People in need who live in the county borough of Wrexham, which covers the community council districts of Cefn Mawr, Penycae, Rhosllanerchrugog (including Johnstown) and Ruabon.

Types of grants: One-off and occasionally recurrent grants of up to £200. Grants are given to schoolchildren towards uniforms/clothing, equipment/instruments and educational visits/excursions.

Exclusions: Loans are not given, nor are grants given to investigate bankruptcy proceedings.

Annual grant total: In 2005 the charity had assets of £70,000, an income of £3,100 and a total expenditure of £2,200. There were 11 grants made totalling £1,100. The trust does not distinguish between educational and relief-in-need grants.

Applications: In writing to the correspondent either directly by the individual or a family member, through a third party such as a social worker or teacher, or through an organisation such as Citizens Advice or a school. Applications are considered on an ongoing basis.

Correspondent: J R Fenner, Secretary, Cyncoed, 65 Albert Grove, Ruabon, Wrexham LL14 6AF (01978 820102; Fax: 01978 821595; e-mail: jamesfenner@amserve.com)

South Wales

The David Davies Memorial Trusts

Eligibility: South Wales mineworkers or their (unemployed) dependants, or redundant or retired mineworkers who have not taken up employment since leaving the coalmining industry.

Types of grants: Grants, ranging from £200 to £500, to enable people to pursue educational courses or other approved studies at university which they otherwise could not afford.

Annual grant total: In 2004, the trust had an income of £12,000 and a total expenditure of £11,000. Grants totalled about £10,000.

Applications: On a form available from the correspondent. Applications can be made directly by the individual and are considered throughout the year.

Correspondent: Andrew Morse, Coal Industry Social Welfare Organisation, Woodland Terrace, Maesycoed, Pontypridd, Mid-Glamorgan CF37 1DZ (01443 485233; Fax: 01443 486226)

The Gane Charitable Trust – see entry on page 18

Correspondent: Mrs R Fellows, The Secretary, c/o Bristol Guild, 68–70 Park Street, Bristol, BS1 5JY (0117 926 5548)

The Glamorgan Further Education Trust Fund

Eligibility: (i) Pupils who have for not less than two years at any time attended a county secondary school in the area of the former administrative county of Glamorgan (or Howell's Glamorgan County School, Cardiff, provided that the candidates attending the said school have lived in the former administrative county of Glamorgan for at least two years while a pupil at the school).

(ii) Female pupils who, in addition, have for not less than two years at any time attended any maintained primary school in the parishes of Llantrisant, Pontypridd, Pentyrch, Llanfabon, Llantwit Fardre, Eglwysilan and that part of the parish of Llanwonno comprising the former Ynysybwl ward of the former Mountain Ash urban district. There is a preference for such girls who while in attendance at any such school lived in the parish of Eglwysilan.

N.B. Applicants are not eligible for assistance if they are in receipt of a central government bursary or a mandatory or discretionary award, or are exempt from the payment of the tuition fee.

Types of grants: (a) Cash grants tenable at any Teacher training college, university or other institution of further education (including professional and technical) approved by the council and governed by rules made by the council.

(b) Financial assistance, outfits, clothing, tools, instruments or books to assist those leaving school, university or other educational establishments to prepare for or enter a profession, trade or calling.

Annual grant total: In 2005/06 it had both an income and a total expenditure of £60,000. Grants to individuals for educational purposes totalled £45,000.

Applications: On a form available from the correspondent. Applications should be submitted before 31 May each year for consideration in July/August.

Correspondent: Mrs Helen Lewis, Student/Pupil Support Section, Department for Education, Leisure and Lifelong Learning, 1st Floor, Aberafan House, Port Talbot SA13 1PJ (01639 763580)

The Gwent Further Education Trust Fund

Eligibility: People over 16 studying part-time who have lived in the former county of Gwent for at least three years or who have attended a secondary school in Gwent. No grants for people who live in Newport.

Types of grants: Grants to help with school, college or university fees, books and equipment. Students on Income Support can receive grants of about £360; employed students receive grants of around £60.

Annual grant total: About £10,000 each year is available for grants to individuals.

Applications: On a form available from the correspondent.

Correspondent: The Trustees, c/o Pupil & Student Services Section, Monmouthshire County Council, Education Department, County Hall, Cwmbran, Gwent NP44 2XH

The Geoffrey Jones (Penreithin) Scholarship Fund

Eligibility: People who have lived in the following parishes or districts for at least 12 months: Penderyn, Ystradfellte Vaynor and Taff Fechan Valley, Merthyr Tydfil.

Types of grants: Grants to students in further or higher education (no upper age limit) to help with the cost of books, fees/living expenses and study or travel abroad.

Annual grant total: About 25 grants are made each year totalling £2,000 to £3,000.

Applications: In writing to the correspondent, including details of any educational grant received. Applications are considered in September/October each year.

Correspondent: Mr Butler, 17–19 Cardiff Street, Aberdare, Rhondda Cynon Taff CF44 7DP (01685 885500; Fax: 01685 885535)

The Monmouthshire Further Education Trust Fund

Eligibility: Students on part-time courses who have attended a local comprehensive/secondary school and have lived in the Greater Gwent area, except Newport, that is, the council areas of Caerphilly (part), Torfaen, Blaenau Gwent and Monmouthshire.

Types of grants: One-off grants, although students can reapply in subsequent years, towards books, fees, travel and equipment. Grants range between £60 and £360, depending on student's circumstances. Full-time students receiving funding from another source are not funded.

Annual grant total: In 2004/05 the trust made grants to 82 individuals totalling £12,000.

Applications: Application forms are available from the correspondent, for consideration throughout the year.

Correspondent: The Further Education Department, The School and Student Access Unit, Floor 5, Monmouthshire County Council, County Hall, Cwmbran, Gwent NP44 2XH (01633 644644)

Caerphilly

The Rhymney Trust

Eligibility: People in need who live in Rhymney.

Types of grants: One-off grants ranging from £30 to £100 to school children and college students. Between 27 and 35 grants are made each year.

Annual grant total: In 2004/05 the trust had assets of £34,000, an income of £1,600 and a total expenditure of £1,500. Grants usually total around £1,500 per year.

Applications: In writing to the correspondent directly by the individual. Applications should be submitted in June for consideration in August.

Correspondent: D Brannan, 11 Forge Crescent, Rhymney, Gwent NP22 5PR (01685 843094)

Carmarthenshire

The Dorothy May Edwards Charity

Eligibility: Former pupils of Ysgol Pantycelyn School, Llandovery who are under 25 and are pursuing a course of higher education.

Types of grants: Grants of £15 to £125 to: provide outfits, clothing, tools,

instruments or books on leaving school, university or other educational establishment to prepare for and to enter a profession, trade or calling; travel in this country or abroad to pursue education; study music or other art; continue education at college or university or at any approved place of learning.

Annual grant total: In 2003/04, the charity gave grants to 18 individuals totalling £1,400.

Applications: Application forms are available from the correspondent. These should be completed and returned by 31 October.

Correspondent: Roger Jones, Director of Resources, Carmarthenshire County Council, County Hall, Carmarthen, Dyfed, SA31 1JP

The Elizabeth Evans Trust see entry on page 74

Correspondent: The Trust Secretary, c/o Ungoed Thomas and King, Gwynne House, 6 Quay Street, Carmarthen, SA31 3AD (e-mail: hazelthorogood@ theelizabethevanstrust.co.uk; website: www.theelizabethevanstrust.co. uk)

The Minnie Morgans Scholarship

Eligibility: People under the age of 25 who have attended any of the secondary schools in Llanelli and who are studying drama and dramatic art at the University of Wales or any school of dramatic art approved by the trustees.

Types of grants: One-off grants usually of £1,000.

Annual grant total: In 2005, the Scholarship had an income of £11,000 and a total expenditure of £7,000. No grant information was available.

Applications: Application forms are available from the correspondent and should be returned by 31 October.

Correspondent: Roger Jones, Carmarthenshire County Council, County Hall, Carmathen, Dyfed, SA31 1JP (01267 224503; Fax: 01267 221692)

The Mary Elizabeth Morris Charity

Eligibility: Past and present pupils of Ysgol Rhys Prichard School and Ysgol Pantycelyn School, who are under 25.

Types of grants: Grants to:

- pupils transferring from Ysgol Rhys Pritchard
- supplement existing grants of beneficiaries in further or higher education
- help towards the cost of education, training, apprenticeships or education for those starting work

- help with the cost of educational travel at home or abroad.

Annual grant total: In 2004/05, the charity had an income of £1,300 and a total expenditure of £1,000. No grant information was available.

Applications: Application forms are available from the correspondent and should be returned in either June (for primary school pupils) or by 31 October (for secondary school pupils).

Correspondent: Roger Jones, Director of Resources., Carmarthenshire County Council, County Hall, Carmarthen, Dyfed, SA31 1JP (01267 234567; Fax: 01267 221692)

The Robert Peel/Taliaris School Charity

Eligibility: People under the age of 25 years who at the time of application live in the ancient parish of Llandeilo Fawr and have done so for a minimum of two years. Preference is given to applicants who are members of or are connected with the Church in Wales. The ancient parish of Llandeilo Fawr was a very large parish extending from Capel Isaac and Taliaris in the north west down to the outskirts of Brynamman in the south east and including the township of Llandeilo.

Types of grants: Awards to promote the educational interests of individuals transferring to a recognised course of further education and also to assist school pupils in need.

Annual grant total: In 2004/05, the foundation had an income of around £700. It gave no grants to individuals this year.

Applications: On a form available from the correspondent to be returned by 31 October.

Correspondent: Alison Williamson, Student Support Manager, Student Support Services, Education Children's Department, Pibwrlwyd, Carmarthenshire SA31 2NH (01267 224503)

The May Price SRN Award

Eligibility: People who have lived in Cardiganshire, Carmarthenshire or Pembrokeshire for at least two years and who are pursuing a course in medical or medically-related studies.

Types of grants: Grants to help with the cost of books or equipment or to supplement existing grants.

Annual grant total: In 2004/05 it had an income of around £1,000 and an expenditure of £600. Grants totalled about £500.

Applications: On a form available from the correspondent, to be returned by 31 October each year.

Correspondent: Roger Jones, Director of Resources, Director of Resources, Carmarthenshire County County, County

Hall, Carmarthen, Dyfed, SA31 1JP
(01267 234567)

City of Cardiff

The Cardiff Caledonian Society

Eligibility: People of Scottish nationality and their families, who live in Cardiff or the surrounding district and are in need.

Types of grants: Grants are made to college students, undergraduates, vocational students and mature students, including those towards fees, books and instruments and equipment. Grants are also made to people starting work.

Annual grant total: In 2004/05 the trust had assets of £25,000, an income of £8,300 and a total expenditure of £6,200. One relief-in-need grant was made totalling £250. No educational grants were made during the year.

Applications: In writing to the correspondent. Applications can be submitted directly by the individual or through a social worker, citizen's advice bureau or other welfare agency at any time. Applications are considered on a regular basis.

Correspondent: Mrs Elizabeth Anne Elsbury, The Dingle, 9 Warren Drive, Caerphilly CF83 1HQ (029 2088 2588; Fax: 029 2088 2588)

The Cardiff Further Education Trust Fund

Eligibility: Young people who are resident in Cardiff and who attended a primary or secondary school in the city and are in need.

Types of grants: Grants in connection with the costs of further education.

Annual grant total: The amount given from the fund varies from year to year.

Applications: In writing to the correspondent.

Correspondent: Rick Zaple, Room 348, County Hall, Atlantic Wharf, Cardiff CF10 4UW (029 2087 2324)

The Howardian Educational Trust

Eligibility: Young people who are resident in Cardiff and who attended a primary or secondary school in the city and are in need.

Types of grants: Grants in connection with the costs of further education.

Annual grant total: In 2004/05, the trust had an income of about £1,000 and an expenditure of £600. Grants totalled about £500.

Applications: In writing to the correspondent.

Correspondent: Rick Zaple, Room 348, County Hall, Atlantic Wharf, Cardiff CF10 4UW (029 2087 2324)

Monmouthshire

Llandenny Charities

Eligibility: Students in full-time higher education who live in the parish of Llandenny and have lived there for more than one year.

Types of grants: Recurrent grants of £54.

Annual grant total: In 2004 the charities had an income £920. Pensions were made to 20 individuals totalling £650. Other grants were made totalling £270 to students in full-time education.

Applications: In writing to the correspondent, to be submitted directly by the individual. Applications should be submitted by 15 January for consideration in February.

Correspondent: Dr G K Russell, Forge Cottage, Llandenny, Usk, Monmouthshire NP15 1DL (01291 690380; e-mail: gsrussell@btinternet.com)

Monmouth Charity

Eligibility: Further education students who live within an eight-mile radius of Monmouth.

Types of grants: One-off grants usually up to a maximum of £500.

Annual grant total: In 2003/04 the charity had an income of £9,800 and a total expenditure of £8,400. Grants are made for education and welfare purposes. During the year about £4,000 was given in educational grants.

Applications: The trust advertises in the local press each September/October and applications should be made in response to this advertisement for consideration in November. Emergency grants can be considered at any time. There is no application form. Applications can be submitted directly by the individual or through a social worker, Citizens Advice or other welfare agency.

Correspondent: A R Pirie, Pen-y-Bryn, Oakfield Road, Monmouth NP25 3JJ

The Monmouthshire Farm School Endowment

Eligibility: Further and higher education agriculture students (and those studying related subjects) living in the former county of Monmouthshire (as constituted in 1956). Preference is given to students who are under the age of 25.

Types of grants: Grants of between £500 and £1,000 to help with the costs of study at the Usk College of Agriculture or any other farm institute, school, university or department of agricultural education approved by the governors. Grants can be

Correspondent: Rick Zaple, Room 348, County Hall, Atlantic Wharf, Cardiff CF10 4UW (029 2087 2324)

for books, equipment/instruments, fees, living expenses and educational outings in the UK.

Annual grant total: In 2004/05 grants were made to 19 individuals totalling £21,000.

Applications: On a form available from the correspondent which can be submitted at any time directly by the individual including an estimate of costs. Applications are considered in October and January.

Correspondent: Directorate of Lifelong Learning and Leisure, The School and Student Access Unit, Floor 5, Monmouthshire County Council, County Hall, Cwmbran, Gwent NP44 2XH (01633 644644; Fax: 01633 644208)

Other information: The trust has previously stated that owing to a shortage of applications, the trust deed is in the process of being revised in an attempt to widen the field of applications. However, the endowment remains open for applications.

The Monmouthshire Welsh Church Acts Fund

Eligibility: People of any age studying at school, university or any other place of study, who live in the boundaries of Monmouthshire County Council and their dependants. Grants are also made to people starting work.

Types of grants: Scholarships, bursaries, loans and maintenance allowances ranging from £50 to £500 for uniforms, other clothing, books, equipment, fees, childcare and travel in the UK and overseas for educational purposes. Grants include those for music or arts courses.

Annual grant total: In 2004/05 the trust had assets totalling £2.3 million and an income of £226,000. Grants to organisations and individuals totalled £161,000.

Applications: On a form available from the correspondent which can be submitted at any time, and must be signed by a county councillor. Applications can be made either directly by the individual, or through his or her school, and are usually considered in June, September, December and March.

Correspondent: Marie Rees, Management Accountancy, Monmouthshire County Council, County Hall, Cwmbran, Monmouthshire NP44 2XH

Other information: Following the reorganisation of local councils the funds from the Gwent Welsh Church Fund were divided and are now administered by five new councils. The above council is the only one which makes grants directly to individuals.

James Powell's Education Foundation

Eligibility: Boys and girls who live in the ancient parish of Llantilio Crossenny and who are 16 years old and over. No grants to students who live outside this area.

Types of grants: Grants are given for books, equipment and other essentials for people starting work, and for students and pupils for maintenance and living expenses.

Annual grant total: In 2004 the foundation had assets of £120,000, an income of £6,000 and a total expenditure of £3,600. Grants were made to 20 individuals totalling £3,200.

Applications: In writing to the correspondent, by a parent of the applicant. Applications should be made by August for consideration in September.

Correspondent: Mrs D M Watkins, Clerk, Park Farm, Llantilio Crossenny, Nr Abergavenny, Monmouthshire NP7 8TD (01600 780218)

Neath Port Talbot

Elizabeth Jones' Charities

Eligibility: People under the age of 25 in further/higher education who live in the old borough of Port Talbot and are in need.

Types of grants: One-off grants ranging from £50 to £400, towards books and study abroad.

Annual grant total: In 2004/05 the charities had an income of £21,900 and a total expenditure of £2,800. Grants totalled about £2,000.

Applications: On a form available from the correspondent. Applications can be submitted directly by the individual.

Correspondent: Ken Tucker, 6 Glandwffryn Close, Port Talbot SA13 2UB (01639 766224)

Pembrokeshire

Wynford Davies Travelling Scholarship

Eligibility: People under 26 years who have attended a secondary school in the Pembrokeshire Education Authority area.

Types of grants: A one-off travelling scholarship of £500 is made each year to a single individual where the travelling will broaden his or her educational, cultural or vocational experience.

Annual grant total: One grant of £500.

Applications: In writing to the correspondent directly by the individual. Applications should be made from the autumn through to February, for consideration in March.

Correspondent: T A L Davies, 3 Picton Close, Crundale, Haverfordwest, Pembrokeshire SA62 4EP (01437 764953)

The Charity of Doctor Jones

Eligibility: People between 16 and 25 who live in Pembroke.

Types of grants: Help towards the cost of education, training, apprenticeship or equipment for students, schoolchildren and those starting work.

Annual grant total: About £3,000 is available each year for grants to individuals.

Applications: Application forms are available from the correspondent.

Correspondent: Cllr D M Davies, Gwaun Derw, Norgans Hill, Pembroke SA71 5EP (01646 682257)

Other information: The charity advertises locally when grants are available, usually twice each year.

Milford Haven Port Authority Scholarships

Eligibility: Undergraduates at British universities in their second or later year of study. Applicants must have resided at some time in Pembrokeshire and have spent the majority of their secondary education in a Pembrokeshire school. Students who have lived in Pembrokeshire but attended secondary schools in nearby counties are also eligible.

Types of grants: Scholarships of £1,000 each.

Annual grant total: Each year the scheme provides four awards of £1,000 each to undergraduates.

Applications: Application forms are available from the port authority and on its website and should be returned by 25 November. All communication should be marked 'Scholarship Scheme'.

Correspondent: Gorsewood Drive, Milford Haven, Pembrokeshire SA73 3ER (01646 696100; Fax: 01646 696125; e-mail: enquires@mhpa.co.uk; website: www.mhpa.co.uk)

Other information: Each year a further grant of £2,000 is made to a postgraduate.

Narberth Educational Charity

Eligibility: People who have lived in the community council areas of Narberth, Llawhaden, Llanddewi Velfrey, Lampeter Velfrey (including Tavernspite and Ludchurch), Templeton, Martletwy (including Lawrenny), Begelly, part of Jeffreyston, Minwere and Reynalton. Applicants must have lived there for at least two years and be aged under 25.

Types of grants: Grants ranging from £100 to £150 to help those at school and those transferring to a recognised course or further or higher education.

Annual grant total: In 2004/05 the charity had an income of £2,900 and a total expenditure of £1,500.

Applications: Application forms are available from the correspondent. They must be returned directly by the individual by August for consideration in November.

Correspondent: M R Lewis, Education Offices, Pembrokeshire County Council, County Hall, Haverfordwest, Pembrokeshire SA61 1TP

Other information: The charity also provides financial assistance for local organisations engaged in youth activities and the promotion of education for young people/children living in the catchment area.

The Tasker Milward and Picton Charity

Eligibility: Former pupils of the Sir Thomas Picton School or the Tasker Milward School in Haverfordwest, Pembrokeshire, who are under the age of 25 and are experiencing financial hardship or other circumstances which could affect their studies.

Types of grants: One-off and recurrent grants ranging from £100 to £1,000. Students in further or higher education can receive grants towards books, living expenses and study or travel abroad.

Annual grant total: In 2004/05 the trust had an income of £41,300 and a total expenditure of £60,000. Further information for the year was not available. In previous years grants to individuals totalled around £10,000, with about £50,000 in grants also made to Sir Thomas Picton School and Tasker Milard School.

Applications: On a form available from the correspondent. Applications should be made directly by the individual or through a school/college/educational welfare agency and should be received by 1st September although individual applications are accepted throughout the year. Applications are considered twice in the autumn term and once in the spring and summer terms.

Correspondent: T A L Davies, 3 Picton Close, Crundale, Haverfordwest, Pembrokeshire SA62 4EP (01437 764953)

Swansea

The Swansea Foundation

Eligibility: People in education who live in Swansea. Preference is given to people who have attended one of the following schools or colleges: Bishop Gore Comprehensive School; Dynevor Comprehensive School; Swansea College; and Swansea Institute Of Higher Education.

Types of grants: One-off and recurrent grants according to need.

Annual grant total: In 2003/04 the foundation had an income of £9,900 and a total expenditure of £380.

Applications: In writing to the correspondent.

Correspondent: The Trustees, City & County of Swansea Council, County Hall, Oystermouth Road, Swansea, SA1 3SN

Torfaen

The Cwmbran Trust

Eligibility: People in need who live in the former urban area of Cwmbran, Gwent.

Types of grants: One-off and recurrent grants, ranging from £125 to £2,500.

Annual grant total: In 2004 grants to 41 individuals totalled £30,000.

Applications: In writing to the correspondent. Applications can be submitted directly by the individual or through a social worker, Citizens Advice, welfare agency or other third party. Applications are usually considered in March, May, July, October and December.

Correspondent: K L Maddox, Arvinheritor HVBS (UK) Ltd, Grange Road, Cwmbran, Gwent NP44 3XU (01633 834040; Fax: 01633 834051; e-mail: cwmbrantrust@ arvinmeritor.com)

Vale of Glamorgan

The Cowbridge with Llanblethian United Charities

Eligibility: People in need who live in the town of Cowbridge with Llanblethian.

Types of grants: Grants are towards clothing, fees, travel and maintenance for people preparing, entering or engaging in any profession, trade, occupation or service.

Annual grant total: In 2004/05 the charities had assets of £613,000 and an income of £27,000. Grants totalled £21,000, of which £20,000 was given in Christmas and summer grants and £1,000 to students.

Applications: In writing to the correspondent. Applications can be submitted directly by the individual or through a school/college or educational welfare agency.

Correspondent: H G Phillips, 66 Broadway, Llanblethian, Cowbridge, Vale of Glamorgan CF71 7EW (01446 773287; e-mail: unitedcharities@aol.com)

4. NORTH EAST

The Christina Aitchison Trust

Eligibility: Young people under the age of 25 years from north east or south west England.

Types of grants: One-off or recurrent grants for up to £300 to support young people in educational music, riding or sailing activities and other educational purposes. Donations are made in the form of books, equipment, fees, bursaries and fellowships.

Annual grant total: In 2004/05 the trust had an income of £1,500 and a grants total of about £1,200.

Applications: On a form available from the correspondent, to be submitted in March or September for consideration in April or November.

Correspondent: A P G Massingberd-Mundy, Secretary, c/o The Old Post Office, West Raynham, Fakenham, Norfolk, NR21 7AD

Other information: Grants are also given to assist people who have an ophthalmic disease or who are terminally ill.

Lord Crewe's Charity

Eligibility: Necessitous clergy, their widows and dependants who live in the dioceses of Durham and Newcastle.

Types of grants: The trust can give grants for a whole range of education needs up to and including first degrees.

Annual grant total: In 2004 the charity's income was £755,000 and its total expenditure was £679,000. Grants to clergy totalled £186,000. Grants are made for welfare and educational purposes.

Applications: On a form available from the correspondent for consideration in March or November.

Correspondent: The Clerk, Durham Cathedral, The Chapter Office, The College, Durham DH1 3EH (0191 375 1226; e-mail: peter.church@durhamcathedral.co.uk)

For the Kids

Eligibility: People who are 19 or under and either live or go to school in the East Yorkshire and Northern Lincolnshire area. This area extends to Mablethorpe in the South, York and Carlton in the West and Flamborough in the North.

Types of grants: Grants are made towards children who are sick, disabled or have learning disabilities.

Annual grant total: About £10,000 a year is given to individuals and organisations. Around £5,000 was given for educational purposes.

Applications: On a form available from the correspondent. They are considered quarterly. Cheques are paid to a charity on the individual's behalf to ensure it is spent for the intended purpose.

Correspondent: Debbie Westlake, c/o Viking FM, Commercial Road, Hull HU1 2SG (01482 593193; e-mail: debbie.westlake@vikingfm.co.uk; website: www.vikingfm.co.uk)

Hylton House Fund

Eligibility: People in the North East with cerebral palsy and related disabilities, and their families and carers. The priority 1 areas cover County Durham, Darlingotn, Gateshead, South Shields and Sunderland. Priority 2 areas are Hartlepool, Redcar, Cleveland, Middlesbrough and Stockton.

Types of grants: Grants of up to £500 towards: education, training and therapy, such as sound and light therapy for people with cerebral palsy to improve quality of life or funding towards further education courses; training and support for carers and self-help groups where no statutory support or provision is available); provision of aids and equipment, particularly specialist clothing, communication and mobility aids; travel costs, such as taxi and rail fares to attend a specific activity if no alternative transport is available; and respite support for an individual when the needs of the person requires them to either be accompanied by an employed carer or by visiting a specialist centre where full-time extensive care is provided.

Exclusions: No grants for: legal costs; ongoing education; medical treatment; decorating and/or refurbishment costs (unless the work is due to the nature of the applicant's disability); building adaptations; motor vehicle adaptations; motor insurance; deposits or running costs; televisions or videos; assessments, such as the costs involved in the Scope Living Options Schemes; or retrospective funding.

Annual grant total: In 2004 a total of £4,200 was given in grants from the fund.

Applications: Applicants can either: use a form available from the correspondent or the website; or write to the correspondent including their name, address, relationship to beneficiary (if applying on somebody else's behalf), how the eligibility criteria is met, what the grant will be used for and why it is important, details of the course and the benefits it will bring (for educational grants), total costs, how much is being asked for, how any shortfall will be met, who else has been approached and details of who any cheque should be payable (usually a supplier or provider rather than directly to the applicant).

All applications must include a reference from a social worker or professional adviser in a related field, with a telephone number and the individual's permission for them to be contacted about an application.

Appeals are considered in January, April, July and October and needed to be received before the start of the month. They can be considered between these dates within a month of application if the need is urgent, but the applicant will need to request this and provide a reason why an exception to the usual policy needs to be made.

Correspondent: Grants Officer, Jordan House, Forster Business Centre, Finchale Road, Durham DH1 5HL (0191 383 0055; Fax: 0191 383 2969; e-mail: info@countydurhamfoundation.co.uk; website: www.countydurhamfoundation.co.uk)

Northern Counties Orphans' Benevolent Society

Eligibility: Children in need through sickness, disability or other causes with a preference for those who live in the counties of Cleveland, Durham, Tyne & Wear, Northumberland and Cumbria. There is a preference for orphaned children.

Types of grants: Both one-off and recurrent grants for education and clothing. The trust has previously stated that assistance takes the form of grants towards school fees, the cost of school clothing and equipment and, in a limited number of cases, the provision of special equipment of an educational or physical nature for disabled children. In almost every case, the need for assistance arises through the premature death of the major wage earner, or the break up of the family unit. Applications are treated in strict confidence and the financial circumstances of each applicant are fully and carefully considered by the trustees before an award is made.

Annual grant total: In 2004/05 the trust had assets of £1.5 million and an income of £114,000. Grants to 56 children for education and relief-in-need purposes totalled £96,000.

Applications: On a form available from the correspondent, for consideration in January, April, July or October.

Correspondent: Ms G Mackie, 29a Princes Road, Gosforth, Newcastle upon Tyne NE3 5TT (0191 236 5308)

The Northumberland Village Homes Trust

Eligibility: Young people under the age of 21 who are in need through poverty, sickness or distress and live in Tyne & Wear, Durham, Cleveland or Northumberland.

Types of grants: One-off and recurrent grants according to need. Grants are given to promote the education and training of young people. Grants are available for a wide range of needs. In the past help has been given towards the costs of books, clothing and other essentials.

Exclusions: Grants are not given for gap year projects.

Annual grant total: In 2004/05 the trust had assets of £1.2 million generating an income of £54,000. Grants totalling £46,000 were made mostly to organisations who work with people under 21. Grants to individuals totalled about £1,000.

Applications: In writing to the correspondent. The trustees meet in November and applications should be submitted in September. No personal applications will be considered unless supported by an accompanying letter from the headteacher or an official from the local authority or other such body.

Correspondent: Derek McCoy, Trustee, Savages Solicitors, Maranar Building, 2nd Floor, 28-30 Mosley Street, Newcastle upon Tyne NE1 1DF (0191 221 2111; Fax: 0191 222 1712)

The Sir John Priestman Charity Trust

Eligibility: Clergy and their families in need who live in the historic counties of Durham and York (especially the county borough of Sunderland).

Types of grants: Grants to help towards the cost of school fees and for gap year activities including Christian mission.

Annual grant total: In 2004 the trust had assets of £7.6 million and an income of £269,000. Grants to clergy and their families totalled almost £12,000.

Applications: In writing to the correspondent. Applications are considered quarterly.

Correspondent: P W Taylor, McKenzie Bell, 19 John Street, Sunderland, Tyne & Wear SR1 1JG (0191 567 4857)

Other information: The trust also assists charities serving County Durham (especially the Sunderland area) and helps maintain Church of England churches and buildings in the above area.

The Provincial Grand Charity

Eligibility: Children (including adopted and step-children) of present and deceased masons who live or lived in North Yorkshire and Humberside.

Types of grants: Grants for those at school, college or university towards school clothing, books, school fees and living expenses depending on the parental circumstances. Grants range from £100 to £3,000.

Annual grant total: In 2004 the fund had net assets of £638,000, an income of £52,000 and a total expenditure of £41,000. The fund gave grants to individuals of £30,000.

Applications: In writing to the correspondent, to be considered at quarterly meetings. Applications must be supported by the relative who is a member of the masons.

Correspondent: M Graham, Provincial Offices, Castlegate House, Castlegate, York YO1 9RP (01428 652236)

Prowde's Educational Foundation

Eligibility: Boys and young men between the ages of 9 and 25 who live in Somerset or the North or East Ridings of Yorkshire. There is a preference for those who are descendants of the named persons in the will of the founder. There is also a preference for boys with serious family difficulties such that the child has to be educated away from home and for those with special education needs.

Types of grants: One-off grants to boys and men in further or higher education, including postgraduates, for fees, uniforms, other school clothing, books, equipment, instruments, fees and study or

travel abroad. The average grant to an individual is £450.

Annual grant total: In 2004/05 the foundation had an income of £22,000 and a total expenditure of £16,000. Grants to individuals total about £10,000.

Applications: Applications can be submitted directly by the individual, parents or occasionally social workers, and should include a birth certificate and evidence of acceptance for a course. They should be submitted in May/June for consideration in July.

Correspondent: R G Powell, Administrative Trustee, Broad Eaves, Hawks Hill Close, Leatherhead, Surrey KT22 9DL (01372 374561)

The Sherburn House Educational Foundation

Eligibility: People aged between 16 and 21 who live in the pre-1972 boundaries of County Durham.

Types of grants: Grants of between £50 and £450 are available to students towards books, equipment, instruments and fees.

Annual grant total: In 2004/05 the trust had assets of £35,600 and an income of £2,600. Grants were made to 12 individuals totalling £2,000.

Applications: Applications should be made through the individual's school/college, educational welfare agency or a third party such as social services or a citizen's advice bureau. They are considered throughout the year.

Correspondent: Stephen P Hallett, Ramsey House, Sherburn Hospital, Sherburn House, Durham DH1 2SE (0191 372 2551; Fax: 0191 372 0035; e-mail: admin@ sherburnhouse.org; website: www. sherburnhouse.org)

Stanhope Castle School Charitable Trust

Eligibility: People aged 24 or under who are, or have been, in local authority care in County Durham, Darlington, Hartlepool, Redcar and Cleveland, Middlesbrough, Stockton, Gateshead, South Tyneside or Sunderland for a minimum of six months.

In exceptional circumstances, the trustees will also consider the provision of equipment, of an educational nature only, for young people with special needs.

Types of grants: One-off grants of between £100 and £500 to support educational and training activities. This includes: educational outings, fees and study aids such as books, subscription fees; training courses; bursaries to pay for young people to participate at a regional, national or international level in their chosen field; and driving or motorbike lessons (maximum contribution £250) where you can prove either an extensive interest in car or motorbike mechanics and/or you have been offered employment for which you will need a driving licence.

Exclusions: No grants for uniforms, large capital items, holiday or hardship funds (educational trips will be considered but not 'Operation Raleigh type support'), or debt clearance. The trust will not fund any activity that is the duty of a local authority to provide. Retrospective grants are not made.

Annual grant total: In 2003/04, the trust had an income of £8,000 and a total expenditure of £10,000. Grants totalled about £7,000.

Applications: On a form available, with guidelines for applicants, from the correspondent, or in writing, providing the information listed in the guidelines. Applications should be made directly by the individual and include a referee. Only one grant can be made per individual in each financial year.

Applicants will need to provide full costings and show that they have researched and sought advice from an appropriate source such as an independent professional adviser, for example, a teacher for specialist equipment and provision or a social worker or home manager.

Applications from a number of young people who wish to undertake educational or training activities together and who can demonstrate why they should be considered as a group application will also be considered.

Applications are considered in February, May, August and November, although urgent requests can be considered between meetings. Applications are processed within four weeks and the trust will usually contact the applicant to discuss their application during this time.

Correspondent: Melanie Caldwell, Suite 2, First Floor, Jordan House, Forster Business Centre, Finchale Road, Durham DH1 5HL (0191 383 0055; Fax: 0191 383 2969; e-mail: info@countydurhamfoundation.co.uk; website: www.countydurhamfoundation.co.uk)

The Yorkshire Training Fund for Women

Eligibility: British women aged 16 or over who live in, or have connections to, Yorkshire and are in higher or further education.

Types of grants: One-off grants of generally about £50, but they can be up to £250, for women undertaking courses of study that should enable them to become self-sufficient financially. Grants are given towards books, equipment and instruments.

Exclusions: People on access courses are not eligible.

Annual grant total: In 2004 the fund had an income of £1,400 and a total

expenditure of £1,800. Around 10 grants are made each year totalling about £1,600.

Applications: On a form available from the correspondent, to be submitted either by the individual or through a social worker, Citizens Advice or other welfare agency. Applicants should provide details of two referees and detailed information of their financial position. Completed forms should be returned by 1 May for the June meeting or by 1 November for the December meeting.

Correspondent: Mrs F M Slater, Hon. Secretary, 5 Bede Court, Wakefield WF1 3RW (01924 373077)

Other information: The trust states that 'there is a great deal of competition for the grants'.

County Durham

The Lady Dale Scholarship

Eligibility: Girls and young women from poorer families going from school to further and higher education and who have attended Branksome, Eastbourne, Haughton, Hummersknott, Hurworth or Longfield comprehensive schools – Darlington.

Types of grants: Scholarships for those going on to colleges of further education.

Annual grant total: In 2004/05 the trust had an income of £1,000 and a total expenditure of £200, with just one grant to an individual.

Applications: In writing to the correspondent, to be submitted through the individual's school by early August, although preferably earlier.

Correspondent: Elaine Sayers, Clerk to the Trustees, Children's Services, Town Hall, Darlington DL1 5QT

The Darlington Education Fund

Eligibility: Persons under the age of 25 who attend or have attended Branksome, Eastbourne, Haughton, Hummersknott, Hurworth or Longfield comprehensive schools, or the Queen Elizabeth Sixth Form College – Darlington.

Types of grants: Grants for: people at school/college/university; people leaving any educational establishment to prepare for and enter a profession, trade or calling; educational travel in this country and abroad and for people to study music or other arts. Financial assistance can be for clothing, training, travel, equipment, books and the like. With the approval of the managing trustees the award of exhibitions tenable at any secondary school, college of education, university or other institution of further education (including professional and technical) can

also be made.

Students currently attending the Darlington College of Technology and who previously attended one of the above mentioned schools are also eligible to apply for grants. Except in exceptional circumstances, assistance will not be given towards the cost of travel expenses within the Darlington area.

Awards are made on a quarterly basis.

Annual grant total: In 2004/05 the trust had an income of £15,000 and a total expenditure of £7,000, all of which was given in grants to 74 individuals.

Applications: Further information and an application form are available from the correspondent. Pupils still in attendance at any of the schools/college listed may discuss the matter with the headteacher in the first instance. Full details of the purpose for which the award is required and some indication of the cost involved should be given. The trustees meet once each term to consider applications.

Correspondent: Elaine Sayers, Clerk to the Trustees, Children's Services, Town Hall, Darlington DL1 5QT

The Sedgefield District Relief-in-Need Charity

Eligibility: College, university, vocational and mature students who live in the parishes of Bishop Middleham, Bradbury, Fishburn, Mordon, Sedgefield and Trimdon in County Durham.

Types of grants: One-off grants are made to undergraduates and mature students for maintenance/living expenses.

Annual grant total: In 2005 the sum of £6,700 was distributed in more than 200 welfare grants. A further £880 was distributed in 4 educational grants.

Applications: On a form available from the correspondent, to be submitted by 30 September each year.

Correspondent: R Smeeton, Clerk, 13 North Park Road, Sedgefield, County Durham, TS21 2AP (01740 620009)

Other information: This trust mostly provides relief-in-need grants to people of any age in the geographical area of benefit.

The Sedgefield Educational Foundation

Eligibility: People who normally live in the civil parishes of Sedgefield, Fishburn, Bradbury and Morden in County Durham and are aged between 18 and 25.

Types of grants: Recurrent grants during period of study. Grants to help with college, university or technical college courses or other vocational courses towards the cost of books and to help with fees/living expenses. The trustees normally only help with education higher than A-level and current policy is to limit aid to courses not available at schools. Grants range from £140 to £300 (depending on the applicant's circumstances).

Students seeking funds for study or travel abroad and mature students over 25 may be referred to the Sedgefield District Relief-in-Need Charities, to which welfare applications are also referred (see separate entry).

Annual grant total: In 2005 the trust had both an income and a total expenditure of around £4,500. Grants were made to 16 individuals totalling £3,800.

Applications: On a form available from the correspondent. Applications must be submitted by 30 September for consideration in October.

Correspondent: R Smeeton, Clerk, 13 North Park Road, Sedgefield, County Durham TS21 2AP (01740 620009)

Durham

The Johnston Educational Foundation

Eligibility: People under 25 who live or whose parents live in the city of Durham and who have attended one of the city's comprehensive schools for at least two years.

Types of grants: One-off and recurrent grants ranging from £50 to £1,000. Grants are made to students in further/higher education to help with the cost of books, equipment/instruments, fees, living expenses and study or travel abroad to help or to assist entry into a profession, trade or calling.

Annual grant total: In 2004/05 the trust had an income of £2,600 and a total expenditure of £1,100, all of which was given in grants to four individuals.

Applications: On a form available from the correspondent. Applications are considered in February, June and October and should be submitted directly by the individual.

Correspondent: Barry Piercy, Clerk to the Trustees, School and Governor Support Service, County Hall, Durham DH1 5UJ (0191 383 4596; Fax: 0191 383 4597)

Frosterley

The Frosterley Exhibition Foundation

Eligibility: People in full-time education, from secondary school age upwards, whose parents live in the parish of Frosterley. Preference is given to college and university students.

Types of grants: Grants are given towards books, uniforms and any other educational requirement deemed necessary.

Annual grant total: In 2004/05 the trust had an income of £1,100 and a total

expenditure of £1,500. Grants were made totalling around £1,000.

Applications: In writing to the correspondent, to be submitted by the applicant's parent, to whom the cheque will be made. Applications should be submitted in August for consideration in September.

Correspondent: Miss Judith Bainbridge, Norton House, 6 Osborne Terrace, Frosterley, Bishop Auckland, County Durham DL13 2RD (01388 527668)

Stanhope

The Hartwell Educational Foundation

Eligibility: People aged between 11 and 21 who live in the civil parish of Stanhope. Eligibility is dependent on parental income.

Types of grants: Grants are primarily awarded on a recurrent basis to students going to college or university for help with fees/living expenses and books. Students from poorer homes receive larger grants. One-off grants, if financial circumstances warrant, are given to younger pupils attending secondary schools. These smaller grants are towards the cost of uniforms, other clothing, books, and so on.

Annual grant total: In 2004/05 grants to six individuals totalled £900.

Applications: Applications should be made by the last Saturday in August, on a form available from the correspondent, for consideration in September/October. Applications can be made either directly by the individual or by a parent/guardian.

Correspondent: Mrs Dorothy Foster, Sowen Burn, Stanhope, County Durham DL13 2PP (01388 528577)

East Yorkshire

Joseph Boaz Charity

Eligibility: People from Hull and East Yorkshire who are in further or higher education, including mature students and postgraduates.

Types of grants: One-off grants of £250 to £500 are given towards books, equipment and instruments.

Exclusions: Grants are not given for course fees or living expenses.

Annual grant total: In 2004/05 the trust had assets of £330,000 and income of £14,000. Total expenditure was £17,000 of which £8,500 went to organisations. No grants were made to individuals during the year.

Applications: In writing to the correspondent to be submitted either directly by the individual or a parent/guardian, through a third party such as a teacher, or through an organisation such as a school or an educational welfare agency. Applications are considered in June and December.

Correspondent: P R Evans, Graham & Rosen Solicitors, 8 Parliament Street, Hull HU1 2BB (01482 323123; Fax: 01482 223542; e-mail: pre@graham-rosen.co.uk)

The Joseph & Annie Cattle Trust

Eligibility: Schoolchildren who have dyslexia and live in Hull or the East Riding of Yorkshire area.

Types of grants: One-off grants of £200 to £500.

Annual grant total: In 2004/05 the trust had assets of £7.6 million and an income of £339,000. Grants totalled £235,000 of which £56,000 went to individuals.

Applications: In writing to the correspondent, only via a welfare organisation, for consideration on the third Monday of every month. Please note, if applicants approach the trust directly they will be referred to an organisation, such as Disability Rights Advisory Service, or social services.

Correspondent: Roger Waudby, Administrator, Morpeth House, 114 Spring Bank, Hull HU3 1QJ (01482 211198; Fax: 01482 211198)

The Leonard Chamberlain Trust

Eligibility: People who live in Selby or the East Riding of Yorkshire and are in further or higher education.

Types of grants: Grants are given towards books.

Annual grant total: Around 10 grants are made each year ranging from £50 to £1,000.

Applications: On a form available from the correspondent. They should be returned in August for consideration in September.

Correspondent: The Secretary, c/o 6 Manor Park, Preston, Hull HU12 8XE

The Hesslewood Children's Trust (Hull Seamen's & General Orphanage)

Eligibility: Young people under 25 who live or have firm family connections with the former county of Humberside and North Lincolnshire, with a preference for children of former seamen who served in the Merchant Navy. The trust also gives to former Hesslewood Scholars.

'Applicants must be in need, but must show their resolve to part fund themselves.'

Preference is given to people with special educational needs.

Types of grants: Grants are given towards: books, school uniforms, educational outings and maintenance for schoolchildren; books for students in higher and further education; and equipment and instruments and clothing for people starting work. Grants are one-off.

Exclusions: Loans are not made.

Annual grant total: In 2004/05 the trust had assets of £2.2 million and an income of £81,000. Grants to individuals totalled £15,000.

Applications: On a form available from the correspondent, accompanied by a letter from the tutor or an educational welfare organisation (or from medical and social services for a disability grant). Applications can be submitted by the individual, through their school, college or educational welfare agency, or by another third party such as the Citizens Advice bureau or health centre. Details of the applicant's and parental income must be included, along with an indication of the amount the applicant will contribute. A contact telephone number would be useful. The deadlines are 16 February, 16 June and 16 September.

Correspondent: R E Booth, Secretary, 66 The Meadows, Cherry Barton, Beverley, East Yorkshire HU17 7SP

Other information: Grants are also made to organisations (£41,000 in 2004/05)

The Hook & Goole Charity

Eligibility: People aged 16 to 25 who are in further or higher education and have lived in the parish of Hook and the area of the former borough of Goole as constituted on 31 March 1974 within the last two years.

Types of grants: Grants of between £150 and £400 are given towards books, living expenses, educational outings and study or travel overseas.

Annual grant total: In 2004 the trust had an income of £11,000 and a total expenditure of £14,000. Grants totalled about £10,000.

Applications: On a form available from the correspondent. Applications should be submitted directly by the individual in July/August for consideration in September.

Correspondent: K G Barclay, 3–15 Gladstone Terrace, Goole, East Yorkshire DN14 5AH (01405 765661)

Humberside Educational Trust

Eligibility: People aged 21 or under in the East Riding of Yorkshire.

Types of grants: One-off grants of £500 to £750 are given to schoolchildren for maintenance and living expenses.

Annual grant total: About four or five grants are given each year totalling £3,000.

Applications: In writing to the correspondent. The AGM is held in November, although applications are also considered at other times.

Correspondent: P S Bennett, Secretary of the Trust, Pocklington School, West Green, Pocklington, York YO42 2NJ (01759 321204; Fax: 01759 306366; e-mail: bursar@pocklington.e-yorks.sch. uk)

The Nancie Reckitt Charity

Eligibility: People under 25 who have, or whose parents have, a minimum of five years' residency and are still living in the civil parishes of Patrington, Winestead and Rimswell in East Yorkshire.

Types of grants: Recurrent grants of £100 to £600 are given to people starting work for clothing and equipment and to students in further or higher education for equipment, books and fees.

Annual grant total: In 2004/05 the trust had assets of £125,000, an income of £6,000 and a total expenditure of £5,800. Grants were made to 15 individuals totalling £5,300.

Applications: On a form available from the correspondent to be submitted directly by the individual. Applications from people starting work should be submitted in April for consideration in May. University and college students should apply in August for consideration in September. Claims for books, materials, tools and so on should have the cost substantiated by forwarding receipts.

Correspondent: Mrs M Stansfield, Clerk, Heath House, 19 Northside, Patrington, East Yorkshire, HU12 0PA (01964 630960)

The Sir Philip Reckitt Educational Trust Fund

Eligibility: People in full-time education who live in Kingston-upon-Hull, the East Riding of Yorkshire, or the county of Norfolk.

Types of grants: Grants are given towards educational travel such as Raleigh International, working in the developing world, outward bound type courses and so on. Travel must be connected with the extracurricular projects of the course. Grants can also be used to help with residence and attendance at conferences, lectures and short educational courses.

Exclusions: Awards will not normally be made to persons under the age of 14 on the date of travel.

Annual grant total: In 2005, the trust had assets of £824,000 and an income of £27,000. Grants to 93 individuals totalled £15,000; a further £7,855 was given to 14 groups.

Applications: Applications can only be made using the trust's official forms which can be completed online at its website. Postal applications can be made using forms available on request or by downloading a printable version.

Contacts:

Kingston-upon-Hull, the East Riding of Yorkshire – The Trustees, Sir Philip Reckitt Educational Trust, Rollits, Wilberforce Court, High Street, Hull HU1 1JY (e-mail: hull@spret.org). **Norfolk** – The Trustees, Sir Philip Reckitt Educational Trust, c/o Mrs J. Pickering, 99 Yarmouth Road, Ellingham, Bungay NR35 2PH (e-mail: jpickering@spretrust. freeserve.co.uk; website: www.spret.com).

Sir Henry Samman's Hull Chamber of Commerce Endowment Fund

Eligibility: Preference to young people of Hull and the former East Riding. Applicants should normally have reached the age of 18, and be studying, or planning to study, at degree level, although consideration will be given to those slightly under this age limit.

Types of grants: The fund provides scholarships to assist young people who wish to spend a period overseas to further their study of 'business methods or a foreign language' with a view to taking up a career in commerce or industry.

'Awards are made for a stay of not less than three months and up to maximum of 12 months. They could be available to those wishing to spend time overseas between leaving school and embarking on a course of further or higher education; to students spending up to three terms abroad as part of their course or using long vacations to improve their knowledge of the language; and to those going straight into employment whose employers may be prepared to release them to study or gain experience in a foreign country, possibly spending time in one of their offices overseas or with an associated company.

'It is desirable for applicants to pursue a course of study in the country concerned. The awards can be used for living expenses during the visit, and could, among other things, enable the young person to travel within the country to an extent that would not otherwise be possible. Award holders are required to submit a letter of report.'

Annual grant total: In 2004, the fund had an income of £7,700 and a total expenditure of £5,500. Grants totalled about £5,000.

Applications: In writing to the correspondent.

Correspondent: Dr I Kelly, Secretary, Hull & Humber Chamber of Commerce, Industry & Shipping, 34–38 Beverley Road, Hull HU3 1YE (01482 324976; Fax: 01482 213962)

Other information: The fund was set up in 1917 originally to encourage the study of Russian in a commercial context, but has since been extended.

The Sydney Smith Trust

Eligibility: Long-term residents of Kingston- upon- Hull and its immediate vicinity who are undertaking further, higher or vocational training or re-training, and are in need. Applicants must be under 35 and have attended secondary school in Hull.

Types of grants: One-off grants to people starting work and students in further/higher education, including mature students under 35, towards equipment and instruments.

Annual grant total: In 2004/05, the trust had an income of £6,000 and a total expenditure of £15,700.

Applications: In writing to the correspondent at any time. Details of schools attended, qualifications obtained and future plans are required.

Correspondent: Brian Smith, HSBC Trust Company (UK) Ltd, Commercial Road, Southampton, SO15 1GX (023 807 22223; Fax: 023 807 22250)

Robert Towries Charity

Eligibility: People in need who live in Aldbrough, East Newton and West Newton.

Types of grants: One-off grants for educational purposes.

Annual grant total: In 2003/04 the charity had an income of £6,300 and a total expenditure of £4,600. Grants totalled about £4,000.

Applications: In writing to the correspondent. Applications should be submitted directly by the individual for consideration in November.

Correspondent: Mrs P M Auty, 6 Willow Grove, Headlands Park, Aldbrough, Hull HU11 4SH

Ann Watson's Trust

Eligibility: People in need under the age of 25 who live in the former borough of Kingston-upon-Hull and the East Riding of Yorkshire.

Types of grants: One-off and recurrent grants according to need.

Annual grant total: In 2005 the trust had both an income and a total expenditure of £335,000. Educational grants to individuals were made totalling £90,000.

Applications: In writing to the correspondent at any time during the year. The trustees meet quarterly.

Correspondent: Mrs Karen Palmer, Flat 4 The College, 14 College Street, Sutton-on-Hull, Hull HU7 4UP (01482 709626; e-mail: awatson@awatson.karoo.co.uk)

The Christopher Wharton Educational Foundation

Eligibility: People who live in the former parish of Stamford Bridge with Scoreby or the parish of Gate Helmsley. Applicants must be under 25 years old.

Types of grants: Grants of about £100 to help with further education, tools, instruments or apprenticeships not normally provided by the local education authorities.

Annual grant total: About £1,000.

Applications: In writing to the correspondent by 31 October.

Correspondent: Mrs E M Catterick, 25 High Catton Road, Stamford Bridge, York YO41 1DL

Barmby on the Marsh

The Blanchard's Educational Foundation

Eligibility: People under the age of 25 living in Barmby on the Marsh.

Types of grants: Grants are available for (a) schoolchildren, including help with the cost of clothing, books and educational outings but not school fees or maintenance; (b) students in further or higher education including help with the cost of books and study or travel abroad, but not for fees/living expenses; (c) people starting work for books and equipment, but not clothing or travel; and (d) mature students (under 25) for books and travel, but not for fees or childcare expenses.

Annual grant total: In 2004/05 the foundation had an income of £2,200 and a total expenditure of £1,800. Grants were made to individuals totalling around £1,500.

Applications: In writing to the correspondent. Meetings are held in July and December.

Correspondent: John Burman, Clerk, Heptonstalls Solicitors, 7-15 Gladstone Terrace, Goole, East Yorkshire DN14 5AH (01405 765661; Fax: 01405 764201)

Beverley

The Christopher Eden Educational Foundation

Eligibility: People under the age of 25 who live in the town of Beverley and the villages in Beverley Rural Ward. People with special educational needs are given preference.

Types of grants: One-off grants of £50 to £400 are given to: (a) schoolchildren and students in higher education to help with books, equipment, clothing, travel, field trips, sports equipment and training and for studying music and the arts, but not for school fees or school uniforms; (b) people in further or higher education towards fees or to supplement existing grants, including grants to travel in connection with education and books; and (c) people starting work to help with the cost of books, equipment, clothing and travel.

Recurrent grants are occasionally given for the duration of the course, but no loans are available.

Annual grant total: In 2004/05 the foundation had an income of £13,300 and a total expenditure of £12,000. Grants to individuals totalled about £11,000.

Applications: On a form available from the correspondent. Applications for assistance with university or college costs should be submitted in September for consideration in October. Applications for any other purposes are considered in January, April, July and October. A parent/guardian should complete the application for those under 16. Applications must also include course details, education details, parents' income, applicant's income and outgoings and the reason why help is needed. Incomplete or incorrectly completed applications will not be considered and are not returned.

Correspondent: Mrs Judy Dickinson, 85 East Street, Leven, Beverley HU17 5NG (01964 542593; e-mail: judydickinson@mac.com)

Other information: The charity has endowed a berth on a sail training schooner and selects a deserving young person for the berth each year.

The James Graves Educational Foundation

Eligibility: Students preferably under the age of 18 who live in the parish of St Martin, Beverley.

Types of grants: Grants for the education of minors (with a particular emphasis on religious education). This means help with the cost of books and other essentials for schoolchildren, particularly those with a church connection. The maximum grant is £500.

Annual grant total: About £1,500.

Applications: In writing to the correspondent. Apparently not many suitable applications are received each year. Applications are considered twice yearly.

Correspondent: Mrs Joy Willson, The Parish Office, Beverley Minster, East Yorkshire HU17 0DP

The Wray Educational Trust

Eligibility: People aged 25 or under who have lived in the parish of Leven in Beverley for at least three years.

Types of grants: One-off grants are given to schoolchildren, people starting work and students in further or higher education towards books, equipment, instruments, fees, educational outings and study or travel abroad.

Annual grant total: In 2003/04 the trust had an income of £5,600 and a total expenditure of £5,100.

Applications: On a form available from the correspondent, who knows many of the people in the village and is always willing to discuss needs. Applications are considered in January, April, July and October.

Correspondent: Mrs J Dickinson, 85 East Street, Leven Beverley, North Humberside HU17 5NG (01964 542593)

Cottingham

Mark Kirby's Charity

Eligibility: People of school age who live and attend, or have attended, school in the parish of Cottingham.

Types of grants: One-off cash grants of £25 to £100 to school pupils to help with clothing (in cases of special need), travel, or special education courses and any travel expenses arising from this. Grants are not given for school fees or to people who have left school (except rarely to students in further or higher education for study or travel abroad).

Annual grant total: In 2004 the trust had assets of £52,000 and an income of £2,200, all of which was given in grants to 10 individuals.

Applications: In writing to the correspondent by the end of April for consideration in May. Applications can be submitted directly by the individual or via a school, social worker or a welfare agency.

Correspondent: Mrs C Worsdall, 19 Queens Drive, Cottingham HU16 4EL (01482 840919)

Hedon

The Hedon Haven Trust

Eligibility: People at any stage or level of their education, undertaking study of any subject, who live in Hedon near Hull. Preference is given to children with special educational needs.

Types of grants: One-off grants ranging from £50 to £500 are given to: schoolchildren for educational outings in the UK and abroad; students in further or higher education towards study or travel abroad and maintenance/living expenses; and mature students for living expenses.

Annual grant total: In 2004, the trust had an income and expenditure of £2,300. Grants are made to organisations and individuals.

Applications: In writing to the correspondent at any time, enclosing an sae. Applications can be submitted directly by the individual or through the school/college or educational welfare agency.

Correspondent: Ian North, Secretary, Burnham House, Souttergate, Hedon, Hull HU12 8JS (01482 897105; Fax: 01482 897023; e-mail: iannorth@ lineone.net)

Horbury

The Daniel Gaskell & John Wray Foundation

Eligibility: People under 25 in full-time education who live in the former urban district council of Horbury.

Types of grants: Grants towards books, equipment, field trips, travel, course expenses, and so on, for those at school, college or university. Grants tend to range from £25 to £150 depending on the number of suitable applications.

Annual grant total: About £1,500 in grants to individuals.

Applications: Applications should be made after advertisements are placed in the local press. The trustees meet annually in September, so applications should be received by the end of August.

Correspondent: Mrs M Gaunt, 22 Westfield Road, Horbury, Wakefield, West Yorkshire WF4 6HP (01924 263166)

Humbleton

Heron Educational Foundation

Eligibility: People living in the parish of Humbleton, under the age of 25.

Types of grants: Grants for clothing and books given on entering primary and secondary school, further education or university.

Annual grant total: In 2004/05 the trust had an income of £7,800 and a total expenditure of £7,900. Grants were made to 13 individuals totalling £1,400.

Applications: In writing to the correspondent.

Correspondent: Mrs S Fleming, Coltsfoot House, Main Road, Humbleton, Hull, East Yorkshire HU11 4NL (01964 671809)

Kingston-upon-Hull

Alderman Ferries Charity

Eligibility: People aged 16 to 25 and live in the city of Kingston-upon-Hull.

Types of grants: One-off grants of about £300 to £500 each. Grants are given to college students and vocational students for books, equipment, instruments, fees, maintenance and living expenses.

Annual grant total: In 2005 the charity had an income of £11,000 and a total expenditure of £14,000. The sum of £11,000 was distributed in 20 grants.

Applications: On a form available from the correspondent. Applications should be submitted directly by the individual or a parent/guardian by 1 November for consideration in December.

Correspondent: Mrs V Fisher, Trust Manager, Hull United Charities, Northumberland Court, Northumberland Avenue, Kingston-upon-Hull HU2 0LR (01482 324135; Fax: 01482 324135; e-mail: office@hulluc.karoo.co.uk)

The Doctor A E Hart Trust

Eligibility: People who live within the city boundary of Kingston-upon-Hull (this does not include students who only live in Hull while at college). Applications are not encouraged from students under 18.

Types of grants: The trust was established for 'the promotion and encouragement of education for needy students'. Assistance may be given towards course fees, maintenance, study or travel overseas, text books, equipment and other essentials for schoolchildren, students, mature students and people starting work. Grants for childcare can also be given to mature students. One-off and recurrent grants are made ranging from £200 to £300, but not loans.

Exclusions: No grants to overseas students studying in Britain or for student exchanges.

Annual grant total: In 2005, the trust had net assets of around £534,000, an income of £26,000, and an expenditure of £23,700. The trust gave grants to individuals totalling £13,100.

Applications: On an application form (seven pages long which must be photocopied four times by the applicant and stapled together) available from the correspondent from June onwards. One academic and one character reference must accompany the form. Applications for awards must be submitted in October each year and are usually considered in December or January. Only in the most exceptional circumstances (e.g. for a course starting in January and of which the applicant had no knowledge the previous June) can applications outside these dates be considered, provided they explain why they are applying at that time.

The grants available from this trust are relatively modest, and are most unlikely to have any significant bearing on an applicant's decision to embark on any given course. In any event, the amount of the award (if any) will not be known until January/February, by which time most courses will have already started. Grants are paid in cheques and applicants must have their own bank accounts.

Correspondent: John Bullock, Secretary, Williamsons Solicitors, Lowgate, Kingston-upon-Hull HU1 1EN (01482 323697; Fax: 01482 328132; e-mail: admin@ williamsons-solicitors.co.uk; website: www. williamsons.solicitors.co.uk)

Kingston-upon-Hull Education Foundation

Eligibility: People over 13 who live, or whose parents live, in the city of Kingston-upon-Hull and either attend, or have attended, a school in the city.

Types of grants: Grants of £80 to £250 towards: (i) scholarships, bursaries or grants tenable at any school, university or other educational establishment approved by the trustees or (ii) financial assistance towards the cost of outfits, clothing, tools, instruments or books to assist such persons to pursue their education or to prepare for and enter a profession, trade, occupation or service on leaving school, university or other educational establishment.

Annual grant total: In 2004/05 the foundation had an income of £4,600 and a total expenditure of £6,200.

Applications: On a form available from August from the correspondent. Applications are considered in November (closing date mid-October) and February (closing date mid-January). A letter of support from the applicant's class or course tutor, plus evidence of their progress and attendance on the course is needed before a grant is made.

Correspondent: K D Brown, Corporate Finance, 2nd Floor Treasury Building, Hanover Square, Guildhall Road, Kingston-upon-Hull, HU1 2AB

Newton on Derwent

Newton on Derwent Charity

Eligibility: Students in higher education who live in the parish of Newton on Derwent.

Types of grants: One-off grants towards fees, usually paid directly to the relevant institution.

Annual grant total: Educational grants usually total around £5,000 per annum.

Applications: In writing to the correspondent, for consideration throughout the year.

Correspondent: The Clerk to the Charity, Messrs Grays, Duncombe Place, York YO1 7DY (01904 634771)

Ottringham

The Ottringham Church Lands Charity

Eligibility: People in need who live in the parish of Ottringham.

Types of grants: Grants are made according to need.

Exclusions: No grants are given which would affect the applicant's state benefits.

Annual grant total: In 2004/05 the trust had an income and a total expenditure of £8,200.

Applications: In writing to the correspondent at any time. Applications can be submitted either directly by the individual, through a third party such as a social worker or teacher, or through an organisation such as Citizens Advice or a school.

Correspondent: J R Hinchliffe, 'Hallgarth', Station Road, Ottringham, East Yorkshire HU12 0BJ (01964 622230)

Rawcliffe

The Rawcliffe Educational Foundation

Eligibility: People who live in the parish of Rawcliffe, who were educated at one of the local schools, and are aged between 16 and 25.

Types of grants: One-off and recurrent grants of up to £600 to assist young people remaining in full-time education beyond normal school leaving age. This includes help with the cost of books and fees/living expenses for students.

Exclusions: It does not include school fees or study or travel overseas.

Annual grant total: In 2004/05, the trust had an income of £17,200 and an expenditure of £11,000. Grants totalled about £8,000.

Applications: Applications should be made in writing, including the type and duration of the course to be studied. Students must affirm that they are not in receipt of any salary. They are considered in September.

Correspondent: Miss Julie Hennessey, 26 Station Road, Rawcliffe, Goole, North Humberside DN14 8QR (01405 839637)

Riston

The Peter Nevill Charity

Eligibility: Young people under 25 who live, or who have a parent who lives, in the parish of Riston.

Types of grants: Grants of £50 to £200 are given towards books, clothing and other essentials for school-leavers taking up employment and for students in further or higher education. (Grants also made to Riston Church of England Primary School and village organisations serving young people.)

Annual grant total: In 2004/05 the charity had both an income and a total expenditure of £4,500. Grants to individuals are made each year totalling about £1,000.

Applications: In writing to the correspondent.

Correspondent: Revd David Perry, The Vicarage, Skirlaugh, Hull HU11 5HE (01964 562259; e-mail: david@ perryskirlaugh.karoo.co.uk)

North Yorkshire

The Beckwith Bequest

Eligibility: People living or educated in the parishes of Easingwold and Husthwaite who are in need of financial assistance.

Types of grants: Cash grants of £100 to £150 for beneficiaries to help with books, equipment, clothing and travel. (Grants are also made towards the provision of facilities not normally provided by the local education authority for recreation, education, and social and physical training for those receiving education.)

Annual grant total: In 2003/04 the trust had an income of £8,700 and a total expenditure of £8,300. Previously, about £2,000 has been distributed to individuals.

Applications: In writing to the correspondent. Applications are considered at quarterly trustees' meetings.

Correspondent: P D Hannam, Solicitor, Hileys Solicitors, Market Place, Easingwold, York YO61 3AB (01347 821234)

Bedale Educational Foundation

Eligibility: People aged between 5 and 25 who live in the parishes of Aiskew, Bedale, Burrill, Cowling, Crakehall, Firby and Leeming Bar. Preference is given to people with special educational needs.

Types of grants: One-off grants in the range of £200 and £600 are given to school children and college students, including those towards books, fees maintenance/ living expenses and excursions.

Annual grant total: In 2005/06 the trust had an income of £1500 and a total expenditure of £850. Grants total about £600.

Applications: On a form available from the correspondent, to be submitted at any time either directly by the individual or a parent.

Correspondent: P J Hirst, 18 Firby Road, Bedale, North Yorkshire, DL8 2AS (01677 423376)

Bedale Welfare Charity

Eligibility: People who live in Bedale and the immediate surrounding area.

Types of grants: One-off grants usually ranging from £50 to £5,000.

Annual grant total: In 2004/05 it had assets of £364,000 and an income of £13,000 all of which was distributed in 94 relief-in-need grants. No educational grants were made during the year.

Applications: On a form available from the correspondent, to be submitted at any time either directly by the individual or through a third party such as a social worker or teacher.

Correspondent: P J Hirst, 18 Firby Road, Bedale, North Yorkshire, DL8 2AS (01677 4423376; e-mail: curlyhirst@aol. com)

Other information: Grants are also made to organisations (£11,000 in 2004/05).

The Gargrave Poor's Land Charity

Eligibility: People in need who live in Gargrave, Banknewton, Coniston Cold, Flasby, Eshton or Winterburn.

Types of grants: One-off and recurrent grants and loans are given to: schoolchildren for uniforms, clothing and outings; people starting work towards childcare; and students in further or higher education towards fees. Grants are also given for relief-in-need purposes.

Annual grant total: In 2004/05 the trust had assets of £346,000 and an income of £41,000. Grants totalled £17,000, of which £2,500 was given to individuals for educational purposes.

Applications: On a form available from the correspondent. Applications can be submitted at any time.

Correspondent: The Trustees, 10 Ivy House Gardens, Gargrave, Near Skipton, North Yorkshire, BD23 3SS

Reverend Matthew Hutchinson Trust (Gilling and Richmond)

Eligibility: People who live in the parishes of Gilling and Richmond in North Yorkshire.

Types of grants: Grants are given to school children for fees, equipment and excursions. Undergraduates, including mature students, can receive help towards books whilst vocational students can be supported for study/travel overseas.

Annual grant total: In 2004 the combined income of the charities was £16,000 and their combined expenditures were £14,000.

Applications: In writing to the correspondent by March or November. Applications can be submitted directly by the individual or through a trustee, social worker, Citizens Advice or other welfare agency.

Correspondent: Mrs C Wiper, 3 Smithson Close, Moulton, Richmond, North Yorkshire, DL10 6QP

Other information: The Gilling and Richmond branches of this charity are administrated jointly, but with separate funding. Grants are also made to local schools and hospitals.

The Kirkby-in-Malhamdale Educational Foundation

Eligibility: People under 25 who have a parent or guardian living in one of the following parishes in the county of North Yorkshire: Airton, Calton, Hanlith, Kirkby Malham, Malham, Malham Moor, Otterburn and Scosthrop.

Types of grants: One-off grants of £100 to £200 to: schoolchildren for uniforms/ clothing, study/travel overseas, books, equipment/instruments and excursions; college students, undergraduates and children with special educational needs for uniforms/clothing, fees, study/travel overseas, books, equipment/living expenses and excursions; and to people starting work for work clothes, fees, books and equipment/instruments.

Annual grant total: In 2005, the foundation had both an income and a total expenditure of around £800.

Applications: In writing to the correspondent. Applications can be submitted either directly by the individual or through the individual's school/college or an educational welfare agency. Applications are considered three times per year.

Correspondent: C Pighills, Cross Stones, Airton, Skipton, North Yorkshire, BD23 4AP

The Rowlandson & Eggleston Relief-in-Need Charity

Eligibility: People who are disabled and in education in the parishes of Barton and Newton Morrell.

Types of grants: One-off grants of £100 to £500 for educational expenses in cases of need. Expenses can include those towards uniforms/clothing, fees, study/travel

abroad, books, equipment/instruments and maintenance/living expenses.

Annual grant total: In 2004/05 the trust had assets of £80,000 and an income of £3,400. Grants to 22 people totalled £2,500. All grants are given for welfare purposes.

Applications: In writing to the correspondent including details of circumstances and specific need(s), for consideration throughout the year. Applications may be submitted directly by the individual, through a social worker, Citizens Advice or other welfare agency or any third party.

Correspondent: P E R Vaux, Chair, Brettanby Manor, Barton, Richmond, North Yorkshire DL10 6HD (01325 377233; Fax: 01325 377647)

Other information: Grants can also be made to organisations.

York Children's Trust

Eligibility: Children and young people under 25 who live within 20 miles of York.

Types of grants: One-off grants of between £100 to £300 and are awarded to schoolchildren for uniforms/clothing, equipment/instruments and excursions, college students for study/travel overseas, equipment/instruments, maintenance/ living expenses and childcare, undergraduates for study/travel overseas, excursions and childcare, vocational students for uniforms/clothing, fees, study/ travel overseas, excursions and childcare, mature students for childcare, and to people starting work and those with special educational needs for uniforms/clothing.

Preference is given to schoolchildren with serious family difficulties so that the child has to be educated away from home and to people with special educational needs who have been referred by a paediatrician or educational psychiatrist.

Exclusions: Grants are not available for private education or postgraduate studies.

Annual grant total: In 2004 the trust had an income of £83,000 and made 99 grants to individuals totalling £29,000.

Applications: Application forms are available from the correspondent and can be submitted directly by the individual or by the individual's school, college or educational welfare agency, or a third party such as a health visitor or social worker. Applications are considered in January, April, July and October, and should be received one month earlier.

Correspondent: H G Sherriff, Clerk/ Treasurer, 34 Lucombe Way, New Earswick, York YO32 4DS

Other information: Grants are also made to youth groups.

Acaster

The Knowles Educational Foundation

Eligibility: People who live in the ancient parish of Acaster.

Types of grants: In the past grants have been given towards swimming lessons for small children, field trips and visits abroad for schoolchildren and students at college and university. Grants have also been given towards books, materials and cost of transport from place of study to lodgings.

Annual grant total: In 2005, the foundation had an income of around £3,000, and a total expenditure of £3,500.

Applications: In writing to the correspondent, including invoices for expenses. As each case is considered on its own merit the more information the applicant can supply, the better. Applications are considered in March, June and October.

Correspondent: J Jenkinson-Smith, The Granary, Mill Lane, Acaster Malbis, York YO23 2UL (01904 706153)

Harrogate

The Haywra Crescent Educational Trust Fund

Eligibility: People who live in the Harrogate Borough Council area and are in any form of post-16 education.

Types of grants: One-off grants towards books, equipment or travel.

Annual grant total: In 2004/05, the trust had an income of £13,000 and a total expenditure of £14,000. The trust gives about 17% of its annual income to individuals and about 68% to organisations with the balance being used for further investment.

Applications: On a form available from the correspondent. Students in post-16 educational courses at secondary schools in Harrogate or at Harrogate College are expected to make their application through their institution. The deadline for applications is 30 November; they are considered in December.

Correspondent: The Student Support Manager, Continuing Education, North Yorkshire County Council, County Hall, Northallerton, North Yorkshire DL7 8AL

Kirkbymoorside

The John Stockton Educational Foundation

Eligibility: Students and apprentices aged 16 to 25 who live in certain parishes in the Kirkbymoorside area and have done so for at least two years.

Types of grants: Grants range from £30 to £60. Apprentices can receive help towards the cost of tools. Vocational students and students at university can receive grants towards books, fees, living expenses and study or travel abroad. Students may apply for three years.

Exclusions: Sixth form students do not qualify for grants.

Annual grant total: In 2004/05 the trust had assets of £17,500, an income of £600 and a total expenditure of £400. Grants were made to eight individuals totalling £360.

Applications: On a form available from the correspondent, to be submitted by the first week of June or December. Applications can be made directly by the applicant or parent.

Correspondent: Mrs Elizabeth Mary Kendall, Clerk, The Sheilings, Chapel Street, Nawton, York YO62 7RE (01439 771575)

Lothersdale

Raygill Trust

Eligibility: Full-time students on a first degree or equivalent course at a university or college who live in the ecclesiastical parish of Lothersdale.

Types of grants: Grants to students in the first three years of their further education.

Annual grant total: In 2004/05 the trust had an income of £9,200 and a total expenditure of £11,000. Grants totalled about £10,000.

Applications: In writing to the correspondent. Applicants who do not send thank you letters will not be considered for future grants.

Correspondent: Roger Armstrong, Armstrong and Bridgmond, 12-16 North Street, Keighley, West Yorkshire BD21 3SE (01535 613660; Fax: 01535 613689)

Newton upon Rawcliffe

Poad's Educational Foundation

Eligibility: People from a poor background who are under 25 and live in the ancient town of Newton upon Rawcliffe.

Types of grants: Grants towards course fees, travel, books, incidental expenses and maintenance costs. Grants are towards a broad range of educational needs including support for courses that are not formal and after-school swimming classes.

Annual grant total: In 2003/04 the foundation had an income of £2,300 and a total expenditure of £2,500. Grants totalled about £1,500.

Applications: In writing to the correspondent by 25 March.

Correspondent: P J Lawrence, Secretary to the Trustees, c/o Pearsons & Ward, 2 Market Street, Malton, North Yorkshire YO17 7AS

Scarborough

The John Kendall Trust

Eligibility: Children under 18 who live in Scarborough and who are orphaned, from single-parent families or whose parents receive income support.

Types of grants: One-off grants of £100 to £1,000 to schoolchildren for uniforms/clothing, fees, study/travel abroad, excursion, books and equipment/instruments

Annual grant total: In the 15 months ending March 2005 the trust had assets of £147,000 and an income of £6,300. Grants to five individuals totalled £2,600.

Applications: In writing to the trustees at 76 Scalby Road, Scarborough, North Yorkshire YO12 5QN for consideration in January, May and September.

Correspondent: Michael J Barrett, 6 Northfield Way, Scalby, Scarborough, North Yorkshire YO13 0PW (01723 378432)

The Scarborough Municipal Charities

Eligibility: People who live in the borough of Scarborough.

Types of grants: Support is given to college, vocational, mature student and undergraduates, including those for books, fees, uniforms, travel, equipment, maintenance/living expenses and excursions.

Annual grant total: In 2005 educational grants to 12 individuals totalled £9,800 and 158 welfare grants totalled £2,400.

Applications: On a form available from the correspondent. Applications are considered quarterly. A sub-committee of three trustees interview each applicant.

Correspondent: Mrs E Greening, Flat 2, 126 Falsgrave Road, Scarborough, North Yorkshire YO12 5BE (01723 375256)

The Scarborough United Scholarships Foundation

Eligibility: People under 25 who live in the former borough of Scarborough and have attended school in the area for at least three years.

Types of grants: Grants range from £100 to £500 a year. Grants are usually given to those at Scarborough Sixth Form College, Yorkshire Coast College or a college of further education 'where a student is following a course which is a non-advanced course'.

Grants are also given to schoolchildren, college students, undergraduates, vocational students, mature students and to people starting work for uniforms/clothing, study/travel overseas, books, equipment/instruments and excursions.

Grants are occasionally given to second-degree students, and loans are sometimes obtainable.

Exclusions: No grants for fees.

Annual grant total: In 2004/05 the trust had assets of £52,300 and an income of £4,200. A total of nine grants were made to individuals totalling £2,800.

Applications: The foundation mostly deals with the local colleges to ensure potential applicants are made aware of when and how to apply.

Correspondent: Anne Morley, 6 Northfield Way, Scalby, Scarborough, North Yorkshire, YO13 0PW (01723 378432)

Swaledale

Muker Educational Trust

Eligibility: People who live in the ecclesiastical parish of Swaledale.

Types of grants: The trust gives one-off and recurrent grants of £15 to £400 to schoolchildren for books, equipment/instruments and travel/study overseas and to college students, undergraduates, vocational students and mature students for fees, study/travel overseas, books and equipment/instruments.

Exclusions: Grants are not given for maintenance, clothing or living expenses.

Annual grant total: Previously around £2,000 to individuals.

Applications: On a form available from the correspondent. Replies are only given if an sae is enclosed. Applications are considered in November and should be submitted in October either directly by the individual or through an organisation such as a school or educational welfare agency.

Correspondent: Michael B McGarry, Secretary, c/o Johnsons Solicitors, Market Place, Hawes, North Yorkshire DL8 3QS (01969 667000)

Wensleydale

Yorebridge Educational Foundation

Eligibility: Students under 25 years of age undertaking full-time courses of further education. Students or parents must live in Wensleydale, North Yorkshire.

Types of grants: One-off grants, typically of £200 a year, towards books, fees and living expenses.

Annual grant total: Grants total around £8,000.

Applications: Applications are considered in September/October each year and should be submitted in writing directly by the individual.

Correspondent: R W Tunstall, Treasurer, Kiln Hill, Hawes, North Yorkshire DL8 3RA

York

The Merchant Taylors of York Charity

Eligibility: People involved in education/training in the area of art and craft who live in Yorkshire, particularly in York and nearby.

Types of grants: On average about eight one-off grants are made ranging between £500 to £2,000 each.

Annual grant total: In 2005 the trust had assets of £314,000, an income of £98,000 and a grant total of £16,000.

Applications: In writing to the correspondent. Applications are considered throughout the year.

Correspondent: Nevil Pearce, Chancellor, 104 The Mount, York YO4 1GR (01904 655626; e-mail: n.pearce@calvertsmith.co.uk)

The Micklegate Strays Charity

Eligibility: Freemen or dependants of freemen, under 25, of the city of York and who are now living in the Micklegate Strays ward. (This is now defined as the whole of the part of the city of York to the west of the River Ouse.) The applicant's parents must be living in the above area.

Types of grants: Grants of £30 a year are given to schoolchildren and people starting work for uniforms, clothing, books, equipment, instruments, fees, maintenance and living expenses. Grants are also given to students in further or higher education towards study or travel abroad.

Annual grant total: About £600 a year.

Applications: Applications can be submitted directly by the individual or by a parent. They must include the date at which the parent became a freeman of the city and the address of the parent. Applications are considered twice a year.

Correspondent: The Clerk, PO Box 258, York, YO24 4ZD

Other information: The trust was created by the 1907 Micklegate Strays Act. The city of York agreed to pay the freemen £1,000 a year in perpetuity for extinguishing their rights over Micklegate Stray. This sum has been reduced due to the forced divestment

of the trust government stock, following the Charities Act of 1992.

York City Charities

Eligibility: People in need who live within the pre-1996 York city boundaries (the area within the city walls).

Types of grants: This trust has three funds. Lady Hewley's Fund gives grants to mature students aged 21 or over for general purposes. The Advancement Branch gives grants to young people aged under 21 for general educational purposes, except school trips. There is also The Poor's Branch which has relief-in-need purposes.

Annual grant total: In 2003/04 the trust had an income of £146,000 and made grants to individuals totalling £1,500.

Applications: In writing to the correspondent, to be submitted by a headteacher, doctor, occupational nurse, social worker, Citizens Advice or other third party or welfare agency. Applications are considered throughout the year.

Correspondent: Mrs Carol Bell, 41 Avenue Road, Clifton, York YO30 6AY (01904 645131; Fax: 01904 645131; e-mail: carol@forthergil15.freeserve.co.uk)

Northumberland

Coates Educational Foundation

Eligibility: People up to the age of 25 who live in the parishes of Ponteland, Stannington, Heddon-on-the-Wall, and the former district of Newburn. Pupils and former pupils of Coates Endowed Middle School are also supported.

Types of grants: One-off grants to help with the cost of books, clothing, educational outings, maintenance and fees for schoolchildren and students at college or university. People starting work can be helped with books, equipment/instruments, clothing or travel.

Annual grant total: In 2004 the foundation had an income of £18,000 and a total expenditure of £4,500.

Applications: On a form available from the correspondent, to be submitted directly by the individual. Applications are considered in February and June.

Correspondent: P Jackson, Secretary, 184 Darras Road, Ponteland, Tyne & Wear NE20 9AF (0191 274 7074)

The Eleemosynary Charity of Giles Heron

Eligibility: Only people who live in the parishes of Simonburn, Wark and Humshaugh in Northumberland.

Types of grants: Help towards the cost of education, training, apprenticeship or equipment for those starting work and for educational visits abroad.

Annual grant total: In 2004/05 the trust had an income of £13,000 and a total expenditure of £11,000. Grants are made to organisations as well as individuals.

Applications: In writing to the correspondent for consideration in May or November.

Correspondent: George Benson, Chair, Brunton House, Wall, Hexham, Northumberland NE46 4EJ

The Rothbury Educational Trust

Eligibility: People aged 18 to 25 who live in the ancient parish of Rothbury, Thropton and Hepple. Applicants must be pursuing a full-time further education course at a technical college, university or similar establishment approved by the trustees.

Types of grants: Cash grants, usually of about £100.

Annual grant total: In 2004/05, the trust had an income of about £4,900 and an expenditure of £5,000. In previous years the trust has given £4,000 in grants to individuals.

Applications: In writing to the correspondent for consideration in late August/ early September. Grants are advertised in the local newspapers.

Correspondent: Mrs Susan Rogerson, 1 Gallow Law, Alwinton, Morpeth, Northumberland NE65 7BQ (01669 650 390)

Allendale

Allendale Exhibition Endowment

Eligibility: People under 25 (on 31 September in year of application) and who live in the parishes of East and West Allendale.

Types of grants: Grants of £50 to £150 to: schoolchildren for educational outings in the UK or overseas; people starting work for books, equipment, instruments, maintenance, living expenses, educational outings in the UK and study or travel abroad; and students in further or higher education for all of the above as well as student exchanges.

Annual grant total: About £5,000 in grants to individuals.

Applications: On a form available from the correspondent. Applications should be submitted directly by the individual and the deadline is usually at the end of October. An advert is placed in the local paper, library and shops in mid-August.

Correspondent: G Ostler, Low House, Allendale, Hexham, Northumberland, NE47 9NX

Blyth

The Blyth Valley Trust for Youth

Eligibility: People who live in the borough of Blyth Valley and are under 21.

Types of grants: Grants to assist people active in the fields of arts, music and physical recreation. Support can be given for uniforms/clothing, fees, books, equipment, instruments and awards for excellence. Applicants should be of amateur status and support may only be given to those who are able to identify specific 'Centres of Excellence' which they will be attending. Grants usually range from £50 to £250 and are one-off.

Annual grant total: In 2004/05, the trust had an income of £2,300 and a total expenditure of £1,100.

Applications: Application forms are available from the correspondent and can be submitted directly by the individual. Full details of the activity and references must be included on the form. The trust advises applicants to apply early (preferably before February each year) in time for the trustees' meeting, usually held in April.

Correspondent: D Earl, Civic Centre, Renwick Road, Blyth, Northumberland NE24 2BX

The Blyth Valley Youth Travel Fund

Eligibility: People under 25 who live in the borough of Blyth Valley, Northumberland, or have attended an educational establishment in the area for at least two years.

Types of grants: Grants to enable deserving students in need of financial assistance to travel in the UK or abroad to further their education. Preference is given to young people who would otherwise not have the opportunity to travel. Grants are one-off and range from £25 to £150.

Annual grant total: In 2003/04, the fund had an income of £390. There was no expenditure during the year.

Applications: Applications can be submitted directly by the individual on a form available from the correspondent, and should include details of: educational establishment, course being undertaken, qualifications, activities/pastimes, support required and references.

Correspondent: D Earl, Civic Centre, Renwick Road, Blyth, Northumberland NE24 2BX

Haydon Bridge

Shaftoe Educational Foundation

Eligibility: Individuals in need who live in the parish of Haydon Bridge.

Types of grants: One-off and recurrent grants of at least £400. Grants are made to schoolchildren for fees and study or travel abroad, people starting work for equipment or instruments, and further and higher education and mature students for fees.

Annual grant total: In 2004/05, the trust had assets of £2.5 million and an income of £116,000. Grants totalled £55,000, of which £17,000 was distributed to 39 individuals.

Applications: In writing to the correspondent, for consideration in March, July and November. Initial telephone calls are welcomed. Applications can be made either directly by the individual or through the individual's school, college or educational welfare agency.

Correspondent: Richard A D Snowdon, Clerk, The Office, Shaftoe Terrace, Haydon Bridge, Hexham NE47 6BW (01434 688871; e-mail: news4shaftoe@aol. com)

Kirkwhelpington

The Kirkwhelpington Educational Charity

Eligibility: People who live in the civil parish of Kirkwhelpington who are under the age of 25, to promote education including social and physical training. (Grants are also given to schools and voluntary organisations in the parish who provide facilities for people under the age of 25.)

Types of grants: Individuals who have gone on to some form of training or further education after school have received help with items such as equipment, books, cost of transport and extra courses where these are not covered by Local Education Authority grants. Schoolchildren have received help with the cost of educational outings and special tuition. Grants are usually one-off and in the range of £50 and £300.

Annual grant total: About £1,000.

Applications: In writing to the correspondent including details of how the money is to be spent, other possible sources of grants and receipts of money spent where possible. Applications are usually considered in February, May and October.

Correspondent: Mrs H Cowan, 11 Meadowlands, Kirkwhelpington, Newcastle upon Tyne NE19 2RX

South Yorkshire

The Aston-Cum-Aughton Educational Foundation

Eligibility: Pupils in the area of Aston-Cum-Aughton and Swallownest with Fence, where needs cannot be met from official sources.

Types of grants: One-off and recurrent grants towards items the LEA cannot provide, such as books and other equipment.

Annual grant total: About £5,100, mostly to schools with any surplus given to individuals.

Applications: In writing to the correspondent or to any trustee either by the individual or their headmaster. Applications are considered in March and September, but special cases will be considered throughout the year. Applications should include some details of what the grant is to be spent on and the total cost.

Correspondent: J Nuttall, 3 Rosegarth Avenue, Aston, Sheffield S26 2DB

The Bolsterstone Educational Charity

Eligibility: People aged between 16 and 25 who live in the parishes of St Mary's – Bolsterstone, St Matthias' – Stocksbridge and St John's – Deepcar.

Types of grants: Grants of between £50 and £200 are given towards books, equipment/instruments and study or travel abroad.

Exclusions: No grants are given to mature students or people starting work.

Annual grant total: In 2004/05, the charity had an income of £8,200 and a total expenditure of £6,400. Grants are made to organisations and individuals.

Applications: On a form available from the correspondent. They should be submitted directly by the individual for consideration at the start of March, July or November.

Correspondent: C A North, 5 Pennine View, Stocksbridge, Sheffield S36 1ER (0114 288 2757; Fax: 0114 288 7404; e-mail: cliff.north@virgin.net)

The Elmhirst Trust

Eligibility: People who live in Barnsley, Doncaster and Rotherham, normally over the age of 30, seeking to develop their life in new directions and who are prevented from doing so by low income. Particular emphasis is given to those whose proposals benefit the community as a whole. Applicants may be undertaking vocational training or retraining in any subject, and must be in need of financial assistance to support them in their training. The trust strongly prefers to support people who have had little or no post-16 education and are involved in the voluntary sector to offer them a second chance of personal or vocational development.

Types of grants: One-off grants range from £100 to £850 which has previously been spent predominantly on fees but also on travel, books, equipment and childcare.

Annual grant total: In 2004/05 the trust had assets of £142,000, an income of £5,400 and a total expenditure of £9,800. Grants were made to 12 individuals totalling £8,500.

Applications: On a form available from the correspondent. 'A response, by telephone or post, is made to all applicants and where applications are considered an assessor visits the applicant. The trust attempts to maintain contact with beneficiaries during their course/activity and thereafter.'

Correspondent: John Butt, 2 Paddock Close, Staincross, Barnsley S75 6LH

The Kirk Sandall Robert Woods Trust

Eligibility: Students in higher education who live in the ecclesiastical parish of Kirk Sandall or Edenthorpe. Applicants must be resident in either parish at date of application.

Types of grants: Grants of £20 to £50 a year to help with the cost of books for first degree students.

Annual grant total: In 2004/05 the trust had both an income and a total expenditure of around £1,000, most of which was given in grants to 43 individuals.

Applications: On a form available from local secondary schools or the correspondent. Applications must be submitted by 30 August, for consideration in September.

Correspondent: D M Telford, Clerk, 15 Woodford Road, Barnby Dun, Doncaster, DN3 1BN (01302 883496)

The Sheffield Bluecoat & Mount Pleasant Educational Foundation

Eligibility: People up to the age of 25 who live within a 20-mile radius of Sheffield Town Hall and have done so for at least 3 years.

Types of grants: One-off and recurrent grants of £100 to £5,000 towards artistic and sporting activities, educational travel, clothing, equipment and private school fees.

Annual grant total: In 2005, the foundation had net assets of £1.3 million and an income of £75,000. Total expenditure was £94,300, of which grants were made to 59 individuals totalling around £49,000.

Applications: In writing to the correspondent or through the school/college or educational welfare agency. Applications are considered in April and September and should be submitted by March and August.

Correspondent: G J Smallman, c/o Wrigleys, Fountain Precinct, Balm Green, Sheffield S1 1JA (0114 267 5588; Fax: 0114 276 3176)

The Sheffield West Riding Charitable Society Trust

Eligibility: Clergy children at school and in further education in the diocese of Sheffield.

Types of grants: Only a small proportion of the grants are educational and are to help with the cost of books, clothing and other essentials.

Annual grant total: Around 20 grants are made each year. In 2004 the trust had an income of £9,300 and a total expenditure of £11,000.

Applications: On a form available from the correspondent.

Correspondent: C A Beck, Secretary and Treasurer, Diocesan Church House, 95–99 Effingham Street, Rotherham S65 1BL (01709 309117; Fax: 01709 512550; e-mail: tony.beck@sheffield-diocese.org. uk)

Other information: Welfare grants are also made to the clergy, house-keepers and disadvantaged families in the diocese.

The Swann-Morton Foundation

Eligibility: Students who live in South Yorkshire.

Types of grants: One-off and recurrent grants according to need.

Annual grant total: In 2004/05, the trust had an income of £46,000. Grants totalled about £43,000, of which £10,000 was given in student grants and electives.

Applications: In writing to the correspondent. In the past the trust has stated that applications have exceeded available funding.

Correspondent: Catherine Briggs, Administrator, Owlerton Green, Sheffield S6 2BJ (0114 234 4231)

Armthorpe

Armthorpe Poors Estate Charity

Eligibility: People who are in need and live in Armthorpe.

Types of grants: One-off and recurrent grants of £50 minimum to schoolchildren who are in need for educational outings and to undergraduates for books.

Annual grant total: In 2004/05 the trust had an income of £15,000. Grants totalled about £2,400 and comprised of £740 to 'welfare bodies', £50 in a single welfare grant and £1,600 in educational grants.

Applications: Contact the clerk by telephone who will advise if a letter of application is needed. Applicants outside of Armthorpe will be declined. Undergraduates are required to complete an application form, available from the correspondent, and return it by 31 August.

Correspondent: Frank Pratt, 32 Gurth Avenue, Edenthorpe, Doncaster DN3 2LW (01302 882806)

Barnsley

The Shaw Lands Trust

Eligibility: People under 25 who live within the former county borough of Barnsley (as defined pre-1974) or are, or have for at least two years at any time been, in attendance at any county or voluntary aided school in the borough.

Types of grants: To provide scholarships/ grants for university, school or other place of learning; assistance for purchase of clothing, tools, books and so on to help beneficiaries enter a profession, trade or calling; travel overseas to enable beneficiaries to further their education; assistance for provision of facilities of any kind not normally provided by the local education authority for recreation and social and physical training for beneficiaries who are receiving primary, secondary and further education; to assist in the study of music and other arts. Grants range from £200 to £750 and may be paid in three instalments.

Annual grant total: In 2005, the trust had assets of 1.1 million with an income of £44,300. The trust made 9 grants to individuals totalling £8,600.

Applications: In writing to the correspondent. Applications are considered in September.

Correspondent: Jill Leece, Newman & Bond, 35 Church Street, Barnsley, South Yorkshire, S70 2AP (01226 213434)

Beighton

Beighton Relief-in-Need Charity

Eligibility: Students in further education who live in the former parish of Beighton and are in need.

Types of grants: One-off grants according to need.

Annual grant total: In 2005 the charity had an income of £8,000 and a total expenditure of £8,200. Grants are made for relief-in-need and educational purposes.

Applications: In writing to the correspondent with proof of acceptance at university or college, if relevant. Applications can be submitted directly by the individual or through a social worker, Citizens Advice, other welfare agency or a third party such as a relative, neighbour or trustee. Applications are considered throughout the year.

Correspondent: Michael Lowe, Elms Bungalow, Queens Road, Beighton, Sheffield S20 1AW

Bramley

The Bramley Poors' Allotment Trust

Eligibility: People in need who live in the ancient township of Bramley, especially people who are elderly, poor and sick.

Types of grants: One-off grants of between £40 and £120.

Annual grant total: About £1,400 is available each year.

Applications: In writing to the correspondent. The trust likes applications to be submitted through a recognised referral agency (social worker, Citizens Advice, doctor, headmaster or minister). They are considered monthly.

Correspondent: Len Barnett, 31 St Oswald's Terrace, Guiseley, Leeds LS20 9BD

Epworth

Epworth Charities

Eligibility: People in need who live in Epworth.

Types of grants: One-off and recurrent grants in the range of £50 and £250. Grants are made to schoolchildren for equipment/ instruments and college students, undergraduates, vocational students and mature students for books.

Annual grant total: In 2004/05 the charities had an income of £1,200. The sum of £450 was distributed in three educational grants. There were two welfare grants made totalling £180.

Applications: In writing to the correspondent to be submitted directly by the individual. Applications are considered on an ongoing basis.

Correspondent: Mrs Margaret Draper, 16 Fern Croft, Epworth, Doncaster, South Yorkshire DN9 1GE (01427 873234; e-mail: margaret.draper@btinternet.com)

Other information: Grants are also made for welfare purposes.

Sheffield

The Church Burgesses Educational Foundation

Eligibility: People up to the age of 25 whose parents have lived in Sheffield for the last three years.

Types of grants: Grants are given towards books, clothing and other essentials for schoolchildren. Grants are occasionally available for those at college or university, although no grants are made where a LEA grant is available. Postgraduates can only receive funding if there is a special need for retraining or education in a different subject. School fees are only paid where there is a sudden, unexpected hardship.

Special grants can also be made to individuals for overseas expeditions, helping churches and missions in UK and abroad, attending summer schools and festivals, artistic and athletic activities and so on.

There is also a 'Music in the City' scheme which supports music tuition.

Annual grant total: In 2004, the foundation had net assets of £200,000, an income of around £300,000 and a total expenditure of £282,000. The foundation gave grants to individuals totalling £108,000

Applications: In writing to the correspondent.

Correspondent: G J Smallman, Church Burgesses Educational Foundation, 3rd Floor Fountain Precinct, Balm Green, Sheffield, S1 2JA (0114 267 5596; Fax: 0114 267 3176)

The Sheffield Grammar School Exhibition Foundation

Eligibility: People who live in the city of Sheffield and have done so for at least three years (this excludes residency for educational purposes).

Types of grants: Grants can be given to people starting work for books, equipment, clothing or travel. Students in further or higher education may be helped with fees, living expenses, study or travel abroad and with the cost of books. Mature students may be provided with money to cover the costs of travel, fees, childcare or books. The trust will occasionally give towards schoolchildren's educational outings.

There is a preference for people who are attending or have attended King Edward VII School. Grants are also given for the benefit of the school.

Annual grant total: In 2004/05 the foundation had assets of £2.5 million and an income of £136,000. Grants to 111 individuals totalled £38,000. A further £5,500 went to organisations.

Applications: In writing to the correspondent. Applications are considered in March, July, October and December and should be submitted either directly by the individual or through their school, college or educational welfare agency.

Correspondent: G J Smallman, Clerk, c/o Wrigleys, Fountain Precinct, Balm Green, Sheffield S1 1JA

Teesside

The Captain John Vivian Nancarrow Fund

Eligibility: People under the age of 25 who live or work in Middlesbrough and who are or have at any time been in attendance at the following schools or colleges: Acklam Grange, Brackenhow/Kings Academy, Hall Garth, Kings Manor, Langbaurgh/Keldholme/Unity City Academy, Middlesborough College and Teesside Tertiary College.

Types of grants: Grants are given for the following: attendance at any approved place of learning; clothing, equipment, and so on needed to prepare for, or enter, a trade or profession; educational travel scholarships; study of music and other arts; educational research; recreational and social and physical training; assistance in the event of sickness, disability and so on to enable full benefit from educational facilities.

Exclusions: No grants where statutory funding is available or to people who have received a grant from Middlesbrough Council in the current financial year.

Annual grant total: Grants are made totalling around £2,000 each year.

Applications: Applications to these charities may be made directly by the individual or by recommendation, where appropriate, from a headteacher. Application forms are available from the correspondent.

Correspondent: Voluntary Sector Team, Middlesbrough Council, Children, Families & Learning, PO Box 69, Vancouver House, Gurney Street, Middlesbrough TS1 1EL (01642 728079 or 01642 728081)

Other information: In the case of educational research, assistance may also be provided to people over 25.

The Teesside Educational Endowment

Eligibility: People under 25 who live or work in the former county borough of Teesside.

Types of grants: Grants for the following: attendance at any approved place of

learning (minimum period one year); the purchase of clothing, equipment or books to prepare for, or enter, a trade or profession; educational travel scholarships; assistance with the provision of facilities for recreation, sport and social and physical training for pupils and students; the study of music and other arts; educational research.

Exclusions: No grants where statutory funding is available or to people who have received a grant from Middlesbrough Council in the current financial year.

Annual grant total: Disposable funds of £2,400.

Applications: Applications to these charities may be made directly by the individual or by recommendation, where appropriate, from a headteacher. Application forms are available from the correspondent.

Correspondent: Voluntary Sector Team, Middlesbrough Council, Children, Families & Learning, PO Box 69, Vancouver House, Gurney Street, Middlesbrough TS1 1EL (01642 728079 or 01642 728081)

Guisborough

The Hutton Lowcross Educational Foundation

Eligibility: People under the age of 25 who live, or whose parents live, in the parish of Guisborough.

Types of grants: One-off and recurrent grants in the range of £50 to £500. Grants are given for the following: (i) attendance at any approved place of learning; (ii) clothing, equipment, etc. needed to prepare for, or enter, a career; (iii) educational travel at home or abroad; (iv) The study of music or the other arts; (v) educational research; and (vi) recreational, social and physical training.

Annual grant total: About £2,500 is available each year. Nine grants were made in 2004/05.

Applications: On a form available from the correspondent to be submitted directly by the individual or a parent/guardian. Applications are considered in October each year.

Correspondent: M Sivills, Director of Children's Services, Student Finance Section, Redcar & Cleveland Borough Council, PO Box 83, Council Offices, Kirkleatham Street, Redcar (01642 444118; Fax: 01642 444251)

Hartlepool

The Preston Simpson Scholarship in Music

Eligibility: People aged 15 to 25 who were either born in Hartlepool or who have had at least one parent living in Hartlepool for the last five years.

Types of grants: Cash grants to help with the cost of the study of music at any school or college or towards instruments.

Annual grant total: About £1,000 is available each year.

Applications: On a form which is available from local schools and on request from the civic centre (see below). Grants are considered once a year, usually just before the start of the school summer holidays.

Correspondent: Pat Watson, Corporate Strategy Division, Hartlepool Borough Council, Civic Centre, Hartlepool TS24 8AY (01429 266522; e-mail: pat.watson@hartlepool.gov.uk)

The Sterndale Scholarships in Music

Eligibility: Women aged between 15 and 25 on 31 July in the year of application who live in the borough of Hartlepool and have done so for at least three years prior to the application.

Types of grants: Scholarships (after audition) in music (vocal or instrumental) for those wishing to make use of their musical ability in their future career. The scholarships range from £150 to £800.

Annual grant total: In 2005 grants totalled £3,300.

Applications: On forms available from the correspondent, Hartlepool secondary schools and sixth form colleges or through an advert placed in the local press.

Correspondent: Chief Financial Officer, Hartlepool Borough Council, Civic Centre, Victoria Road, Hartlepool, Cleveland TS24 8AY (01429 523763; Fax: 01429 523750)

Middlesbrough

Middlesbrough Educational Trust Fund

Eligibility: People under 25 who live or work in Middlesbrough

Types of grants: Grants for the following: attendance at any approved place of learning (minimum period one year); the purchase of clothing, equipment or books to prepare for, or enter, a trade or profession; educational travel scholarships; assistance with the provision of facilities for recreation, sport and social and physical training for pupils and students;

NORTH EAST – TEESSIDE/TYNE & WEAR

the study of music and other arts; educational research.

Exclusions: No grants where statutory funding is available or to people who have received a grant from Middlesbrough Council in the current financial year.

Annual grant total: Disposable funds of £2,400.

Applications: Applications to these charities may be made directly by the individual or by recommendation, where appropriate, from a headteacher. Application forms are available from the correspondent.

Correspondent: Voluntary Sector Team, Middlesbrough Council, Children, Families & Learning, PO Box 69, Vancouver House, Gurney Street, Middlesbrough TS1 1EL

Thornaby-on-Tees

County Alderman Worsley JP Scholarships

Eligibility: Students at university or further education colleges who live in the former borough of Thornaby-on-Tees.

Types of grants: Recurrent grants to a usual maximum of £150 towards books, fees and equipment. Priority is given to families who have a low income.

Annual grant total: In 2005/06 grants were awarded to 17 individuals totalling £2,600.

Applications: On a form available from the correspondent from April, to be returned by 31 August for consideration in September/October. Applications should include two references.

Correspondent: Mrs A Metcalfe, Student Support, Stockton-on-Tees Borough Council, Education Leisure and Cultural Services, PO Box 228, Municipal Buildings, Church Road, Stockton-on-Tees TS18 1XE (01642 526609; Fax: 01642 393525; e-mail: studentsupport@stockton.gov.uk)

Yarm

The Yarm Grammar School Trust

Eligibility: People under 25 years of age who live in the parish of Yarm.

Types of grants: Grants of around £200 are given to schoolchildren for uniforms and other school clothing, books, educational outings and study or travel abroad and to students in further or higher education for books, equipment, instruments, fees, living expenses, educational outings and study or travel abroad.

Annual grant total: In 2004/05, the trust had an income of around £9,000 and a total expenditure of £5,000. Grants totalled about £3,000.

Applications: On a form available from the student support unit or the trust's website. Applications should be submitted directly by the individual by the end of May for consideration in July, or by the end of November for consideration in January.

Correspondent: Student Trust Funds, Stockton Borough Council, PO Box 228, Municipal Buildings, Church Road, Stockton-on-Tees TS18 1XE (01642 526608; e-mail: l student.support@ stockton.gov.uk; website: www.stockton. gov.uk/citizenservices/learning/ financialsupport)

Tyne & Wear

The Cullercoats Educational Trust

Eligibility: People who live in the ecclesiastical parishes of St Paul – Whitley Bay and St George – Cullercoats.

Types of grants: Grants are made towards religious instruction in accordance with the doctrines of the Church of England and to promote the education, including social and physical training, of beneficiaries.

Annual grant total: In 2004/05 the trust had an income of £6,500 and a total expenditure of £6,200. Grants are made to individuals and organisations totalling about £5,000 each year.

Applications: By letter to the correspondent in February or August for consideration in March or September.

Correspondent: Donald J Kean, 40 Parkside Crescent, Tynemouth, Tyne and Wear NE30 4JR (0191 257 1765)

Charity of John McKie Elliott Deceased

Eligibility: People who are blind in Gateshead or Newcastle upon Tyne.

Types of grants: One-off and recurrent grants according to need.

Annual grant total: The trust has about £550 available for grants each year. In recent years it has not always been able to distribute these funds.

Applications: In writing to the correspondent.

Correspondent: R Eager, 3 Dovecote Close, Whitley Bay, Tyne and Wear NE25 9HS (0191 252 4744)

The Newcastle Dispensary Relief-in-Sickness Charity

Eligibility: People who are sick and in need and live in or near the city of Newcastle upon Tyne.

Types of grants: Grants are made up to a maximum of £200 per applicant. Recent

grants have been given towards the cost of a nebuliser, a washing machine and spare bedding.

Grants to other agencies will not be considered, nor are grants given retrospectively.

Annual grant total: About £500.

Applications: On a form available from the correspondent which should be submitted via a social worker, Citizens Advice, or other welfare agency. Applications are considered when received.

Correspondent: Ian Humphreys, 25 Swallowdale Gardens, Newcastle-upon-Tyne, NE7 7TA

The Sunderland Orphanage & Educational Foundation

Eligibility: Young people under 25 who are resident in or around Sunderland who have a parent who is disabled or has died, or whose parents are divorced or legally separated.

Types of grants: (i) Maintenance payments and clothing for schoolchildren.

(ii) Help towards the cost of education, training, apprenticeship or equipment for those starting work.

(iii) Help with travel to pursue education, for the provision of athletic coaching and for the study of music and other arts.

Annual grant total: In 2004/05 the trust had both an income of £23,000 and a total expenditure of £21,000.

Applications: Applications should be made in writing and addressed to: D G Goodfellow, Administrator, 54 John Street, Sunderland SR1 1JG. They are considered every other month.

Correspondent: P W Taylor, McKenzie Bell, 19 John Street, Sunderland SR1 1JG (0191 567 4857)

Houghton-le-Springs

The Kepier Exhibition Trust

Eligibility: Those attending higher education who live in the ancient parish of Houghton-le-Spring.

Types of grants: Cash grants, to a usual maximum of £200, to supplement existing grants. Current policy is to give a one-off grant, payable in the first term at the beneficiary's university, with a preference for students from poorer families.

Annual grant total: About £1,000.

Applications: On a form available from the correspondent from February, to be returned by first post on 1 May.

Correspondent: Rev Dr Ian G Wallis, The Rectory, 5 Lingfield, Houghton-Le-Springs, Tyne and Wear, DH5 8QA (0191 584 2198; e-mail: ian.wallis@sero.co. uk)

Newcastle upon Tyne

The Newcastle upon Tyne Education Prize Fund

Eligibility: People under 25 who live in Newcastle upon Tyne and received a secondary school education in the city are eligible for mandatory or discretionary awards from Newcastle upon Tyne LEA.

Types of grants: Grants of between £100 and £200 to schoolchildren for equipment/instruments, educational outings, study or travel abroad and to people in further education towards equipment/instruments, educational outings, books and study or travel abroad.

Annual grant total: In 2005/06 the fund had both an income and a total expenditure of £1,900, all of which was given in 11 grants to individuals.

Applications: In writing to the correspondent, to be considered at any time. Applications should include details of date of birth, secondary school attended and home address in the city.

Correspondent: Kath Thompson, Room 303, Civic Centre, Barras Bridge, Newcastle-upon-Tyne NE99 2BN (0191 211 5413; Fax: 0191 211 4817; e-mail: kathleen.thompson@newcastle.gov.uk)

South Tyneside

Westoe Educational Charity

Eligibility: People under 25, resident in the Metropolitan Borough Council of South Tyneside (or have a parent resident) and are in financial need.

Types of grants: One-off and recurrent grants for schoolchildren, people with special educational needs, further/higher education students, vocational students, and people starting work towards uniforms/clothing, fees, study or travel abroad, books, equipment/instruments, maintenance/living expenses and excursions.

Annual grant total: In 2004/05 the chartity had a gross income of £17,000 and a total expenditure of £27,000. Grants totalled about £25,000.

Applications: In writing to the correspondent at any time although applications are usually considered in January.

Correspondent: E Campbell, Head of Resources and Strategy, South Tyneside MBC, Lifelong Learning & Lesiure, Town Hall and Civic Offices, Westoe Road, South Shields, Tyne and Wear NE33 2RL (0191 424 7778; Fax: 0191 427 0584; e-mail: website: www.s-tyneside-mbc.gov.uk)

Other information: Due to changes in statutory funding, grants are no longer made for musical instrument tuition.

Sunderland

The George Hudson Charity

Eligibility: People under the age of 18 living in Sunderland whose father is dead or incapacitated, with preference given to children of seafarers.

Types of grants: The trust gives pocket money of £12 a month to children up to the age of 14 and £14 a month to older children. These children may also receive a grant towards clothing.

Annual grant total: In 2004/05 the trust had an income of £35,000 and a total expenditure of £34,000.

Applications: On a form available from: D G Goodfellow, Administrator, 54 John Street, Sunderland SR1 1QH. Applications are considered every other month.

Correspondent: P W Taylor, Messrs McKenzie Bell Solicitors, 19 John Street, Sunderland SR1 1JG

The Mayor's Fund for Necessitous Children

Eligibility: Children in need (under 16, occasionally under 19) who are in full-time education, live in the city of Sunderland and whose family are on a low income.

Types of grants: About £25 grants for provision of school footwear paid every six months.

Exclusions: No grants to asylum seekers.

Annual grant total: In 2004/05 grants totalled about £700.

Applications: Applicants must visit the civic centre and fill in a form with a member of staff. The decision is then posted at a later date. Proof of low income is necessary.

Correspondent: Tony Davey, Pupil, Student and Finance Support Unit Manager, Education Services, Civic Centre, PO Box 101, Sunderland SR2 7DN (0191 553 1458)

West Yorkshire

Boston Spa School

Eligibility: People in need who live in Boston Spa, Collingham, Harewood, Alwoodley, Shadwell, Crossgates, Scholes, Barwichin Elmet, Bardsey, East Keswick, Whinmoor, Aberford, Thomer, Bramham, Clifford, Walton and Thorp Arch in the north east area of West Yorkshire.

Types of grants: One-off grants are usually given for expeditions and explorations or to students on higher education courses where no grants are available, such as postgraduate courses.

Annual grant total: In 2003/04 the trust had an income of £520 and a total expenditure of £2,000.

Applications: In writing to the correspondent, to be considered in March, June and November.

Correspondent: Alun Rees, Boston Spa Comprehensive School, Clifford, Moor Road, Boston Spa, Wetherby, West Yorkshire LS23 6RW (01937 842915)

The Clayton, Taylor & Foster Charity

Eligibility: People in need who live in the city of Wakefield, Thornes with Alverthorpe and Wrenthorpe with Outwood, who are in full-time or higher education.

Types of grants: Small grants to a maximum of about £100 for a variety of educational purposes. As the main purpose of the charity is to administer grants to the over 60s within the area above, educational grants are only given if there are any surplus funds available.

Annual grant total: In 2004 the charity had an income of £1,400 and a total expenditure of £1,100. Grants totalled about £1,000.

Applications: In writing to writing to the correspondent, giving details of the project. Trustees meet in March, September and November.

Correspondent: Mrs Preston, Clerk to the Trustees, 16 Stopford Avenue, Wakefield WF2 6RJ (01924 258660)

Lady Elizabeth Hasting's Educational Foundation

Eligibility: Individuals in need who live in the parishes of Burton Salmon, Thorp Arch, Collingham with Harewood, Bardsey with East Keswick, Shadwell and Ledsham with Fairburn.

Types of grants: One-off and recurrent grants according to need.

Exclusions: Applicants must reside in one of the above parishes to qualify for a grant.

Annual grant total: Grants were made to around 200 individuals totalling £65,000.

Applications: In writing to the correspondent. The trustees meet four times a year, although grants can be made between the meetings, on the agreement of two trustees.

Correspondent: E F V Waterson, Clerk, Carter Jonas, 82 Micklegate, York YO1 1LF

Other information: The trust is managed by, and derives its income from, Lady Elizabeth Hastings Estate Charity.

The Charity of Lady Mabel Florence Harriet Smith

Eligibility: Students in full-time attendance on a first degree course at a British university but who have not yet taken their final first degree examination at the date any awards are payable. Applicants must be ordinarily living in the former West Riding of Yorkshire as constituted on 31 March 1974.

Types of grants: Two grants of about £1,000 each are given towards travelling abroad to further education in a field of study which is the subject of the individual's full-time university course or a directly related field of study. Awards are tenable until 30 June of the year following the year of application.

Annual grant total: About £2,000.

Applications: On a form available from the correspondent. Applications are considered in May and should be submitted by 31 March, including a reference form a university tutor.

Correspondent: Kevin Tharby, Student Support Officer, Student Support Section, Education Offices, County Hall, Northallerton, North Yorkshire DL7 8AE (01609 780780 ext 2225; Fax: 01609 780098; e-mail: kevin.tharby@ northyorks.gov.uk)

Other information: Further information on other trusts administered by North Yorkshire County Council can be obtained from the correspondent.

The Brian Strong Trust for Pudsey Young People

Eligibility: Young people aged between 16 and 21 who live in Calverley, Farsley or Pudsey. Preference is given to children from low-income families.

Types of grants: One-off grants of between £50 and £300 are given to people at school or in further or higher education for books, equipment, instruments, educational outings in the UK and overseas and student exchange. Grants are available to people with special educational needs and people starting work for the same purposes. Personal development, such as organised travel and music, is also supported.

Annual grant total: In 2004, the trust had an income of £620 and a total expenditure of £280.

Applications: On a form available from the correspondent. Applications should be submitted directly by the individual for consideration at any time.

Correspondent: Bridget Strong, 55 Meersbrook Road, Sheffield S8 9HU (0114 255 2350; e-mail: bridgetstronguk@ yahoo.co.uk)

Bradford

The Isaac Holden Scholarships

Eligibility: Male higher education students who have attended maintained schools within the area of the former City of Bradford County Borough Council for not less than three years.

Types of grants: Grants of £120 each.

Annual grant total: In 2004/05, the charity had an income of £1,100. No expenditure has been recorded in recent years.

Correspondent: Deborah Beaumont, Britannia House, Hall Ings, Bradford BD1 1HX

The Frank Wallis Scholarships

Eligibility: Students who have lived within the area of the former Clayton urban district council for at least three years.

Types of grants: Grants range from £50 to £100 and are given for any course of higher education to assist with the purchase of books and equipment.

Annual grant total: In 2004/05, the charity had an income of £430. No expenditure was recorded during the year.

Correspondent: Deborah Beaumont, Britannia House, Hall Ings, Bradford BD1 1HX

Calderdale

The Community Foundation for Calderdale

Eligibility: Primary and secondary school pupils in Calderdale who are in need.

Types of grants: One-off grants (£100) and occasionally small loans are made for the costs of school trips, clothing, books or equipment and so on.

Annual grant total: In 2004/05 the foundation had assets of £4.5 million and an income of £3.3 million. Grants to 94 individuals totalled £6,500 and grants to 396 organisations totalled £1.6 million.

Applications: Individuals must apply through a referring agency, such as Citizens Advice, on an application form available from the correspondent. Grants will only be awarded to individuals in the form of a cheque; cash is not given.

Correspondent: Grants Department, Room 158, Dean Clough, Halifax HX3 5AX (01422 349700; Fax: 01422 350017; e-mail: enquiries@cffc. co.uk; website: www.cffc.co.uk)

Elland

The Brooksbank Educational Charity

Eligibility: People under the age of 25 who live in the former urban district of Elland (as constituted on 31 March 1974).

Types of grants: Grants for people who are moving from junior to secondary schools and to students going on to higher education. Grants are usually £30 per student.

Annual grant total: About £800.

Applications: Application forms are issued through the local junior schools; other students should apply direct to the correspondent. Juniors should apply in May, seniors in September. Trustees meet twice yearly, but can act rapidly in an emergency.

Correspondent: A D Blackburn, Clerk, Ryburn, 106 Victoria Road, Elland, Calderdale HX5 0QF (01422 372014)

Haworth

The Haworth Exhibition Endowment Trust

Eligibility: People who live, or whose parents lived, in the ancient township of Haworth. Candidates must have attended one of the schools (including Oakbank) in the district of Haworth (including Oxenhope and Stanbury, but excluding Lees and Crossroads) for at least three years.

Types of grants: One-off grants ranging from £25 to £75 to people following A-levels and taking up further education, for books and equipment.

Annual grant total: In 2004/05, the trust had an income of £610 and a total expenditure of £640.

Applications: On an application form available from the town hall information desk following an advertisement in the local newspaper. The closing date for applications is 31 August. The trustees meet once a year in October.

Correspondent: Dr Andrew Collinson, 38 Gledhow Drive, Oxenhope, Keighley, West Yorkshire BD22 9SA

Keighley

Bowcocks Trust Fund for Keighley

Eligibility: People in need who live in the municipal borough of Keighley as constituted on 31 March 1974. The trust states that it normally only supports individuals who have been assessed by

Citizens Advice, Disability Advice and similar organisations as being in need.

Types of grants: One-off grants in the range of £50 and £300 are given to disadvantaged families with a child at one of the three upper schools in Keighley for clothing and school trips and to school-leavers who proceed to higher education.

Annual grant total: In 2004/05 the trust had assets of £177,000 and an income of £9,200. Grants totalled £8,100, of which 154 educational grants amounted to £6,800 and six relief-in-need grants totalled £1,200.

Applications: Applications should be made in writing to the correspondent by a social worker, teacher, Citizens Advice or other educational welfare agency, for consideration throughout the year.

Correspondent: Phillip Vaux, Clerk, Old Mill House, 6 Dockroyd, Oakworth, Keighley, West Yorkshire BD22 7RH

Leeds

The Joseph Emmott Scholarship Fund

Eligibility: People who live in the city of Leeds who are at least 17 years old on 1 August of the year of application. They must have lived in Leeds for at least five years and have attended a secondary school in the city.

Types of grants: Grants of £200 a year payable to students at the universities of Oxford or Cambridge or, in exceptional circumstances, at another university.

'Scholars would not normally hold an exhibition or a scholarship from any other source, with the exception of a local authority award under the awards regulations or a student support package under the student support regulations. In this event, either the parental income must be such that a parental contribution is not required or the scholar must be independent. [Furthermore], in awarding the scholarship due regard will be paid to any public examinations which the candidate may have passed.'

Annual grant total: In 2003/04, the fund had an income of £6,300. The sum of £200 was distributed.

Applications: Leeds Education Authority will notify students holding awards who appear to met the criteria of eligibility, and they are invited to apply.

Correspondent: Corporate Services Department, 2nd Floor West, Merrian House, Civic Hall, Leeds LS1 1UR

Peter Bamlett Hayton Scholarship Fund

Eligibility: People who live in the city of Leeds who are at least 17 years of age on 1 April of the year of application. They must not have previously attended a college or institution similar to that at which the

scholarships are to be tenable. They must have lived in Leeds for at least five years and attended a Leeds school.

Types of grants: The scholarships are tenable at the University of Leeds or at other institutions of higher education. One scholarship will be towards study in some branch of engineering, the other in some branch of chemistry. The award is given for the normal duration of the specified course.

'In awarding the scholarship due regard will be paid to any public examinations which the candidate may have passed and to any practical experience they may have had in workshops.' If the interest of the trust allows, additional awards may be offered to the next most deserving candidates.

Annual grant total: In 2003/04 the fund had an income of £1,400. No funds were distributed in the year.

Applications: On a form available from the correspondent.

Correspondent: Corporate Services Department, 2nd Floor West, Merrian House, Civic Hall, Leeds LS1 1UR

The Holbeck Mechanics Institute Trust Fund Scheme

Eligibility: People who live in the city of Leeds south of the River Aire. If no suitable applicant can be found from there, applications from other parts of Leeds will be considered.

Types of grants: Grants for those attending courses of further or higher education to assist with the costs of maintenance and travel but not fees. 'Normally, applications will not be considered where, on the basis of the appropriate regulations, a parental contribution has been assessed or in situations where assistance is available from other sources.'

Annual grant total: In 2003/04, the fund had an income of £850. The sum of £200 was distributed.

Applications: On a form available from the correspondent. Applications may be considered at any time.

Correspondent: Corporate Services Department, 2nd Floor West, Merrian House, Civic Hall, Leeds LS1 1UR

Kirke Charity

Eligibility: People in need who live in the ancient parish of Adel comprising Arthington, Cookridge and Ireland Wood. There must be evidence of real need/poverty.

Types of grants: One-off grants, generally for around £100, towards the educational needs of the poor of the parish.

Annual grant total: In 2004/05 the charity had an income of £6,300 and a total expenditure of £5,900. Grants totalled around £5,000.

Applications: Applications can be submitted directly by the individual or through a social worker, Citizens Advice or other welfare agency or third party. There is a quick response in cases of emergencies. Other applications are considered in January and June.

Correspondent: J B Buchan, 8 St Helens Croft, Leeds LS16 8JY

The Mitchell Memorial Fund

Eligibility: Students in higher/further education who live in Rawdon or Horsforth and do not receive assistance from Leeds City Council.

Types of grants: One-off and recurrent grants according to need.

Annual grant total: In 2003/04, the fund had an income of £1,500. No funds were distributed in the year.

Applications: On a form available from the correspondent.

Correspondent: Corporate Services Department, 2nd Floor West, Merrian House, Civic Hall, Leeds LS1 1UR

Mirfield

The Mirfield Educational Charity

Eligibility: People under the age of 25 who live (or whose parents live) in the former urban district of Mirfield.

Types of grants: 'The policy of the trustees is to apply the income of the charity to schools, youth groups, Scouts, Guides etc. for the benefit of as many qualifying persons as possible rather than to individuals. Applications from individuals are not discouraged but the financial circumstances of the individual and, if applicable, his/her parents will be taken into account.'

Annual grant total: In 2005 the charity had net assets of £1.2 million, an income of £45,000 and a total expenditure of £49,500. The charity gave grants to individuals totalling £42,800.

Applications: In writing to the correspondent. The trustees meet three times a year, in February, May and October.

Correspondent: M G Parkinson, 7 Kings Street, Mirfield WF14 8AW

Rawdon

The Rawdon & Laneshaw Bridge School Trust (Rawdon Endowment)

Eligibility: People under the age of 21 and living in the former urban district of Rawdon.

Types of grants: Grants for people at college or university (typically for books or equipment) and to needy students pursuing education at lower levels, and changing to higher levels of education.

Annual grant total: In 2004/05 the trust had assets totalling £30,200, an income of £1,000 and a total expenditure of £810. Grants were made to six individuals totalling £800.

Applications: In writing to the correspondent. Grants are awarded annually in October after applications have been invited in the local press during September.

Correspondent: Mrs Anthea Hargreaves, Park Dale, Layton Drive, Rawdon, Leeds LS19 6QY

Other information: The correspondent also administers the Charity of Francis Layton. This is for the advancement in life of deserving and necessitous Rawdon residents under the age of 21. It was formerly to assist with apprentice fees, but now tends to support other educational purposes. It gives one or two grants a year totalling £100.

Shipley

The Salt Foundation

Eligibility: People who live in the former urban district council of Shipley (Saltaire or Shipley).

Types of grants: The foundation supports local schools and individuals. One-off grants are given to: schoolchildren for books, equipment/instruments and educational outings in the UK; people starting work for equipment/instruments; and people in higher or further education, including mature students and postgraduates, for books, equipment/instruments and study or travel overseas.

Annual grant total: In 2005, the foundation had assets of £20,400, a total income of £85,300 and an expenditure of £87,300. Grants totalled £21,800 of which £15,000 was given to institutions, and a further £6,800 was awarded to individuals.

Applications: On a form available from the correspondent, it can be submitted either directly by the individual or through their school or college, an educational welfare agency or another third party. Applications should arrive in January or September for consideration in March and October.

Correspondent: Mrs M Davies, Clerk, 17 Springfield Road, Baildon, Shipley, West Yorkshire, BD17 5NA (01274 591 508)

Wakefield

Lady Bolles Foundation

Eligibility: People under 21 who live in the county borough of Wakefield, and who are in full-time education.

Types of grants: Grants are given to schoolchildren towards uniforms, other school clothing, fees and educational outings. Students in further and higher education can receive help towards books and fees.

Annual grant total: Grants total about £5,000 a year.

Applications: In writing to the correspondent, for consideration in February and October.

Correspondent: M E Atkinson, The Beaumont Partnership, 67 Westgate, Wakefield, West Yorkshire WF1 1BW (01924 291234; Fax: 01924 290350)

Feiweles Trust

Eligibility: People at the start of their artistic career. The theme of the bursary changes each year.

Types of grants: One bursary per year.

Annual grant total: Between £10,000 and £12,000 a year.

Applications: In writing to the correspondent, to be submitted directly by the individual. The deadline is January; applications are considered in February/March.

Correspondent: The Trustees, c/o Yorkshire Sculpture Park, Bretton Hall, Bretton, Wakefield, West Yorkshire WF4 4LG (01924 830642; e-mail: aducation@ysp.co.uk; website: www.ysp.co.uk)

5. NORTH WEST

The Bowland Charitable Trust

Eligibility: Young people in need in the north west of England.

Types of grants: One-off and recurrent grants towards educational character-forming activities for young people.

Annual grant total: In 2004, grants made to five individuals £2,600.

Applications: In writing to the correspondent, to be considered at any time.

Correspondent: Ms Carol Fahy, TDS House, Whitebirk Estate, Blackburn, Lancashire, BB1 5TH

Crabtree North West Charitable Trust

Eligibility: Young people up to the age of 18 in education in the North West.

Types of grants: One-off according to need.

Annual grant total: Between £5,000 and £10,000 a year.

Applications: In writing to the correspondent.

Correspondent: Ian Currie, 3 Ralli Courts, West Riverside, Manchester M3 5FT (0161 831 1512)

The Darbishire House Trust

Eligibility: Women who were born in, reside in or work(ed) in Greater Manchester. Preference is given to professional women who are retraining.

Types of grants: Grants towards the costs of education and retraining, including for books, equipment, clothing, uniforms and travel. A one-off contribution to fees may be considered.

Annual grant total: In 2004/05, the trust had an income of £860 and a total expenditure of £820.

Applications: On a form available from the correspondent which must be completed by a sponsor from an educational establishment.

Correspondent: Ms Shirley Adams, Gaddum Centre, Gaddum House, 6 Great Jackson Street, Manchester M15 4AX (0161 834 6069; Fax: 0161 839 8573; e-mail: sma@gaddumcentre.co.uk)

Manchester Publicity Association Educational Trust

Eligibility: People aged 16 or over, living in Greater Manchester and the surrounding area, who are already working in or hoping to enter marketing or related occupations or who are studying marketing communications.

Types of grants: Grants ranging between £200 and £500 towards the cost of books or fees for education or training, usually to cover the second half of the year.

Annual grant total: About £9,500.

Applications: On a form available from the correspondent. Applications must be supported by a tutor and are considered on demand.

Correspondent: Gordon Jones, Secretary, 38 Larkfield Close, Greenmount, Bury, Lancashire BL8 4QJ (01204 886037)

The Bishop David Sheppard Anniversary Trust

Eligibility: People between the ages of 21 and 49 who live in the Anglican diocese of Liverpool (which includes Southport, Kirkby, Ormskirk, Skelmersdale, Wigan, St Helens, Warrington and Widnes) and who are doing second-chance learning at a college or training centre.

Types of grants: Grants are one-off, about £100 and are made to people in second-chance learning such as access courses and training. Priority is given to those who are unemployed or who have difficulty in finding the money for books, equipment, uniforms. Grants cannot be given for fees, travel or childcare. Grants can be for training purposes to enable applicants to get a job, for example, in order to obtain a HGV licence.

Exclusions: No grants to students who have had no break from their education (or schoolchildren), to people with good vocational qualifications or on degree courses, or to organisations.

Annual grant total: In 2005 grants totalled £8,400.

Applications: On a form available from the administrator to be submitted directly by the individual at any time. Applications are usually considered in March, May, September and December.

Correspondent: Mrs Jen Stratford, Administrator, Church House, 1 Hanover Street, Liverpool L1 3DW (0151 709 9722)

Winwick Educational Foundation

Eligibility: Children and young people under the age of 25 who live in the parishes of Winwick, Newton St Peter's, Newton All Saints, Emmanuel Wargrave, St John's Earlestown, Lowton St Mary's and Lowton St Luke's.

Types of grants: One-off or recurrent grants for books, equipment and fees. Grants range from £75 to £100.

Annual grant total: In 2005 the trust had an income of £5,400. Grants to individuals totalled about £1,000.

Applications: On a form available from the correspondent. Applications should be submitted in February and March for consideration in April. They can be made directly by the individual or through a third party such as the individual's school, college or educational welfare agency.

Correspondent: A Brown, Clerk, Davies Ridgway, 17-21 Palmyra Square, Warrington WA1 1BW (01925 654221; Fax: 01925 416527; e-mail: abrown@ daviesridgway.co.uk)

World Friendship

Eligibility: Overseas students studying at universities in the diocese of Liverpool. Preference is given to people in the final year of their course. Students from an EU country, or who are intending to stay in the UK at the end of their course, are not usually supported.

Types of grants: One-off grants towards relieving unexpected hardships which have arisen since the start of the course.

Exclusions: Grants are not given to those whose place of study is outside the diocese of Liverpool.

Annual grant total: In 2004 the trust had an income of £11,000 and a total expenditure of £9,600. Grants totalled about £9,000.

Applications: On a form available from the individual's institution. For details of the relevant contact, or to download a form, applicants should view the trust's website.

Correspondent: The Diocesan Registry, Church House, 1 Hanover Street, Liverpool L1 3DW (website: www. worldfriendship.merseyside.org)

Cheshire

The Sir Thomas Moulson Trust

Eligibility: Students under 25 who live in the villages of Huxley, Hargrave, Tarvin, Kelsall and Ashton in Cheshire.

Types of grants: One-off grants ranging from £100 to £500 to students in further/ higher education towards books, fees/ living expenses and study or travel abroad.

Annual grant total: In 2005, the trust had assets of £154,200 and a total expenditure of £5,600. Grants were given to two individuals costing £500; a further £1,600 was given to an organisation.

Applications: In writing to the correspondent. Applications should be submitted directly by the individual and are usually considered in September.

Correspondent: Mrs Julie Turner, Meadow Barn, Cow Lane, Hargrave, Chester CH3 7RU (01829 781640)

The Thornton-Le-Moors Education Foundation

Eligibility: People under 25 in full-time education who live in the ancient parish of Thornton-Le-Moors which includes the following villages: Dunham Hill, Elton, Hapsford, Ince and Thornton-Le-Moors.

Types of grants: The trust gives grants mostly to students going to university for books and also to the local youth groups, mainly the guides, brownies, scouts and cubs.

Annual grant total: In 2005, the trust had an income of £750 and a total expenditure of £250. No further information was available.

Applications: In writing to the correspondent. Trustees meet twice a year, usually in April and November.

Correspondent: R F Edwards, Trustee, Jesmin, 4 School Lane, Elton, Chester CH2 4LN (01928 725188)

The Wrenbury Consolidated Charities

Eligibility: People in need who live in the parishes of Chorley, Sound, Broomhall, Newhall, Wrenbury and Dodcott-cum-Wilkesley.

Types of grants: Payments on St Marks' (25 April) and St Thomas' (21 December) days to pensioners and students. Grants are also given for one-off necessities. Grants range from £120 to £130.

Annual grant total: In 2004 the charity had an income of £7,800 and a total expenditure of £8,200. Grants totalled about £8,000.

Applications: In writing to the correspondent either directly by the individual or through another third party on behalf of the individual. The Vicar of Wrenbury and the parish council can give details of the six nominated trustees who can help with applications. Applications are considered in December and March.

Correspondent: Mrs M H Goodwin, Eagle Hall Cottage, Smeatonwood, Wrenbury, North Nantwich CW5 8HD

Other information: Grants are also given to churches, the village hall and for educational purposes.

Alsager

The Alsager Educational Foundation

Eligibility: People who live in the urban district of Alsager. People who do not have a permanent home address in Alsager will not be supported.

Types of grants: One-off and recurrent grants are given to schoolchildren, college students, undergraduates, vocational students and to individuals with special educational needs for study/travel overseas, books, instruments/equipment and excursions, and also to schoolchildren for uniforms and clothing.

Exclusions: Postgraduates are not supported.

Annual grant total: In 2004/05 the trust had an income and a total expenditure of £11,000. Grants usually total around £7,500 per year, with about one-third of this total given to individuals.

Applications: In writing to the correspondent directly by the individual. Applications are considered four times per year.

Correspondent: Mrs C Lovatt, Secretary, 6 Pikemere Road, Alsager, Stoke-on-Trent ST7 2SB (01270 873680)

Audlem

Audlem Educational Foundation

Eligibility: People in need who live in the ancient parish of Audlem and are under 25 years of age. Preference is given to people who are attending, or have attended a maintained school for at least two years.

Types of grants: One-off and recurrent grants according to need.

Annual grant total: In 2004/05 the trust had an income of £14,000 and a total expenditure of £12,000.

Applications: In writing to the correspondent.

Correspondent: Richard Wilkinson, Cheshire County Council, Education Department, County Hall, Chester, CH1 1SQ

Chester

The Chester Municipal Charities – Owen Jones Educational Foundation

Eligibility: Young people under 25 years of age (i) whose fathers are (or if dead, were at the date of death) a freeman of the City of Chester and a member of one of the City Companies 20 beneficiaries or, (ii) who attend or have attended a school in Chester and who live in the city. Priority is given to those in category (i).

Types of grants: One-off grants of between £100 and £800 are given to schoolchildren for help with uniforms and other school clothing, and to students in further/higher education for books, living expenses and equipment/instruments.

Annual grant total: About £40,000.

Applications: On a form available from the correspondent. Applications should be submitted directly by the individual for consideration in September and October.

Correspondent: Birch Cullimore Solicitors, 20 White Friars, Chester CH1 1XS

Congleton

The Congleton Town Trust

Eligibility: People in need who live in the town of Congleton (this does not include the other two towns which have constituted the borough of Congleton since 1975).

Types of grants: The principal aim of the trust is to give grants to individuals in need or to organisations which provide relief, services or facilities to those in need. The trustees will, however, consider a grant towards education or training if the applicant is in need. Support can be given in the form of books, tools or in cash towards tuition fees or maintenance.

Annual grant total: In 2004 the trust had assets of £255,000 and an income of £23,000. Grants to organisations totalled £20,000. No grants were made to individuals during the year.

Applications: On a form available from the correspondent, to be submitted directly by the individual or a family member. Applications are considered quarterly, on the second Monday in March, June, September and December.

Correspondent: Ms J Money, Clerk, c/o Congleton Town Hall, High Street, Congleton CW12 1BN (01260 291156)

Other information: The trust also administers several smaller trusts, and has recently taken over the finances of the William Barlow Skelland Charity for the Poor which has been wound up.

Knutsford

Knutsford Educational Foundation

Eligibility: People who live in the urban district of Knutsford and are on courses of higher education or training. There is a minimum age of 18 and maximum age of 24 by 31 August in the year in which the application is being considered.

Types of grants: Grants to help with the cost of books, fees and living expenses, study or travel abroad and assistance with entering a profession or trade. Usually a full grant is only given once to each applicant, although on occasions, a half grant can be made to second-time applicants.

Exclusions: No grants for student exchanges.

Annual grant total: About £1,500.

Applications: On a form available from the correspondent. Completed application forms must be submitted by 24 December. Grants are issued in January.

Correspondent: S D Armstrong, Clerk, Hague Lambert Solicitors, 131 King Street, Knutsford, Cheshire WA16 6EJ (01565 652411)

Vale Royal

The Verdin Trust Fund

Eligibility: People who live in Northwich and surrounding districts.

Types of grants: Most of the trust's funds are given in the form of prizes to local schools, Young Farmers' Associations and courses, gap years and so on.

Annual grant total: In 2004/05 the trust had an income of £1,800. It has about £2,000 a year to distribute in grants.

Applications: In writing to the correspondent.

Correspondent: J E Richards, Rose Cottage, Vale Royal Courtyard, Whitegate, Cheshire CW8 2BA (01606 43746)

Other information: Grants are also made to organisations.

Warrington

The Police-Aided Children's Relief-in-Need Fund

Eligibility: Children of pre-school or primary school age living in the borough of Warrington and whose families are in financial or physical need. Applications from students of secondary school age and

over will be considered in exceptional circumstances.

Types of grants: Vouchers of £30 to £110 (depending on age) to help with the cost of clothing and footwear. Vouchers are only redeemable at selected retailers in the borough.

Annual grant total: About £15,000.

Applications: On a form available from the correspondent.

Correspondent: Warrington Council For Voluntary Services, The Gateway, 89 Sankey St, Warrington, WA1 1SR (01925 246880)

Widnes

The Widnes Educational Foundation

Eligibility: People under the age of 25 who have either lived in the borough of Widnes for at least three years or who have attended college there for at least three years.

Types of grants: The foundation mainly focuses on giving grants to help with educational trips and visits. Cash grants can also be given for books and educational outings for those at school. Very occasionally small grants are given to help with school/college fees or to supplement existing grants.

Annual grant total: In 2004/05, the foundation had both an income and expenditure of £700. Grants totalled about £500.

Applications: On a form available from the correspondent. Applications must be supported by a third party, such as senior teachers.

Correspondent: Miss Wendy Jefferies, Halton Borough Council, Municipal Buildings, Kingsway, Widnes, Cheshire WA8 7QF (0151 424 2061; Fax: 0151 471 7343; e-mail: wendyjefferies@halon-borough.gov.uk)

Wilmslow

The Lindow Workhouse Trust

Eligibility: Children with special educational needs who live in the ancient parish of Wilmslow.

Types of grants: One-off grants of amounts up to £500.

Annual grant total: In 2005 the trust made 40 grants for welfare and educational purposes totalling around £5,000.

Applications: In writing to the correspondent at any time. Applications can be submitted either directly by the individual or a family member, through a third party such as a social worker or teacher, or through an organisation such as Citizens Advice or a school.

Correspondent: Grp Capt J Buckley, 10 Summerfield Place, Wilmslow, Cheshire SK9 1NE (01625 531227)

Cumbria

The Barton Educational Foundation

Eligibility: People who live in Barton, Yanwath, Pooley Bridge, Martindale or Patterdale.

Types of grants: Recurrent grants ranging between £25 and £100 to students at colleges and universities for help with books, fees and living expenses. Help with the costs of books for schoolchildren is also occasionally provided.

Annual grant total: In 2005 the foundation had both an income and total expenditure of £1,100.

Applications: Directly by the individual on a form available from the correspondent. Applications are considered in October.

Correspondent: A Wright, 15 Church Croft, Pooley Bridge, Penrith, Cumbria, CA10 2NL

The Brow Edge Foundation

Eligibility: People in need who live in the area of Haverthwaite and Backbarrow, aged between 16 and 25.

Types of grants: Grants for full and part-time students and those starting apprenticeships. Preference will be given to applications for one-off grants.

Annual grant total: In 2005, the foundation had an income and a total expenditure of £1,400.

Applications: In writing to the correspondent, directly by the individual. Applicants must state the type of course of study or apprenticeship they are about to undertake. Applications are usually considered in September.

Correspondent: Robert William Hutton, 20 Ainslie Street, Ulverston, Cumbria LA12 7JE (01229 585888)

The Burton-in-Kendal Educational Foundation

Eligibility: People aged between 16 and 25 years who live in the parishes of Burton, Beetham, Arnside, Storth and Meathop, Ulpha, Holme, Preston and Patrick and are in need of financial assistance. Applicants must have attended a county or voluntary primary school for no less than two years.

Types of grants: Grants ranging between about £10 and £60 a year are made to schoolchildren, college students, undergraduates and vocational students towards fees, study/travel abroad, books, equipment/instruments and maintenance/

living expenses. Grants are also made to people with special educational needs.

Annual grant total: In 2004/05 the foundation had an income of £2,200 and a total expenditure of £2,300. There were 60 grants to individuals made totalling £2,100.

Applications: On a form available from the correspondent, which should be submitted directly by the individual. Applications are considered in May and October/November and should be received by April and September respectively.

Correspondent: Mrs E M Falkingham, Clerk to the Governors, 7 Hollowrayne, Burton-in-Kendal, Cumbria LA6 1NS (01524 782302; e-mail: liz.falk21@tiscali.co.uk)

The Cartmel Old Grammar School Foundation

Eligibility: People between the ages of 18 and 25 who live in the parishes of Cartmel Fell, Broughton East, Grange-over-Sands, Lower Holker, Staveley, Lower Allithwaite, Upper Allithwaite and that part of the parish of Haverthwaite east of the River Leven.

Types of grants: Cash grants of about £85, usually for up to three years, for students in higher education to help with books, fees/living expenses or study or travel abroad. Help is also given for those studying music and the arts in special cases.

Annual grant total: In 2003/04, the trust gave a total of £3,600 to individuals. The trust also gave £3,400 to local schools.

Applications: On a form available from the correspondent, including schools attended, qualifications and place of higher education. Applications are considered in October/November.

Correspondent: Anthony William Coles, Clerk, 2 Rowan Side, Grange-over-Sands, Cumbria LA11 7EQ (01539 534348)

The Gibb Charitable Trust

Eligibility: People who live in the brough of Copeland, the district of Allerdale (but not the parish of Keswick), and that part of the district of Eden formerly known as the district of Alston with Garrigill, who are over the age of 16 and who have been living or employed in the above area for two years.

Types of grants: Depending on the amount of applications received in any particular year and the amount of income of the trust, grants ranging from £25 to £200 can be made towards the cost of books, clothing and other essentials for students at college or university (including Open University).

Annual grant total: In 2004/05 the trust had an income of £640 and a total expenditure of £400, all of which was given in grants to two individuals.

Applications: On a form available from the correspondent. Applications should be made by the end of August for consideration in September. The charity also does its own research and publicity in local schools.

Correspondent: W F Gough, Treasurer, Kerbank, Beckermet, Cumbria CA21 2YF

The Mary Grave Trust

Eligibility: People in need aged between 11 and 21 who were born in the former county of Cumberland (excluding those whose parents were resident in Carlisle). Applicants must live, study or have studied (for at least two years, in secondary/further education) in one of the following areas, listed in order of priority: (i) the former boroughs of Workington or Maryport, or (ii) the former borough of Whitehaven, (iii) elsewhere in the former county of Cumberland. Applicants should not work for British Steel or National Coal Board.

Types of grants: Grants up to about £1,000 to assist in travel overseas which is of educational value.

Annual grant total: In 2005/06 the trust had an income of £98,000 and a total expenditure of £89,000. Grants were made to 116 individuals totalling £85,000.

Applications: On a form available from the correspondent, submitted through the individual's school or college or directly by the individual. The trustees require a copy of the applicant's birth certificate and information about his/her financial circumstances. Applications should be received by 30 April, 30 September and 31 January.

Correspondent: Jane Allen, Cumbria Community Foundation, Dovenby Hall, Dovenby, Cockermouth, CA13 0PN (01900 825760; e-mail: jane@cumbriafoundation.org)

The Greysouthen Educational Charity

Eligibility: People under 24 who live in Greysouthen or Eaglesfield.

Types of grants: Help with the cost of books, clothing, educational outings, fees and other essentials for schoolchildren. Grants are also available for those at college or university towards books, fees/living expenses, childcare costs and study or travel abroad. Grants for people starting work will be made for books, equipment/instruments, clothing and travel.

Annual grant total: About £2,000 a year.

Applications: In writing to the correspondent either directly by the individual or through his/her school, college or an educational welfare agency. Applications are considered in July/August.

Correspondent: John Chipps, Brunlea, Greysouthen, Cockermouth, Cumbria CA13 0UA (01900 825235)

Kelsick's Educational Foundation

Eligibility: Young people, under the age of 25, who were born or who have lived in Ambleside, Grasmere, Langdale or part of Troutbeck (the Lakes Parish) for at least four years. There is a preference for children/students with special needs.

Types of grants: Grants are given to: (i) schoolchildren towards equipment and educational outings, including study or travel abroad; (ii) students in further or higher education to help with books, equipment, computer hardware and software, maintenance/living expenses, educational outings and study or travel abroad; and (iii) vocational students to help with the cost of books and equipment. Grants are one-off and recurrent and range from £25 to £3,000. There were 150 grants made to individuals during 2004/05.

Annual grant total: In 2004/05 the foundation had assets of £5.1 million, an income of £287,000 and a total expenditure of £249,000. Grants to organisations and individuals totalled £207,000.

Applications: On a form available from the correspondent for consideration in February, May, August and November, although applications are accepted at any time. Applicants must list detailed costs (with receipts) of the items required. Applications should be submitted directly by the individual, or by a parent/guardian if the applicant is under 18.

Correspondent: P G Frost, Clerk, Kelsick Centre, St Mary's Lane, Ambleside, Cumbria LA22 9DG (015394 31289; Fax: 015394 31292)

Lamonby Educational Trust

Eligibility: People who live in the Lamonby area who are under the age of 25.

Types of grants: One-off grants in the range of £20 and £200 to schoolchildren, college students, undergraduates, vocational students including those for clothing/uniforms, study/travel abroad, books, equipment/instruments and excursion. Grants are also made to people starting work and people with special educational needs.

Annual grant total: In 2004/05 the trust had assets of £36,000 and an income of £1,800. Grants were awarded to 15 individuals totalling £1,600.

Applications: On a form available from the correspondent. Applications are considered in October and May.

Correspondent: Lynne Miller, Arbour House, Lamonby, Penrith, Cumbria CA11 9SS (01768 484385)

Northern Counties Orphans' Benevolent Society – see entry on page 121

Correspondent: Ms G Mackie, 29a Princes Road, Gosforth, Newcastle upon Tyne NE3 5TT (0191 236 5308)

Silecroft School Educational Charity

Eligibility: People under 25 who were born in the parishes of Whicham, Millom, Millom Without and Ulpha and are moving away from home to continue their education.

Types of grants: Recurrent grants are given for a wide range of educational needs for people at university or college, from books, clothing, equipment and other supplementary awards to foreign travel and other educational visits. However, the trust does not give grants for travel to and from the applicant's place of residence.

Exclusions: Grants are not given for schoolchildren, people starting work or to students who have not moved away from home to continue their education.

Annual grant total: In 2005, the charity had an income of £2,300 and a total expenditure of £2,800.

Applications: On a form available from the correspondent, to be submitted in September for consideration in November. Applications can be made either directly by the individual, or through their school, college or educational welfare agency.

Correspondent: Janet Pinney, Riber, Main Street, Silecroft, Millom, Cumbria LA18 4NU

The Wiggonby School Trust

Eligibility: People who have left school, are under 25 and live in the parishes of Aikton, Beaumont and Burgh-by-Sands, or are former pupils of Wiggonby School.

Types of grants: Grants, usually of around £200, for people engaged in further education or training, including help with fees/living expenses, books, equipment and so on. People starting work may also receive help.

Annual grant total: In 2004/05 the trust had assets of £600,000, an income of £24,000 and a total expenditure of £23,500. Grants to 37 individuals totalled £7,500. Grants to organisations totalled £15,000.

Applications: Applications are invited annually in answer to an advertisement placed in the Cumberland News in August. They can be made on a form available from the correspondent and are considered in September. Information required includes place of further study and qualification aimed for.

Correspondent: M J Reay, Clerk, 5 Walkmill Crescent, Carlisle, CA1 2WF (016973 42752)

Barrow-in-Furness

The Billincoat Charity

Eligibility: People under 21 who live in the borough of Barrow-in-Furness.

Types of grants: One-off grants towards the cost of education, training, apprenticeship or equipment for those starting work; and books, equipment/instruments, fees, educational outings in the UK and study or travel abroad for schoolchildren and people in further and higher education. Schoolchildren can also be supported for uniforms or other school clothing.

Annual grant total: About £500 a year.

Applications: On an application form available from the correspondent to be submitted in December and June for consideration in January and July. Applications can be submitted by the individual or through their school, college, social services or probation service and so on.

Correspondent: Kenneth J Fisher, Glenside House, Springfield Road, Ulverston, Cumbria LA12 0EJ (01229 583437)

Carlisle

The Carlisle Educational Charity

Eligibility: People (or whose parents) who live in the area of Carlisle city (i.e. north and north east Cumbria), aged under 25.

Types of grants: Grants of £50 to £400 are given to: (i) students due to attend full time courses at a university or institution of further education; (ii) graduates undertaking, or wishing to undertake higher studies or obtaining professional qualifications; (iii) students who have to travel in the UK or abroad as part of their course.

Grants are for general educational costs, such as books and equipment.

Annual grant total: In 2004/05 the charity had an income of £5,100 and a total expenditure of £8,400. Grants were made to 29 individuals totalling £6,500.

Applications: On a form available from the correspondent. Applications are considered in March and October and should be submitted by February and September respectively.

Correspondent: Mrs Elspeth Mackay, The Civic Centre, Carlisle CA3 8QG (01228 817034; Fax: 01228 817048; e-mail: cec@carlisle.gov.uk; website: www.carlisle.gov.uk)

Crosby Ravensworth

The Crosby Ravensworth Relief-in-Need Charities

Eligibility: People in need who have lived in the ancient parish of Crosby Ravensworth for at least 12 months.

Types of grants: One-off and recurrent grants. As well as relief-in-need grants, funds can also be given to local students entering university if they have been educated in the parish.

Annual grant total: In 2005 about £2,000 was distributed to individuals, including £300 for student travel.

Applications: In writing to the correspondent submitted directly by the individual including details of the applicant's financial situation. Applications are considered in February, May and October.

Correspondent: G Bowness, Ravenseat, Crosby Ravensworth, Penrith, Cumbria CA10 3JB

Egton-cum-Newland

Egton Parish Lands Trust

Eligibility: Children and young people in need living in the parish of Egton-cum-Newland. Particular favour is given to parents on low incomes whose children wish to go on educational trips.

Types of grants: One-off and recurrent grants of £100 to £1,000 to schoolchildren for equipment/instruments and excursions and to college and university students for books.

Annual grant total: In 2004/05 the trust had an income of £11,000 and it made grants totalling £6,000, mainly to organisations.

Applications: In writing to the correspondent. Applications should be submitted in April and October for consideration in May and November. They can be made either by the individual or through his/her school, college or welfare agency, or other third party.

Correspondent: Mrs J Ireland, Clerk, Threeways, Pennybridge, Ulverston, Cumbria LA12 7RX (01229 861405)

Sedbergh

Robinson's Educational Foundation

Eligibility: People below the age of 25 who live in the parish of Sedbergh, with a preference for people who live in Howgill.

Types of grants: One-off grants from £15 to £1,000 are given for a wide range of educational needs not covered by the local education authority. Grants can be given to

NORTH WEST – CUMBRIA/GREATER MANCHESTER

schoolchildren towards music lessons. Students in further/higher education can receive help for books, fees/living expenses or study or travel abroad.

Annual grant total: In 2004/05 the foundation had an income of £7,700 and a total expenditure of £4,200.

Applications: In writing to the correspondent, either directly by the individual or through a social worker, citizen's advice bureau, other welfare agency or other third party. Applications are considered in September.

Correspondent: A M Reid, Milne Moser Solicitors, 100 Highgate, Kendal, Cumbria LA9 4HE (01539 729786)

Greater Manchester

The Barrack Hill Educational Charity

Eligibility: People under the age of 21 who live or whose parents live in Bredbury and Romiley.

Types of grants: One-off grants to assist towards educational expenses. Students in full-time and part-time education can receive grants towards books, study or travel abroad and equipment; people in vocational training can be helped with tools, uniform, equipment and so on; and schoolchildren can be given grants towards school uniforms, other school clothing and equipment or instruments.

Annual grant total: In 2005 it had an income of £7,600 and a total expenditure of £7,400.

Applications: On a form available from the correspondent, usually made available from local libraries towards the end of the school year. Applications are considered in September and October.

Correspondent: J H Asquith, 24 Links Road, Romiley, Stockport, Cheshire, SK6 4HU

The Dorothy Bulkeley & Cheadle Lads' Charity

Eligibility: People under the age of 25 living in the former district of Cheadle and Gatley (as constituted on 30 April 1974) or people who are or who have attended school in the above district.

Types of grants: Grants are given for general educational purposes to schoolchildren, students in further/higher education, vocational and mature students and people starting work. This can include assistance for professional training, apprenticeships and schooling costs. Grants usually range from £500 to £1,000 and are usually given to two or three individuals each year.

Annual grant total: In 2004/05, the charity had an income of £1,200 and a total expenditure of £1,600. Grants usually total £1,200 a year; however, due to surplus funds, £1,500 was given in grants to individuals.

Applications: On a form available from the correspondent. Applications are considered in November.

Correspondent: Dr Peter Martin Dooley, Secretary, 48 Chorlton Drive, Cheadle, Cheshire SK8 2BG (0161 491 1816)

The Ann Butterworth & Daniel Bayley Charity

Eligibility: Children and young people aged 25 and under who are of the Protestant religion.

Types of grants: Grants towards the cost of education, training apprenticeships and so on, including for books, equipment, clothing, uniforms and travel. School and university/college fees are not met.

Annual grant total: In 2004/05 the charity had an income of £1,600 and a total expenditure of £600. Grants totalled about £500.

Applications: The charity stated that it receives more applications than it can possibly support

Correspondent: The Trust Administrator, Gaddum Centre, Gaddum House, 6 Great Jackson Street, Manchester M15 4AX (0161 834 6069; Fax: 0161 839 8573)

The Greater Manchester Educational Trust

Eligibility: Young people aged 11 to 18 living within the former Greater Manchester boundary who are attending certain independent schools in the area and have been placed in the top 25% of the entrance exams.

Types of grants: Grants are made for school fees to allow children from low-income families the opportunity of an independent school education. Grants are also available to families who have temporarily fallen on hard times.

Annual grant total: In 2004/05, the trust had net assets of £5.4 million, an income of £250,000. The trust gave grants to 394 pupils who received awards totalling £1.4 million.

Applications: On recommendation of the individual's school, including details of income.

Correspondent: Kevin Curd, Natwest Bank PLC, Brighton Branch, 153 Preston Road, Brighton, East Sussex, BN1 6BD (01273 545119; Fax: 01273 545006)

Mynshull's Educational Foundation

Eligibility: Children and young people aged 25 and under who are at school, university or college, on an apprenticeship or attending another educational/training course, except postgraduates. Applicants must be resident or have been born in the city of Manchester and the following adjoining districts: Reddish, Audenshaw, Failsworth, Chadderton, Middleton, Prestwich, Old City of Salford, Stretford, Sale, Cheadle, Heaton Moor, Heaton Mersey and Heaton Chapel.

Types of grants: Grants towards the costs of education, training, apprenticeship and so on, including books, equipment, clothing, uniforms, travel and so on.

Exclusions: School and university/college fees are not usually met.

Annual grant total: In 2004/05 the foundation had an income of £10,000 and a total expenditure of £9,800. Grants totalled about £9,000.

Applications: On a form available from the correspondent which must be completed by a sponsor from the educational establishment.

Correspondent: The Trust Administrator, Gaddum Centre, Gaddum House, 6 Great Jackson Street, Manchester M15 4AX

The Pratt Charity

Eligibility: Women over 60 who live in or near Manchester and have done so for a period of not less than five years.

Types of grants: Grants are given towards education, health and relief of poverty, distress and sickness.

Annual grant total: About £1,000.

Applications: In writing to the correspondent via a social worker.

Correspondent: Shirley Adams, Gaddum Centre, Gaddum House, 6 Great Jackson Street, Manchester M15 4AX (0161 834 6069; e-mail: sma@ gaddjmcentre.co.uk)

The Rochdale Ancient Parish Educational Trust

Eligibility: People, preferably but not exclusively under 25, who live in Rochdale, Littleborough, Milnrow, Wardle, Todmorden, Saddleworth and Whitworth and who attend or have attended a school in the area of the ancient parish. Preference is given to schoolchildren with serious family difficulties who have to be educated away from home, and people with special educational needs.

Types of grants: One-off grants to schoolchildren and further and higher education students, including mature students and postgraduates, towards the cost of uniforms or other school clothing, books, equipment/instruments, fees, educational outings in the UK, study or travel abroad and student exchanges. Further and higher education students can also receive help with maintenance/living expenses and childcare costs. People starting work can also receive financial assistance. Grants are for up to £1,000 each.

Exclusions: No grants to students studying at a level they already hold a qualification in (such as a 2nd degree course) or to people who have received assistance from either the Hopwood Hall College Access Fund or The Rochdale Educational Trust.

Annual grant total: In 2004/05 the trust had an income of £18,400 and a total expenditure of £21,800. Grants totalled about £20,000.

Applications: On a form available from the correspondent; applications can be submitted directly by the individual or through the school/college or educational welfare agency, and are considered in January, March, July and September.

Correspondent: Gary Edwards, FAO Treasurer, Rochdale Metropolitan, Borough Council, PO Box 70, Rochdale, Lancashire, OL16 1YD (01706 865 422; Fax: 01706 865 450; e-mail: gary.edwards@rochdale.gov.uk)

Other information: The trust also has to maintain several cottages that it owns.

Seamon's Moss Educational Foundation

Eligibility: People aged under 25 who live in the ancient townships of Dunham Massey, Bowden and Altrincham.

Types of grants: One-off grants up to a maximum of £250 each.

Exclusions: People must reside in the ancient townships of Dunham Massey, Bowden and Altrincham.

Annual grant total: In 2004/05 the trust had an income of £1,800 and a total expenditure of £960, all of which was given in grants to six schools. No grants were made to individuals during the year.

Applications: In writing to the correspondent. Applications should be submitted directly by the individual and are considered in August. Ineligible applications will not be responded to.

Correspondent: R Drake, Secretary, 32 Riddings Court, Timperley, Altrincham, Cheshire WA15 6BG (0161 969 7772)

The Stockport Educational Foundation

Eligibility: People under 25 who live in Stockport and the surrounding area.

Types of grants: One-off grants of £100 to £300. Schoolchildren may receive grants for educational outings or school fees. Students in further/higher education can be supported for books, fees/living expenses and study or travel abroad.

Annual grant total: In 2002/03, the trust had an income of £1,400 and an expenditure of £2,600.

Applications: In writing to the correspondent, providing the applicant's date of birth, address, educational career to date, course details and costs and financial situation and resources. Applications are usually considered in April and October.

Correspondent: Anthony Roberts, 32 Sevenoaks Avenue, Stockport, Cheshire, SK4 4AW (0161 4431 314; Fax: 0161 4431 314)

Billinge

John Eddleston's Charity

Eligibility: Persons under the age of 25 years in need of financial assistance who live in, or whose parents live in, the parish of Billinge.

Types of grants: One-off grants for educational purposes including social and physical training.

Annual grant total: In 2004 the trust had an income of £49,000 and an expenditure of £43,000. Grants to individuals totalled £1,000 and £6,300 was distributed to organisations.

Applications: In writing to the correspondent by the end of March. The annual meeting of the trustees takes place after the end of March.

Correspondent: Mrs G Blundell, Greenbank Partnerships, Greenbank House, 152 Wigan Lane, Wigan WN1 2LA (01942 740400; Fax: 01942 740401)

Bolton

The Chadwick Educational Foundation

Eligibility: Schoolchildren and students, under 25 years of age, living in Bolton and, who are in need.

Types of grants: One-off grants of £100 to £250 for text books, uniforms, equipment/instruments, educational outings in the UK and study or travel abroad. The foundation prefers to support the promotion of education in the principles of the Church of England.

Annual grant total: In 2004, the trust had an income of £52,000 and made grants totalling £55,000 of which £1,300 went to five individuals.

Applications: Application forms available from the correspondent, to be submitted by the individual in July for consideration in September. Proof of parental income is essential.

Correspondent: Diane Abbott, Secretary, R P Smith & Co, 71 Chorley Old Road, Bolton, Lancashire, BL1 3JA

Other information: The Marsden and Popperwell Educational Charity is administered by the same correspondent and has the same eligibility.

The James Eden Foundation

Eligibility: Students in or entering full-time further education at universities or colleges, aged under 25, who are bona fide residents of the metropolitan borough of Bolton. Preference is given to people who

have lost either or both parents, or whose parents are separated or divorced.

Types of grants: Cash grants of between £400 and £1,500 are given to assist college students and undergraduates with fees, books, equipment/instruments, maintenance/living expenses, educational outings in the UK and study or travel overseas. Parental income is taken into account in awarding grants.

Annual grant total: In 2003/04 the trust had an income of £16,300 and a total expenditure of £19,700. Grants were made to individuals totalling about £14,000.

Applications: On a form available from the correspondent, to be returned by the individual before September for consideration in October. If an individual has applied previously the trustees are particularly interested to know about his or her progress.

Correspondent: Mrs D P Abbott, R P Smith & Co, 71 Chorley Old Road, Bolton BL1 3AJ (01204 534421; Fax: 01204 535475; e-mail: info@rpsmith.co.uk)

The Marsden & Popplewell Educational Charity

Eligibility: Students under 25 who live in Bolton and are in need; preference is given to 'the promotion of education in the principles of the Church of England'.

Types of grants: Schoolchildren and students in further and higher education may receive grants towards the cost of uniforms or other school clothing, books, equipment/instruments, educational outings in the UK or study or travel abroad. People starting work may receive help towards the cost of uniforms, books, equipment or instruments.

Annual grant total: Information from the Charity Commission was only available for the financial year 2003. In this year, the charity had an income of £1,400 and a total expenditure of around £1,500.

Applications: On a form available from the correspondent to be submitted directly by the individual. Proof of parents' income is essential; Trustees meet in September each year and applications should be submitted in July.

Correspondent: Diane Abbott, Secretary, R P Smith and Co, 71 Chorley Old Road, Bolton, Lancashire BL1 3JA

Other information: The Chadwick Educational Foundation is administered by the same correspondent and has the same eligibility; local schools are also supported.

Provincial Insurance Company Trust for Bolton

Eligibility: People who live in Bolton Metropolitan Borough.

Types of grants: Grants are mainly one-off and are for between £100 and £1,000. Grants are not made for relief-in-need, but are given to individuals towards character development and 'helping others', for example, Operation Raleigh, Health Projects Abroad.

Exclusions: No grants to students or recent ex-students of Bolton School, building works, commercial ventures or for personal loans.

Annual grant total: In 2003/04 the trust had an income of £14,000 and a total expenditure of £15,000. Grants were given to 29 individuals totalling around £7,000.

Applications: On a form available from the correspondent. Applications are usually considered in March/April and September/October and should be submitted at least two to four weeks before those meetings.

Correspondent: Mrs S Riley, Hon. Secretary, 6 Lennox Gardens, Bolton BL3 4NH (01204 63051)

Other information: The trust also makes grants to organisations.

Golborne

The Golborne Charities

Eligibility: People in need who live in the parish of Golborne as it was in 1892.

Types of grants: One-off grants for equipment such as books, school uniforms and instruments, or for excursions. Grants are usually of between £50 and £80, but occasionally of up to £250. They are usually cash payments, but are occasionally in kind.

Exclusions: Loans or grants for the payments of rates are not made. Grants are not repeated in less than two years.

Annual grant total: In 2004/05 the trust had assets of £650 and an income of £4,500. Grants were given to ninety individuals for relief-in-need purposes totalling £3,100. A further five educational grants were made totalling £250.

Applications: In writing to the correspondent through a third party such as a social worker or a teacher, or via a trustee. Applications are considered at three-monthly intervals. Grant recipients tend to be known by at least one trustee.

Correspondent: Paul Gleave, 56 Nook Lane, Golborne, Warrington WA3 3JQ

Other information: Grants are also given to charitable organisations in the area of benefit, and for relief-of-need purposes (£400 in 2004/05).

Leigh

The Old Leigh Educational Endowment

Eligibility: People under the age of 25 who live in the former borough of Leigh, are going on to higher education and have achieved high A-level results.

Types of grants: Grants for students attaining good examination results and proceeding with further training to help with fees and living expenses, books and equipment. Grants are between £250 and £500 per year per student.

Annual grant total: In 2005/06 grants were made totalling around £5,000. Grants are made to about 20 individuals each year.

Applications: Applications should be submitted in September after A-level results are released for consideration in October. Applications must be submitted through the individual's college, which submits a list of suitable applicants for the trustees to choose from.

Correspondent: The Director of Education, Education Department, Progress House, Westwood Park Drive, Wigan WN3 4HH (01942 486123; Fax: 01942 486231; e-mail: education@ wiganmbc.gov.uk; website: www. wiganmbc.gov.uk)

Other information: This trust is currently undergoing changes. It is considering merging with the similar Miss Marsh Foundation, whilst Wigan Borough Council also administers The France Educational Foundation which is currently dormant.

Rochdale

The Heywood Educational Trust

Eligibility: People who live in the Heywood area or the village of Birch or those attending or who have previously attended a school in the area.

Types of grants: One-off grants for schoolchildren and further and higher education students, including mature students, to help with uniforms or other school clothing, books, equipment/ instruments, fees, educational outings in the UK, study or travel abroad and student exchanges.

Annual grant total: In 2004/05, the trust had an income of £1,900 and a total expenditure of £2,200.

Applications: By the individual on a form available from the correspondent for consideration in February and September. Applications should include confirmation that the student is on the course, and details of academic record, family income, previous awards, LEA awards and student loans.

Correspondent: Committee Services Officer, Rochdale Metropolitan Borough Council, PO Box 39, Rochdale OL16 1LQ

The Middleton Educational Trust

Eligibility: People who live or attend or have attended a school in the area of the former borough of Middleton, Rochdale.

Types of grants: Cash grants for schoolchildren with books, equipment/

instruments, uniforms and other school clothing, educational outings in the UK, study or travel abroad and student exchanges. Grants to students in further and higher education, including mature students, postgraduates and foreign students, also include assistance for fees, maintenance/living expenses and childcare. People starting work can also receive financial assistance. Grants are one-off and are up to £300.

Annual grant total: In 2004/05, the trust had an income of £5,700 and a total expenditure of £5,000. No further information concerning grants was available.

Applications: On a form available from the correspondent. Applications can be submitted directly by the individual or through the individual's school/college/ educational welfare agency and they are considered twice yearly in April and September. Applications should be addressed to Donna Parker.

Correspondent: Donna Parker, Commitee Services, Town Hall, Rochdale OL16 1AB (01706 864717; Fax: 01706 864705; e-mail: donna.parker@rochdale.gov.uk)

The Rochdale Educational Trust

Eligibility: People who live, have lived or are studying in the old county borough of Rochdale (excluding Wardle, Milnrow and Littleborough).

Types of grants: Grants to schoolchildren, further and higher education students including mature students and postgraduates, and people starting work towards the cost of uniforms or other school clothing, books, equipment/ instruments, fees, maintenance/living expenses, educational outings in the UK, study or travel abroad or student exchanges. Grants range from £50 to £1,500.

Annual grant total: In 2004/05, the trust had both an income and total expenditure of £7,500. Grants totalled about £6,000.

Applications: On a form available from the correspondent which can be submitted directly by the individual, through the individual's school/college/educational agency or through another third party such as a social worker. Applications are considered in March, July, September and December.

Correspondent: Gary Edwards, FAO Treasurer, Rochdale Metropolitan Borough Council, PO Box 39, Rochdale, Lancashire, OL16 1LQ (01706 647 474; Fax: 01706 865 450; e-mail: gary.edwards@ rochdale.gov.uk; website: www.rochdale. gov.uk)

Other information: Postgraduates may be considered for funding.

Sale

The Sale Educational Foundation

Eligibility: People who have attended/are attending a secondary school in the former borough of Sale, and whose parents have lived in the borough for at least two years prior to the application.

Types of grants: Grants to students undertaking/about to undertake further or higher education, which may be used for books, equipment and travel. The award is £250 a year for up to three years per student.

All grants are in addition to any award made available by the local education authority.

Annual grant total: In 2004/05 the charity had an income of £5,900 and a total expenditure of £5,800.

Applications: On a form available from the correspondent.

Correspondent: P E F Ribbon, Hon. Secretary, 84 Ashton Lane, Sale M33 6WS

Salford

The Salford Educational Foundation

Eligibility: People under 25 who live in Salford.

Types of grants: The trust states: 'The main beneficiaries of this fund are pupils attending schools maintained by the Salford Area Education Authority. Grants are made for the purpose of attending various educational courses, visits or activities e.g. courses for members of the National Youth Orchestra, Outward Bound courses, attendance at interviews for the purpose of obtaining a place on a full-time course of higher education, participation in sporting events at a national or regional level, attendance at sports training courses etc.'

The trust can also give support through scholarships and maintenance allowances tenable at any school, university or other place of learning approved by the city council to help with the cost of outfits, clothing, tools, books, travel expenses and assistance to study music or other arts.

Annual grant total: In 2005/06 the foundation had an income of £1,500 and a total expenditure of £3,200, all of which distributed in seven grants.

Applications: On a form available from the correspondent. Applications are considered quarterly.

Correspondent: Bob McIntyre, Education Office, Minerva House, Pendlebury Road, Swinton M27 4EQ (0161 778 0123; e-mail: robert.mcintrye@salford.gov.uk)

The Salford Foundation Trust

Eligibility: People in residence in the area of Salford of between 5 and 25 years of age. Priority will be given to applicants who have resided in Salford for a minimum of three years.

Types of grants: The trust will consider requests to fund opportunities that will enable a young person to learn and/or develop new skills or take part in a character building experience or activity. Examples of this could be an item of equipment, an activity, a training course; we are keen to hear about the impact the opportunity will have on the applicant and what they hope to achieve from it.

Exclusions: 'Funding will not be considered for the following: driving lessons, childcare costs, higher education course fees, living expenses, remedial intervention i.e. therapies (speech/language/occupational etc), retrospective funding. No consideration will be made on opportunities that have a political or religious focus or should be financed by statutory services.'

Annual grant total: In 2005 the trust made grants totalling £10,000 distributed to 29 individuals.

Applications: Application forms are available from the trust and can be submitted directly by the individual, a family member, a third party such as a teacher or social worker or through an organisation such as a Citizens Advice or school. There six deadlines throughout the year with applications considered every eight weeks.

Correspondent: Grants Administrator, 1st Floor, Charles House, Albert Street, Eccles, Manchester, M30 0PW (0161 787 3834; Fax: 0161 787 8555; e-mail: mail@salfordfoundationtrust.org.uk; website: www.salfordfoundationtrust.org.uk)

Other information: The trust also makes educational grants.

Stockport

James Fernley Scholarship Fund

Eligibility: Pupils of secondary school age who have attended primary school in the borough of Stockport.

Types of grants: Grants to students to help mainly with activities relating to travel and the arts. Sympathetic consideration is given to students undertaking short periods of overseas study, for instance, medical/dental electives. Grants range from £50 to £150.

Exclusions: No grants are given for fees.

Annual grant total: In 2004/05 the fund had an income of £560. No grants were made during the year.

Applications: In writing to the correspondent, including purpose of request, dates when any activity/visit is to take place, and details of approximate cost. Applications can be submitted directly by the individual. They are considered quarterly.

Correspondent: Director of Education, Stockport MBC, Education Division, Stopford House, Town Hall, Stockport SK1 3XE

Sir Ralph Pendlebury's Charity for Orphans

Eligibility: People who have been orphaned and live, or whose parents lived, in the borough of Stockport for at least two years.

Types of grants: Grants for schoolchildren towards the cost of clothing, holidays and books. Grants can be for £5 or £6 a week and recipients also receive a clothing allowance twice a year. The main priority is for relief-in-need (About £16,000 a year).

Annual grant total: About £1,400 a year for educational purposes.

Applications: In writing to the correspondent.

Correspondent: S M Tattersall, Carlyle House, 107 Wellington Road South, Stockport, SK1 3TL

Tameside

The Ashton-under-Lyne United Scholarship Fund (The Heginbottom & Tetlow and William Kelsall Grants)

Eligibility: People under the age of 25 who have attended a secondary school in the former borough of Ashton under Lyne or who live, or whose parents live, in the former borough and who will not have any award or grant other than a local education authority or state grant. Applications from residents in Audenshaw, Denton and the area of the former Limehurst Rural District Council will also be considered.

Types of grants: Grants for those who will be attending university, teacher training college or an institution of full-time technical education.

Annual grant total: In 2004/05 grants were made totalling £3,900.

Applications: On a form available from the correspondent to be submitted directly by the individual by 30 September for consideration in October.

Correspondent: The Director of Education & Cultural Services, Tameside Metropolitan Borough Council, Room 223, Council Offices, Wellington Road, Ashton under Lyne OL6 6DL (0161 342 2878; Fax: 0161 342 2619)

Other information: Various grants are administered under this fund. The above refers to The Heginbottom & Tetlow Grants and William Kelsall Grants. There are also two smaller trusts: Thomas Taylor Grant to those studying full-time for a degree or diploma in electrical engineering;

and J B Reyner Grants to those attending approved colleges of music.

The Dowson Trust and Peter Green Endowment Trust Fund

Eligibility: People aged under 25 who live in the former borough of Hyde.

Types of grants: Grants to those undertaking approved courses at universities or teacher training colleges.

Annual grant total: In 2004/05 grants totalled £500.

Applications: In writing to the correspondent. Applications should be submitted by the individual by 30 September for consideration in October.

Correspondent: The Director of Education & Cultural Services, Tameside Metropolitan Borough Council, Room 223, Council Offices, Wellington Road, Ashton Under Lyne OL6 6DL (0161 342 2878; Fax: 0161 342 2619)

Timperley

The Timperley Educational Foundation

Eligibility: Pupils, students or apprentices under the age of 21 and in need, who have a parent resident in the parish of Timperley. Assistance is also given to educational establishments and youth organisations within the parish.

Types of grants: One-off and recurrent grants to meet general expenses for students in further/higher education, including those being instructed in the doctrines of the Church of England. Schoolchildren may receive assistance on the recommendation of the headteacher only.

Annual grant total: In 2004 the foundation had an income of £7,200. It gave £6,500 in grants to both individuals and organisations.

Applications: On a form available from the correspondent, either directly by the individual or, more usually, through the individual's parent/guardian, school, college or educational welfare agency. Applications are usually considered in August prior to the academic year for which support is needed, although this is not always essential. Application forms for new university entrants, however, must be received by 31 August.

Correspondent: P Turner, Clerk to the Trustees, 103 Sylvan Avenue, Timperley, Altrincham, Cheshire WA15 6AD (0161 969 3919)

Tottington

The Margaret Ann Smith Charity

Eligibility: People who live in the urban district of Tottington, as defined on 23 June 1964.

Types of grants: Grants of about £200 to help towards the cost of overseas exchange visits. There is an emphasis on Commonwealth countries.

Annual grant total: In 2004/05 the charity had an income of £2,800 and a total expenditure of £1,800.

Applications: In writing to the correspondent. Applications should be submitted directly by the individual or through the individual's school/college or an educational welfare agency.

Correspondent: D R Smith, Clerk, Woodcock & Sons, West View, Princess Street, Haslingden, Rossendale, Lancashire BB4 6NW (01706 213356; Fax: 01706 211494)

Trafford

The F W Bates Charity

Eligibility: Pupils who live in Stretford and who have regularly attended a Stretford school.

Types of grants: Grants, to a usual maximum of about £200, to help with college or university fees or to supplement existing grants.

Annual grant total: In 2004/05 the charity had an income of £2,400. Just one grant of £200 was made to an individual. This is the first grant that has been made for several years as the charity has received no applications.

Applications: In writing to the correspondent at any time.

Correspondent: Philip Herd, c/o Financial Services, Trafford Borough Council, PO Box 13, Talbot Road, Stretford, Greater Manchester M32 0EL (0161 912 4790)

The Renshaw Educational Foundation

Eligibility: People under the age of 25 who live in the borough of Stretford.

Types of grants: Grants for school, college or university students to help with books, equipment, clothing, travel fees, educational visits or to supplement existing grants.

Grants are also given towards the cost of education, training, apprenticeship or equipment for those starting work.

Annual grant total: In 2004/05 the foundation had an income of £600. No grants were made as no applications were received.

Applications: In writing to the correspondent at any time.

Correspondent: Philip Herd, c/o Financial Services, Trafford Borough Council, PO Box 13, Talbot Road, Stretford, Greater Manchester M32 0EL (0161 912 4790)

The Urmston British Schools Scholarship Fund

Eligibility: Children of school age who live in Urmston.

Types of grants: Cash grants for school pupils to help with books, equipment, clothing or travel and music study.

Annual grant total: In 2004/05 the fund had an income of around £250. No grants have been made for several years as no applications have been received.

Applications: In writing to the correspondent at any time.

Correspondent: Philip Herd, c/o Financial Services, Trafford Borough Council, PO Box 13, Talbot Road, Stretford, Greater Manchester M32 0EL (0161 912 4790)

Isle of Man

The Manx Marine Society

Eligibility: Young Manx people under 18 who wish to attend sea school or become a cadet.

Types of grants: One-off grants for people about to start a career at sea towards uniforms, books, equipment/instruments and fees.

Annual grant total: About £5,000.

Applications: In writing to the correspondent. Applications are considered at any time and can be submitted by the individual or through the school/college or educational welfare agency.

Correspondent: Capt. R K Cringle, Cooil Cam Farm, St Marks, Ballasalla, Isle of Man IM9 3AG

Lancashire

The Baines Charity

Eligibility: People in need who live in the ancient townships of Carleton, Hardhorn-cum-Newton, Marton, Poulton and Thornton.

Types of grants: One-off grants ranging from £100 to £250. 'Each case is discussed in its merits.'

Annual grant total: In 2005 the charity had assets of £489,000 and an income of £23,000. There were 55 welfare grants made totalling £5,700. There was one educational grant made of £200.

Applications: On a form available from the correspondent, either directly by the individual, or through a social worker, Citizens Advice or other welfare agency. Applications are considered upon receipt.

Correspondent: Duncan Waddilove, 2 The Chase, Normoss Road, Normoss, Blackpool, Lancashire FY3 0BF (01253 893459; e-mail: duncanwaddilove@ hotmail.com)

The Educational Foundation of John Farrington

Eligibility: People under the age of 25 who live, or have a parent who has lived for at least two years, in any of the following areas: the parish of Ribbleton in the borough of Preston, the parishes of Goosnargh, Grimsargh, Haighton, Longridge, Whittingham and part of Fulwood. Residents in the Ribbleton area will be given preference over the residents in other areas. There is a preference for people with special educational needs.

Types of grants: Help with the cost of books and educational outings for people at school. People starting work can receive grants towards equipment/instruments, fees, childcare and educational outings in the UK. Students in further or higher education may be given help towards books and equipment or instruments. Grants range from £25 to £250.

Grants are also made to help people to develop leadership qualities and social awareness, towards, for instance, leadership courses, community development activities, camping expeditions or any other 'suitable' activity.

Exclusions: Grants are not given where the applicant is already in receipt of a local authority grant. Nor are they intended to cover night-school fees for courses which do not lead to some form of educational progression in a young persons career.

Annual grant total: In 2004/05, the trust had an income of £2,100 and a total expenditure of £1,800.

Applications: In writing to the correspondent for consideration in March and October. The foundation has a leaflet outlining the format and contents of any application letter. Applications can be either made by the individual or through a school, college, educational welfare agency or other third party.

Correspondent: D V Johnson, 51 The Pastures, Grimsargh, Preston, PR2 5JW

Fort Foundation

Eligibility: Young people in Pendle Borough and district, especially those undertaking courses in engineering.

Types of grants: One-off grants of £50 to £1,000 to schoolchildren, college students, undergraduates and vocational students for uniforms/clothing, study/travel overseas, books and equipment/instruments and excursions.

Exclusions: Grants are not made for fees.

Annual grant total: In 2003/04 the trust had an income of £20,000 and a total expenditure of £31,000. Grants to individuals totalled £3,700.

Applications: In writing to the correspondent, directly by the individual. Applications are considered at any time.

Correspondent: E S Fort, Trustee, Fort Vale Engineering Ltd, Parkfield Works, Brunswick Street, Nelson, Lancashire BB9 0SG (01282 440000; Fax: 01282 440046)

Other information: Grants are also made to small groups, for example, scouts/guides.

The Harris Charity

Eligibility: People in need under 25 who live in Lancashire, with a preference for the Preston district, who are in further or higher education.

Types of grants: One-off grants of £250 to £1,000 for equipment/instruments, tools, materials and so on.

Exclusions: No grants are available to cover the cost of fees or living expenses.

Annual grant total: In 2004/05 the trust had assets of £2.7 million and an income of £116,000. Grants totalled £104,000, of which £7,100 went to individuals for relief-in-need and educational purposes.

Applications: In writing to the correspondent with information about financial income and outgoings. Applications are considered during the three months after 31 March and 30 September and can be submitted directly by the individual or through a school/ college or educational welfare agency.

Correspondent: P R Metcalf, Richard House, 9 Winckley Square, Preston PR1 3HP (01772 821021; Fax: 01772 259441)

Other information: The charity also supports charitable institutions that benefit individuals, recreation and leisure and the training and education of individuals (£97,000 in 2004/05).

The Khaleque & Sarifun Memorial Trust

Eligibility: People who live in Lancashire (including overseas students studying there).

Types of grants: Grants are made to schoolchildren, further and higher education students and postgraduates towards the cost of uniforms or other school clothing, books, equipment/ instruments and maintenance/living expenses. Foreign students in further and higher education in the UK can also be supported. Grants range from £50 to £1,100.

Annual grant total: The trust gives grants totalling around £1,000.

Applications: In writing to the correspondent directly by the individual with a supporting letter from the individual's school or college. Applications should be submitted in October for consideration in November.

Correspondent: Dr A Zaman, 8 Golden Villas, Oldfield Avenue, Darwen, Lancashire BB3 1PY (01254 778380)

Peter Lathom's Charity

Eligibility: People in need living in West Lancashire.

Types of grants: Cash grants according to need.

Annual grant total: In 2004 it had assets of £985,000 generating an income of £29,000. Grants to six individual students totalled £2,400.

Applications: On a form available from the correspondent, to be submitted by 30 September. Awards in all cases are based on financial need as applications always exceed distributable income.

Correspondent: Mark Abbott, c/o The Kennedy Partnership, 15 Railway Road, Ormskirk, Lancashire L39 2DW

John Parkinson Charity

Eligibility: People starting work and further and higher education students in need aged under 25 who live in the parishes of Goosnargh, Whittingham and part of Barton.

Types of grants: One-off grants of up to £150 for tools, books, outfits or payment of fees towards entering a profession, trade, occupation or service. People who have to travel outside Lancashire to attend an interview for a further education course or a job interview can receive grants towards travel expenses and living expenses. Students in further or higher education can be given help towards books.

Annual grant total: In 2004 the charity had an income of £4,900 and a total expenditure of £1,200.

Applications: On a form available from the correspondent, to be submitted by the individual's parent or guardian. Applications are considered in May and November.

Correspondent: R S B Garside, Fleet House, Fleet Street, Preston PR1 2UT (01772 201117; Fax: 01772 561775)

The Peel Foundation Scholarship Fund

Eligibility: People in need aged 18 to 25 who live in and around Blackburn. This area is defined as: the borough of Blackburn, the whole borough except the civil parish of North Turton; the borough of Hyndburn, those parts of the former urban districts of Rishton and Oswaldtwistle which are close to the boundary with Blackburn; and the Ribble Valley borough, the civil parishes of Balderstone, Billington, Clayton-le-Dale, Dinckley, Mellor, Osbaldeston, Ramsgreave, Salesbury and Wilpshire.

Provided these conditions are met, the trustees will consider granting scholarships to:

(i) Candidates with three A-level passes at A grade gained at one sitting

(ii) Candidates with a BTEC national diploma with three or more of the second year units or modules at distinction level (provided that these represent at least 50% of the second year units or modules).

Other applicants will be considered on their merits as far as funds allow.

Types of grants: Awards of £500 to students entering university or other institutions of higher education for first or second degree courses. Candidates must begin their course in the term following the award of scholarships (usually in September), unless excused by the trustees for sufficient cause. Grants are for general student expenses.

Annual grant total: In 2004/05, the foundation had an income of £3000 and a total expenditure of £2,700.

Applications: On a form available from the correspondent. Candidates must be nominated by the headteacher or principal of the school or college and applicants are called for an interview. Applications are considered in July and August and should be submitted in April and May.

Correspondent: Mrs Catherine Oldroyd, Barnfield, Billinge End Road, Blackburn, BB2 6QB (01254 56573; Fax: 01254 671999)

Superintendent Gerald Richardson Memorial Youth Trust

Eligibility: People under 25 who live within 15 miles of Blackpool Town Hall. There is a preference for people who are physically or mentally disabled.

Types of grants: One-off and recurrent grants are made, typically in the range of £50 to £250. Grants can be made to schoolchildren and further and higher education students to attend character-building courses or training courses in the arts or sports. Grants can also be made to cover the cost of equipment for outdoor courses.

Annual grant total: In 2004/05 the trust had assets of £105,000, an income of £15,000 and a total expenditure of £19,000, all of which went to schools, youth organisations and individuals, with the latter receiving the largest proportion.

Applications: In writing to the correspondent, giving details of the individual's age, the cost of the course and so on. Applications should be submitted at least two months before the amount being requested is required. They are considered

bimonthly from September and can be submitted either directly by the individual, or via a third party such as a school/college welfare agency or carer.

Correspondent: D H Leatham, 2 Paddock Drive, Blackpool FY3 9TZ (01253 762090)

Shaw Charities

Eligibility: People in need who live in Rivington, Anglezarke, Heath Charnock and Anderton.

Types of grants: Grants to students on first degree courses for books.

Annual grant total: In 2004/05 the charities had an income of £2,800 and a total expenditure of £2,500. Grants totalled about £2,000.

Applications: On a form available from the correspondent to be submitted for consideration in March and November.

Correspondent: Mrs E Woodrow, 99 Rawlinson Lane, Heath Charnock, Chorley, Lancashire PR7 4DE (01257 480515; e-mail: woodrows@ tinyworld.co.uk)

Other information: The charities also make grants for relief of need.

Tunstall Educational Trust

Eligibility: Young people under 25 living in Burrow, Tunstall and Cansfield.

Types of grants: One-off and recurrent grants according to need. The trust mainly makes travel grants.

Annual grant total: In 2004 the charity had an income of £4,600 and a total expenditure of £4,000. The trust makes grants to individuals and organisations.

Applications: In writing to the correspondent. Trustees meet in June and November to consider applications.

Correspondent: Mrs Joyce Megan Crackles, Mill Farm, Burrow, Carnforth, Lancashire, LA6 2RJ (015242 74239)

Blackpool

The Blackpool Children's Clothing Fund

Eligibility: Children aged 4 to 16 who live in the Blackpool area and attend an educational establishment there.

Types of grants: Help with providing school clothing for children whose parents cannot afford it. The fund does not give cash grants but letters of authorisation which can be exchanged at designated retailers.

Annual grant total: In 2004/05 the fund had an income of £1,800 and a total expenditure of £5,000, most of which was given in grants.

Applications: In writing to the correspondent, by an education social work service on behalf of the applicant.

Individuals in need identified by the local education authority are also considered.

Correspondent: Mr Alan Rydeheard, 96 West Park Drive, Blackpool, FY3 9HU (01253 736812)

The Swallowdale Children's Trust

Eligibility: People who live in the Blackpool area who are under the age of 25. Orphans are given preference.

Types of grants: One-off grants are given to: schoolchildren, college students, undergraduates, vocational students and people starting work, including those for clothes/uniforms, fees, study/travel abroad and equipment/instruments.

Annual grant total: In 2004/05 the trust had assets of £841,000 and an income of £27,000. There were 98 relief-in-need grants made during the year totalling £13,000. A further £3,000 was given in 4 educational grants.

Applications: On a form available from the correspondent, with the financial details of the individual or family. Applications must be made through a social worker or teacher. They are considered six times per year.

Correspondent: Mrs M Bell, Secretary, 7 Arnold Avenue, Blackpool FY4 2EP (01253 345027)

Other information: Over £10,000 was given to organisations in 2005.

Burnley

The Edward Stocks Massey Bequest Fund

Eligibility: People who live in the borough of Burnley.

Types of grants: Whilst consideration will be given to applications for financial assistance with education courses, this is not seen as the primary purpose of the fund which is to assist individuals and voluntary organisations to promote education and projects in the arts, sciences and general cultural activities.

Exclusions: No assistance will be given to applicants in receipt of a mandatory award from their LEA. Other sources of funding must have been explored.

Annual grant total: In 2004/05, the trust had assets of £976,000 and an income of £38,000. Grants were made totalling £62,000 including about £5,000 to individuals.

Applications: On a form available from the correspondent, either directly by the individual or by the secretary or treasurer of an organisation. Applications are considered in April/May.

Correspondent: Saima Afzaal, Burnley Borough Council, PO Box 17, Burnley BB11 1JA (01282 425011)

Darwen

The W M & B W Lloyd Trust

Eligibility: People in need who live in the old borough of Darwen in Lancashire. Preference is given to single parents.

Types of grants: One-off and recurrent grants according to need. Grants are made to schoolchildren, college students, undergraduates, vocational students and mature students, including those for uniforms/clothing, books, study/travel abroad, equipment/instruments, excursions and awards for excellence.

Annual grant total: In 2004/05 the trust had assets of £1.8 million, an income of £70,000 and an expenditure of £72,000. Grants to 23 individuals for educational purposes totalled £30,000. No welfare grants were made during the year.

Applications: In writing to the correspondent to be submitted either directly by the individual or through a relevant third party. Applications are considered quarterly in March, June, September and December.

Correspondent: Secretary, The Lloyd Charity Committee, 10 Borough Road, Darwen, Lancashire BB3 1PL (01254 702111; Fax: 01254 706837)

Other information: Grants are also made to organisations (£36,000 in 2004/05).

Leyland

The Balshaw's Educational Foundation

Eligibility: People living in the parish of Leyland.

Types of grants: Help with educational needs including the cost of books, clothing and other essentials for schoolchildren. Grants may also be available for those at college or university.

Annual grant total: In 2004, the foundation had an income of £1,200 and a total expenditure of £900. Grants totalled about £500.

Applications: In writing to the correspondent.

Correspondent: J G Demack, 11 Pendlebury Close, Longton, Preston PR4 5YT (01772 612556)

Littleborough

Alexander and Amelia Harvey Scholarship Fund

Eligibility: Students in need under 25 who live or whose parents live in the former urban district of Littleborough.

Types of grants: One-off grants, for instance towards clothing, tools, books, living expenses, fees and overseas Trust.

Annual grant total: In 2005 the trust had assets of £29,000 and an income of £1,300, most of which was given in four grants to individuals.

Applications: In writing to the correspondent during August and September, for consideration in October. Applications can be submitted either directly by the individual, or through a school/college or educational welfare agency.

Correspondent: Mrs Patricia White, 29 Howarth Street, Littleborough OL15 9DW (01706 378360)

Lowton

The Lowton Charities

Eligibility: People in need who live in the parishes of St Luke's and St Mary's in Lowton.

Types of grants: Help with the cost of books, clothing and other essentials for schoolchildren. Grants are also available for those at college or university.

Exclusions: Grants are not given to postgraduates.

Annual grant total: In 2004/05 the charity had an income of £4,900 and al total expenditure of almost £5,000. About half of grants are given at Christmas for relief-in-need purposes and the rest throughout the year.

Applications: Usually through the rectors of the parishes or other trustees.

Correspondent: J B Davies, Secretary, 10 Tarvin Close, Lowton, Warrington WA3 2NX (01942 678108)

Over Kellett

Thomas Wither's Charity

Eligibility: People under 25 who live in the parish of Over Kellett.

Types of grants: 'Apprenticing children of poor and deserving persons, resident in the beneficial area, to some trade or occupation: assisting them by outfits or otherwise upon a trade, profession or occupation, or into service; making payments to enable them to receive instruction in workshops or at classes or otherwise, so as to prepare them for apprenticeships, technical instruction or employment.'

Furthermore, under the 1980 variation of the scheme: 'If and in so far as the income of the charity is not required for application in accordance with the provisions of the above, the trustees may apply the same in otherwise promoting the education (including social and physical training)' of those eligible. Individual grants will not exceed 60% of the trust's available income.

Exclusions: Applications from outside the area of Over Kellett will not be considered.

Annual grant total: In 2005 the trust had an income of £18,000 and a total expenditure of £3,300.

Applications: On a form available from the correspondent, which should be submitted on or before 1 May or 1 November each year.

Correspondent: D J Mills, Clerk, 51 Greenways, Over Kellett, Carnforth, Lancashire LA6 1DE (01524 732194)

Preston

The Roper Educational Foundation

Eligibility: People aged 11 to 25, who live in St. Wilfrid's Parish, Preston or who have, for not less than two years at any time, attended a school in the parish.

Types of grants: The trust will consider supporting any educational need, at any educational level.

Annual grant total: In 2004, the foundation had fixed assets of £651,000 with an income of £62,500 and an expenditure of £52,000. The foundation gave bursaries to individuals totalling £10,000.

Applications: On a form available from the correspondent. Applications should be submitted directly by the individual. They are considered in February, July and October.

Correspondent: M J Belderbos, Messers, Blackhurst, Swainson, Goodier, 10 Chapel Street, Preston, PR1 8AY (01772 253841; Fax: 01772 201713; e-mail: mjb@bsglaw.co.uk)

Other information: Grants are also made to voluntary aided Roman Catholic schools in the county borough of Preston.

Rishton

The George Lawes Memorial Fund

Eligibility: People under the age of 21 who live in the township of Rishton.

Types of grants: One-off grants up to £230 to help schoolchildren and further and higher education students, including mature students, with books, equipment, clothing/uniforms, fees, maintenance/living expenses, educational outings in the UK and study or travel abroad.

Annual grant total: About £500 a year.

Applications: In writing to the correspondent directly by the individual. Applications should be submitted around November/December for consideration in December.

Correspondent: The Trustees, Scaithcliff House, Ormerod Street, Accrington, Lancashire BB5 0PF

Merseyside

The Girls' Welfare Fund

Eligibility: Girls and young women, usually those aged between 15 and 25 years, who were born in Merseyside. Applications from outside this area will not be acknowledged. Preference will be given to those who are pursuing vocational or further education courses rather than other academic courses.

Types of grants: Both one-off and recurrent grants for leisure and creative activities, sports, welfare and the relief of poverty. Grants may be given to schoolchildren and students for uniforms/clothing, college students and undergraduates for uniforms/clothing, study/travel overseas and books, vocational students for uniforms/clothing, books and equipment/instruments and to people starting work for clothing and equipment/instruments. The fund is particularly interested in helping individual girls and young women of poor or deferred education to establish themselves and gain independence. Grants range from £100 to £1,000.

Exclusions: Grants are not made to charities that request funds to pass on and give to individuals.

Annual grant total: In 2005 the trust had both an income and expenditure of £7,300. Educational grants to 15 individuals totalled £6,300, while welfare grants to four individuals totalled £850. Donations to organisations amounted to £550.

Applications: In writing to the correspondent or by e-mail. Applications can be submitted directly by the individual or through a social worker, Citizens Advice, other welfare agency or college/educational establishment. Applications are considered quarterly in March, June, September and December, and should include full information about the college, course and particular circumstances.

Correspondent: Mrs S M O'Leary, West Hey, Dawstone Road, Heswall, Wirral CH60 4RP (e-mail: gwf_charity@hotmail.com)

Other information: The trust also gives grants to individuals in need and organisations helping girls and young women in Merseyside.

The Holt Education Trust

Eligibility: People in need who are studying on a course of higher education and have lived for most of their life on Merseyside and still have a home there.

The trust concentrates on first degree level courses; academic subjects are given preference. Some grants are given to students reading medicine who have already obtained another first degree.

Most awards are given for full-time study, although applicants who can only study part-time because of family circumstances will be considered.

Types of grants: Grants are single payments ranging from £50 to £300 to help with college or university fees, books, equipment, study trips and, increasingly, with childcare, accommodation and travel.

Annual grant total: In 2003/04, the trust had an income of £12,000 and a total expenditure of £17,000. Grants to individuals totalled about £15,000.

Applications: On a form available from the correspondent. Applications should be made by those who have already started the relevant course and must be accompanied by a reference from the tutor. They should be submitted before the meetings held in February, July and November. Applications must include details of previous education, family circumstances, funding for the present course and the reason for seeking help.

Correspondent: Roger Morris, Secretary, Holt Education Trust, India Buildings, Water Street, Liverpool L2 0RB (0151 473 4693)

Other information: An explanatory leaflet available from the trust describes current policy in detail as the criteria for applications can vary from year to year. These can be obtained from the correspondent.

The Sheila Kay Fund

Eligibility: People in need living in Merseyside who have a background in the voluntary sector.

Types of grants: One-off and recurrent grants are made ranging between £50 to £300 for people engaged in social, youth and community work (paid or voluntary) who cannot afford the relevant education or training. Priority is given to those who have left school with few, if any, qualifications. Any of the costs of education, including childcare, fares and so on can be considered. Most grants are for part-time courses, conferences, educational visits and the like.

Exclusions: No grants for postgraduates.

Annual grant total: In 2004/05, the fund had an income of £72,000 and a total expenditure of £84,000. Grants totalled £29,000.

Applications: Applications should be made at least six weeks before the grant is required. Exemptions from this may be made in emergencies. Application forms are available from the correspondent. Applications are considered all year round.

Correspondent: Peter Clark, 60 Duke Street, Liverpool L1 5AA (0151 707 4304; Fax: 0151 707 4305; e-mail: enquiries@skfunding.org.uk)

Other information: As the basic aim of the fund is to promote opportunities for the development of skills for community activists, it also offers education advice.

The John James Rowe Foundation

Eligibility: Girls aged 10 to 24 who live in Merseyside and: (i) have lost one or both parents; (ii) whose parents are separated; or (iii) whose home life is especially difficult.

Types of grants: Assistance is given for those at secondary school, college, university or other institutions of higher education. Grants are made for equipment, clothing, tools, instruments and books to help prepare for, or assist entry into, a profession, trade or calling. Maximum grant is £200. Single payment grants only are given.

Annual grant total: In 2004/05 the trust had an income of £14,000, and an expenditure of about £17,000. Grants totalled about £15,000.

Applications: In writing to the correspondent for consideration at any time.

Correspondent: Mrs Gill Gargan, Personal Service Society, 18–20 Seel Street, Liverpool L1 4BE

The Rushworth Trust – see entry on page 74

Correspondent: The Grants Team, Liverpool CVS, 14 Castle Street, Liverpool L2 0NJ (Helpline: 0151 653 0550; Fax: 0151 258 1153; e-mail: grants@lcvs.org.uk)

The Sylvia Fund

Eligibility: Women usually aged 25 or over who are going back into education and live and study in inner city Liverpool, Bootle, Kirkby, Huyton, Stockbridge Village or the Wirral. Women who are aged between 20 and 25 and have children may be supported. Grants are mainly given to people who receive income support, especially single mothers.

Types of grants: Grants, generally of between £50 and £500, are given for books, travel. uniform, equipment, materials, child care, compulsory residentials that will aid study. Most grants are ongoing to people who are taking a three or four-year course.

Exclusions: No grants are given for postgraduate courses.

Annual grant total: In 2005 the trust had assets of £17,700, an income of £12,000 and an expenditure of £5,400, almost all of which was given in 28 grants to individuals.

Applications: On a form available from the correspondent for consideration in February/March and November/December, and possibly in one other month according to need. Forms are also circulated in colleges in Merseyside. Applications should be made directly by the individual.

Correspondent: Penny Watson, c/o South Moss House, Pasture Lane, Formby, Liverpool L37 0AP

Great Crosby

The Halsall Educational Foundation

Eligibility: Girls who are leaving sixth form education and entering higher education and live or whose parents live in the ancient township of Great Crosby.

Types of grants: One-off towards books, stethoscopes and so on.

Exclusions: Grants are made only to girls living in the ancient township of Great Crosby.

Annual grant total: Small grants to individuals and an annual grant to Halsall School total about £1,000 each year.

Applications: In writing to the correspondent. Applications should be submitted between March and 31 May, including a sae, for consideration in August and September.

Correspondent: Ms Zorina Annette Jones, 8a Cambridge Avenue, Crosby, Merseyside, L23 7XW (0151 924 6082)

Higher Bebington

The Thomas Robinson Charity

Eligibility: People in need who live in Higher Bebington.

Types of grants: One-off grants in the range of £50 to £500.

Annual grant total: In 2004 the charity had assets of £18,000, an income of £2,600 and a total expenditure of £2,200. Grants totalled about £1,000.

Applications: In writing to: The Vicar, Christ Church Vicarage, King's Road, Higher Bebington, Wirral CH43 8LX. Applications can be submitted directly by the individual or a family member, through a social worker, or a relevant third party such as Citizens Advice or a school. They are considered at any time.

Correspondent: Charles F Van Ingen, 1 Blakeley Brow, Wirral, Merseyside CH63 0PS

Liverpool

The Liverpool Council of Education

Eligibility: Sixth form pupils of Liverpool schools studying for A-levels.

Types of grants: Grants of £50 to £350 for pupils to study overseas or advance their education in other ways.

Annual grant total: Previously about £10,000 each year.

Applications: The correspondent writes to the headteachers of every school with a sixth form in Liverpool at the beginning of each school year, giving details of the trust. Applications should be made in writing and must be supported by a letter of recommendation from the headteacher. The closing date for applications is the last week in January.

Correspondent: Cathy Williams, Revenues and Benefits Service, PO Box 2014, Liverpool, L69 2UT

The Liverpool Friends Scholarship Foundation

Eligibility: Young people in need, who live in Liverpool and are aged between 12 and 18.

Types of grants: There are two types of education grants:

(i) Ackworth Scholarships are given to people attending Friends' School, Ackworth.(ii) General Scholarships are given to people attending any secondary school provided by the Liverpool Education Authority or any other secondary school approved by the governors.The holders of scholarships (and their parents) must be of 'narrow means' and of 'good moral character'.

Exclusions: No grants for private school fees, other than for Friends' School, Ackworth.

Annual grant total: In 2004/05, the foundation had an income of around £3,000 and a total expenditure of £1,860.

Applications: In writing to the correspondent, including details of education to date and means. Applicants are personally interviewed.

Correspondent: James Nigel Rodney Taylor, 21 St Anthony's Road, Blundellsands, Liverpool L23 8TN (0151 236 8211; Fax: 0151 236 4485)

The Lower Bebington School Lands Foundation

Eligibility: People over 18 who live in Lower Bebington; other candidates cannot be considered.

Types of grants: Recurrent grants ranging from £200 to £300 for students in higher/further education to help with the cost of books and fees/living expenses, and for mature students towards books, travel and fees.

Annual grant total: In 2004/05, the foundation had an income of around £2,000, and a total expenditure of £1,000.

Applications: By August each year, on a form available from the correspondent. Applications may be considered at other times if funds are available. Each application is considered on its merit.

Correspondent: S R Lancelyn Green, Wirral Grammar School for Boys, Cross Lane, Bebington, Wirral CH63 3AQ

The Melling with Cunscough Educational Charity

Eligibility: People in further or higher education who live in the parish of Melling. Priority is given to people under 25, with funds only available to others after these needs have been met.

Types of grants: One-off grants are given to: (i) schoolchildren for help with books, educational outings and maintenance; (ii) people starting work for books, equipment, instruments and clothing; (iii) students in further/ higher education for books and fees; and (iv) mature students for books and fees.

Annual grant total: In 2003/04, the charity had an income of £6,000 and a total expenditure of £4,900. Grants total around £4,000.

Applications: In writing to the correspondent, to be submitted by the individual at any time.

Correspondent: Bert Dowell, 29 Woodland Road, Melling, Liverpool L31 1EB (0151 547 3142)

Sefton

The S R Hutton Memorial Fund

Eligibility: People who live in Southport and are under the age of 21.

Types of grants: Grants of between £20 and £200 are made for a wide range of activities such as music, drama, Outward Bound courses and VSO, for which there are no public funds available. The charity simply demands that these activities are 'worthwhile'.

Annual grant total: In 2004, the fund had an income of £420 and no expenditure.

Applications: In writing to the correspondent by the individual's parents/guardians or by recommendation of the school. Applications should include full details of the activity and its cost.

Correspondent: Director of Children, Schools and Families, Finance Department – Sefton Council, 4th Floor Merton House, Stanley Road, Bootle, Merseyside, L20 3FD (0151 934 4112)

The Joseph Harley Bequest

Eligibility: People under 25 who live in Formby.

Types of grants: Grants of up to £250 towards the cost of art, drama, dance, music, natural science, and physical, mental and spiritual training. Grants are only awarded for projects for which assistance is not available from public funds.

Annual grant total: About £1,500.

Applications: On a form available from the correspondent. The trustees usually meet twice yearly in July and February.

Correspondent: Director of Children's Services, Sefton Borough Council, Education Department, Bootle Town Hall, Oriel Road, Bootle, Liverpool L20 7AE (0151 934 3257)

Other information: The following trusts, which each have between about £200 and £400 in total to be given in grants, are also administered by Sefton Borough Council. For further infomation please contact the Director of Finance.

(i) The Thomas Davies Scholarship

People under the age of 25 who live in Bootle and are studying engineering and electricity, towards college and university fees.

(ii) The Simon Mahon Memorial Scholarships

Male students over school leaving age who, or whose parents, have lived in Bootle for at least two years, towards full-time further or higher education.

(iii) The Kate Rimmer Trust

People who live in Southport who were educated at a school within the former county borough boundary are eligible to receive grants towards university fees or to supplement existing grants.

(iv) The Matthew Turbitt Trust Fund

People who live in Southport who were educated at a school within the former county borough boundary. Grants to help with university fees or to supplement existing grants.

The Sefton Educational Trust

Eligibility: People under 25 who live in the borough of Sefton.

Types of grants: Grants of up to £250 towards the cost of art, drama, dance, music, natural science, and physical, mental and spiritual training. Grants are only awarded for projects for which assistance is not available from public funds.

Annual grant total: In 2003/04 the trust had an income of £3,000 and a total expenditure of £5,700.

Applications: On a form available from the correspondent. The trustees usually meet twice yearly in July and February.

Correspondent: Director of Children's Services, Town Hall, Lord Street, Southport, PR8 1DA (0151 934 2032; Fax: 0151 934 2277)

Other information: The following trusts, which each have between about £200 and £400 in total to be given in grants, are also administered by Sefton Borough Council. For further infomation please contact the director of finance.

(i) The Thomas Davies Scholarship

People under the age of 25 who live in Bootle and are studying engineering and electricity, towards college and university fees.

(ii) The Simon Mahon Memorial Scholarships

Male students over school leaving age who, or whose parents, have lived in Bootle for at least two years, towards full-time further or higher education.

(iii) The Kate Rimmer Trust

People who live in Southport who were educated at a school within the former county borough boundary are eligible to receive grants towards university fees or to supplement existing grants.

(iv) The Matthew Turbitt Trust Fund

People who live in Southport who were educated at a school within the former county borough boundary. Grants to help with university fees or to supplement existing grants.

St Helens

The Sarah Cowley Educational Foundation

Eligibility: People between 16 and 24 years of age who live in the borough of St Helens. Applicants must be under the age of 25 on 1 September before the start of their course. Postgraduate students can also be considered.

Types of grants: One-off grants ranging from £50 to £500 to assist in education or training to prepare for or enter a trade, calling or profession. The foundation stated that the following are most likely to awarded grants: further and higher education students, vocational students and people with special educational needs for uniforms/clothing, fees, study or travel abroad, books, equipment/instruments and excursions.

Exclusions: The trustees will not normally consider making grants to applicants who have previously embarked on another career.

Annual grant total: In 2005/06 the foundation had an income of £7,100, all of which was given in grants to 32 individuals.

Applications: On a form available from the correspondent. Applications should be submitted before 30 September prior to the academic year in which the course will be starting. Applications must include details of parental or spouses income.

Correspondent: Mrs Janet Taylor, St Helens Council, Children and Young People's Services, Wesley House, Corporation Street, St Helens WA10 1HF (01744 455339; Fax: 01744 455407; e-mail: studentsupport@sthelens.gov.uk)

The Rainford Trust

Eligibility: People in need who are normally resident in the borough of St Helens.

Types of grants: One-off and recurrent grants ranging from £100 to £750 are paid directly to the college or other third party organisation. Grants can be for schoolchildren for equipment/instruments, fees, maintenance/living expenses and educational outings in the UK. Further and higher education students and mature students can receive grants for books, equipment/instruments, fees, childcare and educational outings in the UK.

Annual grant total: In 2004/05 the trust had assets of £6.1 million and an income of £212,000. Grants were made to organisations totalling £110,000. Around £1,000 to £2,000 is given to individuals each year.

Applications: In writing to the correspondent, for consideration throughout the year. Applications can be made directly by the individual, or through his or her school, college or educational welfare agency. The trust sends out a questionnaire, if appropriate, after the application has been made.

Correspondent: William H Simm, Secretary, c/o Pilkington plc, Prescot Road, St Helens, Merseyside WA10 3TT (01744 20574; Fax: 01744 20574)

6. MIDLANDS

The Beacon Centre for the Blind

Eligibility: People who are registered blind or partially sighted and live in the metropolitan boroughs of Dudley (except Halesowen and Stourbridge), Sandwell and Wolverhampton, and part of the South Staffordshire District Council area.

Types of grants: One-off grants up to a maximum of £250 for specific items or improvements to the home.

Annual grant total: In 2005 the charity had assets of £130,000 and an income of £11,000. There were 28 grants made to individuals during the year.

Applications: In writing to the correspondent stating the degree of vision and age of the applicant, and their monthly income and expenditure. Applications can be submitted through a social worker or a school, and are considered throughout the year.

Correspondent: Chief Executive, Beacon Centre for the Blind, Wolverhampton Road East, Wolverhampton WV4 6AZ (01902 880111; Fax: 01902 886795; e-mail: enquiries@beacon4blind.co.uk; website: www.beacon4blind.co.uk)

The Birmingham & Three Counties Trust for Nurses

Eligibility: Nurses on any statutory register, who have practiced or practice in the city of Birmingham and the counties of Staffordshire, Warwickshire and Worcestershire.

Types of grants: One-off grants up to £300 per annum to nurses taking post-registration courses (post-basic nurse training or back-to-nursing course). Grants are made towards books, travel and/or fees.

Annual grant total: In 2004/05 the trust had assets of £285,000 and an income of £19,000. Its total expenditure on grants was £23,000 including educational grants given to seven individuals totalled £1,700. Welfare grants to 65 individuals totalled £21,000.

Applications: On a form available from the correspondent to be submitted directly by the individual. Applications are considered at any time.

Correspondent: Mrs Ruth Adams, Hon. Secretary, 26 Whitnash Road, Leamington Spa, Warwickshire CV31 2HL (e-mail: ruthmadams_45@msn.com)

Burton Breweries Charitable Trust

Eligibility: Children and young people aged 11 to 25 who are involved in activities which build character and develop/improve skills or qualifications. People will only be considered who live, or are in full-time education, in Burton and the East Staffordshire and South Derbyshire district (including a small area of north west Leicestershire). 'The trustees recognise that some individuals are disadvantaged, through no fault of their own, and priority support will be given to undertake training which leads to personal development for such individuals to help them manage their lives more effectively.'

Types of grants: One-off grants ranging from £100 to £500. Grants are only given for extra circular activities.

Exclusions: No support for education where there is provision by the state and grants will not be made for higher or university education.

Annual grant total: In 2005/06 the trust had assets totalling £800,000 and an income of £36,000. Grants to 39 individuals totalled £8,100. A further 15 grants were made to youth organisations totalling £10,000.

Applications: In writing to the correspondent. Awards for the benefit of individuals will not be made direct but will be made, in general, via organisations with a significant youth membership and will normally take the form of a one-off sponsorship for a person nominated by the organisation to the trustees.

The trustees meet in February, June and October and applications should be sent by January, May and September. A copy of the trust's guidelines are available on request.

All applicants are requested to view the website and the current terms and conditions before applying for support.

Correspondent: Brian Edward Keates, Secretary to the Trustees, Gretton House, Waterside Court, Third Avenue, Centrum 100, Burton-on-Trent, Staffordshire DE14 2WQ (01283 740600; Fax: 01283 511899; e-mail: info@ burtonbctrust.co.uk; website: www. burtonbctrust.co.uk)

Other information: Grants are also made organisations.

The Charities of Susanna Cole & Others

Eligibility: Quakers in need who live in parts of Worcestershire and most of Warwickshire and are 'a member or attender of one of the constituent meetings of the Warwickshire Monthly Meeting of the Society of Friends'. Preference is given to younger children (for education).

Types of grants: One-off and recurrent grants for education or re-training.

Annual grant total: In 2005 the charity had an income of £8,000 and a total expenditure of £5,600. Grants are made for welfare and educational purposes.

Applications: In writing to the correspondent via the overseer of the applicant's Quaker meeting. Applications should be received by early March and October for consideration later in the same months.

Correspondent: The Secretary, Warwickshire Monthly Meeting Office, Friends Meeting House, 40 Bull Street, Birmingham B3 6AF

Melton Mowbray Building Society Charitable Foundation

Eligibility: People in need who live in Leicestershire, Lincolnshire, Nottinghamshire and Rutland.

Types of grants: One-off grants, for example, to schoolchildren for books, equipment/instruments and excursions, to college students and undergraduates for books and to vocational students for study/travel abroad. Other requests will be considered.

Exclusions: No grants are made for circular appeals, for projects of a high capital nature or tuition fees.

Annual grant total: In 2004/05 the trust had and an income of £13,000. The sum of £2,300 was distributed in 23 relief-in-need grants with a further £800 distributed in seven educational grants.

Applications: In writing to the correspondent to be submitted either directly by the individual or a family member, through a third party such as a social worker or teacher, or through an organisation such as Citizens Advice or a school. Applications should include details of the cash value sought, the nature of the expense, the reason for application and the location of the applicant. Applications are considered at meetings held on a quarterly basis.

Correspondent: Miss M D Swainston, Leicester Road, Melton Mowbray, LE13 0D3 (01664 414141; Fax: 01664 414040; e-mail: m.swainston@ mmbs.co.uk)

Other information: Grants may also be given to organisations for education, disability, medical needs and safer communities (£13,000 in 2004/05)

Thomas Monke's Charity

Eligibility: Young individuals between the ages of 17 and 21 who live in Austrey in Warwickshire and Mersham, Shenton and Whitwick in Leicestershire.

Types of grants: One-off and recurrent grants in the range of £100 to £500 to college students, undergraduates, vocational students and people starting work for books and equipment/ instruments. Vocational students and people starting work can receive grants for fees.

Exclusions: Expeditions, scholarships and university course fees are not funded.

Annual grant total: In 2004 the charity had assets of £102,000 and an income of £4,100. Grants to 101 individuals for welfare purposes totalled £1,000, with 4 educational grants totalling £700. Organisations received £1,600.

Applications: Application forms are available from the correspondent and should be submitted directly by the individual before 31 March, in time for the trustees' yearly meeting held in April.

Correspondent: C P Kitto, Steward, 20 St John Street, Lichfield, Staffordshire WS13 6PD (01543 262491; Fax: 01543 254986)

The Newfield Charitable Trust

Eligibility: Girls and women (under 30) who are in need of care and assistance and live in Coventry or Leamington Spa. Postgraduate applications are not considered.

Types of grants: Grants towards school uniforms and other school clothing, educational trips, books and childcare costs. Most grants are under £500.

Exclusions: No grants for postgraduate education.

Annual grant total: In 2004/05 the trust had an income of £45,000 and made grants totalling £43,000.

Applications: Write to the correspondent for an application form. Applications are accepted from individuals or third parties e.g. schools, social services, Citizens Advice etc. A letter of support/reference from someone not a friend or relative of the applicant (i.e. school, social services etc.) may be required. Details of income/ expenditure and personal circumstances should also be given.

Applications are considered eight times a year.

Correspondent: D J Dumbleton, Clerk, Rotherham & Co Solicitors, 8–9 The Quadrant, Coventry CV1 2EG (024 7622 7331; Fax: 024 7622 1293; e-mail: j.russell@rotherham.co.uk)

The Norton Foundation

Eligibility: Young people under 25 who live in Birmingham or Warwickshire and are in need of care or rehabilitation or aid of any kind, 'particularly as a result of delinquency, deprivation, maltreatment or neglect or who are in danger of lapsing or relapsing into delinquency'.

Types of grants: One-off grants in the range of £150 to £500. Donations are given to schoolchildren and further and higher education students for uniforms/other school clothing, books, equipment/ instruments, fees, maintenance/living expenses and educational outings in the UK.

Annual grant total: In 2004/05 the trust had assets of £3.4 million and an income of £117,000. Grants to 475 individuals totalled £68,000, with the majority made for relief-in-need purposes. Donations to organisations totalled £30,000.

Applications: By letter which should contain all the information required as detailed in the guidance notes for applicants. Guidance notes are available from the correspondent or the website. Applications must be submitted through a social worker, Citizens Advice, other welfare agency or another third party. They are considered every month.

Correspondent: The Correspondent, PO Box 10282, Redditch, Worcestershire B97 9ZA (e-mail: correspondent@ nortonfoundation.org; website: www. nortonfoundation.org)

Other information: Grants are also made to organisations.

Sir John Sumner's Trust *see entry on page 83*

Correspondent: A C Robson, The Secretary to the Trustees, No. 1 Colmore Square, Birmingham, B4 6AA

The Anthony & Gwendoline Wylde Memorial Charity

Eligibility: People in need with a preference for residents of Stourbridge (West Midlands) and Kinver (Staffordshire).

Types of grants: One-off grants in the range of £50 and £500 are given to college students and undergraduates for clothing, fees, books, equipment/instruments, maintenance/living expenses and excursions.

Exclusions: No grants towards bills or debts.

Annual grant total: In 2004/05 the charity had assets of £932,000 and an income of £46,000. Total expenditure was £42,000 with £29,000 given in grants.

Applications: In writing to the correspondent. Applications can be submitted directly by the individual or a family member and are considered on an ongoing basis.

Correspondent: Mr D J Nightingale, Clerk, Blythe House, 134 High Street, Brierley Hill, West Midlands DY5 3BG (01384 342100)

Derbyshire

Coke's Educational Charity

Eligibility: People under 25 who live in the parishes of Alkmonton, Hollington, Hungry Bently, Longford and Rodsley.

Types of grants: One-off and recurrent grants for educational purposes.

Annual grant total: In 2005 the trust had an income of £3,200 and a total expenditure of £2,500. Grants totalled about £2,000.

Applications: In writing to the correspondent.

Correspondent: E R Hill, Clerk to the Trustees, Old Orchard, Longford Ashbourne, Derbyshire DE6 3DR (01335 330472)

The Dronfield Relief-in-Need Charity

Eligibility: People under 25 who live in the ecclesiastical parishes of Dronfield, Holmesfield, Unstone and West Handley.

Types of grants: One-off grants up to a value of £100 are given, including those for social and physical training.

Exclusions: No support for rates, taxes and so on.

Annual grant total: About £1,000.

Applications: In writing to the correspondent though a social worker, doctor, member of the clergy of any denomination, a local councillor, Citizens

Advice or other welfare agency. The applicants should ensure they are receiving all practical/financial assistance they are entitled to from statutory sources.

Correspondent: Dr A N Bethell, Ramshaw Lodge, Crow Lane, Unstone, Dronfield, Derbyshire S18 4AL (01246 413276)

Other information: Grants are also given to local organisations.

Faith Hope and Enterprise Company

Eligibility: People in need who live in the Derby area who are unable to progress in their education because of hardship.

Types of grants: One-off grants according to need. Donations are also given in the form of direct services.

Annual grant total: Around £2,000 per year.

Applications: In writing to the correspondent directly by the individual, or through a welfare organisation such as Citizens Advice or Social Services, for consideration throughout the year.

Correspondent: Carl Taylor, Lodge Farm, Lodge Lane, Kirk Langley, Derbyshire DG6 4NX (01332 824903)

Other information: The trust also supports Christian projects.

The Hallowes & Hope Educational Foundation

Eligibility: People under 25 who live in the ecclesiastical parishes of Mugginton and Kedleston. Preference is given to people with serious family difficulties or special educational needs.

Types of grants: One-off grants of up to £300 for: (i) books and educational outings for schoolchildren; (ii) books, fees and living expenses for students in further/higher education; and (iii) books, equipment, clothing and travel for people starting work.

Annual grant total: About £1,200 is available each year.

Applications: Applications should include details of need and can be submitted to the correspondent by the individual, through a school/college or educational welfare agency or other third party or parent and are usually considered in December or when necessary.

Correspondent: A J Naylor, Rock House Farm, Dalbury Lees, Ashbourne, Derbyshire DE6 5BS (01332 824277)

Hilton Educational Foundation

Eligibility: Young people aged under 25 in further or higher education, who live, or whose parents live, in Hilton and Marston on Dove.

Types of grants: One-off grants, usually £100 to £150, towards books and/or equipment needed for studies.

Annual grant total: The trust has an annual income of about £5,000 and grants are typically divided as follows: £1,000 to schools, £350 to the playgroup and £3,700 to individuals.

Applications: In writing to the correspondent directly by the individual. Applications should be submitted in March and October, for consideration in the same month.

Correspondent: Sue Cornish, 6 Willow Brook Close, Hilton, Derby, DE65 5JE

The Risley Educational Foundation

Eligibility: People under 25 who live in the parishes of Breaston, Church Wilne, Dale Abbey, Draycott, Hopwell, Risley, Sandiacre or Stanton-by-Dale.

Types of grants: Grants of £150 for books, equipment, educational travel and promoting the instruction of Church of England doctrines. People on music and arts courses can be supported. Grants are also given to schools.

Annual grant total: In 2004/05, the foundation had net assets of £445,500, an income of £47,000 and a total expenditure of £33,400. The foundation gave scholarships and grants to individuals totalling £10,000.

Applications: On a form available from the correspondent. Applications are considered on a quarterly basis.

Correspondent: Mrs V A Lewis, Clerk to the Trustees, 100 Douglas Road, Long Eaton, Nottingham NG10 4BD (0115 849 0529)

Scargill's Educational Foundation

Eligibility: People under the age of 25 who live in the parishes of West Hallam, Dale Abbey, Mapperley and Stanley (including Stanley Common).

Types of grants: The main beneficiary of the charity is Scargill Church of England Primary School. Priority is also given to three other schools in the area. After that, help is available for groups and also for individuals for the following purposes:

(i) Grants, usually up to about £45, for sixth form pupils to help with books, equipment, clothing or travel.

(ii) Grants, usually up to about £175, to help with school, college or university fees or to supplement existing grants.

(iii) Grants to help with the cost of books and educational outings for schoolchildren.

(iv) For the study of music and other arts and for educational travel.

Annual grant total: Around £8,000 to £10,000 is given in educational grants to individuals each year.

Applications: On a form available from the correspondent. The foundation places advertisements in August, and the formal closing date is 29 September, although applications after this date will be considered if funds permit.

Correspondent: S F Marshall, Clerk, 10-11 St James Court, Friar Gate, Derby DE1 1BT (01332 291431)

The Stanton Charitable Trust

Eligibility: People at any stage or level of their education, undertaking study of any subject who are in need and live near Staveley Works in Chesterfield, Derbyshire, namely Staveley, Brimington, Barrowhill, Hollingwold and Inkersall.

Types of grants: Grants can be given to schoolchildren for books, equipment/instruments and excursions and to mature students and people with special educational needs for equipment/instruments and maintenance/living expenses.

Annual grant total: In 2004/05 the trust had assets of £34,000 and an income of £480. There was one educational grant made totalling £280. Three relief-in-need grants totalled £170.

Applications: In writing either directly by the individual or a family member, or through an organisation such as Citizens Advice or a school. Applications should state the specific amount for a specific item.

Correspondent: P R Burrows, Saint-Gobain Pipelines plc, Staveley Works, Chesterfield, Derbyshire S43 2PD (01246 280088; Fax: 01246 280061)

Other information: Grants are also made to schools, churches, scouts, guides and local fundraising events.

Ault Hucknall

The Hardwick Educational Charity

Eligibility: People aged between 16 and 24, inclusive, whose parent(s) live in the civil parish of Ault Hucknall.

Types of grants: Help with with the cost of books for students in further/higher education and with the cost of books, equipment and instruments for people starting work.

Exclusions: Grants are not available for student exchanges, maintenance, fees or mature students.

Annual grant total: About £1,200 a year.

Applications: In writing to the correspondent. Applications are considered in April and October.

Correspondent: Mrs C E Hitch, Stainsby Mill Farm, Heath, Chesterfield, Derbyshire S44 5RW

Buxton

The Bingham Trust

Eligibility: People in need, primarily those who live in Buxton. Most applicants from outside Buxton are rejected unless there is a Buxton connection.

Types of grants: One-off grants ranging from £200 to £1,000. Grants are made to individuals for a wide variety of needs, including further education.

Exclusions: No grants are made for higher education study.

Annual grant total: In 2004/05 it had assets of £1.5 million and an income of £68,000. Grants, mainly to organisations, totalled £67,000.

Applications: In writing to the correspondent in March, June, September or December for consideration in the following months. Applications should be submitted through a third party such as a social worker, Citizens Advice, doctor or minister.

Correspondent: R Horne, Trustee, Blinder House, Flagg, Buxton, Derbyshire SK17 9QG (01298 83328; e-mail: binghamtrust@aol.com)

Derby

The Derby City Charity

Eligibility: People under 25 who live in the city of Derby and are in need.

Types of grants: Grants for education, training, apprenticeships, and for equipment for those starting work.

Exclusions: Assistance is not given where other funds are available or towards books or fees for pupils and students if the LEA already has a scheme covering such items.

Annual grant total: About £2,000 is given in grants each year. At least 5% of the trust's grant total must be used for educational purposes; the rest is used for welfare grants.

Applications: On a form available from the correspondent, on written request.

Correspondent: The Director of Corporate Services, Derby City Council, The Council House, Corporation Street, Derby DE1 2FS

Holmesfield

The Holmesfield Educational Foundation

Eligibility: People living in the parish of Holmesfield, under the age of 25.

Types of grants: Probably help with the cost of books, clothing and other essentials for schoolchildren. Grants may also be available for those at college or university.

Annual grant total: About £2,500.

Applications: In writing to the correspondent.

Correspondent: Mrs Doreen Bertram, 88 Main Road, Holmesfield, Dronfield, Derbyshire S18 7WT

Matlock

The Ernest Bailey Charity

Eligibility: People in need who live in Matlock (this includes Bonsall, Darley Dale, South Darley, Tansley, Matlock Bath and Cromford).

Types of grants: Most applications have been from local groups, but individuals in need and those with educational needs are also supported. Educational grants are one-off and generally of around £100 to £200. Grants are given to students in further/higher education towards books, fees, living expenses and study or travel abroad. Mature students can apply towards books, travel, fees or childcare. People with special educational needs are considered. Each application is considered on its merits.

Annual grant total: In 2004/05 the trust had an income of £7,100 and a total expenditure of £7,700. Around £1,000 is given in grants to individuals per year.

Applications: On a form available from the correspondent. Applications can be submitted directly by the individual and/or can be supported by a relevant professional. They should be returned by the end of September for consideration and award in October. Applications should include costings (total amount required, funds raised and funds promised). Previous beneficiaries may apply again, with account being taken of assistance given in the past.

Correspondent: Head of Corporate Services, Derbyshire Dales District Council, Town Hall, Matlock, Derbyshire DE4 3NN

Spondon

The Spondon Relief-in-Need Charity

Eligibility: People in education who live in the ancient parish of Spondon within the city of Derby.

Types of grants: Grants of amounts up to £500 are made to schoolchildren, college students, undergraduates and mature students, including those towards uniforms/clothing, study/travel abroad, books, equipment/instruments, excursions, awards for excellence and childcare.

Exclusions: This grant is not intended to supplement an LEA grant.

Annual grant total: In 2005 the trust had an income and a total expenditure of £20,000. There were 23 welfare grants made during the year totalling £8,100. A further £4,400 was distributed in 15 educational grants.

Applications: On a form available from the correspondent to be submitted either directly by the individual or a family member, through a third party such as a social worker or through an organisations such as Citizens Advice or a school. Each form must be accompanied by a letter of support from a sponsor such as a doctor, health authority official, social worker, city councillor, clergyman, headteacher, school liaison officer, youth leader or probation officer. The sponsor must justify the applicant's need. The latter is particularly important. The applicant should provide as much information on the form as possible. It is better to ask for a visit by a trustee if possible.

The trustees meet quarterly.

Correspondent: Richard J Pooles, Secretary/Treasurer, 67 Heronswood Drive, Spondon, Derby DE21 7AX (01332 669879)

West Hallam

The Foundation of Ann Powtrell

Eligibility: Students under the age of 25 who live, or whose parents live, in the parish of West Hallam.

Types of grants: Grants of up to £250 have been given for apprentices and educational trips, for instance, Duke of Edinburgh Awards and a trip to a world scout jamboree in Chile.

Annual grant total: In 2004/05 the trust had an income of £13,000 and a total expenditure of £4,600.

Applications: In writing to the correspondent.

Correspondent: Peter Briggs, 12 High Lane East, West Hallam, Ilkeston, Derbyshire DE7 6HW

Herefordshire

The Hereford Society for Aiding the Industrious

Eligibility: People who live in Herefordshire, with preference for Hereford City and its immediate environs, who are 'seeking to better themselves by their own efforts' and are in need. Applicants may be undertaking primary, secondary, further or higher education, non-vocational training or vocational training or re-training, in most subjects.

Types of grants: Normally one-off grants ranging between £50 and £1,000; interest-free loans occasionally. Grants can be made towards: schoolchildren for educational outings; people starting work towards books and equipment/instruments; students in further/higher education towards books, fees and living expenses; and mature students towards books, travel, fees and childcare. Gap year expeditions etc. are rarely successful in obtaining funding.

Annual grant total: In 2004/05 the trust had assets of £673,000, an income of £74,000 and a total expenditure of £78,000. Eight grants to individuals totalled £3,600.

Applications: In writing to the correspondent. If eligible an application form will be sent and the applicant will probably be asked to attend an interview (between 2.00pm and 4.00pm on Thursday). Grants are rarely given directly to the applicant; instead they are given to the bookseller, college and so on. The trust has stated that applications should be 'precise' and 'honest'. Applications are considered every month.

Correspondent: R M Cunningham, 18 Venns Close, Bath Street, Hereford HR1 2HH (01432 274014)

Other information: The trust also makes grants to organisations (Almost £7,000 in 2004/05).

The Herefordshire Community Foundation

Eligibility: People in need who live in Herefordshire.

Types of grants: One-off and recurrent grants according to need.

Annual grant total: About £6,000 a year to individuals.

Applications: In writing to the correpsondent.

Correspondent: David Barclay, Director, The Fred Bulmer Centre, Wall Street, Hereford, HR4 9HP (01432 272550)

Other information: Grants are also made to organisations (£100,000 in 2004/05).

The Herefordshire Educational Charity

Eligibility: People under the age of 25 who live in Herefordshire as constituted on 31 March 1974.

Types of grants: Grants in the range of £100–£150 to school pupils and students in colleges, universities and so on, to help with books, equipment, clothing or travel. Help is also available towards the cost of education, training, apprenticeship, books or equipment for those starting work.

Annual grant total: In 2004/05, the charity had an income of £1,400 and a total expenditure of £850.

Applications: On a form available from the correspondent.

Correspondent: Andrea Franklin, Herefordshire Council, Legal Department, 35 Hafod Road, Hereford, HR1 1SH

Jarvis Educational Foundation

Eligibility: People who live the parishes of Staunton-on-Wye, Bredwardine and Letton in Herefordshire.

Types of grants: One-off grants can be given: to individuals at secondary school, university or college where education authority support is not available, to provide outfits, clothing, tools, instruments or books to help people enter a trade, profession or calling on leaving education; and to enable such people to travel to pursue their education. Grants can range from £100 to £1,000.

Annual grant total: In 2004 the foundation had an income of £33,000, a total expenditure of £7,200 and no donations were made. The accounts stated that the trust was unable to make donations during the year as it was building up its fund for a commitment it had made to a local school. It was also commented in the accounts that the trust was preparing to review its assets in order to increase the funding available in donations in future years.

Applications: In writing to the correspondent for consideration at any time.

Correspondent: The Charity Clerk, 4 Church Street, Hay-on-Wye, Hereford, HR3 5DQ (01497 821023; e-mail: bettymchay@hotmail.com)

The Emma Russell Educational Foundation

Eligibility: People under 25 who live in the parishes of Ledbury Rural and Wellington Heath.

Types of grants: Grants to help people with expenses at university and those undertaking apprenticeships and training generally.

Annual grant total: About £700 is distributed each year.

Applications: On a form available from the correspondent. Awards are made in October.

Correspondent: W H Masefield, Clerk, Messrs R & C B Masefield, Solicitors, Worcester Road, Ledbury, Herefordshire HR8 1PN (01531 632377)

Bosbury

Bosbury Educational Foundation

Eligibility: Young people leaving school who live in the parish of Bosbury and have done so for at least three years.

Types of grants: Grants of up to £250 towards books are given to young people 'on leaving school' going on to further education. Students undertaking university courses of three years or longer are invited to apply for a further grant in their final year. Grants may also be given towards school uniform for children in need.

Exclusions: Only applications from people living in the parish of Bosbury will be considered.

Annual grant total: In 2004 the foundation had an income of £10,000 and a total expenditure of £12,000. Grant to individuals total around £3,000 each year.

Applications: In writing to the correspondent, including details of the course. Applications should be submitted directly by the individual and are considered at any time.

Correspondent: Mrs Susan Sharples, Little Croft, Bosbury, Ledbury, Herefordshire HR8 1QA

Other information: The parish of Bosbury consists of around 500 people. In previous years the trust has stated that it is being inundated by applications from outside the parish which cannot be considered due to the deeds of the trust, and these applications will not be acknowledged.

Hereford

The Hereford Municipal Charities

Eligibility: People in need who live in the city of Hereford.

Types of grants: One-off grants of up to £200. Grants are given to help with the cost of education and starting work.

Exclusions: No grants towards debts or nursery fees.

Annual grant total: In 2004 the trust had assets of £442,000 and an income of £17,000. Grants totalled £12,000, of which 10,000 was given to individuals for relief-in-need purposes and £2,000 for educational purposes. About 75 grants are made each year.

Applications: On a form available from the correspondent to be submitted directly by the individual or through a relevant third party. Applications are considered monthly.

Correspondent: Lance Marshall, Clerk to the Trustees, 147 St Owen Street, Hereford HR1 2JR

Middleton-on-the-Hill

The Middleton-on-the-Hill Parish Charity

Eligibility: People living in the parish of Middleton-on-the-Hill.

Types of grants: One-off and recurrent grants for both welfare and educational purposes.

Annual grant total: About £1,000 a year is given in grants.

Applications: In writing to the correspondent.

Correspondent: Clare Halls, Secretary, Highlands, Leysters, Leominster, Herefordshire HR6 0HP (01568 750257)

North Canon

The Norton Canon Parochial Charities

Eligibility: Young people who live in the parish of Norton Canon.

Types of grants: Grants have been given towards books and educational outings for schoolchildren, books, fees/living expenses and study or travel abroad for students in further or higher education and equipment/instruments, books, clothing and travel for people starting work.

Annual grant total: Grants total around £4,600 a year for educational and welfare purposes.

Applications: In writing to the correspondent at any time.

Correspondent: Mrs M L Gittins, Ivy Cottage, Norton Canon, Hereford HR4 7BQ (01544 318984)

Ross

The Minett & Skyrme Charity Trust

Eligibility: People in need under 25 who live in Ross-on-Wye or in Ross rural parish.

Types of grants: One-off or recurrent grants according to need. The trust's aim is to provide 'special benefits of any kind not normally provided by the education authority for any school substantially serving the area of benefit'. Grants are given to schoolchildren towards books and educational outings; people starting work towards books, equipment/instruments, clothing and travel expenses; and students in further/higher education (including mature students) towards books, fees/living expenses and study or travel overseas.

Annual grant total: Account information from the Charity Commission was only available for the financial year of 1999/2000. During the year the charity had an income of £6,200, and a total expenditure of £6,800. Grants totalled around £6,000.

Applications: In writing to the correspondent directly by the individual. Applications must include details of age, address, how much the grant is for, what it is for and why it is needed. Applications must arrive in time for consideration in April or October.

Correspondent: Mrs Gina Lane, Clerk, Brampton Rise, Greytree, Ross-on-Wye, Herefordshire HR9 7HY (01989 563262)

The Ross Educational Foundation

Eligibility: People under 25 who live in (or whose parents live in) the urban district of Ross and the civil parish of Ross Rural only.

Types of grants: One-off and recurrent grants for those at school to help with equipment/instruments, excursions and study or travel abroad and to vocational students and further and higher education students for books, excursions equipment/instruments and study or travel abroad. Grants range from £25 to £120.

Exclusions: Accommodation costs and day-to-day travel expenses will not be considered.

Annual grant total: In 2004 the trust had an income of £1,600 and a total expenditure of £1,500. Grants were given to 15 individuals totalling £1,100.

Applications: On a form available from the correspondent to be submitted directly by the individual. Grants should be submitted in February and August for consideration in April and October respectively.

Correspondent: Mrs M Bickerton, Secretary, 3 Silver Birches, Ross-on-Wye, Herefordshire HR9 7UX

Leicestershire & Rutland

The Dixie Educational Foundation

Eligibility: People under 25 who live or whose parents/guardians live, or have at any time lived, in the area of the former district of Market Bosworth Rural District Council for a period of not less than two years.

Types of grants: One-off grants in the range of £75 and £150 for clothing, books, equipment/instruments, educational outings in the UK or study or travel abroad.

Annual grant total: In 2005/06 it had assets of £622,000 and an income of £78,000. The sum of £26,000 was distributed to in 77 grants to individuals.

Applications: In writing to the correspondent. Applications can be submitted directly by the individual, through the individual's school, college or educational welfare agency, or through a parent or guardian. Applicants must give their date of birth, residential qualification and brief details of educational background and present course of study/apprenticeship etc. together with details and costs of items against which a grant is sought. Applications must be received at least two weeks before each of the termly meetings which are held on the first Friday of March, June and November.

Correspondent: P Dungworth, Clerk to the Trustees, Children and Young People's Service, County Hall, Glenfield, Leicester LE3 8RF (Fax: 0116 265 6634; e-mail: education@leics.gov.uk)

Other information: The foundation also supports local organisations (£49,000 in 2005/06).

The Leicestershire Coal Industry Welfare Trust Fund

Eligibility: Redundant or retired mineworkers (and their dependants) from the British coal mining industry in Leicestershire, who have not taken up other full-time work.

Types of grants: Grants are given for education, relief-in-need, health and to organisations linked with the mining industry.

Annual grant total: In 2004 the trust had an income of £10,000 and a total expenditure of £11,000. Grants are made to individuals and organisations.

Applications: In writing to the correspondent, including details of mining connections, residence in Leicestershire and dependence on the mineworker (in the case of children).

Correspondent: Peter Smith, Trustee, NUM, Springboard Centre, 18 Mantle Lane, Coalville, Leicestershire LE67 3DW

The Thomas Rawlins Educational Foundation

Eligibility: People under 25 years of age living in Quorn, Woodhouse, Woodhouse Eaves and Barrow upon Soar only (preference is given to the first three villages).

Types of grants: (i) Grants, usually between £50 to £250, for school pupils, to help with books, equipment, school uniform, maintenance or fees, but not other school clothing or educational outings. (ii) Grants, up to about £250, for students in further and higher education, to help with books, equipment, instruments, study or travel abroad or fees, but not for student exchange or for foreign students studying in the UK. (iii) Help towards the cost of books, equipment and instruments, travel and clothing for people starting work.

Annual grant total: In 2004/05, the foundation had an total income of £2,300 and an expenditure of £1,700.

Applications: On a form available from the correspondent, including details of the parent/guardian's financial position. Applications can be submitted through a parent or guardian at any time.

Correspondent: Geoffrey B Gibson, 2 Wallis Close, Thurcaston, Leicestershire LE7 7JS (0116 235 0946; Fax: 0116 235 0946)

The Harry James Riddleston Charity of Leicester

Eligibility: People aged 21 to 34 who live in Leicestershire or Rutland.

Types of grants: 'The prime purpose of this charity is to set up young persons over the age of 21 and under 35 years in business or to further an existing career which can include grants for further education.' The standard award is not a grant but an interest-free loan of up to £4,000 for education and up to £6,000 for business for a period of five years.

Annual grant total: In 2004/05 the trust had an income of £24,000 and a total expenditure of £20,000, all of which was given in grants.

Applications: On a form available from the correspondent, to be submitted directly by the individual. Applications are considered in February, May, August and November.

Correspondent: Mrs M E Bass, Clerk, 44 High Street, Market Harborough, Leicestershire LE16 7AH (01858 463322; Fax: 01858 410214)

The Rutland Trust

Eligibility: People, usually under 35, in need who live in Rutland and are at any level or stage of their education.

Types of grants: One-off grants ranging between £50 and £400. There are no restrictions on how the grants may be spent. In the past, grants have been made towards music and school trips for needy young people, for European exchange trips, and for young people to take part in educational, missionary and life-experience programmes overseas. Grants may also be spent on books, equipment, fees, bursaries, fellowships and study visits.

Annual grant total: In 2005 the trust had an income of £11,000 all of which was distributed in 43 grants totalling £11,000, including 12 grants to individuals totalling £3,000.

Applications: An initial telephone call is recommended.

Correspondent: Richard Adams, Clerk, 35 Trent Road, Oakham, Rutland, LE15 6HE (01572 756706; e-mail: adams@apair. wanadoo.co.uk)

The Marc Smith Educational Charity

Eligibility: Students (usually under 25) living in the ancient parishes of Claybrook Magna, Claybrook Parva and Ullesthorpe.

Types of grants: Help towards the cost of education, training, apprenticeship or equipment for those starting work. A clothing grant is given to pupils moving from the village schools to the high school. Grants are also given to students in further or higher education.

Annual grant total: In 2005, the trust had an income of around £11,000 and a total expenditure of £6,300. Grants totalled about £5,000.

Applications: Applications for clothing grants should be in writing and they are considered in May. Further education applications are considered in September, and should be submitted at a meeting which applicants are invited to through local advertisements near to the time of the meeting.

Correspondent: Mrs Diana Jones, Secretary, Marc Smith Foundation, 21 Highcroft, Husbands Bosworth, Lutterworth, Leicestershire, LE17 6LF (01858 880741)

Sir Thomas White Loan Charity

Eligibility: People aged between 18 and 34 who have lived in the county of Leicestershire for a minimum of five years.

Types of grants: No grants. Nine-year interest-free loans (present maximum of £12,000) to help with starting businesses. Loans up to £5,000 are also given to people with a degree who wish to do further study.

Annual grant total: In 2005 the charity had assets of £2.8 million and an income of £173,000. Grants to 20 individuals totalled £62,000.

Applications: In writing to the correspondent, including a business plan. The trustees meet in February, May, August and November.

Correspondent: Mrs Wendy Faulkner, Charnwood Court, 5B Newalk, Leicester LE1 6TE (e-mail: wf@stwcharity.co.uk; website: www.stwcharity.co.uk)

Other information: Grants are also made to organisations.

The Wyvernian Foundation

Eligibility: People who live in the city or county of Leicester (i.e. those who have been permanently or ordinarily resident in the city or county for at least three years,

excluding those temporarily resident whilst undertaking a period of study).

Types of grants: One-off and recurrent grants, generally for those in further and higher education (including mature students), towards the cost of fees/living expenses, study or travel overseas, and possibly books and equipment where they are an integral part of the course. Childcare expenses may be given. Grants range from £50 to £300.

Exclusions: Grants are not given to those in private education.

Annual grant total: In 2004/05, the foundation had an income of £2,000 and total expenditure of £3,000. Grants totalled about £1,500.

Applications: An application form must be obtained by sending an sae to the correspondent. Applications should be completed by the applicant and supported by the sponsor. An sae and CV should also be submitted. They should be submitted by early February, May, August and December each year for consideration in the following months.

Correspondent: A R York, 11 Knighton Close, Broughton Astley, Leicester LE9 6UG (01455 285028)

Other information: The foundation makes grants to individuals including loans.

Ashby-de-la-Zouch

The Mary Smith Scholarship Fund

Eligibility: People under 25 who live in Ashby-de-la-Zouch.

Types of grants: Maintenance allowances and bursaries for any place of learning that is approved by the governors. Help is given towards the cost of books; educational outings; maintenance; study/travel broad; student exchange; equipment/instruments; protective clothing; and childcare (mature students only). Grants are also given to enable people to prepare for, or to assist entry into, a profession, trade or calling. Grants can be given to study music or the arts, or to travel abroad to pursue education.

Annual grant total: About £2,500 to £3,000 a year.

Applications: On a form available from the correspondent to be considered in April.

Correspondent: D Taylor, Education Finance Room 125, County Hall, Glenfield, Leicester LE3 8RF (Fax: 0116 265 6279; e-mail: e mail: dataylor@leics.gov.uk)

Cossington

Rev John Babington's Charity

Eligibility: People in need in the parish of Cossington.

Types of grants: One-off and recurrent grants according to need.

Annual grant total: About £2,000 a year.

Applications: In writing to: Smith-Woolley, Collingham, Newark, Nottinghamshire NG23 7LG.

Correspondent: G Dickie, Chair, Old Manor House, Cossington, Leicestershire LE7 4UU (01509 812340).

Great Glen

Great Glen Town Charity

Eligibility: People who live in the parish of Great Glen who are in need.

Types of grants: One-off and recurrent grants, for example, to people going to university, people starting work and people undertaking voluntary work in their gap year.

Annual grant total: About £2,000 to local organisations and individuals.

Applications: In writing to the correspondent. Applications from outside the beneficial area will not be acknowledged.

Correspondent: Mrs H M Hill, Secretary, 35 Ashby Rise, Great Glen, Leicester, Leicestershire LE8 9GB

Keyham

Keyham Educational Foundation

Eligibility: People up to 25 who live in the parish of Keyham, Leicestershire, who are in need. People who have strong family connections with the parish can also be considered.

Types of grants: One-off grants ranging between £100 and £1,000.

Annual grant total: In 2004 the foundation had an income of £5,500 and a total expenditure of £9,200. Grants totalled about £8,000.

Applications: In writing to the correspondent, to be submitted directly by the individual, for consideration in March and October. Urgent applications can be considered at other times. If the applicant does not live in Keyham, information about their connection with residents should be provided with the application.

Correspondent: D B Whitcomb, Chair, Tanglewood, Snows Lane, Leicester, Leicestershire LE7 9JS

Other information: If funds are available, grants are made to groups which benefit the parish.

Leicester

Alderman Newton's Educational Foundation

Eligibility: People under 25 years of age who live (or people who have one parent who lives) in the city of Leicester.

Types of grants: Grants are given towards the cost of school uniforms, other school clothing, books, equipment/instruments, fees, educational outings and study or travel overseas.

Annual grant total: In 2004/05 the trust had assets of £2.4 million, an income of £112,000 and gave grants to organisations and individuals totalling £111,000.

Applications: On an application form, available from the correspondent, including details of income from all sources, details of the amount required and at least two references. Applications can be submitted directly by the individual.

Correspondent: P Griffiths, Leicester Charity Link, 20a Millstone Lane, Leicester, LE1 5JN (0116 222 2200)

The W P B Pearson Bequest

Eligibility: Pupils who have received their early education at council or denominational schools in the city of Leicester and who proceed to a training college for teachers or to any university or college of higher education.

Types of grants: A non-recurrent award of £30 to £50 to each eligible student to help with college or university fees, to supplement existing grants, or to help those on teacher training courses.

Annual grant total: In 2004/05 the bequest had a total income of £1,000 and no expenditure.

Applications: Any secondary school in the city of Leicester may write to the correspondent with the names and addresses of recommended students whom they consider meet the criteria (as outlined above). Applications can also be made directly in writing to the correspondent.

Correspondent: Hazel Noakes-Checklin, Education Finance Department, Leicester City Council Education Department, Malborough House, 38 Welford Road, Leicester LE 7AA (0116 252 7756; Fax: 0116 224 1004; e-mail: hazel.noakes-checklin@leicester.gov.uk)

Other information: The correspondent for this trust is likely to change during the lifetime of this guide, however the present correspondent will forward any relevant post.

Loughborough

The Dawson & Fowler Foundation

Eligibility: People who have lived in the borough of Loughborough (including Hathern) for a period of not less than three years and are aged between 12 and 25 years.

Types of grants: Help towards the cost of education, training, apprenticeship or equipment for those undergoing further educational courses.

Exclusions: No grants are given for accommodation, subsistence, day to day travelling costs, tuition, examination fees or creche costs. Applications from groups of students or classes of pupils cannot be considered.

Annual grant total: About 100 grants (from about 150 applications) totalling at least £20,000 each year.

Applications: On a form available from the correspondent or a school office. The trustees only meet quarterly so applications should be made well in advance to avoid disappointment.

Correspondent: The Clerk to the Trustees, c/o PO Box 73, Loughborough, Leicestershire LE11 0GA

John Storer's Educational Foundation

Eligibility: People under the age of 25 at any stage or level of their education, undertaking study of any subject and living in the old borough of Loughborough who are in need.

Types of grants: One-off grants in the form of scholarships, bursaries or maintenance allowances for employment training, further education, educational travel, musical or physical training.

Annual grant total: In 2005 the trust had an income of £6,600 and an expenditure of £6,000. Grants totalled about £5,000.

Applications: In writing to the correspondent.

Correspondent: Mrs K Jamieson, Clerk, 20 Churchgate, Loughborough, Leicestershire LE11 1UD

Oadby

The Oadby Educational Foundation

Eligibility: People with a home address within the former urban district of Oadby and were educated in Oadby.

Types of grants: One-off grants in the range of £50 and £200 are made to schoolchildren, college students and undergraduates, including those towards uniforms/clothing, study/travel abroad and equipment/instruments.

(ii) People of any age can receive one-off grants towards expeditions and voluntary work such as Operation Raleigh or Voluntary Service Overseas.

Grants are in the range of £50 and £200.

Annual grant total: In 2005 the foundation had assets of £1.1 million and an income of £32,000. The sum of £12,000 was distributed in 193 educational grants to individuals with a further £350 distributed in four relief-in-need grants.

Applications: On a form available from the correspondent. They should be submitted either through the individual's school, college or educational welfare agency, or directly by the individual. They are considered on the second Friday in March, June and October (the deadline for grants to undergraduates is 1 October). Applicants must have a home address in the parish of Oadby.

Correspondent: Rodger Moodie, Hon. Secretary, 26 Richmond Way, Oadby, Leicestershire LE2 5TR (0116 271 6279)

Other information: Grants are also made to organisations (£22,000 in 2005).

Peatling Parva

Richard Bradgate's Charity

Eligibility: People living in the parish of Peatling Parva only.

Types of grants: Help for students in further and higher education towards books or help with fees/living expenses or for people starting work for books and equipment/instruments.

Annual grant total: Grants total about £1,000 a year.

Applications: In writing to the correspondent. Applications are usually considered in October/November.

Correspondent: Dr Brian Higginson, The Old Rectory, Main Street, Peatling Parva, Leicester LE17 5QA (0116 247 8240)

Smisby

The Smisby Parochial Charity

Eligibility: People in need who live in Smisby.

Types of grants: Grants are given to schoolchildren, people starting work, further and higher education students, mature students and postgraduates towards books and equipment. Grants are in the range of £10 and £500.

Annual grant total: About £12,000 in 2003/04, mostly for welfare purposes.

Applications: In writing to the correspondent.

Correspondent: Mrs S Heap, Clerk, Cedar Lawns, Forties Lane, Smisby, Ashby-De-La-Zouch, Leicestershire LE65 2SN (01530 414179; Fax: 01530 414171)

Wigston

The Norton, Salisbury & Brailsford Educational Foundation

Eligibility: People under the age of 25 who live in Wigston.

Types of grants: One-off grants towards the cost of books, tools, equipment and travel, including travel abroad.

Annual grant total: In 2004, the foundation had an income of around £2,000, and a total expenditure of £1,800.

Applications: On a form available from the correspondent. Applications are considered three times a year, usually in March, September and November.

Correspondent: Brenda Moore, Bushloe House, Station Road, Wigston, Leicester LE18 2DR (0116 257 2606)

Wymeswold

The Wymeswold Parochial Charities

Eligibility: People in need who have lived in Wymeswold for the last two years.

Types of grants: One-off grants are given for educational and relief-in-need purposes.

Annual grant total: Grants total about £4,000 a year.

Applications: In writing to the correspondent at any time.

Correspondent: The Trustees, 97 Brook Street, Wymeswold, Loughborough LE12 6TT

Lincolnshire

The Alenson & Erskine Educational Foundation

Eligibility: People who live in the parishes of Wrangle, Old Leake and New Leake and are under 25. Applications are only considered from local people who have received at least five years education in the parish.

Types of grants: Grants vary and are given to: (i) school leavers to help with books, equipment, clothing or travel; (ii) college or university students to help with fees or to supplement existing grants, but not to travel or study abroad.

Schoolchildren, other than those with special education needs, are only considered if family difficulties are serious.

Annual grant total: In 2005 the trust had an income of £3,300 and a total expenditure of £4,500. The trust has previously stated that the grant total varies from year to year.

Applications: In writing to the correspondent. Applicants can only claim for what they have bought and not what they would like to buy and so must submit receipts with the application, which are usually considered in October/November.

Correspondent: Margaret Barnett, 29 Saddlers Way, Fishtoft, Boston, Lincolnshire PE21 0BB

Allen's Charity (Apprenticing Branch)

Eligibility: Young people who live in Long Sutton and Sutton Bridge.

Types of grants: Grants for apprentices.

Annual grant total: About £4,000 a year.

Applications: On a form available from the correspondent. The scheme is advertised in the local press and is promoted by local employers.

Correspondent: K Savage, Lenton Lodge, 4 Armitage Close, Holbeach, Spalding, Lincolnshire PE12 7QL

Cowell and Porrill

Eligibility: People under 25 who live or whose parent(s) live in the parishes of Benington and Leverton, at any level or stage of their education and undertaking the study of any subject.

Types of grants: Grants of £250 to £600 for general educational needs.

Annual grant total: In 2005 the trust had an income of £11,000 and a total expenditure of £15,000. Grants were made to 17 individuals totalling £7,000.

Applications: On a form available from the correspondent, to be submitted by the end of July for consideration in September each year. Applications should be submitted directly by the individual.

Correspondent: R J Hooton, 33 Glen Drive, Boston, Lincolnshire PE21 7QB (01205 310088; Fax: 01205 311282)

English Speaking Union Lincolnshire Branch

Eligibility: Students, aged between 16 and 25, who live in Lincolnshire and wish to teach English in an overseas school or to assist in spreading the use of the English language.

Types of grants: Scholarships of between £250 and £1,000 towards the cost of relevant travel.

Annual grant total: In 2005 the trust had assets of £33,000, an income of £1,500 and a total expenditure of £1,400, all of which was given in grants to four individuals.

Applications: In writing to the correspondent, with a supporting letter if possible. Applications should be submitted in March and are considered in April.

Correspondent: Sir Michael Graydon, The Barn, Eagle Hall, Swinderby LN6 9HZ (01522 868058; Fax: 01522 868058; e-mail: mikegraydon@clara.net)

Other information: Applicants will be interviewed.

For the Kids – see entry on page 121

Correspondent: Debbie Westlake, c/o Viking FM, Commercial Road, Hull HU1 2SG (01482 593193; e-mail: debbie. westlake@vikingfm.co.uk; website: www. vikingfm.co.uk)

Gainsborough Educational Charity

Eligibility: People of at least secondary school age and under 25 who live, or whose parents live, in the former urban district council area of Gainsborough or the parishes of Thonock, Morton and Lea and are in need.

Types of grants: Grants are given to schoolchildren, further and higher education students, postgraduates and people starting work, including those for uniforms/other school clothing, books, equipment/instruments, fees, educational outings in the UK and study or travel abroad. Grants can also be made for the study of music or other arts.

Annual grant total: In 2004/05 the charity had an income of £5,500 and a total expenditure of £4,500. Grants totalled about £4,000.

Applications: On a form available from the correspondent for consideration in March and November; applications can be submitted directly by the individual up to three weeks prior to this. References are required.

Correspondent: Mrs Maria Bradley, Clerk to the Trustees, Burton & Dyson Solicitors, 22 Market Place, Gainsborough, Lincolnshire DN21 2BZ (01427 610761; Fax: 01427 616866; e-mail: law@ burtondyson.co.uk)

The Kirton-in-Lindsey Exhibition Endowment

Eligibility: People who live in Kirton-in-Lindsey, Hibaldstow, Redbourne or Manton, Messingham, Blyborough or Waddingham, Grayingham, Northorpe or Scotter and Scotton and have attended one of the following primary schools for at least two years: Kirton-in-Lindsey, Scotter, Messingham, Waddingham or Hibaldstow.

Types of grants: Grants to help with the cost of books and other essentials for schoolchildren/mature students going on to college, university or teacher training.

Annual grant total: In 2004/05 the trust had an income of £2,500 and a total expenditure of £3,400. Grants are made to individuals totalling about £2,500.

Applications: On a form available from the correspondent to be submitted before 1 September.

Correspondent: Mrs P Hoey, 6 Queen Street, Kirton-in-Lindsey, Gainsborough, Lincolnshire DN21 4NS

Kitchings Educational Charity

Eligibility: People under 25 who live in Bardney, Bucknall, Southrey or Tupholme.

Types of grants: Grants to further and higher education students to assist with books, equipment/instruments, fees and other educational expenses.

Exclusions: No support is given to students who choose to take A-levels (or equivalent) at college when they could take the same course at their school.

Annual grant total: In 2004/05 the trust had an income of £6,600 and a total expenditure of £5,000. Grants totalled about £4,000.

Applications: In writing to the correspondent. Applications can be submitted either through the individual's school, college, educational welfare agency or directly by the individual. They are considered in October and should be received by the end of September.

Correspondent: Mrs M Sankey, 50 Station Road, Barnley, Lincolnshire, LN3 5UB

The Kitchings General Charity

Eligibility: Students, especially mature (over 25 years of age), part-time, and vocational students, living in the parish of Bardney (covers Stainfield, Apley, Tupholme and Bucknall).

Types of grants: Grants are given to schoolchildren for playgroup fees and excursions and further and students for books. Grants are in the range of £200 and £500.

Annual grant total: About £1,000 a year.

Applications: In writing to the correspondent giving details of age, course name, college and brief description of education to date. Applications are considered in May, October and January.

Correspondent: Mrs J Smith, Secretary, 42 Abbey Road, Bardney, Lincoln LN3 5XA (01526 398505)

The Kochan Trust

Eligibility: People living in Lincolnshire who are in need of financial assistance for their study of the creative arts, music or veterinary medicine.

Types of grants: One-off grants according to need, e.g. towards concerts or instruments for students of the creative arts and music, or towards research projects or general course expenses for veterinary students.

Annual grant total: In 2005/06 the trust had an income of £21,000, all of which was allocated in grants. Beneficiaries were two churches, nine veterinary students and five musicians.

Applications: In writing to the correspondent initially, either directly by the individual or through the individual's school/college/educational welfare agency, with brief details about who you are and what you would like the grant for. An application form is then sent out. Applications are considered January, April, July and November.

Correspondent: Revd R Massingberd-Mundy, Secretary to the Trustees, The Old Post Office, West Raynham, Fakenham, Norfolk NR21 7AD (01328 838611; Fax: 01328 838698)

The Mapletoft Scholarship Foundation

Eligibility: People who have attended primary school in the parishes of North Thoresby, Grainsby and Waite, for not less than two years.

Types of grants: Grants up to about £150 to help with further/higher education books and fees/living expenses or to supplement existing grants. Travel grants are also available. Grants are recurrent.

Annual grant total: In 2003/04, the foundation had an an income of around £3,000, and a total expenditure of £2,800. Grants totalled around £2,000.

Applications: Applications should be received not later than 30 September for consideration in November.

Correspondent: P M Purves, Solicitor, The Old Vicarage, Church Street, Louth, Lincolnshire, LN11 9DE (01507 602234; Fax: 01507 604807)

Sir Thomas Middlecott's Exhibition Foundation

Eligibility: Students who live in the parishes of Algarkirk, Fosdyke, Frampton, Kirton, Sutterton and Wyberton, who are in further/higher education and are aged under 25. Applicants must have attended a maintained primary school in the area for at least two years.

Types of grants: Grants are given to students in further/higher education towards books, and equipment/instruments. Grants usually range from £140 to £180.

Annual grant total: In 2004/05 the trust had an income of £15,000 and a total expenditure of £23,000. Grants were made to individuals totalling around £12,000.

Applications: On a form available from the correspondent to be submitted directly by the individual. Applications are considered in October and should be submitted by the end of September.

Correspondent: Frank J Wilson, 57a Bourne Road, Spalding, Lincolnshire PE11 1JR (01775 766117; Fax: 01775 766117)

Mary Parnham's Lenton Charity

Eligibility: People under 23 who live in parishes of Lenton, Keisby and Osgodby.

Types of grants: Help with the cost of books, clothing and other essentials for schoolchildren. Help may also be available for those at college or university and those undertaking apprenticeships or other professional training. Preference is given to people with special educational needs and to schoolchildren with serious family difficulties so the child has to be educated away from home. Grants range from £20 to £250.

Annual grant total: In 2004/05 the trust had an income of £500 and no expenditure.

Applications: No grants have been made since 2000/01 as the trust is trying to build up its asset fund so that it 'will continue to survive'.

Correspondent: F P J Grenfell, Lenton House, Ingoldsby Road, Lenton, Grantham, Lincolnshire NG33 4HB

The Phillips Educational Foundation

Eligibility: People living in the parishes of Long Sutton, Little Sutton and Sutton Bridge, aged between 11 and 20.

Types of grants: Grants of up to £200 are given: (i) to schoolchildren for books, equipment, clothing or travel; (ii) to students in further/ higher education towards the cost of books and travel or study overseas; and (iii) for help with the study of music and the other arts, as well as for overseas study.

Exclusions: Grants are not given for school fees or maintenance, student fees/living expenses or for people starting work.

Annual grant total: Around £2,500 a year.

Applications: On a form available from the correspondent. They are considered at trustees' meetings usually held in July and September.

Correspondent: K Savage, Clerk, Lenton Lodge, 94 Wignals Gate, Holbeach, Spalding, Lincolnshire PE12 7HR

The Pike & Eure Educational Foundation

Eligibility: Young people between the ages of 16 and 25 who are in need and live in the parishes of Washingborough and Heighington in Lincolnshire.

Types of grants: One-off grants for students in further or higher education

towards books and equipment/instruments.

Exclusions: People starting work are not eligible.

Annual grant total: In 2005, the income totalled £3,300 with an expenditure £1,500.

Applications: On a form available from the correspondent, submitted directly by the individual, with information about the nature of the course, location, and the occupation of the parent(s). Applications should be submitted in early August for consideration in October.

Correspondent: Mrs Susan Smith, Clerk to the Trustees, 18 Oxford Close, Washingborough, Lincoln LN4 1DT (01522 792406)

The Educational Foundation of Philip & Sarah Stanford

Eligibility: People under 25 who live in the ancient parishes of Aylesby, Barnoldby-le-Beck, Bradley, Irby-upon-Humber and Laceby.

Types of grants: Grants of £60 to £100 towards books, clothing or equipment/instruments for college students and undergraduates.

Exclusions: Grants are not given for subjects and courses available in schools, nor for help with student fees, travel or living expenses.

Annual grant total: In 2005, the foundation had an income of £3,600 and a total expenditure of £3,200.

Applications: On a form available from the correspondent, submitted directly by the individual, including reasons for the application and plans for the future. The closing date is 1 October each year. Applications must be in the applicant's own handwriting.

Correspondent: Mrs E Hine, Clerk, 86 Brigsley Road, Waltham, Grimsby, South Humberside, DN37 0LA

The Sutton St James United Charities

Eligibility: People who live in the parish boundary of Sutton St James, under the age of 25.

Types of grants: (i) Grants, of up to £100, to all pupils living in the village at age 11 when transferring to secondary schools, to help with books, equipment, clothing etc.

(ii) Grants, of up to £100, to help students taking A-levels and further education courses.

(iii) Grants, of up to £600 a year, to students over 18 at university to help with general expenses and to supplement existing grants.

Annual grant total: In 2003/04 the charities had an income of £8,400 and a total expenditure of £10,000. This was

divided between education and relief-in-need grants.

Applications: On a form available from the correspondent. Applications are considered in April/May for primary school children and December/January for A-level and university students.

Correspondent: K Savage, Clerk, Lenton Lodge, 4 Armitage Close, Holbeach, Spalding, Lincolnshire PE12 7QL (01406 490157; e-mail: keithsavage@ btinternet.com)

The Tetford and Salmonby Education Trust

Eligibility: People under 25 who live in Tetford and Salmonby

Types of grants: One-off and recurrent grants are given to: schoolchildren for uniforms/other school clothing and educational outings in the UK; and people starting work and students in further and higher education for clothing, books, equipment/instruments, fees, maintenance/living expenses, educational outings in the UK and study or travel abroad.

Annual grant total: About £1,000 a year.

Applications: On a form available from the correspondent to be submitted directly by the individual. Applications are considered quarterly but are accepted at any time.

Correspondent: P M Purves, 69 Church Street, Louth, Lincolnshire LN11 9BZ

Dame Margaret Thorold's Apprenticing Charity

Eligibility: People aged 18 to 25, who live in the ancient parishes of Sedgebrook, Marston and Cranwell.

Types of grants: Small cash grants (currently £150) to assist students in further or higher education, especially vocational training. Grants may be recurrent or one-off and are towards books, fees/living expenses or study/travel abroad.

Annual grant total: In 2004 the charity had an income of £1,600 and a total expenditure of £2,100. Grants totalled about £2,000.

Applications: Applications should be submitted in writing by the individual or parent/guardian or through the school/college/educational welfare agency, by mid-January for consideration in February. If appropriate, a letter of support from the employer or place of training should be included with the application.

Correspondent: T S Kelway, Clerk, Tallents, 3 Middlegate, Newark, Nottinghamshire NG24 1AQ (01636 671881; e-mail: tim.kelway@ tallents.co.uk)

Barkston

The Barkston Educational Foundation

Eligibility: People under 25 who live or whose parents live in the parish of Barkston.

Types of grants: One-off and recurrent grants for educational purposes, according to need.

Annual grant total: In 2003/04 the foundation had an income of £5,700 and a total expenditure of £14,800. Further information was not available.

Applications: In writing to the correspondent.

Correspondent: T S Kelway, Clerk, Tallents, 3 Middlegate, Newark, Nottinghamshire NG24 1AQ (e-mail: tim.kelway@tallents.co.uk)

Boston

The Sutterton Education Trust

Eligibility: People in need who live in parishes of Sutterton or Ambellhill in Boston.

Types of grants: Grants of between £50 and £200 are available for: (i) uniforms, school clothing, books and educational outings for schoolchildren; (ii) books, fees, living expenses, study or travel aboard for students in further/ higher education, but not overseas students or student exchange; and (iii) books, travel and fees for mature students, but not childcare. Each case is considered individually.

Annual grant total: In 2004/05 the trust had both an income and total expenditure of £1,900. Grants were made to 12 individuals totalling £1,600.

Applications: In writing to the correspondent.

Correspondent: Mrs Deidre Pauline McCumiskey, 50 Hessle Avenue, Boston, Lincolnshire PE21 8DA (01205 366327)

Corby Glenn

The Willoughby Memorial Trust

Eligibility: People under 25 who live in the Corby Glen area of Lincolnshire.

Types of grants: One-off grants are available to schoolchildren for help with books, fees and educational outings, and to students in further/higher education for help with books and fees.

Annual grant total: In 2004 the trust had assets of £776,000 and an income of £31,000. After funding its own projects, a total of £2,400 was given in grants.

Applications: On a form available from the correspondent, to be submitted by the individual's headteacher.

Correspondent: Timothy Paul Clarke, Grimsthorpe House, Grimsthorpe, Bourne, Lincolnshire PE10 0LY (01778 951205; Fax: 01778 951259)

Other information: This trust is set-up to give grants to schools and organisations, although it budgets £750 a year for grants to individuals.

Deeping

The Deeping St James United Charities

Eligibility: College and university students from the parish of St James, Deeping.

Types of grants: Grants are given towards books.

Annual grant total: In 2004 the trust had assets of £1 million and an income of £36,000. Grants were made totalling £21,000. The sum of £2,900 was distributed in books grants. Grants to local schools and individuals totalled £5,700.

Applications: In writing to the correspondent for consideration at the start of March, June, September and December.

Correspondent: R Moulsher, The Beeches, Windmill Way, Empingham Road, Stamford, Lincolnshire, PE9 2RH

Other information: This trust also gives grants to individuals for relief-in-need purposes and local organisations.

Dorrington

Dorrington Welfare Charity

Eligibility: Primary school children who have lived in the village of Dorrington for at least the last year.

Types of grants: One-off grants of amounts up to £200.

Annual grant total: In 2005 the charity had assets of £62,000 and an income of almost £2,000. Out of a total expenditure of £1,700 the sum of £1,100 was distributed in 42 grants to individuals for welfare purposes and £210 in 14 grants for educational purposes.

Applications: In writing to the correspondent or any trustee, directly by the individual. Applications are considered at any time.

Correspondent: Miss K E Griffiths, 59 Main Street, Dorrington, Lincoln LN4 3PX (01526 832802; e-mail: keg@kgriffiths22.freeserve.co.uk)

Fleet

The Deacon & Fairfax Educational Foundation

Eligibility: People who live in the parish of Fleet (Lincolnshire), aged between 16 and 25 and attending further education.

Types of grants: Grants are given to further and higher education students, including those for clothing, books, equipment/instruments and fees.

Annual grant total: In 2004/05, the foundation had an income of £3,700 and a total expenditure of £2,800. Grants totalled about £2,000.

Applications: In writing to the correspondent directly by the individual. Applications are considered in October and should be received in August or September.

Correspondent: Mrs Jill Harrington, Coubro Chambers, 11 West End, Holbeam, Lincolnshire PE12 7LW

Other information: Grants are also made to schools in the area.

Frampton

The Frampton Educational Foundation

Eligibility: People in higher education who have lived in the ancient parish of Frampton for at least five years.

Types of grants: One-off and recurrent grants according to need.

Annual grant total: In 2004/05 the foundation had an income of £5,800 and a total expenditure of £6,300. Grants were made to individuals totalling around £3,000.

Applications: In writing to the correspondent. Applications are considered in early October and students must reapply each year.

Correspondent: The Clerk, 153 Swineshead Road, Frampton, Fen, Boston, Lincolnshire PE20 1SB (01775 711333; e-mail: louise@mooret.co.uk)

Holbeach

The Farmer Educational Foundation

Eligibility: People who live in the parish of Holbeach, South Lincolnshire, and are above the statutory school-leaving age.

Types of grants: Grants, to a usual maximum of about £100, to help students in higher/further education and to assist schools serving Holbeach with projects.

Annual grant total: In 2004/05 the foundation had assets of £486,000, an income of £21,000 and a total expenditure of £17,000. Grants to 39 individuals totalled £3,900, with organisations receiving almost £10,000.

Applications: On a form available from Holbeach Library, to be submitted by the individual at the end of August. Applications are considered in September.

Correspondent: M J H Griffin, Hurdletree Farm, Hurdletree Bank, Whaplode, Spalding, Lincolnshire PE12 6SS

Horncastle

George Jobson's Trust

Eligibility: Young people in need who attend or have attended schools in Horncastle or live in the parish of Horncastle.

Types of grants: Recurrent grants between £50 and £500 for general education costs.

Exclusions: Postgraduate students are not eligible for a grant.

Annual grant total: In 2004/05 the trust had an income of £32,000 and a total expenditure of £52,000, almost all of which was given in grants, mostly to individuals.

Applications: On a form available from the correspondent. Applications can be submitted directly by the individual or through a social worker, Citizens Advice or other welfare agency.

Correspondent: Miss Jacquelina Johns, Clerk, Messrs Chattertons, 5 South Street, Horncastle, Lincolnshire LN9 6DS (01507 522456; Fax: 01507 522445)

Kesteven

The Kesteven Children in Need

Eligibility: Children/young people up to the age of 16 who live in Kesteven.

Types of grants: Grants of up to £500 towards books, clothing and educational outings.

Annual grant total: Grants total around £1,000 a year.

Applications: Generally through local social workers, health visitors, teachers and education officers. Information should include the family situation, the age of the child and his/her special needs. Applications are considered throughout the year.

Correspondent: Mrs Jane Howard, Nocton Rise, Sleaford Road, Nocton, Lincoln LN4 2AF (01522 791217)

Lincoln

The Leeke Church Schools & Educational Foundation

Eligibility: People between 16 and 24 years who live, or whose parents live, in the city of Lincoln. People studying in Lincoln with a home address elsewhere are ineligible.

Types of grants: One-off and recurrent grants in the range of £150 to £500 each term. Grants are given to: schoolchildren for educational outings in the UK, study or travel abroad and student exchanges; and further and higher education students for uniforms, books, equipment/instruments, fees, educational outings in the UK, study or travel abroad and student exchanges. Grants are not given for private education – there must be a financial need.

Annual grant total: In 2005 the foundation gave £20,000 to individuals aged 16-24 and the schools listed in the trust deed.

Applications: On a form available from the correspondent to be submitted by the individual for consideration at any time. Educational costs should be listed, and either the real amount given, or a fair estimate.

Correspondent: Mrs C Goddard, 48 Gray Street, Lincoln LN1 3HL (01522 522058)

Lindsey

The Joseph Nickerson Charitable Foundation

Eligibility: Young people in further education in the old county of Lindsey. Beneficiaries are usually aged 18 or over and are studying at university.

Types of grants: Recurrent grants of about £900 a year, donated in three tranches.

Annual grant total: In 2004/05, grants to organisations and individuals totalled £12,000.

Applications: In writing to the correspondent. Applications for grants starting in September should be made by 30 June for consideration in July.

Correspondent: Eric White, Estate Office, Rothwell, Market Rasen, Lincolnshire LN7 6BJ

Moulton

The Moulton Poors' Lands Charity

Eligibility: People in need, generally older people, who live in the civil parish of Moulton.

Types of grants: Mainly relief-in-need grants, very occasional education grants are available.

Annual grant total: In 2005 the trust had assets of £889,000 and an income of £28,000. Grants to individuals totalled £7,500.

Applications: In writing to the correspondent, usually through a trustee. Applications are considered in April and December.

Correspondent: R W Lewis, Clerk for the Charity, Maples & Son, 23 New Road, Spalding, Lincolnshire PE11 1DH

Navenby

The Navenby Towns Farm Trust

Eligibility: University students and young people doing their A-levels who are in need and live in the village of Navenby.

Types of grants: Recurrent grants while at university, but only following reapplication every year.

Exclusions: No grants can be given outside the village.

Annual grant total: In 2004/05 it had an income of £9,500 and a total expenditure of £8,500. Grants are made to individuals and organisations.

Applications: On a form available from the correspondent, the post office, or Smith and Willows the newsagents. Applications are considered in September. Unsolicited applications are not responded to.

Correspondent: The Secretary, Winton House, Grantham Road, Navenby, Lincoln LN5 0JJ (01522 810868)

North Lincolnshire

The Withington Education Trust

Eligibility: People who live in the area of the new North Lincolnshire Council. Applicants must be under the age of 21.

Types of grants: Grants to help with fees/living expenses, travel and other education needs, but not normally books or equipment. Grants to assist with non-formal education such as music and ballet are also given. Grants range from £50 to £300.

Exclusions: Grants towards fees for private schooling are not given.

Annual grant total: In 2004/05 the trust had an income of £5,800, and a total expenditure of £1,800. Grants totalled about £1,500.

Applications: In writing at any time, preferably supported by the school or college. Applications are considered once per term.

Correspondent: John Irving, Treasurer & Secretary, Education Office, North Lincolnshire Council, PO Box 35, Brigg,

South Humberside, DN20 8XJ
(01724 297200; Fax: 01724 297242;
e-mail: john.irving@northlinc.gov.uk)

Potterhanworth

The Christ's Hospital Endowment at Potterhanworth

Eligibility: People under the age of 25 who live, or whose parent(s) live, in the parish of Potterhanworth, Lincolnshire.

Types of grants: Grants are available for the cost of educational visits for schoolchildren and towards fees for extra-curricular activities such as music, the arts and social and physical training. A block grant only is given to further education students.

Exclusions: Grants are not given for other costs for schoolchildren such as books or for school fees, nor for people starting work, other than for equipment.

Annual grant total: About £10,000 a year.

Applications: In writing to the correspondent, either by the individual, his/her parents, or through the individual's school, college or university. Applications are considered once a year in November and must include valid receipts where applicable. Applications must be received before 31 October.

Correspondent: Mrs Y Woodcock, The Conifers, Barff Road, Potterhanworth, Lincoln LN4 2DU (01522 790942)

Quadring

The Cowley & Brown School Foundation

Eligibility: People under 25 who live in the ancient parish of Quadring.

Types of grants: Grants towards the cost of books, clothing and other essentials for schoolchildren. Help may also be available for students at college or university.

Annual grant total: In 2004, the foundation had an income of £3,300 and a total expenditure of £3,000.

Applications: In writing to the correspondent. Applications are considered in July and November.

Correspondent: K J Watts, Clerk, 99 Hawthorne Bank, Spalding, Lincolnshire PE11 1JQ (01775 760911)

Scunthorpe

The James R Heslam Settlement

Eligibility: People who live in the 'petty session division' of Scunthorpe.

Types of grants: One-off and recurrent grants or loans to help with maintenance/living expenses, books and essential equipment for education purposes for students in further or higher education, including vocational and mature students.

Annual grant total: In 2004/05 the trust had an income of £2,400 and a total expenditure of £4,000. Grants were made to four individuals totalling £3,000.

Applications: In writing to the correspondent. Applications must include a cv and details of the applicant's financial situation.

Correspondent: R J H Sumpter, c/o Symes Bains Broomer, 2 Park Square, Laneham Street, Scunthorpe DN15 6JH (01724 281616)

South Holland

The Moulton Harrox Educational Foundation

Eligibility: People up to 25 who live in the South Holland district council area.

Types of grants: Grants for school pupils and college students, including mature students, to help with books, equipment, fees, clothing, educational outings and study or travel abroad. Preference is given to schoolchildren with serious family difficulties so the child has to educated away from home, and to people with special education needs.

One-off and recurrent grants according to need. Individuals must reapply in order to receive the grant in the following year.

Annual grant total: In 2005, the foundation had net assets of £119,000, an income of £89,000,and a toal expenditure of £118,500. During the year the foundation gave grants to individuals totalling £500.

Applications: On a form available from the correspondent. Applications should be submitted before 31 August for consideration in September.

Correspondent: R W Lewis, Clerk for the Charity, Messrs Maples & Son, Solicitors, 23 New Road, Spalding, Lincolnshire PE11 1DH (01775 722261; Fax: 01775 767525)

The Spalding Relief-in-Need Charity

Eligibility: People in need who live in the area covered by South Holland District Council with priority to residents of the parishes of Spalding, Cowbit, Deeping St Nicholas, Pinchbeck and Weston.

Types of grants: One-off grants in the range of £100 to £400. Normally payments are made directly to suppliers.

Annual grant total: In 2004 the charity had assets of £490,000 and an income of £25,000. Grants to 116 individuals totalled £28,000.

Applications: On a form available from the charity. Applications can be submitted directly by the individual or assisted if appropriate by a social worker, teacher, school, Citizens Advice, other welfare agency or third party. Grants are considered on a weekly basis.

Correspondent: Spalding Relief-in-Need Charity, Dembleby House, 12 Broad Street, Spalding, Lincolnshire PE11 1ES (01775 768774; Fax: 01775 725842; e-mail: p.skells@knipemiller.co.uk)

Other information: Grants can also be made to organisations.

Stickford

The Stickford Relief-in-Need Charity

Eligibility: Schoolchildren in need who live in the parish of Stickford.

Types of grants: School clothing grants. Grants are also made for welfare purposes.

Annual grant total: In 2004 the charity had an income of £14,000 and a total expenditure of £18,000.

Applications: In writing to the correspondent. Applications should be submitted directly by the individual and are considered all year.

Correspondent: Mrs K L Bunting, Clerk, The Old Vicarage, Church Road, Stickford, Boston, Lincolnshire PE22 8EP

Sutton Bridge

Sutton Bridge Power Fund

Eligibility: Adults living, and children living or attending schools, in Sutton Bridge, Lincolnshire (very clearly defined boundaries which incorporate Waldpole Cross Keys, Norfolk, Tydd St Giles, Cambridgeshire, Sutton Bridge, Tydd St Mary, Lincolnshire).

Types of grants: One-off and recurrent grants according to need.

Annual grant total: Each year £15,000 is made available for grants to individuals.

Applications: In writing to the correspondent.

Correspondent: Anthony Gallagher, EDF Energy, 40 Grosvenor Place, London SW1X 7EN

Sutton St Edmund

The Sutton St Edmund Charities United Educational Foundation

Eligibility: Children or young persons who live in the ancient parish of Sutton St Edmund.

Types of grants: Recurrent grants are given to further and higher education students for books, equipment/instruments, fees and maintenance/living expenses. The amount given in individual grants is dependent on the number of applicants and the amount of available income.

Annual grant total: In 2004/05, the charities had an income of £1,400 and a total expenditure of £1,100.

Applications: In writing to the correspondent either directly by the individual, or through a parent or guardian including details of the course attended i.e. A-level, NVQ, degree, and so on. Applications should be submitted by mid-February each year and grants are paid in April.

Correspondent: K Savage, Lenton Lodge, 94 Wignals Gate, Holbeach, Spalding, Lincolnshire PE12 7HR (01406 490157; e-mail: keithsavage@btinternet.com)

Waddingham

James Thompson Educational Charity

Eligibility: People under 25 who live in the parish of Waddingham and are in need.

Types of grants: One-off and recurrent grants ranging from £50 to £250. Grants are given to: schoolchildren towards school uniform, other school clothing, books, equipment/instruments and educational outings; and vocational students and students in further and higher education towards clothing, books, other equipment, fees/living expenses and study/travel overseas or in the UK.

Exclusions: No grants to children below primary school age.

Annual grant total: In 2004/05 the trust had assets of £22,000, an income of £3,100 and a total expenditure of £3,300. Grants were made to 25 individuals totalling £3,000.

Applications: In writing to the correspondent, either directly by the individual or by their parent or guardian, stating who requires the grant and why, the educational establishment attended and the course being studied. Applications are usually considered in September and should be received in the preceding month.

Correspondent: B Milton, Clerk to the Trustees, South View, Moor Road, Snitterby, Gainsborough, Lincolnshire DN21 4TT (01673 818314)

Other information: Grants are also given to schools which serve the parish.

Northampton-shire

Arnold's Education Foundation

Eligibility: People in need who are under 25 and live in the parishes of Stony Stratford, Buckinghamshire; Nether Heyford, Upper Heyford, Stowe-Nine-Churches, Weedon Bec, Northamptonshire; and the ancient parish of St Giles, Northampton. Preference for members of the Church of England.

Types of grants: One-off and recurrent grants for educational purposes (including social and physical training). Grants are made: for schoolchildren towards the cost of clothing, books, educational outings, maintenance and school fees; towards the cost of books, fees/living expenses, travel exchange and study or travel abroad for students in further or higher education; and towards books, equipment/instruments, clothing and travel for people starting work. Grants range from £200 to £500.

Annual grant total: In 2005 grants totalled £8,000, including £3,500 given in grants to 12 individuals.

Applications: On a form available by writing to the correspondent. Applications are considered in April and October.

Correspondent: The Clerk, c/o Messrs Wilson Browne, Solicitors, 60 Gold Street, Northampton NN1 1RS

The Hervey & Elizabeth Ekins Educational Charity

Eligibility: People who (i) have lived in the borough of Northampton or the parish of Great Doddington for not less than three years; (ii) attended a maintained school in Northampton for not less than one year and (iii) attended an Anglican church on a regular basis. Applicants should be under 25 (or in exceptional cases under 30). No grants to non-Anglicans.

Types of grants: Grants are given to schoolchildren, students in further or higher education and to people starting work towards books, equipment and educational outings in the UK and overseas. Grants are also given for music tuition fees.

Grants average around £200, but in exceptional circumstances can be for as much as £500. Other grants are given to a school for larger projects.

There is a preference for those entering the ministry of the Church of England.

Exclusions: Grants are not given for school fees.

Annual grant total: In 2004/05 the charity had an income of £212,000 and a total expenditure of £218,000. These unusually high figures are as a result of the charity selling its investments then reinvesting the proceeds. About £8,000 was distributed in grants to individuals, with about a further £15,000 distributed to schools.

Applications: In writing to the correspondent directly by the individual, including details of school and church attended. Applications are considered in January, March, May, September and November.

Correspondent: Mrs Elizabeth Fisher, 'The Pines' 36 Lower Street, Great Doddington, NN29 7TL (01933 224369)

The Horne Foundation

Eligibility: Schoolchildren and students who live in Northamptonshire and are in need.

Types of grants: Bursaries are made towards living expenses, course fees and so on, to a maximum of £5,000.

Annual grant total: In 2004/05, the foundation had assets of £5.9 million and an income of £238,000. Grants were made totalling £367,000 and included 23 student bursaries totalling £50,000 and four grants to individual students totalling £8,300.

Applications: The bursary scheme is run in conjunction with the local council, and bursaries to schoolchildren are made on the recommendation of schools. If the applicant is at school, he or she should therefore apply through the head teacher of the school. Students can apply to the trust directly, in writing. Applications are considered twice a year.

Correspondent: Mrs R M Harwood, PO Box 468, Church Stowe, Northampton, NN7 4WL

The Isham Educational Foundation

Eligibility: People under 25 who live in the ancient parish of Lamport and Hanging Houghton.

Types of grants: One-off and recurrent grants of between £50 and £1,000 are given to: (i) school pupils, to help with books, equipment, clothing, travel or school fees but not for maintenance; (ii) students in further/ higher education towards fees or to supplement existing grants; and (iii) those leaving school, college or university to prepare for or enter a trade, profession or calling.

Preference is given to schoolchildren with serious family difficulties so the child has to be educated away from home.

'In the allocation of all benefits the trustees

shall have regard to the principles of the Church of England.'

Annual grant total: About £1,000 is given in grants each year.

Applications: In writing to the correspondent. Applications can be submitted by the individual or by parents and are considered in July and November.

Correspondent: David Surtees-Dawson, 10 Church Street, Brigstock, Kettering, Northamptonshire NN14 3EX

The Dorothy Johnson Charitable Trust

Eligibility: People under 25 who were born and are living, have lived or were educated at some time in Northamptonshire.

Types of grants: One-off and recurrent grants in the range of £100 and £500. Grants are made to schoolchildren, college students, undergraduates, vocational students and people with special educational needs, towards clothing/ uniforms, fees, study/travel abroad, books, equipment/instruments, maintenance/ living expenses and excursions.

Annual grant total: In 2004/05 the trust had assets of £460,000, which generated an income of £20,000. Grants totalled £19,000, including 76 grants to individuals totalling £17,000.

Applications: In writing to the correspondent. Applications are considered three times a year.

Correspondent: Miss Z B Silins, Clerk, DNG Dove Naish, Eagle House, 28 Billing Road, Northampton NN1 5AJ (01604 657200; Fax: 01604 232251; e-mail: zinaida.silins@dovenaish.co.uk)

The Kettering Charities (Apprenticing)

Eligibility: People over 16 who live in the town of Kettering or Barton Seagrave and are in training or further education.

Types of grants: Grants are one-off and range from £25 to £200 and are for general educational needs. They are given towards students in further and higher education, vocational and mature students, people starting work and people with special educational needs.

Annual grant total: During 2004/05 six grants of £250 were made.

Applications: Applications should be made by the individual, their parent or guardian or through the individual's school, college or educational welfare agency for consideration in November and February. Details of the applicant's financial situation must be included. Grants are subject to the parents' income if the applicant is under 21, otherwise they are subject to the applicant's income.

Correspondent: Mrs Anne Ireson, Kettering Borough Council, Municipal Offices, Bowling Green Road, Kettering

NN15 7QX (01536 534398; Fax: 01536 534164; e-mail: anneireson@ kettering.gov.uk)

Parson Latham's Educational Foundation

Eligibility: Children 12 aged years and upwards who have lived in the urban district of Oundle and Ashton since birth or have been resident for at least 5 years and have attended a local school. The foundation will consider giving grants to mature students, although prefers to support people under 25.

Types of grants: One-off and recurrent grants of £100 to £250 are given to:

(i) Schoolchildren for uniforms/other school clothing, books, equipment/ instruments, fees and educational outings in the UK.

(ii) People starting apprenticeships for equipment/instruments.

(iii) Further education students for clothing, books, equipment/instruments, fees and maintenance/living expenses.

(iv) Higher education students for fees, books and maintenance/living expenses.

(v) Mature and vocational students for books and fees.

Exclusions: No grants are given to overseas students studying in the UK or for student exchange.

Annual grant total: In 2004/05 the trust had assets of £19,000, an income of £3,100 and a total expenditure of £3,000, all of which was given in grants to 17 individuals.

Applications: On a form available from the correspondent or the local tourist information centre. Applications to be submitted directly by the individual before 20 August for consideration in September. Applications should include: parental annual income; details of whether the applicant will be living at home or at college; and the number and ages of all dependant children.

Correspondent: Mrs M E Slater, Clerk to the Trustees, 24 North Street, Oundle, Peterborough PE8 4AL (01832 273872)

Other information: As a result of changes in the scheme which governs Parson Latham's Hospital, the foundation now receives 10% of its net income. The foundation is hoping to extend its own Almshouses.

The Foundation of Thomas Roe

Eligibility: People in need who are under 25 and live in the parishes of Scaldwell and Brixworth, Northamptonshire.

Types of grants: One-off grants of £50 to £150 to schoolchildren, students in further or higher education and people starting work for school uniform, school clothing, books, educational outings in the UK, study or travel abroad, maintenance, fees,

living expenses and equipment/ instruments.

Annual grant total: In 2005 the foundation had assets of £6,800 and an income and a total expenditure of £1,800. Grants were made to 12 individuals totalling £1,400.

Applications: On a form available from the correspondent to be considered in March and September each year.

Correspondent: Mrs U Morris, Highfield Grange, Highfield Park, Creaton, Northampton NN6 8NT (e-mail: ursula@ enta.net)

Sir Thomas White's Loan Fund

Eligibility: People who live within the extended borough of Northampton.

Types of grants: (i) Nine-year interest-free loans to people aged between 21 and 34 for education and new businesses (and home improvements). (ii) Grants to young people aged between 16 and 25 attending school, college or university.

The fund was originally set up for the provision of tools for people setting up in a trade or profession.

Annual grant total: In 2004 the fund had assets of £2.6 million and an income of £233,000. Grants totalled £18,000.

Applications: Apply in writing for a form in November, following a public notice advertising the grants.

Correspondent: Clerk to the Trustees, Hewitsons, 7 Spencer Parade, Northampton NN1 5AB (01604 233233)

The Wilson Foundation

Eligibility: People aged 14 to 21 who live in Northamptonshire. Preference is given to schoolchildren with serious family difficulties.

Types of grants: 'The passport to a Wilson Foundation Scholarship is firstly to have shown a genuine enthusiasm for a worthwhile activity. It can be in sport, social work, the arts, an outdoor "challenge" activity or in service to others. Secondly, through your own effort and determination, you must have achieved some above average success.'

To this aim grants are given to help towards the cost of Outward Bound courses, Sail Training Association courses, sporting activities and creative arts courses/study.

Grants are also given to schoolchildren for books, uniform and other essentials. Help is given towards the cost of fees for students and essential costs such as books, equipment and clothing for people starting work.

Grants range from £100 to £400 and are one-off.

Annual grant total: In 2004/05 the foundation had an income of £16,000 and a total expenditure of £139,000. Grants totalled about £70,000.

Applications: In writing to the correspondent, suitable applicants will then be sent an application form.

Correspondent: The Trustees, The Maltings, Tithe Farm, Moulton Road, Holcot, Northamptonshire NN6 9SH

Other information: Grants are made to organisations and individuals.

Blakesley

The Blakesley Parochial Charities

Eligibility: People in need who live in Blakesley.

Types of grants: One-off and recurrent grants according to need.

Annual grant total: In 2004 the charities had an income of £5,200 and a total expenditure of £4,900. Grants totalled about £4,000.

Applications: In writing to the correspondent. Applications are considered in September.

Correspondent: Patricia Paterson, Secretary, Quinbury Cottage, 35 Quinbury End, Blakesley, Towcester, Northamptonshire NN12 8RF

Brackley

The Brackley United Feoffee Charity

Eligibility: People under the age of 25 who live in the parish of Brackley.

Types of grants: One-off grants in the range of £100 and £1,000 to: schoolchildren for uniforms/clothing, study/travel abroad, books, equipment/instruments, excursions and childcare; college students and undergraduates for study/travel abroad, books and excursions; and to people with special educational needs for excursions and childcare.

Annual grant total: In 2004/05 the trust had assets of £667,000 and an income of £21,000. The sum of £4,100 was distributed in 65 welfare grants. A further £500 was distributed to one individual for educational purposes.

Applications: In writing to the correspondent either directly by the individual or through the individual's school, college or educational welfare agency. Trustees meet every three to four months.

Correspondent: Mrs R Hedges, 7 Easthill Close, Brackley, Northamptonshire NN13 7BS (01280 702420)

Brington

The Chauntry Estate

Eligibility: People who live in the parish of Brington. Applicants must have lived in the parish for at least five years.

Types of grants: One-off grants for payment of uniforms for children transferring to secondary schools, books and equipment for students in further/higher education or apprentices, and assistance towards items of school equipment not provided by LEA. Grants are also available for mature students.

Annual grant total: About £4,000 is given each year in educational grants and about £5,000 in welfare grants.

Applications: In writing to the correspondent. Ineligible applications are not acknowledged.

Correspondent: Rita Tank, Walnut Tree Cottage, Main Street, Great Brington, Northampton NN7 4JA (01604 770809; Fax: 01604 771003)

Burton Latimer

The Burton Latimer United Educational Foundation

Eligibility: People who live in Burton Latimer (people who live in other parts, or outside, the borough of Kettering are not eligible).

Types of grants: A general grant is made to students in further or higher education, usually to be used for books; grants to people undertaking training with low earnings to be used at their discretion; and a few grants to schoolchildren towards the cost of field study courses for GCSE work.

Grants are also made to mature students undertaking full or part-time training, in the latter case dependent on their income.

Annual grant total: Around £3,000 a year.

Applications: Application forms are available and must be submitted directly by the individual. Applications are usually considered in October. Applications unrelated to educational needs will not be considered.

Correspondent: Mrs C A Chennell, Clerk, 32 Alexandra Street, Burton Latimer, Kettering, Northamptonshire NN15 5SF

Other information: Grants are also given to the three primary schools in the town.

Byfield

The Byfield Poors Allotment

Eligibility: People in need who live in the parish of Byfield.

Types of grants: Grants are given to undergraduates for books and study/travel overseas.

Annual grant total: In 2005 the charity had an income and a total expenditure of £1,200. Grants totalled about £1,000.

Applications: On a form available from the correspondent. Applications can be made directly by the individual or a relevant third party. They can be submitted at any time for consideration in March, June, September and December.

Correspondent: Mrs J M Goddard, 22 Bell Lane, Byfield, Daventry, Northamptonshire NN11 6US (01327 260619)

Chipping Warden

Relief in Need Charity of Reverend William Smart

Eligibility: People in need who live in the parish of Chipping Warden, Northamptonshire.

Types of grants: One-off grants can be given to individuals or organisations. Preference is given to elderly people and young people in education.

Annual grant total: In 2004 the charity had an income of £3,300 and a total expenditure of £2,400. Grants totalled about £2,000.

Applications: In writing to the correspondent either directly by the individual or by another third party such as a social worker. Applications are considered at any time.

Correspondent: N J Galletly, 3 Allens Orchard, Chipping Warden, Near Banbury, Oxfordshire OX17 1LX

East Farndon

The United Charities of East Farndon

Eligibility: Students in need who live in East Farndon.

Types of grants: One-off grants of up to £50 for people starting work, schoolchildren and college students. Grants given include those for books, equipment and instruments, as well as to schoolchildren for excursions.

Annual grant total: In 2005 the trust had an income of £2,500 and an expenditure of £2,800. Grants to 23 individuals were made for welfare purposes totalling £1,000. No grants were made for educational purposes during the year.

Applications: In writing to the correspondent directly by the individual or a family member for consideration as they are received.

Correspondent: C L Fraser, Linden Lea, Main Street, Market Harborough, Northamptonshire LE16 9SJ (01858 464218; e-mail: fraser-cameron@ hotmail.com)

Ecton

The Ecton Educational Charity

Eligibility: People under the age of 25 who live in the parish of Ecton, Northamptonshire.

Types of grants: One-off grants of £100 to £250 are given to schoolchildren towards the cost of school uniforms/clothing, books, equipment/instruments, educational outings in the UK and study or travel abroad; and to students in higher or further education for books, educational outings in the UK, study or travel abroad and student exchange. People starting work may receive help towards the cost of equipment/instruments.

Annual grant total: In 2005 the trust had assets of £72,000 and an income of £2,300. No grants were made to individuals during the year. Grants totalling £1,400 went to Ecton Primary School and other organisations.

Applications: On a form available from the correspondent for consideration in April and December.

Correspondent: Mrs S Saunders, 18 Church View, Ecton, Northamptonshire NN6 0QL (01604 409444)

Harringworth

The Harringworth Parochial Charities

Eligibility: Students under 25 who live in Harringworth.

Types of grants: One-off grants of between £50 and £300 are given to schoolchildren, students in further/higher education and vocational students for books and equipment/instruments.

Exclusions: No grants for school fees or clothing.

Annual grant total: In 2004/05, the charities had an income of £2,800 and a total expenditure of £2,300.

Applications: In writing to the correspondent, either directly by the individual or through the individual's school/college/educational welfare agency. Applications should be submitted in February for consideration in March.

Correspondent: A C Scholes, Lindisfarne, Wakerley Road, Harringworth, Northamptonshire NN17 3AH (01572 747257)

Isham

The Isham Apprenticing and Educational Charity

Eligibility: Young people under the age of 25 who live in the parish of Isham, Northamptonshire.

Types of grants: Help with (a) the cost of books, clothing, educational outings, maintenance and school fees for schoolchildren and (b) books, equipment/ instruments, clothing and travel for people starting work.

Annual grant total: In 2005 the charity had an income of £1,800 and a total expenditure of £890.

Applications: Directly by the individual or their parent/guardian in writing to the correspondent. Applications are considered regularly.

Correspondent: A S Turner, 36b South Street, Isham, Kettering, Northamptonshire NN14 1HP (01536 722500)

Middleton Cheney

The Blue Coat Educational Charity

Eligibility: People in need who are under 25 years old and live in the borough of Northampton.

Types of grants: One-off and recurrent grants to schoolchildren and students for a wide range of educational purposes, including the costs of school clothing, educational outings, books, school fees, study/travel abroad or student exchange. People starting work may also receive help towards equipment/instruments. Grants range from £100 to £400.

Exclusions: No support for mature students or for overseas students studying in Britain.

Annual grant total: In 2005/06 it had an income of £5,900. Grants to church schools totalled £1,200 while individuals received £4,800.

Applications: Application forms are available by writing to the correspondent, they are usually considered in February, July and November.

Correspondent: W G Gee, c/o Messrs Wilson Browne Solicitors, 60 Gold Street, Northampton NN1 1RS

Middleton Cheney United Charities

Eligibility: People who live in Middleton Cheney.

Types of grants: One-off grants are available to schoolchildren for equipment/ instruments, and to students in higher and further education, including mature

students, for books and study or travel abroad. Grants are in the range of £100 to £200.

Annual grant total: In 2005 the charity had assets of £32,000 and an income of £5,000. Educational grants totalled £900.

Applications: In writing to the correspondent. Applications should be submitted directly by the individual and are considered four times a year.

Correspondent: Mrs Elizabeth Watts, 1 Chacombe Road, Middleton Cheney, Banbury, Oxfordshire OX17 2QS

Northampton

The Beckett's & Sergeant's Educational Foundation

Eligibility: People under 25 who either: (a) live in the borough of Northampton and are attending or have attended a school or further education institution in the borough for at least two years; or (b) are attending or have attended for at least two years All Saints Middle School or Becketts & Sergeants School.

Types of grants: Grants can be given for a wide range of educational purposes, including: educational trips; supplementing existing grants; purchasing books and equipment and studying music or the arts.

Annual grant total: In 2004 it had assets of £2.9 million, which generated an income of £154,000. Grants to seven organisations totalled £28,000, whilst grants to individuals totalled £16,000.

Applications: A written request should be made to obtain an application form. Applications are considered four times a year.

Correspondent: Clerk to the Grants Committee, Hewitsons, 7 Spencer Parade, Northampton NN1 5AB (01604 233233)

Other information: Grants may also be given to other Church of England schools and organisations that are connected with the Church of England.

Ringstead

The Ringstead Gift

Eligibility: People up to the age of 25 whose parents live in the parish of Ringstead.

Types of grants: One-off grants in kind to schoolchildren, college students, undergraduates and vocational students, including those for uniforms/clothing, study/travel abroad, books and equipment/ instruments.

Annual grant total: In 2004/05 the charity had assets of £701,000 and an income of £1,400. One grant of £100 was made to an individual for educational purposes. No welfare grants were made during the year.

Applications: In writing to the correspondent, to be submitted either directly by the individual or a family member, through a third party such as a social worker or teacher or through an organisation such as Citizens Advice or a school. Applications are considered in June and November and should be submitted at least two weeks prior to this.

Correspondent: Mrs D Pentelow, 20 Carlow Street, Ringstead, Kettering, Northamptonshire NN14 4DN

Scaldwell

The Scaldwell Charity

Eligibility: People in need who live in the parish of Scaldwell.

Types of grants: Help with the cost of books, clothing and other essentials for schoolchildren; books, fees and travel expenses for students in further or higher education; books, equipment and clothing for people starting work; and books, travel and fees for mature students.

Annual grant total: In 2005, the charity had an income of £3,000 and a total expenditure of £2,900.Grants totalled about £2,500.

Applications: In writing to the correspondent, including details of financial circumstances. Applications are considered in March, July and November.

Correspondent: James Christopher Kearns, Clerk to the Trustees, Wilson Browne Solicitors, Manor House, 12 Market Street, Higham Ferrers, Rushden, Northamptonshire NN10 8BT (01933 410000; e-mail: jkearns@ wilsonbrowne.co.uk)

Towcester

The Sponne & Bickerstaffe Charity

Eligibility: People in need who live in the civil parish of Towcester.

Types of grants: Grants of £50 to £250 are given to schoolchildren for uniforms, clothing and excursions, to college students for books and to mature students for childcare.

Annual grant total: In 2004 a total of £3,000 was given in grants for welfare and educational purposes.

Applications: In writing to the correspondent, through a social worker, Citizens Advice or other welfare agency. Applications are considered on the third Wednesday of every month.

Correspondent: Sue Joice, Moorfield, Buckingham Way, Towcester,

Northamptonshire NN12 6PE (01327 351206)

Welton

The Welton Town Lands Trust

Eligibility: Students of all ages who live in Welton and have done so for at least two years, who are pursuing a recognised course of study or apprenticeship (which may be elsewhere).

Types of grants: Educational grants of up to £75 are given for up to four years for books and equipment.

Exclusions: Grants are not made to school aged children unless they have a mental or physical disability or to individuals pursuing a hobby.

Annual grant total: In 2003/04 the trust had an income of £5,300 and an expenditure of £4,500. Welfare grants to approximately 35 individuals totalled £1,500 and approximately 8 educational grants totalled £700. Donations to organisations in the village totalled £2,500.

Applications: By application form available on-line to the correspondent. Applications are considered on 1 March and distributed in the same month. Only one application is allowed per financial year. The clerk states that details of the trust are well publicised within the village.

Correspondent: Mrs Deborah Taylor, 1 The Ridgeway, Welton, Daventry NN11 5LQ (01327 310439; e-mail: dtadmin@btinternet.com)

Nottinghamshire

The Bristowe Trust

Eligibility: Pupils or former pupils of schools within the administrative area of the former county council of Nottinghamshire (excluding the city of Nottingham) who are aged between 16 and 21.

Types of grants: Grants averaging £100 towards the cost of educational visits abroad.

Annual grant total: Usually £1,000 is available to be distributed each year.

Applications: In writing to the correspondent at any time. Applicants will be interviewed by the trust.

Correspondent: David Litchfield, Student Awards Section, Nottinghamshire County Council, County Hall, Loughborough Road, West Bridgford, Nottingham NG2 7QP (0115 977 3223)

The Midland Orphanage Fund

Eligibility: Girls between 4 and 25 years, living in Nottinghamshire. Preference is given to young girls and those who have lost one or both parents, or who are dependent on one parent. Girls must normally be of school or college age (although consideration may be given to pre-school children in terms of items such as educational play equipment).

Types of grants: One-off grants to a usual maximum of £250 each to cover the cost of meeting specific needs regarding the education and maintenance of applicants. Grants are given to schoolchildren, college students and undergraduates, including those towards clothing/uniforms, fees, study/travel abroad, books, equipment/ instruments, maintenance/living expenses, excursions and awards for excellence.

Exclusions: Grants cannot be given for domestic appliances, household goods, to fund areas that should be funded by government, to boys, to girls who live outside the Nottingham area, pre-school children, organisations or families whose income is not very low.

Annual grant total: In 2004/05 the fund had assets of £23,000, an income of £1,200 and a total expenditure of £1,900. Grants were made totalling £1,900 to seven individuals.

Applications: On a form available from the correspondent to be submitted at any time, either directly by the individual, through a third party such as a teacher or through the individual's school/college/ educational welfare agency. Applications are considered quarterly.

Correspondent: Mrs Barbara Ricks, 30 Cyprus Road, Nottingham NG3 5EB (0115 9603135; Fax: 0115 9603135; e-mail: faricks@aol.com)

Nottingham Gordon Memorial Trust for Boys & Girls

Eligibility: Children and young people aged up to 25 who are in need and live in Nottingham and the area immediately around the city.

Types of grants: Grants are given to schoolchildren and further and higher education students including those for books, equipment, maintenance/living expenses, educational outings in the UK and study or travel abroad. Grants are also given for school uniforms/other school clothing.

Annual grant total: In 2004 the trust had assets of £977,000 and an income of £39,000. Grants totalled £29,000, the majority of which went to individuals for relief-in-need purposes. Around £3,000 per year is given in educational grants.

Applications: On a form available from the correspondent to be submitted through the individual's school, college, educational welfare agency, health visitor, social worker or probation officer. Individuals, supported by a reference from their school/college, can also apply directly. Applications are considered all year round.

Correspondent: Mrs Colleen Douglas, Cumberland Court, 80 Mount Street, Nottingham NG1 6HH (0115 901 5558; Fax: 0115 859 9652)

Other information: The trust also supports organisations in the Nottingham area.

The Nottingham Roosevelt Memorial Travelling Scholarship

Eligibility: People between the ages of 21 and 30 who are engaged in industry, commerce or 'the professions' and live or work in Nottingham and Nottinghamshire.

Types of grants: Grants to help with the cost of visiting the USA for up to three months to investigate a topic of the applicant's and/or employer's choice. The value of each scholarship can be up to about £3,000, plus return flight tickets to New York. 'Scholars are expected to travel widely throughout the USA and learn about the American way of life – an ambassadorial role.'

Exclusions: Grants are not given to students.

Annual grant total: In 2004 the trust had assets of £22,000, an income of £6,300 and a total expenditure of £6,800. The sum of £3,000 was given to one individual. Each year up to two grants can be given, depending on applications.

Applications: Further information and an application form is available from the correspondent. Applications must include reasons for wishing to be considered for a scholarship. They should be submitted in February for shortlisting in March and final selection in April. Detailed guidelines and application forms can be downloaded from the trust's website.

Correspondent: Amanda Roberts, Hon. Secretary, 18 Marlborough Road, Woodthorpe, Nottingham NG5 4FG (0115 926 9996; Fax: 0115 966 1173; e-mail: nigelroberts@ntlworld.com; website: www.rooseveltscholarship.org)

The Puri Foundation

Eligibility: Individuals in need living in Nottinghamshire who are from India (particularly the towns of Mullan Pur near Chandigarh and Ambala). Employees/past employees of Melton Medes Group LTD, Blugilt Holdings or Melham Inc and their dependants, who are in need, are also eligible.

The trust wants to support people who have exhausted state support and other avenues, in other words to be a 'last resort'. Eligible people can receive help at any stage of their education, including postgraduates and mature students.

Types of grants: One-off and recurrent grants according to need. The maximum donation is usually between £150 and £200.

Annual grant total: In 2004/05 the foundation had assets of £3.5 million and an income of £299,000. Grants totalled £636,000.

Applications: In writing to the correspondent, either directly by the individual or through a social worker.

Correspondent: Nathu Ram Puri, Environment House, 6 Union Road, Nottingham NG3 1FH (0115 901 3000; Fax: 0115 901 3100)

Arnold

The Arnold Educational Foundation

Eligibility: People who live in the ancient parish of Arnold, under the age of 25.

Types of grants: Primarily help for those at college or university, for example, for equipment or books. Help with the cost of books, clothing and other essentials for schoolchildren is given, but only in special circumstances.

Annual grant total: In 2004/05 the foundation had an income of £17,000 and a total expenditure of £20,000. In previous years about 100 grants totalling around £15,000 were made.

Applications: In writing to the correspondent. An application form should be completed by those requesting grants for further education. Grants are given post-expenditure on receiving the receipts for items purchased.

Correspondent: B W West, 73 Arnot Hill Road, Arnold, Nottingham NG5 6LN (0115 920 6656)

Bingham

The Bingham Trust Scheme

Eligibility: People under the age of 21 living in Bingham.

Types of grants: Grants in the range of £50 and £150 to help with expenses incurred in the course of education, religious and physical welfare and so on. They are made in January and early July each year.

Annual grant total: In 2004/05 the trust had an income of £810 and a total expenditure of £670.

Applications: Application forms are available from: Mrs R Pingula, 74 Nottingham Road, Bingham, Nottinghamshire NG13 8AW. They can be submitted directly by the individual or a family member by 30 April and 31 October each year.

Correspondent: Mrs Bailey, 20 Tithby Road, Bingham, Nottingham NG13 8GN (01949 838673)

Bingham United Charities

Eligibility: People in need who live in the parish of Bingham.

Types of grants: One-off grants in the range of £50 and £300. Grants are given for a range of educational purposes including school uniforms, books, school trips, Duke of Edinburgh expeditions and music lessons.

Exclusions: Grants are not given to the same person twice.

Annual grant total: In 2004/05 the charities had an income of £8,100 and a total expenditure of £4,100.

Applications: In writing to the correspondent, preferably directly by the individual; alternatively, they can be submitted through a social worker, Citizens Advice or other welfare agency. Applications are considered on the second Tuesday in alternate months, commencing in May. Details of the purpose of the grant and other grants being sought should be included.

Correspondent: Claire Pegg, c/o Bingham Town Council, The Old Court House, Church Street, Bingham, Nottinghamshire NG13 8AL

Other information: Grants are also given to organisations and individuals for educational purposes.

Carlton in Lindrick

The Christopher Johnson & the Green Charity

Eligibility: Schoolchildren in need who live in the village of Carlton in Lindrick.

Types of grants: One-off grants ranging from £10 to £250 for school trips and so on.

Annual grant total: In 2004/05 the charity had assets of £50,000, an income of £6,200. Out of a total expenditure of £3,100, the sum of £2,900 was given to 22 individuals for relief-in-need and educational purposes.

Applications: In writing to the correspondent either directly by the individual or via a third party such as a social worker, local rector, doctor, district nurse or through Citizens Advice or another welfare agency for consideration throughout the year.

Correspondent: C E R Towle, Hon. Secretary and Treasurer, 135 Windsor Road, Carlton in Lindrick, Worksop, Nottinghamshire S81 9DH (01909 731069; e-mail: robin@towle.screaming.net)

Collingham

William and Mary Hart Foundation – see entry on page 42

see entry on page 42

Correspondent: David Marshall, 2 Keats Drive, Hucknall, Nottingham, NG15 6TE (0115 963 5428)

Mansfield

Faith Clerkson's Exhibition Foundation

Eligibility: Boys and girls of school leaving age upwards who have for at least two years lived in the borough of Mansfield or the urban district of Mansfield Woodhouse.

Types of grants: Small cash grants, with no fixed maximum limit, to help students and others leaving school who are undertaking full-time education, with the cost of books, equipment, clothing and travel.

Exclusions: No grants for fees.

Annual grant total: About £2,000 a year.

Applications: In writing to the correspondent, including proof of income and details of any other grant applied for. Applications are considered in early June and early October.

Correspondent: C P McKay, 67 Clumber Avenue, Beeston, Nottingham NG9 4BH

North Muskham

The Mary Woolhouse Foundation

Eligibility: People under 25 who live in the parish of North Muskham and Bathley.

Types of grants: One-off grants are given to schoolchildren and college students towards books and equipment/instruments.

Annual grant total: In 2005 it had both an income and a total expenditure of £10,000. Most of this was given to individuals with £1,000 going to a local school.

Applications: In writing to the correspondent. Applications should be submitted directly by the individual and are considered at any time.

Correspondent: Mrs S M White, 3 Waterside, North Muskham, Newark, Nottinghamshire, NG23 6FD (01636 704409)

Nottingham

The Audrey Harrison Heron Memorial Fund

Eligibility: Girls and women who live in the city of Nottingham and are under the age of 25.

Types of grants: Grants of between £50 and £2,000 to help with books, equipment, clothing or travel, school, college or university fees or to supplement existing grants. Grants can be one-off or recurrent.

Annual grant total: In 2004/05 the trust had an income of £2,800 and a total expenditure of £5,200, most of which is usually given in grants to individuals.

Applications: On a form available from the correspondent. Applications can be submitted directly by the individual, through the individual's school/college/educational welfare agency or other third party, and are considered all year round.

Correspondent: The Manager, Natwest Trust and Estate Services, 153 Preston Road, Brighton BN1 6PD (0602 417536)

The Haywood Scholarships

Eligibility: First year higher education students who are members of the Church of England and have lived in the city of Nottingham for at least six years before the date of application. The applicant should be studying science, maths or technological subjects and not intending to follow a teacher training course.

Types of grants: Cash grants not exceeding £100.

Annual grant total: About £900 a year.

Applications: In writing to the correspondent. Students satisfying the basic eligibility conditions are sent the necessary forms direct. Applications are judged in accordance with a basic means test of parental income.

Correspondent: Student Awards Section, Nottingham City Council, PO Box 7167, Nottingham NG1 4WD (0115 915 4994)

The Peveril Exhibition Endowment Fund

Eligibility: Applicants who (or whose parents) live within the city of Nottingham, aged 11 to 24. There is a minimum residential qualification period within the city of one year and the trustees will give preference to applicants who originate from, or who have long-term ties with, the Nottingham area rather than to those who are merely living there whilst completing an educational course locally.

Types of grants: One-off and recurrent grants tenable at any secondary school, college of education, university or other institution of further (including professional and technical) education approved by the trustees. Grants range from £50 to £1,500 a year. Larger grants may be given in exceptional circumstances.

Annual grant total: In 2004/05 the fund had assets of £176,000, an income of £6,700 and a total expenditure of £12,700. Grants were awarded to 12 individuals totalling £8,500.

Applications: At any time on a form available from the correspondent. Applications should be submitted directly by the individual; parents will be requested to complete a means-test form if the applicant is still a dependant. Applications are considered all year around.

Correspondent: A B Palfreman, Clerk, 84 Friar Lane, Nottingham NG1 6ED (0115 947 2541; Fax: 0115 947 3636; e-mail: apalfreman@fraserbrown.com)

Sedgebrook

Dame Margaret Thorold Educational Foundation

Eligibility: People resident in the parishes of Sedgebrook, Marston and Cranwell.

Annual grant total: In 2004 the foundation had an income of £12,500 and a total expenditure of £10,700. Further information was not available.

Applications: In writing to the correspondent.

Correspondent: T S Kelway, Clerk, Tallents, 3 Middlegate, Newark, Nottinghamshire NG24 1AQ (e-mail: tim.kelway@tallents.co.uk)

Other information: The foundation also gives to organisations.

Sutton-cum-Granby

Granby Educational Foundation

Eligibility: Girls and boys who currently live in the parish of Sutton-Cum-Granby and have done so for the last four years.

Types of grants: One-off grants in the range of £50 and £200 are given to schoolchildren, further and higher education students and vocational students for help with clothing/uniforms, fees, books, equipment/instruments, living expenses, educational outings in the UK, study or travel abroad and student exchanges.

Exclusions: No grants are given to mature students.

Annual grant total: In 2004/05 the foundation had an income of £220. The sum of £190 was distributed during the year.

Applications: In writing to the correspondent directly by the individual.

Correspondent: Education Finance, Nottinghamshire County Council, County Hall, West Bridgford, Nottingham NG2 7QP

Tuxford

Read's Exhibition Foundation

Eligibility: Children and young people, including university students, who have lived in and attended a school in the parish of Tuxford.

Types of grants: Mainly help for students in further or higher education. Help is also given towards the cost of education, training, apprenticeship or equipment for those starting work and towards essentials for schoolchildren.

Annual grant total: In 2004 grants were made to five individuals totalling £600.

Applications: In writing to the correspondent. Invoices for school equipment must be submitted on application before any grant is issued. Applications can be considered at any time.

Correspondent: A A Hill, Sandy Acre, Eagle Road, Spalford, Newark NG23 7HA (01522 778250)

Warsop

The Warsop United Charities

Eligibility: People in need who live in the urban district of Warsop (Warsop, Church Warsop, Warsop Vale, Meden Vale, Spion Kop and Skoonholme).

Types of grants: Grants for those at school, college or university.

Annual grant total: In 2004 the charities had an income of £7,700 and a total expenditure of £5,900. Grants totalled about £5,000.

Applications: In writing to the correspondent. Trustees meet three or four times a year.

Correspondent: Mrs Denise Fritchley, 33 Medan Avenue, Warsop, Mansfield, Nottinghamshire, NG20 0PP

Wilford

Carter's Educational Foundation

Eligibility: People under the age of 25 on 1 September of the year of applying who live in (or whose parents live in) the ancient parish of Wilford who, in the opinion of the trustees, are in financial need. The area in broad terms includes Wilford Village, Silverdale, Compton Acres, part of West Bridgford, mainly west of Loughborough Road, and some of the south of The Meadows.

Types of grants:
1 Schoolchildren for books, equipment/ instruments and educational outings in the UK.
2 People starting work for equipment/ instruments.
3 Further and higher education students for books, equipment/instruments, maintenance/living expenses and study or educational travel abroad.

Annual grant total: In 2005 over £25,000 was distributed in grants.

Applications: Application forms are available from the correspondent and from the foundation's website. They should be submitted directly by the individual by 31 May annually and are considered in June/ July. They should include details of parental income for those who are financially dependent and details of school/ course to be attended.

Correspondent: Mrs S A Rodgers, Pennine House, 8 Stanford Street, Nottingham NG1 7BQ (website: www.wilford-carters-education.org.uk)

Other information: Grants are also made to youth groups in the parish.

Shropshire

The Atherton Trust

Eligibility: People in need who live in the parishes of Pontesbury and Hanwood and the villages of Annscroft and Hook-a-Gate in the county of Shropshire.

Types of grants: One-off grants given towards fees, living expenses or study or travel abroad for students in further and higher education and towards equipment or instruments for people starting work.

Annual grant total: In 2004/05 the trust had assets of £159,000 and an income of £5,900. Grants to individuals totalled £900, with a further £8,000 given in grants to organisations.

Applications: On a form available from the correspondent, which can be submitted directly by the individual. Applications are considered quarterly in February, May, August and November.

Correspondent: The Secretary, Whittingham Riddell LLP, Belmont House, Shrewsbury Business Park, Shrewsbury SY2 6LG (01743 273273; Fax: 01743 273274)

Other information: The trust also supports institutions that give, or agree to give when required, support and services to people who need aid by loss of sight, limb or health by accident or inevitable causes.

Bowdler's Educational Foundation

Eligibility: People under the age of 25 who live in the county of Shropshire, but with a first priority for those living in the Shrewsbury area.

Types of grants: Grants, to a maximum of £100 to £200, for: (i) school pupils, to help with books, equipment, clothing or travel; (ii) help with school, college or university fees or to supplement existing grants; and (iii) help towards the cost of education, training, apprenticeship or equipment for those starting work.

Annual grant total: Between £1,500 and £2,000.

Applications: On a form available from the correspondent.

Correspondent: T Collard, Clerk to the Trustees, c/o Legal Services, Shropshire County Council, The Shire Hall, Abbey Foregate, Shrewsbury SY2 6ND (01743 252756)

The Careswell Foundation

Eligibility: People under the age of 25 who live in Shropshire and have attended certain schools in the county, namely Shrewsbury School, Bridgnorth Endowed School, Adam's Grammar School (Newport), Idsall School (Shifnal), Thomas Adam's School (Wem) and the school or schools of secondary education by which Donnington, Shropshire is served.

Types of grants: Cash grants, to a usual maximum of about £150 a year for three years, to help with the cost of books and equipment, to be used at college or university or other establishments of further education.

Annual grant total: In 2004/05 the trust had assets of £231,000 and an income of £11,000. Grants were made to 60 individuals totalling £9,200.

Applications: On a form supplied by the headteacher of the relevant school to be submitted in August or September for consideration in October.

Correspondent: Mrs B A Marshall, 24 The Crescent, Shrewsbury SY1 1 TJ (01743 351332; Fax: 01743 351844; e-mail: solicitors@turnbullgarrard.co.uk)

The Clungunford Educational Foundation

Eligibility: People under the age of 25 who live in the parish of Clungunford, that part of the parish of Onibury that used to be in Clungunford, and the former hamlet of Broome in the parish of Hopesay.

Types of grants: Help with the cost of books, clothing and other essentials for schoolchildren. Help is also available for students at college or university, and towards books, equipment, clothing and travel for people starting work. Grants range from £20 to £200.

Annual grant total: In 2005, the foundation had an income of £1,300 and a total expenditure of £1,400. Grants totalled about £1,000.

Applications: In writing to the correspondent or any trustee. An information sheet is distributed to each household in the parish at two or three-year intervals and to all newcomers.

Correspondent: Mrs B W Sheaman, Rose Cottage, Hopton Heath, Craven Arms, Shropshire SY7 0QD

Dr Gardner's Charity for Sick Nurses

Eligibility: People involved in nursing who live in Shropshire.

Types of grants: One-off cash grants usually of amounts up to £300.

Exclusions: No grants for loan repayments.

Annual grant total: In 2004, it had an income of £2,400 and a total expenditure of £180.

Applications: On a form available from the correspondent. Applications can be submitted at any time either through a social worker, Citizens Advice or other welfare agency, or directly by the individual or a relevant third party.

Correspondent: Dr P L Boardman, Hon. Secretary, 3 Mayfield Park, Shrewsbury SY2 6PD (01743 232768)

Millington's Charity

Eligibility: Preference for people who live in Shropshire. Applicants must be residents or have been educated in Shropshire, be aged between 15 and 24, and should be members, or their parents/guardian must be members, of the Church of England.

Types of grants: One-off grants ranging from £100 to £400 to help with incidental expenses associated with college or university attendance where there is a special need; to supplement existing grants; or to assist with funding a specific educational project. Grants are given towards the cost of books, equipment/instruments, maintenance/living expenses and study or travel abroad. Grants can also be awarded to people starting work.

Exclusions: Grants are not normally given towards fees.

Annual grant total: In 2005 the charity had assets of £860,000, an income of £124,000 and a total expenditure of £114,000. Grants were made to 14 individuals totalling £3,600.

Applications: Applications should be made on forms available from the correspondent upon written request. Details of parental income irrespective of the age of the applicant are obligatory. Decisions and awards are made at quarterly meetings in early March, June, September and December.

Correspondent: J W Rouse, Clerk to the Trustees, Houlston Cottage, Myddle, Shropshire SY4 3RD (01939 290898; Fax: 01939 290898; e-mail: johnrouse@clara.net)

The Shrewsbury Municipal Charity

Eligibility: People in need who live, work or study in the borough of Shrewsbury and Atcham. 60% of the disposable income is for education/training of people under 25 years of age; the balance is for general relief of need.

Types of grants: One-off grants of £50 to £250 to assist with educational and vocational needs. For example, a voice synthesiser and multi-sensory equipment for children with disabilities and £250 to a young photographer to produce a portfolio needed to take up a college place.

Annual grant total: In 2004/05 the charity had an income of £1,000 and a total expenditure of £600. Grants totalled about £500.

Applications: In writing to the correspondent, either directly by the individual or through a social worker, Citizens Advice, welfare agency or other third party. Applications are considered in January, May, and September, but emergencies can be considered at any time. Please include details of any other charities that have been contacted for assistance.

Correspondent: John Goldsworthy, 21 Eastwood Road, Shrewsbury SY3 8ES

The Shropshire Youth Foundation

Eligibility: People under the age of 25 years who live in Shropshire.

Types of grants: One-off grants, typically of £200, towards education through leisure time activities, such as voluntary service overseas and expeditions, may be given on occasions, so as to develop the physical, mental and spiritual capacities of individuals.

Exclusions: No grants are made towards educational courses.

Annual grant total: In 2004/05 the trust had an income of £7,800 and gave grants to individuals and organisations totalling £6,500.

Applications: Application forms are available from the foundation. The trustees meet twice yearly in June/July and January/February.

Correspondent: D E Wise, Honorary Secretary, Legal and Democratic Services, The Shirehall, Abbey Foregate, Shrewsbury, Shropshire SY2 6ND (01743 252726; Fax: 01743 252713; e-mail: david.wise@shropshire-cc.gov.uk)

The Walker Trust

Eligibility: People who live in Shropshire.

Types of grants: Grants for people in further and higher education, especially medical and veterinary students, where no local authority grant or student loan is available. Assistance to A-level students is

only given in exceptional circumstances. Individual grants rarely exceed £2,000.

Exclusions: Higher education students eligible for help with tuition fees and student loans.

Annual grant total: In 2004/05 it had assets of £4.8 million, which generated an income of £160,000. Grants to 133 individuals totalled £60,400. Grants were made to 26 organisations totalling £52,000.

Applications: On a form available from the correspondent. Applications are considered in January, April, July and October. They must reach the correspondent at least one month before help is required.

Correspondent: Edward Hewitt, Clerk, 2 Breidden Way, Bayston Hill, Shrewsbury SY3 0LN (01743 873866)

Bridgnorth

The Bridgnorth Parish Charity

Eligibility: People living in Bridgnorth parish, including Oldbury and Eardington, who are in need.

Types of grants: One-off grants according to need, including those towards playgroup fees, school visits, funeral expenses and heating costs.

Annual grant total: In 2004 the charity had assets of £36,000 and an income of £3,900. Grants to individuals totalled £1,800 with no grants made to organisations during the year.

Applications: In writing to the correspondent either directly by the individual or through a doctor, nurse, member of the local clergy, social worker, Citizens Advice or other welfare agency.

Correspondent: F Brown, Secretary, 6 Love Lane, Bridgnorth, Shropshire WV16 4HD (01746 762605)

Other information: Grants are also made to organisations.

Ercall Magna

The Ercall Magna Educational Endowment Fund

Eligibility: People who live in the civil parish of Ercall Magna and have done so for at least one year and are aged between 16 and 25.

Types of grants: Recurrent grants of £20 to £40 for those at college or university towards costs such as books, equipment, fees/living expenses, equipment/instruments and study/travel abroad. Applicants must be staying in full-time education for at least one academic year after applying.

Annual grant total: In 2004/05 grants were made to five individuals totalling £420.

Applications: On a form available from the correspondent. Applications should be submitted in time for consideration in September and the application must include an explanation of what the grant would help to achieve.

Correspondent: Mrs P A Lloyd, Secretary, 35 Talbot Fields, High Ercall, Telford, Shropshire TF6 6LY (01952 770353)

Hodnet

The Hodnet Consolidated Eleemosynary Charities

Eligibility: Students in need who live in Hodnet parish.

Types of grants: Grants for books to students in further/higher education.

Annual grant total: In 2004 the charities had an income of £2,500 and a total expenditure of £2,100. Grants totalled about £1,500.

Applications: In writing to the correspondent for consideration throughout the year. Applications can be submitted directly by the individual or through a social worker, Citizens Advice or other welfare agency.

Correspondent: Mrs S W France, 26 The Meadows, Hodnet, Market Drayton, Shropshire TF9 3QF

Other information: This is essentially a relief-in-need charity that also gives money to students for books.

Hopesay

Hopesay Parish Trust

Eligibility: People in any level of education who live in the parish of Hopesay, Shropshire. Priority is given to those under 25 years old.

Types of grants: Grants are typically between £25 and £650 for an educational need. Except in cases of financial hardship, grants will not normally exceed half the cost of any activity. Trustees prefer not to enter into extended commitments, but will look favourably on repeat applications on an annual basis for extended periods of study.

Exclusions: Grants are not made where the funding is the responsibility of central or local government, whether or not the individual has taken up such provision.

Annual grant total: In 2005 the trust had assets of £150,000 and an income of £2,500. Grants were made to eight individuals for educational purposes totalling £2,500. No grants were made for relief-in-need purposes in this year.

Applications: Preferably on an application form, available from the correspondent. The application form covers the essential information required, and the trustees will

ask for further details if necessary. Applications can be made at any time, either directly by the individual, or by a third party on their behalf, such as parent/guardian, teacher or tutor, or through an organisation such as Citizens Advice or a school. They can be submitted at any time.

Correspondent: David Evans, Park Farm, The Fish, Hopesay, Craven Arms, Shropshire SY7 8HG (01588 660545)

Other information: The trust gives priority to educational grants. At the trustees' discretion, any surplus income may be applied for other charitable purposes but only within the parish.

Newport

The Annabelle Lady Boughey Charity

Eligibility: Individuals connected with the civil parish of Newport who require financial assistance with the costs of educational trips connected with non-vocational courses in any subject.

Types of grants: One-off grants for schoolchildren and students in further/higher education for study or travel abroad and instruments/equipment and also to mature students for study or travel abroad.

Annual grant total: In 2003/04 the trust had an income of £1,200 and a total expenditure of £2,800. Grants totalled about £1,500.

Applications: Initial telephone calls are welcomed and application forms are available on request. Applications can be submitted directly by the individual and are usually considered in March, June, September and November; completed applications should arrive in the preceding month.

Correspondent: Stuart Barber, 23 Station Road, Newport, Shropshire, TF10 7EN (01952 814628)

Other information: Grants are also made to organisations.

Shrewsbury

John Allatt's Educational Foundation

Eligibility: People aged 11 to 25 who live in Shrewsbury and its immediate environs, who are in need.

Types of grants: Help is available to schoolchildren for equipment/instruments and educational outings in the UK and further and higher education students for equipment/instruments, fees, books, living expenses, educational outings in the UK, gap year activities and study or travel abroad. Preference is given to: schoolchildren with serious family difficulties so that the child has to be

educated away from home; people with special educational needs to help towards specialist equipment; and for specialist courses of education. Grants are usually one-off and range from £100 to £150.

Exclusions: No grants are made towards first degree courses.

Annual grant total: In 2004/05 the foundation had assets of £22,000, an income of £1,800 and a total expenditure of £1,400. Grants were made to four individuals totalling £650.

Applications: On a form available from the correspondent. Applications are considered in January and July and should be submitted directly by the individual before 1 January and 1 July respectively. All applications must be supported by a letter from the applicant's educational establishment, or, if relevant, a medical practitioner or educational psychologist.

Correspondent: Clerk to the Trustees, The Old Vicarage, Atcham, Shrewsbury SY5 6QE (01743 761598; e-mail: caney@dsl.pipex.com)

Telford

Maxell Educational Trust

Eligibility: Young people aged 9 to 25 years who live, or whose family home is, in Telford, or who attend school or college there. Projects should ideally have an industrial or technological element.

Types of grants: One-off grants for schoolchildren, college students and people with special educational needs, towards books and equipment/instruments.

Annual grant total: About £25,000.

Applications: In writing to the correspondent. Applications are considered throughout the year and should be submitted either by the individual or a parent/guardian, through a third party such as a teacher, or through an organisation such as a school or an educational welfare agency.

Correspondent: I Jamieson, Secretary of the Trust, Maxell Europe Ltd, Apley, Telford, Shropshire TF1 6DA (01952 522222)

Staffordshire

The Burslem Educational Charity

Eligibility: People under 25 who live in and around Burslem, or with at least one parent living in the beneficial area.

Types of grants: Help with the cost of books, clothing, educational outings, fees and living expenses for people at college or university and schoolchildren.

Annual grant total: About £2,000 a year.

Applications: Application forms are available from the correspondent; trustees meet to consider applications in May and November.

Correspondent: Support Officer, Education Finance, Floor 2, Civic Centre, Glebe Street, Stoke-on-Trent ST4 1HH

Consolidated Charity of Burton-upon-Trent

Eligibility: People who live in the former county of Burton upon Trent and the parishes of Branston, Stretton and Outwoods.

Types of grants: Undergraduate bursaries of £500 per annum for three years and one-off grants of £500 maximum.

Exclusions: Grants are not awarded for postgraduate study.

Annual grant total: In 2004 the trust had assets of £9.2 million and an income of £381,000. Grants totalled £176,000 of which £89,000 went to individuals for relief-in-need and educational purposes.

Applications: On a form available from the correspondent accompanied by a letter of support from a school or college.

Correspondent: T J Bramall, Clerk, Messrs Talbot & Co, 148 High Street, Burton upon Trent, Staffordshire DE14 1JY (01283 564716; Fax: 01283 510861)

Lady Dorothy Grey's Foundation

Eligibility: People under 25 who live (or whose parents live) in the parishes of Enville, Bobbington or Kinver, with a preference for Enville.

Types of grants: One-off and recurrent grants to help further and higher education students with the cost of books, equipment/instruments, fees, maintenance/living expenses, educational outings in the UK and study or travel abroad. Grants are in the range of £150 to £500.

Annual grant total: In 2004/05 the trust had assets of £72,000, and both an income and a total expenditure of £8,400. Grants were made to 25 individuals totalling £6,600.

Applications: Directly by the individual or through a parent or guardian on a form available from the correspondent. Applications should be submitted by 31 August for consideration in October.

Correspondent: John A Gloss, Walls Cottage, Kinver Road, Enville, Staffordshire DY7 5HE (01384 873691; Fax: 01384 873691)

The Maddock, Leicester & Burslem Educational Charity

Eligibility: Students who have lived in Stoke-on-Trent or Newcastle-under-Lyme for at least seven years and are aged 15 to 21 inclusive (grants may occasionally be given to people outside this age range). No postgraduates or mature students are supported.

Types of grants: Help with the cost of books and educational outings for schoolchildren. Help is also available towards course fees for those at college or university. Grants are usually up to £200.

Annual grant total: In 2004/05, the charity had an income of around £6,000 and a total expenditure of £4,900. Grants totalled around £4,500.

Applications: On a form available from the correspondent, to be submitted either directly by the individual or through the individual's school or educational establishment, for consideration in June. A circular is sent to over 20 local schools in the area. Applications must include details of what the grant is to be used for, what the student is aiming to achieve and what other funding is available. The school must also make a comment on the application.

Correspondent: Mrs Margaret Jones, Grindey's Solicitors, Christchurch House, Christchurch Way, Stone, Staffordshire ST15 8BZ (01785 810780; Fax: 01785 810789)

The Strasser Foundation

Eligibility: Schoolchildren and students in the local area, with a preference for North Staffordshire.

Types of grants: Usually one-off grants for books, equipment and other specific causes or needs for educational purposes. Usually no grants to people at doctoral level.

Annual grant total: In 2005 the trust had an income of £20,000 and a total expenditure of £26,000. Grants are made to organisations and to individuals for welfare and relief-in-need purposes.

Applications: In writing to the correspondent. The trustees meet quarterly. Applications are only acknowledged if an sae is sent.

Correspondent: Tony Bell, c/o Knight & Sons, The Brampton, Newcastle-Under-Lyme, Staffordshire ST5 0QW

Bradley

The Bradley Trust

Eligibility: People from the parish of Bradley in Stafford who are studying at university.

Types of grants: Variable grants of amounts up to £2,000 are available for students studying for their first degree only.

Annual grant total: In 2004 the trust had assets of £837,000 and an income of £28,000. Grants totalled £6,400, including £2,000 given in six educational grants to individuals.

Applications: On a form available from the correspondent. Applications are considered once a year in September and should be submitted along with proof of acceptance/attendance at university in August. Applications are considered in September.

Correspondent: Mrs C Cartwright, Clerk, 1 Elm Drive, Bradley, Stafford ST18 9DS (01785 780531)

Other information: Village organisations and schools attended by Bradley children may also be supported.

Leigh

Spencer Educational Foundation Trust

Eligibility: People under 25 who live in the village of Leigh. No other applications will be considered.

Types of grants: Grants of around £150 each are given to further and higher education students for books, equipment/instruments and fees.

Annual grant total: In 2004 the trust had an income of £1,500 and a total expenditure of £1,900. Grants totalled about £1,500.

Applications: On a form available from the correspondent. Applications are considered in September and should be received by August. Grants are paid in arrears after a reference from the educational body is received.

Correspondent: J Beaman, Beechside, Church Leigh, Leigh, Stoke-on-Trent ST10 4PT (01889 502401)

Rugeley

The Chetwynd Educational Foundation (part of the Chetwynd Charities)

Eligibility: People going into higher education who live in the ancient parish of Rugeley.

Types of grants: To students who are proceeding to higher education, university, college or technical college. The correspondent states: 'There is no means test. All applications are considered on their merits. The grant is used mainly to buy books and other equipment. Any applicant who needs to purchase musical instruments or such equipment will also be considered for a further grant from our general fund. This would also apply to provision of special clothing.' Grants are also given towards study or travel abroad for students in further/higher education and towards fees for mature students. Grants are one-off and usually for amounts of £40 or £50 each.

Grants are usually made up to degree level, however, if the applicant intends to take a Masters degree further help may be given.

Annual grant total: About £2,500 a year. About 50 grants are made each year.

Applications: In writing to the correspondent. Applications are usually made directly by the individual and are considered in April and October. 'We normally expect to be informed of the applicant's results and the schools attended. Most applicants inform us of the course and subjects. We enjoy learning of their progress and the correspondence is friendly.'

Correspondent: C Bennett, Sherwood, East Butts Road, Rugeley, Staffordshire WS15 2LU

The Rugeley Endowment

Eligibility: People in need who are under 25 and live in the former urban district of Rugeley as constituted on 31 March 1974. Beneficiaries must have attended a voluntary, grant maintained or county school in the area of benefit.

Types of grants: One-off grants up to a maximum of £100 towards the cost of school clothing, books, travel, educational outings and equipment/instruments to schoolchildren or students in higher education.

Annual grant total: In 2004/05 the charity had assets of £1.7 million, an income of £71,000 and a total expenditure of £79,000. The sum of £5,200 was distributed in 46 educational grants to individuals.

Applications: Through the headteacher of the school attended.

Correspondent: The Trustees, c/o Corporate Director Resources, Staffordshire County Council, PO Box 11, County Building, Martin Street, Stafford ST16 2LH (01785 276332; Fax: 01785 276334)

Stafford

The Stafford Educational Endowment Charity

Eligibility: Pupils and former pupils of secondary schools in Stafford who are under 25 years of age.

Types of grants: Small one-off grants for books, travel, educational outings, educational equipment and similar expenses incurred by schoolchildren, students and people starting work. There is a preference to award grants for benefits not normally provided for by the LEA.

Exclusions: Grants are unlikely to be given for course fees or the ordinary living costs of students.

Annual grant total: In 2004/05 the charity had an income of £15,000 and a total expenditure of £18,000.

Applications: Through the headteacher of the secondary school attended.

Correspondent: The Corporate Director, Children and Lifelong Learning Directorate, Tipping Street, Stafford ST16 2DH

Tamworth

The Rawlet Trust

Eligibility: Students aged 18 to 25 who are going into higher education, and who live or have parents who live in Tamworth.

Types of grants: One-off grants towards the cost of books, fees, living expenses, student exchange and study or travel abroad for students in further or higher education. Grants are also given for equipment/instruments, clothing or travel for people starting work. Grants range from £30 to £100.

Annual grant total: In 2004/05 the trust had an income of £17,000 and a total expenditure of £18,000. Grants are also made for educational purposes.

Applications: On a form available from the correspondent, to be submitted either directly by the individual or through a third party such as a social worker or Citizens Advice. They are considered in March, October and December. The clerk or one of the trustees will follow up applications if they need any further information.

Correspondent: Mrs C A Gilbert, Clerk, 47 Hedging Lane, Wilnecote, Tamworth B77 5EX (01827 704815; Fax: 01827 704815; e-mail: christine. gilbert@mail.com)

Trentham

The Lady Katherine and Sir Richard Leveson Charity

Eligibility: People in need under 25 years who live in the ancient parish of Trentham.

Types of grants: One-off grants are given to: schoolchildren for equipment/ instruments, educational outings in the UK and study or travel abroad; people starting work for equipment/instruments; and further and higher education students and postgraduates for books, equipment/ instruments, educational outings in the UK and study or travel abroad.

Annual grant total: In 2005 the charity had an income of £2,600 and a total expenditure of £6,400.

Applications: In writing to the correspondent, either directly by the individual or through a third party such as an educational welfare office or school/ college. Applications can be submitted at any time, though August is most popular.

Correspondent: A Bainbridge, 67 Jonathan Road, Stoke-on-Trent, ST4 8LP

Tutbury

The Tutbury General Charities

Eligibility: Students and people starting apprenticeships or other training who live in the parish of Tutbury.

Types of grants: One-off grants in the range of £40 and £80.

Annual grant total: In 2004/05 about £1,800 was distributed in welfare grants to individuals. No educational grants were made.

Applications: The trust has application forms, available from the correspondent, which should be returned by 1 October for consideration in November. A letter of acceptance from the place of education is required.

Correspondent: Mrs J M Minchin, 66 Redhill Lane, Tutbury, Burton-on-Trent, Staffordshire DE13 9JW (01283 813310)

Other information: The clerk of the trust states that details of the trust are well publicised within the village.

Warwickshire

The Arlidges Charity

Eligibility: People under 25 who live in Kenilworth, Warwick and Leamington (the old county of Warwickshire). Applicants or their parent/guardian should be a member of a Congregational Church or United Reformed Church.

Types of grants: Help towards the cost of books, fees and travel or study abroad for students in further or higher education. Grants are recurrent if appropriate.

Exclusions: Grants are not given to schoolchildren or people starting work.

Annual grant total: About £2,000 a year.

Applications: In writing to the correspondent, including details of the course to be taken and details of any other funding. Applications are considered in October.

Correspondent: Mrs A Pointon, 17 Ferndale Drive, Kenilworth, Warwickshire CV8 2PF

The Dunchurch & Thurlaston Educational Foundation

Eligibility: People under 25 who live in the parishes of Dunchurch and Thurlaston.

Types of grants: One-off grants, rarely of more than £200. Schoolchildren, people starting work and people in further and higher education can receive support for books, equipment and instruments, educational outings in the UK and travel abroad in pursuit of education. In addition, people starting work and further and higher education students can be funded for fees and maintenance or living expenses.

Annual grant total: In 2004/05 it had an income of £2,100 and gave £550 in grants, including just one grant to a student for £100. In previous years grants have been made to individuals for several times that amount and may be again in future years.

Applications: In writing to the correspondent, directly by the individual or their parent/guardian, at any time.

Correspondent: Paul Smith, Clerk, 11 Bilton Lane, Dunchurch, Rugby, Warwickshire CV22 6PY (01788 810635; e-mail: paul.smith6@virgin.net)

Other information: This trust also supports organisations providing benefits to people under 25 in the area.

The Hatton Consolidated Charities

Eligibility: People who live in the parishes of Hatton, Beausale and Shrewley. Applications from outside these areas will not be considered.

Types of grants: One-off grants of £50 to £500 to college students, undergraduates and vocational and mature students towards books and equipment/instruments. People with special educational needs are also supported.

Exclusions: Grants are not given to schoolchildren.

Annual grant total: In 2004/05 the charities had assets of £164,000 and an income of £8,300. There were 40 welfare grants made totalling £4,100. No educational grants were made during the year due to lack of applications.

Applications: In writing to the trustees or the correspondent, directly by the individual or a family member. Applications should include details of the course and envisaged expenditure.

Correspondent: Mrs M H Sparks, Clerk, Weare Giffard, 32 Shrewley Common, Warwick CV35 7AP (01926 842533)

The Leigh Educational Foundation

Eligibility: People in need who are under 26, and who live, or whose parents live, in the parishes of Stoneleigh, Ashow and Leek Wootton, Warwickshire.

Types of grants: One-off or recurrent grants according to need, ranging from £100 to £1,000. Grants are given to schoolchildren, college students, undergraduates, vocational students and people starting work. Grants given include those towards uniforms/clothing, fees, study/travel abroad, books, equipment/instruments and maintenance/living expenses.

Annual grant total: In 2005 the trust had an income of £32,000. A total of 28 grants were given amounting to £17,000.

Applications: On a form available from the correspondent (in hard copy or electronic format). Applications should be submitted directly by the individual. They are considered in February, May, August and November.

Correspondent: J F Johnson, 3 Barford Woods, Barford Road, Warwick, CV34 6SZ (e-mail: johnson.jf@virgin.net)

Leith Holiday Home Association

Eligibility: Children in Leith and north Edinburgh who are aged 16 or under (and occasionally up to 21 years) who are disabled, have experienced abuse, stressful home circumstances or are in financial need.

Types of grants: Grants are one-off and range from £25 to £100. They are primarily to help with holiday costs, including educational outings, and travel expenses, but can also be towards clothing, pocket money and other associated items. On average 30 to 40 grants are made per year.

Annual grant total: In 2005 the association had an income of £2,200. Grants totalled around £2,000.

Applications: On a form available from the correspondent. Applications should be submitted via a third party such as a social worker, Citizens Advice, health visitor, doctor, youth club leader and so on, in time for consideration at the annual general meeting of the trustees in April.

Correspondent: W Mathison, 11 Corrennie Gardens, Edinburgh, EH10 6DG

The Middleton United Foundation Trust

Eligibility: Young people under the age of 25 who are in need and live, or whose parents live, in the parish of Middleton or the immediate vicinity.

Types of grants: One-off and recurrent grants usually of amounts of up to £300 each. Schoolchildren, further and higher education students and postgraduates can be supported for books, equipment/instruments, educational outings in the UK and study or travel abroad. In addition, schoolchildren can be helped with uniforms/other school clothing and students in further and higher education can be supported with maintenance and living expenses. People starting work can be helped with books and equipment/instruments. Grants can also be made towards the costs of developing a hobby.

Annual grant total: In 2005/06 the trust had an income of £5,400 and a total expenditure of £3,800. There were 17 grants made in the year totalling £3,600.

Applications: In writing to the correspondent, giving as many details as possible, for example, the purpose and size of grant requested, the cost of books/equipment, the age of the applicant and a description of the course.

Correspondent: Mrs E Foulkes, Horseshoes, Crowberry Lane, Middleton, Nr Tamworth, Staffordshire B78 2AJ

Other information: Grants are occasionally made to organisations.

Perkins Educational Foundation

Eligibility: People who have been living for at least two years, immediately prior to their application, in Salford Priors, Kings Broom, Bidford-on-Avon, Harvington or Cleeve Prior, and who are aged 16 to 24.

Types of grants: Grants towards the cost of books, fees/living expenses and study or travel abroad for students in further/higher education, postgraduates or mature students under 25. Help may be given towards the cost of books, equipment/instruments or travel for those involved in apprenticeships or those intending to acquire a profession or trade. Grants range from £145 to £185.

Annual grant total: Grants are made each year totalling around £10,000.

Applications: On a form available from the correspondent, to be returned by mid October for consideration in November. Telephone calls will not be accepted. An applicant's first application must be accompanied by a testimonial from his/her headteacher, college principal, employer or other proper person recommending them as a suitable person to whom a grant might be made.

Correspondent: The Clerk to the Governors, c/o Lodders Solicitors, 10 Elm Court, Arden Street, Stratford Upon Avon CV37 6PA

The Watson Scholarship for Chemistry

Eligibility: People who live in Warwickshire who have an A grade in A-level chemistry.

Types of grants: Grants of up to £200, for one year only, to students taking up a university first degree course in chemistry, or one in which chemistry plays a major part.

Annual grant total: In 2004/05 the trust had both an income and a total expenditure of £1,800. Grants of £200 each were made to nine individuals totalling £1,800.

Applications: On a form, available from the correspondent, but usually from the individual's school or college. The closing date for applications is 31 October.

Correspondent: Mary Aitken, Governor Support Officer, County Education Department, 22 Northgate Street, Warwick CV34 4SR (01926 412115; Fax: 01926 412746; e-mail: maryaitken@ warwickshire.gov.uk)

Baginton

The Lucy Price Relief-in-Need Charity

Eligibility: Only people in need who live in the parish of Baginton, Warwickshire and who are under 25.

Types of grants: Grants are made for: (i) attendance at university, living away from home; (ii) attendance at university or colleges of further education, living at home; (iii) attendance at local schools or sixth form college or A-level courses; (iv) school uniforms; (v) travel or visits of an educational nature at home or abroad organised by school or university; (vi) occasionally for equipment, instruments or books specially required for people starting work; and (vii) special education needs requiring special courses or equipment.

Grants made under (i), (ii) and (iii) are for the academic year and are paid in three equal instalments. Grants made under (iv), (v), (vi) and (vii) may be applied for at any time.

Annual grant total: In 2005 the charity had an income of £52,000 and a total expenditure of £54,000. Educational grants to 110 individuals totalled £45,000.

Applications: Application forms can be obtained from the correspondent either directly by the individual or by the applicant's parents if they are under 16 years old.

Correspondent: G Meredith, Clerk, Flat 39, Westbrook Court, Sutherland Avenue, Coventry CV5 7RB

Barford

The Barford Relief-in-Need Charity

Eligibility: Young people who live in the parish of Barford.

Types of grants: Grants for those at school, college or university. Occasional financial assistance is provided for specific purposes such as Operation Raleigh and outward bound type courses.

Exclusions: No loans are given.

Annual grant total: In 2005 the charity had an income of £8,000. The sum of £11,000 was distributed in 52 welfare grants to individuals and £850 in four educational grants.

Applications: In writing to the correspondent, directly by the individual or a family member. Applications are considered upon receipt. One of the trustees will visit to elicit all necessary information. Applications are usually considered in May and October.

Correspondent: Mr and Mrs T Offiler, 14 Dugard, Barford, Warwick, CV35 8DX (01926 624153)

Bilton

The Bilton Poor's Land & Other Charities

Eligibility: People in need who live in the ancient parish of Bilton (now part of Rugby).

Types of grants: This charity is not primarily an educational charity, concentrating rather on the relief of need.

Annual grant total: In 2004/05 the charities had assets of £461,000, an income of £19,000 and a total expenditure of £15,000. The sum of £2,600 was distributed in 263 welfare grants, with £200 distributed in two educational grants.

Applications: In writing to the correspondent, by the individual or through a relevant third party such as a minister, although often applications are forwarded by social services. They are considered in February, May and October.

Correspondent: Mrs A J Parker, Clerk, 2 David Road, Bilton, Rugby CV22 7PX (01788 810930)

Coleshill

The Simon Lord Digby Educational Endowment

Eligibility: Female students of secondary school or higher education age who live in the parish of Coleshill.

Types of grants: One-off grants are given to schoolchildren for school uniforms and other school clothing, books and educational outings, and to students in further/higher education for help with books. Preference is given to schoolchildren with serious family difficulties.

Exclusions: No grants to mature students.

Annual grant total: In 2004 the trust had an income of £15,300 and a total expenditure of £6,700.

Applications: In writing to the correspondent. Applications should be submitted directly by the individual or parent/guardian for consideration in

March or November, and include a breakdown of expenses, the amount requested and details of applications to any other grants.

Correspondent: Mrs Ann Latimer, The Vicarage Office, High Street, Coleshill, Birmingham, B46 3BP (01675 462188)

Exhall

The Exhall Educational Foundation

Eligibility: People under 25 who live or whose parents live in the ancient parish of Exhall.

Types of grants: One-off and recurrent grants for educational purposes.

Annual grant total: About £1,700 a year.

Applications: On a form available from the correspondent. The trust advertises locally and considers applications in March and September.

Correspondent: Mrs Challingsworth, Secretary, c/o Exhall Vicarage, Ash Green, Coventry CV7 9AA (024 7636 2997)

Kenilworth

The William Edwards Educational Charity

Eligibility: People under the age of 25 who live or whose parents live in the town of Kenilworth, and have attended a school in the town.

Types of grants: For educational purposes, each application is considered on its merits.

Annual grant total: In 2004/05, the charity had assets of £5.2 million and an income of £176,000. Grants to individuals totalled £24,000. A further £90,000 was distributed in grants to schools and £25,000 in bursaries for postgraduate study.

Applications: On a form available from the correspondent.

Correspondent: J M P Hathaway, Solicitor, 42 Brook Street, Warwick CV34 4BL (01926 492407)

Shipton-on-Stour

Shipston-on-Stour Educational Charity

Eligibility: People under 25 who live, or whose parents live, in the parish of Shipston-on-Stour only.

Types of grants: Grants are given to students undertaking further and higher education, postgraduates and apprenticeships. Support can be for uniforms/clothing, books, tools, instruments/equipment, educational outings in the UK or study or travel abroad.

Grants are one off and range from £30 to £120.

Annual grant total: In 2005 the charity had an income of £4,000 and a total expenditure of £2,800. Grants were made to 32 individuals totalling £2,000.

Applications: On a form available from correspondent. Applications should be submitted directly by the individual by the first week of September for consideration at the end of that month.

Correspondent: Mrs J Price, 9 Bosley Close, Shipston-on-Stour, Warwickshire CV36 4QA (01608 662443; Fax: 01608 662443)

Stoke Golding

Stoke Golding Boy's Charity

Eligibility: Young men and boys under the age of 25 who live in Stoke Golding. Some preference is given to people with special educational needs.

Types of grants: One-off grants, generally ranging from £150 to £200, depending on availability and circumstances.

Annual grant total: In 2005 the charity had an income of £6,000 and a total expenditure of £4,500. Grants were made to 16 individuals totalling £4,000.

Applications: In writing to the correspondent direcly by the individual. Applications should be submitted by mid-March for consideration in April.

Correspondent: Mrs Ruth Fisher, 21 Hinckley Road, Stoke Golding, Nuneaton, Warwickshire CV13 6DU (01455 212489)

Stratford-upon-Avon

The Stratford-upon-Avon Municipal Charities – Relief in Need

Eligibility: People in need living in the town of Stratford-upon-Avon.

Types of grants: One-off grants up to £500 are given towards the cost of: (i) school uniforms, other school clothing, books, maintenance and school fees for schoolchildren; (ii) books for students in further and higher education; and (iii) books, equipment and instruments for people starting work.

Annual grant total: About £20,000 is given to individuals for educational and welfare purposes.

Applications: On a form available from the correspondent, including details of the course costs and the financial circumstances of the applicant and parent(s) if appropriate. There is a separate form for students. Applications for

schoolchildren must be made through the school.

Correspondent: Mrs Ros Dobson, Clerk to the Trustees, 155 Everham Road, Stratford-upon-Avon, Warwickshire CV37 9BP (01789 293749)

Thurlaston

Thurlaston Poor's Plot Charity

Eligibility: Students in need who live in Thurlaston.

Types of grants: Grants are given for help with the cost of books.

Annual grant total: About £2,000 a year.

Applications: In writing to the correspondent directly by the individual. Applications are considered in January, September and November.

Correspondent: Mrs K Owen, Clerk, Congreaves, Main Street, Thurlaston, Rugby CV23 9JS (01788 817466)

Other information: Welfare grants are also made to older people.

Warwick

The Austin Edwards Charity

Eligibility: People living in the old borough of Warwick.

Types of grants: Grants ranging from £250 to £500 for students and mature students at college or university or for people starting work, towards clothing, equipment, books, travel expenses, course fees, overseas travel etc.

Annual grant total: In 2004/05 the charity had an income of £9,600 and a total expenditure of £12,000. Grants totalled about £5,000. Grants are made to organisations and individuals.

Applications: In writing to the correspondent. Applications are considered throughout the year.

Correspondent: R Ogg, Wright Hassall & Co, 9 Clarendon Place, Leamington Spa, Warwickshire CV32 5QP (01926 886688; Fax: 01926 885588)

The King Henry VIII Endowed Trust – Warwick

Eligibility: People who live in the former borough of Warwick.

Types of grants: Grants are given to college students and undergraduates for study/travel overseas, to vocational students for fees and to schoolchildren for excursions.

Annual grant total: This trust has assets amounting to £25 million. In 2005 the trust distributed £3,200 in 17 relief-in-need grants and £6,800 in eight educational grants.

Applications: On an application form available from the correspondent. Applications can be submitted at any time directly by the individual, a relevant third party or through a social worker, Citizens Advice or educational welfare agency. They are considered bi-monthly.

Correspondent: R J Wyatt, Clerk & Receiver, 12 High Street, Warwick CV34 4AP (Fax 01925 401464)

Other information: Grants are also made to organisations.

Warwick Apprenticing Charities

Eligibility: People aged 16 to 25 who live within the town boundaries of Warwick and are in need.

Types of grants: One-off grants are given for 'advancement in life', especially for the purchase of tools, equipment, books and travel for apprentices and students in further and higher education, and for outward bound courses.

Annual grant total: About £50,000.

Applications: In writing to the correspondent. The trustees meet regularly during the year to approve and allocate grants.

Correspondent: C R E Houghton, Clerk, c/o Messrs Moore and Tibbits, Solicitors, 34 High Street, Warwick CV34 4BE (01926 491181)

Sir Thomas White's Charity, Warwick

Eligibility: People under 35 who are in need who or whose parents are ordinarily resident in the town of Warwick who are undertaking further education or vocational training.

Types of grants: Interest-free loans towards fees and living expenses.

Annual grant total: In 2004 the charity had an income of £194,000 and a total expenditure of £180,000. Grants totalled about £170,000.

Applications: On a form available from the correspondent. Applications are considered upon receipt.

Correspondent: Roger J Wyatt, Clerk and Receiver, 12 High Street, Warwick CV34 4AP (01926 496262; Fax: 01926 401464)

West Midlands

The Annie Bettmann Foundation

Eligibility: People between 21 and 39 years of age who live in the city of Coventry or within three miles of the municipal boundary.

Types of grants: Grants for either people starting in business, or students in further education. Donations are usually in the range of £1,000 and £15,000.

Annual grant total: The amount given in grants is dependent on income received.

Applications: Application forms are available from the clerk from the end of March to the end of May each year. The trust also advertises in the *Coventry Evening Telegraph*.

Correspondent: Mr Kelley, Clerk to the Trustees, c/o R J Kelley Alsters Solicitors, 1 Manor Terrace, Friars Road, Coventry CV1 2NU

The Sir W W Butler Welfare Fund

Eligibility: Students over the age of 11 who live in the city of Birmingham and the borough of Smethwick.

Types of grants: Grants in the range of £150 and £400 are given to: schoolchildren, college students, undergraduates, vocational students, mature students and people with special educational needs. Grants given include those towards uniforms/clothing, fees, books, equipment/ instruments, and maintenance/living expenses.

Annual grant total: In 2004/05 the trust gave £50,000 in 73 grants for educational purposes.

Applications: In writing to the correspondent. There is a preference for applications supported by a letter from a teacher or educational welfare officer etc. Applications are considered in June/July and should be submitted by the end of April.

Correspondent: Martin J Woodward, Cobbetts LLP, One Colemore Square, Birmingham, B4 6AJ (0845 404 2404; Fax: 0845 404 2434)

The Chance Trust

Eligibility: People in need in the rural deaneries of Warley and West Bromwich.

Types of grants: One-off grants ranging from £50 to £400. Occasionally support can be made to university students for up to three years.

Annual grant total: The trust makes grants of between £2,500 and £3,000 a year to individuals for both educational and relief-in-need purposes.

Applications: In writing to the correspondent, outlining the need and the amount required. Applications are considered in January and July.

Correspondent: Revd Michael Dunk, Trustee, St Hilda's Vicarage, Abbey Road, Smethwick, West Midlands B67 5NQ

Other information: Grants are also given to organisations.

The W E Dunn Trust

Eligibility: People who live in the West Midlands who wish to further their education, but have special difficulties which prevent them from doing so. These can include, for example, prisoners who are using education as part of their rehabilitation, or students who are physically disabled or who have lived through particularly difficult circumstances

Types of grants: One-off grants ranging from £50 to £200.

Exclusions: Grants are not made to settle or reduce debts already incurred.

Annual grant total: In 2004/05 the trust had assets of £3.5 million and an income of £126,000. There were 28 grants made to individuals for educational purposes totalling £6,800. A further £32,000 was given to individuals for welfare purposes.

Applications: In writing to the correspondent. Applications for educational grants from mature students should be submitted directly by the individual and other applications should be submitted through the individual's parent/guardian or school/college/ educational welfare agency. They are considered two or three times a month depending on the number of applications.

Correspondent: Alan H Smith, The Trust Office, 30 Bentley Heath Cottages, Tilehouse Green Lane, Knowle, Solihull B93 9EL (01564 773407)

Other information: Grants are also made to organisations (£89,000 in 2004/05).

The Kathleen & Margery Elliott Scholarship Trust

Eligibility: Preference for people who live in the West Midlands.

Types of grants: Travel grants, of about £50 to £500, for educational purposes, with a preference for the study of music.

Annual grant total: In 2004/05, the trust had an income of £14,000 and a total expenditure of £6,800. The trust usually gives a large number of small grants.

Applications: In writing to the correspondent with an sae, full description of proposal, costings, names of referees, and details of financial resources.

Correspondent: C J B Flint, Shakespeares Solicitors, 37 Temple Street, Birmingham B2 5DJ (01789 488401)

Grantham Yorke Trust

Eligibility: People under 25 who were born in what was the old West Midlands metropolitan county area (basically: Birmingham, Coventry, Dudley, Redditch, Sandwell, Solihull, Tamworth, Walsall or Wolverhampton).

Types of grants: One-off grants are given to: (i) schoolchildren for uniforms/other school clothing, books, equipment/ instruments, fees, maintenance/living expenses, childcare, educational outings in the UK, study or travel overseas and student exchange; (ii) people starting work for maintenance/living expenses and childcare; and (iii) further and higher education students and postgraduates for books equipment/instruments, fees, maintenance/living expenses, childcare, educational outings in the UK, study or travel overseas and student exchanges.

Annual grant total: In 2004/05 it had assets of £5.2 million, which generated an income of £225,000. The sum of £318,000 was given to 46 individuals.

Applications: On a form available from the correspondent. Applications can be submitted either directly by the individual or a relevant third party; or through the individual's school, college or educational welfare agency. They are considered in March, June, September and December and should be received before the start of these months.

Correspondent: Mrs Lucy Cooling and David L Turfrey, Appeals Clerks, Martineau Johnson, No 1 Colmore Square, B4 6AA (0870 763 2000)

Other information: Grants are also made to organisations.

The James Frederick & Ethel Anne Measures Charity

Eligibility: The following criteria apply:

1 applicants must usually originate in the West Midlands

2 applicants must show evidence of self-help in their application

3 trustees have a preference for disadvantaged people

4 trustees have a dislike for applications from students who have a full local authority grant and want finance for a different course or study

5 trustees favour grants towards the cost of equipment

6 applications by individuals in cases of hardship will not usually be considered unless sponsored by a local authority, health professional or other welfare agency.

Types of grants: One-off or recurrent grants, usually between £50 and £500.

Annual grant total: In 2004/05 the trust had assets of £1.1 million and an income of £36,000. Grants totalled £43,000, of which around £3,000 went to individuals.

Applications: In writing to the correspondent. No reply is given to unsuccessful applicants unless an sae is enclosed.

Correspondent: Sally Darby, Clerk to the Trustees, Harris Allday, 2nd Floor, 33 Great Charles Street, Birmingham B3 3JN

The Perry Charitable Trust

Eligibility: People in need under 25 whose parents or guardians have been resident in the West Midlands for not less than three years.

Types of grants: Grants for clothing, instruments, tools, books and so on.

Annual grant total: In 2004/05, the trust had an income of £15,600 and a total expenditure of £156,000. No further information concerning grants was available.

Applications: In writing to the correspondent.

Correspondent: Sir Michael Perry, 75 Park Walk, London, SW10 0AZ (020 7351 9533; Fax: 020 7376 3285)

Birmingham

The Birmingham Bodenham Trust

Eligibility: People under 19 years of age who have special educational needs and live in the Birmingham area.

Types of grants: Grants are made for education and training, including for recreation and leisure, with the object of improving the quality of life of the individual.

Annual grant total: About £20,000 is available to be given in grants each year to organisations and individuals.

Applications: In writing to the correspondent. Applications are considered three times a year.

Correspondent: James Watkins, Learning and Culture Finance, Birmingham City Council, 38–50 Orphanage Road, Erdington, Birmingham B24 9HN

Sir Josiah Mason's Relief in Need and Educational Charity

Eligibility: People studying at first degree level or below who are in need and under 25 years old, with a preference for those who live in Birmingham.

Types of grants: The trust usually makes donations of £50 towards the cost of books, and pays the bookshop directly rather than making the grant in cash to the individual.

Exclusions: No grants are made for fees.

Annual grant total: In 2004/05, four grants totalling £1,400 were made to individuals. These were to residents and former residents of the Sir Josiah Mason Care Charity. No grants were made to third parties during the year.

Applications: In writing to the correspondent.

Correspondent: T S Wallace, Mason Court, Hillborough Road, Birmingham B27 6PF (0121 245 1002)

William Piddock Foundation

Eligibility: People aged between 16 and 25 who are at secondary school or in further or higher education and live in Birmingham.

Types of grants: One-off and recurrent grants, usually ranging from £50 to £500, and loans are made to: further and higher education students and mature students to help with books, equipment/instruments, fees and maintenance/living expenses; and to postgraduates to help with study or travel overseas as part of their course.

Annual grant total: In 2004/05 the foundation had assets of £175,000 and an income of £7,500. Grants were made to 24 individuals totalling £7,900.

Applications: Directly by the individual with a reference from a college/tutor on a form available from the correspondent. Applications are considered in August/September and should be submitted by the end of July. Applicants are required to attend an interview.

Correspondent: Andrew Peet, Secretary, c/o Birmingham and Midland Institute, 9 Margaret Street, Birmingham B3 3BS (0121 236 3591; Fax: 0121 212 4577; e-mail: admin@bmi.org.uk)

Joseph Scott's Educational Foundation

Eligibility: People who live and were educated at primary level in the city of Birmingham.

Types of grants: One-off grants are given to students in further/higher education and mature students towards books and fees/living expenses.

Exclusions: No grants are given to postgraduates.

Annual grant total: In 2004/05 the foundation had an income of £1,900 and a total expenditure of £1,400. Grants totalled about £1,000.

Applications: On a form available from the secretary at the address below, for consideration in March, June, September and November.

Correspondent: Mrs J Elder, 26 Aulton Road, Sutton Coldfield, West Midlands, B75 5PY

Castle Bromwich

The Mary Dame Bridgeman Charity Trust

Eligibility: People under 25 who are in need and living in the ecclesiastical parishes of St Mary, St Margaret and St Clement, Castle Bromwich.

Types of grants: One-off grants ranging from £100 to £400 towards clothing, books and educational outings for schoolchildren; and books, fees, living

expenses and study or travel abroad for students in further/higher education. There is a preference for schoolchildren with serious family difficulties so that the child has to be educated away from home and people with special educational needs.

Exclusions: Grants are not given if they will affect any statutory benefits.

Annual grant total: In 2004/05 the trust had an income of £2,500 and a total expenditure of £1,800. Grants totalled about £900.

Applications: In writing to the correspondent either directly by the individual, through the individual's school, college, educational welfare agency or through a parent. The trustees meet twice a year in May and November.

Correspondent: Revd Michael Sears, 67 Chester Road, Castle Bromwich, Solihull, West Midlands B36 0AL

Other information: This entry is an amalgamation of three separate charity funds which are administered as one.

Coventry

The Sir Charles Barratt Memorial Foundation

Eligibility: People who live in the city of Coventry or those in full-time education at a school or place of further education in Coventry. There is a preference for applicants under the age of 18.

Types of grants: Grants to help those wishing to extend their musical education, whether in the UK or abroad. Grants generally range from £50 to £400.

Annual grant total: In 2003/04, the foundation had an income of £2,900 and an expenditure of £2,500.

Applications: The charity is advertised around October/November, usually in the *Coventry Evening Telegraph*. Applicants can then request an application form, which they must submit by the beginning of November. Applications are considered at the next meeting, usually in January.

Correspondent: D Kellam, City Development Finance, West Orchard House 2nd Floor, 28-34 Corporation Street, coventry, CV1 1GF (024 7683 1398; Fax: 024 7683 2695)

The Children's Boot Fund

Eligibility: Schoolchildren in the city of Coventry, aged 4 to 16.

Types of grants: Grants for school footwear for children in need. No other type of help is given. Grants are made direct to footwear suppliers in the form of vouchers.

Annual grant total: In 2003/04 the fund had assets of £57,000 and an income of £21,000. About 500 vouchers for schools were issued totalling £12,000.

Applications: Application forms are available from schools in the area and should be completed, verified and signed by the headteacher of the child's school. Applications are considered four times a year.

Correspondent: Mrs Janet McConkey, 123A Birmingham Road, Coventry CV5 9GR (02476 402837)

The General Charities of the City of Coventry

Eligibility: Students in need living in the city of Coventry aged 18 to 25.

Types of grants: Grants range from between £50 and £70, and are given to students in further education to help with the cost of books or specialised equipment.

Exclusions: Applications for fees or maintenance are never supported. Cash grants are not given.

Annual grant total: In 2004 the trust had an income of about £1.1 million. The total given in grants by the charities was £502,000, with around £25,000 given in grants to individuals. Grants are made to organisations and individuals.

Applications: Application forms can be collected from the correspondent in late August/early September and should be submitted for consideration in November. Replies will be sent out in December.

Correspondent: The Clerk, Old Bablake, Hill Street, Coventry CV1 4AN

Other information: The charities receive income from Sir Thomas White's Charity, including the allocation for the Sir Thomas White's Loan Fund in Coventry.

The Andrew Robinson Young People's Trust

Eligibility: Young people in Coventry who are in need.

Types of grants: One-off and recurrent grants according to need.

Annual grant total: In 2004/05 the trust had an income of £7,000 and a total expenditure of £7,400. Grants totalled about £6,000.

Applications: This trust has previously stated that its funds were fully committed.

Correspondent: Clive J M Robinson, 31 Daventry Road, Coventry CV3 5DJ

The Soothern & Craner Educational Foundation

Eligibility: Women and girls who live in Coventry. There is a preference for daughters of Quakers living in or attending school in Coventry. However, other girls from the city of Coventry, of any denomination, are eligible.

Types of grants: Mainly grants for further education, up to first degree level, to supplement existing grants or where no mandatory award is available. Grants have

also been given towards school uniforms and school fees. Amounts awarded vary according to circumstances, but are generally between £50 and £500.

Annual grant total: In 2004/05, the foundation had an income of £11,000, and a total expenditure of £8,400.

Applications: On a form available from the correspondent.

Correspondent: The Trustees, Mander Hadley & Co Solicitors, 1 The Quadrant, Coventry, CV1 2DZ (0247 663 1212)

Dudley

The Baylies' Educational Charity

Eligibility: People under 25 living in the area of Dudley Metropolitan Borough Council.

Types of grants: One-off grants for amounts of up to £1,000 each are given to schoolchildren for school uniforms and other school clothing, excursions and awards for excellence. Grants are also available to college students, undergraduates and vocational students for fees, study/travel abroad, books, equipment/instruments and maintenance/living expenses.

Annual grant total: In 2004/05 the trust had an income of £32,000 and gave grants to 84 individuals totalling £22,000.

Applications: On a form available from the correspondent to be submitted directly by the individual or a parent.

Correspondent: A Austin, 5 Priory Close, Dudley, West Midlands DY1 3ED (01384 252310; Fax: 01384 252310)

Daniel Parsons Educational Charity

Eligibility: Students up to the age of 25 who live in Dudley and district.

Types of grants: One-off grants in the range of £200 to £500.

Annual grant total: In 2004 the trust had an income of £9,700 and a total expenditure of £5,000. Grants totalled about £4,000.

Applications: On a form available from the correspondent for consideration at any time.

Correspondent: David Hughes, 53 The Broadway, Dudley, West Midlands, DY1 4AP

King's Norton

The King's Norton United Charities

Eligibility: People who live in the ancient parish of King's Norton in Birmingham.

Types of grants: One-off and recurrent grants according to need.

Annual grant total: In 2005, the charities had an income of £7,000 and a total expenditure of £5,200. Grants are made for welfare and educational purposes.

Applications: Grants are made to named individuals only.

Correspondent: Revd M Blood, Chair, 118 Northfield Road, Kings Norton, Birmingham, B30 1DX

Meriden

Meriden United Charities

Eligibility: Young people commencing a university course who have lived in the parish of Meriden for at least two years.

Types of grants: Grants are given to schoolchildren, college students, undergraduates, vocational students and people with special educational needs. They include those for uniforms/clothing, fees, books and equipment/instruments.

Annual grant total: In 2005 the charity had an income of £1,500. There were two welfare grants made totalling £1,100. No educational grants were made during the year.

Applications: Applications can be submitted either directly by the individual or a family member or through a third party such as a social worker or teacher. The existence of the charities is made known by a notice in the Meriden magazine and by a notice in the library.

Correspondent: A Barker, 163 Avon Street, Coventry CV2 3GQ (024 7645 3342)

Oldbury

The Oldbury Charity

Eligibility: Pupils at schools in Oldbury.

Types of grants: Most grants are given to pupils at Warley High School, but pupils at other schools in Oldbury can also apply. Grants up to about £90 are available to help with books, clothing, equipment and travel for those at school, and grants of up to £300 are given to help with school, college or university fees or to supplement existing grants.

Annual grant total: In 2003/04, the foundation had an inocme of £6,500 and a total expenditure of £6,000.

Applications: In writing to the correspondent by September of each year.

Correspondent: Gayle Ditchburn, Somerset House, c/o Shakespeares Solicitors, 37 Temple Street, Birmingham B2 5DJ (0121 632 4199; Fax: 0121 643 2257)

Rowley Regis

The Mackmillan Educational Foundation

Eligibility: People under 25 who live in the ancient parish of Rowley Regis.

Types of grants: Grants to people at school and college.

Annual grant total: In 2004/05 the foundation had an income of aorund £1,000, and a total expenditure of £600.

Applications: In writing to the correspondent.

Correspondent: V J Westwood, Clerk, 18 Westdean Close, Halesowen, West Midlands B62 8UA (0121 602 2484; e-mail: vicwestw@blueyonder.co.uk)

Sandwell

The George & Thomas Henry Salter Trust

Eligibility: Students and mature students in further or higher education who are in need and normally resident in the borough of Sandwell.

Types of grants: Grants to individuals range between £100 and £1,000 and are given towards the cost of books and college and exam fees.

Exclusions: No grants are given for the repayment of debt, items of capital expenditure, childcare or nursery costs.

Annual grant total: In 2005 the trust had assets of £1.4 million and an income of £45,000. The education fund gave £16,000 in total to schools and other organisations and £3,300 to local trainees at colleges and universities. The relief in need fund gave grants ranging from £150 to £1,800, which totalled £17,000.

Applications: Initially by letter to the correspondent. Applicants must provide full written details of their circumstances and study courses. Trustees meet bi-monthly and will occasionally interview applicants.

Correspondent: Mrs J S Styler, Clerk, Lombard House, Cronehills Linkway, West Bromwich, West Midlands B70 7PL

Other information: Grants are also given for relief-in-need purposes and to organisations.

Smethwick

Pinkney Memorial Trust Fund

Eligibility: Children under 18 who are either living in, are attending or have attended school in the county borough of Smethwick.

Types of grants: Grants are made to schoolchildren and people starting work

towards the cost of clothing, books, equipment/instruments, fees and maintenance/living expenses.

Annual grant total: The trust makes a couple of small grants each year totalling about £500.

Applications: On a form available from the correspondent, to be submitted directly by the individual.

Correspondent: Nick Hamer, Education and Children's Service, PO Box 41, Shaftesbury House, 402 High Street, West Bromwich B70 9LT (0121 569 8275; Fax: 0121 569 8222; e-mail: nick_hamer@ sandwell.gov.uk; website: www.lea. sandwell.gov.uk)

Stourbridge

The Palmer & Seabright Charity

Eligibility: People living in the borough of Stourbridge.

Types of grants: One-off and recurrent grants are made to college students, undergraduates and mature students for fees, books, equipment/instruments and maintenance/living expenses. Grants are also given to schoolchildren for fees.

Annual grant total: In 2004 the trust had an income of £32,000 and a total expenditure of £38,000. Grants totalled £11,000.

Applications: On a form available from the correspondent. Applications can be submitted either directly by the individual or a family member, through a third party such as a social worker or teacher, or through an organisation such as Citizens Advice or a school.

Correspondent: Susannah Griffiths, c/o Wall James & Davies, 15–23 Hagley Road, Stourbridge, West Midlands DY8 1QW (01384 371622; Fax: 01384 374057)

The Scott Educational Foundation

Eligibility: People between the ages of 16 and 25 who live in the old borough of Stourbridge (excluding Amblecote).

Types of grants: Grants in the range of £100 and £600 are given to schoolchildren towards school uniform, other school clothing, books, educational outings in the UK, maintenance and fees. Grants to students in further or higher education are given towards books, equipment/ instruments, fees, living expenses and study or travel abroad; and grants to people starting work are for equipment or instruments.

Grants are mainly one-off, for recurrent grants a repeat application has to be made.

Exclusions: Grants are rarely made to postgraduate students.

Annual grant total: In 2004 the foundation had an income of £830 and a

total expenditure of £870. Grants were made to five individuals totalling £800.

Applications: On a form available from the correspondent. Applications can be submitted either directly by the individual or a parent, guardian or local authority; or through the individual's school/college/ educational welfare agency. Preferably they should be received by June or November for consideration in July and January, otherwise there is no requirement.

Correspondent: John V Sanders, Solicitor, 1 Wollaston Court, Stourbridge, West Midlands DY8 4SQ (01384 394859)

Sutton Coldfield

Sutton Coldfield Municipal Charities

Eligibility: People in need under the age of 25 living in the Four Oaks, New Hall and Vesey wards of Sutton Coldfield.

Types of grants: Grants are given to: schoolchildren for uniforms/other school clothing, books, equipment/instruments, fees and educational outings in the UK; and further and higher education students for books, equipment/instruments, fees, maintenance/living expenses, childcare, educational outings in the UK and study or travel abroad. Grants are also given to people with a wide range of special educational needs.

Exclusions: Grants are not given to individuals with a high parental income.

Annual grant total: In 2004/05 the charities had assets of £34 million, which generated an income of £1.5 million. Grants to 32 individuals for educational and personal needs totalled £21,000. A further 420 school clothing grants were made to individuals totalling £14,000. Grants to 58 organisations totalled £845,000.

Applications: On a form available from the correspondent. Applications should be made directly by the individual or through a parent or carer. They are considered every month, except April, August and December. Telephone enquiries are welcomed.

Correspondent: Andrew Macfarlane, Lingard House, Fox Hollies Road, Sutton Coldfield, West Midlands B76 2RJ (0121 351 2262; Fax: 0121 313 0651)

Other information: The principal objective of the charities is the provision of almshouses, the distribution of funds and other measures for the alleviation of poverty and other needs for inhabitants and other organisations within the boundaries of the former borough of Sutton Coldfield.

Walsall

The Fishley Educational & Apprenticing Foundation

Eligibility: People under the age of 25 who live, work or are being educated in Walsall and who are in need.

Types of grants: Grants are available towards any educational need. Grants have been given towards books, fees, educational outings and towards the study of music and the other arts.

Annual grant total: In 2004/05 the foundation had an income of £13,000 and a total expenditure of £3,700.

Applications: On a form available from the correspondent.

Correspondent: Miss Julie Welsh, Administrator, Student Support Services, Education Department, Third Floor Civic Centre, Darwall Street, Walsall WS1 1DQ

The C C Walker Charity

Eligibility: Individuals under the age of 25 (one of whose parents has died) who were born in Walsall.

In certain cases grants are available to individuals whose parents or surviving parent's fixed place of residence has at any time since the birth of the child been in Walsall (further information on eligibility for this specific criteria should be sought from the charity).

Types of grants: Grants according to need for any educational purpose. Grants have been given towards clothing for schoolchildren and books, fees, living expenses and equipment for students in further/ higher education.

Annual grant total: In 2004/05, the charity had an income of £11,000 and a total expenditure of £3,000.

Applications: On a form available from the correspondent. Applications are considered in January, June and October.

Correspondent: Mrs Julie Welsh, Administrator, Student Support Services, Ground Floor, Walsall Metropolitan Borough Council, Civic Centre, Walsall WS1 1DQ

Warley

Palmer Educational Charity

Eligibility: People under 25 who live in the rural deanery of Warley.

Types of grants: Schoolchildren and further and higher education students can receive help with the cost of books directly related to Christianity and religious education.

Annual grant total: In 2003/04 grants to individuals and organisations totalled £4,300. Grants totalled about £1,500.

Applications: On a form available from the correspondent. They should be submitted through the PCC or clergy of Warley Deanery and are considered in March and October.

Correspondent: Miss Emma Lardner, Personal Assistant to the Diocesan Director of Education, Birmingham Diocesan Board of Education, 175 Harborne Park Road, Harborne, Birmingham B17 0BH (0121 426 0419; Fax: 0121 428 1114; e-mail: e.lardner@birmingham.anglican. org)

West Bromwich

The Akrill, Wilson and Kenrick Trust Fund & West Bromwich Educational Foundation

Eligibility: Students under 25 years of age, who are in need and live in West Bromwich.

Types of grants: (i) Scholarships and maintenance allowances for schoolchildren and students. (ii) Grants, clothing, tools, instruments and books for people leaving school or another educational establishment and starting work. (iii) Grants towards educational travel abroad. (iv) Grants for the study of music and other arts.

Annual grant total: In 2004/05 the foundation had an income of £2,800. No grants were made during the year.

Applications: On an application form, available by writing to the correspondent.

Correspondent: F N Summers, Chief Executives Department, Sandwell Council House, Oldbury, West Midlands B69 3DE (0121 569 2000)

Other information: These are two separate trusts with identical criteria.

Wolverhampton

The W H Jones Scholarship Fund

Eligibility: People who have been educated and live in the city of Wolverhampton and are beginning their first degree course in the Arts or Sciences.

Types of grants: One-off and recurrent grants according to need.

Annual grant total: In 2004/05 the fund had an income of around £400 and a total expenditure of about £1,200.

Applications: In writing to the correspondent accompanied by the relevant financial details, bank statements, course details and a letter from the univeristy confirming the amount being applied for.

Correspondent: Mrs Rosemond Jones, Mayor's Parlour, Civic Centre, St Peters Square, Wolverhampton WV1 1SH (01902 554090; Fax: 01902 554427)

Yardley

The Yardley Educational Foundation

Eligibility: Children between the ages of 11 and 16 and young adults going into further education between 16 and 19 who have lived in the ancient parish of Yardley (virtually the whole of the east of Birmingham) for over two years.

Types of grants: Schoolchildren can receive grants towards school uniforms, school clothing, books, educational outings in the UK and study or travel overseas; and further and higher education students can receive grants towards books. Donations are in the range of £50 to £200.

Annual grant total: In 2005/06, the foundation had assets of £3.2 million, an income of £149,000 and made grants totalling £122,000.

Applications: Application forms are available from the correspondent and should be submitted through the individual's school or college in May or June for consideration in July and August.

Correspondent: Derek Hackett, Edzell House, 121 Chester Road, Castle Bromwich, Birmingham, B36 0AE

Worcestershire

The Alfrick Educational Charity

Eligibility: People who live in the parish of Alfrick, Lulsley and Suckley and are under 25.

Types of grants: Grants are given to further and higher education students for books, maintenance/living expenses and educational outings in the UK.

Annual grant total: In 2004/05 the charity had an income of £7,600 and a total expenditure of £9,800. Grants totalled about £8,000.

Applications: In writing to the correspondent directly by the individual. Applications can be submitted at any time and are considered at any time.

Correspondent: Andrew Duncan, Bewell, Alfrick, Worcestershire WR6 5EY (01905 731731; Fax: 01905 22347; e-mail: a.duncan@wwf.co.uk)

The Bewdley Old Grammar School Foundation

Eligibility: People under the age of 25 living in Bewdley, Stourport-on-Severn, and the parish of Rock and Ribbesford.

Types of grants: Help with the cost of books, clothing and other essentials for schoolchildren. Grants may also be available for those at college or university.

Annual grant total: Between £7,000 and £8,000 is given in grants each year.

Applications: In writing to the correspondent.

Correspondent: The Trustees, c/o Morton Fisher Solicitors, Carlton House, Marlborough Street, Kidderminster DY10 1BA

The Ancient Parish of Ripple Trust

Eligibility: Students in higher education who live in the parishes of Ripple, Holdfast, Queenhill and Bushley.

Types of grants: Small cash grants are made.

Annual grant total: In 2004/05 the trust had an income and a total expenditure of £16,000.

Applications: In writing to the correspondent. The trustees meet twice a year to consider applications, and the funds are advertised locally before these meetings.

Correspondent: John Willis, Secretary, 7 Court Lea, Holly Green, Upton upon Severn, Worcestershire WR8 0PE

Other information: Grants are also made to registered charities that serve local people.

The Hugh Walker Mitchell Fund

Eligibility: People aged 16 to 25 who live in the parish of Wolverley and Cookley.

Types of grants: Grants, to a usual maximum of about £250, to help further and higher education students and postgraduates with the cost of books, fees, equipment/instruments, educational outings in the UK and study or travel abroad.

Annual grant total: In 2004/05, the trust had an income of £1,900 and a total expenditure of £1,700. Grants totalled about £1,500.

Applications: Applications can be submitted by the individual on a form available from the correspondent. They are considered in November and should be received by October.

Correspondent: Geoffrey Shilvock, Wolverley Vicarage, Wolverley, Kidderminster DY11 5XD (01562 851133; e-mail: geoffshilvock@hotmail.com)

Walwyn's Educational Foundation

Eligibility: Young people aged 16 and over who are studying up to first degree level, but including vocational courses (for example, studying to be a chef), who live in the parishes of Colwall and Little Malvern. Some professions insist on qualifications beyond first degree (for example, teaching profession); these will be considered on their merits.

Types of grants: Grants of £160 each are given to students in further or higher education, including those for books, fees/living expenses, study and travel abroad.

Exclusions: Support will not be given to sixth form students or to mature students.

Annual grant total: In 2003/04 the foundation had a gross income of £3,800 and a total expenditure of £4,000. Grants totalled about £3,500.

Applications: On a form available from the correspondent. Applications are considered in late September and should be submitted directly by the individual up to 15 September.

Correspondent: S J Widdows, Clerk to the Governors, West Mead, Walwyn Road, Colwall, Malvern, Worcestershire WR13 6QE (01684 540326)

Worcester Municipal Exhibitions Foundation

Eligibility: People who are resident in, or receiving education in, the city of Worcester and the parishes of Powick, Bransford and Rushwick, and the ancient parish of Leigh for at least two years.

Types of grants: One-off grants are given to schoolchildren, people starting work, further and higher education students and mature students for clothing, books, equipment/instruments, fees, maintenance/living expenses, childcare, educational outings in the UK, study or travel overseas and student exchanges. Grants can range from £20 to £1,000.

Exclusions: Help is not usually given to mature students and no grants are made to foreign students studying in the UK or for private education.

Annual grant total: In 2004 grants the charity had assets of £657,000 and an income of £101,000. Grants totalled £64,000 of which £10,000 went to individuals.

Applications: Applications can be submitted by the individual or through a school, college or educational welfare agency on a form available from the correspondent. They are considered every month.

Correspondent: The Clerk to the Trustees, 4- 5 Sansome Place, Worcester WR1 1UQ (01905 726600; Fax: 01905 743366)

Alvechurch

The Alvechurch Grammar School Endowment

Eligibility: People who: (i) have lived in the civil parish of Alvechurch for at least three years; and (ii) are under the age of 25 on the 30th June in the year of application.

Types of grants: Applications are invited from 'those needing help to enable them to pursue an academic or technical course whether at school or in some form of higher education and the governors are anxious to receive applications relating to education in its widest sense: young people undertaking projects designed to assist with their development, examples of which might be Sail Training Association or Outward Bound courses or language study courses abroad'.

In practice grants are given to those in further or higher education rather than schoolchildren, but they can be given for people starting work. Grants can be towards the cost of equipment, books and educational outings or travel in the UK or overseas.

Annual grant total: About £20,000 is donated each year.

Applications: On a form available from the correspondent, including parents' income, schools attended and record of examination results. Applications are considered in January, May and September/October.

Correspondent: David Gardiner, 18 Tanglewood Close, Blackwell, Bromsgrove, Worcestershire B60 1BU

Other information: Grants are also made to youth-based organisations.

Cropthorpe

Randolph Meakins Patty's Farm & the Widows Lyes Charity

Eligibility: People in need who live in the village of Cropthorne (Worcestershire).

Types of grants: As well as general welfare grants, Christmas parcels are also given.

Annual grant total: In 2004/05 the charity had an income of £4,100 and a total expenditure of £3,500. Grants totalled about £3,000.

Applications: In writing to the correspondent.

Correspondent: John Ayliffe, Orchard House, Main Street, Cropthorne, Pershore, Worcestershire WR10 3LT

Evesham

John Martin's Charity

Eligibility: People resident in Evesham in Worcestershire. Applicants or a parent/guardian must have lived in the town for at least 12 months at the date of application.

Types of grants: Further and higher educational or vocational studies – individual students, between the ages of 16 and state retirement age, may apply for educational grants to support study in a wide variety of courses at local colleges in addition to universities and colleges throughout the country and the Open University. Qualifying courses include HND, Degree, Part-time and day release courses.

School uniform costs – grants may be available to assist with the cost of school uniform for children aged 4-18

Educational visits and music, arts and sports activities – grants may be available to students aged 4-18 for activities including school trips, music lessons/ instrument hire, sporting activities.

'Standards of Excellence' awards are also made.

Annual grant total: In 2004/05 the charity had assets of £17 million and an income of £642,000. Charitable expenditure totalled £547,000. £250,000 was given in academic awards to 664 students, £63,000 was given to 559 older people towards heating costs, £59,000 was awarded to individuals for relief-in-need, £42,000 was given to local schools, £39,000 was donated to 26 organisations and £4,700 was given in 45 miscellaneous educational awards.

Applications: On a form available from the correspondent, on written or personal request. Applications are considered from July to September for further and higher education grants.

Correspondent: The Clerk, 16 Queen's Road, Evesham, Worcester WR11 4JP (01386 765440; Fax: 01386 765340; e-mail: enquires@johnmartins.org.uk; website: www.johnmartins.org.uk)

Other information: Grants are also made to organisations.

Feckenham

The Feckenham Educational Foundation

Eligibility: People under 25 who live in the ancient parish of Feckenham.

Types of grants: Grants are given to schoolchildren and students, and towards the cost of outfits, tools and books to people preparing to enter a trade or profession.

Annual grant total: In 2003/04 the trust had both an income and expenditure of £1,500. Grants usually total about £1,500 a year.

Applications: On a form available from the correspondent.

Correspondent: Mrs J Bate, Clerk, Wychway, Droitwich Road, Hanbury, Nr Bromsgrove, Worcestershire B60 4DB

Rock

The Rock Educational Foundation

Eligibility: People under 25 living in the parish of Rock.

Types of grants: (i) Grants for school pupils, to help with books, equipment, clothing or travel. (ii) Grants to help with school, college or university fees, or to supplement existing grants. (iii) Help towards the cost of education and training.

Annual grant total: In 2004/05, the foundation had an income of £500 and an expenditure of £0.

Applications: On a form available annually in October from the correspondent. Trustees meet each year in January.

Correspondent: The Director of Educational Services, Director of Educational Services, Worcestershire County Council, PO Box 73, Worcester WR5 2YA (e-mail: fmorgan@ worcestershire.gov.uk)

Worcester

The United Charities of Saint Martin

Eligibility: People in need who live in the parish of St Martin, Worcester.

Types of grants: One-off grants are given for general educational purposes.

Annual grant total: In 2004/05 the charities had an income of about £6,000 and a total expenditure of £6,500.

Applications: In application to the correspondent.

Correspondent: Keith Johnson, Clerk, 1 Stuart Rise, Worcester WR5 2QQ (01905 357860)

The Worcester Consolidated Municipal Charity

Eligibility: People in need who live in the city of Worcester.

Types of grants: One-off grants of £20 to £1,000, for educational needs such as school clothing and so on.

Annual grant total: In 2004 the trust had assets of £8.4 million and an income of £1.1 million. The educational grants committee awarded 109 grants to individuals totalling £10,000.

Applications: Applications are usually through a social worker, Citizens Advice or other welfare agency. Statutory sources must have first been exhausted. Applications are submitted on a form available from the correspondent and are considered every month.

Correspondent: Mrs Mary Barker, Hallmarks, 4 & 5 Sansome Place,

Worcester WR1 1UQ (01905 726600; Fax: 01905 613302; e-mail: icp@ hallmarkslaw.co.uk)

7. SOUTH WEST

The Christina Aitchison Trust – see entry on page 121

Correspondent: A P G Massingberd-Mundy, Secretary, c/o The Old Post Office, West Raynham, Fakenham, Norfolk, NR21 7AD

Viscount Amory's Charitable Trust

Eligibility: People in need in the south west of England, with a preference for Devon (due to limited funds).

Types of grants: One-off and recurrent grants according to need.

Annual grant total: In 2004/05 the trust had assets of £9.3 million and an income of £308,000. Grants to 21 individuals totalled £12,000, of which £11,000 was given for educational purposes and £1,000 for relief-in-need purposes. Grants to organisations totalled £260,000.

Applications: In writing to the correspondent, for consideration every month.

Correspondent: The Trust Secretary, The Island, Lowman Green, Tiverton, Devon EX16 4LA (01884 254899; Fax: 01884 255155)

Batten Memorial Fund

Eligibility: Further and higher education students who are in need, live in the counties of Somerset and Dorset and are studying or planning to study agriculture (in its broadest possible terms).

Types of grants: Grants ranging from £200 to £600 towards books and equipment/instruments.

Annual grant total: About £5,000.

Applications: On a form which is available from the correspondent between July and September. Applications are considered in October.

Correspondent: Simon Clothier, c/o Symonds & Sampson, 2 Court Ash, Yeovil, Somerset BA20 1HG (01935 23526)

Devon & Cornwall Aid for Girls' Trust

Eligibility: Girls or women between 16 and 23 years of age who live in the counties of Devon and Cornwall. There is a preference for people who have lost either or both parents, but any other girl in need can apply.

Types of grants: One-off and recurrent grants ranging from £100 to £350. Grants are given to help students in higher/further and vocational education with books, clothing, fees, equipment/instruments and living expenses.

Exclusions: Grants are not given for postgraduate, higher or second qualifications, home or part-time studies, mature students, or study outside of the UK.

Annual grant total: In 2004/05 the trust had an income of £10,000 and a total expenditure of £13,000. Grants to 40 individuals totalled £12,000.

Applications: On a form available from the correspondent, submitted directly by the individual. They are considered throughout the year.

Correspondent: F J Webb, 33 Downham Gardens, Tamerton Foliot, Plymouth, Devon PL5 4QF (01752 776612)

The Dyke Exhibition Foundation

Eligibility: People under 25 years of age at the beginning of the latest year for which an award is applied, who were born in Somerset, Devon or Cornwall and who have lived within the area for the past three years or who have been educated in the area for the past two years.

Types of grants: Awards, usually between £100 and £300 per year for up to three years, for educational purposes. Applications are considered on merit, but preference is given to applicants who are, or are about to become, undergraduates of Oxford University or any other university, and those most in need.

Annual grant total: Previously around £1,200.

Applications: Application forms can be obtained by the individual, school or college, parent or guardian by sending an sae to the correspondent. Completed application forms must be submitted by the end of February for consideration in April.

Correspondent: G J O Channer, Clerk, c/o Messrs Bevan Ashford, 41 St James Street, Taunton, Somerset TA1 1JR

The Elmgrant Trust

Eligibility: Individuals living in the South West, especially in Devon and Cornwall. There is a preference for people with special education needs, and for schoolchildren with serious family difficulties causing the child to be educated away from home.

Types of grants: One-off grants of between £200 and £500 are made to schoolchildren for school clothing (not uniforms), books, equipment, fees and educational outings in the UK; people starting work for equipment; and further and higher education students, including mature students, for books, equipment, fees, maintenance/living expenses, childcare and educational outings in the UK.

Exclusions: Grants are not made for postgraduate study, expeditions, travel and study projects overseas, counselling courses, or to large-scale national organisations or overseas students.

People and organisations who have received a grant within the last two years are not eligible to reapply.

Annual grant total: In 2004/05 the trust had assets of £1.7 million and an income of £63,000. Grants totalling £4,000 were made to 12 individuals.

Applications: In writing to the correspondent at least one clear month before the trustees' meetings in March, July and November. Applications can be made directly by the individual, or through a third party such as a parent/guardian, school/college or educational welfare agency. They should include the individual's current financial circumstances (budget helpful), confirmation of place on course, letter in support (tutor, college or welfare worker) and information about the cost of items needed (if appropriate). An sae should also be included.

Correspondent: Angela Taylor, Elmhirst Centre, Dartington Hall, Totnes, Devon TQ9 6EL (01803 863160)

Other information: Grants are also made to local arts and community projects, disability and disadvantaged groups, and to medical causes. In 2004/05 these donations totalled £57,600.

A B Lucas Memorial Awards

Eligibility: People who live in the administrative counties of Cornwall, Devon, Somerset and Dorset, and those parts of Avon that were previously part of Somerset, and are undertaking the study of dairy agriculture.

Types of grants: One-off grants. In practice the people who apply tend to be young people, aged under 30, who wish to study dairy agriculture overseas. However, the trust is not limited to this.

Annual grant total: In 2004/05 the trust had assets of £50,700 and an income of £1,900. Grants were made to individuals totalling £825.

Applications: In writing to the correspondent.

Correspondent: J A Lindley, Nowers Farm, Wellington, Somerset TA21 9NN

Second Chance Trust for Devon and Cornwall (formerly The Elmgrant Fellowship Scheme)

Eligibility: Primarily people living in Devon and Cornwall over the age of 30 who wish to take up or change their career.

Types of grants: One-off grants ranging from £100 to £400 to mature students for books, equipment/instruments, fees, maintenance/living expenses, childcare and educational outings in the UK.

Exclusions: Grants are not made for postgraduate study or for travel abroad.

Annual grant total: In 2004/05 the trust had an income of £25,000 and a total expenditure of £23,000. Grants were made to 69 individuals totalling £18,000.

Applications: On a form available from Nan Bowyer, Administrator, Glencoe Puddaven, Dartington, Totnes TQ9 6EU.

Correspondent: Barton Farmhouse, Dartington Hall, Totnes, Devon TQ9 6ED (01803 849030)

Surplus Funds of the North Devon & West Somerset Relief Fund

Eligibility: Young people, not more than 25 years of age, who live in a specified area (in general terms comprising of North Devon and the western edge of Somerset), and who are preparing for or entering any trade, occupation or profession.

Types of grants: One-off payments to provide tools or books, towards fees for instruction or examination, for travelling expenses or other needs to enable the applicant to earn their own living or advance them in life.

Annual grant total: In 2004/05 the trust had an income of around £6,000 and a total expenditure of £5,000. Grants to individuals total around £2,000 each year.

Applications: In writing to the correspondent for consideration throughout the year.

Correspondent: W F Michelmore, Hon. Secretary, Michelmores, Woodwater House, Pynes Hill, Exeter EX2 5WR (01392 688688; Fax: 01392 360563; e-mail: wfm@michelmores.com; website: www.michelmores.com)

Bishop Wordsworth's Educational Trust

Eligibility: Children who are under 18, members of the Church of England and live in the diocese of Salisbury (that is, most areas of Wiltshire and Dorset), whose parents are in need financially or through sickness, and so on. Children of both clergy and laity of the diocese of Salisbury are eligible.

Types of grants: Grants can be given to help with the cost of books, educational outings, educational tuition and music tuition. There is a preference for schoolchildren with serious family difficulties and schoolchildren with special education needs. Grants are not made for school fees or maintenance costs.

Annual grant total: The trust has an income of about £20,000 a year, all of which is available to be given in grants. About 80% is given to Church of England schools in the diocese and 20% to a small number of individuals.

Applications: Applications should be made by the parent or guardian to the correspondent. Information required includes applicant's name, occupation of guardian/parent, address, date of birth, name of school, educational expenses, details of income of applicant's parent/guardian (i.e. financial status), amount applied for, for how long, source of other funds available, reasons for application, details of other children in family, church affiliation and a reference from the parish priest. Applications are usually considered around March and October. Telephone enquiries are welcomed.

Correspondent: The Clerk, The Salisbury Diocesan Board of Education, Audley House, 97 Crane Street, Salisbury, Wiltshire SP1 2QA (01722 411977)

Other information: Grants are also made to church schools in the diocese for Christian educational resources.

Avon

Bristol Trust for the Deaf

Eligibility: People who are hearing impaired and live in and around the city of Bristol.

Types of grants: The trustees normally make grants to assist in the training of people working with people who are deaf to ensure that the greatest number of people benefit from the limited resources available. In certain circumstances applications from individuals are considered.

Grants range from £50 to £250 and are given for books, equipment/instruments and fees for students, mature students and postgraduates. Schoolchildren can receive grants for equipment/instruments.

Annual grant total: In 2005 the trust had an income and a total expenditure of £5,200. Grants are mostly made to organisations.

Applications: In writing to the correspondent, directly by the individual. Applications are considered in May and November and should be submitted in April and October, but special consideration can be given at other times to urgent needs.

Correspondent: A M Burrows, Clerk, 13 Wellington Walk, Westbury-on-Trym, Bristol BS10 5ET

Other information: This trust mainly supports Elmfield School for Deaf Children, Hearing Impaired Service and Bristol Centre for Deaf People.

Magdalen Educational Foundation

Eligibility: Young people, under 18 years of age, who are in need, are mentally disabled and live in Bath, or within a 30-mile radius of the city

Types of grants: This charity makes grants for the benefit of children (under 18) who are mentally disabled and in need of special educational treatment.

Annual grant total: About £11,000 was given in grants to individuals in 2004.

Applications: In summer 2006, the foundation was in abeyance. Applications were not being accepted.

Correspondent: Mrs C Bayntun-Coward, Almoner, Bath Municipal Charities, 4/5 Chapel Court, Bath BA1 1SL

Nailsea Community Trust Ltd

Eligibility: Grants are made to schoolchildren, college students and undergraduates for study/travel abroad.

Types of grants: One-off grants, usually up to £500.

Annual grant total: In 2004/05 the trust had an income of £4,300 and a total expenditure of £6,800. Grants totalled about £5,000.

Applications: On a form available from the correspondent. Applications can be submitted either directly by the individual or via a relevant third party such as a school, social worker or Citizens Advice. Applications are considered at meetings held every three months.

Correspondent: Phil Williams, 11 Walnut Close, Nailsea, Bristol, BS48 4YT (Fax: phil@christiansurfers.co.uk)

Bath & North East Somerset

BASD Charitable Trust

Eligibility: Children and adults who have dyslexia. Applicants must live within the Bath and North East Somerset area.

Types of grants: Part-funding of psychometric assessments (the trust will only pay for up to half of the costs). The trust will pay its proportion of the fee directly to the educational psychologist carrying out the assessment.

Annual grant total: About £700 each year.

Applications: Further information and an application form is available from the correspondent on written request.

Correspondent: Mrs Hargreaves, 18 Camp View, Winterbourne Down, Bristol, BS36 1BW

Richard Jones Charity

Eligibility: People under 30 who live in the parishes of Chew Magna, Newton St Loe, Stanton Drew, Stanton Prior and Stowey-Sutton, all in the area of Bath and North East Somerset.

Types of grants: One-off and recurrent grants of £30 to £400 for:

(i) college and university students towards books, study or travel abroad, educational outings in the UK and equipment/instruments

(ii) schoolchildren towards school clothing, books and equipment/instruments

(iii) people starting work towards books, equipment/instruments

(iv) mature students and postgraduates up to the age of 30 for books and equipment/instruments.

Grants are also available for individuals in need at Christmas without any restriction of age. Schools, clubs and other organisations benefiting the youth of the above named parishes also receive grants towards equipment.

Exclusions: No grants are made to people attending private schools.

Annual grant total: In 2005 the charity had assets of £88,000, and both an income and a total expenditure of £2,900. Grants were made totalling £2,700.

Applications: On a form available from the correspondent, submitted directly by the individual. Applications should be submitted in September/October and March/April, for consideration in October and April – actual dates of the meetings when applications are considered are advertised in parish magazines and on parish noticeboards. Completed application forms must be submitted to a parish trustee (details supplied on the form) and an interview arranged.

Correspondent: J P Mead, Clerk, Little Meadow, Stanton Drew, Bristol BS39 4DJ (01275 332651; e-mail: jimp@meadstanton.freeserve.co.uk)

Other information: The correspondent states: 'The majority of our beneficiaries are students at universities and colleges of further education. We would like to attract more applications from school leavers starting to learn a trade for grants towards tools and equipment . We do on occasions assist school pupils with the cost of extra music lessons and, if they can exhibit exceptional talent, towards the cost of musical instruments. We have also given grants to children for educational visits, camps etc. organised by their schools but it seems that most of the state schools in the area are able to fund needy pupils from their own resources for such activities. We do not, generally speaking, assist pupils at private schools. Very occasionally grants may be made towards the cost of school uniform. Grants have also been given in the past few years to participants in Operation Raleigh expeditions, Outward Bound courses and other ventures of a similar nature.'

Ralph and Irma Sperring Charity

Eligibility: People in need who live within a five-mile radius of the Church of St John the Baptist in Midsomer Norton, Bath.

Types of grants: One-off and recurrent grants according to need.

Annual grant total: In 2004/05 the foundation had assets of £4.3 million and an income of £183,000. Grants to both individuals and organisations were made totalling £88,000.

Applications: In writing to the correspondent, to be considered quarterly.

Correspondent: Mrs P Powell, Secretary, Thatcher & Hallam Solicitors, Island House, Midsomer Norton, Bath BA3 2HJ (01761 414646; e-mail: ppowell@th-law.co.uk)

Other information: This trust also supports local organisations in the area.

Bristol

Bagshaw Birkin Educational Trust

Eligibility: Young people between the ages of 11 and 25 (preferably 11 to 18) who live within the boundaries of the city of Bristol and are studying at 'any school, university, college of education or other institution of further (including professional and technical) education approved for the purpose by the trustees', in the maintained education system.

Types of grants: Generally one-off cash grants to help with: essential clothing (not uniforms); school trips considered to have an educational or social value; and musical instruments. Grants are usually about £50, but in exceptional circumstances larger payments will be considered.

Again, in exceptional circumstances, applications from parents whose children are in private education will be considered, but there is a preference for children in the maintained education system.

Occasional block grants are given to one specific school based within the original area of benefit for distribution to named children.

Exclusions: No grants will be considered for: year 11 clothing; baby clothing; furniture or other items; university or college fees; fees for children in private education; funding for the dependants of applicants; maintenance allowances for years 12 and 13.

Annual grant total: In 2004/05 the trust's assets totalled £59,000, it had an income of £3,700 and its total expenditure was £4,500. Grants were made to 15 individuals totalling £3,900.

Applications: There are two types of applicant: individuals (usually through their parents), and schools who will make a block application for many pupils. The applicant's parents in each case will be required to complete a financial statement and give details of other children and whether they include wage earners. The applicant's full address must be provided to ensure the child lives within the Bristol city boundaries (the postcode is not necessarily sufficient). The trustees may wish to interview the parents.

Applications are considered at any time, if urgent, but usually at formal trustee meetings held in February, May and November, and applications for consideration at those meetings must be received by 28th of the previous month.

Correspondent: Mrs Una Ebery, Flat 1, 126 Cromwell Road, St Andrews, Bristol BS6 5EZ

The Christ Church Exhibition Fund

Eligibility: (i) Boys and girls over the age of 11 who live in the city of Bristol and are attending fee-paying schools. Assistance is not, however, given on first entry to fee-paying education. Grants for schoolchildren are calculated in relation to family income and actual fees. (ii) Students in higher education up to the age of 25 who have received at least two years' secondary education in Bristol or who have long residential connections with the city.

Types of grants: (i) Grants, generally between £200 and £1,000 a year, for fee-paying secondary education, where parents are unable to maintain payments because of changed family or financial circumstances. Grants are to help with the cost of school uniforms, other school clothing, books and educational outings.

Occasional help is given to talented pupils at state schools who need help to pay for music lessons.

(ii) Grants of between £100 and £300 a year to students unable to obtain discretionary awards or for higher education courses not qualifying for grants. Grants are awarded only for courses in the UK. Grants can be to help with the cost of books and help with fees and living expenses.

Exclusions: Grants are not given for trips abroad, for courses outside the UK or for postgraduate study.

Annual grant total: About £19,000.

Applications: On a form available from the correspondent from Easter onwards. Applications should be submitted directly by the individual (student) or by a parent (schoolchildren). Meetings are held in June/July for junior grants, and in September for seniors. Applications should include length of residence in Bristol, how long in present school (schoolchildren) and whether a definite place offer has been received (student).

Correspondent: Bristol Charities, 17 St Augustines Parade, Bristol BS1 4UL (0117 930 0303)

Edmonds & Coles Scholarships

Eligibility: People under the age of 25 who live in the ancient parishes of Henbury, Westbury-on-Trym or Horfield (Bristol) and have done so for at least three years.

Types of grants: Grants to help with educational expenses for those at school, college or university. This can include help with the study of music and other arts (which is outside the normal curriculum) and vocational training. Grants range from £210 to £1,000 and can be for books, equipment/instruments, maintenance costs, educational outings in the UK and study or travel overseas. Grants can also be made for university fees, but not for school fees.

At primary and secondary school level, grants are not normally given to enable children to enter private education when parents cannot afford the cost. Help may be given in respect of children already in private education when there is a change in financial circumstances through, for example, death of a parent, marriage break-up, unemployment and so on, and there are good reasons for avoiding disruption of the child's education.

Annual grant total: In 2004/05 the charity had an income of £7,000 and a total expenditure of £6,900. Grants totalled about £6,000.

Applications: On forms available from the correspondent, submitted by the individual or a third party if the applicant is under 16. They are usually considered in February, July and September.

Correspondent: Richard Morris, Treasurer, Merchants Hall, The Promenade, Bristol BS8 3NH (0117 970 7555)

Other information: This charity consults and cooperates with Bristol Municipal Charities in some cases.

Anthony Edmonds Charity

Eligibility: Young people up to the age of 25 who live in any of the ancient parishes (as in 1898) of Henbury, Westbury-on-Trym or Horfield.

Types of grants: One-off grants up to £400 can be made for books, uniforms/school clothing, educational outings in the UK, study or travel overseas, equipment/instruments and fees.

Annual grant total: In 2003/04 the trust had an income of £3,300 and a total expenditure of £2,900. Grants are made to individuals totalling around £2,000.

Applications: On a form available from the correspondent, submitted directly by the individual. The trustees meet to consider applications in March and September.

Correspondent: Mrs F E Greenfield, Clerk, 43 Meadowland Road, Henbury, Bristol BS10 7PW (0117 909 8308)

Fast Track Trust

Eligibility: Individuals over 18 who have been living in the Bristol wards listed below for at least one year. Applicants should be wishing to undertake vocational training, in any subject, but be in need of financial assistance to be able to do so.

The beneficial area is the Bristol wards of Ashley, Easton, Lawrence Hill, Henbury, Lawrence Weston and Southmead.

Types of grants: Grants are made of £500 each and may be used for vocational training costs, for example, towards fees, books, materials, transport and childcare. No grants are made towards living expenses.

Annual grant total: In 2004/05 the trust had an income of £8,300 and a total expenditure of £27,000; these figures are significantly less than in previous years. No information on grants was available for the year.

Applications: Initially by telephone (ring and ask to speak to an advice worker) and then a local interview. Application forms are provided after the interview. Applications are assessed on a monthly basis. Detailed guidelines are available on request.

Correspondent: The Clerk, Brunswick Court, Brunswick Square, Bristol BS2 8PE (0117 942 8211; Fax: 0117 907 7127; e-mail: info@fasttracktrust.org; website: www.fasttracktrust.org)

Other information: Clients are also given encouragement and support during training including, when available, a personal mentor. Advice and information on other sources of funding is also provided to people living in the eligible wards.

The Gane Charitable Trust – see entry on page 18

Correspondent: Mrs R Fellows, The Secretary, c/o Bristol Guild, 68–70 Park Street, Bristol, BS1 5JY (0117 926 5548)

The Redcliffe Parish Charity

Eligibility: Schoolchildren in need who live in the city of Bristol.

Types of grants: One-off grants usually of £25 to £50. 'The trustees generally limit grants to families or individuals who can usually manage, but whom are overwhelmed by circumstances and are in particular financial stress rather than continuing need.' Grants can be for children's school trips and school uniforms.

Exclusions: No support for adult education, school fees or repetitive payments.

Annual grant total: In 2004/05 the charity had assets of £153,000 and an income of £7,400. The sum of £6,200 was distributed in 150 grants.

Applications: In writing to the correspondent. Applications should be submitted on the individual's behalf by a social worker, doctor, health visitor, Citizens Advice or appropriate third party, and will be considered early in each month. Ages of family members should be supplied in addition to financial circumstances and the reason for the request.

Correspondent: Mrs M Jardine, Jowayne, Hobbs Wall, Farmborough, Bath BA2 0BJ (01761 471713)

Other information: Grants to schoolchildren occur as part of the trust's wider welfare work.

The Stokes Croft Educational Foundation

Eligibility: People aged 11 to 50 with family connections with the Unitarian Church in Bristol, the Stokes Croft (Endowed) School or the Western Union of Unitarian and Free Christian Churches.

Types of grants: Cash grants for books and clothing on transfer from junior to secondary school. Grants are also given towards the cost of: (i) educational outings, school uniform, other school clothing, and books for schoolchildren, but not for fees or maintenance; (ii) books, fees/living expenses, study or travel abroad and exchange visits for students in further and higher education; (iii) books, equipment and instruments, and clothing, but not travel for people starting work; and (iv) books and fees, but not expenses such as childcare, for mature students. Grants range from £50 to £500.

Annual grant total: In 2005 the foundation had an income of £17,000 and a total expenditure of £8,700. Around 25 grants totalling about £10,000 are made each year.

Applications: Applicants must apply in writing for a form. Applications should be submitted directly by the individual or by a parent. They are considered in March and September.

Correspondent: Revd B M Latham, Secretary, 9 Chakeshill Close, Bristol, BS10 6NX

Wraxall Parochial Charities

Eligibility: Residents of the parish of Wraxall and Failand, Bristol who are at any level of their education, in any subject, and are in need.

Types of grants: One-off grants in the range of £50 and £100.

Annual grant total: In 2005 the charity had an income of £11,000. There were 92 grants to individuals totalling £7,900.

Applications: In writing to the correspondent, directly by the individual. Applications are considered in February, June, September and November.

Correspondent: Mrs A Sissons, Clerk to the Trustees, 2 Short Way, Failand, Bristol BS8 3UF (01275 392691; Fax: 01275 392691)

North Somerset

Charles Graham Stone's Relief-in-Need Charity

Eligibility: Vocational students who live in the parishes of Churchill and Langford, North Somerset.

Types of grants: One-off grants of £50 to £150 towards fees, books, equipment and instruments.

Exclusions: No grants for payment of national or local taxes or rates.

Annual grant total: In 2004 it had an income of £4,700 and a total expenditure of £3,400. Grants to individuals totalled about £3,000.

Applications: In writing to the correspondent with a full explanation of the personal circumstances. Applications should be submitted by the end of February or August for consideration in the following month. Initial telephone calls are not welcomed.

Correspondent: M A Endacott, Hill Cottage, Worlebury Hill Road, Weston-Super-Mare, North Somerset BS22 9TL

Other information: Most of the trust's work involves making welfare grants within the parishes.

South Gloucestershire

Almondsbury Charity

Eligibility: People in need in the old parish of Almondsbury.

Types of grants: One-off grants are made, usually for buying books.

Exclusions: No grants for school or course fees.

Annual grant total: In 2003/04 the trust had assets of £1.6 million and an income of £47,000. Grants distributed included £6,400 to 257 individuals and £600 for the benefit of 3 families.

Applications: On a form available from the correspondent. Cash grants are never made directly to the individual; the grant is either paid via a third party such as social services, or the trust pays for the item directly and donates the item to the individual.

Correspondent: Shaun Davies, 13 Claydon Green, Whitchurch, Bristol, BS14 0NG (01275 543442; e-mail: sd.almondsbury@ blueyonder.co.uk)

Other information: The trust also gives support to local organisations (£30,000 in 2003/04).

The Chipping Sodbury Town Lands

Eligibility: People in need who are aged up to 25 years and live in Chipping Sodbury or Old Sodbury.

Types of grants: One-off and recurrent grants according to need.

Annual grant total: In 2004 the trust had assets of £7.2 million and an income of £270,000. Grants totalled £86,000 including about £40,000 given in grants to individuals.

Applications: On a form available from the correspondent.

Correspondent: Mrs Nicola Gideon, Clerk, Town Hall, 57–59 Broad Street, Chipping Sodbury, South Gloucestershire BS37 6AD

Cornwall

The Blanchminster Trust

Eligibility: People who live (or have at least one parent who lives) in the parishes of Bude, Stratton and Poughill (the former urban district of Bude-Stratton). Current or immediate past pupils of Budehaven Community School living outside the area are also considered.

Types of grants: One-off grants are made to schoolchildren, people starting work, further and higher education students, mature students and postgraduates towards uniforms or other school clothing, books, equipment/instruments, fees, maintenance/living expenses, childcare, educational outings in the UK, study or travel overseas and student exchanges.

Exclusions: Grants are not given to foreign students studying in Britain.

Annual grant total: In 2004 the trust's assets totalled £8 million, it had an income of £383,000 and its total expenditure was £366,000. Educational grants were made to 272 individuals totalling £143,000 with a further £11,000 distributed to 27 individuals for relief-in-need.

Applications: On a form available from the correspondent. Applications are considered monthly and should be submitted directly by the individual. Where possible the application should include a request for a specific amount and be supported with quotes for the costs of items needed and/or written support from a social worker or other welfare agency. Applications must include evidence of financial need.

Correspondent: Owen A May, Clerk, Blanchminster Building, 38 Lansdown Road, Bude, Cornwall EX23 8EE (01288 352851; Fax: 01288 352851)

Other information: Grants are also made to community projects.

The Elliot Exhibition Foundation

Eligibility: People under the age of 19 on 1 July preceding the award of the exhibition, whose parents/guardians live in the city of Truro, the town council areas of Liskeard and Lostwithiel or the parish of Ladock. Preference is given to applicants who have attended a maintained school for at least two years.

Applicants with parents/guardians who live in the county of Cornwall may also be considered if insufficient candidates meeting the above criteria apply.

Types of grants: Awards of up to £150.

Annual grant total: In 2005/06 the foundation had an income of £790 and made 12 grants totalling £1,200.

Applications: On a form available from the correspondent, to be submitted directly by the individual by 30 September for consideration in November.

Correspondent: Samantha Hocking, Student Services, Services for Children, Young People and Families, County Hall, Truro, Cornwall, TR1 3AY (01872 322495; e-mail: shocking@cornwall.gov.uk)

The Ken Thomas Charitable Trust

Eligibility: Young people connected with the agricultural industry who live in Cornwall and the Isles of Scilly, aged from 20 to 30 years.

Types of grants: One-off cash grants, advice and assistance to enable beneficiaries to travel out of the county of Cornwall to further their experience in matters allied to agriculture and horticulture, either in this country or abroad.

Annual grant total: In 2004/05, the trust an income of £960 and a total expenditure of £2,300.

Applications: Submitted by the individual, on a form available from the correspondent. Applications are considered throughout the year.

Correspondent: C P Riddle, Hon. Secretary, Molesworth House, Wadebridge, Cornwall PL27 7JE

Linkinhorne

The Roberts and Jeffery Foundation

Eligibility: All schoolchildren living in the parish of Linkinhorne who are in secondary education and/or training.

Types of grants: Grants are made to every eligible child; there is an option to return the money if it is not needed. Grants are for uniforms, other school clothing and educational outings in the UK.

Annual grant total: In 2004/05 foundation had a total income of £1,600 and an expenditure of £1,300. Grants totalled about £1,000.

Applications: In writing to the correspondent, directly by the individual or his or her parent/guardian; the trust is also sent a list from the primary school of those children who are moving to secondary school. Applications are considered in April and October.

Correspondent: Mrs Valerie Ham, Churchtown, Linkinhorne, Callington, Cornwall PL17 7LY (01579 362 302)

St Newlyn East

The Trevilson Educational Foundation

Eligibility: People under 25 who live in the parish of St Newlyn East.

Types of grants: Help with the cost of books, educational outings and other essentials for schoolchildren and those at college or university. Grants usually range from £50 to £500.

Annual grant total: In 2004/05 the foundation had assets of £500,000, an income of £6,400 and a total expenditure of £12,700. Grants were made to eight individuals totalling £12,200.

Applications: In writing to the correspondent.

Correspondent: Ms Brimacobe, Secretary, 12 Metha Road, St Newlyn East, Newquay, Cornwall TR8 5LP (01872 510869)

Devon

The Adventure Trust for Girls

Eligibility: Girls aged between 11 and 19 who live or attend school within eight miles of Exmouth Town Hall, excluding the areas west of the river Exe and north of the M5 motorway.

Types of grants: One-off grants ranging from £50 to £400 to assist applicants in their quest for adventure. Grants have been given towards Operation Raleigh, TEFL, school trips, ballet summer schools, sea scouts trips and a Department of Education campaigners camp. Grants have also been given to members of local table tennis, gymnastics and hockey teams. People taking part in a school exchange can be supported.

Exclusions: Grants are not given towards organised school ski trips.

Annual grant total: In 2003/04 the trust had an income of £2,500 and a total expenditure of £3,800. Grants were made totalling around £3,000.

Applications: On a form available from the correspondent. Applications should be submitted two months before trustees' meetings, which are held in January, March, May, July, September and November.

Correspondent: Mrs Beryl Cuff, 28 Lovelace Crescent, Exmouth, Devon EX8 3PR (01395 223606; e-mail: ecuff@btinternet.com)

Other information: Grants are also made to groups.

The Albert Casanova Ballard Deceased Trust

Eligibility: Boys entering or attending secondary schools between the ages of 11 and 16 years, who live within a seven-mile radius of Plymouth.

Types of grants: One-off grants are given towards school uniforms, books and equipment/instruments.

Annual grant total: In 2005/06 the trust had assets of just over £1 million and an income of £48,000. Grants to 134 individuals totalled £20,000. A further £22,000 was distributed to organisations.

Applications: In writing to the correspondent directly by the individual or a parent/guardian. Applications are only considered once a year, in June – the deadline for applications is the end of May.

Correspondent: The Chair of the Trustees, Sandpiper, Linkadells, Plympton, Plymouth PL7 4EF (01752 339334)

Bideford Bridge Trust

Eligibility: People in need who live in Bideford and the immediate neighbourhood.

Types of grants: One-off grants ranging from £150 to £500 to: schoolchildren for books and equipment/instruments; people starting work for books; further and higher education students for books, equipment/instruments and fees; and mature students for books and equipment/instruments.

Exclusions: Grants are not given to postgraduates or for computers for personal use.

Annual grant total: In 2005 the trust had an income of £655,000. Out of a total expenditure of £458,000 the sum of £78,000 was distributed in relief-in-need grants and £45,000 in educational grants.

Applications: On a form available from the correspondent, to be submitted at any time during the year by the individual, although a sponsor is usually required. Applications are considered monthly.

Correspondent: P R Sims, 24 Bridgeland Street, Bideford, Devon EX39 2QB (01237 473122)

The Devon County Association for the Blind

Eligibility: People in education who are blind and live in Devon (excluding the city of Exeter and Plymouth).

Types of grants: Grants of up to £250 to cover specific needs including equipment/instruments and excursions.

Annual grant total: £800 in two grants.

Applications: On a form available from the correspondent. Applications are considered quarterly and should be submitted either directly by the individual or through a third party such as a social worker or teacher.

Correspondent: Mrs Sue Auton, Director, Station House, Holman Way, Topsham, Exeter EX3 0EN (01392 876666)

Other information: Grants are also made to organisations.

The Devon Educational Trust

Eligibility: Pupils and students under the age of 25 who live, or whose parents' normal place of residence is, in Devon. Preference is given to applicants from low income families. Applicants, or their parents, must be living in Devon on a permanent basis for at least 12 months.

Types of grants: One-off grants of between £100 and £500 to schoolchildren for uniforms/clothing and equipment/instruments, to college students and undergraduates for special clothing, study/travel costs, books, equipment/instruments and maintenance/living expenses, to vocational students and people starting work for uniforms/clothing, books, equipment/instruments and maintenance/living expenses and to those with special educational needs.

Exclusions: Assistance is not normally given to those embarking on a second or higher degree course. However, in some cases the trustees may make a small grant to assist with living costs or the purchase of books, equipment and so on. No assistance is available for the payment of fees and only in exceptional cases will the trustees consider paying school or boarding fees.

Annual grant total: In 2005 the trust had assets of £930,000 and an income of £31,000. Grants were made to 115 individuals totalling £24,000. Six organisations received grants totalling £4,000. A total of 151 applications were considered.

Applications: On a form available from the correspondent, including details of two references submitted directly by the individual in February, June and October for consideration by the trustees in March, July and November.

Correspondent: The Clerk, PO Box 86, Teignmouth TQ14 8ZT

Exeter Advancement in Life Charity

Eligibility: Schoolchildren and students aged under 25 who are in need and live in the city of Exeter or within 15 miles of the city centre. Preference may be given to schoolchildren with serious family difficulties so that the child has to be educated away from home.

Types of grants: Grants are one-off and recurrent and range from £100 to £500 a year. Schoolchildren may be supported with uniforms/school clothing, equipment/instruments, fees and educational outings in the UK. People starting work can receive help with equipment/instruments. People in further and higher education, mature

students and postgraduates (if under 25 years) can be helped with books, equipment/instruments, fees and study or travel overseas.

Grants towards study or travel overseas are subject to a minimum study period of six months, unless it is an obligatory part of an approved course.

Annual grant total: In 2004 the trust had an income of £7,000 and a total expenditure of £12,000. Grants totalled about £10,000.

Applications: On a form available from the correspondent. Applications can be submitted directly by the individual or through a third party such as a parent/guardian or educational welfare agency. A reference, for example, from a tutor, and details of financial circumstances should be supplied. Applications are considered in February, May, August and November. Applicants or their personal representative must be prepared to attend an interview with the trustees.

Please note, this charity is comprised of two educational trusts: John Dinam School Endowment and Lady Ann Clifford Trust. These two trusts have the same criteria, described above, with the exception that the Endowment can make grants outside of Exeter – up to 15 miles from the city centre. Applicants can only receive a grant from one of these trusts. Those living outside the city should apply to John Dinam School Endowment.

Correspondent: M R King, Clerk, Chichester Mews, Exeter Municipal Charities, 22a Southernhay East, Exeter EX1 1QU (01392 201550; e-mail: properties@cbandm.co.uk)

Other information: This charity is part of Exeter Municipal Charities.

The Heathcoat Trust

Eligibility: Mainly students in secondary and further education who live and study in Tiverton and the mid-Devon area. Occasionally students can be supported for study outside the area if the courses are not available locally. Applicants need to have a personal connection with either the John Heathcoat or the Lowman Companies.

Types of grants: One-off and recurrent grants, normally for three years towards fees.

Annual grant total: In 2004/05 the trust had assets of £16 million and an income of £564,000. Grants to organisations and individuals totalled £88,000. Further grants were made to individuals for education purposes of £156,000.

Applications: In writing to the correspondent. For A-level applicants who attend East Devon College, application forms are available and should be submitted between April and June each year.

Correspondent: E W Summers, Secretary, The Factory, Tiverton, Devon EX16 5LL (01884 254949)

Elize Hele Educational Foundation

Eligibility: Boys and girls aged 16 to 23 years who have lived for five years within the boundaries of the city of Plymouth or the parishes of Bere Ferrers, Brixton, Sparkwell and Yealmton. There is a preference for people from low-income families who are in higher education or leaving school or university and starting work.

Types of grants: One-off and recurrent grants of between £140 and £400 to further/higher education students for help with books, fees, equipment/instruments and living expenses.

Exclusions: No grants for postgraduates, part-time or home study courses, mature students or study outside the UK.

Annual grant total: In 2004/05 the trust had an income of £5,500 and a total expenditure of £6,600, the majority of which was given in grants to 23 individuals.

Applications: On a form available from the correspondent. Applications should be submitted directly by the individual and are considered throughout the year.

Correspondent: F J Webb, 33 Downham Gardens, Tamerton Foliot, Plymouth, Devon PL5 4QF (01752 776612)

Hele's Exhibition Foundation

Eligibility: People under 25 who live, firstly, in the former parishes of Plympton St Maurice, Plympton St Mary and Brixton, and, secondly, in other parts of Devon (excluding Plymouth) if there are insufficient applications from the initial areas. In practice, all grants are given in the first area and applications for grants from further afield in Devon cannot be considered.

Types of grants: Various, probably including at least some of the following if and when funds are available: cash grants for school pupils to help with books, equipment, clothing or travel; grants to help with school, college or university fees or to supplement existing grants; and help towards the cost of education, training, apprenticeship or equipment for those starting work.

Annual grant total: About £1,200 a year to individuals and organisations.

Applications: In writing to the correspondent.

Correspondent: A F Jarvis, 9 Woodford Crescent, Plympton, Plymouth, Devon PL7 4QY (01752 348580)

The Dulce Haigh Marshall Trust

Eligibility: Violin, viola, cello and double bass players who are in need of financial assistance, live in Devon, and are under 25.

Types of grants: Grants of between about £200 and £500 towards buying an instrument or tuition fees.

Exclusions: No grants to people whose parents (or their own) income is sufficient to meet needs. People who do not demonstrate sufficient commitment to learning their instrument will not be supported.

Annual grant total: In 2003/04 the trust had assets of £46,000, and both an income and a total expenditure of £2,500, all of which was given in grants to 10 individuals.

Applications: On a form available from the correspondent, to be returned before 1 July. Grants are usually distributed in August each year. Applications are made directly by the individual and should include a teacher's report. Students may be asked to attend an audition.

Correspondent: Nicholas Marshall, Heathercoombe, Inner Ting Tong, Budleigh Salterton, Devon EX9 7AP (01395 442893)

The Vivian Moon Foundation

Eligibility: People, over 18 years of age, with residential and/or family ties in the North Devon District or Torridge District Council areas. Support is only given to applicants who:

- are likely to return to the beneficial area to practice their profession, ideally with an offer of employment at the end of their training with a company or firm in the beneficial area
- have an offer of a place on a course of higher educational professional or vocational training, leading to employment or improvement in their vocational skills.

Types of grants: One-off and recurrent grants in the range of £50 to £500 and are given to help college students, vocational students, mature students, people starting work and people with special educational needs.

Grants are given for fees, books and equipment/instruments.

Annual grant total: In 2004/05 the foundation had assets of £430,000 and an income of £27,000. Grants were made to 65 individuals totalling £22,000.

Applications: On a form available from the correspondent. Applications should be submitted directly by the individual and are considered at meetings which take place three times a year, in January, May and September.

Correspondent: The Secretariat, c/o Simpkins Edwards, 21 Boutport Street, Barnstaple, Devon EX31 1RP (e-mail: info@vivianmoonfoundation.co. uk; website: www.vivianmoonfoundation. co.uk)

The Pain Trust

Eligibility: Young males aged between 11 and 21 on the day of the expedition or activity, not on the date of application, who live within eight miles of Exmouth Town Hall or in East Devon, excluding the area west of the estuary of the river Exe.

Types of grants: One-off grants towards travel and adventure to further physical development, character building, leadership training or fostering a team spirit.

Exclusions: The grants are not issued during term time for those in full-time education.

Annual grant total: In 2004/05 the trust had an income of £43,000 and a total expenditure of £49,000. Grants to individuals and organisations totalled £43,000 with 42 individuals receiving a grant. Grants totalled about £30,000.

Applications: On an application form available from the correspondent received in the office at least 16 days before a trustees' meeting. You will be informed of the result of your application within one week of the date of the meeting, provided that the Trustees had all the necessary information.

Correspondent: Administrator, 15 Rolle Street, Exmouth, Devon EX8 1HA (01395 275443; e-mail: admin@pain-trust. org.uk; website: www.pain-trust.org.uk)

The Claude & Margaret Pike Charity

Eligibility: Students who live in Devon between the ages of 16 and 21. They should either be at or between school and university.

Types of grants: 70 to 80 grants are given each year for gap year 'overseas ventures' organised by Raleigh International, Sail Training Association and so on.

Annual grant total: The trust is allocated income each year from The Claude & Margaret Pike Woodlands Trust. About £25,000 is available each year to give in grants to individuals.

Applications: In writing to the correspondent.

Correspondent: J D Pike, Trustee, Dunderdale Lawn, Penshurst Road, Newton Abbot, Devon TQ12 1EN (01626 354404)

Other information: The trust stated that this charity may make fewer, but larger, grants in the future.

The Christine Woodmancy Charitable Foundation

Eligibility: Children and young people up to the age of 21, who live in the Plymouth area and are in need.

Types of grants: One-off grants according to need, usually ranging between £50 to £2,500. Grants can be for 'enterprising' events such as a tall ships race.

Exclusions: No grants for holidays.

Annual grant total: Grants total around £15,000 a year, mostly to schools.

Applications: In writing to the correspondent, directly by the individual or via a school or educatonal welfare worker etc. Applications should include background information and provide evidence of financial need.

Correspondent: Graeme Manfield, Foot Anste Sargent, 4–6 Barnfield Crescent, Exeter EX1 1RF

Bovey Tracey

Bovey Tracey Exhibition Foundation

Eligibility: Full-time students in further education, aged 16, who live in Bovey Tracey and have done so for at least three years.

Types of grants: Grants ranging between £65 and £75 for students attending approved places of further and higher education to help with the cost of, amongst other things, books, fees and living expenses, equipment and uniforms. Grants can generally be spent on whatever is required by the recipient. Grants are generally recurrent.

Exclusions: Grants are not given to students on government sponsored schemes.

Annual grant total: In 2005 the trust made grants to 18 individuals totalling £1,400.

Applications: On a form available from the correspondent from 1 April, to be returned by 31 July for consideration in August. Applications should be made directly by the individual.

Correspondent: Mrs E A Crosby, 32 Churchfields Drive, Bovey Tracey, South Devon TQ13 9QU (01626 835524)

Braunton

Chaloner's Educational Foundation

Eligibility: People under 25 who live in the parish of Braunton.

Types of grants: Grants of £100 are made towards equipment/instruments, books, fees, maintenance/living expenses and study or travel overseas for people who are starting work and for further and higher education students. The latter can also be supported for educational outings in the UK.

Annual grant total: In 2004/05 the trust had an income of £3,700 and a total expenditure of £500.

Applications: On a form available from the correspondent, to be submitted directly by the individual for consideration in February, June or October.

Correspondent: Louise Langabeer, Slee Blackwell Solicitors, 2–6 South Street, Braunton, Devon EX33 2AA

Broadhempston

The Broadhempston Relief-in-Need Charity

Eligibility: Children in need who live in the parish of Broadhempston.

Types of grants: One-off or recurrent grants ranging from £40 to £100. Grants are made towards children's educational trips and aids for educational purposes.

Annual grant total: In 2004/05 the charity had an income of £1,300 and a total expenditure of £1,200. Grants totalled about £1,000.

Applications: In writing to the correspondent directly by the individual to be considered in June and December.

Correspondent: Mrs R H E Brown, Meadows, Broadhempston, Totnes, Devon TQ9 6BW (01803 813130)

Colyton

The Colyton Parish Lands Charity

Eligibility: Young people in need in the ancient parish of Colyton.

Types of grants: One-off and recurrent grants in support of education and training.

Annual grant total: In 2004/05 the trust had an income of £31,000 and an expenditure of £33,000. There were four educational grants made to individuals totalling £450. A further, single relief-in-need grant was made totalling £350.

Applications: In writing to the correspondent to be submitted either directly by the individual or a family member, through a third party such as a social worker or teacher, or through a welfare agency such as Citizens Advice. Applications are considered monthly.

Correspondent: A Kenwick, Colyton Chamber of Feoffees, Town Hall, Market Place, Colyton, Devon EX24 6JR (01297 553593)

Combe Martin

The George Ley Educational Trust

Eligibility: People who live in Combe Martin who are in higher education.

Types of grants: Grants for books and equipment, not for main expenses such as fees or living costs.

Annual grant total: About £1,500.

Applications: In writing to the correspondent. A committee meets to consider applications in May and September. Reapplications for future grants can be made by people who have already been supported by this trust.

Correspondent: James Williams, Cormelles, Victoria Street, Combe Martin, Ilfracombe, Devon EX34 0LZ

Cornwood

Reverend Duke Yonge Charity

Eligibility: People in need who live in the parish of Cornwood.

Types of grants: One-off grants according to need.

Annual grant total: In 2004 it had an income of £13,000 and a total expenditure of £10,000. Grants totalled about £5,000.

Applications: In writing to the correspondent via the trustees, who are expected to make themselves aware of any need. Applications are considered at trustees' meetings.

Correspondent: Mrs J M Milligan, 8 Chipple Park, Lutton, Nr Cornwood, Ivybridge, Devon PL21 9TA (01752 837566)

Other information: Grants are also made towards the community bus service, playgroup and village hall, and to individuals in need.

Culmstock

Culmstock Fuel Allotment Charity

Eligibility: Students in need who live in the ancient parish of Culmstock.

Types of grants: Recurrent grants of £20 to £70 for books and equipment.

Annual grant total: In 2004/05 the charity had an income of £4,300. The sum of £3,000 was distributed in 50 welfare grants and £300 in six educational grants.

Applications: In writing to the correspondent, directly by the individual in September or October for consideration in November.

Correspondent: Mrs Elaine Artus, Clerk, Pendle, Culmstock, Cullompton, Devon EX15 3JQ (01884 840577; Fax: 01884 840577)

Great Torrington

The Great Torrington Town Lands Poors Charities

Eligibility: People in need who live in Great Torrington.

Types of grants: Grants are usually made to students towards a year out (voluntary work). Requests are also considered for school uniform costs for schoolchildren and for other costs for mature students.

Annual grant total: The charity has net assets of £4.3 million. About £5,000 a year is given to individuals for welfare and educational purposes.

Applications: In writing to the correspondent, with all relevant personal information.

Correspondent: C J Styles, The Town Hall Office, High Street, Torrington, Devon EX38 8HN (01805 623517)

Other information: Grants are also made to organisations.

Paignton

The Paignton School & Belfield Fund

Eligibility: Children aged 5 to 18 living in the urban district of Paignton; no one outside the area will be considered.

Types of grants: Grants of up to £40 to help schoolchildren with the cost of books, school uniform/clothing, sports kit and stationery.

Annual grant total: In 2005, the trust had an income of £3,300 and a total expenditure of £4,000. Grants totalled about £3,000.

Applications: On a form available from the correspondent, submitted either directly by the individual or through their school or educational welfare agency. Applications are considered in March, July and November and must include weekly income and outgoings and an indication of state benefit or support received.

Correspondent: P G S Ellis, Clerk, 30 Eugene Road, Paignton, Devon, TQ3 2PQ (01803 528727)

Plymouth

John Lanyon Educational Foundation

Eligibility: People in need who live within Plymouth city boundaries and are aged 16 to 23 years, with a preference for people from low-income families who are in higher education or leaving school or university and starting work.

Types of grants: One-off and recurrent grants ranging from £100 to £300, for instance, towards books, equipment/instruments, fees and maintenance/living expenses.

Exclusions: No grants for postgraduates, part-time or home study courses, mature students or study outside the UK.

Annual grant total: In 2004/05 the trust had an income of £900 and its total expenditure was £800. Grants to six individuals totalled £700.

Applications: On a form available from the correspondent, directly by the individual, for consideration in any month.

Correspondent: Frederick J Webb, 33 Downham Gardens, Tamerton Foliot, Plymouth, Devon PL5 4QF (01752 776612)

The Olford Bequest

Eligibility: Young people from Plymouth schools.

Types of grants: Grants of £250 a year to students to help them 'more fully enjoy their stay at university – not for study'.

Annual grant total: In 2004/05 the charity had assets of £90,000, an income of £4,000 and a total expenditure of £3,500, all of which was given in grants.

Applications: On a form available from the correspondent. Applications must be received by 30 June for consideration in August/September.

Correspondent: Robert Hughes Gaskin, Tredeague House, Devonport Hill, Kingsand, Torpoint, Cornwall PL10 1NJ (01752 823044; e-mail: roberthgaskin@btinternet.com)

Orphan's Aid Educational Foundation (Plymouth)

Eligibility: Children who live in the city and county borough of Plymouth of school age and from a one-parent family.

Types of grants: One-off grants (maximum £100) to help with the cost of books, clothing and educational outings for schoolchildren. Applications from young people in secondary school or further education will be considered to assist with their education in a wide sense. Applicants will be expected to show some exceptional need or circumstances in their application.

No grants for school fees or maintenance, for people starting work or for mature students.

Annual grant total: In 2004 the trust had an income of £1,800 and it did not spend any money. Grants may be made every few years, with figures for 2005 unavailable at the time of writing.

Applications: Applications can be submitted directly by the individual including details of applicant's income and expenditure, and the cost of the item. They are considered at any time.

Correspondent: A G Serpell, 15 Athenaeum Street, Plymouth, Devon PL1 2RJ

Plymouth Charity Trust

Eligibility: People living in the city of Plymouth who are under the age of 25.

Types of grants: One-off grants ranging between £50 and £100 are made to people at all levels of education, including those towards school clothing, fees, books and equipment/instruments.

The trust usually makes the donation in the form of vouchers, credit at a relevant shop. They do not to give payments directly to the applicant.

Exclusions: No grants are given to other charities, to clear debts or for any need that can be met by Social Services.

Annual grant total: In 2004/05 the trust made ten relief-in-need grants totalling £1,000 and nine educational grants totalling £900.

Applications: On a form available from the correspondent, to be submitted directly by the individual or through a school, educational welfare agency or other third party. Applications are considered on the first Monday of every month.

Correspondent: Mrs J Gibbons, Charity Trust Office, 41 Heles Terrace, Prince Rock, Plymouth PL4 9LH (01752 663107; e-mail: jg@charity-trust.demon.co.uk)

Sheepwash

The Bridgeland Charity

Eligibility: Young people in need who live in the parish of Sheepwash.

Types of grants: One-off grants ranging from £50 to £500. Loans are also made.

Annual grant total: In 2004/05 the trust had assets of £703,000, its income was £3,000 and its total expenditure was £2,400. One grant of £50 was made for educational purposes.

Applications: In writing to the correspondent through a third party such as a social worker or teacher, for consideration throughout the year.

Correspondent: P M Whittaker, Littlewoods, East Street, Sheepwash, Beaworthy, North Devon EX21 5NW (01409 231534)

Other information: The trust also supports local schools and community projects (£250 in 2004/05).

Sidmouth

Sidmouth Consolidated Charities

Eligibility: People in need who live in Sidmouth.

Types of grants: One-off grants for educational needs such as computers and books for university students.

Annual grant total: Grants for welfare purposes total about £11,000 a year. Educational grants total around the same amount although the figure varies slightly from year to year.

Applications: In writing to the correspondent, either directly by the individual, or through a social worker, Citizens Advice or welfare agency. Applications are considered at monthly meetings.

Correspondent: Mrs Ruth Rose, 22 Alexandria Road, Sidmouth, Devon EX10 9HB (01395 513079; e-mail: ruth.rose@eclipse.co.uk)

Silverton

The Richards Educational Charity

Eligibility: Young people under 25 who live in the parish of Silverton.

Types of grants: Recurrent grants in the range of £5 to £750 are given to schoolchildren and college students for study/travel abroad, books, equipment/instruments, maintenance/living expenses and excursions and to undergraduates, vocational students, mature students, and people starting work for fees, study/travel abroad, books, equipment/instruments, maintenance/living expenses and excursions

Annual grant total: In 2004 the charity had total assets of £885,000, an income of £30,400 and an expenditure of £37,500. The charity made grants to 145 individuals totalling £32,000.

Applications: On a form available from the correspondent. Applications should be submitted directly by the individual or a parent. They are considered monthly.

Correspondent: Geoffrey Knowles, 26 Hederman Close, Silverton, Exeter EX5 4HW (01392 860109; e-mail: john micheal.thomas@lineone.net)

Silverton Parochial Charity

Eligibility: People in need in the parish of Silverton only.

Types of grants: One-off grants, with no minimum or maximum limit.

Exclusions: No grants are made towards state or local authority taxes.

Annual grant total: In 2005 grants to 25 individuals totalled £15,000.

Applications: Application forms can be obtained from the Silverton Post Office or the Community Hall, or prospective beneficiaries can write or speak to the correspondent. Completed forms can be submitted to the correspondent by the individual or by a carer or welfare department, and so on. The trustees will need details of the applicant's financial situation. Applications are considered monthly.

Correspondent: C A Williams, Henbury, Old Butterleigh Road, Silverton, Devon EX5 4JE (01392 860408)

Other information: Grants are also made to people in need who live in the parish and to organisations providing assistance for them (£14,000 given in 2005).

South Brent

The South Brent Parish Lands Charity

Eligibility: Students in further education who live or have lived in the parish of South Brent.

Types of grants: One-off and recurrent grants in the range of £50 and £300.

Annual grant total: In 2005 the trust had an income of £48,000. Welfare grants to individuals totalled £14,000 with a further £9,800 distributed in educational grants. Disposable income for 2006 is about £33,000.

Applications: On a form available from the correspondent which can be submitted at any time either directly by the individual or a family member, through a third party such as a social worker or teacher, or through an organisation such as Citizens Advice or a school.

Correspondent: J I G Blackler, Luscombe Maye, 6 Fore Street, South Brent, Devon TQ10 9BQ (01364 646173; Fax: 01364 73885; e-mail: luscombe@ukonline.co.uk)

Other information: Grants are also made to organisations (£5,000 in 2005).

Sowton

Sowton In Need Charity

Eligibility: People in need who live in the parish of Sowton.

Types of grants: One-off grants for any specific educational or personal need. Grants have been given towards tuition fees.

Annual grant total: In 2005 the charity had an income of £1,900 and a total expenditure of £2,000. Grants totalled about £1,000.

Applications: In writing to the correspondent, to be submitted either directly by the individual or through a social worker, Citizens Advice, other welfare agency or any third party.

Correspondent: N Waine, Meadowsweet, Sowton, Exeter, EX5 2AE

Other information: Grants are also given to organisations.

Dorset

The Ashley, Churchill & Thorner Educational Trust

Eligibility: Young people under 25 who live either within five miles of the county hall in Dorchester, or in the civil parish of Crossways.

Types of grants: One-off grants are given to further and higher education students for uniforms and other school clothing, books, equipment and instruments, fees, educational outings in the UK, study or travel abroad and student exchanges. Apprentices can also receive grants towards materials, tools, travelling and any other support costs.

Annual grant total: In 2004/05 the trust had an income of £4,300 and a total expenditure of £1,600. Grants totalled about £1,500.

Applications: On a form available from the correspondent. Applications are considered in September, January and April, but urgent applications can be considered at any time. Applications should include details of parental income and confirmation from the tutor of the course being taken and how a grant would benefit the student. They can be submitted by the individual, or through the individual's school/college or educational welfare agency.

Correspondent: Jean Wallbridge, Clerk to the Trustees, The Clerk's Office, Whetstone's, West Walks, Dorchester, Dorset DT1 1AW (01305 262662; Fax: 01305 262662; e-mail: dmc@whetstones.freeserve.co.uk)

The Beaminster Charities

Eligibility: Schoolchildren in need who live in Beaminster, Netherbury and Stoke Abbott.

Types of grants: Grants in the range of £50 and £1,000 are made to schoolchildren and college students for study/travel abroad, books and equipment/instruments. About 50 grants are made each year.

Annual grant total: In 2005 the trust had assets of £285,000 and an income of £13,000. Welfare grants totalled £6,200 with a further £5,200 given in educational grants.

Applications: Applications can be submitted in writing to the correspondent by the individual or through a recognised referral agency such as social worker, Citizens Advice or doctor. The trustees meet throughout the year.

Correspondent: J Groves, 24 Church Street, Beaminster, Dorset DT8 3BA (01308 862313 or 01308 862192)

Other information: Grants are also made to organisations.

The Blandford Children's Fund

Eligibility: Children living in the borough of Blandford who were under 12 on 1 January in the year of application.

Types of grants: One-off or recurrent grants, on average of £100 each, for items such as clothing, school uniforms, books, educational outings and maintenance costs.

Annual grant total: Grants are usually made to individuals totalling around £1,500.

Applications: On a form available from the correspondent. Applications are considered in January and must include details of parental occupation, net family income, purpose for which the grant will be used and a birth certificate. The Mayor of Blandford decides who will benefit.

Correspondent: J Feeney, Assistant Manager, NatWest Trust and Estate Services, 153 Preston Road, Brighton BN1 6BD (01273 545035; Fax: 01273 545075)

The Blandford Forum Apprenticing & Educational Foundation

Eligibility: People under the age of 25 who are living, or who have been educated for at least two years, in the borough of Blandford Forum.

Types of grants: (i) Cash grants, to a usual maximum of about £400, for school pupils to help with books, equipment, clothing or travel.

(ii) Grants to a usual maximum of about £400 to help with school, college or university fees or to supplement existing grants.

(iii) Help towards the cost of education, training, apprenticeship, clothing or equipment for those starting work.

Annual grant total: In 2004/05 the trust had assets totalling £44,300, an income of £3,800 and a total expenditure of £3,100. Grants were made to five individuals totalling £1,700.

Applications: In writing to the correspondent.

Correspondent: Clerk to the Trustees, Barnes Homes, Salisbury Road, Blandford Forum, Dorset DT11 7HU (01258 451810)

The Bridge Educational Trust

Eligibility: People in need who were born in, or whose home is in, Dorset. Priority is given to:

- people who are from the parishes of Piddletrenthide, Plush, Piddlehinton and Alton Pancras
- older people who are making a late start after interrupted education
- people with difficult family circumstances (including single mothers)
- children with special education needs.

Types of grants: Grants of £50 to £3,000, which can be one-off or recurrent (for a maximum of three years). Grants given include those towards fees, study/travel abroad, books, equipment/instruments, excursions and childcare.

Exclusions: No loans are made.

Annual grant total: In 2004/05 the trust had assets of £33,000, an income of £7,200 and a total expenditure of £5,900. Grants were made to 14 individuals totalling £5,000.

Applications: In writing to the correspondent, either on an application form which will be provided or by letter if preferred. Full details of the proposed course are required, together with a brief cv, some family background information and details of financial circumstances and costs. Applications should be submitted in May for consideration in June, directly by the individual, or by the parent if the person is under 16 years.

Correspondent: J F McCormack, Executive Trustee, Woodcombe House, 52a Coobe Valley Road, Preston, Weymouth, DT3 6NL (01305 834613)

The Cecil Trust

Eligibility: Young people, aged 10 to 21 years old, who live within a six-mile radius of the parish church at Lytchett Matravers.

Types of grants: Grants, to a usual maximum of about £600 a year, to help with books or equipment, college or university fees and to schoolchildren with serious family difficulties so that the child has to be educated away from home. Other support may also be given to students whose parents are unable to help.

Annual grant total: On average 15 grants are made each year totalling around £9,000.

Applications: An application form is available from the correspondent and can be submitted directly by the individual. Applications are considered in August, November and March.

Correspondent: Mrs J Cogswell, Graddage Farm, Clayhidon, Cullompton, Devon EX15 3TP

Clingan's Trust

Eligibility: People under the age of 25 who live in the old borough of Christchurch which includes parts of Bournemouth and the surrounding areas.

Types of grants: One-off grants of between £100 and £1,000 for any educational need for people under 25. Preference is given to schoolchildren with serious family difficulties where the child has to be educated away from home and people with special educational needs.

Annual grant total: In 2004 the trust had an income of £57,000 and gave grants to individuals totalling £43,000. Grants to organisations totalled just £1,000 during the year.

Applications: On a form available from the correspondent. Applications can be made directly by the individual unless under the age of 14. They are considered quarterly.

Correspondent: John D H Richardson, Clerk, 27 High Street, Christchurch, Dorset BH23 1AJ (01202 486906; Fax: 01202 477870; e-mail: david@ richardsonspurling.co.uk)

Other information: The trust also makes grants to clubs and schools although individual applications are preferred.

The Dixon Galpin Scholarship Trust

Eligibility: People born in Dorset or who have lived in the county for at least 12 months before the application (excluding people from the boroughs of Poole and Bournemouth).

Types of grants: Scholarships to assist people attending summer schools organised by a university; to people attending short courses or weekend schools organised by the Southern and Western Districts of the Workers' Education Association (or other similar body); or to students attending full or part-time courses at universities or other establishments of further education who are to undertake vacation study anywhere, to travel overseas for an educational purpose approved by the college authorities, or to buy books, instruments or equipment to further their education. Grants range from £100 to £150.

Annual grant total: In 2004/05, the trust had an income of £2,800 and a total expenditure of £2,500. Grants totalled about £2,000.

Applications: On a form available from the correspondent, to be submitted either directly by the individual or through the individual's school, college or educational welfare agency. Applications are considered in February, May and October and must include details of the student's financial circumstances, details of the course/expedition/vocation study,

including costs, and what benefits they hope to gain from the course.

Correspondent: Tony McDonnell, Dorset County Council, County Hall, Colliton Park, Dorchester, Dorset, DT1 1XJ

Other information: Dorset County Council also administers The Marras Prize – each year grants totalling up to £1,000 are given to people aged 16 to 19 who are assessed to be the most deserving from the point of behaviour, honesty and truthfulness. Two smaller trusts are also administered, each making grants totalling less than £500 a year.

The Gordon Charitable Trust

Eligibility: Young people over 15 but less than 25 years of age who live in the county of Dorset or the parishes of Ringwood, Burley, Ellingham, Harbridge & Ibsley, New Milton, Sopley & Bransgore in west Hampshire and are undergoing further education or an apprenticeship.

Types of grants: One-off and recurrent grants of up to £500 a year are made to further and higher education students towards books, equipment/instruments and maintenance/living expenses.

Exclusions: No grant is given where there is an education grant unless such a grant is minimal.

Annual grant total: In 2003/04, the trust had an income of £5,700 and a total expenditure of £4,100.

Applications: On a form available from the correspondent, submitted directly by the individual, for consideration in March, June, September and December.

Correspondent: Gerry Aiken, Hon. Clerk, 45 Dunkeld Road, Bournemouth BH3 7EW (01202 768337; Fax: 01202 767595; e-mail: gerry_aitken@ hotmail.com)

Other information: As the trust is reliant upon donations from other sources its income is limited and variable.

Lockyer's Charity Trust

Eligibility: People who live in Lytchett Minster, Upton and Organford, aged up to 25. Applicants must have lived in the parish for two years before applying and it must be their main residence.

Types of grants: Help towards books, equipment and educational outings in the UK for students in further or higher education. Grants usually range up to £150.

Annual grant total: In 2004 the trust had an income of £2,000. Grants were made to eight individuals totalling £700.

Applications: On a form available from the correspondent, submitted directly by the individual or by a parent or guardian. Applications are considered in February, June and November and should be submitted in the preceding month.

Correspondent: Richard J Tattershall, 89 Redwood Road, Upton, Poole BH16 5QG

Lumb's Educational Foundation

Eligibility: People aged 16 to 25 who live in the borough of Cheltenham and surrounding parishes. Students from Gloucestershire, particularly art and music students, are also considered. Students whose permanent residence is elsewhere are ineligible.

Types of grants: One-off grants of £50 to £1,000 to help with uniforms/other school clothing, books, equipment/instruments, fees, educational outings in the UK and study or travel abroad. People starting work can be helped with uniforms, books and equipment/instruments. People embarking on official gap-year projects are also supported.

Exclusions: Grants are not made towards trips that are more of a holiday rather than educational, towards living expenses, or towards school fees.

Annual grant total: In 2005 the trust had assets of £40,000, an income of £12,000 and a total expenditure of £9,100. Grants totalling £8,900 were made to 15 individuals.

Applications: On receipt of a written application a form is sent out, which must be completed and returned with a supporting letter, including details of income, expenditure, parental financial support and the purpose of the grant. The trustees usually meet in February, April, July, September and November. All applicants are interviewed. Each application is assessed according to need and funds available at the time.

Correspondent: Mrs H J Hunter, 18 Western Court, Western Road, Cheltenham GL50 3RH (01242 524704)

Francis Ramage Prize Trust

Eligibility: Young people up to the age of 19 who live in the administrative area of Dorset and attend a school maintained by Dorset County Council.

Types of grants: One-off and recurrent grants according to need.

Annual grant total: In 2004/05 the trust had an income of £2,300 and a total expenditure of £1,200. Grants were made to four individuals totalling £1,000.

Applications: In writing to the correspondent.

Correspondent: Mrs F L Spracklen, Student Support Service, Children's Services, Dorset County Council, County Hall, Colliton Park, Dorchester, Dorset DT1 1XJ (01305 224304; e-mail: studentsupport@dorsetcc.gov.uk)

The William Williams Charity

Eligibility: People in need who live in the ancient parishes of Blandford, Shaftesbury or Sturminster Newton.

Types of grants: One-off grants of £500 to £1,000 for those at school, college or university.

Annual grant total: In 2004 the trust had assets of £5.1 million, an income of £238,000 and a total expenditure of £199,000. Grants to 179 individuals totalled £121,000.

Applications: Applicants should apply directly to one of the trustees; in the first instance contact the correspondent to find which of the trustees is most relevant, and what their address is. Applications should be submitted before the beginning of September.

Correspondent: Ian Winsor, Steward, Stafford House, 10 Prince of Wales Road, Dorchester, Dorset DT1 1PW (01305 264573; e-mail: wwc@kennedylegg.co.uk)

Other information: Grants are also made to organisations (£37,000 in 2004).

Charmouth

The Almshouse Charity

Eligibility: People in further and higher education who, or whose immediate family, live in the parish of Charmouth.

Types of grants: One-off and recurrent grants, generally of £25 to £250 towards school uniforms, overseas voluntary/education work and university books.

Annual grant total: About £2,000 a year for welfare and educational purposes.

Applications: In writing to the correspondent or other trustees. Applications can be submitted directly by the individual or through a third party such as a rector, doctor or trustee. They are usually considered at quarterly periods; emergencies can be considered at other times. Applications should include details of the purpose of the grant, the total costs involved, and an official letter or programme/itinerary.

Correspondent: Mrs M Comley, Secretary, Pebbles, Five Acres, Charmouth, Birdport, Dorset, DT6 6BE

Other information: Grants are also given to individuals for relief-in-need purposes and to youth clubs for specific purposes.

Corfe Castle

Corfe Castle Charities

Eligibility: People in need who live in the parish of Corfe Castle, including the village of Kingston.

Types of grants: One-off grants or interest-free loans to students in further or higher education and on vocational education courses, for books, fees, maintenance/living expenses, educational outings in the UK and study or travel overseas. Schoolchildren may receive one-off grants for uniforms or other school clothing.

Annual grant total: In 2004/05 the trust made grants to individuals totalling £29,000.

Applications: On a form available from the correspondent, to be submitted directly by the individual. The trustees meet monthly, but emergency requests are dealt with as they arise.

Applications made outside the charity's geographical area of interest are not replied to.

Correspondent: Mrs J Wilson, The Spinney, Springbrook Close, Harmans Cross, Dorset BH20 5HS

Other information: Grants are also made to organisations (£5,900 in 2004/05).

Dorchester

Dorchester Relief-in-Need Charity

Eligibility: People in need who live in the ecclesiastical parish of Dorchester.

Types of grants: One-off grants of up to £250 to schoolchildren for uniforms and excursions, they are also given to people starting work for books and equipment and to people with special educational needs for excursions.

Annual grant total: In 2004/05 the charity had an income of £3,200. The sum of £300 was distributed in three educational grants.

Applications: Application forms are available from the correspondent and can be submitted through a school/teacher, social worker, health visitor, Citizens Advice or social services. The grant is paid to the sponsoring organisations to pass onto the individuals. There is a form and applications are considered throughout the year.

Correspondent: R C Burnett, 18 Chesil Place, Somerleigh Road, Dorchester, Dorset DT1 1AF (01305 265496)

Litton Cheney

The Litton Cheney Relief-in-Need Trust

Eligibility: University students and people starting work who live in the parish of Litton Cheney. No grants for people taking A-levels, or for schoolchildren.

Types of grants: Grants of £100 are made each year for 16-year old people who are about to start a career and to 18-year olds who are about to start at university. Grants are towards books and equipment.

Annual grant total: In 2004 the trust had an income of £4,600 and a total expenditure of £2,900. Grants totalled about £2,000.

Applications: Applications, on a form available from the correspondent, should be submitted directly by the individual, and are considered throughout the year.

Correspondent: B P Prentice Esq, Steddings, Chalk Pit Lane, Litton Cheney, Dorchester, Dorset DT2 9AN (01308 482535)

Poole

The Poole Children's Fund

Eligibility: Children up to 18 who are disadvantaged, disabled or otherwise in need and live in the borough of Poole.

Types of grants: Help towards the cost of holidays and other recreational and educational facilities, including grants for educational outings for schoolchildren and for study or travel abroad for students in further and higher education. Grants can be in the range of £10 to £80 and are usually one-off.

Preference for children with behavioural and social difficulties who have limited opportunities for leisure and recreational activities of a positive nature, for schoolchildren with serious family difficulties so the child has to be educated away from home, and for people with special educational needs.

Annual grant total: In 2004 the trust had an income of £2,000 and its total expenditure was £1,400, most of which was given in grants for both welfare and educational purposes.

Applications: On a form available from the correspondent completed by a third party such as a social worker, health visitor, minister or teacher. Applications are considered throughout the year. They should include details of family structure including: ages; reason for application; family income and any other sources of funding which have been tried; what agencies (if any) are involved in helping the family; and any statutory orders (for example, care orders) relating to the child or their family members.

Correspondent: Julia Palmer, Adult Social Services, Civic Centre Annexe, Park Road, Poole BH15 2RT (01202 633623)

Weymouth and Portland

The Sir Samuel Mico Trust

Eligibility: People aged 16 to 25 who are normally resident in the area of Weymouth and Portland Borough Council.

Types of grants: One-off and recurrent grants are made to students in further or higher education. The applicant must show themselves to be in difficult financial circumstances and demonstrate a desire to improve and extend their education. Grants are given towards the cost of books, fees/living expenses, study or travel abroad and for student exchange. Grants are also given to people starting work towards the cost of books, equipment, clothing and travel.

Annual grant total: In 2005, the annual income was about £50,000, with an expenditure of £71,000.

Applications: On a form available from the correspondent.

Correspondent: C Thompson, Clerk, 26 St Thomas Street, Weymouth, Dorset, DT4 8OJ (01305 774666; e-mail: c.thompson@battens.co.uk; website: www.weymouthtowncharities.org.uk)

Gloucestershire

Charlton Kings

Higgs & Coopers Educational Charity

Eligibility: People under 25 who currently live, or were born, in the former urban district of Charlton Kings (as constituted prior to 1974). Preference is given to people in single parent families.

Types of grants: Grants to help with books, equipment/instruments, educational outings in the UK and study or travel overseas. People starting work and people in further and higher education can also be helped with fees.

Annual grant total: In 2004/05 it had assets of £651,000 and an income of £23,000. Grants were made to individuals totalling £8,300. A further £5,300 was given to organisations.

Applications: On a form available from the correspondent, submitted directly by the individual. Applications are considered six times a year.

Correspondent: M J Mitchell, 11 Chestnut Terrace, Charlton Kings, Cheltenham, Gloucestershire GL53 8J2 (01242 572810)

Other information: The trust supports schools, youth clubs, Guide and Scout groups, boys' and girls' brigades, and other voluntary organisations broadly connected with the education or recreational pursuits of young people in the area of benefit.

Cirencester

John Edmonds' Charity

Eligibility: People under the age of 25, who were born of Cirencester parents or currently live in Cirencester or district, or were educated in Cirencester.

Types of grants: Help towards the cost of education, training, apprenticeship or equipment, including grants for schoolchildren, students and people starting work. Grants range from £100 to £500 and are one-off.

Annual grant total: Up to £4,000 is given in total each year to about 10 individuals.

Applications: On a form available from the correspondent.

Correspondent: R R Mullings, Solicitor, 7 Dollar Street, Cirencester, Gloucestershire GL7 2AS (01285 650000)

Highnam

William Andrews Foundation

Eligibility: People in need aged under 25 years who live in the parish of Highnam.

Types of grants: One-off and recurrent grants ranging from £50 to £200 for schoolchildren, students and young people starting work. Help is specifically given towards school uniforms, textbooks, equipment, and educational visits in the UK, travel overseas and fees.

Annual grant total: In 2004 the trust had an income of £600 and a total expenditure of £500. Previously £550 was given in grants to five individuals.

Applications: In writing to the correspondent, directly by the individual or their parent, in time to be considered at the annual general meeting in July. Applications should include the reason for the request, place of residence, details of education, the age of the applicant and general financial information (for example, low income).

Correspondent: David Slinger, Clerk to the Trustees, 1 Wetherleigh Drive, Highnam, Gloucester, GL2 8LW (01452 412936; website: www.glosc.gov.uk/education)

Stroud

The Stroud & Rodborough Educational Charity

Eligibility: People who live in the Stroud area under the age of 25.

Types of grants: Help is primarily for those in further and higher education towards equipment/instruments and foreign travel for educational purposes. Grants are also available for those at school, usually for extra-curricular activities such as special courses and field trips. Grants range from £10 to £500.

Exclusions: No grants for expenditure which, in the trustees' opinion, should be the responsibility of the Local Education Authority, such as travel to and from school or college or towards course fees.

Annual grant total: In 2004/05 the charity had an income of £72,500 and a total expenditure of about £78,000.

Applications: On a form available from the correspondent. Applications are usually considered in February, April, June, September and November.

Correspondent: Mrs S Baker, 14 Green Close, Uley, Dursley, Gloucestershire, GL11 5TH (01453 860379)

Other information: The priority of the charity is to provide financial help to the three secondary schools in the area. Any remainder is given to individuals.

Weston-sub-Edge

Weston-sub-Edge Educational Charity

Eligibility: People under 25 who live, or whose parents live, in Weston-sub-Edge, or who have at any time attended (or whose parents have attended) Weston-sub-Edge Church of England Primary School.

Types of grants: Grants range from £10 to £500. In cases of special financial need grants can be for uniforms or other clothing for schoolchildren. People at any stage of education who fit the criteria listed above (including people starting work) can be supported for books, equipment/instruments, fees, educational outings in the UK and study or travel abroad. Further and higher education may also be supported for maintenance/living expenses.

Annual grant total: In 2004 the trust had an income of £10,300 and a total expenditure of £9,400. Grants were made to 185 individuals totalling £8,200.

Applications: On a form available from the correspondent, including details of the course, its duration and purpose. Applications should be submitted directly by the individual if over 16, or otherwise by the parent/guardian. Applications are considered in January, March, May, July, September and November.

Correspondent: Mrs Rachel Hurley, Longclose Cottage, Weston-sub-Edge, Chipping Campden, Gloucestershire GL55 6QX (01386 841808)

Somerset

Huish's Exhibition Foundation

Eligibility: Pupils of the following schools in the county of Somerset: Richard Huish College, Taunton; King's College, Taunton; Queen's College, Taunton; Taunton School, Taunton; Wellington School, Wellington.

Types of grants: Grants of £300 a year for students when they start at university. The grants are made for the duration of the university course. To qualify for an exhibition the applicant must have a GCSE or A-level in Religious Studies.

Annual grant total: In 2004 the foundation had an income of £4,400 and a total expenditure of £3,700. Grants totalled about £1,000.

Applications: Applications should be made through the various schools.

Correspondent: W P Morris, Porter Dodson Solicitors, 11 Hammet Street, Taunton, Somerset TA1 1RJ (01823 331293)

Ilminster Educational Foundation

Eligibility: People under 25 living in or educated in the ancient parish of Ilminster and the parish of Whitelackington.

Types of grants: The trust gives grants for two purposes: book grants, of up to £200 a year, to students in universities and to postgraduates; and grants, usually one half of the total cost, up to £200, for educational outings for schoolchildren and study or travel abroad for schoolchildren.

Exclusions: Book grants are not available for A-Level courses.

Annual grant total: In 2004/05 the trust had an income of £39,000 and a total expenditure of £36,000. Educational grants were made to 60 individuals totalling £13,000.

Applications: On a form available from the correspondent. The book grant application form requires signed comments by the applicant's ex-headmaster. Applications are considered in October and November. Higher education grants should be submitted in September and October.

Correspondent: E A Wells, Clerk, 20 Silver Street, Ilminster, Somerset TA19 0DN (01460 52293; Fax: 01460 57666)

Other information: Grants are also made to schools.

Keyford Educational Foundation

Eligibility: Young people aged up to 25 who live in the parishes of Frome or Selwood. There is a preference for families in need.

Types of grants: One-off grants from £50 to £100. Schoolchildren and students in further and higher education can be helped with uniforms/other school clothing, books, equipment/instruments, fees, educational outings in the UK and study or travel abroad.

Annual grant total: In 2005 the foundation had an income of £1,100 and a total expenditure was £700, all of which was given in nine grants.

Applications: On a form available from the correspondent, to be submitted either directly by the individual, through the individual's school, college or educational welfare agency or through another third party such as their parent/guardian or social worker or Citizens Advice. The foundation requires a recommendation from the teacher or tutor and a telephone or personal interview. Applications are considered every other month, from January onwards.

Correspondent: Mrs K McCarthy, The Blue House, Market Place, Frome, Somerset BA11 1AP (01373 455338; Fax: 01373 455338; e-mail: kathy@ bhousecharity.go-plus.net)

Other information: This trust incorporates the Ancient Blue Coat Foundation.

The John Nowes Exhibition Foundation

Eligibility: People under 25 who are in need, studying at a further, higher, or postgraduate level and live in the town of Yeovil and the parishes of Alvington, Barwick, Brympton, Chilthorne Domer, East Coker, Limington, Mudford, Preston Plucknett, West Coker and Yeovil Without.

Types of grants: Grants, ranging from £150 to £500, for general educational purposes to those in further and higher education, vocational and overseas students and for special educational needs.

Annual grant total: In 2004/05, the charity had an income of £6,300 and a total expenditure of £5,100.

Applications: By 31 August each year. A form is available from the correspondent and should be submitted with an academic reference.

Correspondent: The Trustees, c/o Battens Solicitors, Mansion House, Princes Street, Yeovil, Somerset BA20 1EP

Prowde's Educational Foundation – see entry on page 122

Prowde's Educational Foundation – see entry on page 122

Correspondent: R G Powell, Administrative Trustee, Broad Eaves, Hawks Hill Close, Leatherhead, Surrey KT22 9DL (01372 374561)

Blackford

Blackford Educational Trust

Eligibility: People in primary, secondary, further or higher education who are aged 25 or under and live in the ecclesiastical parish of Blackford.

Types of grants: Grants are made to schoolchildren for equipment/instruments, educational outings in the UK and study or travel abroad, and to further and higher education students for books.

Annual grant total: In 2003/04 the charity had an income of £8,200 and a total expenditure of £5,500. Grants totalled about £5,000.

Applications: On a form available from the correspondent, submitted by the individual in January, May or September, for consideration by the trust in February, June or October. Applications must be accompanied by receipts, and all expenses must have been incurred before an application can be submitted.

Correspondent: David Cameron, Secretary, c/o Hugh Sexey Middle School, Blackford, Wedmore, Somerset BS28 4ND

Draycott

Card Educational Foundation

Eligibility: People in need in the hamlet of Draycott, aged between 4 and 30 years.

Types of grants: Grants range from £50 to £200 and can be for books, equipment/ instruments, fees and study or travel abroad. Other grants can be made to: schoolchildren for uniforms or other school clothing, educational outings in the UK and student exchanges; people starting work for uniforms, maintenance/living expenses and educational outings in the UK; further and higher education students for maintenance/living expenses; and mature students and postgraduates for maintenance/living expenses, educational outings in the UK and student exchanges.

Exclusions: No grants towards ski trips or school transport.

Annual grant total: In 2004/05 the trust had assets of £2,000, an income of £4,400 and a total expenditure of £2,300. Grants were made to 30 individuals totalling £1,400. Grants were also made to schools totalling £600.

Applications: In writing to the correspondent including a clear statement of residence in the hamlet. Applications can be submitted either directly by the individual or through a third party such as a parent or teacher. They are considered at the end of November and should be submitted at least two weeks before.

Correspondent: Mrs H M Dance, Clerk & Treasurer, Leighurst, The Street, Draycott, Cheddar, Somerset BS27 3TH (01934 742811)

Evercreech

The Arthur Allen Educational Trust

Eligibility: People who were born or who live in the parish of Evercreech and are over 16 and under 25 years of age.

Types of grants: One-off grants in the range of £50 and £300 to college students, undergraduates and vocational students, towards clothing, fees, study/travel abroad, books, equipment/instruments, maintenance/living expenses and excursions.

Annual grant total: In 2005 the trust had an income of £5,000 all of which was distributed in 27 grants.

Applications: Awards are usually made in late October, so applications must be submitted in September. Applications can be submitted directly by the individual, including name, place and duration of course, eligibility, amount of local authority grant and parents' commitment, previous educational achievements and two references.

Correspondent: Allison Dowding, Meadow's Edge, High Street, Stoney Stratton, Shepton Mallett, Somerset, BA4 6DY (01749 831077; e-mail: adowding.epc@virgin.net)

Other information: The trust states: 'Beneficiaries fall into three categories: university students; technical college students; and those post-comprehensive students taking GCSE and A-level courses at sixth form colleges or other technical colleges.'

Ilchester

Ilchester Relief-in-Need and Educational Charity

Eligibility: Students in financial need who live in the parish of Ilchester only.

Types of grants: One-off grants according to need.

Exclusions: Support will not be given to individuals who live outside the parish of Ilchester.

Annual grant total: In 2003 the trust had an income of £22,000 and an expenditure of £20,000. Grants totalled £11,000, about half of which is given to individuals for both welfare and educational purposes.

Applications: On a form available from the correspondent. Applications can be submitted directly by the individual or through a third party such as their school or an educational welfare agency.

Unsolicited applications are not responded to.

Correspondent: Mrs Wendy Scrivener, Milton House, Podimore, Yeovil, Somerset BA22 8JF (01935 840070)

Rimpton

The Rimpton Relief-in-Need Charities

Eligibility: People who live in the parish of Rimpton only.

Types of grants: One-off or recurrent grants according to need. Grants are made to cover student expenses, for exchange visits and to students representing their country at sport.

Annual grant total: In 2004/05 the trust had assets of £59,000 and an income of £2,000. Grants totalled £2,500.

Applications: On a form available from the correspondent, to be submitted either directly by the individual or a family member, through a third party such as a social worker, or through an organisation such as Citizens Advice or another welfare agency. Applications are considered at any time.

Correspondent: J N Spencer, Secretary, Field End House, Home Farm Lane, Rimpton, Yeovil, Somerset, BA22 8AS (01935 850530)

Taunton Deane

Taunton Town Charity

Eligibility: People living within the Taunton Deane Borough area that are of school age (up to the age of 16). Requests from the colleges of further education on behalf on individuals may also be considered, depending on circumstances and need.

Types of grants: Grants to schoolchildren are made according to need, towards school uniforms and educational outings in the UK.

Annual grant total: In 2005 the charity made grants totalling around £15,000 to families and young people.

Applications: Applications can be made throughout the year, via schools, an educational welfare agency, social services or Citizens Advice. Application forms are available from the correspondent.

Correspondent: Sheila Naylor, Clerk to the Trustees, The Committee Room, Huish Homes, Magdalene Street, Taunton, Somerset TA1 1SG (01823 335348 (mornings only))

Other information: The prime role of the charity is to provide sheltered accommodation for older people. Grants are also made for welfare purposes.

Wiltshire

Broad Town Trust

Eligibility: People in need who were born or have lived for at least five years in the county of Wiltshire and are, in order of priority, (i) apprentices or (ii) other young people under the age of 25.

Types of grants: Grants are towards the tools of the trade for apprentices and, if funds allow, towards books or equipment to help young people in their jobs or careers.

Annual grant total: In 2002/03 the trust had an income of £8,400 and a total expenditure of £8,500 of which about £6,500 was given in grants.

Applications: In writing to the correspondent.

Correspondent: John Lakeman, 64 St Edmunds Church Street, Salisbury, Wiltshire SP1 1EQ

William (Doc) Couch Trust Fund

Eligibility: Young people under the age of 18 who have a disability or are otherwise in financial need and live in Wiltshire.

Types of grants: Grants for schoolchildren and young people with special educational needs for lesson fees, books, equipment and educational outings in the UK.

Annual grant total: In 2004/05 it had net assets of £ 3.4 million, an income of around £100,000 and a total expenditure of £130,000, of which £109,500 was given in grants to 39 individuals.

Applications: On a form available from the correspondent. Applications can be submitted directly by the individual or through a social worker, citizen's advice bureau or other welfare agency. They are considered in July and should be submitted by 30 May.

Correspondent: Michelle Noad, Wiltshire County Council, Treasury and Pensions, County Hall, Trowbridge, Wiltshire BA14 8JJ (01225 713617)

R J Harris Charitable Settlement

Eligibility: Individuals in need who live in West Wiltshire, with particular emphasis on Trowbridge, and in North Wiltshire, south of the M4 motorway.

Types of grants: One-off grants where the person is facing extreme difficulties, for instance the trust will consider paying the remainder of a year's school fees when a child is forced to move schools, due to difficult family circumstances, during an examination year. The trust is not able to fund individuals long-term for their education. Other grants could include

those for educational outings, books and school uniform.

Annual grant total: In 2004/05 the charity had assets of £1.6 million and an income of £46,000. Out of a total expenditure of £71,000, grants to 14 individuals for welfare purposes totalled £2,600. No grants were made for educational purposes.

Applications: In writing to the correspondent, either directly by the individual, or through an educational welfare agency or another third party. Trustees meet to consider applications, in May and October/November and should be submitted at the end of April and the end of September respectively. Details should be included of any other funding that has been applied for.

Correspondent: S M Nutt, Secretary, Thring Townsend Solicitors, Midland Bridge, Bath BA1 2HQ (01225 319735)

Other information: Grants are also made for welfare purposes and to organisations.

Col. William Llewellyn Palmer Educational Charity

Eligibility: Children and young people under 25 who are attending schools maintained by the local education authority and grant maintained schools in Bradford-on-Avon.

Types of grants: One-off grants towards school uniforms, school trips and music lessons. Grants are also made for further education.

Annual grant total: In 2004/05 the charity had an income of £46,000 and a total expenditure of £36,000. Payments to beneficiaries totalled £5,500. Grants are made to organisations and individuals.

Applications: Applications should not be made directly to the correspondent. Individual applications should be made on behalf of the child by his or her school, as part of a block application by the school on behalf of all of their pupils who wish to apply. Such block applications should be submitted to the correspondent, by the school, by 25 October, for consideration at a meeting on 20 November. Grants are then distributed via the school.

Correspondent: The County Treasurer, Wiltshire County Council, Finance Department, County Hall, Trowbridge, Wiltshire BA14 8JJ

The Rose Charity

Eligibility: Schoolchildren who live in Warminster and the surrounding villages.

Types of grants: One-off grants towards costs which cannot be met elsewhere, for example, school uniform, other school clothing, books, educational outings and music lessons. Grants range from £50 to £500.

Annual grant total: In 2003/04 the charity had assets of £108,000 and an income of £13,000. Grants to individuals totalled

£2,800. Between 10 and 20 grants are made each year.

Applications: In writing to the correspondent, with the support of the social services or a school/college or other educational welfare agency, and so on. Applications are considered throughout the year.

Correspondent: C Goodbody, Trustee, Middleton & Upsall, 94 East Street, Warminster, Wiltshire BA12 9BG (01985 214444; Fax: 01985 213426)

Salisbury City Almshouse & Welfare Charities

Eligibility: People under 25 who are in need and live in Salisbury and district.

Types of grants: One-off grants of between £100 and £300 to schoolchildren, college students, undergraduates, vocational students, people with special educational needs and people starting work. Grants given include those towards, uniforms/clothing, study/travel abroad, books and equipment/instruments.

Annual grant total: In 2004 the trust had assets of £11 million, an income of £967,000 and a total expenditure of £667,000. A total of 144 grants were made to individuals for relief-in-need purposes totalling £25,000. A further £2,100 was distributed in 14 educational grants.

Applications: Applications are considered in the second week of each month. Application forms should be submitted two weeks before and should be sponsored by a recognised professional who is fully aware of statutory entitlements and is capable of giving advice/supervision in budgeting and so on. Application forms, together with guidance notes, are available from the clerk.

Correspondent: Clerk to the Trustees, Trinity Hospital, Trinity Street, Salisbury SP1 2BD (01722 325640; Fax: 01722 325640; e-mail: clerk@ almshouses.demon.co.uk)

Salisbury City Educational & Apprenticing Charity

Eligibility: Young people under 25 who live in the district of Salisbury (with a preference to those resident in the city of Salisbury, and/or in secondary education).

Types of grants: One-off grants ranging from £100 to £250 are made to schoolchildren for educational outings in the UK and study or travel abroad, and to further and higher education students (but not mature students or postgraduates) for books, equipment/instruments, educational outings in the UK and study or travel abroad.

Interest-free loans are also made towards the cost of tools and equipment needed to start a trade.

The charity interprets the term education

in the widest sense, and offers help towards the cost of expeditions and other educational projects designed to develop character, such as Project Trust, scout jamborees and adventure training.

Exclusions: Grants are not made for school uniform, maintenance/living expenses or student exchanges.

Annual grant total: In 2004 the trust had assets of £81,100, its income was £3,200 and its total expenditure was £2,700. Grants were made to 14 individuals totalling £1,900.

Applications: Application forms and notes and general advice are available from the clerk – you are advised to visit the clerk early to discuss your requirements or needs. Applications are considered monthly and can be submitted through the individual's school, college or educational welfare agency.

Grants are normally conditional upon 'the balance required being raised'.

Correspondent: Clerk to the Trustees, Trinity Hospital, Trinity Street, Salisbury SP1 2BD (01722 325640; Fax: 01722 325640; e-mail: clerk@almshouses.demon.co.uk)

The Sarum St Michael Educational Charity

Eligibility: People undergoing training as teachers, those pursuing higher education and former students of Sarum St Michael College of Education. Applications should be from people who live in the Salisbury diocese and adjoining dioceses.

Types of grants: Grants are for fees and books.

Annual grant total: In 2005 the trust had assets of £4.8 million and an income of £162,000. Grants to 67 individuals totalled £48,000. Grants to organisations totalled £83,000.

Applications: On a form available from the correspondent. Applications are considered in January, April, July, September and November. Deadline dates for receiving applications are five weeks before the trustees' meetings. Applications should be submitted directly by the individual.

Correspondent: The Clerk to the Governors, First Floor, 27A Castle Street, Salisbury, SP1 1TT (01722 422296; e-mail: ssmsarum@waitrose.com)

The Wiltshire Society

Eligibility: Young people (under 25 on the date of application) who are in need and live in Wiltshire and Swindon, had a parent born in the county or resident in it at the time of the applicant's birth, or who have lived in the county for at least five years on the date of their application.

Types of grants: Grants for amounts of up to £500 each. Help is given to students

towards books, equipment, materials, travelling and other essential costs.

Exclusions: No grants for postgraduates, childcare, or any overseas project.

Annual grant total: In 2004 the trust had an income of £8,100 with nine grants totalling £5,300.

Applications: On a form available from the correspondent, to be submitted either directly by the individual or through their school or college, educational welfare department or a third party such as social services or the parent of a young child. Applications are considered at trustees' meetings held three times a year.

Correspondent: Miss Jean Beecham, 28 Greystones, Bromham, Chippenham, Wiltshire SN15 2JT

The Alfred Earnest Withey Trust

Eligibility: Pupils aged 11 to 18 who are 'poor in pocket but rich in merit' and live in Wiltshire.

Types of grants: 50% of the income accrued by the trust is passed over to the chief education officer to distribute. Priority is given towards the cost of school/field trips, games equipment, and so on. Grants are given for up to 80% of the cost, up to £100.

Grants will not be given retrospectively and will only exceed £500 in exceptional circumstances.

Annual grant total: Previously about £5,000.

Applications: On a form available from the correspondent, by or on behalf of the individual and should include details of the applicant's parents' income and expenses (or the applicant's own income and expenses if they are 21 or above) to ensure the 'poor in pocket' criterion is met. All applications must be accompanied by a reference and full educational record to substantiate the 'rich in merit' stipulation.

Correspondent: M Prince, Wiltshire County Council, County Hall, Trowbridge, Wiltshire BA14 8JJ

Chippenham

Chippenham Borough Lands Charity

Eligibility: People in need who are currently living in the parish of Chippenham and who have lived there for a minimum of two years.

Types of grants: Usually one-off grants, according to need, are made to: schoolchildren for equipment/instruments, educational outings in the UK, study or travel overseas and in rare cases for school fees; and further and higher education students, including mature students, towards books, equipment/instruments,

fees, maintenance/living expenses, childcare, educational outings in the UK and study or travel overseas. Grants are only occasionally made to people starting work and rarely to postgraduates.

Students must have taken up all loans available to them.

Exclusions: Grants are not given in any circumstances where the trustees consider the award to be a substitute for statutory provision.

Annual grant total: In 2004/05 the charity had assets of £10.5 million and an income of £1.2 million. Grants for the year totalled £234,000. A total of 164 grants were approved, 85 of which were given to individuals.

Applications: On a form available from the correspondent. Applications are considered every month and can be submitted directly by the individual or through Citizens Advice, a social worker, other welfare agency or other third party such as a teacher.

Correspondent: The Administrator, Jubilee Building, 32 Market Place, Chippenham, Wiltshire SN15 3HP (01249 658180; Fax: 01249 446048; e-mail: cblc@lineone.net; website: www.cblc.org.uk)

Conock

The Ewelme Exhibition Endowment

Eligibility: People who live in the historical counties of Oxfordshire, Buckinghamshire and Berkshire or the Manors of Ramridge in Hampshire and Conock in Wiltshire, who are aged between 11 and 14 years at the time of application.

Types of grants: Grants to assist with private school fees and, exceptionally, educational outings. Grants range from £600 to £1,200.

Annual grant total: In 2004/05, the foundation had net assets of £234,000, an income of around £135,000, and a total expenditure £97,000. The trust gave grants and awards totalling £89,000.

Applications: On a form available from the correspondent. Applications should include attainments at school, details of parental income and a testimonial from the headteacher. They are considered in February and March.

Correspondent: C R Butterfield, 126 High Street, Oxford OX1 4DG (01865 244661)

East Knoyle

The East Knoyle Welfare Trust

Eligibility: People in need who are under the age of 25 and live in the parish of East Knoyle.

Types of grants: Any need is considered, including grants to school leavers for tools, working clothes and books.

Annual grant total: In 2004 the charities had an income of £1,800 and a total expenditure of almost £2,000.

Applications: At any time to the correspondent or any other trustee.

Correspondent: Miss Sabrina Sully, Old Byre House, Millbrook Lane, East Knoyle, Salisbury SP3 6AW (01747 830520)

Swindon

The W G Little Fund

Eligibility: Secondary school pupils who have lived in the Swindon Borough Council area for at least 12 months. The main priority is for pupils who are leaving primary school and transferring to secondary school. At the trust's discretion, support can also be given to students up to the age of 25 who wish to attend local colleges.

Types of grants: Grants are to help with school clothing.

Annual grant total: In 2004/05 the trust had an income of £45,000, all of which was given in grants to 830 individuals.

Applications: On a form available from the correspondent, to be submitted by the end of July. Successful applicants can only reapply every other year. Applicants are means tested.

Correspondent: Mrs Lesley Hodge, Trust Fund Administrator, Student Support, 4th Floor, Premier House, Station Road, Swindon SN1 1TZ (01793 466052)

Other information: Organisations are also supported, provided their service users are aged 11 to 21 and live within the borough boundary.

The Ethel May Trust

Eligibility: Schoolchildren and students under the age of 25 of good character and studious application, who attend school or college full or part-time in the boundary of Swindon Borough Council.

Types of grants: One-off grants according to need. Grants are often £150 towards equipment or dancewear.

Annual grant total: About £1,000 to £1,500.

Applications: In writing to the correspondent.

Correspondent: Mrs Lesley Hodge, Trust Fund Administrator, Student Support, 4th Floor, Premier House, Station Road, Swindon SN1 1TZ (01793 466052)

The Ernest Withey Trust

Eligibility: Primarily secondary school age pupils in elementary education who live the borough of Swindon and are 'poor in pocket but rich in merit'. There is no upper age limit.

Types of grants: One-off grants according to need.

Annual grant total: In 2004/05 the trust had an income of £2,100. Grants were made to five individuals totalling £1,200.

Applications: All applications must include a reference and full educational record substantiating that the pupils are 'rich in merit'. Applicants will also be means tested, to assess the 'poor in pocket' criteria.

Correspondent: Mrs Lesley Hodge, Trust Fund Administrator, Student Support, 4th Floor, Premier House, Station Road SN1 1TZ (01793 466052)

Tisbury

The Educational Foundation of Alice Combes & Others

Eligibility: People under 25 years who live in the ancient parish of Tisbury and West Tisbury. Applications from outside this area will not be considered.

Types of grants: Cash grants for school uniforms, clothing, books, and educational visits for schoolchildren; nursery school fees; books and study or travel abroad for those in further or higher education; and books for mature students. People starting work can be give help towards books, equipment/instruments, clothing and travel to interviews.

Grants range from £20 to £250 and are one-off. Loans are rarely given.

Annual grant total: In 2005 the trust had assets of £42,000, an income of £1,400 and a total expenditure of £1,600, all of which was given in grants to 15 individuals.

Applications: In writing to the correspondent, either directly by the individual or through their school, college or educational welfare agency, vicar, health visitor or any other third party. Applications are considered throughout the year.

Correspondent: Mrs D Carter, Rosebank, Hindon Lane, Tisbury, Wiltshire SP3 6PU (01747 871311; Fax: 01747 871311)

Warminster

The Warminster Old Boys' Fund

Eligibility: People who live in Warminster.

Types of grants: Scholarships tenable at any school, university, college of education or any other institution approved by the trustees, and grants for the purpose of providing financial assistance, outfits, clothing, instruments or books for people starting work or leaving an educational establishment.

Annual grant total: In 2004/05 it had an income of around £800 and a total expenditure of £700.

Applications: On a form available from the correspondent. All applications for more than £100 must be supported by a reference and full educational record.

Correspondent: Michelle Noad, County Treasurer, Finance Department, Wiltshire County Council, County Hall, Trowbridge, Wiltshire, BA14 8JJ (01225 757584; e-mail: studentfinance@wiltshire.gov.uk; website: www.wiltshire.gov.uk/)

Other information: In addition to administering the following trusts, the council administers 12 smaller trusts and also maintains a list of sources of information on other local trusts. Further information is available from the correspondent.

8. SOUTH EAST

Anglia Care Trust

Eligibility: People in need who live in East Anglia and are experiencing or have experienced a legal restriction on their liberty, and their families.

Types of grants: One-off grants towards rehabilitation and education. Grants usually range from £10 to £70 for students in higher/further education to spend on fees, books, equipment or other learning aids. Sums of money are not usually paid direct, but itemised bills will be met directly.

Applicants are usually already being supported by, or are known to, ACT and should have exhausted all possible sources of statutory funds.

Exclusions: No money is available for schoolchildren.

Annual grant total: Up to £5,000 if funds allow.

Applications: In writing to the correspondent. All applications must be supported by a probation officer or other professional person.

Correspondent: E Battle, Chief Executive, 65 St Matthew's Street, Ipswich, Suffolk IP1 3EW (01473 213140; Fax: 01473 219648; e-mail: admin@ angliacaretrust.org.uk)

Other information: For this entry, the information relates to the money available from ACT. For more information on what is available throughout East Anglia, contact the correspondent.

The Blatchington Court Trust

Eligibility: People aged under 31 living in the Sussex area who are visually impaired.

Types of grants: Grants or allowances are made to young people who are visually impaired at any school, university, college of education or other institution of further education (including those providing professional or technical skills) which are approved by the trustees. Grants are also made towards the cost of equipment, mobility aids, books and other study aids (including those for the study of music and the arts) which will assist in the pursuit of the education, training and employment or business development of young people. Grants will also be made in connection

with preparation for entry to a school, profession, trade, occupation or service. One-off and recurrent grants are made as well as loans.

Annual grant total: In 2005/06 the trust had assets of £8.5 million and an income mainly from investments of £470,000. Grants totalled £20,000, of which £150,000 was given in donations directly to young individuals who are visually impaired.

Applications: Applications should be made in writing to reach the correspondent by 1 February, 1 June, 1 August and 1 October each year.

Correspondent: Dr Geoff Lockwood, Clerk to the Trustees, Ridgeland House, 165 Dyke Road, Hove, East Sussex BN3 1TL (01273 722244; e-mail: enquirers@blatchington-court.co. uk; website: www.blatchington-court.co. uk)

Other information: Grants are also given to other bodies and charities in the field of educational aid to young people who are visually impaired.

The Clan Trust

Eligibility: Students of agriculture or horticulture who live or study in Norfolk and the neighbouring counties.

Types of grants: One-off and recurrent grants according to need.

Annual grant total: Grants total around £30,000 a year and are mostly given to colleges.

Applications: In writing to the correspondent, explaining why you want the grant. The trustees meet quarterly to consider applications.

Correspondent: R H C Hughes, Secretary, Brown & Co, Old Bank of England Court, Queen Street, Norwich NR9 5PR (01603 629871)

The Eric Evans Memorial Trust

Eligibility: People who live in East Anglia or London.

Types of grants: Educational grants linked to sport.

Annual grant total: In 2004/05, the trust had an income of £3,100 and a total

expenditure of £15,000. Grants totalled about £12,000.

Applications: In writing to the correspondent, either directly by the individual or through the individual's school, college or welfare agency, or any other third party. Applications are considered quarterly.

Correspondent: J M Kinder, Trustee, 55 Thornhill Square, London N1 1BE

The Ewelme Exhibition Endowment – see entry on page 210

Correspondent: C R Butterfield, 126 High Street, Oxford OX1 4DG (01865 244661)

The Hale Trust

Eligibility: Young people under 25 years of age who live in Surrey, Sussex, Kent or Greater London.

The trust helps children whose disadvantages include:

(i) mental, physical or sensory disabilities

(ii) behavioural or psychological problems

(iii) living in poverty or situations of deprivation

(iv) illness, distress, abuse or neglect.

Bursaries are given to children under the age of 18 where there are medical requirements, family problems, educational needs or limited funding.

Types of grants: Grants are usually one-off and given towards: (i) school fees, educational outings and books for schoolchildren; and (ii) books for students in further and higher education. Bursaries of £400 per term are also available for people under 18, but they cannot exceed £1,200 a year per individual, or last for more than three years. Grants are paid to the school and not the individual.

Exclusions: No grants for unspecified expenditure, deficit funding, the repayment of loans or second degrees/postgraduate work.

Annual grant total: In 2004/05 the trust had assets of £1 million and an income of £60,000. Grants totalled £44,000, of which £28,000 was distributed to organisations and £17,000 in educational bursaries.

Applications: Applications can be submitted through the individual's school, college or educational welfare agency. Applicants for one-off grants should write to the correspondent, at the address below. They should preferably be submitted in time for the trustees' meetings in February, June and October.

Applicants for bursaries should apply to: Mrs S A Henderson, Crouch House, Edenbridge, Kent TN8 8LQ. The trust aims to interview all applicants for bursaries. Grants are paid to the school.

Correspondent: Mrs J M Broughton, Secretary, Rosemary House, Woodhurst Park, Oxted, Surrey RH8 9HA

Other information: This trust also supports charities concerned with the advancement of education of children who are disabled or deprived.

The Walter Hazell Charitable and Educational Trust Fund

Eligibility: 'The advancement of education amongst employees from time to time and past employees within Buckinghamshire and Berkshire of any person, firm or company carrying on the trade of printing, their spouses, widows, widowers, children and remoter issue and persons who in the opinion of the trustees are or were substantially dependent on such employees for financial or material support.'

Types of grants: Grants for those at university towards the cost of books and expenses related to the course.

Exclusions: Does not issue grants for course fees.

Annual grant total: In 2004/05, the trust had both an income and total expenditure of £19,000. Grants totalled about £18,000.

Applications: In writing to the correspondent.

Correspondent: The Trustees, 20 Aviemore Gardens, Northampton NN4 9XJ

Other information: This trust was formed by the amalgamation of The Walter Hazell Charitable Trust and The Walter Hazell Educational Trust.

Kentish's Educational Foundation – see entry on page 19

Correspondent: Mrs M D Roberts, Clerk to the Trustees, 7 Nunnery Stables, St Albans, Hertfordshire AL1 2AS

The Mijoda Charitable Trust

Eligibility: People who live in Buckinghamshire, Bedfordshire and Hertfordshire who are undertaking further, higher or postgraduate education in music, the arts or medicine. Beneficiaries are usually under 40 years of age.

Types of grants: One-off and recurrent grants ranging from £50 to £500 towards fees and study or travel overseas.

Annual grant total: In 2004/05 the trust had an income of £15,000 and a total expenditure of £10,000. Grants were made to five individuals totalling £650.

Applications: In writing to the correspondent. A reply will only be sent if a sae is enclosed.

Correspondent: Mrs J V Hardman, Oak House, Botley Road, Chesham, Buckinghamshire HP5 1XG (01494 783402; Fax: 01494 793306)

The Nichol-Young Foundation

Eligibility: Individuals in need who are in full-time education, with a preference for those who live in East Anglia.

Types of grants: One-off and recurrent grants ranging from £100 to £500 for educational trips, medical electives and other such projects undertaken by individuals, usually during the course of full-time education.

Annual grant total: In 2003/04 the trust had assets of £633,000 and an income of £24,000. Grants to 16 individuals totalled £6,400.

Applications: In writing to the correspondent. Applications are considered quarterly by the trustees. Unsuccessful applicants will only be contacted if an sae is provided. The trust does not accept telephone enquiries.

Correspondent: Mrs A Damant, Clerk, Bates Wells & Braithwaite, 27 Friars Street, Sudbury, Suffolk CO10 2AD

The Rotherwick Foundation

Eligibility: People aged under 25 who live, or whose parents or guardians live, within a 20-mile radius of: Wither Ashdown Park Hotel, Wych Cross, East Sussex; Tynley Hall Hotel, Rotherwick, Hampshire; or The Grand Hotel, Eastbourne, East Sussex. Beneficiaries must also have attended a school or other educational establishment within the beneficial area for at least five years.

Types of grants: Scholarships, bursaries and maintenance allowances for people at school or in further or higher education. Grants for equipment, books and clothing to people starting work.

Annual grant total: In 2004/05 the foundation had an income of £318,000 and a total expenditure of £116,000. Grants were made totalling £99,200, almost all of which was given to organisations.

Applications: In writing to the correspondent.

Correspondent: G C Bateman, Trustee and General Manager, Ashdown Park, Wych Cross, Forest Row, East Sussex RH18 5JR (01342 820227; Fax: 01342 820222; e-mail: rotherwickfoundation@ ashdownpark.com; website: www. rotherwickfoundation.org)

Bedfordshire

Ashton Schools Foundation

Eligibility: People under 25 years old who are in need and live within a radius of six miles from the parish church of the ecclesiastical parish of St Peter, Dunstable, in Bedfordshire

Types of grants: One-off and recurrent grants according to need.

Annual grant total: In 2004/05 the trust had an income of £18,000 and a total expenditure of £19,000. Grants are made to organisations and individuals.

Applications: In writing to the correspondent.

Correspondent: Michelle Bradley, Grove House, 76 High Street North, Dunstable, Bedfordshire, LU6 1NF

The Bedford Charity (Harpur Trust)

Eligibility: People whose permanent address is in the borough of Bedford (consisting of the town of Bedford and North Bedfordshire) and undertaking continuing or further education courses leading to career development. Preference is given to people returning to study or training. In practice, grants are rarely given to people under 21.

Types of grants: Grants are made to allow people to develop skills and experience that will assist their careers.

Exclusions: No grants towards fees, living expenses for students on full-time first degree or professional training in medicine, accountancy or law.

Annual grant total: In 2004/05 educational grants to seven individuals totalled £7,800. A further £8,500 was distributed through the county council to 126 individuals in school uniform vouchers. Grants to organisations totalled £444,000.

Applications: On a form available from the correspondent. Initial requests for forms should be in writing or by telephone. They must be returned by early July for courses starting in the autumn term, although courses starting at other times can be assessed at a more appropriate time. Applicants are interviewed before a decision to make a grant is made.

Correspondent: Community Grants Executive, Princeton Court, The Pilgrim Centre, Brickhill Drive, Bedford MK41 7PZ (01234 369500; Fax: 01234 369505; e-mail: grants@harpur-trust.org.uk; website: www.bedfordcharity.org.uk)

Chew's Foundation at Dunstable

Eligibility: Beneficiaries must be resident in the borough of Dunstable and surrounding villages, borough of Luton or the parish of Edlesborough. Their parents must not be dissenters of the Church of England. Preference will be given to those families in need, whose beneficiaries are under 25. A certificate of baptism is required.

Types of grants: To support children in their education with the cost of books, school uniforms, school trips, equipment etc.

Annual grant total: In 2004/05 the trust had an income of £13,000 and a total expenditure of £11,000. About 20 to 25 grants were awarded to individuals with the amount depending on parental income and the number of dependant children of school age.

Applications: On a form available from the correspondent on request. Completed applications must be received by the end of May. Grants are awarded in July but late applications may be considered in December.

Correspondent: Mrs Michelle Bradley, Grove House, 76 High Street North, Dunstable, Bedfordshire LU6 1NF (01582 890619)

The Oakley Educational Foundation

Eligibility: People between the ages of 16 and 25 who live in the parish of Oakley.

Types of grants: Grants are made to schoolchildren, people starting work, further and higher education students, mature students and postgraduates. Awards include those for books, equipment/instruments, educational outings in the UK and study and travel abroad. Grants range from £30 to £150.

Exclusions: No grants for travel fares.

Annual grant total: In 2004/05 the trust had assets of £27,900, an income of £2,700 and a total expenditure of £1,900. Grants totalling £1,400 were made to 10 individuals.

Applications: In writing to the correspondent requesting an application form. Applications should be submitted by 1 May and 1 November for consideration in those months respectively, and must include receipts of purchase.

Correspondent: Dr Ruth Bender, 7 Station Road, Oakley, Bedford MK43 7RB (01234 824239; e-mail: r.bender@cranfield.ac.uk)

The David Parry Memorial Trust

Eligibility: Schoolchildren, aged 5 to 18, in the areas centred around Leighton Buzzard and Linslade whose families are experiencing severe financial hardship.

Types of grants: Grants ranging to enable pupils to take part in extra-curricular activities and visits. Help towards books may also be given.

Annual grant total: In 2004, the trust had an income of £3,200 and a total expenditure of £100. No further information was given concerning the total of grants made to individuals.

Applications: Applications can only be made on behalf of the families by the head of the school that the pupil attends and not directly by the parents. They are considered all year round.

Correspondent: Mrs Ann Swaby, Brooklands School, Brooklands Drive, Leighton Buzzard, Bedfordshire LU7 8PF (01525 372018; Fax: 01525 853062; e-mail: brooklands@deal.bedfordshire.gov.uk)

The Sandy Charities

Eligibility: People in need who live in Sandy and Beeston.

Types of grants: One-off grants only, ranging from £100 to £1,000. Schoolchildren can receive grants towards school uniforms and other school clothing and educational outings; and college students, undergraduates and vocational students towards books and equipment/instruments.

Annual grant total: In 2004/05 the charities had an income of £6,900 and gave six grants to individuals totalling £1,500.

Applications: In writing to the correspondent who will supply a personal details form for completion. Applications can be considered in any month, depending on the urgency for the grant; they should be submitted either directly by the individual or via the individual's school, college or educational welfare agency.

Correspondent: P J Mount, Clerk, c/o Woodfine Leeds Smith, 6 Bedford Road, Sandy, Bedfordshire SG19 1EN (01767 680251; Fax: 01767 691775; e-mail: peter.mount@leedssmith.co.uk)

Other information: Grants are also made to organisations and to individuals for welfare purposes.

Bedford

Alderman Newton's Educational Foundation (Bedford branch)

Eligibility: People aged 13 to 25 who live in the town of Bedford.

Types of grants: Grants are given to schoolchildren, people starting work and further and higher education students. Grants given include those for school uniforms, books, equipment/instruments and childcare costs.

Annual grant total: In 2004/05 the foundation had assets of £17,000, an income of £3,700 and a total expenditure of £3,100, all of which was given in grant to five individuals.

Applications: On a form available from the correspondent to be submitted directly by the individual to: D Baker, Room 202, c/o Bedford Borough Council, Town Hall, Bedford MK40 1SJ (01234 227203; e-mail dbaker@bedford.gov.uk). Applications can be submitted at any time.

Correspondent: K R Simmons, Clerk, c/o Bedford Borough Council, Town Hall, Bedford MK40 1SJ

Clapham

The Ursula Taylor Charity

Eligibility: Young people who live in the parish of Clapham, between the ages of 13 and 25.

Types of grants: Grants are made to schoolchildren, people starting work and students in further/higher education for books, educational outings, school fees, equipment/instruments and other educational needs.

Exclusions: No grants are given for bus passes.

Annual grant total: Grants each year are made to about 15 individuals totalling £1,000.

Applications: On a form available from the correspondent, submitted either directly by the individual or through the charity's trustees. Applications are considered in February, April, June and October. Applications should include receipts for items purchased.

Correspondent: Mrs D Kitchen, Secretary to the Trustees, 49 Highbury Grove, Clapham, Bedford MK41 6DT (01234 214251)

Clophill

Clophill United Charities

Eligibility: People in need who live in the parish of Clophill.

Types of grants: One-off and recurrent grants according to need. No grants where statutory funds are available (e.g. no school fees).

Exclusions: No grants where statutory funds are available.

Annual grant total: In 2005 the charities had an income of £32,000 and a total expenditure of £29,000.

Applications: On a form available from the correspondent. The trustees meet every two months to consider applications.

Correspondent: Richard Pearson, 8 Little Lane, Clophill, Bedford, MK45 4BG

Flitwick

The Flitwick Town Lands Charity

Eligibility: Students between 18 and 25 who live in the parish of Flitwick.

Types of grants: Grants are awarded to students of around £100 to £250. As a general rule, educational grants are awarded to students at the start of their second year of study in higher education. In exceptional circumstances, one-off grants may be given, for reasons such as providing sports equipment to a youth group.

Annual grant total: In 2003/04 the charity had an income and a total expenditure of £6,400. Grants are given for education and welfare purposes.

Applications: On a form available from the correspondent.

Correspondent: David William Epsom, 28 Orchid Way, Flitwick MK45 1LF

Kempston

The Kempston Charities

Eligibility: People in need who live in Kempston (including Kempston rural).

Types of grants: One-off grants according to need.

Exclusions: No recurrent grants are made.

Annual grant total: In 2004 the trust had an income of almost £7,000 and a total expenditure of £5,100. Grants totalled about £4,500.

Applications: In writing to the correspondent. Applications should be made either directly by the individual or through a social worker, Citizens Advice or other welfare agency. They are considered in March, July and November.

Correspondent: Mrs L Smith, 14 Riverview Way, Kempston, Bedford MK42 7BB

Other information: Grants are also given to local schools and other local institutions.

Luton

The Colin Smith Music Trust Fund

Eligibility: Young people studying music in Luton.

Types of grants: One-off grants for young people's organisations or clubs towards the cost of instruments and tuition.

Annual grant total: In 2005, the trust had an income of almost £8,000 and a total expenditure of £2,600.

Applications: In writing to the correspondent.

Correspondent: David Fraser, Trustee, 6 Cross End, Thurleigh, Bedford MK44 2EE (01234 771370)

Potton

The Potton Consolidated Charities

Eligibility: People between 18 and 25 who live in the parish of Potton.

Types of grants: Book grants of about £200 for students in further or higher education.

Annual grant total: In 2004/05 grants were made to 37 individuals for educational purposes totalling £7,400.

Applications: Directly by the individual on a form available from the correspondent. Applications are considered in November and should be received by 31 October.

Correspondent: Mrs C J Hall, 1a Potton Road, Everton, Sandy, Bedfordshire SG19 2LD (01767 680663; e-mail: pot. concha@tiscali.co.uk)

Berkshire

Crowthorne Trust

Eligibility: People in need who live in the parishes of Crowthorne, Finchampstead, Sandhurst and Wokingham Without, all in Berkshire. Preference is given to applicants under 25.

Types of grants: Grants are towards the spiritual, moral, mental and physical well-being of recipients.

Annual grant total: The trust awards grants totalling around £15,000 a year to individuals.

Applications: In writing to the correspondent from whom an application form may be obtained. Meetings are held three times a year, although in urgent cases applications can be considered between meetings.

Correspondent: The Hon. Secretary, Wellington College, Crowthorne, Berkshire RG45 7PU (e-mail: adtr@ wellingtoncollege.org.uk; website: www. wellingtoncoll.demon.co.uk/ctrust/)

Other information: The trust also gives £5,000 a year to local youth organisations.

The Polehampton Charity

Eligibility: People who live in the ecclesiastical parishes of Twyford and Ruscombe.

Types of grants: (i) Educational grants – these cover the purchase of books, tools, instruments and so on which are essential for the completion of courses or training at universities, colleges of further education and other recognised educational establishments, including apprenticeships. They also cover assistance to allow young people to study music or other arts, and to make provision for recreational and sports training, not normally provided by local authorities. Grants are also given for school uniforms and school educational outings.

(ii) Educational bursaries – these are to assist those who are under 25 and are undertaking courses of further education for which no local authority or similar grants is available.

Grants are in the range of £100 to £250.

Annual grant total: In 2004 the charity had assets of £1.1 million, an income of £44,000 and a total expenditure of £49,000. A total of 61 relief-in-need grants to individuals were made amounting to £8,000 and 12 individuals received educational grants totalling £1,300.

Applications: Applications should be submitted either directly by the individual or a family member, through a third party such as a social worker or teacher, or through and organisation such as Citizens Advice or a school. They should include a list of the books and/or equipment needed and be addressed to: Ms E Treadwell (Assistant Clerk), 114 Victoria Road, Wargrave, Berkshire RG10 8AE. Applications can be made at any time and are considered at trustee meetings.

Correspondent: Peter M Hutt, Clerk, 1 London Street, Reading RG1 4QW (Fax: 0118 951 6322: 0118 950 2704; e-mail: peter.hutt@fsp-law.com)

Other information: Grants are also made to schools (£22,000 in 2004).

The Reading Charities & Reading Municipal Church Charities

Eligibility: People of secondary school age, up to the age of 24, in Reading and Wokingham.

Types of grants: A number of different charities operate from the same address:

(i) Green Girls' Foundation – grants, for general educational needs for women and girls under the age of 24 living in the area covered by Reading Borough Council.

(ii) John Allen's Charity – grants are given for general educational needs living in the area covered by Reading Borough Council.

(iii) Archbishop Laud's Charity – grants, to a usual maximum of £100, to help with books and equipment for boys in the Wokingham and Reading area.

Annual grant total: The three charities together give grants totalling about £7,000 a year.

Applications: On a form available from the correspondent, submitted directly by the individual or by a third party. Applications are considered throughout the year.

Correspondent: The Clerk to the Trustees, St Mary's Church House, Chain Street, Reading, Berkshire RG1 2HX (0118 957 1057; Fax: 0118 958 7041)

Trustees of the Reading Dispensary Trust

Eligibility: People in need who have a physical or mental disability or are infirm and who live in Reading and the surrounding area (roughly within a seven-mile radius of the centre of Reading).

Types of grants: One-off grants towards course fees.

Exclusions: Grants are not made when help is available from statutory sources.

Annual grant total: In 2004 the trust had assets of £1.1 million and an income of £44,000. A total of £23,000 was given in 165 grants to individuals, mostly for welfare purposes.

Applications: On a form available from the correspondent. Applications should be submitted either through a social worker, Citizens Advice or other welfare agency or third party. Applications are considered every month.

Correspondent: W E Gilbert, Clerk, 16 Wokingham Road, Reading RG6 1JQ (0118 926 5698)

Other information: Grants are also made to organisations (£5,800 in 2004).

The Spoore Merry & Rixman Foundation

Eligibility: People under 25 who live in the old (pre-1974) borough of Maidenhead and the ancient parish of Bray.

Types of grants: Grants for (i) school pupils to help with books, equipment, clothing or travel, and for sporting activities, music, drama, dance and so on; (ii) college or university fees or to supplement existing LEA funding; and (iii) books, equipment, clothing and travel expenses for people starting work. People with special educational needs are also supported. Grants are for amounts of up to £5,000 each, although in special cases, such as death of parents, this figure can be exceeded.

Annual grant total: In 2004 the trust had an income of £158,000 and a total expenditure of £107,000. Grants to individuals totalled £53,000 (over 100 grants are made each year).

Applications: On a form available from the correspondent. Applications can be made either directly by the individual or through a school, college or educational welfare agency. Meetings of the trustees are held in mid January, April, July and October.

Correspondent: M J Tanner, Abbott Lloyd Howorth, Minster Court, 22–30 York Road, Maidenhead, Berkshire SL6 1SF

Other information: Grants are also made to organisations (£38,000 in 2004).

Lady Frances Winchcombe's Thatcham Foundation

Eligibility: People who live in the parishes of Thatcham, Bucklebury or Cold Ash whose children have attended a local school for at least two years. Applicants should be aged between 16 and 25.

Types of grants: Grants to (i) three Church of England Sunday Schools, (ii) young people leaving school at 16 and entering further or higher education for books, help with fees or travel or study abroad and (iii) people starting work for books, equipment, clothing, travel etc. Grants are one-off and range from £75 to £200.

Annual grant total: In 2004/05 the foundation had both an income and a total expenditure of £1,800. Educational grants were made to six individuals totalling £800.

Applications: On a form available from the correspondent, to be completed by the parents or guardian. Applications should be submitted by June for consideration in July.

Correspondent: Mrs D Handby, Clerk, Pendennis House, Chapel Lane, Curridge, Thatcham RG18 9DX (01635 200857)

The Wokingham United Charities

Eligibility: School children in need who live in the civil parishes of Wokingham, Wokingham Without, St Nicholas, Hurst, Ruscombe and that part of Finchampstead known as Finchampstead North.

Types of grants: One-off grants between £25 and £150. Grants have been given towards school uniforms and educational visits.

Annual grant total: In 2004 the charity gave grants totalling almost £8,000.

Applications: On a form available from the correspondent. Applications are considered each month (except August) and can be submitted directly by the individual, or through a social worker, headteacher or similar third party.

Correspondent: P Robinson, Clerk, 66 Upper Broadmoor Road, Crowthorne, Berkshire RG45 7DF (01344 762637)

Pangbourne

The Breedon Educational & Vocational Foundation

Eligibility: Children and young people who live in the civil parish of Pangbourne, Berkshire who are in full-time or further education.

Types of grants: One-off and recurrent grants: (i) to help with books, equipment, clothing or travel for schoolchildren, students or people starting work; or (ii) to help with school, college or university fees or to supplement existing grants.

Annual grant total: Grants total about £2,500 a year.

Applications: On a form available from the correspondent. Applications are considered in March, July and December each year.

Correspondent: E S Goddard, c/o RWP Solicitors, Meadow House, 22 Reading Road, Pangbourne, Berkshire RG8 7LY (0118 984 2266)

Reading

The Harry Tee Young People Foundation

Eligibility: Young people aged 14 to 25 who live or work in the borough of Reading.

Types of grants: One-off grants to develop leadership skills through travel overseas, such as international exchanges, overseas expeditions, short-term study projects and overseas community service projects. Grants range from £50 to £200.

Annual grant total: Grants are made totalling about £1,000 each year.

Applications: In writing to the correspondent, including age, where the applicant is going, what the applicant is proposing to do, the total cost, the amount requested, why support should be given and how the balance will be raised. Applications should be made directly by the individual, though in certain circumstances an adult can assist. They are considered in April and September. Please enclose an sae.

Correspondent: Mrs C Charles, Secretary, Civic Offices, Civic Centre, Reading RG1 7TD (0118 901 5209; Fax: 0118 901 5213; e-mail: carol.charles@reading.gov.uk)

Windsor and Maidenhead

The Prince Philip Trust Fund

Eligibility: Young people undertaking voluntary work or training schemes from the royal borough of Windsor and Maidenhead. Support is also given to individual pupils selected to represent their district, county or country in an activity considered worthy of the trust's support.

Types of grants: One-off grants ranging from £100 to £3,000.

Exclusions: Grants are not made for tuition fees.

Annual grant total: In 2005, the fund had net assets of £1 million, an income of £76,000 and an expenditure of £59,000. The fund gave grants to twelve individuals totalling £5,700.

Applications: In writing to the correspondent, including details of the project, the amount of grant sought, amount in hand and the names of two referees. Application deadlines are at the end of February and September for consideration in April and November.

Correspondent: Kevin M McGarry, Secretary, 10 Cadogan Close, Holyport, Maidenhead, Berkshire SL6 2JS (01628 639577; Fax: 01628 639577)

Other information: Grants are also made to organisations.

Buckinghamshire

The Amersham United Charities

Eligibility: People under the age of 21 who live in the parishes of Amersham and Coleshill.

Types of grants: One-off grants for those at school, college or university, or about to start work, to help with the cost of fees (students only), books, equipment, clothing and travel.

Annual grant total: In 2004 the charities had an income of £29,000 and a total expenditure of £23,000. No grants to individuals were made during the year.

Applications: In writing to the correspondent.

Correspondent: The Chairman, 86 High Street, Amersham, Buckinghamshire HP7 0DS (01494 727674)

Other information: The main work of the charity is the administration and management of 13 almshouses.

Norman Hawes Memorial Trust

Eligibility: Young people aged between 15 and 18 who are in full-time education and live in Milton Keynes and north Buckinghamshire.

Types of grants: Grants for international study visits, ranging between £50 and £200.

Annual grant total: In 2004/05 the trust had assets of £76,000, an income of £2,800 and a total expenditure of £3,000, all of

which was given in grants to four individuals.

Applications: On an application form available from the correspondent to be submitted directly by the individual or through the school/college/educational welfare agency. Applications can be submitted in September/October and January/February for consideration in November and February/March.

Correspondent: Sue Bruce, Schools Support Officer, School Improvement Division, 599 Avebury Boulevard, Milton Keynes MK9 3HR (01908 253614; Fax: 01908 253289; e-mail: sue.bruce@ milton-keynes.gov.uk)

The Marlow Educational Foundation

Eligibility: People under 25 who live or were born in the parish of Great Marlow or the urban districts of Marlow, and are attending, or for not less than one year have attended, any school in that parish or urban district.

Types of grants: Grants are given to individuals for a broad spectrum of educational purposes. Grants range from £200 to £700.

Annual grant total: Grants total between £5,000 and £10,000 a year.

Applications: On a form available from the correspondent. Applications can be submitted directly by the individual or a parent/guardian, through a teacher, or an organisation such as a school or an educational welfare agency. They are considered two or three times a year.

Correspondent: P A R Land, Clerk, Cripps & Shone, The Old House, West Street, Marlow, Buckinghamshire SL7 2LX (01628 482115; Fax: 01628 486412)

The Salford Town Lands

Eligibility: People in need who live in the parish of Hulcote and Salford.

Types of grants: Grants are one-off and range from £100 to £200. They will be considered for the following: the cost of school uniforms, school clothing, books, educational outings and maintenance for schoolchildren; books and help with fees/ living expenses for students in further or higher education; books, travel and fees for mature students; and books, equipment/ instruments, clothing and travel for people starting work.

Annual grant total: In 2004 the trust had an income of £6,500 and a total expenditure of £5,700. Grants were made totalling about £5,000, although this was mostly for welfare purposes.

Applications: In writing to the correspondent. Applications can be submitted directly by the individual or through any other parishioner.

Correspondent: Julian Barrett, South Cottage, 18 Broughton Road, Salford, Milton Keynes MK17 8BH

Other information: Grants are also made to organisations supporting the community.

The Saye & Sele Foundation

Eligibility: People under 25 who live in the parishes of Grendon Underwood and Quainton.

Types of grants: One-off grants to help school, college or university students with books, equipment and training costs. Grants have been made towards computers for people from low-income families and equipment for people with disabilities. Grants are generally around £200, but can be for any amount.

Annual grant total: In 2004, the foundation had an income of £13,500 and a total expenditure of £13,000. Grants totalled about £10,000.

Applications: In writing to the correspondent, to be considered in January, April, July and October.

Correspondent: R T Friedlander, Clerk, Messrs Parrot & Coales, Solicitors, 14 Bourbon Street, Aylesbury, Buckinghamshire HP20 2RS (01296 318500; e-mail: law@parrot-coales. co.uk)

The Stoke Mandeville & Other Parishes Charity

Eligibility: People in need who live in the parishes of Stoke Mandeville, Great and Little Hampden and Great Missenden.

Types of grants: Help with the cost of books, clothing and other essentials for schoolchildren, people at college or university and for people starting work. Grants for schoolchildren are up to a maximum of £300 a year and grants for people in further or higher education are up to a maximum of £600 a year. Individuals must reapply each year for additional grants.

Annual grant total: In 2004 the trust's assets totalled £2.3 million and the income was £268,000. Grants totalled £91,000, of which £18,000 was given in student grants.

Applications: On a form available from the correspondent, considered in January, April, July and October.

Correspondent: G Crombie, Secretary, Blackwells, Great Hampden, Great Missenden, Buckinghamshire HP16 9RJ

Other information: The charity also gives grants to organisations.

Aylesbury

William Harding's Charity

Eligibility: People who live in the town of Aylesbury under 25 years of age.

Types of grants: One-off grants are made to schoolchildren for uniforms/school clothing, fees, study/travel overseas, books, equipment/instruments and educational outings in the UK, to college students, undergraduates, vocational students and mature students for fees, study/travel overseas, books, equipment/instruments and maintenance/living expenses and to individuals with special educational needs for uniforms/clothing, books, equipment/instruments and excursions.

Annual grant total: In 2005 the trust had assets of £17 million and an income of £450,000. Grants totalled £260,000, of which £35,000 went to individuals for educational purposes (62 grants) and £900 to individuals for relief-in-need purposes (two grants). Donations to organisations amounted to £224,000.

Applications: On a form available from the correspondent to be submitted directly by the individual or a family member, through a third party such as a social worker or teacher or through an organisation such as Citizens Advice. Trustees meet 10 times each year to consider applications. Applications should include details of family income.

Correspondent: John Leggett, Clerk to the Trustees, Messrs Parrott & Coales, Solicitors, 14 Bourbon Street, Aylesbury HP20 2RS (01296 318500)

Thomas Hickman's Charity

Eligibility: People in need who live in Aylesbury town.

Types of grants: Grants for school uniforms.

Annual grant total: In 2004 the charity made grants to individuals totalling £28,000.

Applications: On a form available from the correspondent. Applications should be submitted either directly by the individual or a family member, through a third party such as social worker or school, or through an organisation such as Citizens Advice or a school. Trustees meet on a regular basis and applications are considered as they arise.

Correspondent: J Leggett, Parrott & Coales, 14–16 Bourbon Street, Aylesbury, Buckinghamshire HP20 2RS (01296 318500)

Other information: The charity also provides almshouses.

Aylesbury Vale

Charles Pope Memorial Trust

Eligibility: People in need who have lived or been educated in the area administered by Aylesbury Vale District Council for at least two years.

Types of grants: Grants are awarded for musical education, including tuition, instruments, scores etc. Grants will not normally exceed £300.

Annual grant total: In 2004/05 the trust had assets totalling £16,000, an income of £1,000 and made grants to individuals totalling £400.

Applications: On a form available from the correspondent, submitted directly by the individual or by a parent or guardian. Applications are usually considered in March, June and November and should be received in the middle of February, May and October. A reference is required from a relevant music tutor. If it is close to the time when applications are to be considered, it is helpful if the reference can be sent with the application. In other cases the secretary will contact the referee direct. Applicants need to show some musical competence and commitment.

Correspondent: Mrs S M Baxter, Secretary, 77 Regent Street, Leighton Buzzard LU7 3JY (01525 854461)

Calverton

Calverton Apprenticing Charity

Eligibility: Young people aged 17 to 21 who have lived in the parish of All Saints, Calverton village for at least five years.

Types of grants: Recurrent grants in the range of £100 to £150 to college students, undergraduates, vocational students and people starting work, including those for uniforms/clothing, fees, books and equipment/instruments.

Annual grant total: In 2004/05 the charity had assets of £36,000, an income of £3,100 and a total expenditure of £2,500. The sum of £1,100 was distributed in 11 welfare grants. A further of £300 was given in two educational grants.

Applications: On a form available from the correspondent to be submitted directly by the individual or a family member. Applications are considered in May and November.

Correspondent: Miss K Phillips, 78 London Road, Stony Stratford MK11 1JH (01908 563350; e-mail: karen.phillips@ virgin.net)

Cheddington

Cheddington Town Lands Charity

Eligibility: People in need who live in Cheddington.

Types of grants: One-off and recurrent grants according to need.

Annual grant total: In 2004/05 the trust had assets of £697,000 and an income of £31,000. Grants totalled £10,000, with 90% given for educational assistance and 10% for hospital transport and specific hardship.

Applications: In writing to the correspondent, directly by the individual or a family member.

Correspondent: W G King, 5 Chaseside Close, Cheddington, Leighton Buzzard, Bedfordshire LU7 0SA (01296 668608)

Emberton

Emberton United Charity

Eligibility: People under 25 in higher education who live in the parish of Emberton.

Types of grants: One-off and recurrent grants, usually of up to £350, towards books and equipment/instruments, but not fees.

Annual grant total: About £5,000 was given in grants to older people as well as young people for educational purposes.

Applications: In writing to the correspondent, directly by the individual.

Correspondent: George Davies, Secretary to the Trustees, 59 Olney Road, Emberton, Olney, Buckinghamshire MK46 5BU (Fax: 0870 164 0662; e-mail: george@ taipooshan.demon.co.uk)

Great Linford

The Great Linford Advancement in Life Charity

Eligibility: People under 25 who live in the civil parish of Great Linford.

Types of grants: Grants are given for education in the form of social and physical training and scholarships or bursaries for entry to university or other educational establishment. It could also include clothing, tools, musical instruments, books, and travel in the furtherance of these studies, or for preparation for entry into a profession, trade or calling upon leaving school, university or other educational establishment. Grants are normally up to £200.

Annual grant total: About £2,000.

Applications: In writing to the correspondent, either directly by the individual or through their school, college or educational welfare agency. Applications must include details of the purpose for which the request is being made and official estimates. They are considered in January, May and September.

Correspondent: M Williamson, Treasurer, 2 Lodge Gate, Great Linford, Milton Keynes, Bucks MK14 5EW (01908 605664)

Other information: Consideration may be given to groups provided that their membership comprises of eligible people.

Olney

The Olney British School Charity & the Olney British School Foundation

Eligibility: People under the age of 25 who live, or whose parents live, in Olney, who are involved in further education after leaving school.

Types of grants: Grants to those 'who are preparing for, entering upon or engaged in any profession, trade, occupation, or service, by providing them with outfits, or by paying fees, travelling or maintenance expenses, or by such means for their advancement in life or to enable them to earn their living'. Students in further/higher education can receive grants for books or study or travel abroad.

Annual grant total: In 2004/05 the charity had assets of £73,000, an income of £3,100 and a total expenditure of £2,400, all of which was given in grants to 22 individuals.

Applications: In writing to: D J Saunders, Treasurer, 17 Long Lane, Olney, Buckinghamshire MK46 5HL. Applications must be received by 31 August for consideration in September.

Correspondent: Mrs C Crouch, Secretary, Owl House, 25 Wellingborough Road, Olney, Buckinghamshire MK46 4BJ (01234 712533)

Pitstone

The Pitstone Town Lands Charity

Eligibility: People in need who live in Pitstone.

Types of grants: One-off and recurrent grants according to need, for example, tools of the trade such as instruments for musicians.

Annual grant total: About £13,000.

Applications: In writing to the correspondent through a social worker, Citizens Advice or other welfare agency or

third party, or directly by the individual. Applications are considered throughout the year and must include full information to support the application.

Correspondent: Mrs C Martell, 22 Chequers Lane, Pitstone, Leighton Buzzard, Bedfordshire LU7 9AG

Other information: The charity also gives grants to organisations in the area.

Radnage

Radnage Poor's Land Educational Foundation

Eligibility: People in need below 25 years, who live in the parish of Radnage.

Types of grants: One-off grants ranging from £100 to £500. Grants are given to schoolchildren and further and higher education students including those for uniforms, books, equipment/instruments, fees, maintenance/living expenses, educational outings in the UK, study or travel abroad and student exchanges. Grants are also given to people starting work for books.

Annual grant total: In 2005 the foundation had an income of £2,400 and gave eight grants totalling £5,000.

Applications: In writing to the correspondent, either directly by the individual or through a school, college or education welfare agency, for consideration in February, June, September and December.

Correspondent: I K Baylock, Clerk to the Trustees, Hilltop, Green End Road, Radnage, High Wycombe, Buckinghamshire HP14 4BY

Stoke Poges

Stoke Poges United Charities

Eligibility: Children in primary and secondary school and apprentices/people starting work who live in the parish of Stoke Poges.

Types of grants: Grants are given for tools, clothing, books and other school equipment.

Annual grant total: In 2004 the charity had an income of £10,000 and a total expenditure of £600. Grants totalled about £500.

Applications: In writing to the correspondent, to be submitted either directly by the individual or through a social worker, Citizens Advice, other welfare agency or any third party.

Correspondent: Mrs J Tulloch, 4 Willow Park, Stoke Poges, Slough SL2 4ES

Other information: This charity consists of five separate funds which provide grants for relief-in-need or educational purposes.

Stokenchurch

The Stokenchurch Education Charity

Eligibility: People under 25 who live in the parish of Stokenchurch.

Types of grants: Grants range from £5 to £500 and are for academic expenses.

Exclusions: No grants are made for private tuition, or where statutory grants are available. Applicants from outside the Parish of Stokenchurch are not supported.

Annual grant total: Grants total around £50,000 a year, most of which goes to individuals.

Applications: On a form available from the correspondent. In August the trustees place an advertisement in the local press, and two public places in Stokenchurch, inviting applications. Educational applications must be received by 30 November of each academic year and grants are paid in April. Applications from outside the parish are not responded to.

Correspondent: Mrs P L Colling, Secretary to the Trustees, Kinda Cool, Wycombe Road, Stokenchurch, High Wycombe, Buckinghamshire HP14 3RR

Other information: Grants are also made to organisations, as any excess in income is given to village groups which benefit local inhabitants.

Stony Stratford

The Ancell Trust

Eligibility: People in need in Stony Stratford.

Types of grants: Grants are given to students for books. They are also occasionally made to individuals for welfare purposes and to organisations.

Annual grant total: In 2003/04 the trust had an income of £8,600 and a total expenditure of £12,000. Grants totalled about £10,000.

Applications: In writing to the correspondent at any time.

Correspondent: Roger Borley, Secretary, 79 High Street, Stony Stratford, Milton Keynes MK1 1AU

Arnold Education Foundation
see entry on page 171

Correspondent: The Clerk, c/o Messrs Wilson Browne, Solicitors, 60 Gold Street, Northampton NN1 1RS

Winslow

Rogers Free School Foundation

Eligibility: People in any stage of education who live in the parish of Winslow.

Types of grants: Grants are given towards help with school uniforms, other school clothing, educational outings in the UK, books and study or travel abroad.

Annual grant total: In 2005 the trust had an income of £2,300 and a total expenditure of £2,800. A total of five grants were made to individuals totalling £1,900.

Applications: On an application form, available from the correspondent. Applications can be submitted either directly by the individual or through a parent.

Correspondent: T B Foley, 16 Buckingham Road, Winslow, Buckinghamshire MK18 3DY (01296 713904; e-mail: g4fyo@tesco.net)

Wolverton

Wolverton Science and Art Institution Fund

Eligibility: People who live in the Wolverton parish which includes all of Wolverton, New Bradwell, Bradville, Stantonbury, Bradwell Common, Bradwell, Stacey Bushes and Hodge Lea.

Types of grants: Recurrent grants in the range of £100 to £500. Grants are given to schoolchildren, people starting work, further and higher education students, mature students and postgraduates for uniforms/other school clothing, books, equipment/instruments, fees and educational outings in the UK.

Exclusions: Grants are not made to cover the salary expenses of a project

Annual grant total: In 2004/05 the fund had assets of £139,000, an income of £6,000 and a total expenditure of £5,000. Grants were made for educational purposes to six individuals totalling £1,000.

Applications: On a form available from the correspondent, either directly by the individual or through a school/college/educational welfare agency. Applications are considered in February, April, August and October and should be received in the preceding month.

Correspondent: Miss Karen Phillips, 78 London Road, Stony Stratford MK11 1JH (01908 563350; e-mail: karen.phillips@virgin.net)

Other information: Grants are also made to educational organisations.

Cambridgeshire

The Hobson & Crane Exhibition Foundation

Eligibility: People aged 13 to 19 who live and go to school in the Cambridge education area (i.e. the city of Cambridge and surrounding villages, not the whole of the county council education area). In exceptional circumstances people up to the age of 23 may be considered for a grant. No grants to people studying for a second degree.

Types of grants: Grants are given to schoolchildren, people starting work and further and higher education students, to help with books, clothing, equipment/instruments or study or travel abroad.

Annual grant total: About £3,500.

Applications: On a form available from the correspondent, to be submitted directly by the individual. Applications should be submitted by 30 June each year, for consideration in July.

Correspondent: Liz Whitcher, Clerk to the Governors, The Guildhall, Cambridge CB2 3QJ (01223 457015; Fax: 01223 457029; e-mail: liz.whitcher@cambridge.gov.uk)

Bishop Laney's Charity

Eligibility: People in need under 25 who live in the parishes of Soham and Ely. Consideration will be given to people under 25 who live in other parts of Cambridgeshire where funds permit.

Types of grants: Grants are given to people starting work for general purposes. Preference is given to apprentices. Grants are also given to students in further/higher education for uniforms/clothing, books and equipment/instruments and the charity will consider grants for study or travel abroad, excursions in the UK and maintenance/living expenses. Support for schoolchildren is also considered for excursions in the UK and maintenance/living expenses. The grants range from £75 to £3,000.

Annual grant total: In 2004/05 the trust had assets of £1.5 million, an income of £68,000 and a total expenditure of £47,000. Grants were made totalling £22,600 to 125 individuals.

Applications: On a form available from the correspondent, submitted directly by the individual, for consideration usually in July, September, October and December. Applications must include a copy of the applicant's birth certificate, proof of attendance at college/university etc. and details of the book shop/music shop etc.

Correspondent: Richard Tayor, Whiting & Partners, 41 St Mary's Street, Ely,

Cambridgeshire CB7 4HF (01353 662595; Fax: 01353 666119)

The Leverington Town Lands Educational Charity

Eligibility: Schoolchildren and people in further/higher education who live in Leverington, Parson Drove and Gorefield.

Types of grants: One-off grants according to need.

Annual grant total: In 2004/05,the charity had an income of £4,000 and a total expenditure of £2,700.

Applications: On a form available from the correspondent for consideration in September.

Correspondent: Mrs C A Gray, 78 High Road, Gorefield, Wisbech, Cambridgeshire, PE13 4NB (01945 870454; e-mail: leveoffees@aol.com)

The Henry Morris Memorial Trust

Eligibility: Students between the ages of 13 and 19 who live or attend school in Cambridge or east or south Cambridgeshire.

Types of grants: Grants in the range of £20 to £200 are given to help finance 'short expeditions or projects with purpose'.

Exclusions: No grants are given towards organised courses, excursions or projects, for example, Raleigh International.

Annual grant total: In 2005 the trust had an income of £3,000, all of which was given in grants to 30 individuals.

Applications: On a form available from local schools or from the trust's website. Applications should be submitted directly by the individual by the end of January for consideration in February/March.

Correspondent: David Farnell, The Old Manse, 7 Chapel Road, Great Eversden, Cambridge CB3 7HP (01223 262717; e-mail: mail@dfarnell.plus.com; website: www.henrymorris.plus.com)

Other information: Grants are not given to applicants who are part of a group organised by any agency or organisation. Applicants must make independent travel and accommodation arrangements.

The Charities of Nicholas Swallow & Others

Eligibility: People in need who live in the parish of Whittlesford (near Cambridge) and adjacent area.

Types of grants: One-off grants according to need.

Annual grant total: In 2004/05 it had assets of £290,000 and an income of £34,000. Educational grants totalled £140. Christmas cash distributions totalled £2,400.

Applications: Directly by the individual in writing to the correspondent.

Correspondent: Nicholas Tufton, Clerk, 11 High Street, Barkway, Royston, Hertfordshire SG8 8EA (01763 848888)

Other information: The principal activity of this charity is as a housing association which manages 11 bungalows and 9 garages.

Elsworth

The Samuel Franklin Fund

Eligibility: People at any level or stage of their education, studying any subject, who live in the parish of Elsworth.

Types of grants: One-off and recurrent grants in the range of £10 to £1,000.

Annual grant total: About £5,000 a year to individuals.

Applications: In writing to the correspondent including brief details of requirements.

Correspondent: Mrs Lynda Hogan, Secretary, 46 Boxworth Road, Elsworth, Cambridge CB3 8JQ (01954 267254)

Hilton

Hilton Town Charity

Eligibility: People who live in the village of Hilton, Cambridgeshire, at any stage or level of their education, undertaking study of any subject.

Types of grants: Only a limited number of grants are given for educational purposes.

Annual grant total: On average about £2,000 is available in grants.

Applications: In writing to the correspondent.

Correspondent: Ms S Sheppard, Treasurer, 20 Chequers Croft, Hilton, Cambridgeshire, PE28 9PD

Other information: Grants are also available for organisations which serve the direct needs of the village.

Little Wilbraham

The Johnson Bede & Lane Charitable Trust

Eligibility: People in need who live in the civil parish of Little Wilbraham.

Types of grants: One-off grants usually between £50 and £150. Grants given include those to schoolchildren and college students, including those towards fees, equipment/instruments, excursions, music lessons and school outings.

Annual grant total: In 2004/05 the trust had an income of £3,300. Welfare grants to

30 individuals totalled £2,700. There was one educational grant made of £70.

Applications: In writing to the correspondent directly by the individual or by a third party such as a social worker, Citizens Advice or neighbour. Applications are considered on an ongoing basis.

Correspondent: Ms P Addecott, 8 De La Mere Close, Six Mile Bottom, Newmarket, CB8 0XF (01638 570372)

Other information: Grants are also made to organisations (£500 in 2004/05).

Sawston

John Huntingdon's Charity

Eligibility: Schoolchildren, college students and people with people with special educational needs who live in the parish of Sawston in Cambridgeshire.

Types of grants: One-off grants, usually ranging from £25 to £250 and occasionally up to £500 or more. About 100 grants are made each year. Grants are given to: Schoolchildren for uniforms/clothing, school trips and books; college students for books and equipment/instruments; and people with special educational needs for uniforms/clothing, books, equipment/instruments and excursions.

Annual grant total: In 2004 the trust had assets of £6.4 million, its income was £273,000 and its total expenditure was £200,000. Educational grants to 46 individuals totalled £13,000, with a further £11,000 to 93 individuals for welfare purposes. Grants to organisations totalled £61,000.

Applications: On an application form available from Sawston Support Services at the address above or by telephone. Office opening hours are 9am to 2pm Monday to Friday. Grants are considered on an ongoing basis.

Correspondent: Revd Mary Irish, Charity Manager, John Huntingdon House, Tannery Road, Sawston, Cambridge CB2 4UW (01223 830599 (Sawston Support Service Tel: 01223 836289); Fax: 01223 830599; e-mail: office@ johnhuntingdon.org.uk)

Other information: Grants are also made for welfare purposes.

Werrington

The Werrington Educational Foundation

Eligibility: People under 25 who live in the parish of Paston (Werrington).

Types of grants: Grants towards the cost of essentials for schoolchildren, books, fees/ living expenses and study or travel abroad for students, and towards books, equipment and clothing for people starting

work. The trustees are required to have regard to the promotion of education in accordance with the principles of the Church of England.

Recently the trust has had few individual applications and has given grants to the schools in the beneficial area. When individual applications are received they are given priority.

Annual grant total: In 2002 the foundation had an income of £750 and a total expenditure of £1,100.

Applications: On a form available from the correspondent. Applications are considered in May and October.

Correspondent: John Burrell, Clerk, 15 Gildale, Werrington, Peterborough, PE4 6QY (01733 577652)

Whittlesey

The Whittlesey Charity

Eligibility: People under the age of 25 who live in the ancient parishes of Whittlesey Urban and Whittlesey Rural.

Types of grants: Any grant is considered, but the trustees say they would have to be satisfied that all alternative sources had been investigated.

Annual grant total: In 2005 the charity had assets of £1.4 million and an income of £48,000. The grant total for the year was £29,000, distributed as follows: Relief in Need (£5,100); Education (£1,800); Public Purposes (£18,000); and Church (£3,600). Grants are made to organisations and individuals.

Applications: Applications can be submitted directly by the individual, school or college, or other third party. Applications are usually considered in February, May and September, but urgent applications could be dealt with at short notice. Please note, the trust will not respond to ineligible applicants.

Correspondent: P S Gray, 33 Bellamy Road, Oundle, Peterborough PE7 1AR (01832 273085)

Wisbech

Elizabeth Wright's Educational Charity

Eligibility: People who live in the ancient parish of Wisbech St Peter, Cambridgeshire.

Types of grants: Grants to help: schoolchildren with the cost of books, musical tuition and educational outings; and students in further and higher education and mature students with the cost of books, equipmment/instruments, fees, living expenses, educational outings in the UK and study or travel abroad.

Exclusions: No grants for people starting work.

Annual grant total: About £700 to individuals.

Applications: In writing to the correspondent. Applications can be submitted directly by the individual at any time.

Correspondent: Mrs Slyvia Palmer, Beechcroft, 124 Fridaybridge Road, Elm, Wisbech PE14 0AT

East Sussex

Isabel Blackman Foundation

Eligibility: People in need who live in Hastings and the surrounding district.

Types of grants: Grants can be made to schoolchildren for educational outings in the UK and further and higher education, mature and postgraduate students for books, equipment/instruments, fees and maintenance/living expenses. Mature students can also be supported towards the costs of childcare.

Annual grant total: In 2004/05 the trust had assets of £4.5 million and an income of £246,000. Grants totalled £223,000, of which £15,000 was distributed in 25 individual education grants.

Applications: In writing to the correspondent, directly by the individual.

Correspondent: D J Jukes, Secretary, Stonehenge, 13 Laton Road, Hastings, East Sussex TN34 2ES (01424 431756)

Other information: The foundation mainly supports organisations.

The Lewes Educational Charity

Eligibility: People in further or higher education of any age or level who live in Lewes and adjacent parishes of Hamsey, Ringmer, Glynde and Iford & Kingston.

Types of grants: Grants to help with books, equipment and educational projects and visits. Grants are also available to students in further/higher education for fees, living expenses and study or travel abroad, and to mature students towards books, travel and fees.

Annual grant total: In 2005/06 the trust gave seven grants totalling £3,200.

Applications: Applications forms to be submitted by the end of June directly by the individual or the individual's school. Meetings of the trustees are convened once a year, usually in July.

Correspondent: Director of Children's Services, East Sussex County Council, PO Box 4, County Hall, St Anne's Crescent, Lewes, East Sussex BN7 1SG (Fax 01273 481261; e-mail: pat.lowne@ eastsussex.gov.uk)

Other information: Grants are also made to schools.

The Catherine Martin Trust

Eligibility: Children up to 21 in full-time education, whose mother and/or father are deceased, or are unable to work (through ill health) to support the family. The young person must be a British-born subject and a child of British-born parents. The parents must have been legally married (not common-law partners). The deceased or disabled parent must have lived in Hove or Portslade for at least one year before his/ her death.

Types of grants: Recurrent grants according to need are made to schoolchildren and further and higher education students. Grants can be for clothing, books, equipment, educational outings in the UK, fees or living expenses.

Annual grant total: About £12,000 to individuals.

Applications: In writing to the correspondent, either by the individual or through the individual's school, college, educational welfare agency, or a third party such as health or social worker, solicitor, friend or relative. Applications are usually considered in March, June, August, September and December. The young person's parent or guardian will be invited to attend a meeting of the trustees, to which he or she should bring documentary evidence to support the application e.g. parents' marriage certificate, parents' and children's birth certificates and a doctor's note if the parent is unable to work through ill-health.

Correspondent: J E Green, 48 Court Farm Road, Hove, East Sussex BN3 7QR

The Mrs A Lacy Tate Trust

Eligibility: Schoolchildren in need who live in East Sussex.

Types of grants: One-off and recurrent grants according to need.

Annual grant total: In 2004/05 the trust had an income of £41,000 and a total expenditure of £42,000. In recent years, up to £16,000 has been given to individuals.

Applications: In writing to the correspondent.

Correspondent: I Stewart, Trustee, Heringtons Solicitors, 39 Gildredge Road, Eastbourne, East Sussex BN21 4RY (01323 411020; Fax: 01323 411040)

Other information: Grants are also made to individuals in need for relief-in-need purposes and to organisations.

Brighton & Hove

The Brighton Educational Trust

Eligibility: People under 25 who live in Brighton and Hove and are pursuing a course of study.

Types of grants: One-off grants between £10 and £250 are available for a whole range of educational needs and activities, including: books, clothing and equipment; the cost of studying music or other arts; and travel and educational visits in UK or abroad.

Exclusions: Grants are not made towards course fees, maintenance or to foreign students studying in the UK.

Annual grant total: In 2004/05, the trust had an income of £3,500 and a total expenditure of £2,100

Applications: Applications should be made on a form available from the correspondent for consideration in September and April. Applicants should provide a letter of support from the place of study.

Correspondent: Mary Grealish, Brighton & Hove City Council, Central Accounting, Kings House, Grand Avenue, Hove, East Sussex BN3 2SR (01273 291259; e-mail: mary.grealish@brighton-hove.gov. uk)

The Brighton Fund

Eligibility: People in need who live in Brighton and Hove administrative boundary.

Types of grants: One-off cash grants are given for nursery childcare costs, excursions and school uniforms.

Annual grant total: In 2004/05, the fund had assets of £900,000 and an income of £31,000. Grants to individuals in need totalled £26,000. A further £3,800 was distributed in 'exceptional awards'.

Applications: On a form available from the correspondent to be submitted either through an organisation such as Citizens Advice or a school or through a third party such as a social worker or teacher. Applications are considered upon receipt.

Correspondent: Elizabeth O'Kane, c/o Welfare Rights Team, 3rd Floor, Bartholomew House, Bartholomew Square, Brighton, BN1 1JP (e-mail: elizabeth.okane@brighton-hove. gov.uk; website: www.brighton-hove.gov. uk)

Other information: In 2006, the fund was in discussions about merging with The Mayor of Brighton and Hove's Welfare Charity.

The Oliver & Johannah Brown Apprenticeship Fund

Eligibility: People under the age of 25 who live in Brighton and Hove and are pursuing a recognised course of study or serving an apprenticeship. They must either have been born there or have lived there for five years immediately before 1 May in the year in which the application is made.

Types of grants: One-off grants of £10 to £600 are made for a wide range of educational needs e.g. clothing, books, tools and travel. Grants are also given for apprenticeships.

Exclusions: No grants towards course fees, maintenance or overseas students studying in Britain.

Annual grant total: In 2004/05 the fund had both an income and total expenditure of £8,000. Grants totalled about £8,000.

Applications: On a form available from the correspondent, submitted by the individual, for consideration in September and April. Applicants should provide a letter of support from the place of study/apprenticeship.

Correspondent: Miss Mary Grealish, Brighton & Hove Council, Education Finance, Kings House, Grand Avenue, Hove, East Sussex BN3 2SU (01273 291 259; Fax: 01273 291 659; e-mail: mary.grealish@brighton-hove.gov.uk)

The Hallett Science Scholarship

Eligibility: Students under 30 who live in Brighton and Hove and are undertaking a course in pure or applied science.

Types of grants: One-off grants are given for fees, study or travel abroad, equipment, student exchange and research, but not childcare. Applicants must demonstrate the research value of the study being undertaken.

Annual grant total: In 2004/05, the trust had an income of £2,100. No grants were made during the year.

Applications: On a form available from the correspondent, submitted directly by the individual. Applications are considered in April and September.

Correspondent: Mary Grealish, Brighton & Hove City Council, Central Accounting, Kings House, Grand Avenue, Hove, East Sussex BN3 2SR (01273 291259; e-mail: mary.grealish@brighton-hove.gov.uk)

Soames Girls Educational Trust

Eligibility: Girls or young women under 25 years of age who are living, or have recently lived in, Brighton or Hove.

Types of grants: One-off grants are usually to a maximum of £500 a year, for school pupils, college students or university undergraduates, to help with books, equipment, specialist clothing or travel.

Exclusions: No grants for course fees or for basic day to day living expenses.

Annual grant total: In 2004/05, the trust had an income of £4,700 and a total expenditure of £2,900.

Applications: On a form available from the correspondent. Applications are considered in April and September.

Correspondent: Mary Grealish, Brighton & Hove City Council, Central Accounting, Kings House, Grand Avenue, Hove, East Sussex BN3 2SR (01273 291259; e-mail: mary.grealish@brighton-hove.gov.uk)

Hastings

The Magdalen & Lasher Educational Foundation

Eligibility: People under 25 who live in the borough of Hastings.

Types of grants: 'The charity supports all the local schools with book and computer grants. Other applications are considered on their merits, but for individuals an application form is required.'

Annual grant total: In 2005, the foundation had net assets of £9.3 million. It had an income of around £950,000 and a total expenditure of £826,400, of which £12,500 was given to 51 individuals.

Applications: On a form available from the correspondent. The trustees meet every two months.

Correspondent: Richard Carlisle Lane, Young Coles & Langdon, 13 Eversley Road, Bexhill-on-Sea, East Sussex TN34 1QT (01424 210 013; Fax: 01424 218 728)

Mayfield

The Mayfield Charity

Eligibility: Schoolchildren in need who live in the ancient parish of Mayfield.

Types of grants: One-off grants of £50 to £1,000 to: schoolchildren for uniforms, clothing, equipment, instruments and excursions; college students for study/travel abroad and equipment/instruments; and undergraduates for study/travel abroad.

Annual grant total: In 2005 the charity had assets of £120,000, an income of £5,000 and a total expenditure of £4,500. Grants are made for relief-in-need and educational purposes and total about £2,000 each year.

Applications: In writing to the correspondent at any time either directly by the individual or a family member, through a third party such as a social worker or teacher, or through an organisation such as Citizens Advice or a school. Proof of need should be included where possible.

Correspondent: John Logan, Little Broadhurst Farm, Broad Oak, Heathfield, East Sussex TN21 8UX

Newick

The Lady Vernon (Newick) Educational Foundation

Eligibility: Girls living in and/or attending school in Newick only.

Types of grants: One-off and recurrent grants of £100 to £200 to help any girl satisfying the residential/school requirements with her education or starting work. This includes help towards the cost of school uniforms, other school clothing, books, educational outings and study/travel abroad for schoolchildren; fees, books, and study or travel abroad for students in further education and books for students in higher education, mature and vocational students, postgraduates and people starting work. The foundation normally sponsors one girl per year on an outward bound course.

Annual grant total: In 2004/05 the foundation had assets of £85,000, an income of £4,100 and a total expenditure of £3,600. A total of £2,000 was distributed in 10 educational grants to individuals.

Applications: In writing to the correspondent, either directly by the individual if aged 18 or over, or by the parent/guardian for girls under 18 or through an organisation such as a school or educational welfare agency. Details of the purpose of the grant and the amount anticipated to be spent should be included in the application. They are considered in April and October and should be received in the preceding month.

Correspondent: G P Manvell, Jenners, 7a Allington Road, Newick, Lewes, East Sussex BN8 4NA (01825 722732)

Rotherfield

Henry Smith (Rotherfield share)

Eligibility: People in need who live in the ancient parish of Rotherfield (Rotherfield and Crowborough civil parishes).

Types of grants: One-off and recurrent grants according to need.

Annual grant total: In 2003/04 the trust had assets of £5,000, an income of £1,400 and a total expenditure of £200.

Applications: In writing to the secretary to be submitted either directly by the individual, through a third party such as a social worker, or through an organisation such as a Citizens Advice or other welfare agency. Applications are considered upon receipt.

Correspondent: M S Tollit, Secretary, Ghyll Mead South, Ghyll Road,

Crowborough, East Sussex TN6 1SU
(01892 664922; e-mail: rotherfieldpc@gms.
waitrose.com)

Warbleton

Warbleton Charity

Eligibility: People living in the parish of Warbleton who are either taking part in vocational training courses in further education, or starting apprenticeships.

Types of grants: One-off grants towards books.

Exclusions: Students on academic courses are not eligible.

Annual grant total: In 2005 the trust had assets of £7,200 and an income of £1,300. Just one educational grant of £1,000 was made during the year. A further £1,050 was distributed in 47 grants for welfare purposes (£650 on hampers and £400 in fuel grants).

Applications: In writing to the correspondent either directly by the individual or a family member, through a third party such as a social worker or teacher, or through an organisation such as Citizens Advice or a school. Applications are considered every other month.

Correspondent: J A Leeves, Needleview Cottage, Church Street, Ticehurst, East Sussex TN5 7AH (Fax: 01580 200077; e-mail: leeves@freenetname.co.uk)

Essex

The Hervey Benham Charitable Trust

Eligibility: Individuals whose home is in Colchester or North East Essex, who have exceptional artistic talent (especially in music) and are disadvantaged in a way which affects their development.

Types of grants: One-off and recurrent grants ranging from £250 to £2,000. Schoolchildren can be supported for equipment/instruments and fees; further and higher education students can receive grants for equipment/instruments, fees and study or travel abroad; and postgraduates may be supported for fees and study or travel abroad.

Exclusions: Applications are not accepted from outside the beneficial area, or for mainstream education.

Annual grant total: In 2004/05 the trust had assets of £951,000 and an income of £35,000. Grants were made to twelve individuals totalling £9,700. Grants to organisations totalled £12,000.

Applications: On a form available from the correspondent, submitted directly by the individual in time to be considered by the trustees in January, April, July and October. Applications should include information about total funds needed and all other sources of funding available, including from the individual's family.

Correspondent: J Woodman, Clerk to the Trustees, 3 Cadman House, off Peartree Road, Colchester CO3 0NW (01206 561086; Fax: 01206 561086; e-mail: jwoodman@aspects.net)

Billericay Educational Trust

Eligibility: University students under the age of 25 years who live within a six-mile radius of Billericay town centre and are in need.

Types of grants: Recurring grants may be given for up to three years for a variety of purposes including tuition fees, clothing, tools, musical instruments, artistic equipment, books etc. Grants may also be given for travel for educational purposes in the UK or abroad.

Annual grant total: About £8,000 per year.

Applications: Application forms can be downloaded from the trust's website.

Correspondent: Richard Lambourne, Clerk to the Trustees, Brentwood School, Ingrave Road, Brentwood, Essex CM15 8AS (01277 243252; e-mail: richardlambourne@brentwood.essex.sch.uk; website: www.billericayeducationaltrust.co.uk)

The British School Charity – Saffron Walden

Eligibility: Schoolchildren and students in further and higher education aged between 4 and 25 who live, or whose parents/guardians live, in Saffron Walden and neighbourhood.

Types of grants: For the promotion of education but not to relieve public funds.

Annual grant total: About £13,000.

Applications: In writing to the correspondent by the individual or through the school or parent/guardian. including the names and addresses of two referees. Applications are considered throughout the year. Please enclose an sae.

Correspondent: Charles Crawford, Director, The British and Foreign School Society, Maybrook House, Godstone Road, Caterham, Surrey CR3 6RE (01883 331177; website: www.bfss.org.uk/grants)

Other information: Grants are also awarded to schools and educational establishments within the beneficial area.

The Butler Educational Foundation

Eligibility: People who live in Boreham and Little Baddow.

Types of grants: Grants have been awarded mostly after parental application towards the cost of items as diverse as school visits, music lessons, examination fees and special equipment for projects required on certain courses. Grants are also available for students in higher education for general needs.

Annual grant total: In 2004/05 the foundation had assets of £190,000, an income of £9,700 and a total expenditure of £10,300. Grants were awarded to 30 individuals totalling £8,000. A further £1,300 was distributed to local schools and organisations.

Applications: On a form available from the correspondent. The trustees meet three times a year, usually in January, April and October. One of the trustees normally visits the applicant.

Correspondent: N Welch, Duffield Stunt, 71 Duke Street, Chelmsford, Essex CM1 1JU (01245 262351; Fax: 01245 492821)

George Courtauld Educational Trust

Eligibility: People under the age of 21 who live in, or have attended a school in, the parishes of Braintree or Bocking.

Types of grants: One-off grants in the range of £200 to £400. Grants are given to schoolchildren and further and higher education students for uniforms/other school clothing, books and equipment/instruments. Grants given include those in the areas of music and other arts.

Annual grant total: In 2004 the trust had assets of £50,000, an income of £1,600 and a total expenditure of £1,500. Grants were made to individuals totalling £960.

Applications: On a form available from the correspondent. Applications can be submitted at any time, directly by the individual, including an independent letter of support and a written quotation.

Correspondent: Ms K Sharman, c/o Cunningtons, Great Square, Braintree, Essex CM7 1UG (01376 332771; Fax: 01376 326471)

The Marion Ruth Courtauld Educational Trust

Eligibility: People of any age, but preferably under 25, who live in the urban districts of Braintree and Bocking, and Halstead, and the rural districts of Braintree and of Halstead.

Types of grants: Help is given to schoolchildren, further and higher education students and postgraduates, for educational outings in the UK and study and travel abroad. Particular reference is given to geography and history. Donations are in the range of £50 to £400.

Annual grant total: In 2004/05 the trust had assets of £159,000 and an income of £6,800. Grants were made to eight individuals totalling £3,200.

Applications: On a form available from the correspondent, including an independent letter of support and full details of trip, dates, costs etc. Meetings are held in January, March, June and October. If possible, applications should be received a minimum of three weeks prior to a meeting.

Correspondent: Ms K Sharman, c/o Cunningtons, Great Square, Braintree, Essex CM7 1UD (01376 332771; Fax: 01376 326471)

The Earls Colne & Halstead Educational Charity

Eligibility: People up to the age of 25 who either live or have attended school, or lived for at least one year, in the former catchment areas of Halstead & Earls Colne grammar schools.

Types of grants: One-off grants are made to: schoolchildren for educational outings in the UK and study or travel abroad; and further and higher education students and postgraduates for books, equipment/instruments, education outings in the UK and study or travel abroad.

Grants previously awarded include purchase of a cello for a young musician, residential training courses for a footballer and travel to a forestry project in Uganda. Grants range from £100 to £250.

Annual grant total: In 2005/06 the charity had assets of £1 million, an income of £32,000 and a total expenditure of £49,000. Grants were made to about 40 individuals totalling around £12,000

Applications: On a form available from the correspondent, which must include the signature of a relevant person in authority. Applications are considered in February, May, October and December.

Correspondent: Mrs Regina Brook, 3 Hamlet Court, Bures, Suffolk CO8 5BD (01787 227635)

Other information: Voluntary organisations offering opportunities to young people can also receive grants. The following parishes were in the former Halstead & Earls Colne grammar schools catchment areas: Alphamstone, Ashen, Birdbrook, the Bumpsteads, Bures, Coggeshall, the Colnes, Foxearth, Gestingthorpe, Gosfield, Greenstead Green, Halstead Rural, the Hedinghams, the Henns, Lamarsh, the Maplesteads, Middleton, Pebmarsh, Pentlow, Ridgewell, Stambourne, Stisted, Sturmer, Toppesfield, Twinstead, Wickham St Paul, the Yeldhams and the town of Halstead, all in the district of Braintree; and the parishes of Chappel, Mount Bures and Wakes Colne, all in the district of Colchester.

The Fawbert & Barnard's Educational Foundation

Eligibility: People under the age of 25 who live in Harlow and surrounding villages.

Types of grants: (i) Grants, to a usual maximum of about £25, for school pupils to help with books, equipment, clothing or travel. Grants are not given for school fees.

(ii) Grants, to a usual maximum of about £25, to help with school, college or university fees, books or equipment or to supplement existing grants.

(iii) Help towards the cost of education, training, apprenticeship or equipment for those starting work.

Annual grant total: In 2004/05 the charity had assets of £40,000, and both an income and a total expenditure of £1,200, all of which was given to Fawbert & Barnard School. No grants were made directly to individuals during the year.

Applications: In writing to the correspondent. The trustees usually meet in February, June and October.

Correspondent: B Burge, 20 Seeleys, Harlow, Essex CM17 0AD (01279 427244)

Other information: Larger grants are given to schools within the beneficial area.

Hart's & Nash's Education Foundation

Eligibility: Schoolchildren and students who live in the parishes of Great Chesterford and Little Chesterford.

Types of grants: One-off and recurrent grants to schoolchildren towards uniforms, other school clothing, books, educational outings, maintenance and extra-curricular activities, and to students in further/higher education towards books.

Annual grant total: Grants are made to around 10 individuals each year totalling about £2,000.

Applications: In writing to the correspondent.

Correspondent: P Bricknell, Tee Stonehams, Solicitors, 68 High Street, Saffron Walden, Essex CB10 1AD (01799 527299)

The Canon Holmes Memorial Trust

Eligibility: Young people aged 7 to 13 living in the Roman Catholic diocese of Brentwood or the Anglican diocese of Chelmsford, Essex.

Types of grants: Fees for schoolchildren only. Grants are awarded to parents whose children are currently being educated within the independent sector and who, having satisfactorily begun to fund their children, have met with financial difficulty.

Annual grant total: In 2004/05 the trust had an income of £12,800 and a total expenditure of £5,400. No further information was available.

Applications: On a form available from the correspondent. Applications should be submitted by the individual's parent/guardian including full details of their

financial situation. They are mainly considered at a meeting held in May, but also whenever necessary.

Correspondent: The Revd Canon John D Brown, 556 Galleywood Road, Chelmsford CM2 8BX (01245 358185; Fax: 01245 268209)

Ann Johnson's Educational Foundation

Eligibility: People living or educated in Chelmsford and the surrounding parishes, who are under 25.

Types of grants: Help with the cost of books, clothing and other essentials for schoolchildren, including school fees. Grants are also available for those at college or university and towards the cost of books, equipment and instruments, clothing and travel for people starting work.

Annual grant total: About £20,000 per year.

Applications: On a form available from: Ravenscroft, Stock Road, Galleywood, Chelmsford, Essex CM2 8PW (01245 260757). Applications are considered in January, April, July and November.

Correspondent: J P Douglas-Hughes, Clerk, Gepp & Sons, 58 New London Road, Chelmsford, Essex CM2 0PA (01245 493939; Fax: 01245 493940)

The Paslow Common Educational Foundation

Eligibility: People under the age of 25 who are in need and live in the parishes of Blackmore, Bobbingworth, Doddinghurst, Fyfield, High Ongar, Kelvedon Hatch, Magdalen Laver, Moreton, Ongar, Stondon Massey and Willingale, or who have attended a county or voluntary school in any of the above parishes for at least two years.

Types of grants: One-off grants are made to secondary school children, college students, undergraduates, vocational students and people starting work, including those for fees, books, study/travel abroad, equipment/instruments, maintenance/living expenses and excursions.

Annual grant total: The sum of £1,300 was distributed in five grants in 2004/05.

Applications: On a form available from the Student and Pupil Financial Support Service. Applications are considered at meetings held in March, July and November, the deadlines for which are 15 February, 15 June and 15 October respectively.

Correspondent: The Service Manager, Student and Pupil Financial Support Service, PO Box 5287, County Hall, Chelmsford, CM1 1LT (01245 245900;

Fax: 01245 245939; e-mail: student. support@essexcc.gov.uk)

Pilgrim Educational Trust

Eligibility: People aged between 16 and 20 who attend a Braintree or Bocking senior school, namely Alec Hunter High School, Tabor High School, Notley High School or Braintree College of Further Education.

Types of grants: One-off grants are given to costs incurred in connection with A-level courses.

Annual grant total: In 2004/05 the trust had assets of £41,000, an income of £1,300 and a total expenditure £1,700. Just one grant of £600 was made to an individual.

Applications: On a form available from the correspondent, to be submitted by the individual at any time. Applications must include an independent letter of support.

Correspondent: The Trustees, Cunningtons, Great Square, Braintree, Essex CM7 1UD (01376 332771; Fax: 01376 326471)

Canewdon

The Canewdon Educational Foundation

Eligibility: People under 25 who live in the parish of Canewdon only.

Types of grants: Grants to assist with the purchase of books, travel, tuition in music, dance, swimming and so on for both secondary and further education. Help is also given to youth clubs and organisations, together with some assistance to Project Trust type schemes.

Exclusions: Individuals from outside the parish of Canewdon will not be supported.

Annual grant total: In 2004, the foundation made grants totalling £29,000 of which £19,000 went to individuals.

Applications: In writing to the correspondent. Information sheets have been delivered to each household in the parish giving details of how, and to whom, applications should be made. The trustees meet 11 times a year. Unsolicited applications will not be responded to.

Correspondent: C W Aldridge, School House, Anchor Lane, Canewdon Essex SS4 3PB

Other information: Grants are also made to organisations (£7,200 in 2004) and the Canewdon Poor's Charity.

Chelmsford

The Chelmsford Educational Foundation

Eligibility: People who live, and those educated in, the borough and rural district of Chelmsford.

Types of grants: Grants, to a usual maximum of about £500, are given to students – no upper age limit – to help with books, equipment, clothing or travel; to help with college or university fees; or to supplement existing grants, plus travel grants.

Exclusions: Grants are not given for school fees.

Annual grant total: In 2005, the foundation had an income of £13,000 and a total expenditure of £20,000. Grants are made to individuals and organisations.

Applications: On a form available from the correspondent. Initial applications are considered in December/January, Easter and August/September. Candidates are then interviewed before a decision is made.

Correspondent: W C Down, 8 Elms Drive, Chelmsford, Essex CM1 1RH (01245 269598; e-mail: billydown@cmllrh. freeserve.co.uk)

Coggeshall

Sir Robert Hitcham's Exhibition Foundation

Eligibility: Students under the age of 25 who are either in or starting higher education courses and are resident in Coggeshall.

Types of grants: Grants in the range of £50 to £150 are given towards books and equipment/instruments.

Annual grant total: In 2004/05 the foundation had assets of £100,000 and an income of £3,800. Grants were made to 20 individuals totalling £1,600.

Applications: On a form available from the correspondent. Applications are considered in early September and should be submitted by the end of August.

Correspondent: C D Sansom, 76 Church Street, Coggeshall, Essex CO6 1TY (01376 561277)

Finchingfield

Sir Robert Kemp's Education Foundation

Eligibility: People in need who are under 25 and live, or whose parents live, in the parish of Finchingfield.

Types of grants: Grants can be towards books, equipment, educational trips, music and so on for individual students. Grants can also be made to organisations providing an educational element in their activities, as well as educational providers if the benefits of the grants relate directly to under 25 year olds.

Annual grant total: In 2004 the trust had an income of £2,200 and a charitable expenditure of £1,900. Grants were given

to individual students and organisations. Grants to students totalled around £500.

Applications: On a form available from the correspondent. Applications should be submitted in April and October for consideration in May and November respectively.

Correspondent: Shirley Richardson, No.3 Mill End Cottage, Spains Hall Road, Finchingfield, Braintree, Essex CM7 4NH

Other information: Grants are also made to organisations.

Gestingthorpe

The Gestingthorpe Educational Foundation

Eligibility: People who live in the ancient parish of Gestingthorpe, preference being given to those under 25.

Types of grants: One-off grants are given to: schoolchildren and further education students for books equipment/ instruments, fees, educational outings in the UK and study or travel abroad; to mature and vocational students for books and fees; and to higher education students for books. Grants are in the range of £10 to £225.

Annual grant total: In 2005 the foundation had assets of £3,400, an income of £1,000 and a total expenditure of £1,200. Grants were made to 15 individuals totalling £880.

Applications: In writing to the correspondent directly by the individual, including receipts for any payments made. Applications are usually considered in April and October.

Correspondent: Mrs J Winmill, The Secretary, The Dower House, Gestingthorpe, Halstead, Essex CO9 3BL (01787 460631)

Other information: Grants are also made to organisations for educational purposes.

Ongar

Joseph King's Charity

Eligibility: People under 25 years of age who live in the civil parish of Ongar.

Types of grants: Help with the cost of books, clothing and other essentials for schoolchildren. Help may also be available for students at college or university. Preference is given to the advancement of the Christian religion.

Annual grant total: In 2004 the trust had a total expenditure of £58,000. Grants were made to individuals totalling £11,200. The first call on funds is for the upkeep and maintenance of trust property from which the income is derived.

Applications: In writing to the correspondent.

Correspondent: Mrs C E M Kenny Maat, 36 Coopers Hill, Ongar, Essex CM5 9EF (e-mail: ckenny@cm59ef.freeserve.co.uk)

Thaxted

Lord Maynard's Charity

Eligibility: People under 25 who live in the parish of Thaxted.

Types of grants: Help towards the cost of education, training, apprenticeship or equipment for those starting work.

Annual grant total: In 2004/05 the trust had both an income and a total expenditure of £2,300. Grants totalled about £2,000.

Applications: In writing to the correspondent. Applicants traditionally queue in the local church on 1 August for the money to be handed out, but postal applications prior to this are accepted.

Correspondent: Mr Chapman, Messrs Wade & Davies, Solicitors, 28 High Street, Great Dunmow, Essex CM6 1AH (01371 872816)

Other information: The correspondent also administers the Epping and Theydon Garnon charity.

Hampshire

Aldworth Trust Foundation

Eligibility: Residents and former residents of, and former pupils of schools in Basingstoke and Deane.

Types of grants: (i) Grants for school pupils to help with educational outings, uniforms and equipment but not for fees, maintenance or books.

(ii) Grants to students to help with books and study or travel abroad, but not for fees/living expenses or for student exchanges.

(iii) Grants to people starting work for books, equipment and clothing, but not for travel.

(iv) Grants to mature students for books, fees, travel and other expenses such as childcare.

Annual grant total: In 2004/05 the foundation had an income of £1,800, all of which was given in grants to 29 individuals.

Applications: On a form available from the correspondent. Applications are considered in February, June and October.

Correspondent: Mrs D M Reavell, Clerk, 25 Cromwell Road, Basingstoke, Hampshire RG21 5NR (01256 473390; Fax: 01256 473390)

The Ashford Hill Educational Trust

Eligibility: People who live in the parish of Ashford Hill with Headley or the surrounding area.

Types of grants: Grants are generally given to promote social and physical education. They are given towards the cost of formal education, enhancement of employment prospects, group activities, music, adult education and sporting and recreational activities.

Annual grant total: Around £3,000 to £5,000 a year.

Applications: On a form available from the correspondent. Applications are considered in January, March, July and October.

Correspondent: Graham Swait, The Cedars, Ashford Hill Road, Headley, Thatcham, Berkshire RG19 8AB

Bramshott Educational Trust

Eligibility: People under 25 who live or have a parent who lives in the parish of St Mary the Virgin, Bramshott and Liphook.

Types of grants: Grants up to £200. Grants are given for educational needs including physical, social, musical education and travel and equipment necessary in the pursuit of such aims. Some travel scholarships of up to £250 may also be awarded for adventurous or educational travel such as Outward Bound-type courses or Raleigh International.

Annual grant total: The trust gives about £5,000 in grants each year.

Applications: On a form available from the correspondent. Applications are considered in July and November, with the closing dates for applications being 30 June and 31 October each year. Applications should include full details of courses/projects and an sae.

Correspondent: Richard Weighell, 12 Locke Road, Liphook, Hampshire, GU30 7DQ

The Cliddesden & Farleigh Wallop Educational Trust

Eligibility: People under 25 who live within the original boundaries of the parishes of Cliddesden and Farleigh Wallop only.

Types of grants: One-off and recurrent grants. Education is considered in its broadest sense, from help with school projects and trips to college/university courses to music lessons.

Annual grant total: Previously about £2,500 to individuals.

Applications: In writing to the correspondent. Applications should be submitted through a school or directly by the individual or their guardian to reach the secretary by the end of April, August or

December, accompanied by fully documented receipts.

Correspondent: Mrs Nicola Bealing, 16 Southlea, Cliddesden, Basingstoke, Hampshire, RG25 2JN

Dibden Allotments Charity

Eligibility: People in need who live in the parishes of Fawley, Hythe and Marshwood.

Types of grants: One-off grants and recurrent grants ranging from £10 to £2,000 towards the cost of school uniforms, other school clothing, books and educational outings for schoolchildren; books, equipment, instruments, clothing and travel for people starting work; books and fees/living expenses for students in further or higher education; and books, travel, fees and childcare for mature students. There is a preference for people with special educational needs.

Exclusions: No grants for second degrees.

Annual grant total: In 2004/05 grants totalled £187,000. There were 15 grants made for educational purposes totalling £6,300.

Applications: On a form available from the correspondent, with a reference from a professional. Applications are considered weekly.

Correspondent: Barrie Smallcalder, 17 Drummond Court, Hythe, Southampton, Hampshire S045 6HD (023 8084 1035; Fax: 023 8084 1305; e-mail: dibdenallotments@btconnect.com)

Other information: Grants are also made to charitable and voluntary organisations.

The Gordon Charitable Trust – see entry on page 204

Correspondent: Gerry Aiken, Hon. Clerk, 45 Dunkeld Road, Bournemouth BH3 7EW (01202 768337; Fax: 01202 767595; e-mail: gerry_aitken@ hotmail.com)

The Hampshire & Isle of Wight Educational Institute for the Blind

Eligibility: People who are registered partially sighted or blind and are residents of Hampshire or the Isle of Wight.

Types of grants: Grants are given to students in higher or further education towards the cost of books, computer/equipment, fees and living expenses; to mature students towards the cost of books and fees; and possibly to schoolchildren towards the cost of books, educational outings and maintenance. The maximum grant is £300.

Annual grant total: About £3,000 a year.

Applications: On a form available from the correspondent, either directly by the individual, or through a school, college, educational welfare agency or other third party on behalf of the individual.

Correspondent: M A O'Neill, Secretary, The Covers, Green Lane, Hambledon, Waterlooville, PO7 4SS (023 9363 2180)

The Robert Higham Apprenticing Charity

Eligibility: People aged between 16 and under 25 who live in the parishes of Kingsclere, Ashford Hill and Headley, Hampshire.

Types of grants: Grants towards books, specialist equipment or travelling expenses for those preparing for or engaged in any profession, trade, occupation, service or towards books, study or travel abroad for those studying for A-levels. Grants can be one-off or recurrent and are given according to need.

Annual grant total: In 2004 the charity had an income of around £7,000, and a total expenditure of £6,400. Grants totalled about £5,000.

Applications: On a form available from the correspondent. Applications must include a letter outlining the applicant's further education plans. Applications are not accepted from parents. The trustees meet five times a year, applications must be with the correspondent by 31 January, 31 March, 30 May, 31 August and 31 October.

Correspondent: C R Forth, Rostaq, Winston Avenue, Tadley, Hampshire, RG26 3NN (0118 9811602)

The Foundation of Sarah Rolle

Eligibility: Schoolchildren, people starting work and further and higher education students under 25 who live, or whose parents live, in the parishes of East Tytherley and Lockerley.

Types of grants: Grants for uniforms/ other school clothing, books, equipment/ instruments, educational outings in the UK and study or travel abroad. Grants range from £50 to £250.

Exclusions: Grants are not given for school or college fees or living expenses.

Annual grant total: In 2005 it had assets of £278,000 and an income of £10,000. Grants were made to three individuals totalling £780. A further £5,000 went to organisations.

Applications: On a form available from the correspondent, to be submitted either directly by the individual or through a parent. Applications should be submitted by January or July for consideration in February or August respectively.

Correspondent: P L Bullock, 'Tean', Newtown Road, Awbridge, Romsey, Hampshire SO51 0GG (01794 340553)

The Earl of Southampton Trust

Eligibility: People in need who live in the ancient parish of Titchfield (now subdivided into the parishes of Titchfield, Sarisbury, Locks Heath, Warsash, Stubbington and Lee-on-the-Solent).

Types of grants: One-off grants ranging from between £25 and £1,000 to schoolchildren, college students, mature students and to people with special educational need towards fees, uniforms and books.

Exclusions: Grants are not given for study or travel abroad, student exchange, tertiary and postgraduate education.

Annual grant total: In 2004/05 the trust had assets of £1.4 million and an income of £66,000. There were 76 grants made totalling £20,000 for welfare and education purposes.

Applications: In writing to the correspondent through a school, other educational establishment, an educational welfare agency or another third party. Applications must include details of the extent of the need and the full address of the applicant or nominee. Applications are considered on the last Tuesday of every month.

Correspondent: Mrs S C Boden, Clerk to the Trustees, 24 The Square, Titchfield, Hampshire PO14 4RU (01329 513294; Fax: 01329 513294; e-mail: earlstrust@ yahoo.co.uk)

Other information: The trust runs 16 almshouses and a day centre for old people.

Sir Mark and Lady Turner Charitable Settlement

Eligibility: People in need, with a preference for those in further education who live in north London and Hampshire

Types of grants: One-off and recurrent grants up to £300 for fees, books and equipment/instruments.

Annual grant total: About £5,000 in grants to individuals.

Applications: In writing to the correspondent, including either a telephone number or email address. Applications must be received by the end of April or October for consideration in early June or December. Only successful applicants are notified of the trustees' decision.

Correspondent: The Trustees, PO Box 191, 10 Fenchurch Street, London EC3M 3LB (020 7475 5086)

Other information: Grants are also made to organisations.

Alverstoke

The Alverstoke Trust

Eligibility: People in need who live in Alverstoke or nearby.

Types of grants: One-off grants, usually of amounts of up to £200, to college students, undergraduates, vocational students and people with special educational needs. Grants given include those for fees, study/ travel abroad and books.

Exclusions: The trust does not make loans, grants to other charities or recurring awards.

Annual grant total: In 2005 the trust had assets of £45,000 and an income of £1,200. Relief-in-need grants to eight individuals totalled £1,500 with a further £600 distributed in three educational grants.

Applications: In writing to the correspondent, either directly or through a third party such as a Citizens Advice, social worker, welfare agency or other third party. Applications are considered at any time.

Correspondent: Mrs Jane Hodgman, 5 Constable Close, Gosport, Hampshire PO12 2UF (023 9258 9822)

Andover

Miss Gales Educational Foundation

Eligibility: Children and young people under the age of 25 who live in or are being educated in the Andover district. Preference is given to schoolchildren with serious family difficulties.

Types of grants: Grants are given towards the cost of: (i) school uniforms, other school clothing, books and educational outings for schoolchildren; (ii) books and study or travel overseas for students in further and higher education; and (iii) books, equipment and instruments for people starting work. Grants range from £10 to £300 and are one-off.

Exclusions: Grants are not given for school or college fees or living expenses.

Annual grant total: In 2004 the trust had an income of £10,000 and a total expenditure of £11,000. Grants totalled about £10,000.

Applications: In writing to the correspondent, either directly by the individual or through the individual's school, college or an educational welfare agency. Applications should include information on what the grant is required for, the applicant's date of birth and the circumstances which make it impossible for the family to provide for themselves. Applications are considered quarterly.

Correspondent: John Bucknill, The Grange, Grateley, Andover, Hampshire, SP11 8TA

Basingstoke

The Rodges Trust

Eligibility: People between the ages of 16 and 25 who live or who have attended school in Basingstoke.

Types of grants: Grants to help with the cost of training or equipment for music, art, drama and dance leading to a career in one of the visual or performing arts. Grants range from £100 to £500 and are usually one-off.

Annual grant total: In 2004/05, the trust had an income of £3,600 and a total expenditure of £1,000, all of which was given in grants to individuals.

Applications: On a form available from the correspondent, including a reference from a present or recent tutor. Applications are considered as they arrive.

Correspondent: M Rodges, 178 Portsmouth Walk, Basingstoke, Hampshire RG22 6HE (01256 472255; e-mail: martin.rodges@lineone.net)

Fareham

The William Price Charitable Trust

Eligibility: The benefit area consists of the town parishes of Fareham in Hampshire, namely those of St Peter & St Paul, Holy Trinity with St Columba and St John the Evangelist (note that this area does not cover the larger area of Fareham borough as a whole). Only those under the age of 25 living in the Fareham benefit area, or schools substantially serving that area, are eligible for grants.

Types of grants: To help with the education of individuals who are in financial need, under 25 and resident in the benefit area, with fees, travel, outfits, clothing, books etc. Also promoting education in the doctrines of the Church of England and providing schools in or substantially serving the benefit area with educational benefits not normally provided by the local education authority.

Exclusions: Grants can not be given to persons living outside the area of Fareham town parishes or to any organisation or establishment other than the above schools.

Annual grant total: In 2004/05 the trust had an income of £162,700 and a total expenditure of £118,400. Grants were made totalling £110,400, mostly to schools and churches. Grants to individuals totalled £13,300.

Applications: Whenever possible applications should be made through the establishment concerned. Applications forms are used and can be sent on request. Larger grants are considered by trustees twice each year, with the closing dates being 1 March and 1 September. Smaller grants for individual assistance are considered more quickly and normally in less than one month.

Correspondent: Cdr J A Bagg, Clerk, 59 Kiln Road, Fareham, Hampshire PO16 7UH (01329 280636)

Gosport

Thorngate Relief-in-Need and General Charity

Eligibility: People in need who live in Gosport.

Types of grants: One-off grants mostly between £100 and £500.

Exclusions: No grants are made towards legal expenses.

Annual grant total: The charity's income was £16,000, and the total expenditure was £12,000. Grants totalled about £11,000.

Applications: On a form available from the correspondent. Applications can be made either directly by the individual or through a social worker, Citizens Advice, Probation Service or other welfare agency.

Correspondent: Mrs Kay Brent, 21 Alvara Road, Gosport, Hampshire PO12 2HY (023 9250 2558)

Isle of Wight

The Broadlands Home Trust

Eligibility: Girls and young single women from the Isle of Wight (under the age of 22) in need who are at school, starting work or are in further or higher education.

Types of grants: One-off grants to schoolchildren, vocational students, people with special needs and people starting work, including those for uniforms/clothing, books, equipment/instruments and educational trips.

Exclusions: No grants for married women or graduates.

Annual grant total: In 2004/05 the trust had assets of £233,000, an income of £10,000 and an expenditure of £6,800. Grants to 11 individuals for relief-in-need purposes totalled £4,000, with a further £2,000 distributed to 27 individuals for educational purposes.

Applications: On a form available from the correspondent, to be submitted either directly by the individual or a family member. Applications are considered quarterly in January, April, July and October.

Correspondent: Mrs M Groves, 2 Winchester Close, Newport, Isle of Wight PO30 1DR (01983 525630)

Portsmouth

The Zurich Insurance Travelling Scholarships

Eligibility: (i) Pupils attending school in Portsmouth who are studying at least one modern foreign language to A Level and who wish to go to a country of that language. (ii) Students as in (i) but who left a Portsmouth school within the preceding 12 months and who are under 20.

Types of grants: Grants to help with the costs of travel and educational visits abroad, and to help with the cost of study at an overseas educational institution for those studying a foreign language. Examples of scholarships include attending an organised course abroad, attending a foreign school as a full-time pupil for a short period, undertaking a work placement or preparing a project to discover some aspect of life in a foreign country. There is usually a maximum of two scholarships awarded each year of between £750 and £1,000 each.

Annual grant total: The scholarship has an income of about £2,700 and a total expenditure of about £1,400.

Applications: On a form available from the correspondent, to be submitted directly by the individual, including statements on the intended project and how the scholarship will contribute to their studies. Applications should be received by the end of November for consideration in February/March.

Correspondent: Director of Corporate Services, Civic Offices, Portsmouth City Council, Guildhall Square, Portsmouth PO1 2AL (023 9283 4056; Fax: 023 9283 4076)

Wield

The Wield Educational Trust

Eligibility: People aged 5 to 18 who live in the parish of Wield.

Types of grants: One-off and recurrent grants are given towards books and educational outings for schoolchildren. Preference is given to people with special education needs.

Exclusions: Grants are not given for school fees or maintenance.

Annual grant total: In 2004/05 the trust had an income of £6,000 and a total expenditure of £7,000.

Applications: On a form available from the correspondent.

Correspondent: Mr D Cresswell, 1 Wield Grange, Upper Wield, Alresford, Hampshire SO24 9RT

Hertfordshire

The Fawbert & Barnard School Foundation

Eligibility: People between 16 and 25 years of age who live, or have attended a school, within three miles of Sawbridgeworth for at least four years.

Types of grants: Grants to assist those students wishing to continue their studies by way of full-time education at either a college or university. The bursary is awarded for use by the student to purchase books or materials associated with the course. Grants are usually in the range of £100 to £200.

Annual grant total: The foundation has an income and expenditure of about £10,000 each year. In 2005 grants were made to 24 individuals totalling £5,300. Local schools received grants totalling £4,500.

Applications: On a form available from the correspondent. The closing date for applications is 30 September and they are considered in October.

Correspondent: Mrs J Rider, Clerk, 22 Southbrook, Sawbridgeworth, Hertfordshire CM21 9NS (01279 724670; e-mail: jrider@freeuk.com)

Other information: As the grant is awarded once only, students who do not apply during their first year can apply at any time during their period of study.

The Hertfordshire County Nursing Trust

Eligibility: Education for community nurses, either practising or retired, who work or have worked in Hertfordshire.

Types of grants: One-off and recurrent grants for course fees and expenses.

Annual grant total: In 2004/05, the trust had an income of £46,000. Grants totalled £4,800.

Applications: In writing to the correspondent.

Correspondent: Alasdair Shand, Timber Hall, Cold Christmas, Ware, Hertfordshire SG12 7SN (01920 466086)

The Hertfordshire Educational Foundation

Eligibility: Pupils and students up to 21 years who have a home address in Hertfordshire.

Types of grants:

1 Travel scholarships to individuals aged 17 to 21 to undertake approved courses of study, expeditions and other projects in overseas countries. The usual duration is for a minimum of one month. The maximum scholarship is £650.

2 Grants for school visits. Help for pupils in exceptional circumstances, whose parents have difficulty in paying the board and lodging cost of visits arranged by their schools.

3 The Sir George Burns Fund. Grants to enable young people who are disabled or underprivileged aged 16 to 21 to participate in expeditions, educational visits and so on, or to purchase special items of equipment needed for them to become involved in recreational and educational activities. Grants are usually in the range of £50 to £500.

Annual grant total: In 2005 the foundation had a total income of £38,000. Awards were provided for:

1 Travel scholarships and expeditions: 9 grants totalling almost £3,700.

2 School visits: 819 grants totalling £4,000.

3 Sir George Burns Fund: 11 grants totalling about £2,500.

Applications: On forms available from the correspondent. Applications should be submitted at least a month before the individual travels. The deadlines for travel scholarships and Sir George Burns Fund applications are the end of February, May and October. Guidelines and application forms are available from the foundation's website.

Correspondent: Claire Cook, c/o Children, Schools and Families, County Hall, Hertford, Hertfordshire SG13 8DF (website: www.hersdirect.org/hef)

Other information: Awards are made to individuals and not to groups. The amount of any award will depend to some extent on the number and nature of applications.

The Hertfordshire Society for the Blind

Eligibility: Discretionary grants to children and young people who are still in school and are visually impaired.

Types of grants: Small, one-off grants.

Annual grant total: About £500 a year.

Applications: In writing to the correspondent. The society often has far more applicants than it can support and often funds are unavailable so applicants are advised to check with the correspondent before applying.

Correspondent: The Trustees, Leahoe House, County Hall, Pegs Lane, Hertfordshire SG12 8BZ

The Hitchin Educational Foundation

Eligibility: People who live in the former urban district of Hitchin and surrounding villages, aged under 25. The grants are means tested so income and size of family are taken into account.

Types of grants: One-off grants are given towards the cost of uniforms, other school clothing and educational outings for schoolchildren; equipment and clothing for people starting work; and studying and travelling aboard for people in further/higher education. Preference is given to children with serious family difficulties, and people with special educational needs.

Exclusions: Grants are not available for books, fees, travel, living expenses or mature students.

Annual grant total: About £80,000, mostly to organisations.

Applications: On a form available from the correspondent, either directly by the individual, or through the individual's school, college, educational welfare agency or any third party. They are considered monthly.

Correspondent: Brian Frederick, c/o Chaplin Frobisher Welling, Ickneild House, Eastcheap, Letchworth, Hertfordshire SG6 3YY (01462 631717)

Other information: Grants are also made available to three local secondary schools.

The James Marshall Foundation

Eligibility: People under 25 who live in Harpenden and Wheathampstead and are in financial need.

Types of grants: Grants to help with the cost of education, training, apprenticeships or work-related expenses. The awards are very wide ranging in scope, and have included all of the following courses, occupations and activities: GCSE; A-levels; acting; art and design; beauty therapy; BTEC; business studies; carpentry; conservation; electrician; fashion design; hairdressing; law; GNVQ; first degrees; postgraduate studies; medicine; motor mechanics; music; nursing; painting and decorating; plumbing; teaching; theology; and travel and tourism.

Grants are given to schoolchildren, people starting work, further and higher education students, mature students and postgraduates. Grants given include those for uniforms/other school clothing, books, accommodation, equipment/instruments, fees, educational outings in the UK and study or travel abroad. No grants are made towards university tuition fees.

All applications are based on family income, unless the applicant is fully self-supporting.

Grants generally range from £50 to £2,000, but can be for up to £4,000.

Exclusions: Grants are not given for university tuition fees.

Annual grant total: In 2004/05 the trust had assets of £2.1 million, an income of £151,000 and a total expenditure of £138,000. A total of £98,000 was distributed in 195 grants to individuals.

Applications: On a form available from the correspondent which can be submitted directly by the individual at any time; they are considered every six to eight weeks. Applicants must give details of their parental or other income and confirmation of the purpose for the requested grant.

Correspondent: Mrs T Whittle, Clerk to the Trustees, Trustees Office, 17 Leyton Road, Harpenden, Hertfordshire AL5 2HY (01582 760735; e-mail: jmfoundation@ btconnect.com)

The Platt Subsidiary Foundation

Eligibility: People under the age of 25 who live in the parishes of St John the Baptist, Aldenham, and Christ Church, Radlett.

Types of grants: The charity aims in particular to provide:

(i) 'financial assistance, outfits, clothing, tools, instruments or books to assist such people to pursue their education (including the study of music and other arts), to undertake travel in furtherance thereof and to prepare for and enter a profession, trade or calling on leaving school, university or other educational establishment.' (ii) 'facilities not normally provided by the local education authority for recreation and social and physical training including the provision of teaching in athletics, sports and games for such persons who are receiving primary, secondary or further education.'

Annual grant total: In 2004, the foundation had an income of £8000 and a total expenditure of £5,600.

Applications: On a form available from the correspondent. Applications are considered in January, May and September.

Correspondent: Alan Taylor, Secretary, 57a Loom Lane, Radlett, Hertfordshire WD7 8NX (01923 855197)

The Ware Charities

Eligibility: Schoolchildren, college students and people starting work who live in the area of Ware Town Council, the Parish of Ware side and the parish of Tunbridge.

Types of grants: Grants are given to schoolchildren, college students, people with special educational needs, people starting work and overseas students including those for uniforms/clothing, fees, study/travel abroad, books, equipment/ instruments and excursions. Grants are also made to undergraduates and vocational students for uniforms/clothing.

Annual grant total: In 2004/05 the charities had assets of over £1 million and an income of £49,000. Grants to individuals totalled £6,800.

Applications: In writing to the correspondent at any time, to be submitted directly by the individual or a family member. Applications must include brief details of the applicant's income and savings and be supported and signed by a head teacher, doctor, nurse or social worker.

Correspondent: A Errington, Clerk to the Trustees, 28 Bengeo Mews, Hertford, Hertfordshire SG14 3TL (01992 304434)

Other information: Grants are also made to local organisations.

Berkhamsted

Bourne's Educational Foundation

Eligibility: People under the age of 25, who live in the ecclesiastical parish of Berkhamsted St Peter.

Types of grants: Grants to help: schoolchildren with the cost of school uniforms and other school clothing, books, equipment/instruments, educational outings in the UK and study or travel abroad; and further and higher education students with books, equipment/ instruments and study or travel abroad and in the UK.

Exclusions: No grants for people starting work, mature students or maintenance and school fees for schoolchildren.

Annual grant total: In 2004/05 the trust had an income of £1,200 and a total expenditure of £460. Grants were made to nine individuals totalling £320.

Applications: On a form available from the correspondent. Applications can be submitted directly by the individual or through a social worker, Citizens Advice or other welfare agency and should include information on parental income. Applications are usually considered in March and October.

Correspondent: Miss P M Watt, Flat 11, Cavalier Court, Chesham Road, Berkhamsted HP4 3AL (01442 863804)

Salter's Educational Foundation

Eligibility: People under the age of 25, who live in the ancient parish of Berkhamsted St Peter.

Types of grants: Grants in the range of £100 to £200 to help: schoolchildren with the cost of school uniforms and other school clothing, books, equipment/ instruments, educational outings in the UK and study or travel abroad; and further and higher education students with books, equipment/instruments and study or travel abroad and in the UK.

Exclusions: No grants for people starting work, mature students or maintenance and school fees for schoolchildren.

Annual grant total: In 2004/05 the trust had an income of £1,800 and a total expenditure of £1,100. Grants were made to 13 individuals totalling £1,000.

Applications: On a form available from the correspondent. Applications can be submitted directly by the individual or through a social worker, citizen's advice bureau or other welfare agency and should include information on parental income. Applications are usually considered in March and October.

Correspondent: Miss P M Watt, 11 Cavalier Court, Chesham Road, Berkhamsted, HP4 3AL (01442 863804)

Cheshunt

Robert Dewhurst's School Foundation

Eligibility: People who live in the ancient parish of Cheshunt, between the ages of 5 and 24. Preference is given to people who have studied for at least two years at Dewhurst St Mary's Church of England Primary School, although any applicant from the parish will be considered.

Types of grants: One-off grants to schoolchildren and further and higher education students to help with with the costs of books, equipment, clothing, travel, fees and educational outings in the UK.

Annual grant total: In 2004/05 the trust had an income of £4,500 and a total expenditure of £3,500. Grants totalled about £2,000.

Applications: In writing to: P H Hutchinson, 88 Church Lane, Cheshunt, Hertfordshire EH8 0EA. Applications can be submitted directly by the individual or through a school or welfare agency or another third party e.g. social services or headteacher. Applications are considered throughout the year and should state details of hardship.

Correspondent: D A Cracknell, 53 Hillside Crescent, Cheshunt, Waltham Cross, Hertfordshire EN8 8PN

Dacorum

The Dacorum Community Trust

Eligibility: People in need who live in the borough of Dacorum.

Types of grants: Generally one-off grants up to £500 to schoolchildren for uniforms/ clothing, equipment/instruments and excursions, to college students, undergraduates and people starting work for clothing and equipment/instruments and to vocational students, mature students and those with special educational needs for uniforms/clothing, equipment/ instruments and childcare.

Exclusions: Grants are not normally given for the costs of further or mainstream education and only in exceptional circumstances for gap-year travel.

Annual grant total: In 2004/05 the trust made 62 grants to individuals totalling £14,000.

Applications: On a form available from the correspondent. Applications can be submitted by the individual, through a recognised referral agency (such as Social Services or Citizens Advice) or through an MP, doctor or school. Applications are considered in March, June, September and December. The trust asks for details of family finances. A preliminary telephone call is always welcome.

Correspondent: The Trust Manager, 48 High Street, Hemel Hemstead, Hertfordshire HP1 3AF (01442 231396; e-mail: admin@dctrust.org.uk; website: www.dctrust.org.uk)

Hertford

The Newton Exhibition Foundation

Eligibility: Young people between the ages of 5 and 25 attending, or having attended, any school in the town of Hertford, with preference for members of the Church of England. Grants may also be awarded to young people under 25 who are, or have been, resident in the town of Hertford but who, by virtue of special learning difficulties or other disability, are attending or have attended schools outside the town.

Types of grants: Grants in the range of £20 to £400 are given to schoolchildren, further and higher education students and postgraduates. Grants given include those for uniforms/other school clothing, books, equipment/instruments, educational outings in the UK and study or travel overseas.

Annual grant total: In 2004/05 the foundation had an income of £8,600 and a total expenditure of £9,900. Grants were made to 81 individuals totalling £7,900.

Applications: On a form available from the correspondent, including name(s) of schools attended, details of educational project, including cost, for which application is being made, and information as to other grants obtained or applied for. Applications should be submitted through the individual's school or welfare agency, directly by the individual, or through a social worker. They are considered in February, May, July and October, and at other times when necessary.

Correspondent: Mrs Ann Kirby, Molewood End, Molewood Road, Hertford SG14 3LT (01992 558634)

Wellfield Trust

Eligibility: People in need who live in the parish of Hatfield and are undertaking vocational courses, such as computer or hairdressing training. Schoolchildren in the parish may also be supported.

Types of grants: One-off grants of £100 to £500 to schoolchildren, college students, mature students, people with special educational needs and people starting work, including those towards, the cost of uniforms/clothing, fees, books, equipment/ instruments, excursions and childcare.

Exclusions: Grants are not made for council tax arrears, rent or funeral costs.

Annual grant total: In 2004/05 the trust distributed £11,000, mostly in welfare grants.

Applications: On a form available from the correspondent only via a third party such as social services or Citizens Advice. Most of the local appropriate third parties also have the application form. Applications are considered monthly and should be received by the first Monday of every month.

Correspondent: Mrs Karen Richards, Birchwood Leisure Centre, Longmead, Hatfield, Hertfordshire AL10 0AS (01707 251018; e-mail: wellfieldtrust@aol.com)

Hertingfordbury

Walter Wallinger Charity

Eligibility: People aged 6 to 24 who lived, or were educated, for at least two years in the ancient parish of Hertingfordbury, Hertford and are in need of financial assistance in the opinion of the trustees.

Types of grants: (i) Grants to help with books or educational outings for schoolchildren and towards books and study or travel abroad for students.

(ii) Help towards the cost of education, training, apprenticeship or equipment for those starting work.

Grants to a usual maximum of £300.

Annual grant total: In 2004 the charity's income was £2,200 and the total expenditure was £2,000. Grants totalled about £1,500.

Applications: On a form available from the correspondent to be submitted by the individual or a parent/guardian. For consideration in May and November.

Correspondent: G J Field, Clerk, 24 Castle Street, Hertford SG14 1HP (01992 300333)

Hexton

The Hexton Village Trust

Eligibility: People who live in the parish of Hexton.

Types of grants: The trust 'supports individuals and community activities within its charitable objects'. This probably includes help with the cost of books, clothing and other essentials for schoolchildren. Grants may also be available for those at college or university.

Annual grant total: In 2004/05 the trust had an income of £6,600 and a total expenditure of £500. Grants total around £500 each year.

Applications: In writing to the correspondent.

Correspondent: J A Cooper, Hexton Manor, Hitchin, Hertfordshire SG5 3JH (Fax: 01582 881220)

Letchworth Garden City

The Letchworth Civic Trust

Eligibility: Schoolchildren and students attending college or university who are in need and have lived in Letchworth Garden City for two years or more.

Types of grants: Grants are one-off and range from £50 to £500; loans are also made. Schoolchildren can receive help with the cost of educational trips and study or travel abroad where their parents cannot afford the whole amount. People starting work may be supported for equipment/ instruments. Further and higher education students, mature students and postgraduates can be helped with books and equipment/instruments.

Annual grant total: In 2004/05 the trust had an income of £48,000 and a total expenditure of £44,000. The trust gave: 71 grants totalling £21,000 to university students for educational learning materials; 72 grants totalling £3,900 to school students with disadvantaged home backgrounds; and 11 grants to individuals for educational or medical support totalling £5,500. Grants to nine organisations totalled £9,100.

Applications: By letter or on an application form available from the correspondent. Applications can be made at any time, either directly by the individual or through a third party such as a headteacher, probation officer or social worker.

The trust does not respond to applications made outside of its area of interest.

Correspondent: Peter Jackson, Secretary, Broadway Chambers, Letchworth Garden City, Hertfordshire SG6 3AD (01462 484413; e-mail: peterjackson32@ntlworld.com)

Other information: Grants are also made to people who are in need, sick or requiring accommodation, and to groups and societies, but not religious or political groups.

Royston

The Leete Charity

Eligibility: People under 25 who are seeking further education and live or attend a school in Royston.

Types of grants: One-off and recurrent grants to help with books, equipment/instruments, fees and travel expenses for students in further or higher education. Grants range from £50 to £150.

Exclusions: No grants are given for people starting work or mature students.

Annual grant total: In 2004/05 the charity had an income of £4,600 and a total expenditure of £3,000, all of which was given in 16 grants to individuals.

Applications: On a form available from the correspondent. Applications can be submitted directly by the individual at any time.

Correspondent: Town Clerk, Royston Town Council, Town Hall, Melbourn Street, Royston, Hertfordshire SG8 7DA (01763 245484; Fax: 01763 248016)

Wormley

The Wormley Parochial Charity

Eligibility: Students of any age in the parish of Wormley as it was defined before 31 March 1935.

Types of grants: Grants to schoolchildren or college students, people undertaking training or apprentices, towards essential clothing, equipment, instruments or books.

Exclusions: The trust does not give loans.

Annual grant total: About £3,000.

Applications: In writing to the charity either directly by the individual or through a social worker, Citizens Advice, welfare agency or a third party such as a friend who is aware of the situation. Applications are considered in April and October.

Correspondent: Mrs S White, PO Box 281, Broxbourne, EN11 1AR

Kent

The Reverend Tatton Brockman's Charity

Eligibility: People under the age of 25 who are in full-time education and live in the ancient parishes of Brenzett, Cheriton, and Newington-next-Hythe in the county of Kent.

Types of grants: One-off grants to help with the cost of fees, study or travel abroad, books, equipment and instruments for schoolchildren, students in further/higher education, vocational students and people with special educational needs. Grants are in the range of £100 to £500.

Annual grant total: In 2004/05 the trust had an income of £17,400 and a total expenditure of £12,000. Grants to individuals totalled about £2,500. In previous years around £6,000 was distributed to organisations for educational purposes.

Applications: In writing to the correspondent, directly by the individual. Applications are considered in May and November.

Correspondent: Mrs J Salt, Greatfield House, Ivychurch Road, Brenzett, Romney March, Kent, TN29 0EE

Other information: The charity's main financial concern is its support of four Church of England primary schools in the area of benefit. However, the correspondent states: 'We would very much like to make a greater number of grants to individuals but efforts to encourage more applications have, so far, met with very limited success.' Furthermore, 'it should be stated that in allocating grants the trustees shall have regard to the principles and doctrines of the Church of England'.

The John Collings Educational Trust

Eligibility: Children up to the age of 14 who are in need.

Types of grants: Help with the cost of books, fees and other essentials for schoolchildren.

Exclusions: No grants are available for those at college or university.

Annual grant total: In 2004/05, the trust had net assets of £87,000, and a total income of £28,000. The trust assisted individuals with grants through a direct expenditure of £29,000.

Applications: In writing to the correspondent, however, the trust states that income is accounted for and new applicants are unlikely to benefit.

Correspondent: A Herman, Messrs Berry & Berry, 11 Church Road, Tunbridge Wells, Kent TN1 1JA (01892 526344)

The Mike Collingwood Memorial Fund

Eligibility: Young people who live within a 20-mile radius of "The Who'd a Thought It" pub in Grafty Green, Kent.

Types of grants: Grants or loans according to need to provide further experience in, or facilities for, education or vocational training and for similar purposes. The fund aims to give learning opportunities which may not be essential for a course, but are a good learning experience. For example, supporting a trip for a doctor who wants to travel abroad to carry out research. Applications for assistance with Outward Bound or similar courses can also be considered.

Annual grant total: About £1,500 a year.

Applications: In writing to the correspondent including a brief cv, details of the course or activity the candidate wishes to attend and an sae. Applications must be submitted before 31 December each year for consideration in the following month.

Correspondent: P R Green, Trustee, 12 The Platt, Sutton Valence, Maidstone, Kent ME17 3BQ (01622 843230)

Wykeham Stanley Lord Cornwallis Memorial Fund

Eligibility: Any person who lives in Kent who is attending or intending to attend a course of study at a school, college or university to pursue their sporting ambitions, or serving or intending to serve an apprenticeship relating to agriculture or horticulture.

Types of grants: One-off grants or recurring grants in the range of £100 to £500. Grants are given to schoolchildren, further and higher education students, mature students and postgraduates for fees.

Annual grant total: Around £6,500.

Applications: On a form available from the correspondent, on receipt of an sae. Applications can be submitted either directly by the individual, or via the individual's school or college or another third party. Sporting applications should be submitted via Kent County Playing Fields Association. Applications are considered in March and should be submitted four weeks in advance.

Correspondent: R D Bushrod, Honorary Secretary, c/o Beech Cottage, Lidwells Lane, Gouldhurst, Kent, TN1 7EP (01580 211875)

Headley-Pitt Charitable Trust

Eligibility: Individuals in need who live in Kent, with a preference for Ashford.

Types of grants: One-off grants in the range of £100 and £300. Grants are made to schoolchildren, college students, undergraduates, vocational students, mature students, people with special educational needs, people starting work and overseas students.

Annual grant total: In 2004/05 it had assets of £2.3 million and an income of £56,000. There were 35 educational grants made totalling £8,800. A further 25 welfare grants were made totalling £6,300.

Applications: In writing to the correspondent at any time.

Correspondent: Mrs Thelma Pitt, Old Mill Cottage, Ulley Road, Kennington, Ashford, Kent, TN24 9HX (01233 626189)

Other information: Grants are also made to organisations (£28,000 in 2004/05).

Holme's Southborough Foundation

Eligibility: People living in the ancient parishes of Tonbridge, Bidborough and Speldhurst; this includes three parishes and most of Tunbridge Wells, including Southborough, Rusthall and Langton. Candidates must be between 17 and 24 years old, have attended a state school for not less than two years and be able to show proficiency in the knowledge of the Bible and of the doctrines of the Church of England.

Financial need is not a prerequisite.

Types of grants: Up to £500 a year for three years to people undertaking a full-time course in further or higher education.

Annual grant total: The amount given depends upon the availability of funds in any given year.

Applications: In writing to the correspondent, including details of education and service given to the church and/or school and community. Applications are considered from September to 30 November, with interviews held in March for the following academic year.

Interviews test one Anglican service from the prayer book and one small section of the Bible, both of which the candidates have been told about beforehand.

Correspondent: John Fowle, 42 Claremont Road, Tunbridge Wells, Kent TN1 1TA (01892 527425)

The Hothfield Educational Foundation

Eligibility: People under the age of 25 who live in, or attended the primary school at, the parish of Hothfield and the part of the parish of Westwell which forms part of, or nearly adjoins, Hothwell Heath.

Types of grants: One-off and recurrent grants to help with the cost of books, school clothing and other essentials for schoolchildren; and books, fees, living expenses and study or travel abroad for those at college or university. Grants have been given for music and other university courses. People starting work may receive grants towards books, equipment, instruments and clothing.

Annual grant total: In 2005, the foundation had an income of £7,500 and a total expenditure of £5,600. Each year a distribution is made to Hothfield School, with the remainder going to individuals.

Applications: In writing to the correspondent. Applications are considered on an on-going basis.

Correspondent: C P Oliver, Hurst Hill Farm, Hothfield, Ashford, Kent TN26 1ER

The Hugh & Montague Leney (Travelling) Awards Trust

Eligibility: Children and young people aged 16 to 19 who attend, or have attended within the previous 12 months, any county, voluntary or independent school in Kent (as constituted on 31 March 1965).

Types of grants: Bursaries or maintenance allowances to enable travel to all parts of the world for educational and humanitarian purposes. Grants are for amounts of up to £2,500.

The purpose is to extend the knowledge of young people in subjects related to their future occupations by travel or expeditions arranged by recognised bodies in the UK or abroad, or to broaden their general knowledge and confidence before they go on to higher education or employment.

Annual grant total: In 2004/05 the trust had an income of £5,400 and the sum of £5,000 was given in five grants to individuals.

Applications: On a form available from the correspondent. Applications should be submitted by a headteacher, or come through an educational welfare agency. The closing date is 31 January each year.

Correspondent: Lynn Edwards, Kent County Council, Bishops Terrace, Bishops Way, Maidstone, Kent ME14 1AF (01622 605101)

The William Strong Foundation

Eligibility: People under the age of 25 who live in the former borough of Tunbridge Wells, the former urban and rural districts of Tonbridge, and the former urban district of Southborough.

In accordance with the will of the founder in 1713 preference is given to beneficiaries who intend to take up a nautical career or occupation.

Types of grants: Mainly one-off grants in the range of £60 to £250 are given to: (i) schoolchildren for uniforms/other school clothing, books and equipment/instruments; (ii) people starting work for books and equipment/instruments; and (iii) further and higher education students for books, equipment/instruments and maintenance/living expenses.

Exclusions: No grants given for 'year out' activities.

Annual grant total: In 2004/05 the trust has an income of £1,200 with expenditure totalling £560.

Applications: Applications can be submitted in writing directly by the individual or a parent, including details of the applicant's (and parents') total income and annual outgoings. Applications are considered in June and July and should be submitted between January and March.

Correspondent: Norman Smail, Clerk, 25 Walton Road, Tonbridge, Kent TN10 4EF (01732 770504)

Tomorrow's Child Trust

Eligibility: Women who are undertaking midwifery or nursing courses, which they will use in their work to benefit people living in the Medway and Swale districts.

Types of grants: One-off grants according to need.

Annual grant total: In 2003/04 the trust had an income of £3,700 and a total expenditure of £1,400. The trust makes grants to individuals and organisations.

Applications: This trust has previously stated that due to a very low income, grants were not being issued.

Correspondent: Mrs Kathryn Jane Taylor, Chair, 34 Carisbrooke Road, Rochchester, Kent, ME2 3SN (07957 339 008)

Richard Watts and The City of Rochester Almshouse Charities

Eligibility: Students who live in Rochester city or Strood town.

Types of grants: One-off grants towards school uniforms, books, tours, musical equipment and other 'indirect' support.

Annual grant total: In 2004 the charity had assets of £15 million and an income of £892,000. Grants to 197 individuals for education and welfare purposes totalled £59,000.

Applications: In writing to the correspondent, directly by the individual or a family member. Applications can be submitted at any time and are considered on a monthly basis.

Correspondent: Mrs B A Emerry, Watts Almhouses, Maidstone Road, Rochester, Kent ME1 1SE (01634 842194; Fax: 01634 409348)

Other information: Grants are also given to local organisations which benefit the local community (£16,000 in 2004). The charity also runs an almshouse.

The Yalding Educational Foundation

Eligibility: Former pupils of schools in Yalding, Laddingfield and Courier Street who attended for at least two years.

Types of grants: One-off grants towards anything necessary for study at college or university. Grants are also given to local schools.

Annual grant total: In 2004, the foundation had assets totalling £118,000, an income of £5,300 and a total expenditure of £6,000. 17 individual grants were given totalling £3,560.

Applications: In writing to the correspondent giving details of the school attended in the parish, the college or university to be attended, course to be taken and length of the course. Applications should be received by 31 October for a December meeting.

Correspondent: Ivor Hughes, Little Addlestead, Benover Road, Yalding, Maidstone, Kent ME18 6EY (01892 730238)

Other information: The foundation gives prizes totalling £270 for spoken English competitions in the local primary schools. It also donates capitation grants to the primary schools eligible.

Benenden

The Gibbon & Buckland Charity

Eligibility: People under 25 who have lived in Benenden for three years.

Types of grants: Grants are given to students entering further and higher education only.

Annual grant total: About £16,000.

Applications: In writing to the correspondent in September. The charity is advertised locally.

Correspondent: P J Blockley, Clevelands, The Street, Benenden, Cranbrook, Kent TN17 4DB

Borden

William Barrow's Eleemosynary Charity

Eligibility: People in need who live in the ancient ecclesiastical parish of Borden or have lived in the parish and now live nearby.

Types of grants: One-off grants and twice-yearly allowances may be given to schoolchildren for uniforms/clothing, study/travel overseas, books, equipment/ instruments and excursions, to college students and undergraduates for study/ travel overseas, books, equipment/ instruments and maintenance/living expenses, to vocational students for books, students with special educational needs for equipment/instruments and people starting work for clothing, books and equipment. Grants typically range from £350 to £500.

Annual grant total: About £15,000 to individuals for welfare and educational purposes. Grants are also made to organisations.

Applications: On a form available from the correspondent. Applications are considered in January, April, July and October.

Correspondent: S J Mair, Clerk, c/o George Webb Finn, 43 Park Road, Sittingbourne, Kent ME10 1DX

Canterbury

The Canterbury United Municipal Charities

Eligibility: People in need who have lived within the boundaries of what was the old city of Canterbury for at least two years.

Types of grants: One-off and recurrent grants are made to further and higher education students for books and equipment/instruments.

Annual grant total: In 2004 the charities had an income of £6,800. There were 110 welfare grants made totalling £3,200 with a further £200 distributed in 2 educational grants.

Applications: In writing to the correspondent through the individual's school/college/educational welfare agency or directly by the individual. Applications are considered on an ongoing basis and should include a brief statement of circumstances and proof of residence in the area.

Correspondent: Aaron Spencer, Furley and Page, 39 St Margaret's Street, Canterbury, Kent CT1 2TX (01227 763939; e-mail: aas@furleypage.co.uk)

Other information: Grants are also given to individuals for welfare purposes and to organisations with similar objects.

Streynsham's Charity

Eligibility: Young people who live or attend school in the ancient parish of St Dunstan's, Canterbury, and are under the age of 21.

Types of grants: One-off grants up to a maximum of about £300. Help with the cost of books, clothing, educational outings, maintenance and other essentials can be given to schoolchildren. Grants are also available for those at college or university, (including mature students), for books, fees, travel and living expenses. People starting work can receive help towards books, equipment/instruments, clothing and travel.

Annual grant total: In 2004 about £6,000 was given in educational grants to individuals.

Applications: In writing to the correspondent. Applications can be made directly by the individual, through the individual's school/college/educational welfare agency or through other third party on behalf of the individual. They are usually considered in March and October but can be made at any time and should include an sae and telephone number if applicable.

Correspondent: Ms J Killeen, 67 Starle Close, Canterbury, Kent CT1 1XJ (01227 769456)

Dover

The Casselden Trust

Eligibility: People in need who live in the Dover Town Council area.

Types of grants: One-off and recurrent grants, up to a maximum of £250.

Annual grant total: About £1,500 to individuals for both educational and welfare purposes and a further £1,000 to organisations.

Applications: In writing to the correspondent.

Correspondent: Leslie Alton, 26 The Shrubbery, Walmer, Deal, Kent CT14 7PZ (01304 375499)

Fordwich

The Fordwich United Charities

Eligibility: People who live in the parish of Fordwich, aged 16 to 25.

Types of grants: One-off grants of £150 are given towards towards books for college students.

Annual grant total: In 2005, the sum of £750 was distributed in five relief-in-need grants. No educational grants were made during the year.

Applications: In writing to: M R Clayton, Ladywell House, Fordwich, Canterbury CT2 0DL. The deadline for applications is 1 September and a decsion will be made within a month.

Correspondent: A A Spencer, Furley Page Solicitors, 39 St Margaret's Street, Canterbury CT1 2TX

Godmersham

Godmersham Relief in Need Charity

Eligibility: Schoolchildren and students at a further or higher level, who live in the ancient parish of Godmersham in Kent.

Types of grants: Schoolchildren can receive help with the costs of equipment/ instruments, study or travel overseas and extra curricular activities, such as music lessons and sports coaching. Students and mature students can receive more general grants for example towards books or other course materials. Any request for help would be considered.

Annual grant total: In 2005 the charity had assets of £173,000 and an income of £8,000. The sum of £5,000 was distributed in 19 educational grants, with a further £2,000 distributed in 12 welfare grants.

Applications: In writing to the correspondent, directly by the individual, at any time.

Correspondent: David T Swan, Feleberge, Canterbury Road, Bilting, Ashford, Kent TN25 4HE (01233 812125)

Hawkhurst

Dunk's & Springett's Educational Foundation

Eligibility: People under 25 who live in the ancient parish of Hawkhurst.

Types of grants: One-off and recurrent grants to students on any full-time educational course.

Annual grant total: In 2005 the trust had an income of £5,700 and a total expenditure of £7,200. Grants totalled about £5,000.

Applications: In writing to the correspondent after the grants are advertised in a local newspaper.

Correspondent: Mrs B Van Winkelen, Rydale Water, Coptall Avenue, Hawkhurst, Cranbrook TN18 4LR

Hayes

Hayes (Kent) Trust

Eligibility: Students who live in the parish of Hayes and can demonstrate that they are in need.

Types of grants: One-off grants of £75 to £1,500 according to need.

Annual grant total: In 2004/05 the trust had assets of £868,000 and an income of £27,000. Out of a total expenditure of £13,000 there were 12 educational grants made totalling £4,000.

Applications: In writing to the correspondent, for consideration bi-monthly. Applications should include the full name of the applicant, postal address in Hayes (Kent), telephone number and date of birth. Applications can be made either directly by the individual, or through a third party such as the individual's college, school or educational welfare agency.

Correspondent: Ramon Smith, Hon Secretary, 41 Chatham Avenue, Hayes, Kent BR2 7QB (020 8462 2229)

Hythe

Anne Peirson Charitable Trust

Eligibility: People who live in the parish of Hythe who are at any level of their education, in any subject, who are in need.

Types of grants: One-off grants ranging between £50 and £600 given mainly to early years children and schoolchildren for books, educational outings, fees and equipment.

Exclusions: No grants are made where statutory support is available.

Annual grant total: In 2005 the trust's assets totalled £247,000 and it had an income of £11,000. Educational grants to 12 individuals totalled £2,500, with a further £400 distributed to 4 individuals for relief-in-need.

Applications: In writing to the correspondent via either Citizens Advice, a social worker, health visitor, school headteacher or other third party. Grants are considered at quarterly meetings of the trustees, but emergency applications can be considered in the interim.

Correspondent: Mrs Ina Tomkinson, Trustee/Secretary, 34 Sene Park, Hythe, Kent CT21 5XB (01303 260779; Fax: 01303 238660)

Other information: Grants are also made to organisations (£2,900 in 2005).

Medway

Arthur Ingram Trust

Eligibility: People aged between 14 and 21 and in full time education who are in need and live in the Medway council area.

Types of grants: Grants are made from three funds:

(i) The general grant scheme is for students aged between 14 and 16 whose parents are on a low income and need assistance with school uniform, books and towards school trips which are identified as being linked to exam-related studies. The maximum general grant is £300.

(ii) The continuing education scheme is for students aged between 16 and 18 and in financial need but who are continuing at school or in further education establishments/training. Grants are dependent on the applicant having attendance of at least 90% unless there are exceptional reasons for absence, such as long term illness (proof is required). The maximum continuing education grant is £400. Students aged 19 to 21 can also be considered.

(iii) Advanced payments in kind can be made to schools/colleges for students whose courses have been recognised as requiring specialist equipment. The maximum grant is £150.

Independent students can be supported if parental assistance is not possible or appropriate and the student is independent through no fault of their own.

Bursary grants are also given to sixth form students. These students are nominated by the school and applications cannot be requested directly from the trust.

Annual grant total: In 2004/05 the trust had an income of £71,000 and made grants totalling £63,000.

Applications: On a form available from the correspondent. Applications can be

made by the individual, through a third party such as a teacher or through a school, college, or educational welfare agency. Continuing education applications should be submitted between July and March; bursaries can be applied for from April to June. General grants can be submitted at any time and are considered on an ongoing basis. Each application is means tested and evidence of income is required with every application.

Correspondent: Margaret Taylor, Charities/Treasury Management Officer, Medway Council, Finance & Corporate Services, Civic Centre (Annex A), Strood, Rochester, Kent ME2 4AU (01634 332144; Fax: 01634 732835; e-mail: margaret.taylor@medway.gov.uk)

New Romney

Southland's Educational Foundation

Eligibility: People who live in the parish of New Romney under the age of 25.

Types of grants: Grants are given towards the cost of books, equipment, instruments, fees, maintenance/living expenses, educational outings in the UK and study or travel overseas for students in further and higher education. Grants are in the range of £100 to £500.

Annual grant total: In 2004/05 the foundation had an income of £3,900 and a total expenditure of £4,500. Grants were made to 13 individuals totalling £3,600.

Applications: On a form available from the correspondent. Applications are considered in October.

Correspondent: Mrs U Whiting, Clerk, c/o Town Hall, High Street, New Romney, Kent TN28 8BT (01797 362348)

Rochester

Cliffe at Hoo Parochial Charity

Eligibility: People in need who live in the ancient parish of Cliffe-at-Hoo and Rochester.

Types of grants: One-off grants of around £50 for any educational need.

Annual grant total: In 2003/04 the trust had assets of £60,000 and an income of £8,000. A total of £6,000 was distributed in 30 relief-in-need grants and £1,000 in three educational grants.

Applications: In writing to the correspondent, to be submitted either directly by the individual or a family member, through a third party such as a social worker or teacher, or through an organisation such as Citizens Advice or a school. Applications are usually considered at quarterly intervals throughout the year.

Correspondent: P Kingman, Clerk, 52 Reed Street, Cliffe, Rochester, Kent ME3 7UL (01634 220422)

Sandgate

The James Morris Educational Foundation

Eligibility: Young people who live within the boundaries of Sandgate on a permanent basis.

Types of grants: Grants of about £75 to £275 to help further and higher education students with fees/living expenses, books, equipment/instruments and maintenance/living expenses; towards the cost of school uniform, books and equipment/instruments for schoolchildren; and towards books and fees for people starting work. Mature students can receive help towards books, fees and maintenance/living expenses and vocational students can receive help towards fees. Grants can be one-off or recurrent.

Annual grant total: In 2004/05 the foundation had an income of £1,900 and a total expenditure of £2,200. Grants were made to six individuals totalling £1,900.

Applications: In writing to the correspondent, either directly by the individual or through their school, college or educational welfare agency. Applications should include particulars of the university or college that the applicant is attending or planning to attend, together with details of the course of study and ultimate ambitions. Applications should be submitted by 15 September for consideration in October.

Correspondent: Mrs M R Wells, Trustee, 4 Bybrook Field, Sandgate, Folkestone, Kent CT20 3BQ (01303 248092)

Sevenoaks

The Kate Drummond Trust

Eligibility: Young people, especially girls, living in Sevenoaks.

Types of grants: One-off grants are given towards education, recreation or training.

Annual grant total: In 2003/04 the trust had an income of £7,000 and a total expenditure of £2,300. Grants totalled about £2,000.

Applications: In writing to the correspondent, with an sae if a reply is required.

Correspondent: The Rector, St Nicholas' Rectory, Rectory Lane, Sevenoaks, Kent TN13 1JA (01732 740340)

Wilmington

The Wilmington Parochial Charity

Eligibility: People in need, living in the parish of Wilmington, who are receiving a statutory means-tested benefit, such as Income Support, Housing Benefit or help towards their council tax.

Types of grants: One-off grants according to need. Grants are awarded to: (i) schoolchildren for books and educational outings but not clothing, uniforms or fees; (ii) students in further/higher education for books, fees, living expenses and study and travel abroad, but not to foreign students or for student exchange; and (iii) mature students for books and travel but not fees or childcare.

Annual grant total: Welfare grants to individuals total about £10,000 a year. Educational grants total about £2,000 a year.

Applications: Applications should be submitted by the individual, or through a social worker, Citizens Advice or other welfare agency. The trustees meet in February and November. Urgent applications can be considered between meetings in exceptional circumstances.

Correspondent: S J Stringer, 13 Meadow Walk, Wilmington, Dartford, Kent DA2 7BP

Other information: Grants are also given to local schools at Christmas.

Norfolk

Anguish's Educational Foundation

Eligibility: Permanent residents of Norwich and the parishes of Costessey, Hellesdon, Catton, Sprowston, Thorpe St Andrews and Corpusty, aged under 25. Applicants must be on a low income.

Types of grants: The main beneficiaries are pupils of state schools. A small proportion of grants are made to college or university students under the age of 25, mostly for books and equipment, but also for small maintenance grants. A few grants are made each year for educational travel including school trips and occasional overseas visits, for example, attending the world scout jamboree. Grants are made for the costs of music, other arts or sports studies. The trustees believe, however, that the most urgent need of parents is help with the cost of school clothing and the majority of grants are made for this purpose.

Exclusions: Postgraduates are not supported.

Annual grant total: In 2004/05 the foundation had assets of £10.8 million and an income of £547,000. Grants were made totalling £321,000, of which £232,000 was given to individuals. Grants to individuals were broken down as follows:

- School clothing, including foundation grants (£171,000)
- Educational travel (£34,100)
- Further education (£11,400)
- Books, equipment and trade tools (£8,600)
- Music training (£3,700)
- Dyslexia training etc. (£3,200)

Applications: In writing to the correspondent directly by the individual. Applications are considered at five meetings held throughout the year. Parents or individuals will generally be required to attend the office for a short interview.

Correspondent: David Walker, Clerk to the Trustees, 10 Golden Dog Lane, Magdalen Street, Norwich NR3 1BP (01603 621023; Fax: 01603 767025; e-mail: david.walker@nch-charities.co.uk)

The Brancaster Educational & Almshouse Charity

Eligibility: People living in the ancient parishes of Brancaster, Titchwell, Thornham, and Burnham Deepdale only.

Types of grants: Grants to schoolchildren for excursions and to undergraduates for books.

Annual grant total: About £5,000.

Applications: In writing to the correspondent.

Correspondent: Mrs D E Wooster, Treasurer, Strebla, Mill Road, Brancaster, Norfolk PE31 8AW (01485 210645)

Other information: Grants are also given to Brancaster School towards the cost of equipment.

The King's Lynn Educational Charity

Eligibility: People aged between 16 and 25 who have lived in the borough of King's Lynn and West Norfolk for not less than two years, or those who have attended school in the borough for not less than two years.

Types of grants: One-off and recurrent grants in the range of £75 to £200 are made to people starting work for equipment/instruments, and to further and higher education students for books, equipment/instruments and fees.

Annual grant total: In 2005 the charity gave about £800 in four grants.

Applications: On a form available from the correspondent to be submitted between March and July; applications are considered in September. The application should be supported by the applicant's current or previous educational establishment.

Correspondent: R Pannell, 21 Baldwin Road, King's Lynn, Norfolk PE30 4AL (01553 775724; e-mail: bob.pannell1@ btopenworld.com)

The Norfolk (le Strange) Fund & Provincial Charities

Eligibility: Children of poor or deceased Freemasons of the Province of Norfolk.

Types of grants: Help with the cost of books, clothing and other essentials for schoolchildren. Grants may also be available for those at college or university. The trust will ensure that all eligible people will be supported throughout their education.

Annual grant total: Income is above £20,000, but not all of this is given in education grants. No further information was available.

Applications: In writing to the correspondent. Applications should be received by end of April and September for consideration in May and October. The correspondent would prefer applicants to apply and enquire by post rather than by telephone.

Correspondent: A J Brooke, Ford Cottage, Dereham Road, Mattishall, Norfolk NR20 3NP (01362 858052)

The Norwich French Church Charity

Eligibility: Children and young people primarily of French Protestant descent who are under the age of 25 and live in Norwich. Applicants from Norfolk can also be considered.

Types of grants: Grants, ranging from £250 to £500, for schoolchildren and college students for uniforms/other school clothing, books, equipment/instruments, maintenance/living expenses, childcare, educational outings in the UK, study or travel abroad, etc. A preference is given to applicants with a Huguenot descent.

Annual grant total: In 2005 the trust had assets of £280,000, an income of £11,000 and a total expenditure of £8,200. Educational grants were made to nine individuals totalling £1,900.

Applications: On a form available from the correspondent which can be submitted directly by the individual or through the individual's college or educational welfare agency, or another third party, at any time.

Correspondent: G H Smith, Clerk, Hansells Solicitors, 13 Cathedral Close, Norwich NR1 4DS (01603 615731; Fax: 01603 275828)

Red House Youth Projects Trust
see entry on page 24

The Charity of Joanna Scott & Others

Eligibility: People under the age of 25 who are being educated or live within five miles of Norwich City Hall. Preference is given to families in financial need.

Types of grants: Grants are given to schoolchildren for the costs of uniforms/other school clothing, books, equipment/instruments, fees, maintenance/living expenses, childcare, educational outings in the UK, study or travel abroad and student exchanges. Grants range between £15 and £2,000. The trust also offers interest-free loans.

Annual grant total: In 2004/05 the trust had assets of £1.6 million and an income of £70,000. Grants to individuals totalled £28,000, whilst £25,000 was given to organisations.

Applications: On a form available from the correspondent. Applications are usually considered in March, July, September and November, but smaller applications are considered daily. Please supply a copy of the appropriate circular from the school or college to assist the trustees.

Correspondent: G H Smith, Clerk, Hansells, 13 Cathedral Close, Norwich NR1 4DS (01603 615731)

The Shelroy Trust

Eligibility: Youth of East Norfolk and Norwich for voluntary services overseas. This must be for social purposes rather than recreational.

Types of grants: One-off grants, ranging from £200 to £250.

Annual grant total: In 2004/05 the trust had assets of £382,000 and an income of £14,000. Grants to individuals and organisations totalled £16,000.

Applications: In writing to the correspondent. Individuals applying for grants must provide full information and two referees are required. Applications can be made directly by the individual or through a social worker, Citizens Advice or other third party. They are considered at the trustees' quarterly meetings in March, June, September and December.

Correspondent: R Wiltshire, 4 Brandon Court, Brundall, Norwich NR13 5NW

West Norfolk and King's Lynn Girls' School Trust

Eligibility: Girls and young women over the age of 11 who are at a secondary school or in their first years after leaving school or further education, who live in the borough of King's Lynn and West Norfolk and the parishes of Beeston with Bittering, Beetley, Brisley, Great Dunham, Gressenhall, Horningtoft, Kempstone, Langham, Lexham, Litcham, Little Dunham, Mileham, Narborough, Rougham,

Stanfield, Tittleshall, Weasenham All Saints, Weasenham St Peter, Wellingham, Wendling and Whissonsett.

Types of grants: One-off and recurrent grants of between £100 and £1,000 are given to (i) schoolchildren for help with school uniforms, other school clothing, books equipment/instruments and educational outings in the UK and overseas, but not for maintenance or fees; (ii) students in further/higher education for help with books, fees, equipment, instruments, living expenses, study or travel overseas and student exchange but not for foreign students; and (iii) mature students for books, travel, fees, living expenses and childcare. Grants are also available for music, sports and creative arts education. The trustees hope the trust can enable a girl to undertake some course or venture of an educational nature that she would otherwise not have been able to do.

Annual grant total: In 2004/05 the trust had an income of £20,000 and a total expenditure of £22,000. Grants were made to 18 individuals totalling £20,000.

Applications: On a form available from the correspondent. Applications should include parental income, details of course or educational need, two references including one from a teacher or lecturer, and a supporting letter from the applicant. They are considered in January, April and September.

Correspondent: Mrs M Aldous, Clerk to the Trustees, The Goodshed, Station Road, Little Dunham, Kings Lynn PE32 2DJ (01760 720617)

Other information: This trust also gives grants to secondary schools within the area.

Burnham Market

The Harold Moorhouse Charity

Eligibility: Individuals in need who live in Burnham Market in Norfolk only.

Types of grants: One-off grants are made ranging from £50 to £200 for education equipment and school educational trips.

Annual grant total: In 2003/04 the charity had an income and a total expenditure of £16,000. Grants totalled about £15,000.

Applications: In writing to the correspondent. Applications should be submitted directly by the individual in any month.

Correspondent: R J Utting, Trustee, Angles House, Station Road, Burnham Market, King's Lynn, Norfolk PE31 8HA

Burnham Thorpe

Richard Bunting's Educational Foundation

Eligibility: People who live in the parish of Burnham Thorpe who have not yet had their 25th birthday.

Types of grants: Grants of up to £400 are made to help schoolchildren with the cost of uniforms, books, equipment/instruments, fees, educational outings in the UK, study or travel abroad and student exchanges. Grants are also made to help towards clothing costs for people starting work, further and higher education students and mature students.

Annual grant total: In 2004/05 the foundation had assets of £8,000, and both an income and a total expenditure of £3,100, all of which was given in grants to 27 individuals.

Applications: In writing to the correspondent either directly by the individual (if over 18) or by a parent/guardian. Applications are considered in February and September, but emergencies can be dealt with on an ongoing basis.

Correspondent: Mrs M A Heather, Meadway, Creake Road, Burnham Thorpe, King's Lynn, Norfolk PE31 8HW (01328 738224; e-mail: mary.heather@tiscali.co.uk)

Buxton with Lammas

Picto Buxton Charity

Eligibility: People in need who live in the parish of Buxton with Lamas.

Types of grants: One-off grants of £100 to £200 to schoolchildren for uniforms/clothing, books and excursions and to college students, undergraduates, vocational students, mature students and people starting work towards books.

Annual grant total: In 2005/06 the trust had an income of £19,000 and a total expenditure of £7,900. In the year only one grant of £25 was made to an individual.

Applications: In writing to the correspondent directly by the individual or a family member, or through a third party such as a social worker or teacher. Applications are considered at any time.

Correspondent: Dick W Smithson, Clerk, Avandix, Crown Road, Buxton, Norwich NR10 5EN (01603 279203)

Other information: Grants are also available for relief-in-need purposes and to organisations or groups within the parish boundary.

Diss

The Diss Parochial Charities Poors Branch

Eligibility: People in need who live in the town and parish of Diss.

Types of grants: One-off grants to schoolchildren towards fees, books and excursions and to college students and undergraduates towards fees and books. Grants range from £30 to £200.

Annual grant total: In 2005 the charity had assets of £110,000 and an income of £21,000. There were two educational grants made totalling £300. A further £2,900 was distributed in 26 welfare grants.

Applications: In writing to the correspondent directly by the individual, through the individual's school/college/educational welfare agency or through another third party on behalf of the individual. They are considered upon receipt.

Correspondent: J H Scoggins, 2 The Causeway, Victoria Road, Diss, Norfolk, IP22 4AW (01379 650630)

East Tuddenham

The East Tuddenham Charities

Eligibility: People in further and higher education who live in East Tuddenham.

Types of grants: Help with the cost of books, clothing and other essentials.

Annual grant total: Grants of £1,800 a year, mostly for welfare purposes.

Applications: In writing to the correspondent.

Correspondent: Mrs Janet Guy, 7 Mattishall Road, East Tuddenham, Dereham, Norfolk NR20 3LP

Feltwell

Sir Edmund Moundeford's Educational Foundation

Eligibility: Individuals in need who live in Feltwell.

Types of grants: One-off cash grants and grants in kind are made to schoolchildren, college students and vocational students, including those for clothing/uniforms, books and equipment/instruments.

Annual grant total: In 2004 the fund's income was £84,000 and it had a total expenditure of £19,000. The sum of £4,500 was distributed in 140 grants to individuals for welfare purposes and £1,900 in 35 grants for education,

Applications: In writing to the correspondent either directly by the individual or through an organisation such as Citizens Advice or a school.

Applications are considered at meetings held quarterly.

Correspondent: B L Hawkins, The Estate Office, Lynn Road, Downham Market, Norfolk PE38 9NL (01366 387180; Fax: 01366 386626; e-mail: info@barryhawkins.co.uk)

Garboldisham

The Garboldisham Parish Charities

Eligibility: People under 25 who have lived in Garboldisham for at least two years.

Types of grants: One-off and recurrent grants including gifts in kind are made to schoolchildren, college students, undergraduates, vocational students, people with special needs and people starting work. Grants given include those for uniforms/clothing, study/travel aboard, books, equipment/instruments and maintenance/living expenses. Grants are in the range of £30 to £600.

Annual grant total: In 2004/05 the charities had an income of £5,600 and a total expenditure of £4,500. About £1,000 was distributed in educational grants.

Applications: Applications can be submitted directly by the individual including specific details of what the grant is required for. They are usually considered in July and December.

Correspondent: P Girling, Treasurer, Smallworth, Garboldisham, Diss, Norfolk IP22 2QW (01953 681646)

Harling

Harling Town Lands Educational Foundation

Eligibility: Young people resident in Harling who are in need.

Types of grants: Awards of exhibitions or grants may be at any secondary school, training college for teachers, university, or other institution of further education (including professional and technical education) approved by the trustees. Grants may also be given for outfits, clothing, tools, instruments or books to people leaving school, university or any other educational establishment, to prepare for, or to enter a profession, trade or calling.

Otherwise assistance may be given for the promotion of education (including social and physical training).

Annual grant total: In 2004/05 the foundation made grants totalling £1,400 to four individuals.

Applications: In writing to the correspondent at any time from any source, a brief financial statement will be required.

Correspondent: David Gee, Clerk, Hanworth House, Market Street, East Harling, Norwich NR16 2AD (01953 717652; Fax: 01953 717611; e-mail: gee@harlingpc.org.uk)

Hempnall

The Hempnall Town Estate Educational Foundation

Eligibility: People who live in Hempnall and have done so for a year.

Types of grants: Grants to help with: (i) costs of educational outings for schoolchildren; (ii) expenses incurred while at college or university such as books, help with fees and study or travel abroad; and (iii) help with the cost of vocational courses. Grants are also available for a wide range of other activities, including athletic expenses and the study of the arts.

Grants to individuals are usually made on a percentage basis on production of receipts for courses, books and so on, with a maximum ceiling which is reviewed annually. Each application is considered entirely on merit, but if a grant is made to one person everyone making an application for the same course receives exactly the same amount or percentage.

Annual grant total: About £10,000 is given in educational grants to individuals and to village organisations.

Applications: In writing to the correspondent, including evidence of the course being taken and relevant receipts. Applications are considered in March, July and November and should be received before the 1st of these months. The foundation stated that 'if you do not live in the parish of Hempnall there is no point in applying'.

Correspondent: Secretary, 17 Roland Drive, Hempnall, Norfolk NR15 2RB (01508 499460)

Other information: Further information on the foundation and how to make an application is available in the Parish News Letter, published annually in January.

Hilgay

The Hilgay Feoffee Charity

Eligibility: People starting an apprenticeship or work who live in the parish of Hilgay.

Types of grants: One-off and recurrent grants according to need, including fuel vouchers and help towards costs of apprenticeship or training.

Annual grant total: Around £500, although the grant total varies each year.

Applications: In writing to the correspondent, directly by the individual.

Applications are considered in June each year.

Correspondent: Mrs P Golds, Reeve Cottage, Wards Chase, Stow Bridge, King's Lynn, Norfolk PE33 3NN

Horstead with Stanninghall

The Horstead Poor's Land

Eligibility: People in need who live in Horstead with Stanninghall.

Types of grants: One-off grants up to a maximum of £2,000 can be made for any purpose.

Annual grant total: In 2004/05 the charity had an income of £8,000 and made 20 grants totalling £4,000.

Applications: Applications can be submitted directly by the individual, through a school or college, or other third party giving details of the applicant's financial resources. Applications are considered at any time.

Correspondent: W B Lloyd, Watermeadows, 7 Church Close, Horstead, Norwich NR12 7ET (01603 737632)

Other information: This trust also makes grants for relief-in-need purposes and to support village amenities.

King's Lynn

The King's Lynn General Educational Foundation

Eligibility: People aged under 25 who have lived in the borough of King's Lynn for not less than two years, or those who have attended school in the borough for not less than two years, who are going on to further education.

Types of grants: One-off grants to people at school, college or university or any other further education institution towards the cost of books, equipment, fees and living expenses.

Annual grant total: In 2004 the trust had assets of £42,000, an income of £1,600 and a total expenditure of £1,800, all of which was given in grants to nine individuals.

Applications: On a form available from Mr R G Pannell, 21 Baldwin Road, King's Lynn, Norfolk PE30 4AL, to be submitted by 30 August each year. The application should be supported by the applicant's previous educational establishment.

Correspondent: A J Cave, Wheelers, 16 North Street, Wisbech, Cambridgeshire PE13 1NE

Norwich

Norwich Town Close Estate Charity

Eligibility: Freemen of Norwich and their dependants.

Types of grants: Grants are given to schoolchildren, further and higher education students, mature students and postgraduates for fees and maintenance/living expenses.

Annual grant total: In 2004/05 the charity had assets of £17 million and an income of £638,000. Grants to 233 individuals totalled £227,000, educational donations totalled £82,000. A further £253,000 was given to organisations, £137,000 in pensions, £4,700 for television licenses and £3,700 for relief-in-need causes.

Applications: In writing to the correspondent by June/early July each year. Applications are considered in August.

Correspondent: David Walker, 10 Golden Dog Lane, Magdalen Street, Norwich NR3 1BP (01603 621023; e-mail: david.walker@nch-charities.co.uk)

Sir Peter Seaman's Charity

Eligibility: Young men and women up to the age of 21 who live in Norwich.

Types of grants: One-off and recurrent grants generally between £100 and £300. Grants can be towards all kinds of educational purposes, including starting a new job/career or to help with educational trips such as Duke of Edinburgh Award Scheme, Raleigh International etc.

Annual grant total: In 2003/04 the charity had an income of £3,500 and a total expenditure of £3,200. Grants to individuals totalled around £3,000.

Applications: In writing to the correspondent. Applications can be submitted directly by the individual and are considered quarterly in March, June, September and December.

Correspondent: The Administrator, The Great Hospital, Bishopsgate, Norwich NR1 4EL (01603 622022; Fax: 01603 766093)

Outwell

The Owen Jones Charity

Eligibility: People in need who live in Northop, Northop Hall and Sychdyn.

Types of grants: One-off and recurrent grants according to need.

Annual grant total: In 2004/05 the charities had an income of £9,500 and a total expenditure of £40.

Applications: In February 2006 the charities were in the process of changing their governing documents. Changes were hoping to be finalised by early 2007.

Correspondent: Jack Wolstenholme, Hon. Secretary, 18 St Peter's Park, Northop, Flintshire CH7 6DP

The Outwell Town Lands Educational Foundation

Eligibility: People who live in the ancient parish of Outwell.

Types of grants: Recurrent grants are usually made to: (i) those staying at school beyond normal school-leaving age; (ii) those attending courses of further education at technical colleges, other colleges (e.g. agricultural and teacher training) and universities; and (iii) those taking an apprenticeship course or other work leading to a trade qualification. Grants range from £50 to £200 and are for general educational purposes.

Annual grant total: In 2005, the foundation had a gross income of £4,000, and a total expenditure of £3,700.

Applications: On a form available from the correspondent. Applications should be submitted directly by the individual in September for consideration in October. Proof of satisfactory attendance may be requested. Grants are paid at the end of January.

Correspondent: Mrs Debbie Allen, 90 Wisbech Road, Outwell, Wisbech, Cambridgeshire PE14 8PF (01945 773381; e-mail: outwellpc@tiscali.co.uk)

Oxborough

The Hewars Educational Charity

Eligibility: People who live in the ancient parish of Oxborough who are under the age of 25.

Types of grants: Grants to help with education costs incurred by those at school, college or university. The average donation is for £200.

Exclusions: Grants are only made to people who live in the ancient parish of Oxborough.

Annual grant total: In 2004 the trust had an income of £686. No grants were made to either individuals or organisations during the year, yet there was still an expenditure of £487.

Applications: Applications are usually considered in November.

Correspondent: Mrs E W Wilson, The Lodge, Brookville, Thetford, Norfolk IP26 4RB (01366 727185; Fax: 01366 727340)

Saxlingham

The Saxlingham United Charities

Eligibility: People under 21 who have lived in Saxlingham Nethergate for at least five years.

Types of grants: Grants of £50 to £100 towards the cost of books, clothing or tools to young people starting work or in further or higher education.

Annual grant total: In 2004/05 the charities had an income of £2,600 and a total expenditure of £1,600. Grants are made for welfare and educational purposes.

Applications: In writing to the correspondent. Applications can be submitted directly by the individual and are usually considered in October.

Correspondent: Mrs Jane Turner, 4 Pitts Hill Close, Saxlingham, Nethergate NR15 1AZ

Snettisham

Halls Exhibition Foundation

Eligibility: People in need who are aged 11 to 25 and live in the village of Snettisham (and have been there for at least one year).

Types of grants: One-off grants up to a maximum of about £2,500. Recent grants have included those to students for gap-year activities and to people moving on to secondary, further and higher education.

Exclusions: No grants for the purchase of computers or for musical instruments.

Annual grant total: In 2004/05 it had an income of £672,000 and a total expenditure of £55,000. Grants to 92 individuals totalled around £50,000.

Applications: On a form available from the correspondent. Applications can be submitted either directly by the individual or a parent/guardian, through a third party such as a teacher, or through an organisation such as a school or an educational welfare agency.

Correspondent: Christopher Holt, 4 Bewick Close, Snettisham, King's Lynn, Norfolk PE31 7PJ (01485 541534; website: www.hallsfoundation.fsnet.co.uk)

Other information: Grants are also made to organisations (£3,000 in 2004/05).

South Creake

The South Creake Charities

Eligibility: People in further or higher education who are in need and live in South Creake.

Types of grants: One-off grants range from £100 to £200 and are given to help

schoolchildren and further and higher education students with the cost of books, equipment/instruments, fees and educational outings in the UK.

Annual grant total: In 2004/05 the charities had an income of £4,300 and a total expenditure of £3,000.

Applications: In writing to the correspondent. Applications should be submitted directly by the individual and are considered in November; they should be received before the end of October.

Correspondent: The Vicar, The Vicarage, Front Street, South Creake, Fakenham, Norfolk NR21 9PE (01328 823433)

Other information: Grants can also be given to schools and playgroups.

South Walsham

Harrold's Charity

Eligibility: People aged 13 to 25 who live in the parish of South Walsham.

Types of grants: Grants are given towards the cost of school uniform, school clothing, books, equipment, educational outings and study or travel abroad for schoolchildren. Students in further/higher education, apprentices and students on training courses can receive grants towards general education costs. Grants can be one-off and recurrent and range from £25 to £250.

Annual grant total: In 2004/05 the trust had an income of £3,000 and a total expenditure of £2,300. Grants totalled about £2,000.

Applications: In writing to the correspondent. Applications are considered in January, April and September and must include receipts for any expenditure incurred, or confirmation of college course and so on.

Correspondent: Mrs James, Beech Farm, Marsh Road, Upton, Norwich, NR13 6BP (01493 751070)

Walpole

The Walpole St Peter Poor's Estate

Eligibility: People in need aged 16 and over who are at college or university and live in the old parishes of Walpole St Peter, Walpole Highway and Walpole Marsh.

Types of grants: Recurrent grants ranging from £10 to £50 to help buy books.

Annual grant total: The trust distributes about £1,300 to £1,400 a year in grants.

Applications: In writing to the correspondent. Applications should be submitted directly by the individual and are considered in November.

Correspondent: P C Lambert, Holmleigh House, Francis Road, Walpole St Andrew, Wisbach, Cambridgeshire, PE14 7JF

Other information: Grants are also made to older people.

Wiveton

The Charities of Ralph Greenway

Eligibility: Young people living in the parish of Wiveton or associated closely with it, up to university age, including young people who are starting work.

Types of grants: One-off grants are given towards books, equipment, clothing, study/travel abroad, excursions and so on.

Annual grant total: In 2004/05 the trust had assets of £74,000 and an income of £2,400. No educational grants were made during the year. The sum of £950 was distributed in 72 welfare grants.

Applications: Applications, on a form available from the correspondent, should be submitted directly by the individual and are considered twice a year. However, if a need arises, a special meeting can be convened.

Correspondent: Mrs Margaret L Bennett, 4 The Cottages, Blakeney Road, Wiveton, Holt, Norfolk NR25 7TN (01263 741384)

Other information: Grants are also available for individuals in need who are over 60 and live in the village.

Woodton

Woodton United Charities

Eligibility: People in need who live in the parish of Woodton.

Types of grants: One-off and recurrent grants according to need for books and equipment. Recent grants include tools for an apprentice (£270) and books for an A-level student (£35).

Annual grant total: In 2005 the charities had an income of £2,700 and a total expenditure of £2,100. Grants totalled about £1,500.

Applications: In writing to the correspondent directly by the individual, including details of the nature of the need. Applications can be submitted at any time.

Correspondent: P B Moore, 6 Triple Plea Road, Woodton, Bungay, Suffolk NR35 2NS (01508 482375)

Oxfordshire

The Bampton Exhibition Foundation

Eligibility: People under 25 who live in Bampton, Aston, Cote, Weald or Lew and are in need.

Types of grants: Grants are given to schoolchildren, people with special educational needs, students in further/higher education, vocational students and postgraduates for projects/courses which would be otherwise beyond the means of applicants. Support that can be given includes books, equipment/instruments, fees, maintenance/living expenses, educational outings in the UK, study or travel abroad and so on.

Annual grant total: Grants totalling up to £2,000 are made each year to individuals.

Applications: In writing to the correspondent at any time, including details regarding the proposed project/course, any expenses involved and relevant references. Applications can be submitted either directly by the individual, through the individual's school, college or educational agency, or through another third party such as a teacher or parent.

Correspondent: Marion Dowling, Bursaries Administrator, Bay Tree Cottage, Rosemary Lane, Bampton, Oxfordshire OX18 2NF (01993 850167)

The Bartlett Taylor Charitable Trust

Eligibility: Students from Oxfordshire.

Types of grants: Grants in the range of £100 and £750.

Annual grant total: In 2004/05 the trust had assets of £1.5 million which generated an income of £55,000. There were 21 grants made to individuals for medical and welfare purposes totalling £5,900 and 7 for educational purposes totalling £2,100.

Applications: In writing to the correspondent. The trustees meet every two months.

Correspondent: The Trustees, c/o 24 Church Green, Witney, Oxfordshire OX8 6AT

Other information: Grants are also made to organisations (£47,000).

The Culham Educational Foundation

Eligibility: Priority is given to teachers and clergy, studying or working in the Oxford diocese, who are wishing to study at postgraduate level in the fields of religious education, theology or religious studies. Endorsement by a diocesan or LEA officer is required, or in the case of clergy, the area bishop or archdeacon.

Types of grants: Grants up to a maximum of £1,000 are made towards books, fees and living expenses. A few grants are made to corporate bodies; the main work of the foundation is the support of the Culham College Institute.

Exclusions: Applicants must be living or working in the diocese of Oxford.

Annual grant total: Around £5,000 to individuals.

Applications: On a form available from the correspondent. Applications must be submitted by 31 March for courses commencing in the autumn.

Correspondent: Revd Dr John Gay, 15 Northham Gardens, Oxford, OX2 6PY (01865 284885; Fax: 01865 284886; e-mail: cef@culham.ac.uk)

Ducklington & Hardwick with Yelford Charity

Eligibility: People in need or hardship who live in the villages of Ducklington, Hardwick and Yelford.

Types of grants: Grants of £75 to £200 to: schoolchildren for educational outings in the UK; people starting work for equipment; people in further/higher education for books and study or travel overseas and vocational students for books.

Annual grant total: In 2005 the trust had assets of £70,000 and an income of £4,300. Welfare grants to 14 individuals totalled £2,600 and 3 educational grants totalled £230.

Applications: In writing to the correspondent. Applications are considered in March and November, but emergency cases can be dealt with at any time.

Correspondent: Mrs J Parry, 16 Feilden Close, Ducklington, Witney, Oxfordshire OX29 7XB (01993 705121)

Other information: Grants are also made to organisations such as clubs, schools and so on.

The Faringdon United Charities

Eligibility: People in need who live in the parishes of Faringdon, Littleworth, Great and Little Coxwell, all in Oxfordshire.

Types of grants: One-off grants to: schoolchildren for study/travel abroad, equipment/instruments and excursions; mature students for books; people with special educational needs for equipment/instruments; and people starting work for equipment/instruments.

Annual grant total: In 2004/05 the charities had assets of £238,000 and an income of £16,000. There were 15 educational grants made totalling £2,500.

Applications: In writing to the correspondent throughout the year. Applications can be submitted either through Citizens Advice, a social worker or other third party, directly by the individual or by a third party on their behalf for example a neighbour, parent or child.

Correspondent: W R Jestico, Clerk, Bunting & Co, 7 Market Place, Faringdon, Oxfordshire, SN7 7HL (01367 243789; Fax: 01367 243789)

Other information: Grants are also made to organisations helping people in need.

The Henley Educational Charity

Eligibility: People under the age of 25 who live in the town of Henley or parishes of Bix, Rotherfield Greys or Remenham, or attend a publicly, maintained school or college in the region, or have done so for at least two years.

Types of grants: Grants are awarded to school children for uniforms, educational outings, pre-school fees, music lessons and educational extra-curricular activities on an income-based assessment. Young people under 25 can apply for assistance with books, studying or voluntary work abroad but not for university courses or accommodation costs. Assistance may be provided for people starting work to buy equipment.

Annual grant total: In 2004/05, over £16,000 was given to individuals.

Applications: Application forms can be submitted by the individual, or through their school/college, parent/guardian, educational welfare agency or social services, and are considered throughout the year. An information leaflet is also available from the correspondent.

Correspondent: Mrs D Carter, Holy Trinity Vicarage, 16 Church Street, Henley-on-Thames RG9 1SE (e-mail: hedcharity@hotmail.com)

Other information: One third of the trust's income may be given in special benefits to publicly maintained schools in the region. The charity states: 'You may need help in some other way not mentioned. The charity would like to assist you if it possibly can. Do not be afraid to ask!'

The Hope Ffennell Trust

Eligibility: People under the age of 25 years who live in the parishes of Wytham and North Hinksey.

Types of grants: Help towards outings and educational visits, books and the study of music.

Annual grant total: About £5,500.

Applications: In writing to the correspondent.

Correspondent: The Secretary, Louis Letourneau, Church End, Wytham Abbey, Wytham, Oxon, OX2 8QE

Dr South's Educational Foundation

Eligibility: People who live in the parish of Islip and adjoining parishes, under the age of 25.

Types of grants: The chief object of the foundation is the assistance of Doctor South's School, Islip. However, individuals in the eligible parishes are also supported.

Grants may be given to: (i) schoolchildren for uniforms/other school clothing, books, equipment/instruments, educational outings in the UK, study or travel overseas and student exchanges; (ii) people starting work for uniforms and equipment/instruments; (iii) further and higher education students for books, educational outings in the UK, study or travel overseas and student exchange; and (iv) postgraduates for books and equipment/instruments. Grants range from £50 to £500.

Annual grant total: In 2003/04 the foundation had an income of £6,300 and a total expenditure of almost £10,000. Grants totalled about £9,000.

Applications: In writing to the correspondent, either through the individual's school, college or educational welfare agency, or directly by the individual. Applications can be considered at any time.

Correspondent: Edward Stephenson, The Confessors Gate, High Street, Islip, Kidlington, Oxfordshire OX5 2SN (01865 848331)

The Stevens Hart & Municipal Educational Charity

Eligibility: People who live in the parishes of Bix and Rotherfield Greys and the town of Henley-on-Thames.

Types of grants: Help with the cost of books, clothing and other essentials for schoolchildren. Help may also be available for students at college or university. Grants can range from £60 to £1,500, but £300 is more common.

Annual grant total: In 2004/05, the charity had an income of £3,700 and a total expenditure of £4,000.

Applications: On a form available from the correspondent.

Correspondent: Mrs J E Pickett, Henley Municipal Charities, Rear, 24 Hart Street, Henley-on-Thames, Oxon, RG9 2AU (01491 412360; Fax: 01491 412360)

The Thame Welfare Trust

Eligibility: People in need who live in Thame and immediately adjoining villages.

Types of grants: One-off grants of amounts up to £1,000 are given to help towards a wide variety of needs to schoolchildren, college students, undergraduates, vocational students, mature students, people with special

educational needs and people starting work.

Annual grant total: In 2004/05 the trust had an income of £19,000 and a total expenditure of £17,000. Grants usually total about £2,000. This money is given to individuals and organisations for relief-in-need and education.

Applications: In writing to the correspondent mainly through social workers, probation officers, teachers, or a similar third party, but also directly by the applicant.

Correspondent: J Gadd, Pearce Court, Windmill Road, Thame, Oxfordshire OX9 2DJ (01844 212564)

Banbury

The Banbury Charities – Countess of Arran's Charity

Eligibility: People under 25 who live in the former borough of Banbury, as it was in 1974.

Types of grants: Grants are given to people preparing for or entering a profession or trade and students in higher and further education.

Annual grant total: In 2004 the charities had net assets of £4.3 million; income totalled £300,000, with a total expenditure of £270,000. The charities gave grants to 392 individuals to a total of £127,000.

Applications: In writing to the correspondent.

Correspondent: A Scott Andrews, Clerk, 36 West Bar, Banbury, Oxfordshire OX16 9RU (01295 251234; Fax: 01295 270948)

The Banbury Charities – The Banbury Arts & Educational Charity

Eligibility: People under 25 who live in the Banbury area of Oxfordshire.

Types of grants: (i) Grants to promote the study of literature, the arts and sciences. (ii) Help towards the cost of further education and training.

Annual grant total: In 2004 the charity had both an income and a total expenditure of £53,000. Grants totalled about £50,000.

Applications: In writing to the correspondent.

Correspondent: A Scott Andrews, Clerk, 36 West Bar, Banbury, Oxfordshire OX16 9RU (01295 251234)

Barford

The Shepherd & Bakehouse Charity

Eligibility: Young people under 25 who live or whose parents live in the parish of Barford St John and Barford St Michael and have done so for at least three years.

Types of grants: Help towards the cost of education, training, apprenticeship or equipment for those starting work. Grants range from £150 to £300.

Exclusions: Grants are not made for schoolchildren.

Annual grant total: In 2004/05 grants were made to eight individuals totalling £1,400.

Applications: Applications can be submitted directly by the individual by 30 September.

Correspondent: Mrs B Greenwood, 7 Robins Close, Barford St Michael, Banbury, Oxfordshire OX15 0RP (01869 338677)

Bletchington

The Bletchington Charity

Eligibility: People in need who live in the parish of Bletchington.

Types of grants: Grants to students and apprentices to help with the purchase of books, instruments or tools necessary for their course.

Annual grant total: In 2004, the charity had an income of £7,900 and a total expenditure of £7,100.

Applications: Applications can be made in writing to the correspondent by the individual.

Correspondent: John Smith, Quarry Bank House, Gibraltar Hill, Enslow, Oxon OX5 3AZ

Other information: The charity also seeks to support any medical and social needs that will benefit the village community as a whole.

Charlbury

The Charlbury Exhibition Foundation

Eligibility: Students in higher/further education who live in the ancient township of Charlbury.

Types of grants: Recurrent grants of about £100 per applicant per annum (depending on income), paid in the first and then subsequent years to students on three-year courses to be spent on books, equipment and so on.

Exclusions: No grants to schoolchildren.

Annual grant total: In 2003/04 the foundation had an income of £7,900 and a total expenditure of £5,200. The grant total varies from year to year and is for educational purposes only.

Applications: In writing to the correspondent by 1st October to be considered annually.

Correspondent: Mrs Kate Gerrish, Secretary, 62 Ticknell Piece Road, Charlbury, Oxford OX7 3TW (01608 811899)

Eynsham

Bartholomew Educational Foundation

Eligibility: People under 25 who live in the parish of Eynsham and are in need.

Types of grants: The foundation makes one-off grants to schoolchildren, people starting work, further and higher education students and postgraduates for general education needs. Donations are usually in the range of £50 and £200 and include those for uniforms/other school clothing, books, equipment/instruments, fees, maintenance/living expenses, educational outings in the UK, study or travel abroad and so on.

Annual grant total: In 2004 the trust had both an income and a total expenditure of £2,400. Educational grants were made to 10 individuals totalling £870.

Applications: In writing to the correspondent, to be submitted directly by the individual or through the individual's school, college or educational welfare agency. Applications should include costings, particulars of need and date of birth. Applications are considered in February, May, September and November and should be received in the month preceding each meeting.

Correspondent: R N Mitchell, Clerk, 20 High Street, Eynsham, Witney, Oxfordshire OX29 4HB (website: www.eynsham.org)

Oxford

The Thomas Dawson Educational Foundation

Eligibility: Children and young people in need who have lived in the city of Oxford (postcodes OX1 to OX4) for three years.

Types of grants: Help with the cost of books, clothing, fees and other essentials for schoolchildren and for people at college or university. Grants also for people preparing for entering or engaging in a profession, trade, occupation or service. Grants generally range from £40 to £1,500, although most grants are under £500.

No grants are given for medical

sponsorships or electives, or towards accommodation, travel or living expenses.

Annual grant total: In 2004, the charity had net assets of £7.7 million. For the same year the charity's income was £342,000 with an expenditure of about £321,000. The charity made grants to individuals totalling £5,100 and grants to institutions of £18,100.

Applications: In writing to the correspondent, with evidence regarding course fees. Please note: applicants can only apply for one degree course.

Correspondent: Mrs K K Lacey, Clerk, 56 Poplar Close, Garsington, Oxford, OX44 9BP (01865 368259)

The City of Oxford Charities

Eligibility: Students under 25 who have lived in the city of Oxford for at least five years.

Types of grants: One-off grants are given to: schoolchildren for uniforms, fees, books, equipment and school trips; students for books and equipment/instruments; undergraduates for books and equipment/instruments; and mature students under 25 for fees, books and equipment/instruments. Grants are also made for childcare.

Annual grant total: In 2004 the charity made 24 educational grants to individuals totalling £3,600.

Applications: Application forms are available from the correspondent, to be submitted either directly by the individual, or through the individual's school, college or educational welfare agency. Applications are considered quarterly.

Correspondent: David Wright, 11 Davenant Road, Oxford OX2 8BT (01865 553043; Fax: 01865 553043; e-mail: david@oxfordcitycharities.fsnet.co.uk; website: www.oxfordcitycharities.org)

Other information: Grants are also made to organisations.

The Saint Mary Magdalen Apprenticing & Educational Foundation

Eligibility: People under the age of 24 who live in the city of Oxford.

Types of grants: (i) Grants for school pupils to help with books, clothing, educational outings, maintenance, school fees or travel.

(ii) Grants to help students in further or higher education with books and fees/living expenses.

(iii) Help towards the cost of equipment/instruments, books, clothing and travel for those starting work.

Grants range from £50 to £750.

Annual grant total: About £3,700.

Applications: In writing to the correspondent either directly by the individual or by their parent or guardian if they are under 16; no telephone calls or other approaches will be taken. Applications are usually considered in March and October and must include details of the applicant's age, financial circumstances and educational history to date.

Correspondent: Dr W B Stewart, Clerk, SMM Charities, Exeter College, Oxford OX1 3DP

Rotherfield Greys

The Rotherfield Greys Educational Charity

Eligibility: People aged between 5 and 25 who live in the ecclesiastical parish of St Nicholas, Rotherfield Greys.

Types of grants: One-off grants are available to schoolchildren and further and higher education students to cover the cost of books, equipment/instruments, fees, educational outings in the UK, and study and travel abroad. There is a preference for Church of England-oriented education. Grants are given in the range of £100 to £250.

Annual grant total: In 2004 the trust had an income of £1,000 and a total expenditure of £600.

Applications: On a form available from the correspondent for consideration in March and September. Applications must include proof of residential qualification.

Correspondent: R Ovey, Hernes, Henley-on-Thames, Oxfordshire RG9 4NT (01491 574646; Fax: 01491 574645)

Wallingford

The Wallingford Municipal & Relief-in-Need Charities

Eligibility: Schoolchildren who live in the former borough of Wallingford.

Types of grants: Help with the cost of books, clothing and other essentials. The trust gives one-off grants only.

Annual grant total: In 2004/05 the charity had an income of £5,900 and a total expenditure of £5,200. Grants totalled about £5,000.

Applications: On a form available from the correspondent, submitted either directly by the individual or through a local organisation. Trustees meet about every three months, although emergency cases can be considered. Urgent cases may require a visit by a trustee.

Correspondent: A Rogers, Town Clerk, 9 St Martin's Street, Wallingford, Oxfordshire OX10 0AL

Wheatley

The Wheatley Charities

Eligibility: People who are under 25 and live in the parish of Wheatley.

Types of grants: Grants are given to help young people prepare for any trade or occupation or to promote their education.

Annual grant total: In 2004 the charities had both an income of about £2,200 and a total expenditure of £1,400. Grants totalled about £1,000.

Applications: In writing to the correspondent.

Correspondent: R F Minty, 24 Old London Road, Wheatley, Oxford, OX33 1YW (01865 874676)

Other information: This charity is an amalgamation of The Dame Eliza Curzon and The Joseph Sims Charities.

Wootton

The Parrott & Lee Educational Foundation

Eligibility: People under the age of 25 who attended Wootton-by-Woodstock Primary School and/or live in Wootton-by-Woodstock.

Types of grants: Annual grants of about £200, in particular towards course fees, maintenance, travel, outfits, books and equipment to people in tertiary education.

Annual grant total: In 2005 a total of £1,200 was given in grants to six individuals.

Applications: On a form available from the correspondent, which should be submitted directly by the individual. They are considered half yearly, normally in March and September.

Correspondent: Charles Ponsonby, Woodleys House, Woodstock, Oxford OX20 1HJ (01993 811717; Fax: 01993 812966; e-mail: ponsonby@ woodleyswoodstock.freeserve.co.uk)

Other information: In 2005 the sum of £205,000 was given to Wootton-by-Woodstock Primary School, which is the foundation's principal beneficiary.

Suffolk

The Calthorpe & Edwards Educational Foundation

Eligibility: People between the ages of 18 and 25 who live in the parishes of Ampton, Great Livermere, Little Livermere, Ingham and Timworth, Troston, Ixworth, Culford, Great Barton, West Stow, Wordwell, Fornham St Genevieve and Fornham St Martin.

Types of grants: Grants for university students to help with the cost of books and study or travel overseas.

Exclusions: No grants for schoolchildren, A-level students, people starting work or mature students.

Annual grant total: In 2003/04, the foundation had an income of £7,900 and a total expenditure of £520.

Applications: Applications can be submitted directly by the individual. They are usually considered in October.

Correspondent: Miss D Potter, Clerk, 5 Oakeyfield Road, Thurston, Bury St Edmunds, Suffolk IP31 3RX (01359 230054)

The Fauconberge Educational Foundation

Eligibility: Children and young people between the ages of 11 and 19 who live within a five-mile radius of Beccles Town Hall, and who are 'engaged in a course of study intended to prepare them for higher or further education or for an advanced qualification'.

Types of grants: Grants for schoolchildren and further education and vocational students to help with school fees, books, equipment, educational outings in the UK and study or travel abroad. Schoolchildren can also receive help for uniform and clothing. The grants are given as one-off payments and range from £50 to £500.

Exclusions: University students are not eligible.

Annual grant total: In 2004/05 the trust had assets of £37,000, an income of £1,800 and a total expenditure of £1,200. Grants were made to two individuals totalling £1,000.

Applications: Vacancies are advertised in local papers and area noticeboards, and application forms are available from the correspondent. Applications are considered at any time. They can be submitted directly by the parent/guardian or through a teacher and should include the family's financial position and number of children.

Correspondent: D A Simpson, Clerk, 8 The Spinney, Beccles, Suffolk NR34 7DF

Other information: The trust also makes occasional grants to local secondary schools.

The Gippeswyk Educational Trust

Eligibility: People under 21 who live in Ipswich and the surrounding area.

Types of grants: One-off grants are made. Schoolchildren can receive grants towards the cost of school uniforms, other school clothing, books, educational outings, maintenance costs and school fees. Students in further or higher education can be given grants towards books, fees/living expenses and study or travel abroad. Preference can be given to schoolchildren with serious family difficulties.

Annual grant total: Up to about £11,000 a year.

Applications: On a form available from the correspondent, submitted through the individual's school, college or educational welfare agency. Applications are considered throughout the year.

Correspondent: Mrs S Maskell, Clerk, St Mildred's Chambers, 6 Cornhill, Ipswich, Suffolk IP1 1DE

The Mills Educational Foundation

Eligibility: Children and young people up to the age of 24 who live in Framlingham and the surrounding district, or attend a school there.

Types of grants: One-off grants ranging from £50 to £550. Schoolchildren and further/higher education students can be supported for uniforms, other school clothing, books, equipment, instruments, educational outings in the UK and study or travel abroad. People starting work can receive grants for uniforms, other clothing, equipment and instruments.

Annual grant total: In 2004/05 the trust had an income of £5,900 and a total expenditure of £4,000. Grants to individuals totalled around £1,500.

Applications: In writing to the correspondent, either directly by the individual or through a third party such as a social worker or the individual's school/college/educational welfare agency. Applications are considered every two months, unless it is an emergency situation.

Correspondent: Neil J Ackerman, 10a Market Hill, Framlingham, Suffolk IP13 9AN (01728 621621; Fax: 01728 621621; e-mail: office@ ackermans.co.uk)

The Stowmarket Educational Foundation

Eligibility: People in need who are under 25 and live or attend a school or other educational establishment, or whose parents live, in the town of Stowmarket and the civil parishes of Badley, Combs, Greeting St Peter, Great Finborough, Haughley, Old Newton with Dagworth, Onehouse and Stowupland, all in the county of Suffolk.

Types of grants: One-off grants of £50 to £200 towards uniforms, clothing and educational outings for schoolchildren. Students, including mature students, in further/higher education can receive assistance with books, equipment and instruments.

Annual grant total: In 2004/05 the foundation had assets of £10,800, an income of £2,000 and a total expenditure of £1,700, all of which was given in two educational grants to individuals.

Applications: On a form available from the correspondent, for consideration throughout the year. Applications should be submitted by a school or college, a social worker or other professional.

Correspondent: C Hawkins, Clerk to the Trustees, Kiln House, 21 The Brickfields, Stowmarket, Suffolk IP14 1RZ (01449 674412; Fax: 01449 677595)

Annie Tranmer Charitable Trust

Eligibility: Young people in education who live in within a 15 mile radius of Woodbridge in Suffolk.

Types of grants: One-off and recurrent grants according to need, towards for example, educational outings, fees, equipment/instruments and travel overseas. Grants range from £70 to a few hundred pounds.

Annual grant total: In 2004/05 the trust had assets of £3.2 million and an income of £113,000. Grants totalled £99,000, of which £13,000 went to 25 individuals and the remainder to organisations.

Applications: In writing to the correspondent, including details of the specific need, finances and alternative funding sources.

Correspondent: Mrs M R Kirby, Clerk to the Trustees, 51 Bennett Road, Ipswich, Suffolk IP1 5HX

Brockley

The Brockley Town & Poor Estate (Brockley Charities)

Eligibility: Schoolchildren who live in Brockley village.

Types of grants: Grants of about £25 are given for the purchase of uniforms for students going up to middle and upper schools. An educational book is also given to all students in the village on reaching the age of 15.

Annual grant total: In 2005 the trust had an income of £1,800, the sum of £1,100 was distributed in 17 relief-in-need grants. A further £95 was distributed in four educational grants.

Applications: In writing to the correspondent to be submitted directly by the individual or a family member. Applications should be submitted by 1 February, for books and 1 June, for uniforms.

Correspondent: Mrs M A Morley, Fundin, Chapel Lane, Brockley, Bury St Edmunds, Suffolk IP29 4AS (01284 830543)

Bury St Edmunds

Old School Fund

Eligibility: Persons under 25 who live in, or whose parents live in, Bury St Edmunds and are undertaking further or higher education in any subject and are in need.

Types of grants: One-off and recurrent grants (for example for the duration of a university degree course) of between £100 and £250 towards the cost of books, fees and living expenses.

Exclusions: Grants are not made for benefits which are normally provided by the local education authority.

Annual grant total: In 2004 the fund had an income of £4,900 and a total expenditure of £5,000. Grants totalled about £4,000.

Applications: An introductory letter and reference to the correspondent is preferred, requesting an application form. Deadlines for applications are subject to dates of trustee meetings.

Correspondent: M C Dunn, 121 Southgate Street, Bury St Edmunds, Suffolk IP33 2AZ (01284 769483)

Dennington

The Dennington Consolidated Charities

Eligibility: Grants are awarded to those embarking on tertiary education and vocational training living in the village of Dennington.

Types of grants: One-off and recurrent grants.

Exclusions: The trust does not make loans, nor does it make grants where public funds are available unless they are considered inadequate.

Annual grant total: About £500 is given each year for educational purposes and £3,000 for welfare.

Applications: In writing to the correspondent. Applications are considered throughout the year and a simple means test questionnaire must be completed by the applicant.

Grants are only made to people resident in Dennington (a small village with 500 inhabitants). The charities do not respond to applications made outside this specific geographical area.

Correspondent: W T F Blakeley, Clerk, Thorn House, Saxtead Road, Dennington, Woodbridge, Suffolk IP13 8AP

Dunwich

Dunwich Pension Charity

Eligibility: People in need who live in the parish of Dunwich.

Types of grants: One-off grants are usually of around £250 towards the costs of higher education.

Annual grant total: In 2004 it had assets of £480,000 and an income of £34,000. Grants to individuals for welfare totalled £3,900 and grants to individuals for education totalled £3,700.

Applications: In writing to the correspondent, including reasonable proof of need, hardship or distress. Applications can be made directly by the individual or family member and are considered every two months.

Correspondent: John W Saunders, The Old Smithy, Dursham Road, Westleton, Saxmundham, Suffolk IP17 3AX (01728 648259)

Earl Stonham

Earl Stonham Trust

Eligibility: People in need who live in the parish of Earl Stonham.

Types of grants: One-off grants up to a maximum of £200.

Annual grant total: In 2004/05 the trust had an income of £4,000 and a total expenditure of £3,300. Educational grants to individuals totalled £670, with a further £730 being given for relief-in-need purposes.

Applications: In writing to the correspondent, to be submitted directly by the individual.

Correspondent: S R M Wilson, College Farm, Forward Green, Stowmarket, Suffolk IP14 5EH

Gislingham

The Gislingham United Charity

Eligibility: Children up to the age of 18 who live in Gislingham. Preference is given to schoolchildren.

Types of grants: Grants are given to schoolchildren for excursions and to college and mature students for books.

Exclusions: No regular payments are made.

Annual grant total: In 2005 the charity had assets of £416,000 and an income of £13,000. A total of £480 was given in five educational grants and £1,100 in 12 welfare grants.

Applications: Applications can be submitted directly by the individual or verbally via a trustee. They are considered on the third Friday of alternate months; January, March, May, July, September and November. Applications must include reasons for the application, the amount requested and the applicant's address.

Correspondent: R Moyes, 37 Broadfields Road, Gislingham, Eye, Suffolk IP23 8HX (01379 788105; Fax: 01379 788105; e-mail: rmoye@onetel.net.uk)

Other information: The charity also gives grants to individuals in need and supports village organisations and ecclesiastical causes.

Hadleigh

Ann Beaumont's Educational Foundation

Eligibility: People aged up to 25 years and in need, who live in the parish of Hadleigh.

Types of grants: Grants to help with course books, equipment or travel for people at school, college, university or for those starting work.

Annual grant total: In 2003/04 the foundation had an income of £19,000 and gave grants to individuals and organisations totalling £13,500.

Applications: In writing to the correspondent, together with evidence of the cost of the books or equipment required. Applications are considered four times a year.

Correspondent: Mrs S Self, 104B High Street, Hadleigh, Suffolk IP7 5EL (01473 822718)

Halesworth

The Halesworth United Charities

Eligibility: People in need who live in the ancient parish of Halesworth.

Types of grants: One-off grants according to need. Recent examples include travel abroad for educational purposes, medical equipment or tools needed for a trade.

Annual grant total: About £1,500.

Applications: In writing to the correspondent, directly by the individual or through a social worker, Citizens Advice or other welfare agency. Applications can be submitted at any time for consideration in January, July and December, or any other time if urgent.

Correspondent: Janet Staveley-Dick, Clerk, Hill Farm, Primes Lane, Blyford, Halesworth, Suffolk, IP19 9JT

Hundon

The Hundon Educational Foundation

Eligibility: People under 25 living in the parish of Hundon.

Types of grants: Grants are given to schoolchildren and further and higher education students including those for uniforms, books, equipment/instruments, fees, maintenance/living expenses, educational outings in the UK and study or travel abroad.

Grants are given to people starting work for books and equipment/instruments.

Donations are in the range of £50 to £500.

Annual grant total: In 2005, the foundation had an income of about £6,000 and a total expenditure of £7,500. Grants totalled about £5,000.

Applications: On an application form available from the correspondent, either directly by the individual or by their parent/guardian. Applications are considered in March, July and November and should be received in the preceding month.

The foundation is well advertised in the village. It does not respond to applications made outside of its area of interest.

Correspondent: Bernard Beer, Beauford Lodge, Mill Road, Hundon, Suffolk CO10 8EG (01440 786942)

Lakenheath

The Charities of George Goward & John Evans

Eligibility: People under 25 in the parish of Lakenheath in Suffolk.

Types of grants: Grants in the range of £25 and £300, for school leavers and students in further and higher education to help with living expenses and books. Schoolchildren can receive grants towards uniforms, clothing and educational outings. Grants are also given to people starting work for books and equipment.

Annual grant total: In 2005 the charities had an income and total expenditure of £14,000. Educational grants to 28 individuals totalled £7,600. A further six relief-in-need grants totalling £1,500 were made.

Applications: In writing to the correspondent. Applications can be submitted either directly by the individual or a family member, through a third party such as a social worker or teacher, or through an organisation such as Citizens Advice. They should be received by February and August for considered in March and September respectively. Applications should include a brief financial situation and receipts are required for book grants.

Correspondent: Mrs Mary Crane, 3 Roughlands, Lakenheath, Brandon, Suffolk IP27 9HA (01842 860445)

Other information: Grants are also made to organisations (£3,200 in 2005).

Lowestoft

The Lowestoft Church and Town Educational Foundation

Eligibility: People in need aged between 5 and 25 who have either lived or attended school in the area of the old borough of Lowestoft for at least three years.

Types of grants: One-off grants of £150 each are given to: schoolchildren towards the cost of uniforms/other school clothing, childcare, educational outings in the UK, and study and travel abroad; and students in further/higher education towards the cost of books, equipment/instruments, maintenance/living expenses and study or travel abroad.

Annual grant total: In 2004/05 the foundation had both an income and a total expenditure of £13,000. Grants were made to 70 individuals totalling around £11,000.

Applications: Applications, on a form available from the correspondent, should be submitted directly by the individual. Forms need to be verified by the applicant's place of education; the closing date is 30 November. Grants are paid in the following January.

Correspondent: J M Loftus, Clerk, 148 London Road North, Lowestoft, Suffolk NR32 1HF (01502 718700)

Other information: Grants are also made to local schools.

Mendlesham

The Mendlesham Education Foundation

Eligibility: People under 25 who live in the parish of Mendlesham.

Types of grants: One-off and recurrent grants of £50 to £260 are given towards pre-school fees for children with serious family difficulties, and books and equipment for students in higher education or apprenticeships. Also annual grant support is given to Mendlesham youth organisations and Mendlesham CP School.

Exclusions: Grants are not given for school fees or maintenance. They are not normally available towards the cost of school educational outings or for special education needs.

Annual grant total: In 2005 the trust had an income of £32,000 and a total expenditure of £29,000. Grants were made

to 64 individuals totalling £15,000. Grants were also made to organisations and Mendlesham CP School totalling £10,000.

Applications: On a form available from the correspondent, including details of education to date, details of course to be taken, other grants applied for, estimated expenditure, parents' financial position and other dependent children in the family. Applications can be made by the individual or through a parent/guardian at any time.

Correspondent: Mrs P Colchester, Clerk to the Trustees, Ashes Farm, Mendlesham Green, Stowmarket, Suffolk IP14 5TE (01449 766330; Fax: 01449 766330)

Pakenham

The Pakenham Educational Trust

Eligibility: Students on further or higher education courses who are in need and who live in Pakenham.

Types of grants: Grants are given to people attending university and college courses for a variety of educational needs. Mature students may receive help towards fees. Grants are also given towards activities such as Duke of Edinburgh Award Scheme, cathedral camps, sports scholarships etc. Grants can be one-off or recurrent and range from £50 to £300.

Annual grant total: In 2005, the trust had an income of £3,300 and a total expenditure of £3,000. No information was available concerning grant total.

Applications: Applications should be sent directly by the individual to the correspondent by 31 October. They are considered in November.

Correspondent: Maggie Cohen, Clerk, 5 St Mary's View, Pakenham, Nr Bury St Edmunds, Suffolk IP31 2ND (01359 232965)

Other information: Grants are also given to local organisations.

Risby

The Risby Fuel Allotment

Eligibility: People in need who live in the parish of Risby.

Types of grants: Grants are given to higher education students.

Annual grant total: Around £9,000 is given to individuals, primarily for relief-in-need purposes.

Applications: In writing to the correspondent. Applications can be submitted by the individual and are considered in March and October. Applications made outside the specific area of interest (the parish of Risby) are not acknowledged.

Correspondent: Mrs P Wallis, 3 Woodland Close, Risby, Bury St Edmunds, Suffolk IP28 6QN (01284 810649)

Stutton

The Charity of Joseph Catt

Eligibility: People in need who live in the parish of Stutton only.

Types of grants: One-off grants and loans according to need.

Annual grant total: In 2005 the charity had an income of £9,800 and a total expenditure of £8,100. Grants totalled about £8,000.

Applications: Applications can be submitted by the individual, or through a recognised referral agency (e.g. social worker, Citizens Advice or doctor) and are considered monthly. They can be submitted to the correspondent, or any of the trustees at any time, for consideration in May and November.

Correspondent: K R Bales, 34 Cattsfield, Stutton, Ipswich, Suffolk IP9 2SP

Other information: The charity also supports local almshouses.

Walberswick

The Walberswick Common Lands

Eligibility: People in need who live in Walberswick village.

Types of grants: Grants are given in the range of £35 and £1,200 to schoolchildren for maintenance/living expenses and to college students for study/travel abroad and maintenance/living expenses.

Annual grant total: In 2004 the charity had an income of £56,000 and a total expenditure of £48,000. There were seven educational grants made totalling £5,400 with £4,500 distributed in 60 relief-in-need grants.

Applications: In writing to the correspondent, either through the individual's school/college/educational welfare agency, or directly by the individual or through a parent or relative. Applications are considered in February, April, June, August, October and December.

Correspondent: Mrs Jayne Tibbles, Lima Cottage, Walberswick, Southwold, Suffolk IP18 6TN (01502 724448; Fax: 01502 722469)

Other information: Grants are also made to individuals for relief-in-need purposes and to organisations (£24,000 in 2004).

Surrey

The Archbishop Abbot's Exhibition Foundation

Eligibility: People aged between 11 and 24 inclusive who (i) live in the area administered by the Guildford Borough Council or the Waverley Borough Council (except that part of Waverley formerly within the urban district of Farnham), or (ii) attend, are about to attend or have for at least three years attended a school in the borough of Guildford as constituted on 1 April 1974. Preference is given to male applicants.

Preference is given to low-income families, to schoolchildren with serious family difficulties so that the child has to be educated away from home and to people with special educational needs.

Types of grants: One-off grants are given to: schoolchildren towards books, equipment, instruments and fees; and people starting work or at any level of further or higher education towards equipment, instruments, books, fees and living expenses. Students in further or higher education can also be supported in their study or travel abroad. Grants are given to assist students in their future careers.

Grants range from £250 to £800 and are one-off.

Annual grant total: In 2005 the foundation had an income of £4,600 and an expenditure of £5,900. Grants were made to 14 individuals totalling £5,000.

Applications: On a form available from the correspondent which requests details of information about parents'/guardians' income and expenditure and details of any savings. Applications can be submitted directly by the individual, through the individual's school, college or educational agency or through a relative or friend. Applications are considered in January, May and September and should be received in the preceding month.

Correspondent: Colin E Fullagar, 7 Southway, Guildford, Surrey GU2 8DA (01483 533184)

The Dyslexia Institute

Eligibility: In practice, school-aged children who have dyslexia, live in England and Wales and are from families on a low income. Applicants from families where joint annual income is in excess of £22,000 will not be considered without evidence of exceptional circumstances.

Types of grants: Grants are made for assessments and for specific periods of tuition based on educational needs related to dyslexia. Grants for assessments are for about £300 each; grants for one term's tuition are for about £500, totalling about £3,000 for six terms' tuition. A contribution from the individual's family is required at a minimum of £25 for an assessment and £5 a week for tuition.

The majority of bursary-funded pupils attend the nationwide centres of Dyslexia Action for 1.5 or 2 hours multi-sensory tuition each week during the academic year.

Annual grant total: During the 18 month period to August 2005 grants were made to individuals totalling £191,000. These were in the form of tuition fees (£183,000) and assessment fees (£7,000).

Applications: In writing via the Dyslexia Action Centre (network of centres throughout England and Wales), at which the applicant wishes to have assessment/tuition. Applications are considered by the Bursary Allocations Committee three times a year (one meeting each academic term). Grants are awarded on the basis of educational need. Applicants for grants for assessments should indicate difficulties experienced and family income; applicants for tuition grants should indicate family income and severity of dyslexia – a full educational psychologist's assessment is required.

Please note that whilst a bursary is awarded to an individual, the payment of fees for assessment or tuition is made directly to the consulting psychologist or Dyslexia Action.

Correspondent: The Administration Manager, Park House, Wick Road, Egham, Surrey TW20 0HH (01784 222335; Fax: 01784 222333; e-mail: info@ dyslexiaaction.org.uk; website: www. dyslexiaaction.org.uk)

The Egham Education Trust

Eligibility: People under 25 who have lived in the electoral wards of Egham, which is now Egham, Engerfield Green, Virginia Water and Hythe, for at least five years.

Types of grants: One-off and recurrent grants in the range of £100 and £500 are made to schoolchildren, undergraduates, vocational students, mature students and people with special educational needs. Grants may also be given for activities such as the Duke of Edinburgh Award Scheme.

Annual grant total: Between £6,000 and £7,000 each year in about 70 educational grants.

Applications: On a form available from the correspondent. Applications must include details of other grants and loans. The deadline for applications is the 15th of each month.

Correspondent: Max Walker, 33 Runnemede Road, Egham, TW2 9BE (01784 472742)

The Pilgrim Band Trust

Eligibility: Young musicians who are in need in Reigate and the surrounding area.

Types of grants: Grants are given towards tuition fees.

Annual grant total: In 2004/05, the trust had net assets of £1.8 million, an income of £86,000 and a total expenditure of £69,000. It gave scholarships to individuals totalling £6,700.

Applications: In writing to the correspondent.

Correspondent: Keith Donachie, Trustee, 8 Ridgeway Road, Redhill, Surrey RH1 6PH (01737 763865)

The Mary Stephens Foundation

Eligibility: People under the age of 25 who live in the ancient parish of Chipstead and Hooley, or who have attended Chipstead County First School.

Types of grants: One-off and recurrent grants up to a maximum of £1,200 a year. Help to people in further education is in the form of books, uniforms and travel expenses. Limited help is given towards fees on a scholarship basis.

Grants are given to those qualifying to obtain further education in the broadest possible way, such as for music lessons and field courses.

Exclusions: The trust does not issue grants to pre-school children or provide loans.

Annual grant total: In 2004/05, the foundation had an income of £22,000 and a total expenditure of £11,200. Grants totalled about £10,000.

Applications: Applications are considered at quarterly meetings and should be made directly by the individual, or by the individual's head of school or church leader.

Correspondent: Mr Simon Kolesar Frics, Hon. Secretary, Herons Croft, How Lane, Chipstead, Coulsdon, Surrey, CR5 3LT (01737 552869)

Witley Charitable Trust

Eligibility: Children and young people aged under 20 who are in need and who live in the parishes of Witley and Milford.

Types of grants: One-off grants ranging from £25 to £300.

Exclusions: The trust does not give loans or for items which should be provided by statutory services.

Annual grant total: In 2005 the trust had an income of £3,900 and an expenditure of £3,800. Grants totalled about £2,500.

Applications: In writing to the correspondent, to be submitted through social workers, schools, Citizens Advice and so on but not directly by the individual. Applications are usually considered in early February and September, although emergency applications can be considered throughout the year.

Correspondent: Daphne O'Hanlon, Triados, Waggoners Way, Grayshott,

Hindhead, Surrey GU26 6DX
(01428 604679)

Charlwood

John Bristow and Thomas Mason Trust

Eligibility: Only people who live in the ancient parish of Charlwood (as constituted on 17 February 1926). Applicants not living in the area of benefit at the time of application cannot be considered.

Types of grants: Grants are given to schoolchildren, college students, undergraduates, vocational students, mature students, people with special educational needs and to people starting work. Help is given for the cost of uniforms/other school clothing, books, equipment/instruments, fees, maintenance/living expenses, childcare, education outings in the UK, study or travel abroad and student exchanges.

Annual grant total: In 2005 the trust had assets of £2.3 million and an income of £86,000. There were five relief-in-need grants made totalling £2,500. The sum of £400 was given in a single educational grant. A further £165,000 was given to organisations.

Applications: On a form available from the correspondent. Applications can be submitted directly by the individual or through a third party. They are considered five times per year.

Correspondent: Mrs P J Assender, Trust Secretary, 54 Churchfield Road, Reigate, Surrey RH2 9RH (01737 226008; Fax: 01737 226008)

Other information: This trust is an amalgamation of the Thomas Alexander Mason Trust and Revd John Bristow's Charity.

Chertsey

The Chertsey Combined Charity

Eligibility: People in need who live in the electoral divisions of the former urban district of Chertsey.

Types of grants: Grants are often given to help towards the cost of books, clothing and other essentials for those at school. Grants may also be given to people at college or university.

Annual grant total: In 2004/05 the trust had an income of £46,000 and a total expenditure of £25,000. Grants to individuals for education and welfare purposes totalled £4,700. A further £3,900 was given to organisations.

Applications: On a form available from the correspondent.

Correspondent: M R O Sullivan, Secretary, PO Box 89, Weybridge, Surrey KT13 8HW

Chessington

The Chessington Charities

Eligibility: People in need who live in the parish of St Mary the Virgin, Chessington. Applicants must have lived in the parish for at least one year.

Types of grants: Recent grants included those for grants for school uniforms, shoes and school trips. Grants are given in the range of £30 to £250 and are usually one-off.

Exclusions: Grants are not given to pay debts. Applicants must live in the Parish of St Mary the Virgin, this excludes those that live in the rest of the Chessington postal area.

Annual grant total: In 2005 the charities had an income of £3,800 and a total expenditure of £3,300. Grants totalled about £1,500.

Applications: On a form available from the correspondent to be submitted either directly by the individual or through a social worker, Citizens Advice or other agency. Christmas gifts are distributed in November. Other applications are considered throughout the year. A home visit will be made by a trustee to ascertain details of income and expenditure and to look at the need.

Correspondent: Mrs A M Hollis, 26 Bolton Road, Chessington, Surrey KT9 2JB

Other information: Grants are also given to local organisations which help people who are elderly or disabled such as Chessington Voluntary Care and Arthritis Care. Individual welfare grants are also available.

East Horsley

Henry Smith's Charity (East Horsley)

Eligibility: Children from poor or disadvantaged backgrounds who have lived in East Horsley for at least two years.

Types of grants: Grants can be given to children to support them through their schooling and to orphaned children for small scholarships.

Annual grant total: Each year the trust receives about £1,000, allocated by Henry Smith's (General Estate) Charity which is divided according to need between welfare and educational grants.

Applications: In writing to the correspondent through a third party such as a social worker, teacher or vicar. Applications are considered in December.

Correspondent: Mr R Deighton, East Horsley Parish Council Office, Kingston

Avenue, East Horsley, Surrey KT24 6QT
(01483 281148)

Elmbridge

The R C Sherrif Rosebriars Trust

Eligibility: Composers, craftspeople, curators, designers, directors, film-makers, musicians, performers, producers, promoters, theatre technicians, visual artists, writers and other individual arts practitioners in Elmbridge.

Types of grants: Grants and bursaries to assist with:

- Professional development and training (including travel grants) e.g. short courses in specific skills, work placements with other artists, specified periods of travel and/or study
- Research and development for arts projects
- The publication or production of a specific piece of work
- Capital items e.g. equipment.

Exclusions:

- Arts activities or events taking place outside Elmbridge (except in the case of attendance at training courses/development opportunities for individuals)
- Activities that are not arts-related
- Fundraising events, e.g. special performances in aid of a local charity
- Activities that provide no potential benefit to the public
- Activities that have already taken place; goods or services that have been bought or ordered before receiving an offer letter
- Commercial ventures that could recoup their costs from their profits (other than underwriting grants for performances)
- Costs that are already covered by other funding
- Core costs i.e. ongoing overheads such as salaries, insurance, and maintenance budgets for equipment or buildings
- Higher education courses, long-term vocational training e.g. Drama School, or ongoing training programmes (e.g. piano lessons, regular dance classes).

Annual grant total: In 2004 the trust had assets of £3.2 million and an income of £175,000. Grants for the year totalled £23,000, with around £10,000 awarded to individuals and about £13,000 awarded to local organisations. It also gave £36,000 towards various arts initiatives.

Applications: On a form available from the correspondent or the trust's website. The trustees meet at least five times a year to consider applications.

Correspondent: Mrs S M Thompson, The Administrator, Case House, 85-89 High Street, Walton on Thames, Surrey

KT12 1DZ (01932 235990; e-mail: arts@ rcsherrifftrust.org.uk; website: www. rcsherrifftrust.org.uk)

Other information: Grants are also made to organisations.

Epsom

The Epsom Advancement in Life Charities

Eligibility: People under 25 who live in the ancient parish of Epsom.

Types of grants: One-off and recurrent grants according to need are given to: schoolchildren, college students, undergraduates, vocational students, mature students, people starting work and people with special educational needs, including those towards clothing/ uniforms, fees, books, equipment/ instruments maintenance/living expenses and excursions.

Annual grant total: Previously £600 a year. Between two and three grants are made a year.

Applications: On a form available from the correspondent, to be submitted directly by the individual. Applications are considered in March, June, September and December and should be submitted in the preceding month.

Correspondent: Mrs T Vanstone-Walker, Clerk to the Trustees, 'Farm View Suite', 42 Canons Lane, Burgh Heath, Tadworth, Surrey, KT20 6DP (01737 361243)

Gatton

The Henry Smith Charity (Gatton)

Eligibility: People in need who live in the parish of Gatton.

Types of grants: Grants are available for uniforms and school clothing for schoolchildren, tools of the trade for apprentices and money towards books for students in further/higher education.

Exclusions: Grants are not given for rates or taxes.

Annual grant total: The trust receives £2,300 income, allocated by Henry Smith's (Worth Estate) Charity. However, the charity receives more money than it can give in grants and always has much more money available.

Applications: In writing to the correspondent either directly or through a third party such as a doctor, minister of religion, councillor and so on. Applications are generally considered twice a year, but urgent applications can be considered within four weeks. The charity advertises before Christmas, whilst the trustees are well known within the community and know of people who are in need.

Correspondent: M S Blacker, Chair, 6a Orpin Road, Redhill, Merstham, Surrey RH1 3EZ

Leatherhead

The Leatherhead United Charities

Eligibility: People in need who live in the area of the former Leatherhead urban district council.

Types of grants: One-off grants in the range of £100 and £750. This charity does not deal with educational needs only, 'grants are made for the relief of need generally'.

Annual grant total: In 2004 the charity had assets of £3.7 million, an income of £227,000. Out of a total expenditure of £156,000, there were 33 grants made to individuals totalling almost £6,000.

Applications: On a form available from the correspondent to be submitted directly by the individual or a family member. Applications are considered throughout the year.

Correspondent: David Matanle, Homefield, Fortyfoot Road, Leatherhead, Surrey KT22 8RP (01372 370073)

Merstham and South Merstham

Henry Smith Charity (Merstham)

Eligibility: Students who live in the parish of Merstham and South Merstham.

Types of grants: One-off and recurrent grants typically of £50 each, including those for the purchase of books.

Annual grant total: In 2002/03 the charity had both an income and total expenditure of £3,450. Grants to individuals totalled around £3,000.

Applications: On a form available from the correspondent to be submitted directly by the individual. Applications are considered in December/January.

Correspondent: Mrs L Sanderson, 186 Radstock Way, Redhill RH1 3NS

Tadworth and Walton

Tadworth & Walton Overseas Aid Trust

Eligibility: Gap year students from Tadworth and Walton who are known to the trustees and are undertaking volunteer work in 'some of the poorest parts of the world' (developing countries).

Types of grants: One-off grants of around £100 to £200 for involvement in gap year projects where there is a clear benefit to the community which the gap year student is visiting.

Exclusions: No grants are made to gap year students applying for funding. Please see the applications section for clarity about this.

Annual grant total: In 2003/04 the trust had an income of £8,600 and a total expenditure of £10,600. Grants are mainly made to organisations although a couple of individuals are supported each year.

Applications: The trust stated that in practice it does not give grants to gap year students. As a network of development organisations in its local area it becomes aware from time to time of local people who are undertaking voluntary work overseas and makes a proactive decision to support them rather than reacting to people's requests for help. Therefore, applications to this trust will not be supported – if they want to support people they will do so from their own local knowledge.

Correspondent: Mike Fox, 49 Shelvers Way, Tadworth, Surrey KT20 5QJ (01737 350452; e-mail: mike.fox@iclway. co.uk; website: www.walkintadworth.com/ twoat/index.htm)

Tandridge

The Henry Smith Charity (Tandridge)

Eligibility: People in need who live in the parish of Tandridge.

Types of grants: One-off grants of about £100.

Annual grant total: About £3,000 a year.

Applications: In writing to the correspondent. Applications should be submitted in October either directly by the individual or through another third party if the individual is unable to apply. Applications should include the address and the amount of money needed; they are considered in November.

Correspondent: Mrs C Scott, Goulds Farm, Hare Lane, Lingfield, Surrey RH7 6JA (01342 832376)

Other information: The charity mainly makes relief-in-need grants to individuals and also makes grants to organisations providing education, health and social services to residents.

Thorpe

The Thorpe Parochial Charities

Eligibility: People in need under 21 years who live in the ancient parish of Thorpe.

Types of grants: Grants are occasionally given towards books for students in further or higher education. Relief-in-need grants are also available.

Annual grant total: In 2003/04 the trust had assets of £800,000, an income of £2,100 and made 37 grants totalling £1,900.

Applications: In writing to the correspondent by the end of October. Applications are usually considered in November. The grants are usually given out at Michaelmas.

Correspondent: Mrs D Jones, 9 Rosefield Gardens, Ottershaw, Chertsey, Surrey, KT16 0JH

Woking

The Deakin Charitable Trust

Eligibility: People studying music who are living in the immediate Woking area.

Types of grants: Bursaries are given to students of music.

Annual grant total: In 2003/04, the trust had assets of £681,000, an income of £57,000 and made grants totalling £50,000. Music and arts bursaries totalled £9,300.

Applications: In writing to the correspondent.

Correspondent: W A Hodgetts, Herbert Parnell, Kingsway House, 123–125 Goldsworth Road, Woking, Surrey GU21 1LR

West Sussex

The Hooper & Downer Educational Foundation

Eligibility: People under 25 who live, or whose parents live, in the area of benefit, which is the parishes of Amberley with Stoke, Ashington with Buncton, Ashurst, Bramber with St Botolphs, Greatham, Parham, Pulborough, Steyning, Storrington, Sullington, Thakeham with Warminghurst, Upper Beeding, Washington, West Chiltington, Wiggonholt and Wiston, all in West Sussex.

Types of grants: One-off grants according to the nature of assistance requested. Grants can be given towards books, tools, equipment, travel expenses, course fees and so on.

Annual grant total: In 2004 the trust had assets of £240,000, an income of £15,000 and a total expenditure of £21,000. Grants were made to 60 individuals totalling £8,700.

Applications: On a form available from the correspondent. An endorsement by a teacher or tutor is required if applicable, and also information on family circumstances.

Correspondent: Mrs V Stuart, Secretary to the Trustees, Rectory Office, Rectory Road, Storrington, West Sussex RH20 4EF (01903 742888)

Other information: Funds are also used to maintain and improve the Old School in Storrington, the trust's historic property, which is in use for educational and cultural purposes.

The Betty Martin Charity

Eligibility: People in need who live in West Sussex.

Types of grants: Grants are given to people, including mature students, in further/higher education towards the cost of books, fees, living expenses, study and travel overseas, travel and childcare. Grants range from £100 to £500.

Annual grant total: In 2004/05, the trust had an income of £12,000 and its total expenditure was £50,000.

Applications: An application form is available from the correspondent which is then submitted directly by the individual along with a reference.

Correspondent: Madeleine Crisp, 46 Guillards Oak, Midhurst, West Sussex GU29 9JZ (01730 813769; e-mail: madeleine.crisp@tesco.net)

The Bassil Shippam and Alsford Charitable Trust

Eligibility: Students in need who live in West Sussex.

Types of grants: One-off grants for projects undertaken voluntarily, such as gap year activities, for example, Operation Raleigh.

Exclusions: No grants for expenses related to academic courses.

Annual grant total: In 2004/05 it had assets of £3.6 million and an income of £156,000. Grants were made to 27 individuals totalling £7,400. A further £144,000 was given in grants to organisations.

Applications: In writing to the correspondent, for consideration at any time. Applications should indicate the nature and location of the project and should give as much notice as possible.

Correspondent: S A E MacFarlane, Trustee Administrator, Messrs Thomas Eggar, The Corn Exchange, Baffins Lane, Chichester, West Sussex PO19 1GE (01243 786111)

Angmering

William Older's School Charity

Eligibility: People aged 23 or under who live in the ecclesiastical parish of Angmering. The applicant's parents must reside in Angmering.

Types of grants: One-off and recurrent grants up to £500, towards the cost of equipment/instruments and fees for schoolchildren and towards books, equipment/instruments, childcare and educational outings in the UK for students in further or higher education.

Grants/loans are also given to local schools, pre-school playgroups and other educational foundations towards the rent of premises, provision of books, equipment etc.

Annual grant total: In 2004 the trust had assets of £365,000, an income of £14,800 and a total expenditure of £12,300. Grants were awarded to 26 individuals totalling £3,300. A further £8,700 was given to organisations.

Applications: In writing to the correspondent giving details of income and expenditure, course being studied and residence in Angmering. Applications are considered in January, May and October.

Correspondent: Mrs Andrea C Wood, Larks Rise, Rectory Lane, Angmering Village, West Sussex BN16 4JU (01903 771247)

9. LONDON

The Aldgate & Allhallows Barking Exhibition Foundation

Eligibility: Young people under the age of 25 who are permanent residents of Tower Hamlets or City of London (and have been for at least 3 years) and are from financially disadvantaged backgrounds.

Types of grants: On average between 10 and 20 grants are made each year ranging between £500 and £2,500. Most grants are made by way of undergraduate bursaries to students at Queen Mary, University of London. A small number of other grants are made to individuals studying at other colleges and universities.

Annual grant total: In 2004/05 the foundation had assets of £5.9 million, an income of £230,000 and a total expenditure of £297,000. Grants to 37 individuals totalled £41,000. A further £223,000 was distributed to organisations for educational purposes.

Applications: Initially in writing to the correspondent by the individual, through a third party such as a teacher or through an organisation such as a school or educational welfare authority detailing circumstances and purpose of grant. Those meeting the correct criteria are then sent an application form to complete and return. Applications are considered throughout the year.

Correspondent: 31 Jewry Street, London EC3N 2EY (020 7488 2518; Fax: 020 7488 2519; e-mail: contactus@sirjohncass.org)

Sir William Boreman's Foundation

Eligibility: Full or part-time students under the age of 25 who live either in the London boroughs of Greenwich or Lewisham, and have been resident there for at least the last three years. Parental joint residual income must be in the region of £25,000 gross taxable income per annum.

Types of grants: The main aim of the foundation is to make educational grants to students at secondary school and institutions of further and higher education. This includes grants towards the costs of books, educational outings, travel fares, equipment/stationary, maintenance, student fees/living expenses and costs for mature students such as

childcare. The average grant is about £500, the maximum in the region of £2,500.

The foundation rarely gives assistance with private school fees and then only in cases of unexpected and considerable hardship that have arisen since the child's entry to the school and where the child is due to sit either GCSEs or A-levels in the current academic year.

Grants may only be made to UK citizens or Home Office recognised refugees (who have been resident in the UK for a minimum of three years). Grants are not usually given to help with the cost of study or travel abroad or exchange visits.

Preference will be given to the children of parents who have served in the armed forces, particularly those who followed a seafaring career.

Annual grant total: In 2004/05 the foundation had assets of £2.8 million, an income of £91,000 and a total expenditure of £172,000. Grants to 18 individuals totalled £34,000. Grants were also made to 27 organisations totalling £137,000.

Applications: On a form available from the correspondent, together with proof of income and parental income, evidence of age, an academic reference and for non-UK citizens only, proof of refugee status. Applicants are expected to have applied for a grant from their Local Education Authority and to have received a decision on this before applying to the foundation. Some applicants will be asked to attend a brief interview with the governors. Applications are considered at meetings which take place four times a year, usually in January, March, July and October.

Correspondent: Miss D J Thomas, Clerk to the Governors, Drapers' Hall, London EC2N 2DQ (020 7588 5001; Fax: 020 7628 1988; e-mail: charities@thedrapers.co.uk; website: www.thedrapers.co.uk)

The British and Foreign School Society Trust Fund

Eligibility: Students who have been living in the London boroughs of Bermondsey, Bethnal Green, Poplar, Southwark and Stepney for two years and need financial assistance for one year of a course. This must be the student's first qualification and they must not be in receipt of a mandatory award.

Types of grants: Grants to help with school, college or university education.

Exclusions: Grants are not given for private education.

Annual grant total: In 2004 the trust had an income of £6,800 and a total expenditure of £7,100. Grants total around £6,000 each year.

Applications: Applications should be made in writing to the correspondent, either directly by the individual or through their college or educational welfare agency, enclosing an sae.

Correspondent: J Kidd, Director, Maybrook House, 97 Godstone Road, Caterham, Surrey CR3 6RE (01883 331177)

Other information: Most grants are awarded through universities/colleges in the area of benefit

Sir John Cass's Foundation

Eligibility: People in need aged under 25 who, for the last three years, have been a permanent resident for Inner London (namely Camden, City of London, City of Westminster, Greenwich, Hackney, Hammersmith and Fulham, Islington, Kensington and Chelsea, Lambeth, Lewisham, Newham, Southwark, Tower Hamlets and Wandsworth). Preference is given to people aged over 19.

Applicants must be on one of the following courses: further education courses above GSCE/NVQ Level 2 standard, such as BTEC, City and Guilds, A-Level and foundation courses; higher education courses: at the current time, the foundation's only support for HE students is through its scholarship programme, which has 12 bursaries available each year at City University (awards are also available for students studying acting at RADA and City & Guilds of London Art School). However, grants can also be made to undergraduate medical students studying for an intercalated degree or undertaking electives; postgraduate courses: these awards are for students undertaking taught postgraduate science, technology and engineering qualifications, and professional vocational courses, e.g. Legal Practice Certificate or Bar Finals. Scholarships are available for study at the following institutions: City University, Guildhall School of Music & Drama, Imperial College, London Metropolitan University, Queen Mary College, University of East London and Royal College of Art.

Types of grants: Grants are made towards maintenance and/or fees for one year (although applicants are free to reapply in subsequent years). All grants are means tested with those in greatest financial need given priority. However, academic achievement can be taken into account to distinguish between people of equal financial needs.

Exclusions: No grants are made towards one year courses, which only offer qualifications at a level already attained from a different course or repeating/resitting a year of study.

Annual grant total: In 2004/05 the foundation had assets of £52.2 million, which generated an income of £2.1 million. Grants were made to 78 individuals totalling £182,000. Grants to organisations totalled £2 million.

Applications: In writing to the correspondent, at any time. Initial letters should include age of candidate, course, address (with details of which borough it is in), details of why a grant is required and how you heard about the foundation. If appropriate, an application form will be sent. Possible beneficiaries will then be interviewed before a final decision is made.

Correspondent: Richard Foley, Grants Manager, 31 Jewry Street, London EC3N 2EY (020 7480 5884; Fax: 020 7481 2519; e-mail: contactus@sirjohncass.org; website: www.sirjohncassfoundation.org)

Other information: This trust also administers The Aldgate and Allhallows Barking Exhibition Foundation with identical criteria except being open only to people in the City of London and the borough of Tower Hamlets.

For further information on the grants made to organisations, please see *A Guide to the Major Trusts Volume One*, also published by DSC.

The Castle Baynard Educational Foundation

Eligibility: People in need with a connection to the City of London or the former county of Middlesex.

Types of grants: Grants in the range of £100 and £500 for those at school, college or university, people starting work and people with special educational needs. Grants are more suited towards meeting expenses such as specific books, items of equipment or events.

Exclusions: Grants are not normally for course fees or general maintenance.

Annual grant total: In 2003/04 the foundation had a total income of £9,500

and a total expenditure of £3,000. Grants are made totalling around £2,500.

Applications: In writing to the correspondent. Applications should include: details of the purpose for which the grants is requested; a cv setting out age, schools and colleges attended and educational attainments to date; proof of financial need; a written reference in support of the application confirming current educational status and financial need; and an sae. Applications are considered in March, June, September and December.

Correspondent: Catherine McGuiness, Clerk, c/o Member's Room, Guildhall, London EC2P 2EJ (020 7359 0145; Fax: 020 7354 9225; e-mail: csmcguiness@ aol.com)

The City & Diocese of London Voluntary Schools Fund

Eligibility: Any person under 25 who has attended a Church of England voluntary aided school in the diocese of London (i.e. north of the river) for at least two years.

Types of grants: Grants are given towards educational activities which do not form part of the usual school day or curriculum. Pupils still at school can receive support for music, dance, specialist sport (such as national team places), field trips and other forms of educational enrichment, and for pupils whose personal circumstances are difficult. Occasional grants are given for special needs.

Grants are also given to students in further/higher education for books, fees and travel abroad, and to people starting work for books, equipment and occasionally clothing. Grants range from £50 to £500 and are usually one-off, but are sometimes recurrent.

Exclusions: Grants are not given for school fees or other costs for schoolchildren except those above.

Annual grant total: In 2004/05 the trust had assets of £352,000 and an income of £16,600. Grants were made to 55 individuals totalling £25,000.

Applications: On a form available from the correspondent by written request. Applications should include references and details on the proposed purpose of the grant. They are considered quarterly.

Correspondent: John Richard Thurley, London Diocesan Board for Schools, 36 Causton Street, London SW1P 4AU (020 7932 1163; e-mail: dee.thomas@ london.anglican.org; website: www. london.anglican.org/schools)

The Isaac Davies Trust

Eligibility: People of the Jewish faith who live in London.

Types of grants: Grants for those at school, college or university. Priority is

given to applicants studying Jewish-related subjects/projects.

Exclusions: Grants are not given for educational study abroad.

Annual grant total: The trust's income is about £11,000. Most of the income is given in grants to organisations, but around £2,000 is given to individuals, some of which is for general welfare purposes.

Applications: In writing to the correspondent.

Correspondent: The Secretary, United Synagogue, Adler House, 735 High Road, London N12 0US (020 8343 8989)

Archibald Dawnay Scholarships

Eligibility: Inner London borough residents (former London County Council area) who are studying engineering full-time at schools, or further/higher education institutions. Preference is given to civil engineering or structural engineering as opposed to building, surveying and allied fields.

Types of grants: One-off grants of between £25 and £400 may be given for uniforms, books, equipment/instruments, maintenance costs, course or conference fees, travel or other expenses.

Exclusions: Previous beneficiaries are ineligible to reapply.

Annual grant total: In 2004/05 the trust had an income of £3,100 and total expenditure of £5,300.

Applications: On a form available from the correspondent, submitted either directly by the individual, or through their school/college/educational welfare agency with a recommendation from a course tutor, an LEA award letter (where applicable) and evidence of residential status. Applications should be made before the first Friday of November and they are considered in December. Candidates will be advised whether their application has been successful within 10 weeks of the closing date. In approved cases, payment will be made by cheque after the activity has been completed, on receipt of a report (one side of A4) and receipts or other proof of expenditure.

Correspondent: The Assistant Education Officer, Corporation of London, PO Box 270, Guildhall, London EC2P 2EJ (e-mail: education@corpoflondon.gov.uk; website: www.cityoflondon.gov.uk)

John Edmonds Charity

Eligibility: People under 25 who live in the former metropolitan borough of Battersea, with a preference for those whose families have lived in Battersea for a long time.

Types of grants: One-off and recurrent grants of £50 to £500. Schoolchildren can receive help towards uniforms, school clothing, books, equipment, instruments, educational outings in the UK and study or travel abroad. Students in further and higher education, including postgraduates and vocational students can receive grants towards books, equipment, instruments, excursions, fees, maintenance and childcare.

Annual grant total: In 2004/05 the charity had assets of £67,000, an income of £4,000 and a total expenditure of £1,900. Grants to four individuals totalled £1,800.

Applications: On a form available from the correspondent, to be submitted at any time directly by the individual or through their school, college or university. Applications are considered bi-monthly.

Correspondent: Roger Coton, Battersea United Charities, Battersea District Library, Lavender Hill, London SW11 1JB

The Eric Evans Memorial Trust – see entry on page 213

Correspondent: J M Kinder, Trustee, 55 Thornhill Square, London N1 1BE

Francon Trust

Eligibility: People in need aged up to 20, who were born or brought up in London and still live there, particularly those studying in the professions of medicine, architecture, accountancy, insurance, banking, law or other professional business or trade fields, including science and engineering. Applicants must have expected (or obtained) grades of at least one A and two Bs for their A-levels.

Types of grants: Grants range between £10,000 and £15,000 in the form of interest-free loans which become gifts on completion of the course after six months of employment in a related occupation. Grants can be spent on the costs of university training. Grants awarded are not necessarily restricted to course fees, but may cover other aspects of necessary expenditure including living expenses (all items should be listed in the detailed financial analysis to be provided). Grants may be in the form of a single payment, or a series of successive payments, depending upon circumstances.

Annual grant total: In 2004/05 the trust had an income of £19,000 and a total expenditure of £17,000. Grants totalled about £15,000.

Applications: The trust does not invite 'unsolicited applications' and states that 'all funds are committed'.

Correspondent: Col. Derek Ivy, Smithtown, Kirkmahoe, Dumfries DG1 1TE (01387 740455; Fax: 01387 740152)

Higher Education Research and Special Expenses Fund – Clause 1 (HERSEF Junior)

Eligibility: People aged 14 to 18 who are in need and are following special technical courses full-time at secondary schools or

establishments of further education in the area formerly under the control of the London County Council (ex-ILEA area). Priority will be given to courses related to civil engineering and construction, but other branches of engineering, building studies, manufacturing, IT and design will also be considered. A list of approved courses is available from the correspondent.

Types of grants: Support may take the form of: a bursary over an academic year, with possible renewal for further years during the period of eligibility (living, travel and/or tuition expenses); specific grants to assist in the completion of short course or educational project work; help with the costs of attendance at courses or conferences in the UK or overseas.

Annual grant total: Each year about £3,000 is available in total to be distributed in grants.

Applications: On a form available from the correspondent, submitted either directly by the individual, or via his or her school, college or educational welfare agency. Applications must show evidence of financial hardship and be accompanied by a covering letter of support from the head of the institution. Applications should be submitted before 31 December for consideration in January or February.

Correspondent: Stephen Denny, Education Officer, Corporation of London, PO Box 270, Guildhall, London EC2P 2EJ (020 7332 1750; Fax: 020 7332 1621; e-mail: education@corpoflondon.gov.uk; website: www.cityoflondon.gov.uk)

The Hornsey Parochial Charities

Eligibility: People under 25 who have lived for at least one year in the ancient parish of Hornsey (that is the London postal area of N8, and parts of the London postal areas of N4, N6, N10 and N16 in Haringey and Hackney).

Types of grants: Grants for students to help with books, equipment, clothing or travel. Grants to help with school, college or university fees or to supplement existing grants. Help towards the cost of education, training, apprenticeship or equipment for those starting work.

Annual grant total: In 2004 it had assets of £1.2 million and an income of £39,000. Grants totalled £31,000 and were made to individuals and organisations.

Applications: Individuals can write requesting an application form that, on being returned, can usually be dealt with within a month.

Correspondent: Lorraine Fincham, PO Box 22985, London N10 3XB (020 8352 1601; Fax: 020 8352 1601; e-mail: hornseypc@blueyonder.co.uk)

Inner London Fund for the Blind and Disabled

Eligibility: People who are blind, partially sighted or disabled who live or are regularly employed in the borough of Greenwich, and people who are blind or partially sighted who live within the London area. Preference will be given to applicants who live alone.

Types of grants: Grants to assist with tuition fees.

Exclusions: No grants towards rent arrears, rates, food, clothing/footwear, heating or lighting, except in exceptional circumstances. No application will be considered where an alternative statutory source of funding is available.

Annual grant total: In 2003/04 the fund had an income of £10,000 and a total expenditure of £4,400. Grants to individuals totalled around £4,000.

Applications: On a form available from the correspondent. Applications can be made directly by the individual or through a social worker. Details of income/expenditure and charitable assistance received within the past year must be included.

Correspondent: Sybil King, 89 Frederick Place, London, SE18 7BH

The Island Health Charitable Trust

Eligibility: People who are involved in providing primary healthcare and live in the London boroughs of Tower Hamlets and Newham.

Types of grants: One-off grants and recurrent grants according to need for up to three years.

Exclusions: Grants are not made where statutory funding is available.

Annual grant total: The total grant allocation each year is just over £100,000 to organisations and individuals. Grants to individuals usually total around £25,000.

Applications: In writing to the correspondent. See the trust's website for further details.

Correspondent: Sonia Lapwood, 43 Caledonian Wharf, London E14 3EN (020 7538 1494; e-mail: info@ islandhealthtrust.org; website: www. islandhealthtrust.org)

Other information: Grants are also made to postgraduate students taking courses related in some way to primary healthcare.

Neale's Educational Foundation

Eligibility: Young men under the age of 26 who attended school in the City of London or the London borough of Westminster for at least two years. Preference is given to people who propose to train for the Merchant or Royal Navy.

Types of grants: One-off grants are given towards any education or experiences of a nature to aid the individual's development.

Annual grant total: Over £3,000 is available each year.

Applications: In writing to the correspondent.

Correspondent: David Powell, 32 Westminster Palace Gardens, Artillery Row, London SW1P 1RR

Need & Taylor's Educational Charity

Eligibility: Children, under the age of 21, who live in the former boroughs of Brentford and Chiswick.

Types of grants: One-off grants to schoolchildren towards uniforms and other school clothing, equipment, instruments, fees and educational outings in the UK.

Annual grant total: In 2004/05 the charity had an income of £11,000 and a total expenditure of £15,000. Grants totalled about £14,000.

Applications: In writing to the correspondent either directly by the individual or through the individual's school/college/educational welfare agency, social services or by his/her parent/guardian or headteacher. Applications are considered at any time.

Correspondent: Ms Julia Cadman, 5 The Dell, Brentford, Middlesex TW8 8DY

Other information: Grants are also made to schools.

The Philological Foundation

Eligibility: People aged 16 to 25 who attended a secondary school in the London borough of Camden or the City of Westminster, including those who are living elsewhere for their studies.

Types of grants: One-off and recurrent grants of £150 to £1,000 are given to: schools and young people for educational outings in the UK, student exchange and study or travel abroad; further and higher education students for books, equipment, fees, living expenses, study or travel overseas and student exchange; and postgraduates (but not people undertaking research degrees) for books, fees, living expenses and study or travel abroad.

Exclusions: The foundation does not give bursaries, scholarships or loans.

Annual grant total: In 2004/05 the foundation had assets of £788,000 and an income of £55,500. Grants were made to 25 individuals totalling £10,000, with a further £26,500 being given to schools.

Applications: On a form available from the correspondent. Applications are considered in February, April, July, September and December and completed forms must be submitted a month before these meetings. Applicants must provide:

(i) proof of attendance at a Westminster or Camden school; (ii) support for the figures quoted in the amount of grant requested; (iii) exam results; and (iv) details of income and expenditure. Applicants should also have applied for a statutory loan.

Correspondent: Mrs A Millar, Clerk, Flat 4, 24 Carlton Hill, St John's Wood, London NW8 0JY (020 7624 4849)

Other information: The correspondent stated: 'If non-eligible students apply (for example, those aged over 25 or those who did not attend a secondary school in Westminster or Camden) the application will not be acknowledged.'

The Pocklington Apprenticeship Trust (Acton, Ealing and Hammersmith and Fulham branch)

Eligibility: Young people aged 25 or under who have lived in Acton, Ealing or Hammersmith and Fulham for at least five years. Special consideration is given to people who have a disability or special educational needs.

Types of grants: Grants in the range of £100 and £300 are given towards tools, equipment, training course fees, textbooks, stationary, computer accessories, special clothing etc.

Annual grant total: About £1,000 is available each year.

Applications: On a form available from the correspondent, for consideration in May/June. Applicants should provide evidence of financial hardship; this could be being in receipt of state benefits or because of personal circumstances. Applicants can apply on their own behalf or through a sponsor who might be a teacher, tutor, youth leader or social worker.

Correspondent: Mrs M C Church, 48 St Dunstans Avenue, Acton, London, W3 6QB, 42 Creswick Road, Acton, London W3 9HF (020 8992 8311; Fax: 020 8992 6385)

Other information: Although it is primarily for the benefit of young people, the fund has stated that it will also be worth older people applying who, because of a disabling condition later in life, have had to consider an alternative job to that which they have been used to.

Richard Reeve's Foundation

Eligibility: Applicants must be under the age of 25 (in exceptional cases this maybe extended to 40) and either (i) they or their parent(s) must have lived or worked for the last 12 months, or for at least 2 of the last 10 years, in the City of London or London boroughs of Camden and Islington, or (ii) they must be students of, or have been accepted as students of,

educational institutions in the area of benefit.

Types of grants: One-off grants of between £100 and £750 to schoolchildren for school uniforms and other school clothing, books, educational outings and maintenance. Students in further/higher education are supported towards the cost of equipment, books, fees, living expenses and travel, but no grants towards study or travel abroad, student exchange, foreign students, childcare costs, school outings, school meals or independent school fees (except for choir schools or where serious social, medical or physical needs suggest this is the best option). Grants are also available towards the cost of special tuition or treatment such as music or dyslexia classes. Grants are only given for second degrees where the qualification is essential, such as law. People starting work can be helped with the costs of equipment and instruments.

Exclusions: No grants for independent school fees.

Annual grant total: In 2004/05 it had assets of almost £11 million and an income of £350,000. Grants to 508 individuals totalled £257,000. Grants to organisations totalled £54,000.

Applications: In writing to the correspondent with an outline of the need to request an application form. Applications are normally considered at meetings in March, June, September and December. Applications should be received well in advance and the cut-off date is two weeks before each meeting. Applications can be submitted by either the individual or through one of the following: City and Islington College, London Institute, Birkbeck College, LSE or Guildhall School of Music and Drama.

Correspondent: Clerk to the Governors, 31 Jewry Street, London EC3N 2EY (020 7488 2496; e-mail: reevesfoundation@ sirjohncass.org)

Other information: 'The foundation sometimes helps with maintenance payments for local college and university students whose parents fail to make up their grants as well as giving them book grants for their courses.

'The foundation will consider any request for a grant which can be considered educational where the beneficiary is under the age of 25 (and satisfies the other criteria set out in Eligibility above).' Furthermore 'if a request for help cannot be considered by the trustees then it is normally passed on to someone who is in a position to consider the applicant's request'.

Discretionary awards are only made where the local authority has a policy in accordance with the requirements of the Education Acts.

Grants to students in higher education are only made when statutory provision, including student loans, have been taken up in full. Students who do not live within the area of benefit (or whose parent does not qualify on employment grounds) may only apply for assistance once they have completed 12 months of their course at an institution within the area of benefit.

The Royal Scottish Corporation (also known as The Scottish Hospital of the Foundation of King Charles II) – see entry on page 99

Correspondent: Willie Docherty, Chief Executive, 37 King Street, Covent Garden, London WC2E 8JS (020 7240 3718 (UK helpline 0800 652 2989); Fax: 020 7497 0184; e-mail: enquiry@ royalscottishcorporation.org.uk; website: www.royalscottishcorporation. org.uk)

The Sheriffs' & Recorders' Fund

Eligibility: People on discharge from prison, and families of people imprisoned. Applicants must live in the Metropolitan Police area or Greater London area.

Types of grants: One-off grants for education and training at any level.

Annual grant total: In 2004/05 the fund made 436 grants totalling £113,000. There were 52 grants totalling £14,000 made for education and training purposes.

Applications: Must be on a form available from the correspondent, submitted through probation officers or social workers. They are considered throughout the year.

Correspondent: Mrs Richard Saunders, Chair, c/o Central Criminal Court, Old Bailey, London EC4M 7BS

St Clement Danes Educational Foundation

Eligibility: After meeting the needs of St Clement Danes Primary School, grants are awarded to, in order of priority: (i) ex-pupils of St Clement Danes Church of England Primary School. (ii) people who are under 25 years of age and have lived within the diocese of London, with preference for the City of Westminster, for the majority of their education.

Types of grants: Grants to assist with the costs of books, materials, travel, uniform and associated costs for study at college or university.

Exclusions: Grants towards fees are not usually given to pupils in primary and secondary education. No grants to overseas students.

Annual grant total: Previously £15,000.

Applications: On a form available from the correspondent. Applications can be submitted directly by the individual, or by a parent/guardian if the individual is under 18, for consideration in February, May, October or November. They need to be submitted six weeks before the committee meeting.

Correspondent: Jean Rymer, Clerk, St Clement Danes Church of England Primary School, Drury Lane, London WC2B 5SU (020 7641 6593; Fax: 020 7641 6589)

Sir Walter St John's Educational Charity

Eligibility: People under 25 who live in the boroughs of Wandsworth and Lambeth and have lived there for at least six months. There is a preference for those who live in the Battersea area. All applicants must provide evidence that they and their parent(s) are in receipt of benefit or very low income.

Grants will only be awarded to students who are following a validated, approved or recognised course.

Types of grants: Grants are one-off and are for a range of educational needs; this can include social and physical training as well as study on school and college courses. Student grants are towards costs that are necessary for attendance on the course, such as registration fees, travel, books and equipment. The normal upper limits for grants are £500 for students aged 16 to 18, and £750 for students aged 19 to 24. Lone parents who are in receipt of benefit can receive grants of up to £1,800 towards childcare. People with special educational needs can be given help towards buying special equipment.

Grants are made to schoolchildren and students under 18 and to full-time students on university degree courses only in exceptional or unforeseen circumstances.

Exclusions: Grants are not made to pupils at independent schools or to students on postgraduate courses. Grants are not given towards general living expenses, study or travel abroad or student exchanges.

Annual grant total: In 2004/05 the charity had assets of £3.2 million, an income of £124,000 and made grants totalling £101,000, including £8,800 to 28 individuals.

Applications: All applicants must provide evidence that they have a good prospect of successfully completing the course. Students attending courses at South Thames College should apply to their college student advice service.

Students attending courses at other colleges should write or telephone, providing their full name, date and place of birth, present address and length of time they have lived there, the name of their college or school and the title of the course of study or training, including start and finish dates. Applicants who then appear eligible for an award will be asked to complete an application form.

Correspondent: Melanie Griffiths, Unit 11, Culvert House, Culvert Road, London SW11 5DH (020 7498 8878 – Tuesdays and Wednesdays; e-mail: manager@swsjcharity. org.uk)

Other information: The charity mainly makes grants to organisations (£92,000 in 2004/05).

The Truro Fund

Eligibility: Young men under the age of 21 living or attending school or college in the area previously within the Inner London Education Authority. Female applicants cannot be considered.

Types of grants: The fund's policies are laid out in a clear and simple leaflet, a model for other charities to follow. Small grants may be awarded for the purchase of tools, books or other equipment for young men intending to start their own business, follow a trade or profession or enter an apprenticeship. The trust also gives bursaries or scholarships to help those wishing to further their education. Grants to individuals rarely exceed £500 and are non-renewable.

The trustees take a strong personal interest in all applicants and prefer to make small grants to individuals rather than organisations. No grants for school fees, maintenance or travel costs. Grants to organisations will only be made where the organisation can identify the young men who will be assisted by funding. The aim has to be to improve the employment prospects or the education of the beneficiaries.

Annual grant total: In 2004/05 the total income for the fund was about £7,700 and the expenditure was around £3,800.

Applications: On a form available from the correspondent and must include: three references, at least one of which should be from college; evidence of date of birth; full financial details, and any information concerning immigration status if necessary. Applications are considered in May and November.

Correspondent: Colonel John C M Ansell, The Clerk to the Trustees, 401 Salisbury House, London Wall, London, EC2M 5RR (0207 638 8358; Fax: 0207 638 9681)

Sir Mark and Lady Turner Charitable Settlement – see entry on page 229

Correspondent: The Trustees, PO Box 191, 10 Fenchurch Street, London EC3M 3LB (020 7475 5086)

The Turner Exhibition Fund

Eligibility: Girls and women who are members of the Church of England, have attended a school wholly or partly maintained out of public funds for at least two years and are now living in the diocese of London or that part of the diocese of Southwark which lies within the London boroughs of Greenwich, Lambeth, Lewisham, Southwark and Wandsworth.

Types of grants: Small cash grants, from £250 to £1,000, to assist candidates in meeting the expenses of, and incidental to, their education or training at any stage after leaving primary school, such as fees, and the purchase of books and equipment. Grants are also made for travel costs to and from college. The fund prefers to award grants to those undertaking a first course of education or training, rather than postgraduate students.

Annual grant total: In 2003/04 the fund had an income of £2,300 and a total expenditure of £1,000.

Applications: In writing to the correspondent, including the nature of the course of education and training which the applicant intends to pursue and availability of other funding. Applications are usually considered in June and October and application forms are issued on request approximately two months before each meeting.

Correspondent: Mrs J M Cuxson, Vizards Tweedie, 42 Bedford Row, London, WC1R 4JL (0207405 1234; Fax: 0207 405 4171; e-mail: judith.cuxon@visardstweedie.co.uk)

Vacher's Endowment

Eligibility: People in need live or have lived in Greater London, and their dependants. Preference has to be given to those who have been engaged in some trade or profession on their own account in Greater London, and residents in the parish of St John Westminster.

Types of grants: Quarterly allowances and one-off grants in the range of £50 and £500.

Annual grant total: In 2004 the charity had assets of £584,000 and an income of £20,000. Out of a total expenditure of £22,000, the sum of £13,000 was distributed in relief-in-need and educational grants to individuals.

Applications: Further information may be obtained from the correspondent in writing.

Correspondent: Roger Walker, United Westminster Almshouse Foundation, Palmer's House, 42 Rochester Row, London SW1P 1BU (020 7828 3131)

Other information: Grants are also made to organisations.

The Wiseman & Withers Exhibition Foundation

Eligibility: People who live in the London borough of Greenwich and that part of the London borough of Newham which was formerly in the metropolitan borough of Woolwich. Applicants must be under the age of 26.

Types of grants: Grants, of between £50 and £200, to provide equipment needed

for courses of further education. No grants towards travel or major awards to finance full-time education.

Annual grant total: The trust had an income of about £1,500 and a total expenditure of £2,000. Grants totalled about £1,500.

Applications: In writing to the correspondent. The trustees meet twice a year.

Correspondent: D Fisher, Clerk, 5 Upton Road, Bexleyheath, Kent, DA6 8LQ (020 8306 0278; Fax: 020 8331 8126; e-mail: d.c.fisher@gre.ac.uk)

The Chris Woodroofe Trust Fund

Eligibility: Children and young people aged 10 to 18 years who are either attending schools in Havering and Barking or are living in the area and wish to pursue outdoor activities, for example, rock climbing, caving and canoeing.

Types of grants: One-off grants, usually for £50, for equipment/instruments, educational outings in the UK and study or travel abroad.

Annual grant total: In 2003/04 the trust had an income of £400 and gave grants to five individuals totalling £250.

Applications: On a form available from the correspondent, submitted directly by the individual.

Correspondent: D A Bowler, 41a Cricketers Lane, Herongate, Brentwood, Essex CM13 3QB (01277 810633; Fax: 01277 810637; e-mail: david_bowler@msn.com)

Barking & Dagenham

The Catherine Godfrey Association for those with Learning and other Disabilities

Eligibility: People who have learning difficulties and/or other disabilities, including physical disabilities, and people with mental health problems. Applicants must be in financial need and live in Barking and Dagenham and the surrounding areas. Support is also given to carers.

Types of grants: Grants for outdoor activities and holidays in Britain to those who cannot afford them.

Annual grant total: Grants total around £3,500 a year.

Applications: In writing to the correspondent. Applications need to be co-signed by a social worker or similar and have to be submitted between September

and December for consideration in January.

Correspondent: Kathryn Pettitt, c/o Aldersey Gardens, Barking, Essex IG11 9UG (01279 505148)

Barnet

The Elizabeth Allen Trust

Eligibility: People in need, under 25, who live in the borough of Barnet and who have not already gained a first degree. Priority is given to applicants from the pre–1965 urban district of (High) Barnet.

Types of grants: One-off grants of up to £300 are made for specific needs (such as books, equipment and fees) and maintenance grants of up to £250 a term are paid for an academic year. Grants for educational outings in the UK are considered in exceptional circumstances.

Exclusions: No grants are made towards private school fees, for gap year activities or for purposes funded by the LEA.

Annual grant total: In 2004/05 the trust had assets of £601,000 and made grants totalling £16,000 to 40 individuals.

Applications: On a form available from the correspondent upon receipt of an sae. Forms can also be obtained by leaving a message (including telephone number) on the trust's answerphone. Applications must include details of parental finances and the use of the applicant's student loan. The trustees meet five times a year to consider applications.

Correspondent: Clerk to the Trustees, 28 Hillside Gardens, Barnet, Hertfordshire EN5 2NJ (Tel: 020 8440 7130)

Other information: The trust states that the trustees' April meeting is realistically the last at which applications for the current year can be considered.

The Milly Apthorp Charitable Trust

Eligibility: Young people who live in the London borough of Barnet.

Types of grants: Grants towards adventurous expeditions and character-building activities.

Annual grant total: In 2004/05 the trust had assets of £10 million and an income of £636,000. Grants were made to organisations and individuals totalling £552,000, including £15,000 towards adventure holidays.

Applications: On a form available from the correspondent. Applications are considered in March, June, September and December and should be made through a registered charity in the preceding month. The trust does not invite applications, and will not reply to unsuccessful applicants.

Correspondent: Secretary, Borough Treasurer's Department, London Borough of Barnet, Town Hall, The Boroughs, London, NW4 4BG

The Mayor of Barnet's Benevolent Fund

Eligibility: Schoolchildren who live in the London borough of Barnet and have done so for at least six months and whose parents are on an income-related benefit.

Types of grants: One-off grants of up to £100 can be given towards school uniforms.

Annual grant total: Variable, but rarely exceeding £4,000.

Applications: Applications should preferably be submitted directly by the individual, but may also be made directly by a supporting agency. All requests should include a quotation for the items required.

Correspondent: The Grants Unit, London Borough of Barnet, Town Hall, The Burroughs, Hendon, London NW4 4BG (020 8359 2020; Fax: 020 8359 2685)

The Hyde Foundation

Eligibility: People in education up to first degree level in the ancient parishes of Chipping Barnet and Monken Hadley.

Types of grants: One-off grants in the range of £100 and £6,000. Grants are given to college students, undergraduates, vocational students, mature students, people with special educational needs and people starting work. Grants given include those for music lessons, fees, travel abroad, books, equipment and maintenance/living expenses.

Annual grant total: In 2005 the trust had assets of £574,000 and an income of £53,000. Out of a total expenditure of £38,000, grants to 22 individuals totalled £16,000. The sum of £11,000 was given to organisations.

Applications: In writing to the correspondent, who will forward an application form. Trustees meet quarterly in January, April, July and October to consider applications and applications should be received at the end of December, March, June and September respectively.

Correspondent: C A R Marson, Clerk to the Trustees, Claverdon, 19 Bedford Avenue, Barnet, Hertfordshire, EN5 2EP (020 8449 3032; Fax: 020 8449 3032)

The Valentine Poole Charity

Eligibility: Young people in need under the age of 26 who live in the former urban districts of Barnet and East Barnet (approximately the postal districts of EN4 and EN5).

Types of grants: One-off grants to schoolchildren for uniforms and people starting work for books, equipment and instruments.

Annual grant total: In 2005 the trust had assets of £541,000 and an income of £60,000. Grants totalled £39,000, of which £23,000 went to individuals.

Applications: On a form available from the correspondent for consideration in March, July and November. Applications should be submitted by a school, welfare agency or other relevant third party, not directly by the individual.

Correspondent: Mrs M G Lee, The Forum Room, Ewen Hall, Wood Street, Barnet, Hertfordshire EN5 4BW (020 8441 6893)

Other information: Grants are also made to local organisations (£16,000 in 2005).

Bexley

Bexley United Charities

Eligibility: People under the age of 25 who live in the borough of Bexley.

Types of grants: Grants of between £100 and £1,000 are given towards books for students at school, college or university, and towards books, equipment and instruments for people starting work.

Annual grant total: In 2004/05 the trust had both an income and a total expenditure of £20,000. Grants to individuals totalled about £2,000.

Applications: In writing to the correspondent.

Correspondent: Kenneth Newman, 13 High Street, Bexley, Kent DA5 1AB (01322 525543)

Camden

Bromfield's Educational Foundation

Eligibility: People under 25 who live (or whose parents or guardians live) in the Holborn area of the London borough of Camden.

Types of grants: Annual grants of £600 for clothing, books, equipment/instruments and maintenance/living expenses.

Exclusions: No grants for school, college or university fees.

Annual grant total: In 2004/05 the trust had both an income and a total expenditure of £15,000, all of which was distributed in grants to individuals.

Applications: On a form available from the correspondent, to be submitted directly by the individual or through a school/college/educational welfare agency or a parent or guardian. Details of income and expenditure and personal information are required, supported by documentary evidence which will be treated in the strictest confidence. Applications can be submitted at any time, and will be considered within 21 days.

Correspondent: The Grants Officer, St Andrew's Holborn, 5 St Andrew Street, London EC4A 3AB (020 7583 7394)

Hampstead Wells & Campden Trust

Eligibility: People in need who live in the former metropolitan borough of Hampstead.

Types of grants: Grants are given to people at any stage of their education, or who are entering a trade or profession, for uniforms and other clothing, books, equipment, instruments, maintenance, living expenses, childcare and educational outings in the UK.

Exclusions: Grants cannot be made towards the payment of taxes, including Council Tax, nor the payment of fines. The trustees are also unable to offer assistance with course or school fees.

Annual grant total: In 2003/04 the trust had assets of £13 million, generating an income of £484,000. Grants totalled £274,000 of which £3,800 was given to 12 individuals for educational puroses. Welfare grants and pensions are also made.

Applications: Applications may be made by letter or on the trust's application form which can be downloaded from its website. Applications by letter will only be accepted if they include the following details: the client's name, date of birth, occupation, address and telephone number, details of other household members, other agencies and charities applied to, result of any applications to the Social Fund, household income, and details of any savings and why these savings can not be used. Applications should be supported by a statutory or welfare agency. Decisions are made within two weeks.

Correspondent: Mrs Sheila A Taylor, Clerk to the Trustees, 62 Rosslyn Hill, London NW3 1ND (020 7435 1570; Fax: 020 7435 1571; e-mail: grant@hwct.fsnet.co.uk; website: www.hwct.org.uk)

Other information: There is a leaflet available from the above address which further outlines the objectives and procedures of the trust.

City of London

Thomas Carpenter's Trust

Eligibility: People under 25 who live, or whose parents have lived or worked for three years, in Bread Street and adjoining wards in the City of London.

Types of grants: Grants of £500 to £3,000 to people at school, college or university towards costs which are directly related to the course, including fees, books, equipment, instruments, uniforms, travel abroad to pursue their education and help with the costs of studying music or other arts.

Exclusions: No grants are given towards electives or field trips which are not part of a full-time study course.

Annual grant total: In 2004/05 the trust had an income of £24,000 and a total expenditure of £20,000.

Applications: On a form available from the correspondent. Applications should be submitted before 31 July by the individual's parent or guardian, details of whose financial circumstances should be provided.

Correspondent: Thomas F Ackland, Secretary, 59 Broadfields Avenue, Winchmore Hill, London N21 1AG (020 8360 5296; Fax: 020 8360 5296; e-mail: bushhill@onetel.net)

The Farringdon Within Ward Trust

Eligibility: People under the age of 25 and in need who meet one of the following criteria: (i) people who live or work, or one or both of whose parents live or work in the ward of Farringdon Within. (ii) people who live or attend schools or other educational establishments in the City of London. (iii) people who work, or one or both of whose parents work, in the City of London.

Types of grants: 'To promote the education (including the social and physical training) of persons eligible by awarding scholarships, exhibitions, bursaries, grants and maintenance allowances tenable at schools, colleges of education or other institutions of further (including professional and technical) education approved by the trustees.' In practice, most grants are towards school fees.

Annual grant total: In 2003/04, the trust had an income of £7,100 and a total expenditure of £5,400.

Applications: Individuals or their parents should write in the first instance to the correspondent. Applications for the next academic year must usually be submitted by mid-April.

Correspondent: John Hughesdon, 44 Christchurch Road, Sidcup, Kent, DA15 7HQ

The Charity of John Land for Widows & Children (Apprenticing Branch)

Eligibility: Children under the age of 25 of Freemen of the City of London, who are in need and people in need under the age of

25 whose parents have lived in the City of London for at least five years.

Types of grants: One-off or recurrent grants may be given for educational purposes and apprenticing (training) for any trade, profession or vocation. Grants can be for living expenses.

Annual grant total: Around £1,000 is given each year, although more funds are available.

Applications: In writing to the correspondent.

Correspondent: David Powell, 32 Westminster Palace Gardens, London, SW1P 1RR

The Mitchell City of London Educational Foundation

Eligibility: People aged 11 to 19 who are either attending a City of London school or whose parents have lived or worked there for at least five years.

Types of grants: Grants ranging from £1,200 to £1,400 each are given as sixth form bursaries for A-level students or grants for school fees for children from single parent families.

Annual grant total: In 2004/05 the foundation had assets of £687,000 and an income and total expenditure of £65,000. Grants to 39 individuals totalled £54,000.

Applications: On a form available from the correspondent, to be submitted either directly by the individual or a parent/guardian, or through an organisation such as a school or an educational welfare agency. They are considered in March and September.

Correspondent: John Keyte, Clerk, Fairway, Round Oak View, Tillington, Hereford HR4 8EQ (01432 760409; Fax: 01432 760409)

City of Westminster

William Shelton's Educational Foundation

Eligibility: Children up to the age of 11 living or being educated in the ancient parishes of St Giles in the Fields, St Martin in the Fields and St Paul, Covent Garden.

Types of grants: Grants to help with the cost of books, clothing and other essentials for schoolchildren.

Annual grant total: In 2004 the foundation had assets of £3.1 million and an income of £139,000. Grants to organisations and individuals totalled £42,000.

Applications: In writing to the correspondent.

Correspondent: Mrs P Nicholls, The Rectory, 15a Gower Street, London WC1E 6HW (020 7323 1992; Fax: 020 7323 4102; e-mail: pam.nicholls@london.anglican.org)

Croydon

Church Tenements Charity – Education Branch

Eligibility: People under the age of 25 who are living or studying in the London borough of Croydon, including people from overseas studying in Croydon.

Types of grants: 'The trustees have a limited amount of funds at their disposal. They are therefore inclined to apply the trust income to exceptional or extraordinary cases of hardship or circumstance. They will generally favour an application below £500 where a grant has not been given previously by the local education authority. Grants are wide ranging but mainly cover primary, secondary or post-school education and training. Grants may also be given towards the cost of uniforms, equipment, musical instruments etc.' Grants can also be for books, school fees, educational outings in the UK and study or travel abroad. They range from £50 to £500.

Whilst no preference is given to any type of application, the trustees will be encouraged to give grants if the applicant has made some effort to raise some finance him/herself.

Annual grant total: In 2004/05 the charity had assets of £573,000, an income of £23,000 and a total expenditure of £19,000. Grants were made to 45 individuals totalling £11,000.

Applications: On a form available from the correspondent. Applications are considered quarterly in January, April, July and October. The trust asks for as much supporting information as possible.

Correspondent: Hilary Bowles, Clerk to the Trustees, c/o Nunappleton Way, Hurst Green, Oxted, Surrey, RH8 9AW (e-mail: hilary.bowles@tiscali.co.uk)

Frank Denning Memorial Charity

Eligibility: Full-time students at colleges of further education who live or whose parents/guardians live in the London Borough of Croydon. Applicants must be between the ages of 19 and 25 on 1 March in the year the application is considered.

Types of grants: One-off travelling scholarships of up to £750 each for travel abroad to carry out projects which have specific educational objectives. Beneficiaries must have every intention of returning to the UK at the end of their overseas visit.

Annual grant total: In 2004/05 the trust had an income of £6,000 and a total expenditure of £6,500. Grants were made to 15 individuals totalling £5,000. In 2005/06 grants were made to nine individuals totalling £4,800.

Applications: On a form available from the correspondent. Forms are available from June and must be returned by the individual by 1 March for consideration in March/April. Please note that it is the latter date that the age qualification mentioned above refers to. A handout is sent to all Croydon students giving information on the charity. Interviews are held each year during the Easter holidays.

Correspondent: Gerry Hudson, Assistant Honorary Secretary, Democratic and Legal Services Division, Policy and Corporate Services Department, London Borough of Croydon, Taberner House, Park Lane, Croydon CR9 3JS (020 8726 6000; e-mail: gerry.hudson@croydon.gov.uk; website: www.croydon.gov.uk)

Ealing

Acton (Middlesex) Charities

Eligibility: Students whose home residence is in the former ancient parish of Acton. They must be over 18 years of age and have entered a full-time course in the UK, usually of at least three years, which will lead to a recognised qualification.

Types of grants: Grants of £200 per year to assist with books or equipment.

Annual grant total: In 2004 the trust had assets of £342,000 and an income of £12,000. There were 18 educational grants made to individuals totalling £3,600. A further £2,900 was distributed in 11 relief-in-need grants.

Applications: On a form available from the correspondent or the rector. Proof that the student is entered on an educational course is required.

Correspondent: Miss L Dodd, Clerk, St Mary's Parish Office, 1 The Mount, Acton High Street, London W3 9NW

Other information: The trust also provides welfare and arts grants and supports local schools and carnivals.

The Francis Courtney Educational Foundation

Eligibility: People under 25 who live in Southall.

Types of grants: One-off grants are given to assist in further education only. Help may be given towards books, fees/living expenses and study or travel abroad.

Mature students may also receive help in special circumstances.

Exclusions: No grants for clothing, equipment or childcare.

Annual grant total: About £1,500.

Applications: On a form available from the correspondent, indicating the size of contribution the individual can make and an indication of what the grant is for. The applicant's place of study must approve the completed form, which should be submitted directly by the individual. Applications are considered before the individual begins further education.

Correspondent: E Vickers, Clerk, 1 Vine Cottage, Tentelow Lane, Norwood Green, Southall, Middlesex UB2 4LG (020 8574 3973)

The Educational Foundation of William Hobbayne

Eligibility: Schoolchildren from low-income families who live in Hanwell (W7 area) in the London borough of Ealing. There is a preference for children in junior school.

Types of grants: Grants generally of up to £100 for the costs of school trips and educational outings.

Exclusions: No grants to university students.

Annual grant total: In 2004/05 the charity had both an income and a total expenditure of £5,500, all of which was given in grants. Educational grants to 32 individuals totalled £3,700, with the remainder going to organisations

Applications: In writing to the correspondent. Applications must be supported by a sponsor (usually the school, Scout or Guide group and so on), and are considered monthly.

Correspondent: Mrs C Lumb, Clerk, 25 Golden Manor, Hanwell, London W7 3EE (020 8579 2921; Fax: 020 8579 2921)

Other information: Grants are also made to organisations.

Enfield

The Enfield Church Trust for Girls

Eligibility: Young women in need (under the age of 25) who live, work or attend school, college or university in the ancient parish of Enfield.

Types of grants: Grants to help individuals to lead as fulfilling lives as possible by helping with the costs of their education, recreation, leisure and social welfare. For example, the trust bought a radio-linked hearing aid to enable a deaf 12-year-old girl to continue normal schooling.

Grants have also been given towards course fees when local education authority grants are not available and to students for books and study or travel abroad. Grants for childcare and other child costs have been given to single-parents who are studying, training or early on in their careers, and the trust will consider grants for books, equipment and clothing for women starting work. The trustees are particularly concerned to help disadvantaged young women and girls. Grants usually range from £70 to £300. Grants are generally one-off although beneficiaries are free to re-apply each year.

Exclusions: No grants for mature students or for school fees, though grants for school uniform, books, educational outings and maintenance are considered for schoolchildren.

Annual grant total: About £2,500.

Applications: On a form available from the correspondent. Applications are considered all year.

Correspondent: Revd Michael M Edge, Enfield Vicarage, Silver Street, Enfield, Middlesex, EN1 3EG

The Old Enfield Charitable Trust

Eligibility: People in need who live in the ancient parish of Enfield.

Types of grants: For students and other residents who are undertaking education or training, help is given with living costs, equipment, stationery, childminding and other general expenses during their course of study.

Exclusions: The trust cannot help with costs that are the responsibility of the local authority or central government.

Annual grant total: In 2004/05, the trust had assets of £5.2 million and an income of £645,000. A total of £181,000 was given in 393 grants to individuals. A further £79,000 was given to organisations

Applications: On a form available on written request from the correspondent. Applicants are then interviewed by a committee.

Correspondent: Mrs P Taylor, Clerk, The Old Vestry Office, 22 The Town, Enfield, Middlesex EN2 6LT (020 8367 8941; Fax: 0208 366 7708; e-mail: enquiries@toect.org.uk; website: www.toect.org.uk)

Other information: The Enfield Parochial Charities and the Hundred Acres Charity were merged to form this charity on 1 April 1994.

Greenwich

The Greenwich Blue Coat Foundation

Eligibility: Young people up to 25 years of age who live, or who are being educated in, the borough of Greenwich.

Types of grants: One-off and recurrent grants towards educational needs.

Annual grant total: The amount given in grants varies around £1,000 from year to year.

Applications: In writing to the correspondent.

Correspondent: M I Baker, Clerk, 136 Charlton Lane, London SE7 8AB (020 8858 7575)

Hackney

The Hackney District Nursing Association

Eligibility: Nurses and midwives who work in the London borough of Hackney.

Types of grants: Grants towards training for nurses and midwives and the provision of comforts during their study.

Annual grant total: In 2005 the trust had an income of £6,900 and a total expenditure of £5,200. Grants are made for welfare and educational purposes.

Applications: An application form, available from the correspondent, should be submitted through an organisation such as Citizens Advice or school by April for consideration in May.

Correspondent: Charlotte Ashburner, c/o Homerton University Hospital, Homerton Row, Homerton, London E9 6SR

Other information: Homes for nurses and midwives, clinics for child welfare and other relief and assistance can also be given to people in need in the area of benefit.

The Hackney Parochial Charities

Eligibility: People in need who live in the former metropolitan borough of Hackney (as it was before 1970).

Types of grants: Help towards the cost of books, tools and examination fees for apprentices and young people at college or university who are not in receipt of a full grant. Grants are one-off (although applicants can re-apply annually).

Annual grant total: In 2004/05 it had an income of £145,000 and a total expenditure of £207,000. Grants totalled £137,000. Grants are made to organisations

and individuals. Further information was not available from this year.

Applications: In writing to the correspondent. The trustees meet in March, June, September and November and as grants cannot be made between meetings it is advisable to make early contact with the correspondent.

Correspondent: Robin Sorrell, Craigen Wilders & Sorrell, 2 The Broadway, High Street, Chipping Ongar, Essex CM5 9JD

Hammersmith & Fulham

Dr Edwards' & Bishop King's Fulham Charity

Eligibility: People undertaking vocational training who live in the old metropolitan borough of Fulham.

Types of grants: One-off grants are made to people starting work for uniforms/ clothing and to vocational students for fees, books and equipment/instruments. Cash grants are not given (unless they are to be administered by an agency).

Exclusions: Grants are not normally given to people who are homeowners. Arrears on utility bills are not paid, nor are grants given retrospectively.

Annual grant total: In 2004/05 grants to individuals totalled £132,000. A further £125,000 went to organisations.

Applications: On a form available from the correspondent submitted either directly by the individual or through social welfare agencies. The Relief in Need Committee, which considers relief-in-need applications, including education grant applications, meets 10 times a year, roughly every 4-5 weeks.

Correspondent: Ms Vivienne Robb, Clerk to the Trustees, Percy Barton House, 33–35 Dawes Road, London SW6 7DT (020 7386 9387; Fax: 020 7610 2856; e-mail: clerk@debk.org.uk; website: www. debk.org.uk)

Other information: This charity gives money to both individuals and organisations, with its main responsibility being towards the relief of poverty rather than assisting students.

Haringey

Tottenham Grammar School Foundation

Eligibility: People under 25 who, or whose parents, normally live in the borough of Haringey, or who have attended a school in the borough.

Types of grants: Awards are available for one year only, normally the first year of college or equivalent course, for former pupils of Haringey maintained secondary schools proceeding to university. Awards are also available for other post-school courses, excluding GSCEs and A-levels, but occasionally including postgraduate courses. People embarking on educational journeys and voluntary work overseas can also be supported. People with special educational needs can be supported for any specialist equipment which will assist their education.

Annual grant total: In 2004/05 it had assets of £20 million and an income of £995,000. Grants to individuals totalled £465,000. Grants to organisations totalled £477,000.

Applications: An application form is available from the headteacher of the individual's secondary school. Applicants going to a non-university education can also receive a form from the clerk.

Correspondent: Graham Chapple, Clerk, PO Box 34098, London N13 5XU (020 8882 2999; e-mail: info@tgsf.org.uk)

Other information: The trust also donates money to schools in Haringey and other voluntary organisations in Haringey for equipment and activities not provided by the local authority.

The Wood Green (Urban District) Charity

Eligibility: People in need who have lived in the urban district of Wood Green (as constituted in 1896, roughly the present N22 postal area) for at least three years.

Types of grants: Assistance to schoolchildren, college students, undergraduates, vocational students, children with special educational needs, people starting work and overseas students for clothing (including uniforms), books and equipment/instruments.

Annual grant total: In 2004/05 the charity had assets of £60,000, an income of £7,800 and a total expenditure of £7,600. No educational grants were made during the year.

Applications: On a form available from the correspondent, to be submitted by a school, social worker, Citizens Advice or other welfare agency or third party. Applications are considered all year round.

Correspondent: Mrs Carolyn Banks, Clerk, c/o River Park House, High Road, Wood Green, London N22 4HQ (020 8489 2965; Fax: 020 8489 2662)

Hillingdon

Uxbridge United Welfare Trusts

Eligibility: People in need who live in the Uxbridge area (bordered by Harefield in the north, Ickenham in the east, Uxbridge in the west and Cowley/Colham Green in the south).

Types of grants: One-off grants for people in school or further or higher education. Grants can be towards books, uniforms and equipment and sometimes living expenses and so on.

Exclusions: No grants for school fees.

Annual grant total: Between £40,000 and £50,000 a year; about £5,000 of this is given for educational purposes and a small amount to organisations.

Applications: On a form available from the correspondent. Applications can be submitted directly by the individual or through a social worker, Citizens Advice or educational welfare agency. They are considered each month.

Correspondent: Mrs S M Pritchard, Chair, Trustee Room, Woodbridge House, New Windsor Street, Uxbridge UB8 2TY (01895 232976)

Islington

Dame Sarah Temple's Educational Foundation

Eligibility: Schoolchildren (aged 5 to 16) living in the parish of Islington, that is, not Clerkenwell or Finsbury.

Types of grants: One-off grants of £30 to £100 are made to schoolchildren for items such as school uniforms, clothing, equipment, educational outings in the UK and books. Grants are to help the child benefit from state education.

Exclusions: No school fees are paid and no grants are given for further education. Applications may ONLY be made by educational welfare officers.

Annual grant total: About £2,500 a year.

Applications: Applications may ONLY be made by educational welfare officers. Requests from any other individual, members of public, or any other third party will not be considered or acknowledged. Members of the public may not apply directly.

Correspondent: Judy Hackney, St Mary's Church Office, Upper Street, Islington, London N1 2TX

The Worrall & Fuller Exhibition Fund

Eligibility: People living in the former metropolitan borough of Finsbury who are aged between 5 and 25.

Types of grants: The fund covers a wide range of educational purposes giving grants towards, for instance, school, college or university fees and books, travel and other equipment expenses, for people wishing to study music and the arts and for those preparing to start work.

Annual grant total: In 2004/05, the fund had an income of about £15,000 and an expenditure of about £12,000. Grants totalled about £6,000.

Applications: On a form available from the correspondent.

Correspondent: Mrs C Shephard, 32 Clerkenwell Close, London EC1R 0AU

Other information: The trust gives grants to individuals and organisations.

Kensington & Chelsea

The Campden Charities

Eligibility: People in need who live in the old parish of Kensington, north of the Fulham Road. Applicants must have lived in Kensington for at least two years and normally must be under the age of 30, although exceptions may be made.

Types of grants: Recipients can vary from primary schoolchildren with dyslexia to postgraduate students. Grants cover all subjects including music, art and sports, and are towards tools, books and equipment for people who are studying or for those starting work.

Annual grant total: In 2004/05, the charities had assets of £69 million and an income of £2.4 million. Grants to organisations and individuals totalled £1.6 million.

Applications: Preliminary enquiries should be made by telephone or in writing to the education assistant, who will then informally interview applicants. The trustees of the education committee, who meet monthly, then make final decisions, based on the formal interviews of the applicants.

Correspondent: C Stannard, Clerk, 27a Pembridge Villas, London W11 3EP (020 7243 0551; website: www. campdencharities.org.uk)

The Pocklington Apprenticeship Trust

Eligibility: Young people in need, aged 21 years or younger who were either born in Kensington and Chelsea or who have lived there for at least 10 years.

Types of grants: One-off grants, usually of between £200 and £300 are awarded to schoolchildren, students in further/higher education, vocational students, people starting work and special educational needs for books, equipment, instruments and commuting expenses. People starting work may also receive support for uniforms and clothing.

Exclusions: Help is only given to attend classes outside the borough if the classes are unavailable within it.

Annual grant total: In 2004/05 the trust had an income of £5,000 and a total expenditure of £1,500. Grants totalled about £1,500.

Applications: On a form available from the correspondent, for consideration at any time.

Correspondent: Graham Taylor, The Royal Borough of Kensington & Chelsea, Room 907, Town Hall, Hornton Street, London W8 7NX (020 7361 2257; e-mail: graham.taylor@rbkc.gov.uk)

Lambeth

The Walcot Educational Foundation

Eligibility: People who live in the London borough of Lambeth who are aged 4 to 29.

Types of grants: Grants are given to students to assist with course fees, travel to college, university or other educational establishments and books and equipment required for their course of study. Grants are considered for mature students towards the cost of books, travel and fees. People starting work can receive help towards books, equipment/instruments and clothing.

Grants are given to schoolchildren to assist with school uniforms and occasionally towards fares to school and school meals. Grants for school fees are made in very exceptional circumstances.

Grants are usually from £100 to £150 per term. A small number of larger grants are also available through the Walcot and St Thomas' Bursary.

Annual grant total: In 2004 the trust made grants totalling £56,000 to 208 pupils and students. Voluntary-Aided Schools Fund received £135,000 and other schools received £145,000.

Applications: Students should write a letter of application stating their name and address, date of birth, the length of time that they have lived in Lambeth and brief details of the proposed course and the financial help required. Applicants who are eligible will then be sent an application form and will be interviewed by the director of charities before an award is made.

Applications for schoolchildren should be made on a form available from the correspondent. They must be made through a recognised agency such as educational social work, social services, Citizens Advice, a doctor or minister of religion.

For further help or advice contact the correspondent or Victor Willmott, Fieldworker or Gillian Broaders, Student Grants Administrator, at the address below. Applications are considered throughout the year.

Correspondent: Robert Dewar, Director and Clerk, 127 Kennington Road, London SE11 6SF (020 7735 1925; Fax: 020 7735 7048)

Lewisham

Lewisham Education Charity

Eligibility: People aged 26 or under who are in need and live in the ancient parish of Lewisham (which does not include Deptford or Lee).

Types of grants: One-off grants for any educational need. There are no specific restrictions except where statutory bodies should be responsible. Applications are preferred for specific items rather than contributions to large fee costs.

Annual grant total: In 2004/05 the charity had an income of £880 and a total expenditure of £1,300. Grants totalled about £1,000.

Applications: On a form available from the correspondent, either directly by the individual, or via their school, college or educational welfare agency. Applications are considered regularly.

Correspondent: Mrs Alison Murdoch, Clerk, Lloyd Court, Slagrove Place, London SE13 7LP (020 8690 8145)

Other information: Some support is also occasionally given to local schools.

Merton

A & H Leivers Charity Trust

Eligibility: Young people in need up to the age of 18 who have lived in the London borough of Merton for at least five years.

Types of grants: One-off and recurrent grants to help with the cost of books, clothing, educational outings and other essentials for those at school.

Annual grant total: In 2004/05 the trust had assets of £429,000 and an income of £11,500. Grants were made to individuals totalling £5,000.

Applications: On a form available from the correspondent. Applications can be submitted by the individual, his/her head teacher or a social care worker. Applications should include full details of what funds are requested, and are usually considered between April and June although urgent cases can be considered at any time.

Correspondent: Mrs Joan Young, PO Box 112, Worcester Park, Surrey KT4 7YY

Richmond-upon-Thames

The Barnes Relief-in-Need Charity and The Bailey & Bates Trust

Eligibility: People in need who live in the London SW14 postal district.

Types of grants: Grants in the range of £250 and £1,000 are made to college students, undergraduates, vocational students and mature students, including those for fees, books, equipment/ instruments, maintenance/living expenses and childcare.

Exclusions: Grants are not made to children of statutory school age. No grants for school fees.

Annual grant total: In 2004/05 the charity had assets of £142,000 and an income of £4,800. There were seven relief-in-need grants made totalling £1,500. No educational grants were made during the year.

Applications: On a form to be submitted directly by the individual or a family member. They are considered on an ongoing basis.

Correspondent: The Clerk to the Trustees, c/o Richmond Parish Lands Charity, The Vestry House, 21 Paradise Road, Richmond, TW9 1SA

Other information: Grants are also made to organisations (£4,000 in 2004/05).

The Barnes Workhouse Fund

Eligibility: Students in need in the ancient parish of Barnes (in practice SW13).

Types of grants: One-off grants of up to £1,000 are available for students in further education where local or national authority assistance is unavailable.

Annual grant total: In 2004 the trust had assets of £4.4 million and an income of £160,000. Welfare grants to 78 individuals totalled £17,000 and 16 educational grants totalled £6,200.

Applications: On a form available through the fund's website, to be submitted directly by the individual. Applications are considered upon receipt. If students apply for more than £750 this will be considered at bi-monthly trustee meetings held in January, March, May, July, September and November.

Students under the age of 25 must provide details of their parents'/carers' income.

Correspondent: Mrs M Ibbetson, PO Box 665, Richmond TW10 6YL (e-mail: barnesworkhousefund@tiscali.co. uk; website: www.barnesworkhousefund. org.uk)

Other information: Grants are also made to organisations (£92,000 in 2004).

The Hampton Wick United Charity

Eligibility: People under 25 who are in need and live in Hampton Wick and most of South Teddington, within the parishes of St John the Baptist, Hampton Wick and St Mark, South Teddington.

Types of grants: One-off cash grants (with the possibility of future reapplication) to help with the cost of, for example, books, equipment, clothing and course fees.

Annual grant total: Over £20,000 a year in educational and welfare grants.

Applications: In writing to the correspondent. The trustees normally meet three times a year to consider applications.

Correspondent: Roger Avins, 241 Kingston Road, Teddington, Middlesex TW11 9JJ

The Petersham United Charities

Eligibility: People under 25 who live in the ecclesiastical parish of Petersham, Surrey as constituted in 1900.

Types of grants: One-off grants of £75 to £500 are given for any educational need.

Annual grant total: In 2004 the trust had an income of £370 and one educational grant was made totalling £200.

Applications: In writing to the correspondent. Applications are considered in January, April, July and October and can be submitted either directly by the individual or through a social worker, Citizens Advice or other welfare agency.

Correspondent: R M Robinson, Clerk, Dixon Ward, 16 The Green, Richmond, Surrey TW9 1QD (020 8940 4051; Fax: 020 8940 3901)

Other information: Grants are also given for relief-in-need purposes.

The Richmond Parish Lands Charity

Eligibility: Students above school age who are in need and have lived in Richmond, Kew, Ham, Petersham, North and East Sheen or Central Mortlake (NOT the whole borough of Richmond) for at least six months prior to application and have no other possible sources of help.

Types of grants: The education fund is available to students to follow a course of study or training. Grants may be awarded for fees, books, equipment, instruments, educational outings in the UK, study or travel abroad or childcare costs.

The maximum award is £5,000 but such sums are entirely exceptional. Assistance is not given for private school fees.

Exclusions: No grants to schoolchildren.

Annual grant total: In 2004/05 it had assets of £48 million and an income of £1.7 million. Grants to individuals consisted of £77,000 for education (about 70-80 grants), £29,000 in heating vouchers to older people through its WARM campaign and £50,000 in small grants to individuals in severe need.

Applications: On a form available from the Clerk to the Education Committee, to be submitted directly by the individual. This includes details of current employment, income and expenditure, details of the course/expenses applied for and a statement in support of the application. Two references are required and applicants are usually asked to attend an interview. Applications should be based on financial need and parental income is taken into account up to the age of 25 years. Applications are considered every month except February, August, December and April.

Correspondent: The Clerk to the Trustees, The Vestry House, 21 Paradise Road, Richmond, Surrey TW9 1SA (020 8948 5701; Fax: 020 8332 6792)

Other information: Education grants form a small part of this charity's activities. Grants are also made to organisations (£600,000 in 2005).

The Thomas Wilson Educational Trust

Eligibility: People under 25 who live in Teddington and neighbourhood.

Types of grants: Grants are given to schoolchildren towards clothing, books, educational outings and fees (only in exceptional circumstances) and to students in further or higher education, including overseas students (depending on how long they have been a resident in Teddington), towards books, fees, living expenses and study or travel abroad. Help may also be given to mature students under 25.

Annual grant total: In 2005 the trust had an income of £52,000, all of which was given in grants to individuals.

Applications: On a form available from the correspondent. Applications can be submitted directly by the individual or by a parent or guardian. They are considered throughout the year.

Correspondent: Mrs Karen Hopkins, 23 Tranmere Road, Whitton, Middlesex TW2 7JD

Southwark

The Christchurch Church of England Educational Foundation

Eligibility: People aged 19 to 25 who live in the following areas (in order of priority): (i) the parish of Christchurch, Southwark; and (ii) the former borough of Southwark.

Types of grants: Grants are for promoting education 'in accordance with the principles of the Church of England'. Grants are made towards (i) school uniforms, other school clothing, books and educational outings for schoolchildren, (ii) books, study or travel abroad and student exchanges for students in further and higher education, (iii) books, equipment and instruments, clothing and travel for people starting work and (iv) books and travel for mature students. Grants range from £50 to £150 and are one-off.

Preference is given to schoolchildren with serious family difficulties so the child has to be educated away from home and to people with special education needs.

Grants are not made for fees or maintenance costs for shoolchildren or for fees/living expenses for students.

Annual grant total: In 2005, the fund had an income of £3,800 and a total expenditure of £1,800.

Applications: In writing to the correspondent, including details of other applications made. Applications are considered in May and November.

Correspondent: The Administrator, Christchurch Industrial Centre, 27 Blackfriars Road, London SE1 8NY (020 7928 4707; e-mail: admin@ christchurchsouthwark.org.uk; website: www.christchurchsouthwark.org. uk)

Charity of Thomas Dickinson

Eligibility: Young people aged 25 or under and in financial need who are living in, studying in or have at least one parent working in the ancient parishes of: St Giles, Cripplegate; St Sepulchre, St George the Martyr, Southwark; or St Mary Magdalene, Bermondsey.

Types of grants: One-off grants ranging from £100 to £500 are given to:

schoolchildren for uniforms and educational outings in the UK and overseas; students in further or higher education for books; vocational students for equipment and instruments; and to individuals with special educational needs for uniforms/clothing.

Annual grant total: In 2004 the trust had an income of £3,000 and a total expenditure of £2,500.

Applications: On a form available from the correspondent, submitted either directly by the individual or via their school/college/educational welfare agency. Applications are considered in February/ March, June/July and October/November.

Correspondent: Revd A S Lucas, Chair of Trustees, St George's Church, Borough High Street, London SE1 1JA (020 7407 2796; e-mail: tonyslucas@ btinternet.com)

The Newcomen Collett Educational Foundation

Eligibility: People under the age of 25 who live in the London borough of Southwark. There is a preference for those living in the parish of St Saviour's.

Types of grants: Grants are made: (i) towards fees or expenses while attending college or university; (ii) towards buying tools, books, materials and so on for a college course or to prepare for or enter a profession, trade or occupation; (iii) to enable persons to travel to pursue their education; and (iv) to study music or any other of the arts or for social or physical training. Grants are one-off and of up to £1,000, but are usually below £500.

Exclusions: No grants for school fees, domestic bills, childcare or debts.

Annual grant total: In 2004/05, the trust had assets of £2.9 million, an income of £202,000 and gave £149,000 in grants to both individuals and organisations.

Applications: In writing to the correspondent requesting an application form, giving brief details of your background and what you wish to apply for. Every application must be accompanied by a supporting statement from the school headteacher or a tutor or other suitably qualified instructor or supervisor. The statement need not exceed 50 words and should give an opinion of the suitability of the applicant for a grant. Applications are considered in March, June, September and December.

People on courses of further education beyond school leaving age must have lived in the borough of Southwark for two years before the start of their course and still be living in Southwark when making the application.

Correspondent: Richard Goatcher, Clerk, Marshall House, 66 Newcomen Street, London Bridge, London SE1 1YT (020 7407 2967; Fax: 020 7403 3969)

St Olave's United Charity, incorporating the St Thomas & St John Charities

Eligibility: People under the age of 24 who live in the ancient parishes of Southwark St Olave and St Thomas, and Bermondsey Horsleydown St John. In practice this means residents of Bermondsey (part SE1 and all SE16).

Types of grants: Grants for schoolchildren for items such as clothing, travel and fees are only given in very exceptional circumstances. Grants to college students and mature students for books.

Annual grant total: In 2004/05 the charity had assets of £9.8 million and an income of £360,000. Educational grants to individuals totalled £30,000.

Applications: In writing outlining the need. Applications should be made through a school or similar organisation.

Correspondent: Mrs A O'Shaughnessy, 6–8 Druid Street, off Tooley Street, London SE1 2EU (020 7407 2530)

Other information: Grants are also made to organisations.

Tower Hamlets

Stepney Relief-in-Need Charity

Eligibility: People in need who live within the old Metropolitan Borough of Stepney.

Types of grants: One-off grants of £200 to £500, including those for uniforms/clothing, books and fees for attendance at college or university.

Annual grant total: In 2003/04 the charity had assets of £348,000 and an income of £15,000. There were 15 relief-in-need grants made totalling £5,500, with a further £2,000 distributed in 11 educational grants.

Applications: An application form is available from the correspondent and may be submitted either directly by the individual or through a relative, social worker or other welfare agency. The trustees usually meet four times a year, but some applications can be considered between meetings at the chair's discretion.

Correspondent: Mrs J Partleton, Clerk to the Trustees, Rectory Cottage, 5 White Horse Lane, Stepney, London E1 3NE

The Tower Hamlets and Canary Warf Further Education Trust

Eligibility: Students (but not schoolchildren) who have lived in the London borough of Tower Hamlets for at least three years. Applicants must be ordinarily resident in the UK, have been granted exceptional leave to remain in the UK or have refugee status. The three year

residency is waived for people with full refugee status, or people whose parents have lived in the borough for the last three years and have returned home.

Types of grants: The trust gives grants for fees and maintenance, paid in three termly instalments. There is a means-tested system for deciding which applicants qualify for help with fees, maintenance support and those who can claim for both. Grants also cover books and equipment/instruments. Grants to a maximum of £3,000.

Exclusions: Students eligible for an education maintenance allowance are not considered. Courses of religious study are not supported, regardless of religion.

Annual grant total: In 2003/04 grants totalled £106,000.

Applications: On a form available from the correspondent with full guidelines. Completed forms must be submitted directly by the individual and include details of family income, proof of residency in the borough and confirmation by the college or university of intention to study. The closing date is usually in June in the preceding academic year for the grant to be made when the course commences. Forms are normally available from March each year.

Correspondent: Nizam Uddin, London Borough of Tower Hamlets, Mulberry Place, 5 Clove Crescent, London E14 2BG (020 7364 4419; e-mail: nizam.uddin@towerhamlets.gov.uk)

Waltham Forest

The Henry Green Scholarship Fund

Eligibility: People under 25 who live in Waltham Forest and are studying at the universities of Cambridge, London or Oxford and attended one of the following schools: Connaught Girls' High School, Norlington Boys' High School, Leyton Sixth Form College, George Mitchell High School, Tom Hood Senior High School and Leytonstone School.

Types of grants: Grants ranging from £50 to £200 to help with books, equipment or living expenses.

Annual grant total: Between £1,000 and £5,000.

Applications: On a form available from the correpsondent. Applications must be submitted directly by the individual by the end of May for consideration by August.

Correspondent: The Student Services Manager, Sycamore House, Forest Road, Walthamstow, London, E17 4SY

Sir William Mallinson Scholarship Trust

Eligibility: People under 21 who live in the London Borough of Waltham Forest.

Types of grants: Grants of £150 to £500 to people starting work for equipment, instruments and travel expenses and students in further or higher education for study or travel overseas and student exchange.

Annual grant total: In 2004/05, the trust had an income of £1,400 and a total expenditure of £780.

Applications: On a form available from the correspondent, to be submitted by the end of February through the individual's school, college or educational welfare agency for consideration in March/April.

Correspondent: The Student Services Manager, Sycamore House, Forest Road, Walthamstow, London E17 4SY

The Sir George Monoux Exhibition Foundation

Eligibility: Further and higher education students aged under 25 who live in the London Borough of Waltham Forest and are pupils or former pupils of the following schools: Holy Family College, Highams Park Grant Maintained School, McEntee School, Sir George Monoux Sixth Form College, Warwick School, Aveling Park School, Walthamstow Girls' School, Willowfield School, Kelmscott School and Rushcroft School.

Types of grants: One-off awards ranging from £50 to £100 are available for activities not normally covered by local authority grants. Such activities include student exchanges and other educational visits overseas, as well as educational visits in the UK. The fund also aims to 'encourage students to develop their project work'.

Annual grant total: In 2004 the foundation had an income of £1,400 and a total expenditure of £2,900.

Applications: On a form available from: Deputy Chief Education Officer, Education Department, London Borough of Waltham Forest, Municipal Offices, Leyton, London E10 5QJ. Applications should be submitted directly by the individual by the end of May for consideration from May to September.

Correspondent: The Student Services Manager, Sycamore House, Forest Road, Walthamstow, London, E17 4SY

The Walthamstow Fund

Eligibility: Students in further or higher education who are under 25, live in Walthamstow and attended the following schools: Aveling Park, Highams Park Grant Maintained, Kelmscott, McEntee, Holy Family College, Rushcroft, Monoux College, Walthamstow, Warwick and Willowfield.

Types of grants: One-off grants ranging from £50 to £100 for books, equipment, instruments and maintenance costs.

Annual grant total: In 2004/05 the fund had an income of £400 and an expenditure of about £500.

Applications: In writing directly by the individual to: Deputy Chief Education Officer, London Borough of Waltham Forest, Municipal Offices, High Street, Leyton E10 5QJ.

Correspondent: The Student Services Manager, Sycamore House, Forest Road, Walthamstow, London, E17 4SY

Wandsworth

Charlotte Despard Charity

Eligibility: Women over the age of 25 who have lived in the former metropolitan borough of Battersea for at least three years who are wishing to return to work after a career break.

Types of grants: One-off and recurrent grants of £100 to £500 are given towards books, equipment, instruments, fees, living expenses and childcare for women re-entering education at any level. People starting work can also be supported.

Annual grant total: In 2004/05 the charity had assets of £7,800 and an income and a total expenditure of £500, all of which was given in three grants.

Applications: On a form available from the correspondent, to be submitted directly by the individual. Applications are considered bi-monthly.

Correspondent: Roger Coton, Battersea United Charities, Battersea District Library, Lavender Hill, London SW11 1JB

The Peace Memorial Fund

Eligibility: Children aged 16 or under who live in the borough of Wandsworth.

Types of grants: Grants of £40 to £75 towards the cost of holidays and educational visits (mainly in the UK).

Annual grant total: About £6,000 a year.

Applications: Through a welfare agency on a form available from the correspondent. Applications should be submitted in February/March and May/June.

Correspondent: Gareth Jones, Town Hall, Room 153, Wandsworth High Street, London SW18 2PU (020 8871 7520)

Supporting Children of Wandsworth Trust (SCOWT)

Eligibility: Children aged between 3 and 18 who live in the borough of Wandsworth and have lived there for at least two years.

Types of grants: Grants to a maximum of £200 towards items such as musical instruments, sporting equipment, special clothing and educational trips. Grants are made for educational and welfare purposes to 'help children to achieve their full potential'.

Annual grant total: In 2003/04 the trust had an income of £1,100 and a total expenditure of £3,500.

Applications: On a form available from the correspondent. Applications should include recommendation letters from clubs, social workers and so on if possible. The trustees meet every two to three months, although urgent applications can be considered between meetings.

Correspondent: Adrian Butler, Education Department, Town Hall, High Street, Wandsworth, London SW18 2PU (020 8871 7895; Fax: 020 8871 6609; e-mail: abutler@wandsworth.gov.uk)

Tooting Graveney Educational Charity

Eligibility: People under 25 in need whose home is in the Tooting area, which is roughly SW17, and who are in full-time further or higher education at a recognised establishment.

Types of grants: One-off and recurrent grants ranging from £25 to £600, although individuals tend to reapply each year for ongoing grants. Help can be towards books, equipment, fees and study or travel overseas.

Exclusions: No grants are given towards part-time education, which includes evening classes or to people who are starting work.

Annual grant total: In 2004 the charity had an income of £11,000 and a total expenditure of £9,600. The charity gives grants and loans to individuals.

Applications: On a form available from the correspondent, with information about the individual's date of birth, home address, nature of education and details of the establishment, and with some indication of the financial need. Applications should be submitted during August or the first two weeks of September for consideration at the end of September. They can be submitted directly by the individual, or through his or her college or educational welfare agency.

Correspondent: Mrs P Fennell, 6 Burtonwood Grange Road, London SW18 3JX (0208 870 0133)

Other information: One-third of the trust's income is designated to a Sunday School.

Westminster

The Forrest & Grinsell Foundation

Eligibility: People under 25 who have their permanent family home in the City of Westminster.

Types of grants: Exhibitions are made to people on completion of secondary education to attend university or other institutes of higher education. People preparing for entry into any trade, profession or calling can be supported for outfits, clothing, tools, instruments or books.

Annual grant total: In 2005 the foundation made 29 grants to individuals totalling almost £7,000 and gave exhibitions amounting to £24,000.

Applications: In writing to the correspondent. Applications for grants can be made directly by the individual or through a school or youth club. Applications for exhibitions are made through the staff or governors of Westminster secondary schools.

Correspondent: Roger Walker, Palmer's House, 42 Rochester Row, London SW1P 1BU (020 7828 3131; Fax: 020 7828 3138; e-mail: uwa@londoncharities.com)

The Hyde Park Place Estate Charity (Civil Trustees)

Eligibility: People under 25 who are residents of the borough of Westminster and are studying at schools or colleges in Westminster.

Types of grants: Grants in the range of £50 and £500, including those to schoolchildren, college students and vocational student towards clothing, books, living expenses and excursions.

Exclusions: Refugees, asylum seekers and overseas students are not eligible.

Annual grant total: In 2003/04 the civil trustees had an income of £140,000 and made grants totalling £101,000 of which £83,000 went to organisations and £18,000 to individuals.

Applications: All applications should be made through a recognised third party/ organisation and include a case history and the name, address and date of birth of the applicant. Applications are considered on an ongoing basis.

Correspondent: James McKeran, Clerk, The Vestry, 2a Mill Street, London W1S 1FX (020 7629 0874; Fax: 020 7629 0874)

The Paddington Charitable Estates Educational Fund

Eligibility: People aged under 25 for the duration of their course who live in the former metropolitan borough of

Paddington (roughly the north west corner of the City of Westminster bounded by the Edgeware Road and Bayswater Road).

Types of grants: The fund has a number of schemes that support both individuals and organisations.

The pocket money scheme allocates a block grant to the admissions and benefits office of the education department of Westminster City Council, which then distributes about 25 to 30 grants to individuals nominated by schools and educational welfare officers, of £2 per week for children aged 11 to 14 and £2.50 for children aged over 14.

Long-term recurrent grants are made for school and course fees for children who are particularly gifted, or in need of special tuition, to enable them to attend special schools.

One-off grants are also made towards one-off course fees and maintenance, travel, clothing and other expenses.

Scholarships and bursaries are available towards educational trips and to allow people to enter into a trade or profession or to study music and other arts.

Annual grant total: In 2004, the trust had an income of £62,000 and an expenditure of £49,600.

Applications: Applications should be made in writing by a social services or welfare organisation on behalf of an individual. If in doubt a telephone call to the correspondent would be useful to establish whether a case is eligible.

Correspondent: Mick Steward, 17th Floor, Westminster City Hall, 64 Victoria Street, London SW1E 6QP (0207 641 3134; e-mail: dbenjafield@westminster.gov.uk)

Other information: For further information on the grants to organisations, please see *A Guide to Local Trusts in Greater London*.

The Saint Marylebone Educational Foundation

Eligibility: People aged between 8 and 25 who, for at least two years, have lived or been educated in the former borough of St Marylebone and the City of Westminster.

Types of grants: Generally recurrent grants for school pupils to help with fees. Grants range from £500 to £4,500.

Exclusions: No tertiary grants are made.

Annual grant total: In 2004/05 the foundation had assets of £515,000 and an income of £127,000. Grants to 41 individuals totalled £114,000, with a further £84,000 distributed to organisations.

Applications: Initially by writing to the correspondent, requesting an application form. These should be completed by the applicant's parent/guardian or by the individual if aged over 18. Applications can also be made by a third party such as a teacher, or come through an organisation such as a school or welfare agency. Applications are considered in January and July.

Correspondent: Ms P Le Gassick, c/o St Peter's Church, 119 Eaton Square, London SW1W 9AL

STATUTORY GRANTS & STUDENT SUPPORT

Please note that a comprehensive guide to benefits is beyond the scope of this book. There are a number of organisations which provide comprehensive guides, information and advice to students wishing to study in the UK and overseas. Contact details for these organisations can be found in the *Sources of Further Information* section of this guide.

The following is a basic guide to the statutory entitlements for people in education. The situation is extremely complex and changes constantly, but the state is still the largest provider of educational support and will continue to be so. Potential applicants should check the situation before applying.

This chapter covers the following:

- Schoolchildren (aged 16 and under) – free school meals, school clothing grants, education travel passes and back to school grants (Northern Ireland only)

- Educational Maintenance Allowances

- Learning Support Funds

- Income Support and Jobseeker's Allowance entitlements

- Housing benefit entitlements

- Local Education Authority (LEA) support for students in further and higher education

- Access funds

- Hardship loans

- Teacher training

- Funding and bursaries for NHS courses

- Help for students studying on approved social work course.

Schoolchildren (aged 16 and under)

The following benefits are all separately administered by individual local education authorities who set their own rules of eligibility and set the level of grants. What follows is the basic general criteria for benefits, but you should contact your LEA directly for further information and advice (a list of LEAs can be found starting on page 283).

Free school meals

In England and Wales, Local Education Authorities maintained schools must provide a free midday meal to pupils if they or their parents receive Income Support or income-based Job Seeker's Allowance, or if they are receiving support as asylum seekers. The school must also provide a free meal if a pupil's parents receives Child Tax Credit and their income is below a certain level or if they get the guarantee part of the State Pension Credit.

Statistics from the Child Poverty Action Group indicate that only one in five children are currently eligible to receive a free school meal, yet 20% of these children do not take them due to reasons including fear of social stigma, parents not being aware of their entitlement to this benefit and parents' concern that the meals provided by the school are not nutritional and balanced. Furthermore one million children living in poverty are not entitled to free school meals and 10% of children are deterred from paying for school meals by costs.

It is worth noting that the value of free school meals to a parent or parents on a low income is significant, maybe adding up to £400 per year in total for a single child.

School clothing grants

It is often at the discretion of the LEA in your county whether help is given with the cost of school clothing. Policies on who and what they support varies greatly. Some, for example, restrict their help to school uniforms, some pay a one-off grant when the pupil starts school, while others pay regular grants as the pupil grows and needs new clothing. Some give help in cash grants, while others give vouchers to be used at local shops and others give actual items of clothing.

Some LEAs do not giving financial help to buy school uniforms on the grounds that there is no legal basis for a pupil to wear a school uniform. You may therefore have to challenge your LEA if the school requires a pupil to wear a uniform and you cannot afford the cost. Information on challenging a LEA can be found on the Advice Guide website (www.adviceguide.org.uk).

It is worth remembering that many schools address the issue of the cost of school uniforms by selling good quality second-hand items directly to parents. Some schools also have hardship funds to enable parents to purchase uniforms, while others run schemes for purchasing uniforms through the school, paying for uniforms in weekly instalments. Contacting the school before buying new items may significantly help to reduce the cost.

Education travel passes

Education authorities must provide free transport to children up to the age of 16 living more than three miles away (two miles if aged under 8 in England, Scotland or Wales, or 11 in Northern Ireland). This is the case even when a child is attending a school in a different LEA, or a grant-maintained school other than the one the LEA has designated as serving his or her home address.

In cases where pupils are not eligible for free transport, LEAs may help by paying all or part of their travelling expenses. They may take account of parental means in deciding whether or not to do so, but this is at the individual LEA's discretion.

Discretionary grants may be available from LEAs to cover travel expenses for parents visiting children at special schools.

Students aged 16 to 18, or 19 and over if continuing a course started before the age of 19, may also be entitled to discounted or free travel. Individuals should contact their local LEA. Further information is available on the Department for Education and Skills website at: www.dfes.gov.uk/financialhelp/16-19transport.

Back to school grant (Northern Ireland only)

The Back to School Grant is a scheme run by the Northern Ireland Memorial Fund to help parents/guardians who have been affected by the Troubles and cannot afford the cost of school uniforms, books and other costs associated with the start of the school year. To qualify for the grant, you must have a child in full-time education who is living at home and must either:

- Have lost either a parent, partner or child.

- Have been injured yourself.

- Be the primary carer for an immediate family member who has been injured.

- Be currently receiving Income Support, Income-based Jobseeker's Allowance, or Housing Benefit.

To apply for a grant, contact: The Northern Ireland Memorial Fund, Grants Administration, 1st Floor, Albany House, 73-75 Great Victoria Street, Belfast BT2 7AF (028 9024 5965; Fax: 028 9024 5048; e-mail: nimfgoa@belfast.org.uk).

Education maintenance allowance

Education Maintenance Allowances (EMA) provide a weekly allowance up to £30 per week dependent on household income (£30,810 in 2006/07) to students who stay on in education at school or college after taking GCSEs. EMAs are available for any academic or vocational course which involves at least 12 hours of guided learning per week. From April 2006, EMA has been extended to young people on Learning and Skills Council-funded E2E courses or taking a learning programme that leads to an apprenticeship. The cash can cover items such as travel costs, books or equipment. A student will receive an EMA as long as they turn up to their classes, and it will be paid for the duration of their studies.

The student may also be entitled to bonuses of £100 depending on progress made with their studies and if they come back for a second year.

Information on EMAs can be found on the Department for Education and Skills website at www.dfes.gov.uk/financialhelp/ema, which includes details of criteria, and how and when to apply. Application forms are available from schools, online or by telephoning 080 8101 6219.

Learning support funds

Learner Support Funds are available in colleges or school sixth forms to help towards costs of starting or following a course. They can be paid in addition to EMA. These costs include:

- Help with living, learning or personal circumstances.

- Books and equipment.

- Extras, like visits or field trips.

- Emergencies affecting your living or learning arrangements.

- Accommodation costs where it is necessary to take up a course further away than a daily travelling distance.

- Transport, including fares to and from school, college or a training centre.

- Childcare and associated transport costs.

Further information on this fund and details on how to apply should be available through college via a Student Support or Welfare Officer, or if a sixth form via a year tutor, or Student Awards or Student Support Officer.

Income support and jobseeker's allowance

Income Support is one of the main statutory benefits for people on low incomes who are not working or who work on average less than 16 hours a week. Job Seeker's Allowance is for those who are actively seeking work. Generally students are not eligible for Income Support or Job Seeker's Allowance but there are exceptions.

For up-to-date information and advice on benefit entitlement it is worth contacting your local job centre or Citizens Advice.

Income support

For those under 19 and at school or college

Income support cannot be claimed by those under 16. This is the same for those aged 16 to 18 in full-time non-advanced education (this means attendance at a school, college or similar establishment for education up to and including GCE/A-Levels, Scottish Certificate of Education (Higher level) or equivalent), however there are some exceptions. This means they can claim a maintenance grant and free school meals (until their 19th birthday) on the basis of their own benefit. You may be able to claim income support if:

- You are the parent of a child who lives with you.

- You are an orphan and not being looked after by someone acting as your parent.

- You have a severe mental or physical disability which means that you would be unlikely to find work within 12 months if you left school.

- You are of necessity living away from your parents or any person acting in place of a parent because you are estranged from them, or in physical or moral danger, or there are serious risks to your physical or mental health.

- You are living apart from your parents or from people acting as your parents and they are in prison, or chronically sick or mentally or physically disabled,

or prohibited from entering or re-entering Great Britain.

- You have just left care and have to live independently.

Unless you are in one of the listed groups, you cannot normally claim Income Support immediately after you leave education if you are under 19. You are excluded from claiming until around the end of the holiday following your final term.

For those 19 and over in full-time education:

Those studying on a full-time course are classified as students and therefore not able to claim Income Support. Exceptional cases are when:

- You are a lone parent and are responsible for a child under 16.

- You are a lone foster-parent and are responsible for a child under 16.

- You are disabled and qualify for the Disability Premium

- You qualify for a local education authority disabled student's allowance because of deafness.

- You have been in receipt of Income Support at any time in the previous 18 month as a disabled student.

- You are a student who has been ill and incapable of work for a period of not less than 196 days.

- You have been granted refugee status and are attending an English language course for more than 15 hours a week and when that course started you had been in Great Britain for under a year (Income Support will only be paid for a maximum of 9 months).

For those 19 and over in part-time education:

Part-time students can claim for Income Support if they satisfy other rules for receiving Income Support.

Jobseeker's allowance

If you are attending a full-time non-advanced course, you are counted as being in 'relevant education'. As such, you cannot normally qualify for Job Seeker's Allowance, however there are some exceptions.

Students in full-time relevant education:

If you are a full-time student, you can claim Job Seeker's Allowance if:

- You are one of a couple who are both full-time students and either one or both of you is responsible for a child, this exception only applies during the summer vacation.

- You are aged 25 or over and have been unemployed for two years or more, you may be able to do a full-time employment-related course for up to a year.

Students in part-time education:

If you are studying part-time, but are still available for and actively seeking work, you may be able to get Job Seeker's Allowance. This will also depend on the number of hours you study and your other circumstances.

Housing benefit

Most full-time students are not entitled to claim Housing Benefit during the whole of their course, including the summer vacations and any periods of temporary absence from the course of study. However, if you are a part-time student or if you are in one of the exempt categories (see below), then you may be able to get help with rent.

Full-time students who can claim Housing Benefit are:

- Lone parents.
- Students with disabilities.
- Students aged under 19 following a course of further education but not higher education.
- Students with a partner who is also a full-time student, and who have dependent children.
- People aged 60 or over.

If you are in one of the above categories, your local council will be able to give you further details.

Local education authority support for students in further and higher education

The single largest source of student finance are the local education authorities (LEAs). The financial support available from the LEAs is described below; the information relates to people studying in 2006/07.

Grants towards tuition fees

From September 2006 universities in England will be allowed to vary the fees they charge new students for tuition. Universities will be able to charge up to £3,000 per year. The maximum fee chargeable will not rise by more than the rate of inflation before 2010 at the earliest. Amounts charged may vary between courses, as well as between different universities and colleges.

Students will not have to pay fees before they start university or whilst they are studying. Instead eligible students will be able to apply for a Student Loan for Fees to cover these costs. This means that they won't have to find the money before they start their course or whilst they are studying, and the fees will be paid direct to their university or college, on their behalf.

Students will repay these loans once they have left university and are earning over £15,000.

There are no upper age limits imposed for students loans for fees.

Help with living costs

New Maintenance grant

From 2006, new full-time students from lower income households will be eligible for the new non-repayable Maintenance Grant which is worth up to £2,700 a year. How much a student will get will depend on their income and that of their household. If that income is £17,500 or less they will receive the full £2,700 grant. A partial grant will be payable where household income is between £17,501 and £37,425.

Around half of all new full-time students are likely to be eligible for a full or partial grant. Grants are payable in three instalments – one at the start of each term.

Bursaries

Universities and colleges wishing to charge more than £2,700 a year for a course will have to provide at least £300 a year in non-repayable financial support, such as bursaries, to students on these courses who are receiving the full £2,700 Maintenance Grant.

Some students will get more than this, as many universities and colleges are expected to offer financial help worth more than £300. It will be important to speak to the university or college that you're interested in and find out what it offers. Contact their student advice service for information.

Student loans for maintenance

Maintenance loans to help with living costs are available. The interest on the loan is linked to inflation, this means that the amount you pay back will be roughly the same value in real terms as that which you borrowed. Full-time, sandwich and part-time initial teacher training students are entitled to receive a loan. They are available to all full-time, English and EU citizens who have been resident in the UK for three years. In 2006 the maximum age limit for application was 54, although this was under review by the Department for Education and Skills.

The maximum loan available for a full year is £4,505 (£6,170 for students living in London, £3,415 for students living at home). Loans are reduced in the final year of a course as it does not cover the summer holidays. They are paid in three instalments.

75% of the loan is available to everyone, the remaining 25% is means-tested (assessed on the students' or their families' income).

Maintenance loan entitlement for maintenance grant recipients will be reduced by up to £1,200 as up to £1,200 of the maintenance grant is paid in substitution for part of the maintenance loan (which has the effect of reducing the debt for lower income students by up to £1,200 a year).

The amount you repay will be linked to your income. Under the existing arrangements, once you are earning over £15,000 a year you will be obliged to begin repayment of your loans, usually the April after you graduate (providing you are earning enough). Deductions are usually made through the PAYE tax system by your employer in the same way as tax and National Insurance contributions. Someone earning £20,000 a year would repay £8.65 a week or £37.50 a month. If you stop working, or your earnings fall below £15,000, then your repayments will cease.

For students taking out their first loan in September 2006 or later, the Government will write off student loan balances (except for arrears) which are left unpaid 25 years after their liability to repay commenced, which is the April after the course finished. This will cover both student loans for fees as well as student loans for maintenance.

Applying for a loan

Applications should be made through your LEA. It is provided by the Student Loans Company and is normally paid by cheque or directly into your bank account in three instalments – one at the beginning of each term. Your LEA assesses your entitlement each year, so you must remember to reapply every year of your course.

Further information: The Student Loan Company Ltd can be contacted at 100 Bothwell Street, Glasgow G2 7JD (0800 405010; Website: www.slc.co.uk).

Supplementary grants

Some students are entitled to extra help:

- The Parents' Learning Allowance. This allowance is to help with course-related costs for students who have dependant children. How much you get depends on your household income, including your husband, wife or partner.

- Child Tax Credit from the Inland Revenue. Students with dependant children are eligible for this credit, with students receiving the maximum amount are entitled to free school meals for their children. The money you get depends on your circumstances. To find out whether you are eligible call 0845 300 3900 or visit www.hmrc.gov.uk/taxcredits.

- Childcare grant. This grant can be applied for by full-time students with dependant children in registered or approved childcare. How much you get is based on your actual childcare costs and will depend on you household income.

- Adult Dependants' grant. If you have a husband, wife or partner or another member of your family who depends on you financially, you maybe eligible.

- Students who are disabled or who have a specific learning difficulty can apply for grants from the Disabled Student Allowances (DSA). A booklet about DSAs called 'Bridging the Gap' is available from your LEA or from the Department for Education and Skills on 0800 731 9133, by textphone on 0800 328 8988 or can be downloaded from the website at: www.studentsupportdirect.co.uk

- Care Leavers' Grant. This grants can offer up to a £100 a week to students who have been in care.

- Assembly Learning Grant. Funded by the Welsh Assembly Government and paid through LEAs, this grant provides support to help people from low-income families to access and remain in further and higher education. It is intended to help cover the cost of books, equipment, travel and childcare whilst studying. It can be applied for in addition to student loans and some other forms of support and it does not need to be paid back. (www.learning.wales.gov.uk)

Further information

The above information only provides a brief outline. There are free booklets available from the Education Departments. They are probably the easiest basic guide to funding your course. They are updated each year, so make sure you get the latest copy.

For students in England: information can be obtained from the Department for Education and Skills (Website: www.dfes.gov.uk/studentsupport).

For students in Wales: information can be obtained from Student Finance Wales (Website: www.studentfinancewales.co.uk).

For students in Scotland: Information can be obtained from: Student Awards Agency for Scotland (Website: www.student-support-saas.gov.uk).

For students in Northern Ireland: Information can be obtained from the Department for Employment and Learning (Website: www.delni.gov.uk).

Advice is available from your LEA (the addresses are printed in the chapter entitled *Local Education Authorities* later in this guide). However, please note that the busiest time for LEAs is the period between mid-August (when A-level results come out) and about mid-November (by which time most awards have been). It is probably best not to contact your LEA for detailed advice at this time unless absolutely necessary.

Further advice and information services are listed in the *Sources of further information and advice* section of this publication.

Access funds

Access to Learning funds (or Financial Contingency Funds in Wales) are administered by the individual college or university. They are there to help students with financial difficulties and do not have to be repaid. Each college will have its own policy on distributing the funds. The sizes of the grants given will therefore vary, but will depend on your circumstances, how many other applications they have received and how much funds the college has. They can be paid as a short-term loan but would usually be a grant. Some colleges may offer bursaries from these funds (a grant for each year of the course) for mature students or others who may be prevented from completing their course because of financial problems. Ask if your college operates a bursary scheme before you start the course. To apply you must be studying full-time or part-time (at least 50% of a full-time course) and on an undergraduate or postgraduate course. Further education students at university or higher education college can also apply. Students will be assessed according to individual needs.

For students eligible for a loan you must have already applied for your full entitlement before applying to the Access funds. You can apply more than once through the year. You will need to provide evidence of your financial circumstances. The college will deal with any appeals if you are not satisfied with the decision.

Please note that Access funds are not tied to Access courses.

Hardship funds

Like Access funds, hardship funds are administered by the individual college or university. Hardship funds provide extra support for students who experience unforeseen or higher than expected costs. They can be used to help with general living costs such as rent, and also course-related costs such as books and equipment or travel, or childcare. Hardship fund payments can range between £100 and £3,500 according to need. These can be either non-repayable grants or repayable loans. Whether you receive a payment, and how much, is up to the individual college or university to decide and will depend on your circumstances. They will also decide whether to pay you in a lump sum or in instalments. Contact your student services department for more details.

Teacher training

The following information was taken from the Training and Development Agency for Schools website at: www.tda.gov.uk/. Please refer to this site for further information and up-to-date advice.

To address the problem of the current shortage of teachers the government is offering training salaries to trainee teachers in England and Wales. There are also a number of financial incentives available to those doing subjects where there is a particular shortage. Shortage subjects include design and technology, information and communications technology, mathematics, modern languages, music, religious education or science, and also Welsh and English in Wales.

The information below relates to details for the year 2006/07, for up-to-date information on these schemes please refer to www.tda.gov.uk

For England, support for trainee teachers on approved postgraduate routes for 2006/07 has been announced. Student support has been devolved to Wales with effect from 2006/07. For further information about the academic year 2006/07 please visit www.learning.wales.gov.uk

Undergraduates

If you take an undergraduate course of Initial Teacher Training (ITT) in England

These courses do not automatically attract any special funding. From September 2006, the DfES will provide a means-tested grant of up to £2,700 each year for all undergraduate students.

Priority subjects in England are currently:

- design and technology
- information and communications technology
- mathematics
- modern languages
- music
- religious education
- science.

Your eligibility for such an award will be assessed by your university or college, but bear in mind that the amount you receive could vary significantly, and you are not guaranteed to receive anything.

If you take an undergraduate course of ITT in Wales

If you are an undergraduate training in Wales to be a secondary teacher, you may be eligible for a Secondary Undergraduate Placement Grant to support you during your school-based placement. These grants amount to £1,000 for trainees in priority subject areas and £600 in all other secondary non-priority subject areas.

This funding is provided through your ITT provider. Priority subjects in Wales are currently:

- English (including drama)
- design and technology
- information and communications technology
- mathematics
- modern languages
- science
- Welsh.

Postgraduates

If you take a postgraduate course of ITT in England or Wales

From September 2006, students in England will be eligible for a non-means tested grant of £1,200 and to apply for an additional means-tested grant of £1,500.

On 23 September 2005, The Welsh Assembly Government announced the package of teaching incentives available to PGCE students in Wales from September 2006. The new incentives package takes account of the fact that tuition fee finances in Wales are different from those in England and the value of individual incentives differ accordingly, however, the overall level of support available (the combination of incentives and funding toward tuition fees) is the same in both countries.

Visit the DfES student support website for full details of funding available for home students and how you can apply. Separate arrangements have been put in place for EU students. Please check the DfES EU website for full details of funding available to students from the EU.

In addition, eligible postgraduate trainee teachers are entitled to a tax-free bursary while they train, the value of which will depend on where you train, the subject you are training to teach, and when you start your course.

The Welsh medium incentive supplement

Trainees undertaking secondary ITT postgraduate courses in Wales and training through the medium of Welsh may also be eligible for the £1,200 Welsh Medium Incentive Supplement. This is aimed at trainees who need extra support to raise confidence in their ability to teach effectively through the medium of Welsh.

Decisions on eligibility for the Welsh Medium Incentive Supplement are made by the individual ITT providers involved in the scheme; information on courses that qualify for this supplement can be obtained from the ITT providers.

If you take an employment-based programme of ITT

Trainee teachers on the Graduate Teacher Programme (GTP), the Registered Teacher Programme (RTP) and the overseas trained teacher programme (OTTP, England only) all receive a salary from their school. This will be at least equal to the minimum point on the unqualified teacher pay scale, but your school may choose to pay you more.

In general, if you undertake an employment-based route into teaching in England, the TDA will pay your school to cover the cost of your training.

In Wales, state-maintained schools supporting a trainee on the GTP are eligible to receive a grant of £13,000 towards the cost of the trainee's salary and an additional grant of £4,000 to cover training costs.

'Golden hellos' and other financial incentives

If you complete your ITT you may also be eligible to receive an additional payment – a 'golden hello' in England or a teaching grant in Wales – once you complete your induction year. Golden Hellos apply to postgraduate routes only and do not apply for those qualifying through GTP or RTP.

Not strictly speaking funding, these payments and other related schemes are designed to encourage people to enter the profession and teach particular priority subjects.

England

If you complete a postgraduate ITT and take up an NQT position in a maintained school or non-maintained special school in England, you may be eligible to receive a one-off, taxable 'golden hello' payment of between £2,500 and £5,000 at the start of your second year of teaching, after successfully completing your induction period.

Golden hellos are available to eligible NQTs who have trained to teach English (including drama); information and communications technology; design and technology; modern foreign languages; religious education; music; mathematics; or science.

The amount you receive will depend on your subject, with mathematics and science attracting £5,000 and all other priority subjects £2,500.

Wales

Like the golden hellos available in England, the teaching grant for mathematics and science teachers amounts to £5,000. However, if you teach English (including drama); information and communication technology; modern foreign languages;

design and technology; or Welsh, you may be eligible to receive £4,000.

Further Information

Further information on any teacher training issues contact the Teaching Information Line on 0845 6000 991, or the Welsh Language Teaching Information Line on 0845 6000 992. If you are an FE teacher, contact The Further Education National Training Organisation (FENTO) on 020 7332 9535 or refer to the Training and Development Agency for Schools website at www.tda.gov.uk

Funding and bursaries for NHS courses

NHS bursaries for medical and dental courses

Undergraduate medical and dental students living in England on standard 5 to 6 year courses in any UK country, and who joined their course from September 1998 onwards, will be eligible for NHS bursaries and help with tuition fees in their fifth and further years of study. They can also receive 50% of the full loan in their fifth and further years of study. For the first four years on the medical or dental course their support will be on the same basis as for other higher education students.

Students living in England on the four-year graduate entry medical programmes will be eligible for NHS bursaries and help with tuition fees in years two to four of the course. They can also receive 50% of the full loan in years two to four of the course. In the first year of the course their support will be on the same basis as other graduate entry higher education students, except there is no income assessed tuition fee support.

National Health Service bursaries for health professional courses

NHS bursaries are available for full-time or part-time pre-registration courses in England in the following subjects:

- Audiology
- Chiropody
- Dental hygiene
- Dental therapy
- Dietetics
- Nursing
- Midwifery
- Occupational therapy
- Operating department practice
- Orthoptics
- Physiotherapy
- Prosthetics and orthotics
- Radiography
- Speech and language therapy

To be eligible for an NHS bursary you must be accepted for an NHS-funded place. NHS funded students are also eligible for payments from the Access to Learning Fund.

Further Information

For students in England: The 'Financial Help for Health Care Students' booklet explains NHS funding for students in more detail. You can get a copy of the booklet on-line at www.nhsstudentgrants.co.uk or for information on NHS bursaries contact The Customer Services Team, The NHS Student Grants Unit, Hesketh House, Fleetwood FY7 8LG (0845 358 6655; e-mail: enquiries@nhspa.gov.uk.

For students in Wales: The NHS Wales Student Awards Unit, National Leadership and Innovation Agency for Healthcare (NLIAH), 2nd Floor Golate House, 101 St Mary Street, Cardiff, CF10 1DX (029 2026 1495; www.nliah.wales.nhs.uk)

For students in Scotland: The Student Awards Agency for Scotland, Gyleview House, 3 Redheughs Rigg, Edinburgh EH12 9HH (0845 111 1711; www.saas.gov.uk/home.htm).

For students in Northern Ireland: Student Finance ni, Customer Support Office (0845 600 0662)

Help for students studying an approved social work course in England

The General Social Care Council (GSCC) provides bursaries to students studying approved degree or diploma courses in social work. Applicants must meet the eligibility criteria set out in the GSCC bursary application form and guidance notes which can be downloaded from the Bursaries page of the GSCC website (www.gscc.org.uk/Home/). If your question is not answered on the website, please e-mail your enquiry to bursaries@gscc.org.uk. You can also write to GSCC Bursaries, General Social Care Council, Bursaries Office, Goldings House, 2 Hay's Lane, London SE1 2HB (020 7397 5835).

Social work bursary for students on full-time undergraduate or non-graduate courses

If you are not subject to variable tuition fees The General Social Care Council (GSCC hereafter) can offer you the grant rate below, which is paid in three instalments:

- Students studying full-time at a London-based university or college – up to £3,475 for a 52-week period.
- Students studying full-time at a London-based university or college outside London – up to £3,075 for a 52-week period.

If you are subject to variable tuition fees they will offer you the grant rate below, which is also paid in three instalments.

- Students studying full-time at a London-based university or college – up to £4,975 for a 52-week period.
- Students studying full-time at a university or college outside London – up to £4,575 for a 52-week period.

As the grant contains a tuition fee contribution, the GSCC are not responsible for paying any tuition fee to your university or college. How you use the grant is up to you. You do not have to use it towards your tuition fees if you choose.

Social work bursary for students on part-time undergraduate, non-graduate or postgraduate courses

If you are studying on a part-time postgraduate course or you are a continuing student studying on a part time undergraduate or non-graduate course, in general the GSCC can offer you the grant rate below, which is paid in three instalments.

- Students studying part-time at a London-based university or college – up to £1,737.50 for a 52-week period.
- Students studying part-time at a university or college outside London – up to £1,537.50 for a 52-week period.

If you are starting your part-time undergraduate or non-graduate course for the academic year 2006/07, in general we will offer you the grant rate below, which is paid in three instalments.

- Students studying part-time at a London-based university or college – up to £2,487.50 for a 52-week period.
- Students studying part-time at a university or college outside London – up to £2,287.50 for a 52-week period.

Postgraduate for students on full-time postgraduate courses

- Students studying full-time at a London-based university or college – up to £3,475 for a 52-week period.
- Students studying full-time at a university or college outside London – up to £3,075 for a 52-week period.

Additional applications for students on full-time postgraduate courses:

Income-assessed childcare allowance

If you are on an undergraduate or non-graduate course and have children, contact your local authority for possible assistance with your childcare costs.

Disabled students' allowances

If you are on an undergraduate or non-graduate course and have a disability, or develop a disability during your course, contact your local authority for possible support.

Further Information

For students in Wales: Care Council for Wales (CCW), South Gate House, Wood Street, Cardiff CF10 1EW (029 2022 6257; email info@ccwales.org.uk; www.ccwales.org.uk/)

For students in Scotland: Scottish Social Services Council (SSSC), Compass House, 11 Riverside Drive, Dundee, DD1 4NY (01382 207101; e-mail enquiries@sssc.uk.com; www.sssc.uk.com/Homepage.htm)

For students in Northern Ireland: Social Services Inspectorate (SSI), The Department of Health, Social Services and Public Safety, Castle Buildings, Stormont, Belfast, BT 4 3SJ (028 90520500; www.dhsspsni.gov.uk/index/ssi.htm).

Company sponsorship & Career development loans

This chapter looks at two possible sources of finance for some students:

- **Company sponsorships** – which apply particularly to people in their last year at school who are intending to study a business-related, engineering, or science-based subject at university.

- **Career development loans** – which can be a useful means of helping finance vocational courses for periods of up to two years, particularly if the course holds out the prospect of obtaining a steady, reasonably well-paid job at the end.

Company sponsorships

Sponsorship of degree courses

A number of companies sponsor students taking degree courses at universities, usually in business, engineering, technology or other science subjects. These are generally for students resident in the UK taking a first degree course, or a comparable course.

Sponsorship generally takes the form of cash support (i.e. a bursary/scholarship) whilst at university, with a salary being paid during pre-university and vacation employment or periods of industrial training at the company concerned. (If the sponsorship is for a sandwich course the placements will be for longer than the vacation and will form an integral part of the course.) Sponsorships are highly competitive but can be of great value to students who, for any reason, do not receive the full grant. They may also help students avoid having to take out a loan.

Each company has its own sponsorship policy. Some sponsorships are tied to a particular course or institution; others are only given for specific subjects. The value of the sponsorship also varies. Additional help can be available in the form of discretionary educational gifts or degree prizes.

Sponsorships do not necessarily offer a permanent job at the end of the course (unless the student is classed as an employee). Equally, the student does not usually have to take up a job if offered one by the company, although there may be at least a moral obligation to consider one.

Students should not decide on a course simply because there may be sponsorship available, they should choose the course first and seek sponsorship afterwards if appropriate.

In most sponsorships it is the student, not the company, who has to make arrangements to get on the course. Indeed some companies will only sponsor students who have already been accepted on a course. However, most university departments have well established links with industry and actively encourage students seeking sponsorship.

Students should apply for sponsorships as early as possible in the autumn term of the final academic year before moving to university.

Year in Industry

This is an option for students to take a year between school and university to earn money and gain work experience. It can help you to clarify which course you want to take, and to decide what you want to do once you have completed it.

The Year in Industry is an education charity which finds placements for students in the high performance engineering industry during this year. It offers the chance of sponsorship or paid vacation work, is available nationwide and is open to any students interested in a career in industry. The package includes "off the job" training to develop interpersonal skills and business awareness.

Applications for pre-degree places in industry can be made directly to the company or through the scheme. It is recommended that applications are made as early as possible in the final year of A-levels, Highers, Advanced GNVQ and so on. There is a non-refundable £25 registration fee for applying.

For further information you should contact one of the regional centres which administer the scheme. Details can be found by visiting the website at www.yini.org.uk.

Further information

The main guide on company sponsorships is *Engineering Opportunities*. This is published by the Institution of Mechanical Engineers, 1 Birdcage Walk, London, SW1H 9JJ (020 7222 7899; Website: www.imeche.org.uk). It is published annually and is available free of charge.

Details of company sponsorship for other industries is a little sketchy. Individuals are best advised to identify major institutions working in the industry they intend following and see what schemes are available.

Career development loans

Career Development Loans (CDLs) are available through an arrangement between the Learning and Skills Council (LSC) and three high street banks. They incur no interest or repayments until the course is completed. The interest during the duration of the course (and one month afterwards) is met by the LSC. The loan is then repaid to the bank over an agreed period at a fixed rate of interest.

To be eligible, you must meet the following criteria:

- be aged 18 or over at time of application

- be unable to pay for the course yourself

- be ordinarily resident in England, Scotland or Wales with an unlimited right in the UK

- intend to work in the European Union (which includes Iceland, Liechtenstein and Norway) once the course is finished.

CDLs can not be given for courses financed through another publically-funded source, student loans or non-means tested NHS bursary. Employed people receiving a grant from their employer are also ineligible.

Amount available

The amount available ranges from £300 to £8,000. Loans, and deferments, can be made for up to two years (three if a year's practical experience is included as part of the course). Therefore, for courses lasting longer than this, it is recommended that the CDL is only taken for the final two years to avoid repayments starting whilst still studying. For part-time courses, the loans can be used for up to 80% of the course fees (or up to the full amount if the applicant has been unemployed for at least three months), whilst full-time students can claim up to 100% of their living expenses as well as the course fees entitlement. As CDLs can affect benefit claims, it is worth considering the full implications of a loan before agreeing to one. However, people claiming as full-time students are entitled to work for up to 30 hours a week during their study without eligibility for a CDL being affected (provided they do not have the means for financing their study from these wages).

For course fees, payment is paid directly to the learning provider as and when needed. For living expenses, payments are only made once the bank has received notification from the provider that the individual has started the course. Living expenses are normally paid in instalments rather than in full at the start of the course. There is no obligation to bank with the financial institution providing the CDL, the only benefit of already being a customer is that it sometimes involves having less forms to fill in rather than affecting the outcome of the application.

Repayments

Repayments begin one month after the completion of the course. This is interpreted as the intended finishing date at the start of the course, the day the learner withdraws from the courses or extensions provided due to ill health or similar unforeseen circumstances. Extensions given for other reasons, such as late submission of a dissertation, are not accepted as a new finishing date. Similarly, submitting a dissertation before a deadline, for example, does not affect the referral date.

There are options to postpone the start of repayments if you are receiving a statutory means-tested benefit at the end of the course, although this must be agreed by the bank. Therefore, people actively looking for employment and receiving Jobseeker's Allowance, for instance, may be able to defer, whereas people opting to spend a year travelling before looking for work cannot.

The rate of interest is agreed when the loan is taken out and a plan for repayments is made. These can be spread over one to five years. Banks can offer different interest rates within the scheme.

Further information

A booklet on the scheme, including the literature from each of the participating banks, is available by: telephone on 0800 585 505 (8am to 10pm seven days a week); or via the internet at www.lifelonglearning.dfes.gov.uk/cdl. Repayment details can be obtained from branches of the three participating banks:

Barclays Bank PLC (0845 60 900 60).

The Co-operative Bank (08457 212 212).

The Royal Bank of Scotland (0800 121 127).

INDEPENDENT & BOARDING SCHOOLS

Many children in the UK are educated away from home. Often this is a result of parental choice, but sometimes it is an educational or social necessity. This chapter looks at some of the options available for independent and boarding school education. It is divided into four sections:

- Maintained schools with boarding provision
- Useful contact for information on boarding schools
- Music, dance and stage schools
- Other possible sources of help with fees

Please note this section does not include information on independent boarding schools in the UK. Further information on these schools, including a publication called 'Choosing a Boarding School – a Guide for Parents' is available free of charge from: The Boarding Schools Association, Grosvenor Gardens House, 35–37 Grosvenor Gardens, London SW1W 0BS (020 7798 1580; e-mail: bsa@boarding.org.uk; Website: www.boarding.org.uk).

Maintained schools with boarding provision

For some children, education away from home (more commonly known as boarding education) is a desirable alternative to day school; for others it is an educational or social necessity. A report by the Boarding Schools Association identified 13 categories of children who may be in boarding need, including the following:

- Children with a parent in HM Forces (liable to posting)
- Children of UK parents working overseas
- Children for whom there is no nearby school
- Children whose parents move frequently
- Children whose family background is unstable (such as through parental illness, overcrowding, relationship break-up)
- Children with behavioral difficulties for whom boarding is the best option
- Children for whom boarding is desirable for religious reasons
- Children with special talents (such as in music or ballet), for which there is no local provision.

Under the terms of the 1980 Education Act, any parent can opt for a boarding education at a maintained school for their child, whether this is for educational or social reasons or a combination of both.

The local education authority (LEA) maintains schools with boarding provision; the fees payable at these schools are in two parts: the boarding fees and the tuition fees. Boarding fees are paid by (or for) the parent(s); tuition fees are paid by the local LEA (where the child is normally resident). Therefore, maintained schools are a much cheaper way for parents wishing their children to have a boarding education than independent schools.

Maintained boarding schools range from schools where the majority of pupils are boarders to normal day schools with one or two boarding houses. Many of the schools are now providing weekly as well as full boarding. Boarding fees vary between schools; the average cost is £5,909 and £3,107 for day fees per term. Some local authorities will help with boarding fees and a few schools have their own funds to help families on low incomes.

There are currently 32 maintained schools with boarding provision, with one school in Wales, the rest in England. While the majority of schools are mixed, there are 11 single sex schools of which nine are boys only and two are girls only. There are over 4,000 boarding places available in maintained schools.

Applications procedure

There is no central application system; parents wanting to place a child in a maintained school should contact the individual schools to see if there are any vacancies (remembering that you are not restricted to a local school, rather you can apply to any maintained school with boarding provision anywhere in the country). The school will send a prospectus and arrange an interview. Parents should then contact the local authority to tell them of the decision and establish what they should do next (the procedure varies from authority to authority).

A directory, published by the Boarding Schools Association, is available free of charge, giving further information about each school (see below). It is probably worth getting hold of this directory before contacting the school that interests you. Further information contact DfES by e-mail: info@dfes.gsi.gov.uk, or by ringing 0870 000 2288 for a full list of relevant publications that are available free of charge.

Useful contacts for information on boarding schools

The Boarding Schools Association

For further information on boarding schools including maintained schools with boarding provision contact Adrian Underwood, Secretary, the Boarding Schools Association, Grosvenor Gardens House, 35–37 Grosvenor Gardens, London SW1W 0BS (020 7798 1580).

Mr Underwood can give more detailed advice on the workings of state maintained boarding schools and the procedures for applying both to the school and the local authority (although he cannot recommend individual schools). Information on boarding schools can also be found on the Association's website at: www.boarding.org.uk, or e-mail: bsa@boarding.org.uk.

The Independent Schools Council Information Service (ISCis)

ISCis, Grosvenor Gardens House, 35–37 Grosvenor Gardens, London SW1W 0BS (020 7798 1500; Fax: 020 7798 1501; e-mail: office@isc.co.uk; Website: www.iscislse.co.uk).

ISCis is the main source of information on independent schools. Its website contains lots of detailed information to enable families to select the right school and find possible sources of funding.

There are also eight ISCis/ISIS regional offices. Each publishes a regional handbook of schools and has a detailed knowledge of regional schools. Many offices also organise exhibitions attended by member schools. Contact addresses and services provided by the offices are as follows:

ISCis London & South East

Deborah Yonge, Regional Director, ISCis London & South East, 14 Buckingham Palace Road, London, SW1W 0QP (020 7798 1560; Fax: 020 7798 1561; e-mail: southeast@iscislse.co.uk; Website: www.iscislse.co.uk).

More than 500 schools are in membership. Its main function is to provide the public with information and advice about independent schools in the region. The office distributes 30,000 free regional handbooks to parents each year and school exhibitions are organised where parents can meet ISCis staff and school head teachers. Families can also take advantage of the professional consultation and placement services.

ISCis South and West

Quentin Edwards, Regional Director, ISCis South and West, Cools Farm, East Knoyle, Salisbury, Wiltshire SP3 6DB (01747 830761; Fax: 01747 830859; e-mail: southwest@isc.co.uk; Website: www.iscis-sw.co.uk).

This region has over 200 schools in membership, and covers the whole of the southwest peninsula including Bristol, the M4 corridor as far as Reading, and eastwards as far as Portsmouth. The offices distribute 16,000 free copies of the regional handbook each year. Information and advice is available free of charge from office staff.

ISCis East

Mark Filler, Regional Director, ISCis East, Pipanbrig, Shortgrove Lane, Hopton, Diss, Norfolk IP2 22RP (01953 688 242; Fax: 01953 688 245; e-mail: info@iscis-east.co.uk Website: www.iscis-east.co.uk).

The office is open between 9am and 4.30pm on Tuesdays, Wednesdays and Thursdays. The region has 110 member schools.

ISCis Central

Robin Barlow, Regional Director, ISCis Central, 5 Barby Road, Rugby, Warwickshire CV22 5DT (01788 570537; Fax: 01788 575889; e-mail: office@isciscentral.info; Website: www.isciscentral.info).

The region has about 240 member schools, and covers the area from Shrewsbury and Hereford in the west to Lincoln, Peterborough and Bedford in the east, Swindon and the line of the M4 in the south, and Nottingham and Derbyshire in the north. It includes OX and MK postcodes.

ISCis Wales

Ian Brown, Regional Director & ISC Political Officer, ISCis Wales, Regional Director & ISC Political Officer, ISCis Wales, Hazelhurst, Ledbury Road, Dymock, Gloucestershire GL18 2AG (Tel / Fax: 01531 890150; e-mail: ibrwn6@aol.com).

A free handbook is available on request.

ISIS North

Don Hutton, Regional Director, ISIS North, Southwick Grange, Finghall, Nr. Leyburn, North Yorkshire DL8 5NB (01677 450139; Fax: 01677 450140; e-mail: regionaldirector@isis-north.co.uk; Website: www.isis-north.co.uk).

The region covers the area from Berwick to Carlisle, and North Wales to Hull. Staff are available to assist parents with queries about potential schools. There are a number of local exhibitions that provide parents with an opportunity to hear about schools in their region. A regional handbook is available free of charge.

Scotland

Fiona Valpy, SCIS/ISIS Assistant Director, 21 Melville Street, Edinburgh EH3 7PE (0131 220 2106; Fax: 0131 225 8594; e-mail: information@scis.org.uk; Website: www.scis.org.uk).

There are over 100 independent schools in Scotland, 70 of which belong to the Scottish Council of Independent Schools (scis). For further information a free handbook is available.

Northern Ireland and Irish Republic

Palmer Carter, Regional Director, ISC Ireland, 5 Sandycove Avenue East, Sandy Cove, County Dublin, Eire (00 353 1 280 9545; e-mail: palmercarter@eircom.net).

Music, dance and stage schools

Choir schools

The Choir Schools' Association is a group of 44 schools attached to cathedrals, churches and college chapels around the country. Pupils have unlimited access to a first-class schooling and musical training.

Further information (for example about age restrictions, voice trials and so on) can be obtained by contacting the CSA Information Officer, Windrush, Church Road, Market Weston, Diss, Norfolk IP22 2NX (01359 221333; Fax: 01359 221835, or email: info@choirschools.org.uk).

Alternatively contact the CSA Administrator, Wolvesey, College Street, Winchester, Hampshire SO23 9ND (01962 890530, Fax: 01962 869978, or email: admin@choirschools.org.uk).

Music schools

Parents should contact one of the following specialist schools directly: Chetham's School of Music, Manchester; The Purcell School, Bushey, Hertfordshire; Wells Cathedral School, Wells; Yehudi Menuhin School, Cobham; and St Mary's Music School, Edinburgh.

Dance schools

Information on vocational training in dance and drama can be obtained from the Council for Dance, Education and Training (CDET), Council for Dance Education and Training, Old Brewer's Yard, 17-19 Neal Street, Covent Garden, London WC2H 9UY (0207 240 5703; Fax: 020 7240 2547; e-mail: info@cdet.org.uk; Website: www.cdet.org.uk).

Stage schools

Although no specific national organisation exists to give advice in this area. The National Council for Drama Training (NCDT) primarily provides information for those wishing to start higher education courses in acting and stage management. It can however provide some information on drama schools for those aged 18 or above. Their address is: 1–7 Woburn Walk, London WC1H 0JJ (020 7387 3650; Fax: 020 7387 3860; e-mail: info@ncdt.co.uk), they will send information to you on receipt of a stamped addressed envelope. Information is also available from the organisation's website at: www.ncdt.co.uk/

Many independent schools offer scholarships and bursaries to one or a few applicants. Scholarships vary in value but rarely cover the whole fees; minor scholarships might be worth as little as 10%. Many schools supplement scholarships with bursaries based on parental means. For historical reasons, there can be various restrictions on eligibility, for example they may only be given to children of Church of England clergy. They can be subject to fierce competition, and are often awarded on the basis of academic merit as well as individual need.

Music scholarships

A number of independent schools also offer music scholarships. Children aged 7 to 18 can qualify, but often children have to be under 14 when they apply (contact the Director of Music at the individual school for more details). Scholarships can vary from 10% to full fees paid (including free musical tuition). There is strong competition for places and candidates often have to offer two instruments (or one instrument and voice). Usually schools expect Associated Board Grades 6 – 8 on the main instrument, although again the individual school will give more precise details.

Useful publications and points of contact

The Independent Schools Yearbook is published by A & C Black, 37 Soho Square, London W1D 3QZ (020 7758 0200) and is available in most public libraries. It has good information on entrance and music scholarships and information on all school.

For information on music awards at independent schools please contact The Music Masters and Mistresses Association, MMA Awards Book, Way Faring, Smithers Lane, East Peckhan, Tonbridge TN12 5HT. Details are also available on the association's website at www.mma-online.org.uk, or email Carol Hawkins, the MMA administrator for further information at cjh@stedmunds.org.uk.

Comprehensive lists of academic, music and arts scholarships are also available from the Girls Schools Association (GSA), Tel: 0116 254 1619, email: office@gsa.uk.com; or from the Headmasters' and Headmistresses' Conference (HMC) schools, Tel: 0116 285 4810, email: hmc@hmc.org.uk.

The website www.dfes.gov.uk/mds, which is run by the DfES, provides details on scholarships and grants for young people interested in specialising in music and dance. It includes details of participating schools and centres that offer training, and explains how to apply for a place. It is also piloting a new national grants in music and dance scheme, details of which can be found on the website.

Other possible sources of help with fees

Allowances for Crown servants

Children whose parent(s) are serving overseas in the diplomatic service are eligible for grants from their government department to contribute to the cost of fees. The grants are set at a fixed rate for junior and senior school, day and boarding fees.

For further information contact: Education Unit, Foreign and Commonwealth Office, 1 Palace Street, London SW1E 5HE (020 7270 1500).

Allowances for armed forces personnel

Children whose parent(s) are members of Her Majesty's Forces are also eligible for an allowance towards boarding education, whether their parent is serving at home or abroad.

Further information can be obtained from the education or personnel officers on the unit or from: HQSCE (UK), Service Children's Education, Trenchard Lines, Uphaven, Pewsey, Wiltshire SN9 6BE (01980 618244).

Multinational companies

Some multinational companies and organisations help with school fees if parents have to work overseas. A few firms make grants, run scholarship schemes, or provide low interest loans for employees resident in the UK. You should consult your employer.

Local authorities

Local authorities vary in the way they make grants to parents of children attending independent schools. However, if you can demonstrate a need for boarding education (possibly based on the reasons set out in the section on maintained schools with boarding provision above) and also show how the maintained schools cannot meet that need, then the local authority may help with the costs of boarding and/or tuition fees.

Apply to the Director of Education or Chief Education Officer for the area in which you live or, if you live outside the UK, with which you have most connection.

EDUCATION AUTHORITIES

This section provides a list of council offices or education departments for Britain. A list of the four main government education departments is also included. Please note that a list of Local Education Authorities (LEAs) can be found on the DfES Student Support website at: www.dfes.gov.uk/studentsupport/.

Government departments

Department for Education and Skills: Sanctuary Buildings, Great Smith Street, Westminster, London SW1P 3BT (08700 002288; Fax: 01928 794248; e-mail: info@dfes.gsi.gov.uk; Website: www.dfes.gov.uk).

Welsh Office Education Department: Crown Buildings, Cathays Park, Cardiff CF10 3NQ (029 2082 5111; Website: www.learning.wales.gov.uk).

Department of Education for Northern Ireland: Rathgael House, 43 Balloo Road, Bangor, Co. Down BT19 7PR (028 9127 9279; Fax: 028 9127 9100; e-mail: mail@deni.gov.uk; Website: www.deni.gov.uk).

Scottish Education Department: Victoria Quay, Edinburgh EH6 6QQ (0131 556 8400; Fax: 0131 244 8240; e-mail: ceu@scotland.gov.uk; Website: www.scotland.gov.uk).

Local Education Authorities

England

Bath & North East Somerset Council: PO Box 25, Guild Hall, High Street, Bath BA1 5AW (01225 477000; Fax: 01225 394011; Website: www.bathnes.gov.uk).

Bedfordshire County Council: Arts and Libraries, County Hall, Cauldwell Street, Bedford MK42 9AP (01234 363222; Fax: 01324 228619; Website: www.bedfordshire.gov.uk).

Blackburn with Darwen Borough Council: Town Hall, Blackburn, Lancashire BB1 7DY (01254 585585; Fax: 01254 698388; Website: www.blackburn.gov.uk).

Blackpool Borough Council: PO Box 77, Town Hall, Blackpool FY1 1AD (01253 477477; Fax: 01253 476504; Website: www.blackpool.gov.uk).

Bournemouth Borough Council: Town Hall, Bourne Avenue, Bournemouth BH2 6DY (01202 451451; Fax: 01202 451000; e-mail: enquiries@bournemouth.gov.uk; Website: www.bournemouth.gov.uk).

Bracknell Forest Borough Council: Easthampstead House, Town Square, Bracknell RG12 1AQ (01344 352000; Fax: 01344 352810; Website: www.bracknell-forest.gov.uk).

City of Bradford Metropolitan District Council: Flockton House, Flockton Road, Bradford BD4 7RY (01274 751840; Fax: 01274 740612; Website: www.bradford.gov.uk).

Brighton & Hove Council: King's House, Grand Avenue, Hove BN3 2LS (01273 290000; Website: www.brighton-hove.gov.uk).

Bristol City Council: PO Box 57, The Council House, College Green, Bristol BS1 5TR (0117 922 2000; Fax: 0117 903 7963; Website: www.bristol-city.gov.uk).

Buckinghamshire County Council: County Hall, Walton Street, Aylesbury HP20 1UA (0845 370 8090; Fax: 01296 383367; Website: www.buckscc.gov.uk).

Calderdale Metropolitan Borough Council: Town Hall, Crossley Street, Halifax HX1 1UJ (01422 357257; Fax: 01422 343102; Website: www.calderdale.gov.uk).

Cambridgeshire County Council: Shire Hall, Castle Hill, Cambridge CB3 0AP (01223 717970; Fax: 01223 717201; Website: www.cambridgeshire.gov.uk).

Cheshire County Council: County Hall, Chester, Cheshire CH1 1SF (01244 602424; Fax: 01244 603821; e-mail: info@cheshire.gov.uk; Website: www.cheshire.gov.uk).

Cornwall County Council: County Hall, Treyew Road, Truro, Cornwall TR1 3AY (01872 322000; Fax: 01872 270340; e-mail: childrenservices@cornwall.gov.uk; Website: www.cornwall.gov.uk).

Cumbria County Council: Education Offices, 5 Portland Square, Carlisle CA1 1PU (01228 606060; Fax: 01228 606237; Website: www.cumbria.gov.uk).

Darlington Borough Council: Education Dept, Town Hall, Darlington DL1 5QT (01325 388807; Fax: 01325 382032; e-mail: student.support@darlington.gov.uk; Website: www.darlington.gov.uk).

Derby City Council: Derby City Education Service, Student Support Section, Middleton House, 27 St Marys Gate, Derby DE1 3NN (01332 716924; Fax: 01332 716709; Website: www.derby.gov.uk).

Derbyshire County Council: Education Offices, County Hall, Matlock DE4 3AG (01629 580000; Fax: 01629 585401; Website: www.derbyshire.gov.uk).

Devon County Council: County Hall, Topsham Road, Exeter EX2 4QD (01392 382000; Fax: 01392 382830; Website: www.devon.gov.uk).

Doncaster Metropolitan Borough Council: Doncaster MBC, 2 Priory Place, Doncaster DN1 1NB (01302 734444; Fax: 01302 737223; Website: www.doncaster.gov.uk).

Dorset County Council: Libraries and Art, County Hall, Colliton Park, Dorchester DT1 1XJ (01305 251000; Website: www.dorsetforyou.com).

Dudley Metropolitan Borough Council: Council House, Priory Road, Westox House, 1 Trinity Road, Dudley DY1 1HF (01384 812345; Fax: 01384 814216; Website: www.dudley.gov.uk).

Durham County Council: County Hall, Durham DH1 5UL (0191 383 4567; Fax: 0191 383 4500; Website: www.durham.gov.uk).

East Riding of Yorkshire: County Hall, Beverley HU17 9BA (01482 393939; Fax: 01482 393375; Website: www.eastriding.gov.uk).

East Sussex County Council: County Hall, St Anne's Crescent, Lewes BN7 1SG (01273 481000; Fax: 01273 481261; Website: www.eastsussex.gov.uk).

Essex County Council: County Hall, Market Road, Chelmsford CM1 1LX (01245 492211; Fax: 01245 492759; Website: www.essexcc.gov.uk).

Gateshead Metropolitan Borough Council: Civic Centre, Regent Street, Gateshead NE8 1HH (0191 433 3000; Fax: 0191 4901168; Website: www.gateshead.gov.uk).

Gloucestershire County Council: Education Department, Shire Hall, Westgate Street, Gloucester GL1 2TG (01452 425300; Website: www.gloucestershire.gov.uk).

Halton Borough Council (formerly Cheshire): Municipal Building, Kingsway, Widnes, Cheshire WA8 7QF (0151 424 2061; Fax: 0151 471 7301; Website: www.halton-borough.gov.uk/).

Greater Manchester

Bolton Borough Council: Pupil and Student Services, PO Box 53, 3rd Floor, Paderborn House, Civic Centre, Bolton BL1 1JW (01204 333333; Fax: 01204 365492; Website: www.bolton.gov.uk).

Bury Borough Council: Bury MBC, Town Hall, Knowsley Street, Bury, Lancashire BL9 OSW (0161 253 5000; Fax: 0161 253 5653;Website: www.bury.gov.uk).

Manchester City Council: Town Hall, Albert Square, Manchester M60 2LA (0161 234 5000 Fax: 0161 234 7007; Website: www.manchester.gov.uk).

Oldham Borough Council: Education and Leisure Services, Civic Centre, West Street, Oldham OL1 1UG (0161 911 3000; Website: www.oldham.gov.uk).

Rochdale Borough Council: Education Department, PO Box 39, Municipal Offices, Smith Street, Rochdale OL16 1LQ (01706 647474; Fax: 01706 658560; Website: www.rochdale.gov.uk).

Salford City Council: Civic Centre, Chorley Road, Swinton, Salford M27 5DA (0161 794 4711; Fax: 0161 728 6068; Website: www.salford.gov.uk).

Stockport Borough Council: Stockport Town Hall, Edward Street, Stockport SK1 3XE (0161 480 4949; Fax: 0161 953 0012; Website: www.stockport.gov.uk).

Tameside Borough Council: Tameside Borough Council: Education and Leisure, Council Offices, Wellington Road, Ashton-under-Lyne OL6 6DL (0161 342 8355; Fax: 0161 342 3070; Website: www.tameside.gov.uk).

Trafford Borough Council: Trafford Town Hall, Talbot Road, Stretford, Manchester M32 OYT (0161 912 2000; Fax: 0161 912 1354; Website: www.trafford.gov.uk).

Wigan Borough Council: Town Hall, Library Street, Wigan WN1 1YN (01942 244991; Fax: 01942 828811; e-mail; education@wiganmbc.gov.uk; Website: www.wiganmbc.gov.uk).

Hampshire County Council: Education County Office, The Castle, Winchester SO23 8UJ (01962 846452; e-mail: enquiries@education.hants.gov.uk; Website: www.hants.gov.uk).

Hartlepool Borough Council: Civic Centre, Victoria Road, Hartlepool TS24 8AY (01429 266522; Fax: 01429 523777; Website: www.hartlepool.gov.uk).

County of Herefordshire Council: Brockington, 35 Hafod Road, Hereford, Herefordshire HR1 1SH (01432 260900; Fax: 01432 260957; e-mail: education@herefordshire.gov.uk; Website: www.herefordshire.gov.uk).

Hertfordshire County Council: County Hall, Pegs Lane, Hertford SG13 8DQ (01923 471555; Website: www.hertsdirect.org).

Hull City Council: Guildhall, Alfred Gelder Street, Hull HU1 2AA (01482 300300; Website: www.hullcc.gov.uk).

Isle of Wight Council: Education Dept, County Hall, High Street, Newport PO30 1UD (01983 821000; Fax: 01983 826099; Website: www.iwight.gov.uk).

Council of The Isles of Scilly: Town Hall, St Mary's, Isles of Scilly TR21 0LW (01720 422537; Fax: 01720 422202; Website: www.scilly.gov.uk).

Kent County Council: Sessions House, County Hall, Maidstone, Kent ME14 1XQ (01622 696565; Website: www.kent.gov.uk).

Lancashire County Council: PO Box 78, County Hall, Fishergate, Preston PR1 8XJ (0845 053 0000; Fax: 01772 533533; Website: www.lancashire.gov.uk).

Leicester City Council: New Walk Centre, Welford Place, Leicester LE1 6ZG (0116 254 9922; Fax: 0116 233 9922; Website: www.leicester.gov.uk).

Leicestershire County Council: County Hall, Glenfield, Leicester LE3 8RA (0116 232 3232; Fax: 0116 265 6634; e-mail: childrenservices@leics.gov.uk; Website: www.leics.gov.uk).

Lincolnshire County Council: Education Department, County Offices, Newland, Lincoln LN1 1YL (01522 552222; Fax: 01522 553257; e-mail: education@lincolnshire.gov.uk; Website: www.lincolnshire.gov.uk).

London

Barking & Dagenham: Civic Centre, Dagenham RM10 7BN (020 8592 4500; e-mail: enquiries@lbbd.gov.uk; Website: www.barking-dagenham.gov.uk).

Barnet: Hendon Town Hall, The Burroughs, Hendon NW4 4BG (020 8359 2000; Website: www.barnet.gov.uk).

Bexley: Education and Community Services, Hill View, Hill View Drive, Welling, Kent DA16 3RY (020 8303 7777; Fax: 020 8319 4302; Website: www.bexley.gov.uk).

Brent: Town Hall, Forty Lane, Wembley HA9 9HD (020 8937 1234; Fax: 020 8937 3040; Website: www.brent.gov.uk).

Bromley: Education Department, Civic Centre, Stockwell Close, Bromley BR1 3UH (020 8313 4088; Fax: 020 8313 4145; Website: www.bromley.gov.uk).

Camden: Camden Town Hall, Judd Street, London WCH1 9JE (020 7278 4444; Fax: 020 7911 1536; Website: www.camden.gov.uk).

Corporation Of London: Economic Development and Education Office, PO Box 270, Guildhall, London EC2P 2EJ (020 7606 3030; Website: www.cityoflondon.gov.uk).

Croydon: Education Offices, Taberner House, Park Lane, Croydon CR9 3JS (020 8686 4433; Fax: 020 8760 5514; Website: www.croydon.gov.uk).

Ealing: 5th Floor, Percival House, 14–16 Uxbridge Road, Ealing W5 2HL (020 8825 5599; Website: www.ealing.gov.uk).

Enfield: Civic Centre, Silver Street, Enfield EN1 3XY (020 8379 1000; Fax: 020 8379 4453; Website: www.enfield.gov.uk).

Greenwich: Town Hall, Wellington Street, Woolwich, London SE18 6PW (020 8854 8888; Fax: 020 8356 2185; Website: www.greenwich.gov.uk).

Hackney: Town Hall, Mare Street, London E8 1EA (020 8356 3000; Fax: 020 8356 2080; Website: www.hackney.gov.uk).

Hammersmith & Fulham: Town Hall, King Street, London W6 9JU (020 8748 3020; Fax: 020 8576 5686; Website: www.lbhf.gov.uk).

Haringey: Education Dept, Civic Centre, High Road, Wood Green, London N22 8LE (020 8489 0000; Website: www.haringey.gov.uk).

Harrow: Civic Centre, Station Road, Harrow HA1 2XF (020 8863 5611; Fax: 020 8863 1966; Website: www.harrow.gov.uk).

Havering: Havering Education, The Broxhill Centre, Broxhill Road, Harold Hill, Romford RM4 1XN (01708 434343; Website: www.havering.gov.uk).

Hillingdon: Youth and Leisure Services, Civic Centre, High Street, Uxbridge UB8 1UW (01895 250111; Fax: 01895 273636; Website: www.hillingdon.gov.uk).

Hounslow: Civic Centre, Lampton Road, Hounslow TW3 4DN (020 8583 2600; Fax: 020 8583 2613; Website: www.hounslow.gov.uk).

Islington: 222 Upper Street, Islington, London N1 1XR (020 7527 2000; Website: www.islington.gov.uk).

Kensington & Chelsea: The Town Hall, Hornton Street, London W8 7NX (020 7361 3000; Fax: 020 7938 1445; Website: www.rbkc.gov.uk).

Kingston-upon-Thames: Royal Borough of Kingston Education, Guildhall, High Street, Kingston-upon-Thames, Surrey KT1 1EU (020 8547 5757; Website: www.kingston.gov.uk).

Lambeth: Education Dept, International House, Canterbury

Crescent, London SW9 7QE (020 7926 1000; Website: www.lambeth.gov.uk).

Lewisham: Directorate for Education and Culture, 3rd Floor, Laurence House, Catford SE6 4RU (020 8314 6000; Website: www.lewisham.gov.uk).

Merton: Merton Civic Centre, London Road, Morden, Surrey SM4 5DX (020 8274 4901; Website: www.merton.gov.uk).

Newham: Education Dept, Broadway House, 322 High Street, Stratford, London E15 1AJ (020 8430 2000; Fax: 020 8430 1066; Website: www.newham.gov.uk).

Redbridge: London Borough of Redbridge, Town Hall, PO Box 2, High Road, Ilford, Essex IG1 1DD (020 8554 5000; Website: www.redbridge.gov.uk).

Richmond-upon-Thames: Education and Children's Services, First Floor, Regal House, London Road, Twickenham TW1 3QB (020 8891 7500; Fax: 020 8891 7714; Website: www.richmond.gov.uk).

Southwark: Town Hall, Peckham Road, London SE5 8UB (020 7525 5000; Website: www.southwark.gov.uk).

Sutton: London Borough of Sutton, Civic Offices, St Nicholas Way, Sutton SM1 1EA (020 8770 5000; Website: www.sutton.gov.uk).

Tower Hamlets: Education and Community Services, Mulberry Place, 5 Clove Crescent, London E14 2BG (020 7364 5000; Website: www.towerhamlets.gov.uk).

Waltham Forest: Town Hall, Forest Road, London E17 4JF (020 8496 3000; Fax: 020 8496 3301; Website: www.lbwf.gov.uk).

Wandsworth: Education Dept, Town Hall, Wandsworth High Street, London SW18 2PU (020 8871 8275; Website: www.wandsworth.gov.uk).

Westminster: Westminster City Hall, 64 Victoria Street, London SW1E 6QP (020 7641 6000; Fax: 020 7245 5510; Website: www.westminster.gov.uk).

Luton Borough Council: Town Hall, George Street, Luton, Bedfordshire LU1 2BQ (01582 546000; Website: www.luton.gov.uk).

Medway Council: Civic Centre, Strood, Rochester, Kent ME2 4AU (01634 306000; Website: www.medway.gov.uk).

Merseyside

Knowsley Borough Council: Education Offices, Huyton Hey Road, Huyton, Merseyside L36 5YH (0151 443 3232; Website: www.knowsley.gov.uk).

Liverpool City Council: Municipal Buildings, Dale Street, Liverpool L69 2DH (0151 233 3000; Website: www.liverpool.gov.uk).

St Helens Borough Council: Town Hall, Victoria Square, St. Helens, Merseyside WA10 1HP (01744 456789; Website: www.sthelens.gov.uk).

Sefton Borough Council: Education Dept, Town Hall, Oriel Road, Bootle, Merseyside L20 7AE (0845 140 0845; Website: www.sefton.gov.uk).

Wirral Borough Council: Town Hall, Brighton Street, Wallasey, Wirral CH44 8ED (0151 606 2000; Website: www.wirral.gov.uk).

Middlesbrough Borough Council: PO Box 99A, Town Hall, Middlesbrough TS1 2QQ (01642 245432; Website: www.middlesbrough.gov.uk).

Milton Keynes Council: Saxon Court, 502 Avebury Boulevard, Milton Keynes MK9 3HS (01908 691691; Fax: 01908 253289; Website: www.mkweb.co.uk).

Norfolk County Council: County Hall, Martineau Lane, Norwich NR1 2DH (0844 800 8020; Fax: 0844 800 8012; Website: www.norfolk.gov.uk).

North East Lincolnshire Council: 7 Eleanor Street, Grimsby DN32 9DU (01472 323208; Fax: 01472 323251; Website: www.nelincs.gov.uk).

North Lincolnshire Council: Pittwood House, Ashby Road, Scunthorpe, North Lincolnshire DN16 1AB (01724 296296; Website: www.northlincs.gov.uk).

North Somerset Council: Town Hall, Walliscote Grove Road, Weston-Super-Mare BS23 1UJ (01934 888888; Fax: 01934 418194; Website: www.n-somerset.gov.uk).

North Yorkshire County Council: County Hall, Northallerton, North Yorkshire DL7 8AD (01609 780780; Fax 01609 778199; Website: www.northyorks.gov.uk).

Northamptonshire County Council: County Hall, Northampton NN1 1DN (01604 236236; Fax: 01604 236652; Website: www.northamptonshire.gov.uk).

Northumberland County Council: Education Department, County Hall, Morpeth NE61 2EF (01670 533000; Fax: 01670 534117; Website: www.northumberland.gov.uk).

Nottingham City Council: The Guildhall, South Sherwood Centre, Nottingham NG7 4BT (0115 915 5555; Fax: 0115 915 4580; Website: www.nottinghamcity.gov.uk).

Nottinghamshire County Council: County Hall, West Bridgford, Nottingham NG2 7QP (0115 982 3823; Fax: 0115 981 2824; Website: www.nottinghamshire.gov.uk).

Oxfordshire County Council: County Hall, New Road, Oxford OX1 1ND (01865 792422; Fax: 01865 815224; Website: www.oxfordshire.gov.uk).

Peterborough City Council: Town Hall, Bridge Street, Peterborough PE1 1QT

(01733 747474; Fax: 01733 452645; Website: www.peterborough.gov.uk).

Plymouth City Council: Civic Centre, Plymouth PL1 2AA (01752 668000; Fax: 01752 304880; Website: www.plymouth.gov.uk).

Borough of Poole Council: Education Dept, Civic Centre, Poole, Dorset BH15 2RU (01202 633633; Website: www.poole.gov.uk).

Portsmouth City Council: Education Dept, Civic Offices, Guildhall Square, Portsmouth PO1 2BG (023 9282 2251; Website: www.portsmouth.gov.uk).

Reading Borough Council: Civic Offices, Civic Centre, Reading RG1 7TD (0118 939 0900; 0118 958 9770; Website: www.reading.gov.uk).

Redcar & Cleveland Borough Council: Redcar & Cleveland House, Kirkleatham Street, Redcar TS10 1YA (01642 444121; Website: www.redcar-cleveland.gov.uk).

Rutland District Council: Department of Education, Youth & Culture, Catmose, Oakham, Rutland LE15 6HP (01572 722577; Fax: 01572 758307; Website: www.rutnet.gov.uk).

Shropshire County Council: Education Services Directorate, Shirehall, Abbey Foregate, Shrewsbury SY2 6ND (0845 678 9000; Fax: 01743 252827; Website: www.shropshire.gov.uk).

Slough Borough Council: Education Office, Town Hall, Bath Road, Slough SL1 3QU (01753 475111; Website: www.slough.gov.uk).

Somerset County Council: County Hall, Taunton, Somerset TA1 4DY (0845 345 9122; Website: www.somerset.gov.uk).

South Gloucestershire Council: Education Services, Bowling Hill, Chipping Sodbury BS37 6JX (01454 868008; Website: www.southglos.gov.uk).

South Yorkshire

Barnsley Borough Council: Education Offices, Berneslai Close, Barnsley S70 2HS (01226 773500; e-mail: education@barnsley.gov.uk; Website: www.barnsley.gov.uk).

Doncaster Borough Council: 2 Priory Place, Doncaster, South Yorkshire DN1 1NB (01302 734444; Website: www.doncaster.gov.uk).

Rotherham Borough Council: Civic Building, Walker Place, Rotherham S65 1UF (01709 822563; Website: www.rotherham.gov.uk).

Sheffield City Council: Education Dept, Town Hall, Sheffield S1 2HH (0114 272 6444; Website: www.sheffield.gov.uk).

Southampton City Council: Education Learning Services, 5th Floor, Frobisher House, Nelson Gate, Southampton SO15

1BZ (023 8022 3855; Website: www.southampton.gov.uk).

Southend-on-Sea Borough Council (formerly Essex): Civic Centre, Victoria Avenue, Southend-on-Sea SS2 6ER (01702 215000; Website: www.southend.gov.uk).

Staffordshire County Council: Education Dept, County Buildings, Martin Street, Stafford ST16 2LH (01785 223121; Fax: 01785 215153; Website: www.staffordshire.gov.uk).

Stockton-on-Tees Borough Council: Education, Leisure & Culture Services, Church Road, Stockton-on-Tees TS18 1TX (01642 393939; Website: www.stockton-bc.gov.uk).

City of Stoke-on-Trent Council: Education Dept, Civic Centre, 2nd Floor, Glebe Street, Stoke-on-Trent ST4 1RN (01782 234567; Website: www.stoke.gov.uk).

Suffolk County Council: Suffolk County Council Headquarters, Endeavour House, 8 Russell Road, Ipswich, Suffolk IP1 2BX (01473 583000; Website: www.suffolkcc.gov.uk).

Surrey County Council: County Hall, Penrhyn Road, Kingston-upon-Thames KT1 2DJ (08456 009009; Fax: 020 8541 9004; Website: www.surreycc.gov.uk).

Swindon Borough Council: Education Department, Sanford House, Sanford Street, Swindon SN1 1QH (01793 463902; Fax: 01793 488597; Website: www.swindon.gov.uk).

Telford and Wrekin Council: Education and Training, Civic Offices, Telford TF3 4LD (01952 202100; 01952 293946; Website: www.telford.gov.uk).

Thurrock Council (formerly Essex): Education Department, PO BOX 118, Civic Offices, New Road, Grays, Thurrock, Essex RM17 6SL (01375 652652; Fax: 01375 652359; Website: www.thurrock.gov.uk).

Torbay Borough Council (formerly Devon): Children's Services, Oldway Mansion, Paignton, Devon TQ3 2TE (01803 208208; Fax: 01803 208225; Website: www.torbay.gov.uk).

Tyne & Wear

Gateshead Borough Council: Education Offices, Civic Centre, Regent Street, Gateshead NE8 1HH (0191 433 3000; Website: www.gateshead.gov.uk).

Newcastle upon Tyne City Council: Education and Libraries, Civic Centre, Barras Bridge, Newcastle upon Tyne NE9 1RD (0191 232 8520; Fax: 0191 211 4908; Website: www.newcastle.gov.uk).

North Tyneside Borough Council: Education Service, Stephenson House, Stephenson Street, North Shields, Tyne and Wear NE30 1QA (0191 200 5006;

Fax: 0191 200 6090; Website: www.northtyneside.gov.uk).

South Tyneside Borough Council: Education Dept, Town Hall & Civic Offices, Westoe Road, South Shields NE33 2RL (0191 427 1717; Fax: 0191 427 0584; Website: www.s-tyneside-mbc.gov.uk).

Sunderland Borough Council: Education and Community Services, PO Box 100, Civic Centre, Sunderland SR2 7DN (0191 553 1000; Website: www.sunderland.gov.uk).

Warrington Borough Council: Education and Lifelong Learning, New Town House, Buttermarket Street, Warrington WA1 2NH (01925 442915; Website: www.warrington.gov.uk).

Warwickshire County Council: Education Department, 22 Northgate Street, Warwick CV34 4SP (01926 412268; Website: www.warwickshire.gov.uk).

West Berkshire Council: Avonbank House, West Street, Newbury RG14 1BZ (01635 42400; Website: www.westberks.gov.uk).

West Midlands

Birmingham City Council: Education Office, The Council House, Victoria Square, Birmingham B1 1BB (0121 303 9944; Website: www.birmingham.gov.uk).

Coventry City Council: Earl Street, Coventry CV1 5RS (024 7683 1547; Fax: 024 7683 1568; Website: www.coventry.gov.uk).

Dudley Borough Council: Student Support Section, Westox House, 1 Trinity Road, Dudley DY1 1JQ (01384 814200; Website: www.dudley.gov.uk).

Sandwell Borough Council: Education and Lifelong Learning, PO Box 41, Shaftesbury House, 402 High Street, West Bromwich B70 9LT (0121 569 2200; Fax: 0121 553 1528; Website: www.lea.sandwell.gov.uk).

Solihull Borough Council: Education & Children's Department, PO Box 20, Council House, Solihull B91 3QU (0121 704 6000; e-mail: education@solihull.gov.uk; Website: www.solihull.gov.uk).

Walsall Borough Council: Education Dept, Civic Centre, Darwall Street, Walsall WS1 1TP (01922 650000; Fax: 01922 720885; Website: www.walsall.gov.uk).

Wolverhampton Borough Council: Education Department, Civic Centre, St Peter's Square, Wolverhampton WV1 1SH (01902 554140; Website: www.wolverhampton.gov.uk).

West Sussex County Council: Education Department, County Hall, Chichester PO19 1RQ (01243 777100; Website: www.westsussex.gov.uk).

West Yorkshire

Bradford District Council: Education and Schools Dept, Flockton House, Flockton Road, Bradford BD4 7RY (01274 385500; Website: www.bradford.gov.uk).

Calderdale Borough Council: Education Department, Halifax HX1 1UJ (01422 392511; Fax: 01422 393102; Website: www.calderdale.gov.uk).

Kirklees Council: Education Service, Oldgate House 8th Floor, 2 Oldgate, Huddersfield HD1 6QW (01484 225242; Website: www.kirkleesmc.gov.uk).

Leeds City Council: Civic Hall, Calverley Street, Leeds LS1 1UR (0113 234 8080; Fax: 0113 395 0219; Website: www.leeds.gov.uk).

Wakefield District Council: Room 229, Chantry House, 123 Kirkgate, Wakefield WF1 1ZS (01924 305674; Website: www.wakefield.gov.uk).

Wigan Borough Council: Town Hall, Library Street, Wigan WN1 1YN (01942 224991; Fax: 01942 828811; Website: www.wiganmbc.gov.uk).

Wiltshire County Council: Education Dept, County Hall, Bythesea Road, Trowbridge, Wiltshire BA14 8JB (01225 713678; Website: www.wiltshire.gov.uk).

Windsor and Maidenhead: Education Dept, Town Hall, St Ives Road, Maidenhead SL6 1RF (01628 796712; Website: www.rbwm.gov.uk).

Wokingham District Council: Education and Cultural Services, Shute End, Wokingham RG40 1BN (0118 974 6000; Website: www.wokingham.gov.uk).

Worcestershire County Council: Education and Lifelong Learning, County Hall, Spetchley Road, Worcester WR5 2NP (01905 763763; Website: www.worcestershire.gov.uk).

City of York Council: The Guildhall, York YO1 9QN (01904 613161; Website: www.york.gov.uk).

Scotland

Aberdeen City Council: Summerhill Education Centre, Stronsay Drive, Aberdeen AB15 6JA (01224 522000; Website: www.aberdeencity.gov.uk).

Aberdeenshire Council: Education and Recreation, Woodhill House, Westburn Road, Aberdeen AB16 5GB (08456 081207; Website: www.aberdeenshire.gov.uk).

Angus Council: Education Department, County Buildings, Market Street, Forfar DD8 3WE (01307 461460; Fax: 01307 461848; Website: www.angus.gov.uk).

Argyll & Bute Council: Education Dept, Kilmory, Lochgilphead, Argyll PA31 8RT

(01546 602127; Website: www.argyll-bute.gov.uk).

Clackmannanshire Council: Education and Community Services, Lime Tree House, Castle Street, Alloa FK10 1EX (01259 450000; Fax: 01259 452440; Website: www.clacksweb.org.uk).

Comhairle nan Eilean Siar: Council Offices, Sandwick Road, Stornoway, Isle of Lewis HS1 2BW (01851 703773; Fax: 01851 705349; Website: www.w-isles.gov.uk).

Dumfries & Galloway Council: Education Dept, 30 Edinburgh Road, Dumfries DG1 4NW (Information Services: 01387 260000; Fax: 01387 260385; Website: www.dumgal.gov.uk).

Dundee City Council: Education Dept, 8th Floor, Tayside House, Crichton Street, Dundee DD1 3RZ (01382 433111; Fax: 01382 433080; Website: www.dundeecity.gov.uk).

East Ayrshire Council: Council Headquarters, London Road, Kilmarnock KA3 7BU (0845 724 0000; Website: www.east-ayrshire.gov.uk).

East Dunbartonshire Council: Tom Johnston House, Civic Way, Kirkintilloch G66 4TJ (0845 045 4510; Website: www.eastdunbarton.gov.uk).

East Lothian Council: Education and Community Services, John Muir House, Haddington EH41 3HA (01620 827827; Website: www.eastlothian.gov.uk).

East Renfrewshire Council: Council Offices, Education Dept, Eastwood Park, Rouken Glen Road, Glasgow G46 6UG (0141 577 3001; Website: www.eastrenfrewshire.gov.uk).

Edinburgh City Council: Education Dept, Wellington Court, 10 Waterloo Place, Edinburgh EH1 3EG (0131 469 3000; Website: www.edinburgh.gov.uk).

Falkirk Council: Education Services; McLaren House, Marchmont Avenue, Polmont FK2 0NZ (01324 506600; Fax: 01324 506601; Website: www.falkirk.gov.uk).

Fife Council: Fife House, Education Dept, Rothesay House, North Street, Glenrothes, Fife KY7 5PN (01592 414141; Website: www.fife-education.org.uk).

Glasgow City Council: Education Dept, 25 Cochrane Street, Glasgow G1 1HL (0141 287 2000; Website: www.glasgow.gov.uk).

Highland Council: Glenurquhart Road, Inverness IV3 5NX (01463 702000; Fax: 01463 702111; Website: www.highland.gov.uk).

Inverclyde Council: Education Services, 105 Dalrymple Street, Greenock PA15 1HT (01475 712824; Fax: 01475 712875; Website: www.inverclyde.gov.uk).

Midlothian Council: Schools and Community Learning and Development,

Fairfield House, 8 Lothian Road, Dalkeith EH22 3ZG (0131 271 3718; Fax: 0131 271 3751; Website: www.midlothian.gov.uk).

Moray Council: Educational Services, Council Offices, High Street, Elgin IV30 1BX (01343 563397; Website: www.moray.gov.uk).

North Ayrshire Council: Cunninghame House, Friars Croft, Irvine KA12 8EE (0845 603 0590; Website: www.north-ayrshire.gov.uk).

North Lanarkshire Council: Education Dept, Municipal Buildings, Kildonan Street, Coatbridge ML5 3BT (01236 812222; Website: www.northlan.gov.uk).

Orkney Islands Council: Council Offices, School Place, Kirkwall, Orkney KW15 1NY (01856 873535; Website: www.orkney.gov.uk).

Perth & Kinross Council: Education and Children's Services, Pullar House, 35 Kinnoull Street, Perth PH1 5GD (01738 476211; Fax 01738 476200; Website: www.pkc.gov.uk).

Renfrewshire Council: Education and Leisure Services, Cotton Street, Paisley PA1 1LE (0141 842 5663; Fax: 0141 842 5655; Website: www.renfrewshire.gov.uk).

Scottish Borders Council: Lifelong Learning, Council Headquarters, Newtown St Boswells, Melrose TD6 0SA (01835 825090; Fax: 01835 825091; Website: www.scotborders.gov.uk).

Shetlands Islands Council: Education Services, Hayfield House, Hayfield Lane, Lerwick, Shetland ZE1 0QD (01595 744000; Fax: 01595 692810; Website: www.shetland.gov.uk).

South Ayrshire Council: County Buildings, Wellington Square, Ayr KA7 1DR (01292 612000; Fax: 01292 612143; Website: www.south-ayrshire.gov.uk).

South Lanarkshire Council: Education Dept, 5th Floor, Council Offices, Almada Street, Hamilton ML3 0AA (01698 454444; Website: www.southlanarkshire.gov.uk).

Stirling Council: Viewforth, Stirling FK8 2ET (0845 277 7000; Website: www.stirling.gov.uk).

West Dunbartonshire Council: Learning and Education, Council Offices, Garshake Road, Dumbarton G82 3PU (01389 737000; Website: www.west-dunbarton.gov.uk).

West Lothian Council: Education Services, Lindsay House, South Bridge Street, Bathgate EH48 1TS (01506 776000; Website: www.westlothian.gov.uk).

Wales

Blaenau Gwent County Borough Council: Education/Lifelong Learning, Municipal Offices, Civic Centre, Ebbw Vale NP23

6XB (01495 355340; Website: www.blaenau-gwent.gov.uk).

Bridgend County Borough Council: Education, Leisure and Community Services, Civic Offices, Angel Street, Bridgend CF31 4WB (01656 643643; Website: www.bridgend.gov.uk).

Caerphilly County Borough Council: Directorate of Education & Leisure, County Offices, Caerphilly Road, Ystrad Mynach, Hengoed CF82 7EP (01443 864956; Fax: 01443 863070; Website: www.caerphilly.gov.uk).

The City and County Council of Cardiff: Education Dept, County Hall, Atlantic Wharf, Cardiff CF10 4UW (029 2087 2087; Fax: 029 2087 2086; Website: www.cardiff.gov.uk).

Carmarthenshire County Council: County Hall, Carmarthen SA31 IJP (01267 234567; Fax: 01267 221692; Website: www.carmarthenshire.gov.uk).

Ceredigion County Council: Education Dept, County Offices, Aberystwyth SY23 2DE (01970 633569; Fax: 01970 633663; Website: www.ceredigion.gov.uk).

Conwy County Borough Council: Education Dept, Government Buildings, Dinerth Road, Colwyn Bay LL28 4UL (01492 575051; Fax: 01492 541311; Website: www.conwy.gov.uk).

Denbighshire County Council: Council Offices, Wynnstay Road, Ruthin LL15 1YN (01824 712659; Fax: 01824 712664; Website: www.denbighshire.gov.uk).

Flintshire County Council: Education and Children's Services, County Hall, Mold CH7 6NB (0845 607 7577; Website: www.flintshire.gov.uk).

Gwynedd Council: Schools, Service Development Directorate, Council Offices, Caernarfon LL55 1SH (01286 672255; Fax: 01286 673993; Website: www.gwynedd.gov.uk).

Isle of Anglesey County Council: Dept of Education and Leisure, Park Mount, Glanhwfa Road, Llangefni, Anglesey LL77 7EY (01248 752900; Fax: 01248 752999; Website: www.anglesey.gov.uk).

Merthyr Tydfil County Borough Council: Civic Centre, Castle Street, Merthyr Tydfil CF47 8AN (01685 725000; Website: www.merthyr.gov.uk).

Monmouthshire County Council: Lifelong Learning and Leisure, County Hall, Cwmbran NP44 2XH (01633 644644; Website: www.monmouthshire.gov.uk).

Neath Port Talbot County Borough Council: Education Dept, Civic Centre, Port Talbot SA13 1PJ (01639 763333; 01639 763444; Website: www.neath-porttalbot.gov.uk).

Newport County Borough Council: Education Dept, Civic Centre, Newport

NP20 4UR (01633 656656; Website: www.newport.gov.uk).

Pembrokeshire County Council: Education Dept, County Hall, Haverfordwest SA61 1TP (01437 764551 ext.5860; Fax: 01437 775303; Website: www.pembrokeshire.gov.uk).

Powys County Council: Education Dept, County Hall, Llandrindod Wells, Powys LD1 5LG (01597 826000; Website: www.powys.gov.uk).

Rhondda Cynon Taff County Borough Council: Education and Lifelong Learning, Ty Trevithick, Abercynon, Mountain Ash, Porth CF45 4UQ (01443 744000; e-mail: support@rctednet.net; Website: www.rhondda-cynon-taff.gov.uk).

City & County of Swansea: Education Dept, County Hall, Swansea SA1 3SN (01792 636000; e-mail: education.department@swansea.gov.uk; Website: www.swansea.gov.uk).

Torfaen County Borough Council: Education Department, County Hall, Croeyceiliog, Cwmbran, Torfaen NP44 2WN (01633 648164; Website: www.torfaen.gov.uk).

The Vale of Glamorgan County Borough Council: Education Dept, Civic Offices, Holton Road, Barry CF63 4RU (01446 700111; 01446 745566; Website: www.valeofglamorgan.gov.uk).

Wrexham County Borough Council: Education and Leisure Services, Ty Henblas, Queens Street, Wrexham LL13 8AZ (01978 297401; Website: www.wrexham.gov.uk).

Northern Ireland

Belfast: Education & Library Board, 40 Academy Street, Belfast BT1 2NQ (028 9056 4000; Fax: 028 9033 1714; Website: www.belb.org.uk).

Western: Education & Library Board, Campsie House, 1 Hospital Road, Omagh, Co. Tyrone BT79 0AW (028 8241 1411; Fax: 028 8241 1400; Website: www.welbni.org).

North Eastern: Education & Library Board, County Hall, 182 Galgorm Road, Ballymena, County Antrim BT42 1HN (028 2565 3333; Website: www.neelb.org.uk).

South Eastern: Education & Library Board, Grahamsbridge Road, Dundonald, Belfast BT16 2HS (028 9056 6200; 028 9056 6266; Website: www.seelb.org.uk).

Southern: Education & Library Board, 3 Charlemont Place, The Mall, Armagh BT61 9AZ (028 3751 2200; Website: www.selb.org).

CCMS (Council for Catholic Maintained Schools): 160 High Street, Holywood, County Down BT18 9HT (028 9042 6972; Fax: 028 9042 4255; e-mail: info@onlineccms.com).

SOURCES OF FURTHER INFORMATION & ADVICE

Many schoolchildren and students need financial advice and help from time to time. It is usually best to contact the following as a starting point:

- your school careers officer (if you have one)
- your student union
- your local education authority (addresses are in the previous section of this guide)
- your local Citizens Advice or other welfare agencies.

These should point you in the right direction for more specialist advice if you need it. However, the following organisations and publications may be useful and should be available from all main libraries. Readers should also look at the specialist sections of this guide where relevant.

Financial advice for students

Educational Grants Advisory Service (EGAS)

EGAS, 501–505 Kingsland Road, London E8 4AU (020 7254 6251; Website: www.egas-online.org).

EGAS is part of the Family Welfare Association which gives support to poor families in the community (for further information see www.fwa.org.uk). EGAS offers guidance and advice on funding for those studying for post-16 education and training. Enquires regarding student funding should be initially made through completing a *Student Questionnaire* which is available from the organisation's website or by sending a stamped addressed envelope to EGAS. Further details can be found on the website.

The National Union of Students (NUS)

NUS, 2nd floor, Centro 3, Mandela Street, London NW1 ODU (0871 221 8221; Website: www.nusonline.co.uk).

Department for Education and Skills – Student Support Website

Website: www.dfes.gov.uk/studentsupport

The website includes information about help available to higher education students in England and Wales. A number of publications are available to download, including those offering advice to mature students, students with disabilities and part-time students.

Further and higher education advice

The following organisations provide information about further and higher education.

Northern Ireland: Department of Education for Northern Ireland, Further Education Branch, Rathgael House, Balloo Road, Bangor, County Down BT19 7PR (028 9127 9279; Fax: 028 9127 9100; e-mail: mail@deni.gov.uk; Website: www.deni.gov.uk).

Scotland: Student Award Agency for Scotland, Gyleview House, 3 Redheughs Rigg, Edinburgh EH12 9HH (0845 111 1711; Fax: 0131 244 5887; e-mail: saas.geu@scotland.gsi.gov.uk; Website: www.student-support-saas.gov.uk).

North West, North East, West Midlands and Yorkshire: CENTRA (Education & Training Services) Ltd, Duxbury Park, Duxbury Hall Road, Chorley, Lancashire PR7 4AT (01257 241428; Fax: 01257 260357; e-mail: enquiries@centra.org.uk; Website: www.centra.org.uk).

Eastern Region: ACER, Association of Colleges in the Eastern Region, Suite 1, Lancaster House, Meadow Lane, St Ives, Cambridgeshire PE27 4LG (01480 468198; Fax: 01480 468601; e-mail: general@acer.ac.uk; Website: www.acer.ac.uk).

South West England: Learning South West, Bishops Hull House, Bishops Hull, Taunton, Somerset TA1 5RA (01823 335491; Fax: 01823 323388; Website: www.learning-southwest.org.uk).

Southern England: AOSEC, Building 33, University of Reading, London Road, Reading, Berkshire RGI 5AQ (0118 378 6325; Fax: 0118 378 6324; Email: enquiries@aosec.org.uk; Website: www.aosec.org.uk).

Further and higher education admissions

University and Colleges Admissions Service (UCAS)

UCAS, Rose Hill, New Barn Lane, Cheltenham, Gloucestershire GL52 3LZ (01242 222444; e-mail: enquiries@ucas.ac.uk; Website: www.ucas.ac.uk).

Applications for full-time university degree courses must be made through UCAS (part-time degree courses and the Open University are not covered by UCAS – apply directly to the university).

The Open University (OU)

The Open University, PO Box 197, Milton Keynes MK7 6BJ (0870 333 4340; e-mail: general-enquiries@open.ac.uk; Website: www.open.ac.uk).

The Open University is the only university in the country where you can study without any prior qualifications. It has both degree and non-degree courses and students can spread their learning over a period of years with breaks in between if necessary. Whilst it is best known for its part-time and distance learning courses, full-time courses are available at its Milton Keynes campus. Costs are very low compared with other universities. There are funds which are set up particularly to make grants to Open University students who are in severe financial need. Contact the university for further information.

Schoolchildren – statutory benefits

Child Poverty Action Group (CPAG)

Child Poverty Action Group, 94 White Lion Street, London N1 9PF (020 7837 7979; Fax: 020 7837 2501; Website: www.childpoverty.org.uk).

The CPAG publishes a number of guides which include information on state benefit and entitlements both for schoolchildren and students.

Adult education

National Institute of Adult Continuing Education (NIACE)

Renaissance House, 20 Princess Road West, Leicester LE1 6TP (0116 204 4200; e-mail: enquiries@niace.org.uk; Website: www.niace.org.uk).

National Institute of Adult Continuing Education Wales

Ground Floor, 35 Cathedral Road, Cardiff CF11 9HB (0292 037 0900; Fax: 0292 037 0909; e-mail: enquiries@niacedc.org.uk; Website: www.niace.org.uk or www.niacedc.org.uk).

NIACE is the national organisation for adult learning. It works with national and local government, educational institutions, Learning and Skills Councils, employers and so on to promote equal opportunities of access to learning for all adults. It also advises on developments in policy and practice.

Students with disabilities

Skill – National Bureau for Students with Disabilities

Skill, Chapter House, 18–20 Crucifix Lane, London SE1 3JW (Tel & Minicom: 020 7450 0620; e-mail: skill@skill.org.uk; Website: www.skill.org.uk).

Skill in Scotland, Norton Park, 57 Albion Road, Edinburgh EH7 5QY (Tel & Minicom: 0131 475 2348; e-mail: admin@skillscotland.org.uk).

Skill in Northern Ireland, Unit 2, Jennymount Court, North Derby Street, Belfast BT15 3HN (Tel & Minicom: 0123 228 7000; e-mail: admin@skillni.demon.co.uk).

Skill in Wales, Students Services Department, University of Glamorgan, Pntypridd, Mid Glamorgan CF37 1DL (01443 654 317; e-mail: rpass@glam.ac.uk; Website: www.skill.org.uk/wales/index.asp).

Skill is a national charity which promotes opportunities for young people and adults with any kind of disability in post-16 education, training and employment across the UK. It gives advice on opportunities, facilities and financial assistance available for students with disabilities and produces a range of information sheets and publications.

Study overseas

British Council

10 Spring Gardens, London SW1A 2BN (0161 957 7755; Fax: 0161 957 7762; e-mail: general.enquiries@britishcouncil.org; Website: www.britishcouncil.org).

Advice and publications on educational trips overseas.

UK Socrates – Erasmus

UK Socrates – Erasmus Council, Rothford, Giles Lane, Canterbury, Kent CT2 7LR (01227 762712; Fax: 01227 762711; e-mail: info@erasmus.ac.uk; Website: www.erasmus.ac.uk).

Information on educational programmes overseas and other educational advice.

Overseas students

The British Council

British Council Educational Information Centre, Bridgewater House, 58 Whitworth Street, Manchester M1 6BB (0161 957 7755; Fax: 0161 957 7111; e-mail: general.enquiries@britishcouncil.org).

United Kingdom Council for Overseas Students' Affairs (UKCOSA)

9–17 St Albans Place, London N1 0NX (020 7288 4330; e-mail: enquiries@ukcosa.org.uk; Website: www.ukcosa.org.uk).

UKCOSA provides information for overseas students on entering the UK, as well as general advice.

Education International (also known as World University Service (UK)/ Refugee Education & Training Advisory Service)

Education Action International, 14 Dufferin Street, London EC1Y 8PD (020 7426 5820).

RETAS (Advice Line: 020 7426 5801, Tuesdays & Thursdays 2.30–5.00pm; e-mail: info@education-action.org (please note no advice services are accessed via this e-mail).

This organisation offers an education advisory service to refugees in the UK. There is also an Employment Team who run training courses to help refugees find work in the UK.

Index